INFORMATION SYSTEMS
IN PUBLIC ADMINISTRATION

INFORMATION SYSTEMS IN PUBLIC ADMINISTRATION

and their Role in Economic and Social Development

*Proceedings of an International Seminar held in
Chamrousse, France, 17-23 June, 1979*

organized by
the Data for Development International Association

under the auspices of
the United Nations Educational, Scientific
and Cultural Organization (UNESCO),
and the International Federation
for Information Processing (IFIP)

edited by

David EADE
*United Nations Centre for
Science and Technology for Development
New York
U.S.A.*

John HODGSON
*Data for Development
Marseille
France*

NORTH-HOLLAND PUBLISHING COMPANY – AMSTERDAM · NEW YORK · OXFORD

Published by:
NORTH-HOLLAND PUBLISHING COMPANY – AMSTERDAM • NEW YORK • OXFORD

Sole distributors for the U.S.A. and Canada
ELSEVIER NORTH-HOLLAND, INC.
52 Vanderbilt Avenue
New York, N.Y. 10017

PRINTED IN THE NETHERLANDS

INTRODUCTION

This collection of papers arises out of an international seminar organized by the Data for Development Association with the co-sponsorships of Unesco and the International Federation for Information Processing (IFIP). The seminar took place from 17-23 June 1979 in Chamrousse near Grenoble, France. Its aim was to discuss, under the general theme of "information systems in public administration and their role in economic and social development" the organization of information and the management of data resources in government, with special attention to the needs of development planning.

The seminar sessions were of two sorts: plenary sessions of which papers of a general nature were presented and discussed; and parallel working group sessions. The results of working group discussions were reported back and commented on in plenary session. The working groups were given as themes certain key development issues, either sectoral (industrial development, traditional sector development...) or technical (bibliographic and documentary services, use of new computer communication technologies). The eight themes chosen were:

- human factors: information systems on population, health and education;

- information systems for agriculture and food production;

   - natural resource information systems;

   - industrial information systems;

   - access to "know-how" information systems on technologies;

   - urban and regional information systems in developing countries;

   - information systems for the traditional sector;

   - use of new computer and communication technologies in
     developing countries.

The proceedings are presented in two parts, part 1 containing the contributed papers presented in plenary session, and part 2 the contributed
papers presented in the working group sessions, together with the final
reports prepared by the working groups.

The wide range of subjects treated in these papers and working group
reports reflect the multidisciplinary approach that is essential in any
attempt to manage the information resources - in the widest sense - of
public administration in a global way.   Advocacy of the global approach,
and research into practical methods of realizing it, is the central concern
- indeed the *raison d'être* - of Data for Development.   The seminar provided an occasion to bring together professionals in the relevant disciplines from many parts of the world to work together on the problems
facing public administration, especially in developing countries, of mas-
tery of their information and data resources.   No one would claim that
the problems have all been solved, but we believe that the papers presented here make a valuable contribution to the continuing research.

What cannot - inevitably but unfortunately - be reflected in the published papers are the equally valuable personal exchanges and inter-
actions which were a notable feature of the Chamrousse seminar.   The
fruitfulness of this aspect of the seminar was in large measure due to the
fact that the participants attended as individuals rather than representatives of organizations.   Formal meetings and organizational dialogues are
of course also necessary but the development of ideas by exchange and

cross-fertilization seem to happen most readily at the kind of informal event that non-governmental organizations - like Data for Development - are ideally placed to promote.

Data for Development is therefore proud to have been at the origin of this seminar; but no such event could have been mounted as a solo effort by such a small organization, and our thanks go to all those who contributed to the success of the seminar.   Firstly our co-sponsors Unesco and the International Federation for Information Processing who worked with us on the conception and planning of the seminar.   Second, those who made the seminar possible by providing the money to pay for it; we are greatly indebted to the United Nations Fund for Population Activities, Unesco, the United Nations Development Fund, the U.S. Agency for International Development, the Mission à l'Informatique (Ministère de l'Industrie, Paris) and the Institut de Recherche en Informatique et Automatique (Paris) for their generous support.

Next we would like to thank the seminar participants, especially those who contributed papers, led working groups, drafted group reports or otherwise took on extra responsibilities; the seminar success owes a great deal to their unstinted efforts.   Thanks are also due to the secretariat support staff at the seminar, and especially to Miss Sue Bazeley and Miss Pauline Shard, who retyped all the papers for this publication, and finally mention must be made of the outstanding behind the scenes work of Melle Christiane Tonini in the material organization of the seminar.

Our heartfelt thanks go to all these people, and this volume of papers - the partial fruit of their work - is dedicated to them.

EXPLANATORY NOTES

References to dollars ($) are to United States dollars unless otherwise stated.

A full stop is used to indicate decimals.

A comma is used to distinguish thousands and millions.

Mention of firm names and/or commercial products does not imply the endorsement of Data for Development.

The designations employed and the presentation of the material in this publication do not imply the expression of any opinion whatsoever on the part of Data for Development.

The views expressed in the papers are those of the authors and do not necessarily reflect those of the organizations with which they are associated or of Data for Development.

"Program" and " programme" are two alternative spellings for the concept of "a plan to be followed". In this publication the spelling "program" indicates a set of instructions and data specifying a computational or data processing plan. For other plans, the spelling "programme" is used - for example, an educational programme.

TABLE OF CONTENTS

PART TWO: WORKING GROUP PAPERS

Working Group 1
Human Factors: Population, Health and Education

Working Group 2
Food and Agriculture

Working Group 3
Natural Resources

Working Group 4
Industry

Working Group 5
Expertise

Working Group 6
Urban and Regional Development

Working Group 7
The Traditional Sector

Working Group 8
New Computer and Communication Technologies:
Their Use in Developing Countries

ANNEXES

PART ONE
PLENARY PAPERS

INFORMATION SYSTEMS IN PUBLIC ADMINISTRATION
D. Eade, J. Hodgson (editors)
North-Holland Publishing Company
© *DFD, 1981*

THE BOLIVIAN APPROACH TO THE DEVELOPMENT OF A
NATIONAL INFORMATION SYSTEM

Warren Crowther*

Gonzalo Riveros**

Abstract

The 1½ years of operational experience and the promising programme of
Bolivia's national information system are instructive for other developing
countries. This frank exposition compares Bolivia's rather unique approach
with that of other developing countries in dealing with serious information
problems which are common among many of these countries. The Bolivian
approach emphasizes

(a) a broad training programme on the functioning, research,
design and implementation of information systems, and on data-handling
techniques;

(b) work by inter-institutional commissions on general instruments of
co-ordination of decentralized activities intended to facilitate access to
national intellectual production and to pertinent documentation from abroad;
and

(c) demonstration projects for sector information systems or networks.

This article cites the practical difficulties with each of these foci of the
national information system and some specific strategic characteristics of the
Bolivian approach which have evolved.

---

* Resident Adviser, Bolivian National Development Information System and
Fund (SYFNID), and Project Official, International Development Research Centre,
Canada.

** Director, SYFNID.

The authors are grateful for the comments on an earlier draft by
Hugo Loaiza.

W. Crowther and G. Riveros

Figure I. Integration of information activities

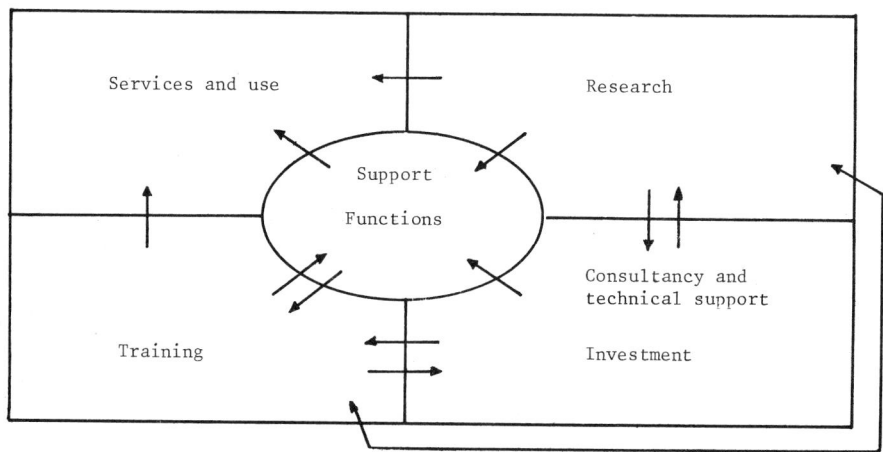

Examples of services

(functions directly related to user)

Loan
Dissemination
Retrieval
Reference
Translation
Reprography

Examples of support functions

(other functions in information-handling)

Acquisition of information
Technical processes
Storage of information
Purchase of Equipment
Personnel Operations

A. Introduction

As a unique national information system, considering its wide scope of responsibilities encompassing all types of scientific, technological and socio-economic information, Bolivia's National Development Information System and Fund (SYFNID), two years after being created and after 1½ years of operation, can be fairly described as a promising programme. Certainly, the experience of SYFNID during this interval is useful for developing countries in general, and this unique approach merits a frank appraisal of its initial achievements and the problems encountered.

The most general objective of SYFNID has been that of implementing, sustaining and promoting a permanent, pertinent and flexible infrastructure for analyzing and solving the information problems related to Bolivia's development.

This has required co-ordination in a number of senses and has meant the consolidation of the presently discontinuous and narrowly-focussed activities in the information field into a sustained and joint effort. For example, the activities in training, in research, and those intended to create or reinforce services and support functions are made to be mutually reinforcing (See figure I). The overspecialized fields of archivology, cybernetics and computer science, documentation, library science and statistics are interrelated in order to assure unified system developments, choosing the most adequate technologies available and addressing the multifaceted and complex demands for the information handled by these specialties. The conditions are created for the transfer of information from one productive or social sector to another, in order to facilitate converg-ence and co-ordination of development projects. The activities in the information field of the private sector are examined in terms of public interest and made to be consistent with public policies.

In order to meet these responsibilities for developing and co-ordinating a national information infrastructure, SYFNID has been assigned the following tasks:[1]

(a) To co-ordinate and rationalize the use of human and material resources of the nation in scientific, technological and socio-economic information for development;

(b) To adapt those information resources to national development needs and to assure that the activities of the public institutions regarding such information are consistent with decision-making requirements for the National Development Plans;

(c) To promote the consolidation and improvement of the existing bibliographical and numerical information units in the country, as well as the creation of others as needed;

(d) To help such units by means of financial and technical assistance based on the joint use of national and foreign resources;

(e) To intensify and make operative connexions with world and regional information systems;

(f) To co-ordinate, channel and regulate the technical and financial assistance, both national and foreign, in this field, so that it can be rationalized and utilized optimally.

---

[1] Decreto Supremo No. 14502, 22 April, 1977

The more specific functions undertaken by SYFNID to meet these responsibilities, in general order of priority are: training, research, creation of basic instruments of co-ordination, technical assistance, promotion and financing of information projects.2/

In this paper a brief description will be made of the key information problems of Bolivia, and of the general strategy and unique characteristics of this country's approach to its information problems. For comparative purposes, some references will be made to the experiences of other developing countries, especially Chile, Colombia, Kenya and Mexico, based on reports and documents available to us.3/

B. General Information Deficiencies

SYFNID's research has discovered that in Bolivia there is very limited organization of national intellectual production. National bibliographical control during recent years is limited to publications of large private editors, an estimated 60 per cent of documents produced in agricultural field, published studies in geology and health, and the documents included in a smattering of very specialized bibliographies. There is a multiplicity of decrees which are contradictory and largely ineffective regarding the obligatory deposit of national intellectual production. There is also a multiplicity of separate, discontinuous and often unreliable data-gathering activities and of administrative registers regarding projects and on-going administrative functions and objects. The more reliable data-gathering is undertaken in periodic or special censuses, sample surveys and special research projects, which in any case must deal with three major spoken languages and large cultural variations in a very dispersed population (five million inhabitants in a territory twice the size of France). Most data are inaccessible, except in aggregated form, and even those arriving at The National Institute of Statistics are poorly stored for later reference or retrieval.

As a whole, there are very poor facilities for the acquisition of information important for Bolivia's development from international and foreign sources and a generally poor understanding among information workers of the mechanisms, other than direct purchase, for obtaining such information and for collection development. There is a paucity of technical information from other countries, even from other Spanish-speaking countries. The typical library or documentation centre, for example, receives a few technical journals and very occasionally an already outdated reference work. Many collections include large numbers of documents which are never consulted, often because they are not pertinent to the tasks of the institution or interests of the users.

The information that is acquired becomes accessible or known to only a small portion of the potential users. University and secondary school students exhaust not only university and public library capacity but that of specialized public sector libraries as well, yet many of the university students in key

---

2/ The original programme is contained in documents submitted by the Government of Bolivia to the International Development Research Centre, Canada, on 27 July 1976 and 5 April 1977.

3/ For Chile and Colombia see Betty Johnson V., "Los sistemas nacionales de informacion: las experiencias de Colombia y de Chile", paper presented at the meeting on Information for Development in Latin America and the Caribbean, Cali, Colombia, 23-28 October 1977. For Kenya, see the publications on the African projects of Data For Development. For Mexico, the major source of information is Antonio Ayesterán; also Myla Goldman, "Technical information services in Mexico", Special Libraries, Vol. 69, No. 9 (September 1978), pp. 355-60.

professions, and the professionals themselves, lack any contact with journals or reference works. Most depressing is the very low motivation of large segments of these groups to improve their technical information utilization, reflecting a basic deficiency in their professional education.

Low public consciousness regarding the key role of information for development leads to inadequate budgets for the purchases of documents or for a continuous work on designing and implementing adequate data flows and files. There is no real rationalization of the flows of statistical information and little relationship in many fields between data handling and decision making. Urgent or important data requirements are met on an ad hoc basis and considerable duplication and transcribing takes place.

Information units and systems (with some notable exceptions) tend to emphasize data processing and document holding more than services tailor-made to user needs and the fostering of working relationships with key information sources. They generally lack the basic elements required for effective participation in international networks or specialized data bases, and even in the important information flows within the country (for example, those flows which bring information to bear on decision making). They tend to overspecialize by type of information.

Very few information units in the country have adequate or continuous executive backing and a plan or programme for development of its services.

A few ministries and the most important public enterprises in this largely state corporative economy, have set up or are setting up computerized systems for a few management controls. Some computer installations, including those of the universities, are used partly in research projects. It is common for commitments to equipment purchases to be made before there is a clear idea of their future use. The ministries vary considerably in their commitment to library and documentation system developments. The large public enterprises tend to rely on costly and unsystematic contacts with international counterparts for obtaining technical information. The technical information generated internally in the ministries, the public enterprises and the development corporation of each department is dispersed. The universities are in considerable tension regarding the library centralization/decentralization issue, and the scarce resources for library development are scattered in too many unco-ordinated activities. There are some serious efforts to maintain historical archives, but in general the public sector archives are in over-all chaos since the move in 1898 of the national governmental offices (except the National Archives) from Sucre to La Paz, and the problem is compounded by the unco-ordinated and illusory efforts in some sectors to focus on large-scale data bases instead of a simple organization of their data files and flows.

New operations or units are mounted without a systematic perspective regarding the entire flow of the information to be handled from original source to final user. Parallel systems are set up to deal with a sector or group or sources/users, based rather haphazardly on initiatives of public executives (usually in office a short time) or an international organization mission or a consultant. Even though the existing units are deficient and have problems obtaining adequate support to overcome these deficiencies, at times they can lead a vehement opposition against modernization proposals for information systems in their sector.

Most personnel that work in the information units are self-taught. Those that have received formal training have mostly received a packaged training more appropriate for working conditions in other countries where there is much more institutional and professional support in favour of developing adequate information services and products. The university educational programme in the information field are separately developed for different specializations (computer science, library science, mass communications and statistics) and most have tended to adopt quite traditional or theoretical curricula, in any case not based on a study of the job market and evidently inadequate for professional development commensurate with Bolivia's real needs.[4]

Since recognition and financial rewards are very poor, information personnel turnover can be very rapid. Meanwhile, public executives are prone to contract the services of expensive foreign consultants to provide data and set up information systems, generally with overly-sophisticated data-processing equipment, or with equipment for which soft-ware adequate to the needs is not available. A cycle of technological dependence is maintained, given the lack of prepared local personnel and the usual necessity to make considerable adaptations of the transferred systems.

In setting up these systems, inadequate attention is given to the reliability of the data which will be processed, to the importance of adopting standardized classification and codes suitable for national realities and development goals, and to setting out institutional (rather than personal) criteria of confidentiality for assuring access for those needing the information.

When an occasional information system or unit has been set up applying technical criteria and adapted to institutional needs, there has been a constant danger of discontinuity as a result of change of government or executives. Unfortunately, some model systems of administrative data collection and retrieval and libraries have been disbanded or abandoned.

However, some units and systems have been developed and maintained with great effort by Bolivians, with results that could be important case studies or even functioning prototypes for future creations. These commendable programmes include documentation centres for health, general technology and geology; libraries for agriculture, mining/metallurgical research, cartography and education; general population census; commercial documentation and facilitation regarding transit of foreign commerce through neighbouring countries; railway management information systems; inventory control and financial reporting systems for public enterprises; etc.

Until recently, no serious research had been carried out on the Bolivian experiences with information systems. SYFNID's initial programme was based on some seriously mistaken premises which could only be corrected on a trial-and-error basis and as its own research results became available.

4/ Ana S. de Gutierrez and Warren Crowther, "La profesionalizacion de las ciencias de la informacion en Bolivia", _Presencia_, vol. 18 (February 1979).

C. The Bolivian Approach

Vaguely conscious of these deficiencies and experiences and intent on dealing with them in a systematic manner, a number of Bolivians in key positions (especially the Director of the National Documentation Centre) were receptive to proposals by the Information Sciences Division of the International Development Research Centre (IDRC) of Canada, that Bolivia become a pilot project of a bottom-up strategy, as opposed to the top-down strategy, of information systems developments among developing countries. It was evident that the commonly-mentioned "territorial formula" of assigning responsibilities in international networks required substantial development of the national information infrastructure in many countries.[5]

The general sequence of activities to be undertaken in the Bolivian case is not unlike that of the Data for Development projects in developing countries, although from the very outset much more emphasis has been placed in Bolivia, as in other Latin American cases, on a broad training programme on the functioning, research, design and implementation of information systems, and on data-handling techniques, apart from the training which is normally inherent in the outside consultant/local counterpart relationship during project implementation.

Figure II summarizes the resulting sequence. Rather than engage each step in this sequence at a time, SYFNID is now undertaking activities in different stages of systems development, depending on the programme or sector involved. The experience of a few sectors or programmes becomes instructive for work in others. The research and diagnostic phases are complete[6] and the design, programming and budgeting are now underway for the implementation of specific projects during the 18-24 month period beginning July 1979.

The Bolivian approach to development of a national information system is admittedly very ambitious and difficult. Bolivia's system encompasses three areas: Archives, Bibliographical and Numerical. SYFNID's Board includes the Planning Minister, SYFNID's Director, the Director of the National Documentation Centre (also Technical Secretary of SYFNID), and the Directors of the National Computing Centre, the National Statistics' Institute, the National Academy of Sciences, the major university library, and the National Archives. SYFNID is at the same hierarchical level in the Planning Ministry as the Scientific and Technological Policy Division.

In Chile, Colombia, Mexico and other Latin American countries, the national information systems have historical ties to the university system and are presently dependent on the national science and technology agencies. These national systems tend to concentrate on the Bibliographical Area, giving rise to other nation-wide systems for other types of scientific, technological,

---

[5] Elizabeth Miller and Kate Wild, "A strategy for international information systems", Special Libraries, Vol. 69, No. 11 (November 1978), pp. 435-442. John Woolston, "The importance of international information systems for building national capabilities", International Forum on Information and Documentation, Vol. 2, No. 2 (1977), pp. 16-21. John Woolston, "International information systems for development", paper presented at the meeting on Information for Development in Latin American and the Caribbean, Cali, Colombia, 23-28 October, 1977.

[6] For example, in the field of geology, the publications thus far are: SYFNID, "La geología en Bolivia frente a la problemática de la información. Resultados de un estudio y propuestas de acciones a ser tomadas", February 1979; SYFNID, "Directorio de geólogos en Bolivia", May 1979; SYFNID, "Fuentes nacionales e internacionales de información geológica", 1979.

Figure II. Information system development activities

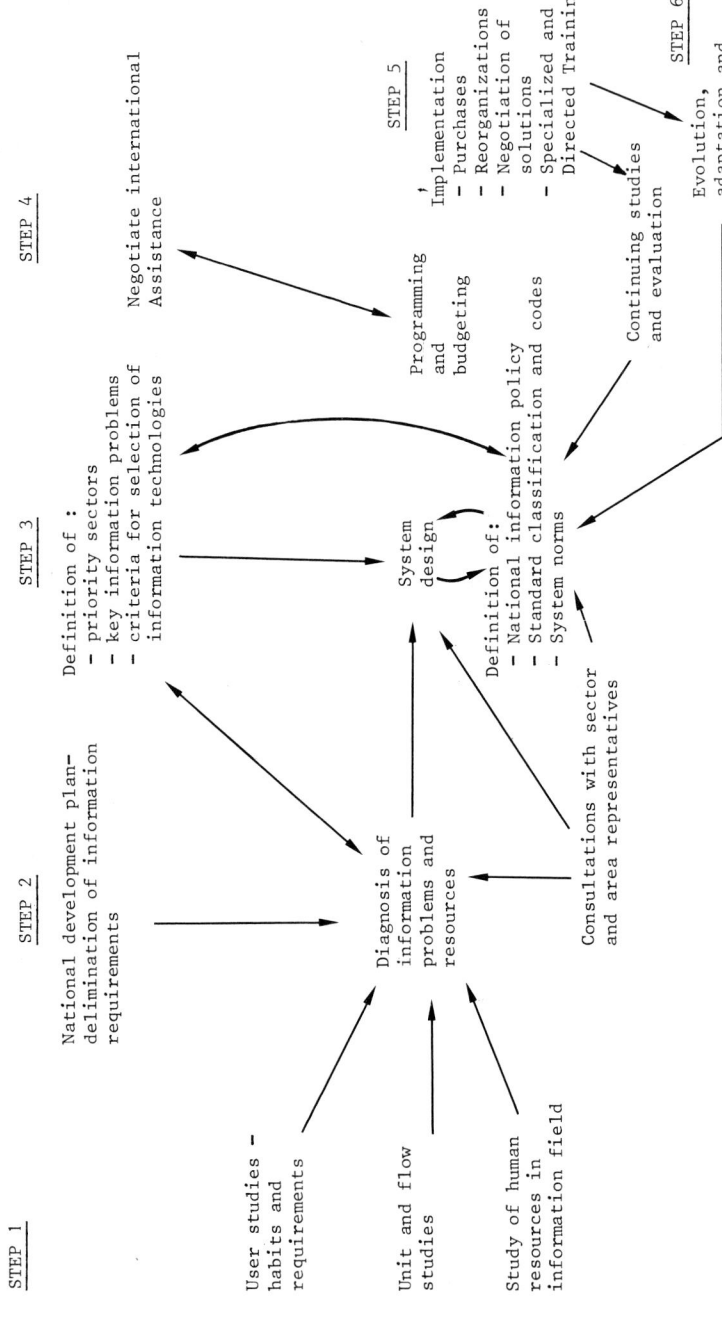

General training on functioning, research, design and implementation of information systems

educational and socio-economic information. The Bolivian system, by comparison, is not dependent on the varying degrees of importance which a national science and technology agency might lend to different types of information system developments, but must convince others of its importance on its own terms. This separation is logical in the sense that in comparison with policies oriented to scientific and technological development, information system developments must be subject to less imposition and to much more careful negotiation with all the parties involved. However, a very close co-ordination is required between those two areas of development.

Nor is the Bolivian system restricted by ties to one information processing unit, as in Kenya. The Kenyan System was to consider all types of data, but the actual phase 1 work has concentrated on statistical and administrative data, in line with its dependence on the Central Bureau of Statistics.

The SYFNID Council has approved a general outline of the scope which Bolivia's national information policy should encompass 7/ and this is a guideline for programming. Other criteria for setting priorities for the short and medium-term programme, as in Kenya, are development priorities, consideration of important activities which are already underway and a logical attack on the inter-related information problems. The projects fall into three general categories and are given appropriate priority rankings therein.

1. Training

Early experiences of SYFNID demonstrated the necessity of distinguishing among different levels of training. 8/ For the many persons without any formal training, elementary courses are considered, for example, an adaptation and updating of the basic United Nations Education, Scientific, and Cultural Organisation (UNESCO) audio-visual library course and basic reference courses in key sectors. For those persons with substantial experience and formal training, advanced courses in continuing education are being carried out, for example, courses on data bases and advanced reference courses. For university students in information programmes, joint courses (bringing together the library science, computer science, mass communication and statistics students) are needed on information science in general, on information system design and implementation, on information policies, and on data bases. (The first of these courses is now underway.) User education is also considered. Elements of the basic reference courses are to be extracted for presentation to

---

7/ Council of SYFNID, "Bases para la formulación de la política nacional de información", 1978.

8/ Pernot Wersing and Thomas Seeger, "Future main trends of information systems and their implications for specialization of information personnel", International Forum on Information and Documentation, vol. 3, No. 4 (1978), p. 13. The Chilean system sponsors a large series of advanced courses in continuing education. The Mexican system sponsors continuing education and reinforces the university programmes.

specialized groups of users. Case studies of Bolivian experiences with
information systems development will be used for the university courses and for
seminars for public executives. Of secondary importance is a programme of
training abroad, on-the-job training in specialized information centres and
masters programmes for outstanding candidates. Training within Bolivia accounts
for the bulk of the training which is required. The programme is meant to
complement the training on data-handling techniques and system design by the
National Computing Centre and the National Institute of Statistics.

In order to carry out such a broad training programme certain key problems
had to be faced: (a) some facultys and students were concerned that the
graduates of their regular university programmes would face undue employment
competition from the students receiving certificates from the SYFNID
elementary and advanced courses; (b) on the other hand, tying SYFNID's
training programme to that of the university led to postponements due to the
frequent university closures for political reasons; (c) one of the information
programmes in the university asserted that all information science courses
should logically be administrated by that specialty alone; (d) there was concern
that foreign consultants would displace national teachers, whereas in one
concrete case the latter demonstrated that they could achieve better results;
(e) it is very difficult to assure a priori that the right people are taking
the right course, resulting in conflicting pressures on the teachers to
simplify or upgrade the level of each course; (f) the ability of foreign
consultants to adjust their instruction down to the appropriate level while
maintaining a challenge for the more interested students (a quality difficult
to assess on the candidate's résumé alone); (g) many consultants abroad are
slow to reply to inquiries and they are not always available when needed;
(h) the rotation of personnel in SYFNID entailed extra instruction for those
more recently hired, while trying to maintain the programmed sequence of
courses; (i) despite the careful preparation of terms of reference for the
students and agreements with the host institutions abroad, the training abroad
was generally, but not always, disappointing. In part, the host
institutions did not give the anticipated attention to the Bolivian students.
And it was seen that special courses abroad for more recently hired personnel
has not been satisfactory; (j) many Bolivian institutions are reluctant to
give personnel leave for attending long courses. A vicious circle exists
whereby the institutions, not having trained personnel, do not understand the
benefits of the training; (k) the original idea of selecting as SYFNID
technicians the best students from the first courses, proved unworkable. The
more promising professionals from different fields had to be hired in order to
induce them to enter the information field, prior to the initial training;
(1) finally, there were debates on the instruction methods. Some
misunderstandings arose among promoters of international information systems
when they noted that the Bolivians were encouraged during the training to
adopt a critical appraisal of the technical work of such systems, not
realizing that this was primarily a didactic exercise, although it could
result in some supplementary measures to adapt the systems to national output
requirements without altering the systems' own basic norms. Also, there was
a great deal of discussion as to whether the instruction should be based
on ideal-type models of information systems or geared to the resource levels
and reasonable expectations for Bolivia's level of information system
developments in the near future.

For all these reasons, the training programme faced an unexpected amount
of controversy and delay.

2. Area co-ordination projects

These are projects intended to increase interaction and a rational division of work among information units which already exist or as they are created. The selection of projects depends greatly on an assessment of the key bottlenecks to the adequate flow and organization of information in the country, and of the problems which are being created by current unco-ordinated system developments. In Bolivia, as in Chile, Colombia, Mexico and other Latin American countries, special attention is given to certain key instruments for co-ordination: legal deposits system to conserve and exercise bibliographical control on national intellectual documental production; a union serials catalogue; deposit accounts in foreign documentation services; a national consulting service (connected to UNEP/INFOTERRA, the international referral system of the United Nations Environment Programme); standardization of specialized classifications and codes; newspaper indexing, etc. The general procedure is to organize an inter-institutional working group, usually with a foreign adviser, at least in the research and diagnostic stages of work. SYFNID's Resident Adviser assures continuing technical assistance during the elaboration of the instrument.

The needs are so great and it is so difficult just to keep up with the separate initiatives of different institutions (for example, to automate their archives or set up a specialized classification scheme for ordering documents), that the major problem has become one of choosing where to concentrate efforts. While there has been some unfortunate institutional jealousy and initial resistance to co-operation with SYFNID (at least until it could be explained that SYFNID does not intend to centralize data collections but rather give support to co-ordinated and decentralized activities), it has also been most surprising that huge expectations have developed well beyond the capacity of the system. With regard to individual projects, for example that of the legal deposits, whereas SYFNID has tried to respect the political, legal and technical arguments in favour of a decentralized system, this has given rise both to pressures to have the system functioning overnight and to delaying counterpressures as different institutions vie for more significant roles in the system. Since the emphasis is on using these projects as training vehicles in the design and implementation of information systems, and not just on the solution of an immediate information problem, there are bound to be greater delays than would be the case if there were more reliance on foreign consultants. However, there is more likelihood of suitability of the product for the country, and even of technical innovation, when the Bolivians themselves undertake the primary work. Of the three areas (archives, bibliographical, numerical) of SYFNID responsibility, the most difficult to analyze is that of archives, given the lack of personnel (foreign or national) who have a broad enough background to understand and consolidate all the archival reorganization activities (O & M, data bases, historical archives, management data systems, etc.) into a coherent programme.

3. Priority sector information networks

The major idea is to set up demonstration projects of effective sector information systems or networks. Priority has been given by Bolivian Government to the following five sectors: planning (with emphasis on project control); agriculture; education; geology; and health. The problem to be attacked is somewhat different in each case, but the general methodology has been the same (in line with the sequence shown in figure II). Again, the emphasis here is not just on producing a workable showpiece product, but on using the projects as training material for information specialists.

To carry out this work SYFNID has selected technical professionals such as geologists, teachers or agronomists, or information specialists such as librarians or communication experts. This combination has generally worked well but the substantive field professionals have not always been accepted easily by the librarians, statisticians, etc., of other institutions.

A key problem during SYFNID's first year was a tendency of its technicians to bounce uneasily between assertions of authority and feelings of unpreparedness for the tasks to be undertaken. It is evident that these technicians are not prepared to give ample technical assistance to individual units, unlike the experience of the Mexican system. As the SYFNID technicians have come to realise that their role is merely a co-ordinating one and that the sectors can and will assume a great deal of the required effort and intellectual investment, and as the less motivated or capable technicians leave SYFNID, a more balanced attitude has developed. As the technicians acquire more experience and formal training there will undoubtedly be an evolution of their terms of reference.

There have been many debates on the number and scope of sector projects which SYFNID undertake at one time. Originally, eight sector specialists from as many fields were hired, and 13 different sectors were assigned among them. Since most of them were substantive field professionals, their motivation for commiting themselves to information work was thought to be greater if they were able to work in their own sphere. At the same time, there was some reluctance to make the difficult policy choice of selecting priority sectors. The choice of a few sectors as demonstration projects was difficult, given the considerable differences in key problems from one sector to another. The result was too many projects being undertaken at once and the development of too many expectations. Also, progress in the different sectors depended greatly on individual capacities, and some of the professionals considered themselves held back (since they worked in parallel on methodological tools) by the slower staff. Finally, it became apparent that a single Resident Adviser could not give adequate assistance to so many concurrent projects and that the programme had to be cut back. The sectors which are displaced for future attention are not set aside altogether as the sector specialists have been invited to participate in the commissions working on the area projects.

There has been a gradual evolution of the administrative structure of SYFNID following the lines of this programme, as shown in Figure III. The staff positions and logistical support have largely been financed from national funds, while the International Development Research Centre of Canada has contributed to the financing of costs of consultants, research and training.

The first two Directors of SYFNID were chosen for their administrative background and interest in leading the country in this pioneer endeavour. The present Director does have an information background (as Deputy Director of the National Institute of Statistics). As the familiarity of the staff with the information field has increased, and as programming and administrative functions have been sharpened in light of a constant evaluation of SYFNID's experience, the role of the Resident Adviser has gradually been reduced to conform to his most important task, that of lending technical advice to key projects. SYFNID has passed from a pilot project status to that of a regular Bolivian governmental programme, calling for technical and financial assistance from a variety of sources for its various projects.

Figure III. Structure of SYFNID

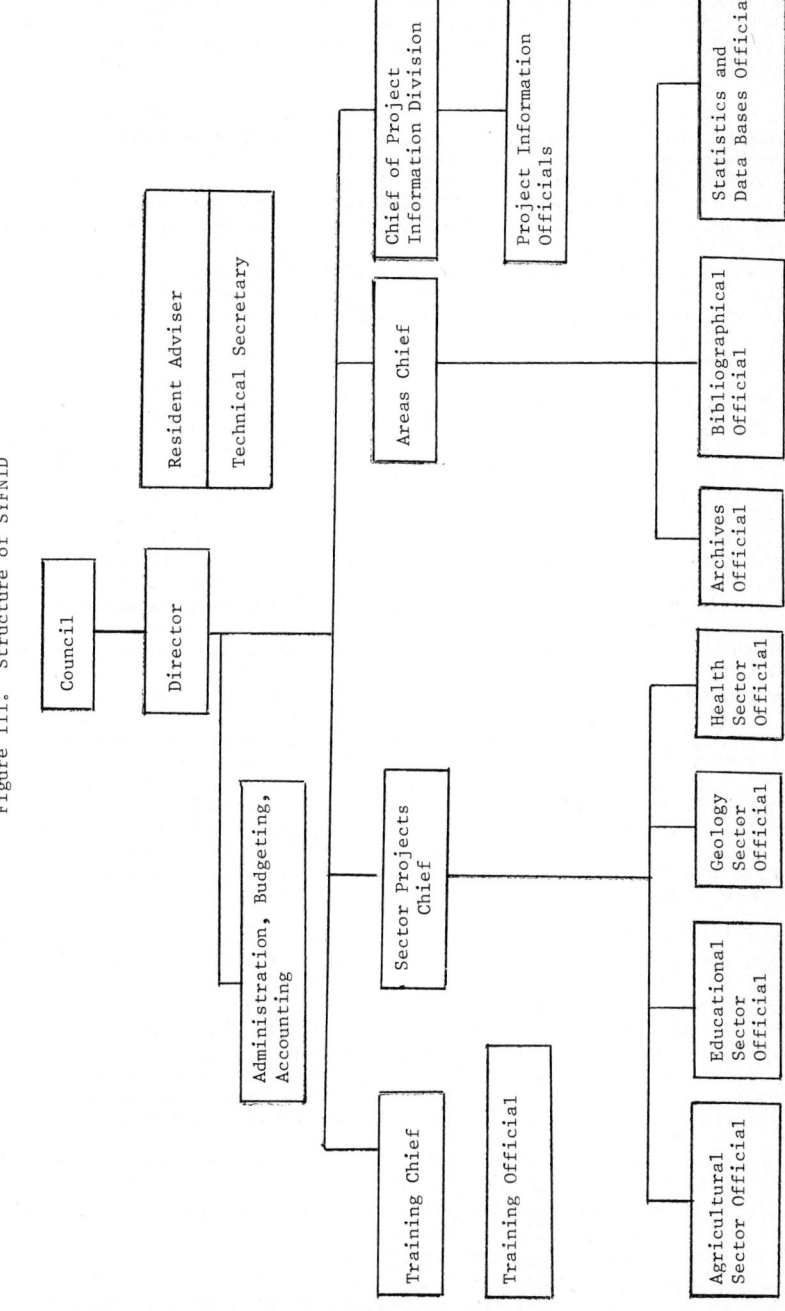

D. Specific characteristics of the Bolivian approach

Aside from the types of projects which are undertaken, there are other characteristics of the Bolivian approach which are worthwhile considering on a comparative basis.

(a) The Bolivian approach attempts to give balanced treatment to the problems of organizing and making accessible locally generated information, and to obtaining and disseminating technological information from outside the country. This compares with some African systems which tend to be concerned almost exclusively with local data gathering, and with some Latin American systems which, by emphasizing already organized documentation sources, tend naturally to favour foreign sources of information. In Bolivia, the organization of local information has been advanced through the reorganization of legal deposists, a more extensive preparation of the national bibliography, the extension of the work of the National Institute of Statistics to include the rationalization of statistical flows throughout the public administration sector (and not just data gathering for its own processing), the extension of the work of the National Computing Centre to include the organization of data for retrieval (and not just processing) and the organization of a plan of archival development. The organization of access to useful foreign information sources is reinforced through the development of specialized documentation centres, the union serials catalogue, deposit accounts, and other mechanisms.

(b) The Bolivian approach is user-oriented. Thus the studies of invisible colleges and other users' habits and requirements are as basic to the programming of SYFNID's activities as the studies of information flows and units and the national development plans. Another example is the work on standardization of classifications and codes, which is based on user information requirements in the first instance, rather than on the materials of present collections. This contrasts with the Kenyan methodology, which compares the results of the studies on data and data-handling by national institutions with projections of information requirements based on development goals.

(c) SYFNID places emphasis on conceptual and terminological integration and leaves the work on more complete forms of logical or physical integration to other institutions.[9/] This is consistent with the more bibliographically-oriented national systems of Latin America, and is less rigorous than what is sought by most statistically-oriented national systems in Africa and Latin America. This means that SYFNID works largely by negotiating a concensus among affected institutions, and at times delegating responsibilities to institutions which may or may not comply with expectations.

(d) If there is a bias regarding technological alternatives, the Bolivian approach attempts to bring more attention to manual and semi-automatic technologies for analyzing and processing data, in part to counterbalance the modern tendency to consider the computer as a panacea for information problems. It is not just a case of protecting labour-intensive work, which is a concern in Kenya, but of avoiding unnecessary expenditures in automated systems which at times are less efficient than manual systems in delivering up-to-date and pertinent information. The main point is to encourage the careful study and justification of needs before introducing new technologies.

[9/] Data for Development International Association, Data and Development, DFD, Marseille, France, 1978, pp. 118-21.

(e) As with the Kenyan system, the Bolivian approach is concerned both with supply-oriented systems and functional or problem-oriented systems.[10] However, to data more work has been carried out in SYFNID itself on data base and reference systems than on systems intended to respond to specific administrative decisions. SYFNID is anticipating system developments which could be supply-induced or demand-induced.[11] However, as with other Latin American systems, the emphasis tends to be on supply in the first instance, to assure a minimum offer of materials before encouraging greater demand for their use. SYFNID is also concerned with non-traceable as well as traceable sectors,[12] given that much of the important economic and social activity of the country is not regularly registered and data on such activities must be obtained in special surveys and studies.

(f) SYFNID has adopted a rather cautious approach with regard to two of its functions, both of which are assumed more actively by the Mexican system. One of these is the co-ordination of contacts with international information systems and bases. When implementing national systems of document-handling, integration into regional and international networks is certainly an important consideration. Given the serious problem at the international level of co-ordination of such systems and data bases which complicates the design choice for developing countries, SYFNID has prepared criteria for evaluating the manner by which Bolivia can participate most constructively in such international networks. The principle of balancing the advantages of international co-operation and national information requirements has been respected in contacts with UNEP/INFOTERRA, given the usefulness of relating that system's procedures to SYFNID's inventory of information units and flows,[13] and also in contacts with AGRINTER, following the advanced state of development of Bolivia's participation (through the Agricultural Ministry Library) in that regional network.[14]

The other function which needs to receive considerable attention in the future is the financing of new and expanding information units and systems. As the demand for such financing is much greater than the availability of national or international resources, the SYFNID Council will have to decide on the most promising projects to be aided. Otherwise, the assistance by SYFNID to a sector or programme requires that the sector or programme itself

---

[10] Op. cit., pp. 31-32.

[11] An example of a dynamic supply-incentive system, which uses information dissemination to generate user interest, is DOCPAL, the Latin American Population Documentation System, described in Notas de Poblacion: Revista Latinoamericana de Demografía, vol. 4, No. 10 (April 1976), pp. 95-110. Demand-incentive systems are based on user studies and respond to explicit user requirements.

[12] Republic of Kenya, Ministry of Finance and Planning, Central Bureau of Statistics, and Data for Development International Programme, "The data network in the Government of Kenya, phase 1: analysis of the present situation", revised April 1977, pp. 8-9.

[13] SYFNID, "Proposal for the regional organization of IRS in Latin America"; paper presented at the meeting of National Focal Points of IRS, Nairobi, November 1977; "Inventario de flujos y unidades de información", ACTUALIDADES, vol. 3, No. 3 (October 1977), pp. 19-22.

[14] Documentación e Información para el Desarrollo Agrícola, vol. vi, Nos. 3-4 (1978).

takes the initiative regarding funding.

(g) One of the most unique features of the Bolivian approach is the
emphasis placed on providing favourable conditions for information specialists
of different backgrounds to consult and work together. This is important with
respect to the system requirements of developing countries which do not fit
neatly into any single information specialization, but rather are of an
inter-disciplinary nature. Examples are a project control information retrieval
system which will produce bibliographies and statistical summary reports on
investment projects in the public sector, and an agricultural information
network which is concerned not only in bringing information of this sector under
bibliographical control, but also in facilitating the access to simplified forms
of this information by the agricultural producers. Such projects would ideally
merge concepts and techniques of documentation, statistics, computer science
and social communication.

(h) The success of the Bolivian approach is not only contingent upon
convincing the major interest groups in the country of the importance of a
national information system and on a realistic and coherent programming of the
implementation of this system, but upon adaptations of the strategy of
implementation to cultural and institutional realities. The Bolivians working
in and with the system are dedicated to adopting techniques which are suitable
for the country's development goals. It is also evident that the different
cultures of Bolivia have very distinct traditions of thought, with sharply
divergent points of view regarding what is acceptable or valid information
to represent an idea, fact or event. Fortunately, the values and perspectives
of Bolivia's various cultures are represented in the national public
administration and are present in the working commissions of SYFNID. It would
be counterproductive if those wishing to support the country in this
endeavour did not appreciate or understand the importance of this rich
cultural mixture or of the institutional traditions which are derived from it.

E. Conclusion

SYFNID has undertaken a monumental task and the unique Bolivian approach
to problems which are common to many developing countries deserves continuous
evaluation. This frank exposition of the problems of information in Bolivia
and the difficulties in dealing with these problems by means of the strategy
which has been evolving during the last $1\frac{1}{2}$ years, is a contribution towards a
dialogue among developing countries and a realistic appraisal of the challenge
ahead.

INFORMATION SYSTEMS IN PUBLIC ADMINISTRATION
D. Eade, J. Hodgson (editors)
North-Holland Publishing Company
© *DFD, 1981*

SETTING PRIORITIES FOR INFORMATION SYSTEMS DEVELOPMENT PROJECTS
IN PUBLIC ADMINISTRATION

Aarno Laihonen*

A. Introduction

The paper considers a systematic framework of priority setting for
information systems or information service development projects in public
administration. It does so by proposing a situation whereby a public body
or a non-profit organization produces or co-ordinates the production of a
great number of different information services to a great number of users.

The paper aims at a general framework or model which applies to priority
setting for different kinds of information services. Possible fields of
application of the general framework are development of library services,
development of the services of information and reference centres, directing
and priority setting of research programmes and development of national
statistical services.

In this paper the framework and principles presented are exemplified
by examining a case of priority setting of statistical development projects
by a central statistical authority in connexion with medium-term planning of
official statistics.

---

* Planning Officer, Central Statistical Office, Finland.

The general framework presented in the paper reflects the research work
carried out in the Central Statistical Office and especially the work of a
research project of the Finnish Academy, led by O.E. Niitamo.

B. The general framework

A public or non-profit body is presupposed whose task is directing the
production of certain kinds of information services at the national level. The
number of services and their users is assumed to be large.

The information services are produced free of charge or at prices which
do not reflect their actual cost. Thus, an ordinary supply-demand model is
not applicable in directing the production of these services.

The raison d'être of the directing body in pursuing its task is assumed
to be promoting the production of the information services in question in
accordance with the needs of the users, so that the services are produced
at the lowest possible cost to the society.

Thus, in order to pursue its task, the directing body has to identify
users of the information services, evaluate their needs and priorities and
assess the costs to the society of the production of the services needed.

Information is a commodity which has a limited value as such unless
used directly or indirectly to promote a user's ability to perform different
activities. The concept of need for information may therefore be defined as
follows: The user has a need for information if the use of it will improve
the results of his actions or provide better opportunities for action.

The demand for information, on the other hand, is a user's expressed desire
to acquire specific information. Thus, by definition, the need for information
does not necessarily require awareness on the part of the user. But the
demand presupposes conscious action, an expression of a desire.

The over-all social need of information cannot be evaluated safely on
the basis of the conscious needs of individual users; the directing body must
also continuously analyze the functions of society in order to find new
potential uses for the information concerned and evaluate the importance of
these uses for the functions through which the socio-economic goals are
attained.

Because users do not always have an unbiased conception of their real
needs, the demand is not necessarily part of the need. On the other hand,
the directing body is not capable of an unbiased assessment of the real needs
of users by its knowledge alone. That is why the supply of information does
not necessarily reflect the real need. The relation between need, demand
and supply at a certain point in time can be expressed as follows:

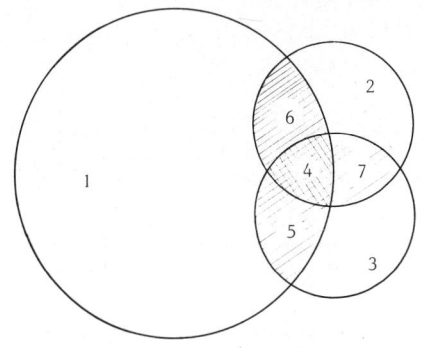

1 = need

2 = supply

3 = demand

4 = supply which satisfies both
      need and demand

5 = both need and demand exist,
      but there is no supply

6 = supply which corresponds to
      unconscious needs

7 = supply which satisfies biased
      demand

In the long run, the directing body should aim at adjusting the supply and
demand as near to the need (actual and potential) as possible while maximizing
the value of information within given resources.

Let us next consider the value of information. As was mentioned previously,
information is important to the user because it enhances opportunities for
action.

The value of information therefore is realized in the additional
benefits derived from users' activities when the information is
used.

The value of information depends not only on the properties of the information
itself, but also on the characteristics of its users, the use situations and the
nature of activities thus affected. In principle, evaluation of the value of a
piece of information requires examination of the whole chain:

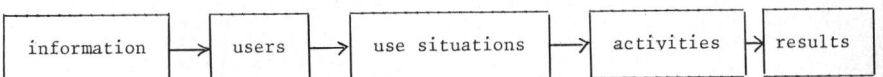

However, there is a tendency to over-emphasize the beginning of the chain
because of the difficulties in measuring and evaluating the effects of
information at the end of the chain. That is why it is seldom possible to
measure the financial benefits derived.

Often the only way is to evaluate the significance of the information on
more or less indirect and subjective grounds by the central properties of
information which affect its value. Such properties are for example, the
relevance of contents, timeliness, reliability, form, etc. These properties
are the utilities of information and the value of the information can be
considered as a function of these utilities.

Instead of evaluating the significance of the information directly on the
basis of these properties, an evaluation can be made easier by defining the

the value of information using the following formula:[1]

AVI = VPI − MU

AVI = the actual value of information

VPI = the value of "perfect",[2] optimal information

MU = deficiencies in the properties of the information

It is clearly easier to evaluate the deficiencies of the information (the lack of utilities) than all its useful properties. In practice it would suffice to examine the deficiencies of the most important properties which affect the value of the information.

It is impossible to measure the value of perfect information in financial terms. But the above-mentioned method can be used for a systematic, subjective evaluation of the relative benefits. The perfect information is then given the value 1, whereby the relative values of all the alternative imperfect pieces of information on the same object can be compared when the respective imperfections have been deducted from 1.

This so-called Bayesian approach is well suited to our purposes because it fits the concept of need defined earlier. As the reader may recall, need was defined from the point of view of the potential uses of information, which directly refers to the concept of perfect information.

The previous paragraphs have presented the basic definitions, assumptions and starting points on which the general framework for priority setting will be based. Because monetary measurements on the value of information cannot be made, the framework aims at helping in organizing and processing all the qualitative information and evaluations needed in making systematic decisions on priority setting. The aim is not to mechanize the decision-making process, but to provide the kind of conceptual framework and means which will make the choices easier and more systematic.

The ultimate aim is to enable priority setting of individual development projects which concern individual information services. Hereafter, an individual information service is called an information product or, simply, a product.

The development needs of information services ultimately concern individual products and more specifically the central properties of the products. Identification of these central properties for the type of information concerned is the first step in outlining the priority setting framework.

However, it is assumed that the number of individual products is large; therefore the number of products times the number of central properties is very

---

1/ The same kind of approach in information evaluation has been suggested by for example, Roman R. Andrus, in "Approaches to information evaluation", MSU Business Topics (Summer 1971).

2/ Information is perfect when its properties (relevance timeliness, form, reliability, etc.) are optimal from the point of view of all potential uses.

large. It is obvious that an over-all examination of development needs cannot be managed at product level. The products should be aggregated, that is, an appropriate product classification is required. This classification has to be a classification of subject matter, which is the principal dimension of information. Forming of a proper subject matter classification for the type of information concerned is the second step in outlining the framework.

The development needs are ultimately drawn from users' demands on improved products on the one hand, and from the analyses of the potential uses of information on the other. As the number of users was assumed to be large, it is obvious that an over-all analysis of the development needs cannot cover in detail all the actual and potential users. Therefore an appropriate classification of the actual and potential users of information is needed.

It must be borne in mind that the forming of the user classification implicitly includes weighing the significance of the users and groups of users. For this reason, special attention must be paid in forming the classification and the criteria used therein. Forming of an appropriate user classification for the information concerned is the third step in outlining the framework.

The significance of information, at the moment of its use, depends on how it affects the results of users' activities. This on the other hand depends on various characterisitics of the use situations as was pointed out earlier. In order to systematize the examination of the importance of different products to different users, an appropriate classification of central purposes of use which adequately reflects the main features of use situations, is needed. Forming of an appropriate purpose of use classification for information concerned is the fourth step in outlining the framework.

Having examined all the elements of the framework needed to effect a systematic analysis of development needs, the analysis will proceed as follows.

The Bayesian approach previously outlined is applied by first putting the subject matter classes of the information in order of priority according to their potential social significance. This is done by ranking the groups of users according to the social significance of their activities and to the significance to them of the information concerned. The priorities of the user groups are then used with the analysis of the actual and potential uses of information in putting the subject matter classes in order of priority according to their potential social significance.

In the second phase, the development needs are analyzed by examining the deficiencies of the central properties of products by subject matter class from the point of view of their optimal state. The development needs are then put in order of priority using the priority order of the subject matter classes.

The order of priority the development needs forms the basis for setting the order of priority of individual development projects. This happens by comparing uniform project descriptions with the set priorities of development needs. The final order of priority will be reached by taking into account the costs of the projects. Uniform project descriptions would include information on the development plans in a form which is as comparable with the information from development need analysis as possible. Creating the format for the project descriptions completes the fifth step in the outlining of the general framework. The whole process of priority setting is illustrated in figure IV.

Figure IV. Priority setting process of the development projects

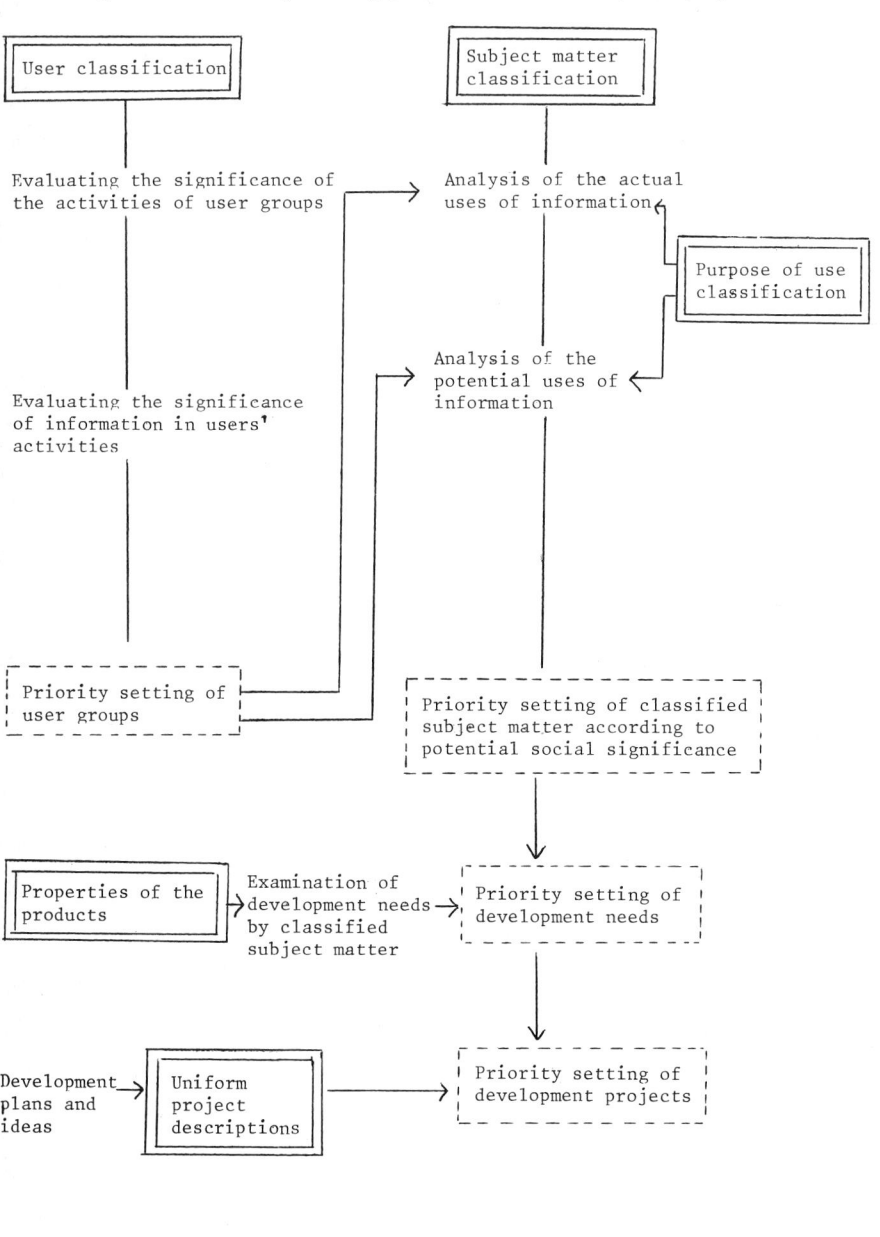

            = conceptual framework
- - - - - - - - - -   = priority setting decisions

C. Application to the setting of priorities in the national statistical service

In the 1970s, the over-all planning of government or official statistics gained ground in several countries. This trend stems from the growing tendency to regard the production of economic and social statistics as a whole. The development of this whole in a balanced way, by taking into account the interaction of its various parts and functions, is considered of increasing importance, even on an international level.[3/]

Finland is one of the pioneers in the over-all planning of government statistics on account of the medium-term planning system introduced in 1971 called Programme for the Development of Government Statistics, which system was compiled annually by the Central Statistical Office for the following five years.

The application of the general framework outlined in the previous section will be treated next in connexion with the medium-term planning of the official statistics. The examination of the application is made within the framework of the Programme for the Development of Government Statistics. The Programme is currently being fundamentally revised in Finland. Actually, some of the basic ideas of the general framework developed here will be tested in the context of the Programme revision. In its revised form the Programme will be drafted at three-year intervals and the needs and guidelines for the development of government statistics will be laid down for the next five years. It will further comprise an annual report for the follow-up of the implementation of the Programme. The report will be based on current actions and on the medium-term plans of the statistical bodies (including the Central Statistical Office itself).[4/]

In the context of the annual report, the development projects of different statistical bodies will be put in order of priority. This priority setting aims to affect the implementation and budgeting decisions concerning these projects.

The concepts of value and benefits of statistical information, which are vital for the evaluation of its significance, will be examined first. One of the properties of statistical data is that in use it does not wear physically, even though its significance as a function of time usually diminishes. Further, a particular branch of statistics comprises not only the annual or other periodical production of statistical data at a certain point in time, but also the previously produced data, that is, the whole data base of the branch up to that time.

When estimating whether it is worth starting to produce a new branch of statistics, it is not enough to evaluate the significance of the annual production of the branch only, but of the whole stock of products (time series) to be produced. The value of the branch of statistics is related to this stock.

3/ This view is reflected for example, in a United Nations document, "Statistical organization: the organization of national statistical services: a review of major issues", report of the Secretary-General (E/CN.3/495), 15 June, 1976.

4/ The Programme for the Development of Government Statistics in Finland aims at directing all the statistics produced by about 30 different governmental bodies. The revision of the Programme as mentioned above aims at linking it more closely to the ordinary annual governmental medium-term planning process. This process is based on annual medium-term resource and action plans of all separate government bodies.

When the statistical data is actually used, its value is realized as benefit to the user. Benefit is thus a flow concept. The following mathematical relation could be assumed between benefit and the value, if the value of a new branch of statistics is examined at a certain point in time before its implementation.[5/]

$$A(0) = \left[\sum_{t=0}^{n} (1+i)^{-t} \right] \cdot \int_{0}^{\theta_k} \lambda_k(t,q)\,dq$$

$A_k(0)$ = the value of the statistics k at time point 0

n = the period during which the branch of statistics k is produced in the same form and with the same content

i = the discount rate of the benefits

θ_k = a period of time when older data of statistics k is no longer useful

$\lambda k\ (t,q)$ = the benefits of statistics k at point q of the data produced at point t (a decreasing function of q)

Further, it can be assumed that $\lambda k(t,q) = f\ (p_1, p_2,,,p_m)$ whereby p_1, p_2, ... p_m are properties or utilities of the statistics produced at point t and used at point q.

Such properties of statistical information are for example:

(a) Contents (relevance, coverage);

(b) Timeliness;

(c) Reliability (unbiasedness and statistical accuracy);

(d) Form (the suitability of the form in which statistics are delivered to users);

(e) Harmony (the comparability and conceptual combinability of the information with other statistical information);

(f) Flexibility (the technical opportunities for combining and rearranging the data);

(g) Regionality.

These properties are the utilities of statistical information, and the value of statistical information is a function of these utilities.

The development needs of statistics are thoroughly analysed every third year and entered into the Programme as guidelines for the development of government statistics. The annual follow-up report of the Programme registers its implementation at project level and a check of current development needs is also made. In conjunction with the follow-up report, the development projects are given an order of priority in order to direct the on-going co-ordination

---

5/ It is clear that the formula has only conceptual value because of operational difficulties.

activities of the Central Statistical Office with other statistical bodies.
The priority setting of the development projects is based on the Programme
and the analyses of development needs made in conjunction with it.

When the Programme is being drafted, the development needs are put into
order of priority, which again provides the basis for the priority setting of
the projects. The situation is clarified in figure V.

Figure V. Priority setting in conjunction with medium-term
planning of official statistics

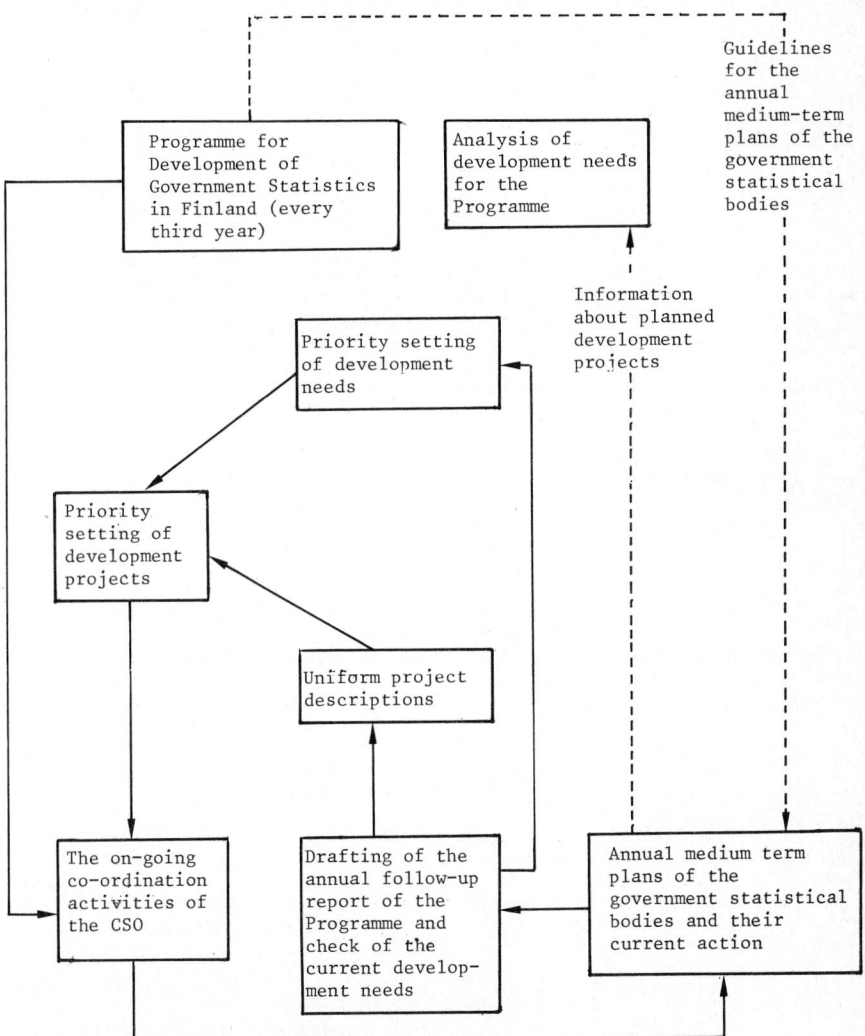

If necessary and on the basis of the background analyses, the priority setting of the development needs can be made at greater depth than as presented in the Programme itself.

Classification of the subject matter or groups of statistics and user classification, which could be used in the over-all need analysis, are described in annexes I and II.6/ The classification of the purposes of use of statistics could be as follows:

    (a) Decision-making;

    (b) Planning;

    (c) Follow-up;

    (d) Research and development work;

    (e) Teaching and education;

    (f) General information.

The general framework for priority setting outlined in the previous section can be applied as follows. At first the groups of statistics (see annex I) are put in order of priority according to their potential social significance. Then, in order to find out central development needs, the extent to which the central properties of the products in each group of statistics satisfy the needs of the users is examined. Finally, the development needs are put in order of priority by groups of statistics, using the ranking of the potential significance of these groups.

The groups of statistics can be put in order of priority, basing upon their potential significance, in the following way:

    (a) The significance of various user groups is evaluated on the ground of the social significance of their activities and the general role of statistics in those activities;

    (b) The actual and potential uses of different groups of statistics are examined. This is done as follows:

      (i)   The most important user groups for each group of statistics are identified. How large a share of each group uses, or could potentially use, the statistics in question must also be ascertained;

    (ii)   The purpose and level of use, or potential use, by groups of statistics and groups of users is examined, as well as the share of statistical information in relation to other information;

    (c) On this basis the groups of statistics are put in order of priority according to their potential social significance.

After this it will be evaluated how well the central properties of statistical products (contents, timeliness, etc.) satisfy the needs of user

---

   6/ The subject matter classification of the kind presented in annex I has actually been used in the Programme since 1971.

groups by examining the deficiencies of these properties from the point of view of their optimal state.

Due to the fact that the priority setting of development needs is being examined in connexion with the medium-term planning, the changes in information needs over the planning period should also be taken into account.

The results of the analysis can be drawn together and presented in matrix form, in which the development needs of groups of statistics are described by properties of statistical products. Based on this résumé and on the priorities given to the potential significance of groups of statistics, the following decisions about resource allocation and priority settings can be made:

(a) Resource allocation between ongoing statistical production and development work. This decision can be based on the total number and importance of development needs revealed by the analysis and on the general financial (budget) possibilities during the planning period in question;

(b) Resource allocation between development work for separate products and functional development work. This is done by examining the distribution of the development needs between content and other properties of statistical products as well as the general concentration of development needs on groups of statistics on the one hand and on the properties of statistics on the other;

(c) Development needs can be put in order of priority by groups of statistics with the help of the priorities, given the potential significance of the groups of statistics and by drawing together the development needs of different properties within each group of statistics;

(d) The needs for functional development work can be put in order of priority by drawing together the needs for development using the properties of statistical products. When drawn together, needs should be weighed against the priorities of respective groups of statistics.

The situation can be illustrated by the scheme set out in figure VI. The exposition given above on development needs can be called an over-all need analysis of official statistics. Information about development needs can be gathered in different ways. However, it is essential that the information is based both on users' knowledge of their own conscious needs and on the analysis of possible potential uses of statistics made by producers. Further, it is essential from the point of view of systematic priority setting that gathered information on needs is examined within a systematic framework.

The systematic and active part of gathering information on needs is composed of:

(a) Examination of the present use of the statistical products;

(b) Investigation of society, its structures and information flows in order to ascertain the potential uses;[7]

---

[7] This kind of investigation is realized for example in the development of systems of statistics (system of national accounts, framework for social and demographic statistics, system of environmental statistics, etc.).

Figure VI.   Decisions about resource allocation and priorities
             made within the priority setting framework

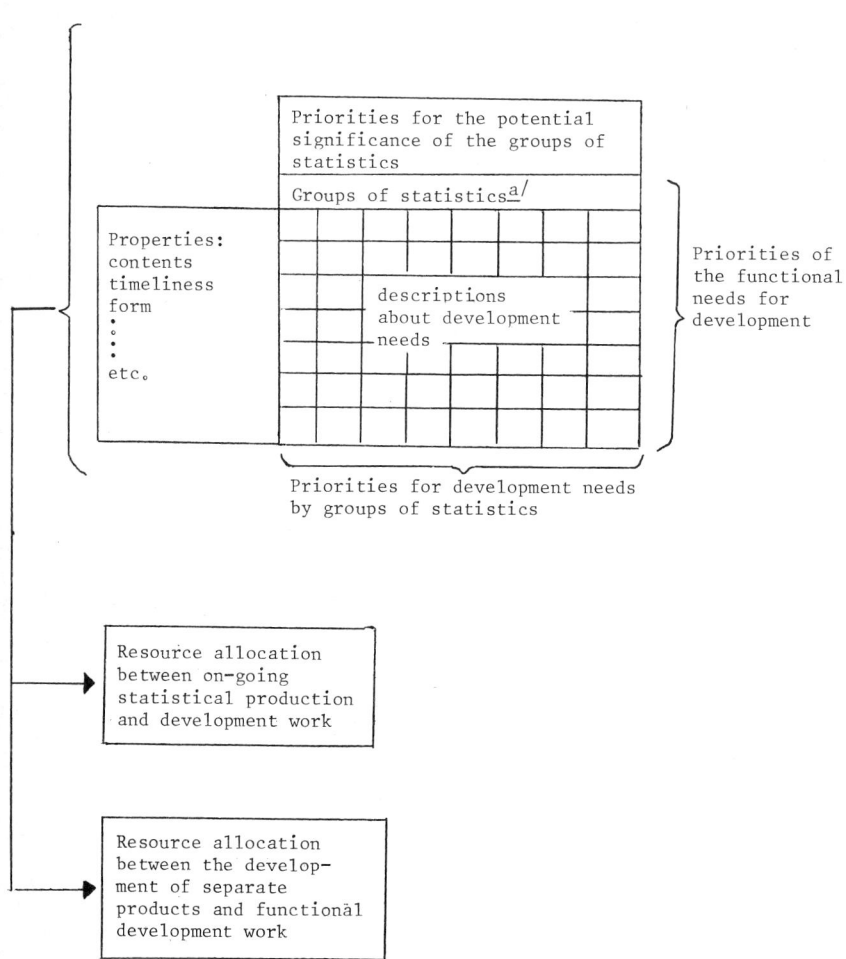

Priorities for the potential
significance of the groups of
statistics

Groups of statistics[a]

Properties:
contents
timeliness
form
etc.

descriptions
about development
needs

Priorities of
the functional
needs for
development

Priorities for development needs
by groups of statistics

Resource allocation
between on-going
statistical production
and development work

Resource allocation
between the develop-
ment of separate
products and functional
development work

a/ See annex I.

(c)   Inquiries for needs directed towards groups of users.

Further, information about development needs can be acquired:

(a) By following the stands taken by various interest groups on statistics and statistical policy in the mass media;

(b) By investigating the information policy programmes of the various interest groups;

(c) By following the work of government committees, boards and working groups, and by ascertaining the demands made by them concerning production of statistics.

Finally, the development projects are put in order of priority in the following way. When drafting the follow-up report of the Programme, uniform project descriptions of the current and planned development projects for the Programme period are made. These project descriptions are compared with the development needs in connexion with the Programme. In this way, the relative importance of the different projects can be evaluated. The final priority order will be reached by taking into account the costs of the projects.

The uniform project descriptions would include at least the following information:

(a) The most important users and purposes of use of the product under renewal or the new product introduced (for a product project);

(b) Exposition of the deficiencies in the properties of the products (contents, timeliness, reliability, etc.) that can be removed by the project;

(c) The costs of implementation of the project.

D. Conclusions

The general framework of setting priorities for information systems development projects was developed in conjunction with the development of planning methods of the national statistical service. However, the basic principles of the framework should be applicable for development of different kinds of information services with similar features, that is, free service with a great number of different information products and a great number of users.

The main feature of the framework presented is that it enables systematic handling, organizing and also utilizing so-called soft or qualitative information in decision making, planning and development work in a situation where quantitative planning methods cannot be used or are insufficient.

Annex I

The classification of statistics in the programme for the development of official statistics in Finland

1. General social and demographic conditions

2. Population

3. Labour force and working conditions

Annex I (continued)

The classification of statistics in the programme for the
development of official statistics in Finland

4.   Health

5.   Education

6.   Research

7.   Culture, leisure and the use of time

8.   Social services

9.   Judicial system

10. Social participation

11. Housing

12. The income, consumption and wealth of households

13. Other data materials on living conditions

14. General economic conditions (national accounting, etc.)

15. Agriculture, forestry, fishing and hunting

16. Industry, mining and supply of energy

17. Construction

18. Trade, hotel and catering trade

19. Transport

20. Financing, insurance and real estate

21. Social and personal services

22. Other statistics and data materials related to economic life

23. Environment (environment statistical system, etc.)

24. Other statistics and data materials related to environment

Annex II

Classification of users of statistics

1.   General administration of state

1.1. Parliament, government, parliamentary committees

1.2. Ministries

1.3. Central offices, governmental bodies

2.   Regional administration

2.1. Regional administration of state

Annex II (continued)

Classification of users of statistics

2.2. Regional planning associations

3. Communes and communal organizations, local administration

3.1. Communal organizations

3.2. Communes and local administration

4. Educational and research institutes

4.1. Universities and self-governing research institutes

4.2. Other educational institutes

5. Enterprises and their organizations

5.1. Organizations of enterprises

5.2. Financial institutions

5.3. Other corporate enterprises

6. Private persons and their organizations

6.1. Political parties and party organizations

6.2. Trade unions

6.3. Other organizations and private persons

7. Means of communications

8. International organizations, foreign countries and other foreign users

INFORMATION SYSTEMS IN PUBLIC ADMINISTRATION
D. Eade, J. Hodgson (editors)
North-Holland Publishing Company
© DFD, 1981

AN APPROACH TO THE DESIGN OF NATIONAL INFORMATION SYSTEMS
FOR DEVELOPING COUNTRIES

Martin J. Shio*

A. Introduction

The information revolution has created problems for both the developing and developed world and has resulted in a number of countries developing new information processing institutions and systems to cope with the unprecedented quantities of new information. It has also been recognized that scientific and technological information constitutes an important resource for economic and social development comparable to other major categories of resources such as money, labour and capital. It is this awareness that has prompted both developed and developing countries to put considerable effort into establishing national information systems. International organizations such as the United Nations are playing a significant role in encouraging countries to establish national information systems. The United Nations efforts have been supplemented by those of the regional inter-governmental organizations such as the former East African Community, the Economic Community of West African States (ECOWAS), the European Communities and the International Centre for Scientific and Technical Information in Moscow. So far, many countries in the developed world have been able to establish some sort of a national information system. These systems have provided valuable information to decision makers. Despite these successes in the developed world, very few developing countries have been able to establish national information systems. Apart from a few pilot projects which have been sponsored by the United Nations Education, Scientific and Cultural Organization (UNESCO), there has not been any meaningful progress and in fact it is now believed that much more effort is required before the concept of national information systems for developing countries will be realized.

* Consultant in electronic data processing, East African Management Institute, Arusha, United Republic of Tanzania.

B. Problems hindering the development of national information systems in developing countries

Despite the potential and the reported success of the development of national information systems in developing countries, there has been very poor progress. Several factors which have contributed to this lack of success are described below.

1. Lack of national information policies

Although many developing countries have accepted the idea of setting up national information systems, in practice very few countries have taken any positive action to support such a move. There has been a general lack of national information policy to govern the design and implementation of these systems, resulting in many unco-ordinated and futile efforts. In a few cases where Governments have attempted to draw up national information policies, the success has not been very encouraging. In certain instances government policies have been rejected by the participants concerned because it is alleged that the policies have been imposed without consultation. Information systems that have been designed without co-ordination are usually inefficient and wasteful of resources. In one country for example there are four information centres which are based in different government ministries, but there exists a very limited amount of co-ordination between these four centres. There is a great deal of duplication of effort which could otherwise have been used to foster the development of a national system. Such duplication would not have occurred had there been a national policy to govern the development of information systems.

2. Failure of the designers to identify the information needs of the users

Very often some of the national information systems have been designed without first determining the information needs of the users (a pre-requisite of an acceptable system), and have been rendered useless by not being able to supply those needs. Determining information needs is not an easy task because the users for whom a system is being designed are sometimes not even sure of what information they want. Designers themselves may therefore try to determine user needs, which does not always result in accurate requirements. Systems so designed will more than likely provide information that is neither relevant nor useful.

3. Lack of proper equipment for acquiring and storing information

Development of information systems assumes extensive use of computers and it is believed that an effective and efficient information system requires advanced computer hardware and software not readily available in many developing countries. Those who favour extensive use of computers base their argument on the ability of the computer to collect, store, process and distribute data and information at great speed. A national information system would certainly require quite a large data base which would be very difficult to operate without the help of a computer. But even a well-designed system's usefulness can be diminished because of delays in processing the data, resulting in much of the information being out of date and of little value to the users.

Adequate software should also be provided to support national systems. Although software is sometimes too expensive for some developing countries, international organizations such as the International Development Research Centre, the International Labour Organization, etc. have very powerful software which is usually available free of charge to developing countries. Unfortunately, some developing countries are not aware of these free packages.

4. Poor dissemination of the available information to the users

Dissemination of available information to users is inadequate, either because there are no appropriate means or the channels are poorly designed. For example, one developing country with a very good national agriculture information system finds itself serving only a very small portion of the farmers in the country because of poor dissemination techniques. Much of the dissemination of agriculture information is done through a technical journal published within the country. The circulation of this journal is restricted to the rich land holders who are the minority. The information published in the journal is often irrelevant or above the head of the common farmer who might not be able to read, let alone comprehend. Some of the articles are of use only to the large-scale farmers whose information requirements are very different from those of the small farmer. One half of an issue for example was devoted to discussing various aspects of combine harvesters. The common farmer has not even seen one.

Another dissemination technique commonly used in agriculture information systems is to use extension officers to travel to the rural areas and pass on agriculture information to the farmers. A recently conducted study on the usefulness of this technique has revealed a gap in education between the common farmer and the extension officer so large as to preclude useful communication.

Associated with the problem of dissemination is the problem of documentation. Some developing countries are losing research findings because they are not documented anywhere. Those countries that have tried to document their findings have later found it difficult to retrieve them because of inadequate filing techniques. This further complicates a dissemination problem which is already acute in developing countries.

5. Present national information systems are catering for elite scientist groups

Too frequently we hear of information systems being developed solely for scientific and technical information. Most people in developing countries cannot make good use of such information. A common feature in many developing countries is that the majority of the population is rural; they depend mainly on agriculture or on agro-based cottage industries. This means that sophisticated scientific and technical information will not meet their needs. National information systems are sometimes regarded merely as being of help to a few elite scientist groups to which the common man has limited access. The information requirements of an average farmer are far different from those elite scientists.

6. Control measures and evaluative criteria have not been included in the design of national information systems

Developing countries are not by definition the richest group. They have the most serious financial problems and obviously want the best return from any investment. Many information systems have not been easy to evaluate and no cost-benefit analysis has been possible. This problem of evaluation is also common in the developed world. Dickson admits that:

> "Other than few non-operational approaches there is no way
> to evaluate the information provided by the system in relation to
> the cost of systems development and operation." [1]

---

[1] G.W. Dickson, "Management information – decision systems", Business Horizons, December 1968.

Further problems associated with cost-benefit analysis for information systems include incomplete identification of all alternatives, cost accounting problems, problems with assigning benefits, the cost of performing cost-benefit analysis and the difficulty of simple realities such as the political and social environment surrounding the analysis. As has been indicated, most national information systems have a number of pitfalls which have led to a number of failures, thereby contributing to the reluctance of some developing countries to try to establish such systems. The point to appreciate is that information systems must be properly designed if they are to be successful. In the following pages a number of recommendations are suggested which it is believed if followed will help developing countries to design workable national information systems and enable those countries to reap the potentials thereof. The recommendations are based on the author's experience in designing a national agriculture information system. However, it should be pointed out that these suggestions should not be taken as a panacea for all problems in the development of national information systems. The economic, social and political conditions in each country will more or less dictate the approach that each country will follow.

C.   Recommendations

There is an urgent need for developing countries to set up national information systems policy

Information systems activities and services in any country should be co-ordinated at a national level. This means that each country should have its own national policy and body for governing the development of information systems. The reasons for having a national body have been stated in a UNESCO document as follows:

"Countries, particularly developing countries, are in great need of national programmes to guide the development of their information service infrastructure (manpower information resources, delivery systems, libraries, etc.). A national focal point is essential to the planning, co-ordinating and promoting of infrastructure development. A national focal point is essential for the co-ordination of sectoral information resources and services."

What then should be the main aims of a national policy? Artheron proposes some general aims:

(a) Ensure optimum accumulation of knowledge in science and technology economics and social sciences in order to achieve national objectives for the betterment of society;

(b) Ensure the availability of adequate information for decisions for management and for policy both in government and private enterprise;

(c) Focus the attention of Governments and private organizations on the problems of information availability and use;

(d) Provide information services relevant to present needs, together with a capability for developing services to meet the future needs of generators, processors, disseminators and users of information;

(e) Promote national and international co-operation on the exchange of information and expertise.[2]

A national policy for the development of information systems designed along such lines is likely to be very efficient. Once the national body for governing the development of information systems has been established, the next task is to carry out an analysis of the priorities in the development of information systems. These priorities should reflect the economic, social and scientific considerations of the particular country. Highest priority should be given to information gaps needed for solving important development problems. There is no one model that can be suggested for the determination of priorities but an examination of the priorities drawn up for an Indian national science information policy in 1973 may help in the determination.

Priority List for an Indian national science information policy

1. Natural resources information and data

2. Meteorological and atmostpheric information and data

3. Rural and urban development planning information

4. Engineering and industrial information

5. Council of Scientific and Industrial Research complex; information facilities upgrading

6. National Medical Library facilities upgrading

7. Patent Information Centre

8. Statistical Information Centre

9. Promotion of information technology

10. Augmenting facilities for education and training in information science and technology

Information requirements should be clearly determined at all levels as a prerequisite for a workable national information system

If we accept the proposition that the aim of any national information system is to provide the various groups in a country with the right information that will enable them to make the right decision that will facilitate economic development, then a prerequisite for designing a national information system is the identification of national information requirements. Once the national priorities have been established as outlined above, a survey of the specific needs of the various categories should take into consideration the present information needs of the users, the present and estimated figures of potential users, and their classification according to qualification and specialization. This classification is essential because a global system may not be able to satisfy the needs of the group.

Assessing the information requirements of the users is a time-consuming and complex task. Usually a comprehensive process of analytical interaction

---

[2] P. Atherton, Handbook for Information Systems and Services (Paris, UNESCO, 1977).

between users, information systems specialists, statisticians and economists will help in determining the information requirements and contribute to the design of a system that will be able to provide the required information. This should be followed by a critical analysis of existing information and information flows with the aim of pointing out the main problems faced by data producers and information users.

Avoid doing too much too quickly

Many developing countries, fascinated with the idea of national information systems, have embarked on projects that are too ambitious. Very often some of these projects have been abandoned or have taken too long to complete; the sponsors have sometimes lost hope or have not been patient enough to wait for the final results. To avoid these problems we should follow Axelrod's advice by "moving the mountain one teaspoonful at a time", that is, little by little[3/]. The aim should be to design a minimum, easily attainable system that has the possibility of producing quick and significant results. This minimum system should be chosen in such a way that it will be indicative of the social situation and take into consideration the priorities that will have been established earlier. The systems designer will therefore be able to satisfy the financial sponsors of the project while gaining the confidence of the users.

There should be efficient dissemination methods

If an information system is to be effective it must have efficient methods of disseminating the information that has been acquired and stored. A prerequisite for effective information dissemination is the establishment of a national documentation centre. A national documentation centre is likely to encourage the publication of the results of most of the research work conducted in many of the developing countries. This would further ensure the co-ordination of data centres and library services. The main functions of a documentation centre would include:

(a) Leading the user towards the information source he needs or acquiring information not readily available;

(b) Keeping an up-to-date inventory of all research projects carried out in the country.

A documentation centre with these aims would provide a very useful starting point for proper dissemination of national information. Information dissemination for the elite scientist groups is usually not a problem because these groups are adequately catered for through various scientific and technical journals that already exist in many developing countries. The main problem is getting vital information to the rural areas. As was indicated earlier, the majority of the people in developing countries live in rural areas. These are the people to whom the information systems should cater. Several

---

3/ Axelrod, "14 rules for building an MIS", Journal of Advertising Research, June 1970.

techniques have been used by some developing countries, among them the use of extension officers to maintain contact with the rural population. The Government of Tanzania, for example, has established regional agriculture extension officer posts for the purpose of recommending new agricultural techniques to the farmers in the rural areas. The Government has also tried to establish direct contact between farmers and researchers by means of "the field day". On this day farmers come to the research station and see for themselves the developments that are being made. These techniques have proved to be quite successful and there is no reason why they should not also be successful in other developing countries with features similar to those of Tanzania.

Further efforts to reach the common man in the rural areas should be explored through the use of radio and other communication techniques. The Government of Rwanda, for example, has embarked on a number of radio programmes aimed at giving farmers technical agricultural information and advice; these 90 minute programmes are broadcast weekly. The programmes are prepared by the Ministry of Agriculture in collaboration with the Ministry of Broadcasting. This technique is proving very useful now that radio sets are so easily affordable. The experience of various countries is the use of other dissemination techniques should prove valuable.

It is believed that these recommendations will be useful to developing countries in designing national information systems that will be efficient and appropriate.

D. Conclusions

As has been seen from the experiences of the developed world, national information systems have a great deal of potential for stimulating social and economic development but many developing countries have not been able to develop them. Those that have tried have not always been successful. A number of reasons have been given for this poor rate of success, some of which have been examined in this paper. It is hoped that the recommendations given will go some way towards solving some of the problems. Many will realize that blanket-wide recommendations would not suffice; the social and economic conditions of each country should dictate which of the recommendations are applicable.

A much more effective way of dealing with these problems would be to carry out studies in each country which would result in appropriate recommendations. The pilot projects for the development of national information systems now being sponsored by UNESCO are providing useful insights. Other international organizations should follow UNESCO's example and sponsor similar pilot projects in developing countries. The results of these pilot projects would not only be useful to the countries concerned but would also provide valuable experiences from which other developing countries could benefit.

For those developing countries having difficulty initiating development of national information systems on their own, either because of lack of personnel or reluctance to accept the concept, it is suggested that a government agency be set up that would be charged with the task of guiding, stimulating and co-ordinating the development of information systems and services. This assistance could come from countries in the developed world and from international organizations.

This is not an easy task and a great deal of effort is needed before developing countries can succeed in developing their own national informatio systems. It is hoped that if the recommendations are followed, and help is forthcoming from developed countries and international organizations, the task will succeed.

INFORMATION SYSTEMS IN PUBLIC ADMINISTRATION
D. Eade, J. Hodgson (editors)
North-Holland Publishing Company
© *DFD, 1981*

PROJECT NIDAS: DEVELOPMENT OF AN
INTEGRATED DATA SYSTEM IN MALAYSIA

Kamal Salih*

A. Background

Since 1976, the Centre for Policy Research (CPR) at Universiti Sains
Malaysia has been conducting a three-year pilot project to develop a national
integrated data system (NIDAS) for the Malaysian Government. Its basic aim was
to demonstrate the technical, administrative and financial feasibility of an
information system for public administration at various levels of government,
as well as of a data management system for planning, monitoring and evaluation
of development by the central and operating agencies involved in the
implementation of Malaysia's development plans under the New Economic Policy
(Outline Perspective Plan, 1970-1990). In its development phase, NIDAS is part
of the five year plan itself, aimed at improving the administrative machinery
for planning and implementation (Third Malaysia Plan, 1976-1980, p.267).

The pilot project, undertaken in northern Peninsula Malaysia covering the
State of Penang and two administrative districts in the neighbouring states of
Perak and Kedah (see figure VII for the study area), is being developed under
the aegis of the Socio-economic Research and General Planning Unit (GPU) of thd
Prime Minister's Department. An initial allocation of 1.56 million Malaysian
dollars ($US 1.00 = $M 2.22, approximately), was made which after the mid-term
review of the project was increased to $M 2.2 million (Mid-term Review, Third
Malaysia Plan, 1979). A number of government agencies have participated in the
pilot project which is monitored by a Steering Committee which consists of these
participating agencies and is chaired by the Director-General of the GPU. The
plan is that, after submission of the final report and a briefing for the
National Action Council, which includes Cabinet Ministers, scheduled for late
September this year, the NIDAS pilot system will be handed over in its entirety
to the Implementation and Co-ordination Unit (ICU) of the Prime Minister's
Department, and extended to the rest of the country after the Cabinet gives its
decision to go ahead. The full implementation of NIDAS over the Fourth
Malaysia Plan (1981-85) will then be co-ordinated by a new Steering Committee
headed by the ICU which will probably consist of operating agencies and of
other potential users of the system.

The concept of NIDAS was developed in the Centre in the last quarter of
1975, arising from discussions concerning the enormous amount of data generated
in various CPR projects then being conducted, namely the MADA/USM Land Tenure
Study and the UDA/USM Urban Land Ownership Study. The initial impetus to

---

* Centre for Policy Research, Universiti Sains Malaysia

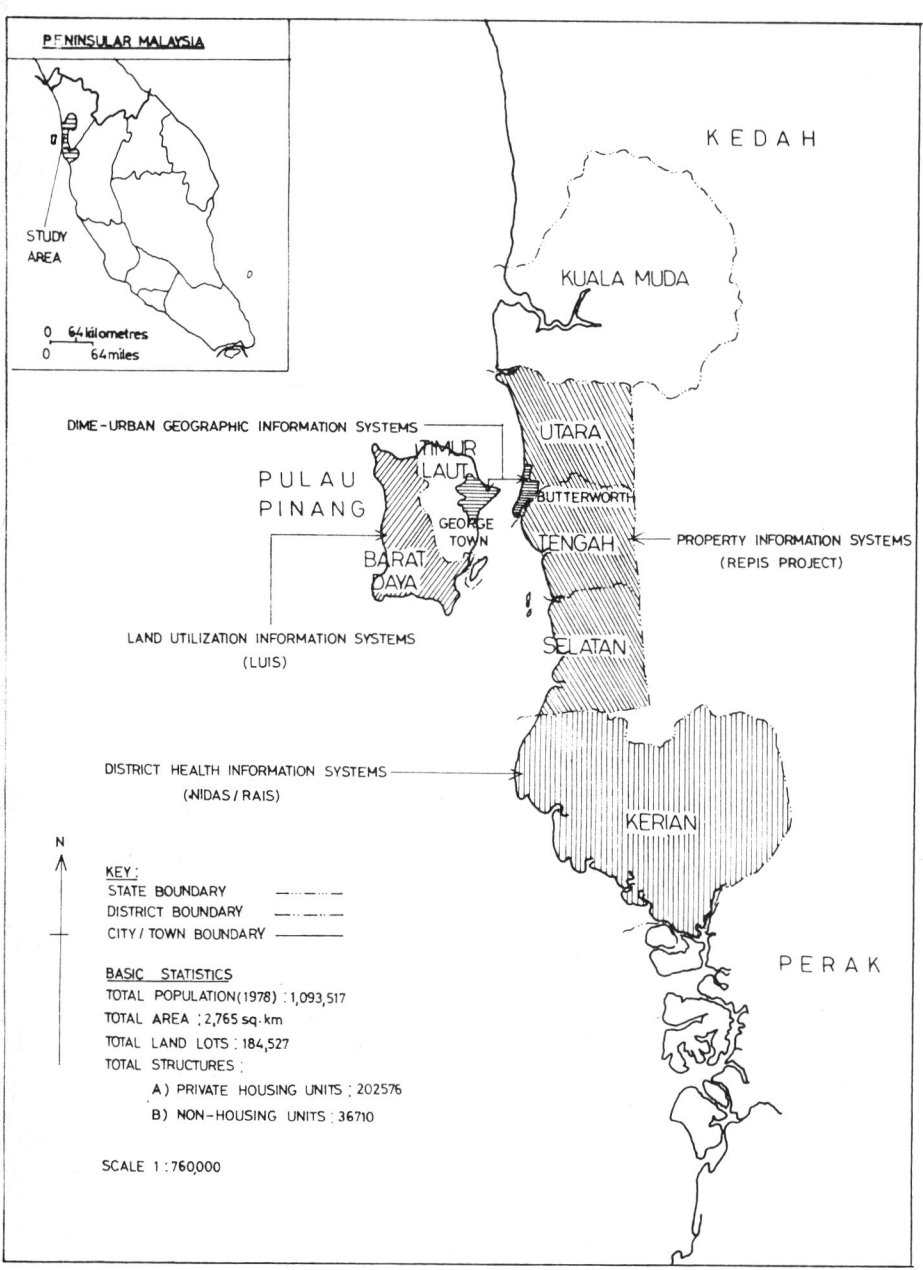

Figure VII. NIDAS Pilot Study area and location of subsystems –
State of Penang, Districts of Kuala Muda (Kedah) and Kerian (Perak)

mobilize this experience and to devise an information system for planning
purposes, particularly in relation to the needs of the New Economic Policy, came
from consideration of data requirements of the Project on Evaluation of Regional
Policy in Malaysia. The whole idea, encouraged by discussions with the then
Ministry of General Planning and Socio-economic Research, culminated in a
proposal submitted to the Ministry for the development of a national integrated
data system (see NIDAS report N-MTR-8(78). The proposal was accepted in early
1976, and was incorporated as a three-year study into the Third Malaysia Plan.
Initial work on NIDAS, in co-operation with the Statistics Department, took the
form of a pre-pilot test in Butterworth (see NIDAS report N-MTR-7(78). The
material and prototype computer system was presented to a briefing in Penang
in June 1976, at which point NIDAS was officially launched.

As a result of the pre-pilot briefing, interest was generated among a
number of organizations in participating in the NIDAS project. The Penang State
Government took special interest in the Land File and independently sponsored a
Land Data Bank project for Penang, which was dovetailed into NIDAS. The local
government authority for Seberang Perai, the mainland part of the State of
Penang, took the initiative to support a separate study aimed at the revaluation
of properties and the creation of a Property Information System through Project
REPIS (Revaluation of Property Information System)) which provided for NIDAS an
opportunity to test a data system for local government needs. The Statistics
Department participated from the beginning, not only because it was first
planned to be the eventual recipient of the NIDAS system, but also to use the
NIDAS census as a pre-test for its own 1980 national Census. The NIDAS work
plan envisages from that point as well to seek the co-operation of as many
government agencies as possible; making initial contacts and ensuring publicity
set the pace for subsequent work.

As a demonstration of the feasibility of an integrated data system, NIDAS
had to first identify the various registers to be included in the system. These
consisted of two types, basic registers and secondary registers, and a geographic
information system. The basic and special registers consist of the following:

Basic Registers: 1. Land Data Bank

2. Census and Population Register

3. Building/Property Register

Secondary or
Special Registers: 1. Health File

2. Education and Manpower File

3. Industry/Business File

4. Land Utilization File

5. Development Projects File

The next three sections of this report outline the three basic aspects of
the work of NIDAS, namely, data base development, the geocoding work, and systems
development. The final sections in turn describe the financial and personnel
aspects of the project, further work to be done, and some concluding remarks on
implications and further development of NIDAS. This paper summarizes the
detailed technical and conceptual material which is contained in the various
reports which form part of the NIDAS documentation work (see annex).

B. Data base development

1. Basic tasks

The data base development work in NIDAS involves several tasks.

(a) Identification of existing data

This involves the identification of available data existing in various
government agencies that are relevant as producers of data and which will
therefore serve as data sources to NIDAS. This work is made through contacts
with various bodies beginning with the most obvious, the Statistics
Department. The data produced by these agencies may be special surveys
conducted by them, or may be generated during the process of administration
(that is, process-generated data). These would be typical of agencies such as
those concerned with land registration, local authority rate payments, motor
vehicle registration, birth and deaths registration, hospital or clinical
records, school records, Labour Exchange data, etc. As a result of this initial
determination, undertaken over the period of the first year, gaps in data
necessary for NIDAS were identified.

(b) The NIDAS census and other special censuses

In many cases, data are simply not available for the creation of data base
files for NIDAS experimentation. For this purpose, a special NIDAS census was
undertaken between June 1977 and June 1978, which incorporated in the
questionnaire schedules as much data as was necessary to build up the initial
data bases. At the same time, the NIDAS special census was used in order to
test some innovations in preparation for the 1980 National Census, which would
itself form one of the bases for the extension of NIDAS to the whole country
after the pilot phase.

The NIDAS census was conducted in two stages, the first stage coinciding
with the assessment unit listing and measurement for the REPIS Project, which
provided the data base for the Project, which provided the data base for the
Property Information System. The second stage involved a 20% sample survey of
the total households and incorporated various items of information which were
used to update the 1970 Population and Housing Census.

Besides the data that was initially captured, which was then redistributed
to the various data files in NIDAS, the census geo-listing stage conducted prior
to the census also enabled NIDAS to obtain data for its geocoding system, which
is described later. Among innovations introduced was the use of aerial
photographs as fieldmaps, and as part of the geocoding exercise.

NIDAS in this instance undertook work to capture data in the various Land
Registries and district Land Offices in order to create the data base for the
Land Data System (NIDAS/LDS). In addition, in conjunction with the Ministry of
Health, a basic health survey was undertaken in the Krian district.

Besides the NIDAS census which forms the bulk, a number of other data
capture activities were undertaken (for example through the Penang Land Data
Bank Project). A proposal to undertake an agricultural census for NIDAS was
shelved due to cost considerations and overlapping work with the Statistics
Department's 1977 Agricultural Census. From another project, data were also
obtained concerning small businesses in Butterworth town.

It should be noted that in devising the schedules for these censuses and
surveys, discussions were held with the various agencies and departments
concerned to ensure that data produced would be useful and meaningful to the

end-users.

(c) Rationalization and data base implementation

The merging of available departmental data with the data from the NIDAS census and other special surveys constituted the third element in NIDAS data base work. This involved not only uniformity in data definition, but also in the use of codes, etc. It also involved reducing overlapping surveys. The basic rationale for an integrated data system is efficiency in the production and use of data through sharing of data.

A number of files or data bases in NIDAS involve matching of the NIDAS census data and other available data sets with existing records kept by agencies. This is so in the case of the Industry/Business Register, the Agricultural File and the Education File. It also applies to the population update exercise by matching 1970 census data and the 1977 NIDAS census data. Much of the matching sequences were done through the geocoding system, as NIDAS is essentially a geographically based data system.

Data base implementation is a process of cleaning, editing and loading the data into the various NIDAS system files maintained in the computer. A considerable amount of rationalization of the file/data base structure had to be performed in the latter part of the project, particularly as individual files are merged into the final system. This will be discussed further below.

(d) Development of operational data systems

NIDAS recognizes that integration of data is simple if operational data systems (for example Land Data, Property Data, Educational Information) are already fully functioning, in which case, the remaining task of NIDAS would merely be to build a system of data sharing and transport through standardization of procedures and codes, and devising an integration facility, (the geocoding system), and the other data management requirements of a computerized data system. For this reason, the project team also got involved with various agencies, not merely to extract data but also to modernize their own operations. This is an important learning and educative task, particularly for the subsequent acceptance and operation of NIDAS. In this context, the pilot project undertook to create a land data system (NIDAS/LDS) for the State Government of Penang (through the Penang Land Data Bank Project), and the Property Information System (through Project REPIS), and work in the Health Ministry (through the Risk Approach Project).

The various agencies involved in these and other activities in NIDAS are listed in table 1.

Table 1. Database development in NIDAS and co-operating agencies

File	Co-operating government agency
Land Data System	Ministry of Land and Regional Development Penang, Perak and Kedah State Governments MAMPU
Census and Population Register	Department of Statistics (Census Division)
Property Information System	Seberang Perai Local Council
Health	Ministry of Health (Maternal and Child Health Division)
Education	Ministry of Education (EPRD)
Labour and Manpower	Penang Labour Office

Table 1. (Continued)

File	Co-operating government agency
DEVPRIS	Penang State Government, EPU, ICU
Business	Department of Statistics (Industries Division)
Geocoding System	National Directorate of Mapping, Department of Surveys

2. Status of data base development

(a) Land Data Base

The Land Data Base is one of several application subsystems in the NIDAS Project. It includes facilities for inquiry, retrieval and analysis of various land-related data and represents one of the basic registers since NIDAS is essentially a land-based system. The Land Data Base is designed to meet certain objectives, namely:

(a) It must contain information which will lead to efficient land management by the state authorities and the National Land Council;

(b) It must contain data which will integrate with other data bases in NIDAS such that the land data can be used in conjunction with other data in physical and socio-economic planning; and

(c) It must be dynamic, and contain not merely a static register, but also information on the status of titles and encumbrances which will serve as the basis of an updating procedure.

The structure of the Land Data Base is summarized in canonical form in figure VIII. There are two identifiers. The first identifier consists of the unique title number which is a primary key. The second identifier is the root key, and consists of the concatenation of the state code, district code, mukim or town/town section number and lot number.

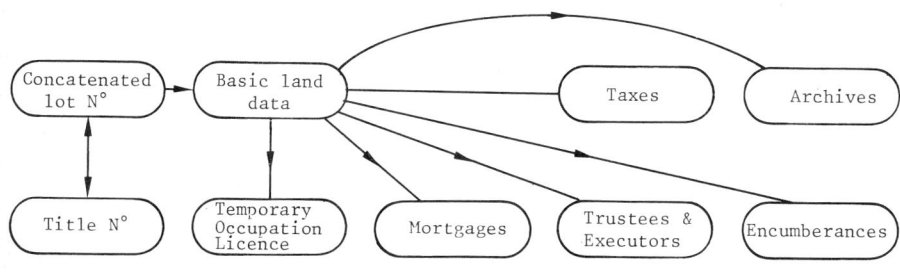

Figure VIII. Data base structure for land

(b) Property Data Base

The second application subsystem in the NIDAS project is the Property
Data Base. This data base is designed with three basic objectives in mind:

(a) To provide for the rationalisation of the property assessment
procedures, thus leading towards a more equitable assessment of properties;

(b) To provide timely and up-to-date management information to various
service departments within the local governing authority for planning purposes;
and

(c) To provide an automatic billing system for the collection of
assessment rates on properties.

The canonical structure for the Property Data Base is given in figure IX.
The many-to-many relationship between assessment units and land lots is worth
noting; it is possible to have an enumeration unit (structure or building)
comprising multiple assessment units, and also a single assessment unit covering
multiple enumeration units.

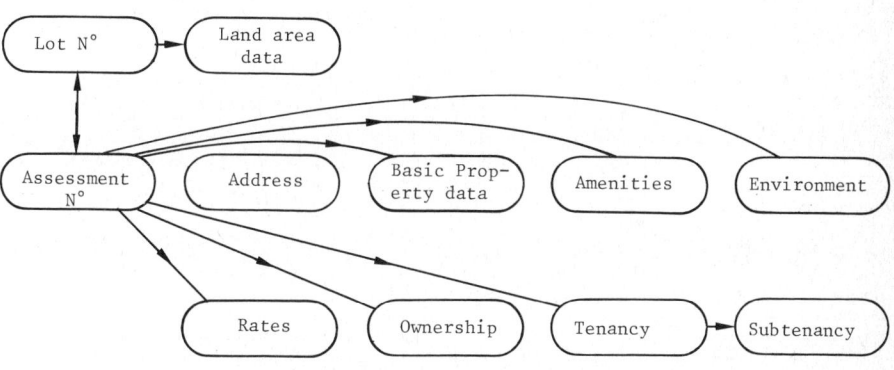

Figure IX. Data base structure for properties

(c) Census Data Base

The census or population data form the bulk of the data in the NIDAS
Project. Basically, the data base consists of data related to all private
housing units as well as all non-private housing units. For each private
housing unit, the data base contains data on households, families and
individuals. The data structure is strictly a hierarchy as represented in
figure X.

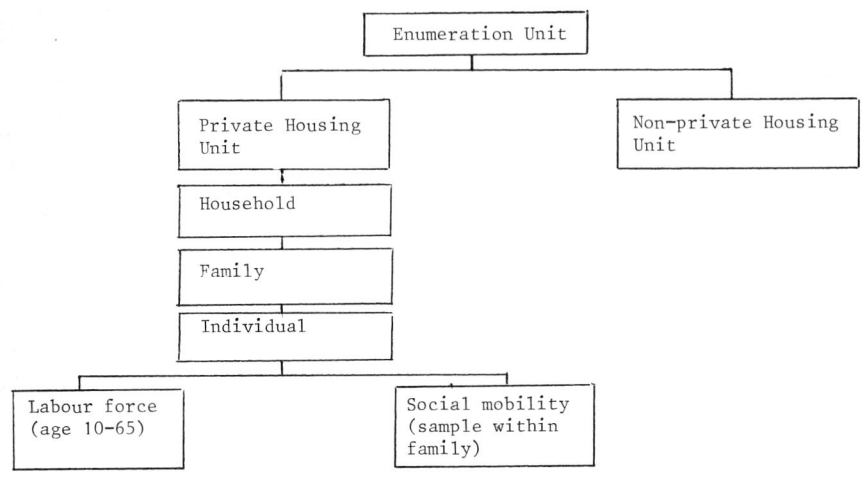

Figure X.   Census data hierarchy

At the household level, data on health, food, income and housing unit ownership/rental are included. Data at the individual level include education, occupation and other personal details. Details of employment, under-employment and unemployment are included for all individuals between the ages of 10 and 65. A sampling of social mobility data is also included for each family.

Census data are identified by unique numeric key made up of a fieldwork block number, sector number, enumeration unit geoaddress, household number, family number and person number. Census type data are not continuously updated en masse when a new census is conducted. Hence, it suffices to use the artificial numbers as the identifiers. On the other hand, these artificial identifiers allow for easy aggregate updates at the enumeration unit level. This is useful in that sample surveys on population can be conducted between censuses such that mini-censuses can be conducted as the need arises, based on the comparison between aggregated data from the surveys and data from the census data base.

In actual fact we have two sets of data, 1. the 1970 Population and Housing Census data, and 2. the NIDAS Stage II population data based on the 1978 exercise. Both of these sets of data are at the moment kept separate. Further work is aimed at merging the two sets to form a comprehensive population data base linked to the other data files.

(d)   Industry and Business File

A complete enumeration of non-housing units (including business establishments) was made in the NIDAS Stage I census, and geocoded. This file has to be linked with data from the Industries Division of the Statistics Department. The residual after matching (using the ADMATCH facility in NIDAS) will form the basis of the small business file. The data from the Butterworth Small Scale Industries Study, which has been geocoded, will then be merged into this file for the use of the Majlis Perbandaran Seberang Perai. This will also demonstrate how data maintained by other operational agencies can be integrated with Statistics Department data and therefore made available for small area analysis and planning for local and other authorities.

The Business Data Base has a simple straightforward structure. Basically, it contains data related to all businesses conducted in non-private housing units. It has two identifiers, namely the artificial concatenation of the fieldwork block number, sector number and enumeration geoaddress as used in the census, and the business registration number. As shall be seen later on, geoaddresses are uniquely identified with street addresses.

(e)   Health File

The original intention was to build this up from data in the NIDAS Stage II census. Then, after contacts already made in 1976, a follow-up with Ministry of Health data will be carried out. A WHO/Ministry of Health sponsored survey was completed in November 1978 in Krian: with the co-operation of the Ministry of Health, this data will be used together with health records generated from the Ministry's own Stage I and II survey to form the prototype District Health Information System.

(f)   Educational and Manpower File

This file is also to be built from NIDAS census data as initial data base, and later integrated with the Educational Planning, Research and Development Unit of the Ministry of Education (EPRD) data files and other school records (for example through the Examination Syndicate) in order to form a prototype Education Information System. In addition, the data bases for the education and manpower file will also be drawn from the Statistics Department and Ministry of Labour and Manpower. There are five sets of data (dated 1973) requested from EPRD, on teachers, pupils and school characteristics, but access has not been given to NIDAS in respect of school finance and physical facilities. An initial commitment has however been made and follow-up action will be undertaken to merge these records to the NIDAS data bases later.

(g)   Development Projects File

The conceptual development of this file is almost complete. A list of development projects under the Third Malaysia Plan for the whole of Penang has been made available. The system work will commence as soon as the conceptualization is completed. The final aim of the development work of the Development Project Monitoring and Evaluation System (DPMES) is to link it with the Census File, the initial test of which will be conducted using the 1970 census. Parallel work is also being done by the Pahang Tenggara Regional Development Authority, but outside of NIDAS work. The system being planned,

RIDAS, replicates NIDAS, but concentrates more on land use and environment, which should serve as a prototype for a similar system in the full NIDAS later on. Approaches are now being made to link up with the Economic Planning Unit (EPU), Prime Minister's Department and ICU work on project monitoring.

3. Further data base development work

All work on data capture has been completed. The project team is at the moment in the process of "cleaning" the data, particularly of the operational data files (for example, land).

The next phase is the rationalization of the file structure. Whole prototype systems have been developed to handle the data bases so far developed; experimentation on the full data base structure, that is, their integration, for the entire NIDAS pilot study area is still to be attempted. So far the full complement has been implemented in this sense only for one administrative district (Northern Seberang Perai), or the full system for individual registers only (as for example the Population Register, both the 1970 Population and Housing Census and NIDAS 1978 census and the Penang Land Data System). At the moment a full implementation has not been possible because of hardware limitations, since the NIDAS pilot system development work is not being done on a dedicated basis and the computer capacity itself is only of medium scale (an IBM 370/135 of 256K storage and an IBM 370/148 of 512K storage). Efficient use is made of peripheral storage (tapes) and reorganized file structures, as for instance the 35-tape 1970 census data from the Statistics Department which is now reduced to four tapes.

Further work in data base development includes the splitting of the comprehensive Population Register, which as it now stands takes the form of an extended record block, into subfiles to be individually merged into the other "functional" registers. In the process, the independently developed data bases can then be "structured" as a prototype integrated data system. But the latter cannot be undertaken until the geocoding system, that is, the basic integration system, is completed, decisions are taken on what data system to adopt and the general data base management system for NIDAS is fully developed.

C. Geocoding system for NIDAS

1. Development of the Geographic Base File

In NIDAS the geographic information system plays a critical role in not only providing the capability for integrating various data files in NIDAS but serves also as basic data base for mapping of processed output from individual or integrated files. In order to generate the geographic information system for NIDAS, one must create a geographic base file which contains geographic references in machine readable form, or geocodes. Geocodes exist in different forms depending not only on the type of geographic data (namely, point data, line data, aerial data), but also on different levels of organization. The most basic or elemental, which provides the flexibility necessary not only for retrieval/integration but also for computer mapping, is the co-ordinate referencing system. In devising the geographic information system for NIDAS, several geocoding tasks therefore have to be undertaken for each component of the system. The co-ordinate referencing of geographic data is obtained through digitization, using special digitizer equipment. These geographic references are then organized into a system as described in the NIDAS Geographic Information System Report (N-MTR-1(78)). Basic referencing work in NIDAS involves the geocoding of structures, the geocoding of land lots, the building up of an address directory and the assignment of numerical codes to standard geographic references such as mukim, villages, town sections, towns, etc. The work schedule for the creation of the geographic base file which began in August 1977 is given in table 2.

Table 2. Time Frame for geocoding work

Tasks	August	November	December 77	January	May	July	December 78
Production of field maps	Seberang Perai — Krian and Kuala Muda — Penang Island						
Digitizing of structures		Digitizing at the Survey Department					
Digitizing networks		Manual digitizing at CPR	Continuation work				
Digitizing/coding lots			Penang			Krian and Kuala Muda	
Digitizing EBs							
Development of lot match programs							
Network file organization							
Experiment with access routines							

Systems input

The co-ordinate references which are used to translate actual data points on the ground to geographic locations in map form are usually recorded from maps in the national topographic series. Such topographic references are derived using the Rectified Skewed Orthomorphic (RSO) projection which represents a standard map projection specialized to Malaysia's national mapping environment. Geocoding information derived from direct digitizing, which, because of the technical constraints are co-ordinate references taken from an artificial and therefore varying origin (from base map to base map, so to speak), has to be transformed into standard national grid references, aligned as it were to a common origin point.

A special aerial photo cover was obtained for the NIDAS area with the co-operation of the Survey Department, and this served as a most up-to-date source for mapping structures. The procedure involved in the production of field maps, geolisting of structures, reconstituting the field maps and then digitization of structures is shown in figure XI.

Critical in this respect is the data collection for the NIDAS census and property information field work which was carried out in typical fashion; but to relate the enumerated units to the map or aerial photograph used, series of geoaddress numbers were assigned to each structure visible on the map. As enumerators visit each structure the same geoaddress number is used as an identifier for the data collected in the census. At the same time, the co-ordinate references are accordingly recorded to each visible (and geoaddressed) structure on the aerial photograph. In this respect geoaddresses form the link between the co-ordinate references and the data.

For the NIDAS land file, lot numbers are used to form this link. Although co-ordinate references of land records can simply be similarly recorded from a land lot map or cadastral sheet, an attempt was made to obtain these from existing records maintained by the survey department so as to tie in the co-ordinate referencing with the normal administrative mechanism of land transactions.

A secondary form of geocoding was developed in the NIDAS project which does not relate directly to collecting co-ordinate references to complement file data but mainly to support the NIDAS Geopak with various analytical capabilities. For instance an address coding guide was devised to facilitate matching of the system to externally defined files which have civic addresses. Also, a system of DIME-like segment geocoding was attempted to enable semi-automatic aggregation of data by ad hoc random areas (the SIME system).

Finally, a co-ordinate referencing of 1970 enumeration blocks was done to enable linkage between the NIDAS data, especially the census file, and the 1970 census data. For this a manual or hand approach was followed to demonstrate how such co-ordinate referencing can be done without sophisticated equipment.

It should be noted that while digitizing required rectification of aerial photographs, the NIDAS Committee decided that rectification was to be dispensed with since it was necessary to speed up operations. Therefore there exists approximately 25 per cent distortion on the edges of the photographs. These distortions may be due in part to the enlargement process. In certain cases this has resulted in the distortion of the location of structures and the mis-matching of structures and lots.

2. NIDAS linkage mechanism

At the centre of the various operational data bases lies the Geographic Data Base. In NIDAS, this data base consists of three directories, namely the

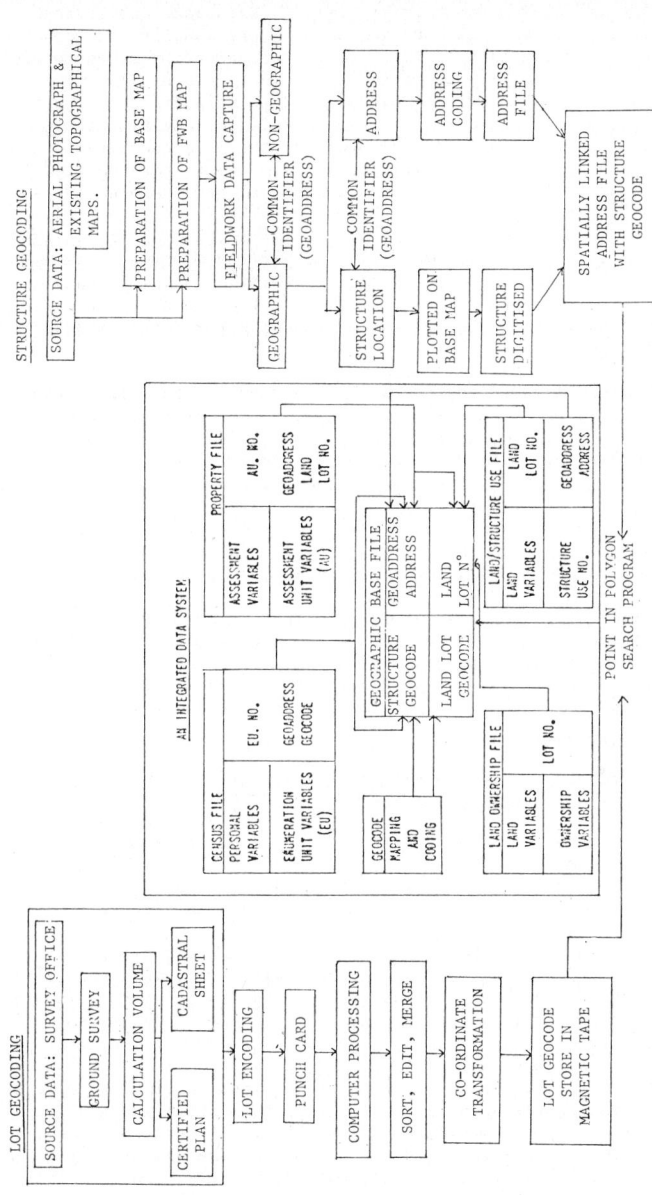

Figure XI. Geocoding of structure and landlots (procedure)

Lot Geocode Directory, the Geoaddress Directory and the Address Directory. Each directory contains a record for each known spatial unit. Each record contains a list of references by which the operational data are identified as well as a geocode. The 12-digit co-ordinate geocode (six for the X-axis and 6 for the Y-axis) conforms with the national grid. The grid which is derived from an RSO projection represents various positions on the ground by the number of metres east (X-axis) and the number of metres north (Y-axis) from a predetermined starting point located at the lower left-hand corner of the grid frame.

By means of any one of the three directories, it is then possible to relate different operational data via its referencing identifiers to the common denominator of co-ordinate goecodes. A whole field of expertise has developed which addresses itself to the problem of locational references which serves not only as an integration key of separate operational data but also as a basis for computer graphics and mapping.

Basically, the directory files of NIDAS encompass three categories. The first covers the street and network segment level. It contains location reference (geocode) information of nodes at each end of network segments, together with the corresponding addresses. The Address Directory is built for each urban and suburban centres within the study area. The second category consists of structures base files covering the whole study area. The Geoaddress Directory treats all structures as point structures and relates the geoaddress to point geocodes. The third category covers large grain files at block or block group level, primarily for rural areas where street features are sparse. The Lot Geocode Directory is considered to come under this third category and relates land lot numbers to the lot centroid geocodes, together with a variable-length string of geocodes for every vertex of a lot. In order to reduce computer search time, it is envisaged that other directories related to the third category will be built for commonly referenced spatial units at the block or block group level such as census enumeration blocks and administrative districts.

The system development for this linking/integration mechanism is examined in the following section.

D.   System development

1.   Data management

From the beginning it has been agreed that for the NIDAS project some form of data base management system would be most appropriate. Although a data base management system was in fact used in the pre-pilot study as illustrated in figure XII (with data bases structure as shown in figure XIII), the restricted hardware resources available at the time the NIDAS project was officially launched in the third quarter of 1976 resulted in the bold decision being taken to develop the prototype system without the initial use of any data base management system. This was made possible by the use of the MARK IV data management system whose automatic system function and powerful file handling capabilities make it well suited for the purpose. MARK IV also has the advantage of being capable of providing the flexibility required for an experimental project of the type discussed.

Any detailed description on the use of the MARK IV facilities in the prototype design is beyond the scope of this paper. However, some of the special features, because of their relevance, need mentioning.

Since most of the data need essentially be stored in coded form, a table look-up capability is mandatory. The generalized systems interface enables

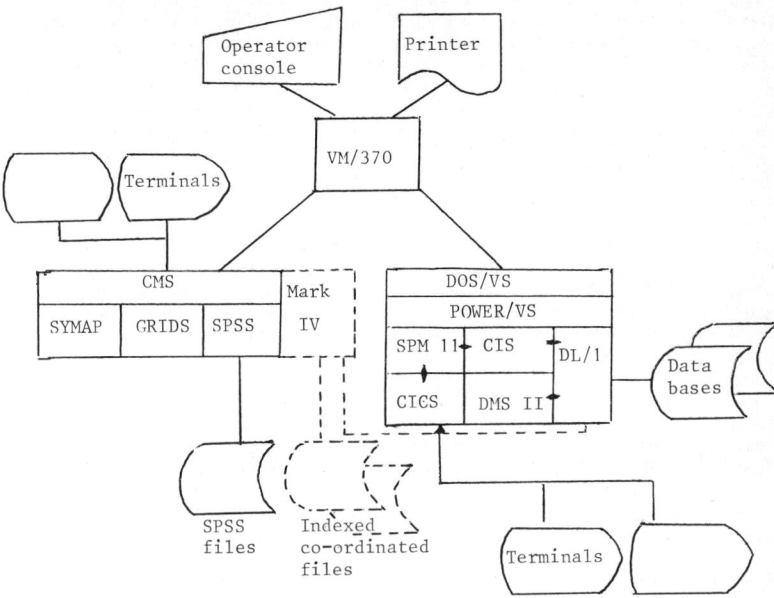

Figure XII. System schematic for pre-pilot study

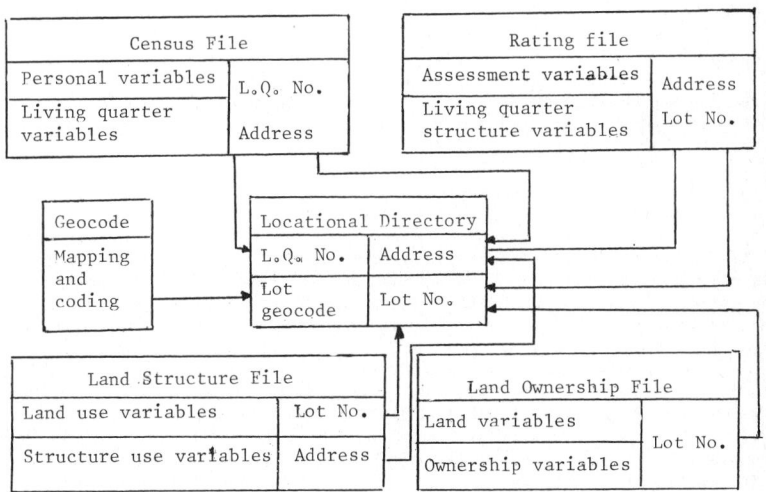

Figure XIII. Data base structure of pre-pilot study

subroutine calls to be made to user routines written in Assembler, COBOL and FORTRAN. This is important in that it now becomes possible for data to be extracted and stored temporarily in subfiles for further processing by many of the statistical and mapping packages that are being used in the study. Since MARK IV provides the ability to co-ordinate up to nine multiple files with a master file, it becomes possible to postpone file linkage until execution time, thus providing an extremely flexible means for the experimentation of such linkages. With the use of indexed co-ordinated files, records can be directly accessed via the run-time definition of the co-ordinating fields enabling processing of co-ordinated files which are not in the same sequence as the master file. Furthermore, the chained co-ordinated file structure allows hierarchical relationships to be established among the co-ordinated files, again at processing time. Finally, the extended file processing feature provides added capabilities to control and process transactions, which are extremely useful in an experimental environment.

Although a data base management system has not been used initially, data bases can be created at a later stage if it becomes essential and practicable. MARK IV has the ability to handle complex data base structures with its extended segment processing facilities and can be interfaced to a number of existing data base management systems of both the hierarchical and network types.

As a matter of fact, with the recent enhancement of the University computer system, it has become possible to extend data base facilities to NIDAS. A decision was made to adopt an IMS/VS data base approach for the NIDAS Land Data System.

2.   Centralized or decentralized data bases

Three different approaches have been considered in the integration of the operational data bases, two of which involve the use of a data base management system, while the third involves only the use of file management software. Following the enhancement of the University computer system, the decision to adopt a data base approach leaves the NIDAS project with two possible alternatives: a centralized data base approach or an approach based on decentralized operational data bases.

The centralized data base approach has been successfully implemented in the pre-pilot study of the Butterworth area. Basically, an integrated data base approach is adopted with the data model consisting of various operational "physical data bases" and a geographic "physical data base". The advantage of this method is that data redundancy and data inconsistency can be easily reduced to a minimum. However, this method may not be very workable in the real environment in that it basically requires that all operational data, be it under the jurisdiction of a federal, state or local authority, be centralized at one physical location. Furthermore, the single data base that results is very large and complex and requires that great care be taken in the selection of suitable storage structures to ensure reasonable performance.

The other approach is basically an extension of the non-data base approach where the MARK IV data management software is used. In this decentralized approach, the MARK IV indexed co-ordinated files are replaced by separate individual operational data bases, the advantage being that even though a data base approach has been adopted, integration of the individual data bases is only carried out at processing time. This means that essentially, the operational data bases can be maintained and operated upon separately at different locations, even though a logically integrated user's view of data from across functional boundaries is presented at processing time as required by the NIDAS objectives. It appears that the decentralized approach would be more likely to be accepted from the administrative viewpoint.

MARK IV interfaces with various data base management software and it is being used as before for integrating the operational data bases at processing time. With the use of the MARK IV data management software jointly with IMS/VS, the selected data base management software appears to provide one alternative that would be hard to surpass. Indeed, the MARK IV offers a powerful online query, transaction processing, table look-up features together with the data base advantages, reduced data redundancy and inconsistency, and the availability of flexible storage structures which forms the basic features of the NIDAS system structure. A prototype integrated data base structure for NIDAS which has been implemented in one administrative district is shown in figure XIV.

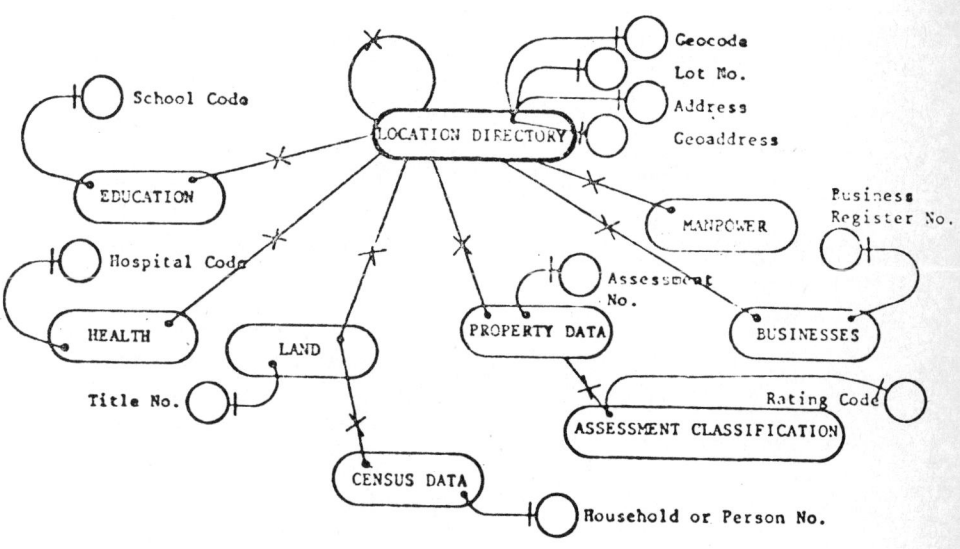

Figure XIV. NIDAS prototype integrated data base structure

3. NIDAS geoprocessing phases

In using geoprocessing techniques in NIDAS, three distinct phases can be
identified, as shown in figure XV.

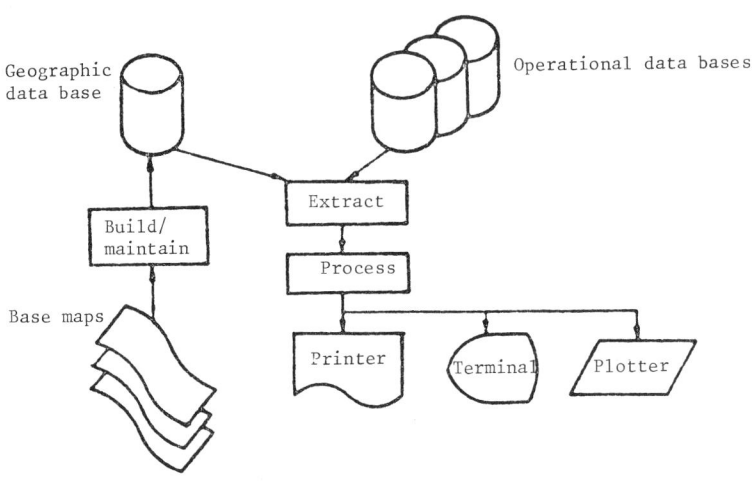

Figure XV. NIDAS geoprocessing system

(a) Build/maintain phase

This phase has the function of constructing, editing and updating the
geographic data base. The geocodes for the point structures are obtained from
the digitization of aerial photographs. With the help of three RSO reference
points, the TRANP program is used to convert the digitized machine co-ordinates
to RSO co-ordinates. In the case of the land lot geocodes, no digitization is
necessary. Instead, the DABTOC program is used to convert distances and
bearings provided by the Survey Department to Cassini co-ordinates. At the same
time, the centroid of each land lot is also calculated using the CENTROID program.
The Cassini codes are then converted to RSO co-ordinates by means of the
CONVERT program, giving a directory consisting of lot numbers, vertice geocodes,
centroid geocodes and areas.

(b) Extract phase

The extract phase performs the function of selecting the appropriate data
in the Geographic Data Base and correlating it with existing operational data
bases. The correlation is performed by matching the appropriate location
identifiers, which appear in both the Geographic Data Base and the operational
data bases, that is, by matching the appropriate integration keys.

The Geographic Data Base is used against the operational data bases via either standard or non-standard retrieval. Standard retrieval refers to retrieval of data within a spatial unit such as an administrative district whose boundaries have already been pre-defined in the Geographic Data Base. For a non-standard retrieval, operational data within any arbitrary boundary may be extracted. Where land lots are concerned, it is very likely that lots may not fit into the query polygon exactly at the boundaries. The approach adopted is that the query polygon would be automatically redefined to incorporate all lots whose centroids lie within the original polygon, but exclude those lots whose centroids lie outside. A point-in-polygon algorithm was developed to conduct this search procedure.

The extract process is illustrated in figure XVI. The LINK 1 program for matching street addresses is based to a large extent on the ADMATCH system.

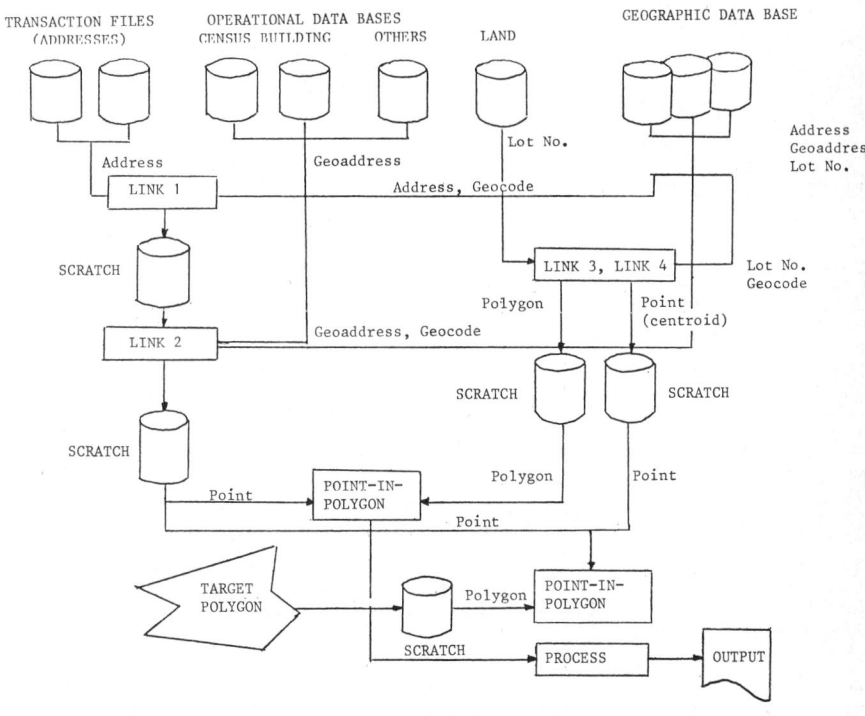

Figure XVI. The NIDAS geoprocessing extract phase

(c) Process phase

The process phase organizes the data into the desired format and displays the result. The output can be graphic (maps), alphanumeric (statistical tabulations) or interactive. The process can include a model for the "what if" questions, or may simply involve straightforward statistical analysis of data correlated in the extract phase.

In NIDAS, facilities are available for mapping on a line printer using SYMAP (from A-conformolines) and GRIDS (from points). Offline mapping is also available on an incremental plotter. Exits to various application packages such as SPSS and BMDP are provided.

4. Other issues in system development

In addition to general system development work, the project has been experimenting with different data security measures (logical as well as physical) and protection of privacy (minimum aggregation of individual data, as well as the possibility of automatic "random error" options).

Another aspect of the system work, particularly in the final phase, is the development of user-oriented facilities in order to minimize programmer intervention. This is in addition to the development of the operational data systems which are geared to the administrative functions of particular agencies, in particular for the computerized land data system and the property information system. These include terminal-based data retrieval features such as predetermined output format, free-format query, updating facilities, interactive statistical analysis as well as computer graphics, including mapping. NIDAS also utilizes standard software packages for both statistical and mapping applications such as SPSS, BMD, SYMAP, GRIDS and special routines such as ADMATCH. In order to simplify and therefore increase user access to the facilities available, NIDAS is working on its own utility programs for statistical and mapping applications, both for on-line as well as batch-processing, which incorporates the programmer-oriented standard software packages. A Data Dictionary and an Area Reference Guide are provided to users for this purpose.

Besides work on software development, the project team has also been giving consideration to alternative hardware configurations for the system. In anticipating a decentralized data base system for NIDAS, if and when it is extended to the rest of the country, a national computer network such as that shown in figure XVII is contemplated. Discussions with relevant government bodies, including ICU which operates the central National Operations Room computer, suggest that such a network may be feasible.

E. Organization of work, personnel and costs of development

The NIDAS pilot project has been an interesting exercise in technology transfer since most of the experiences in development of information systems for public administration are located in Western Europe and North America. The fact is that the NIDAS pilot project is undertaken entirely by local professionals who are attached to the Centre for Policy Research and who also have several research project responsibilities. However, two of the principal investigators undertook a technical tour to assess similar projects, one in Canada and the other in Western Europe. Another aspect in the use of personnel is the fact that many of the support staff, even in technical matters such as geocoding and so on, are relatively inexperienced graduates and programmers as is also the case of lower-level personnel, many of whom are school leavers who were in fact trained on the job. It has therefore been a tremendous learning experience for all those involved in the project.

Figure XVII. A possible national computer configuration for NIDAS

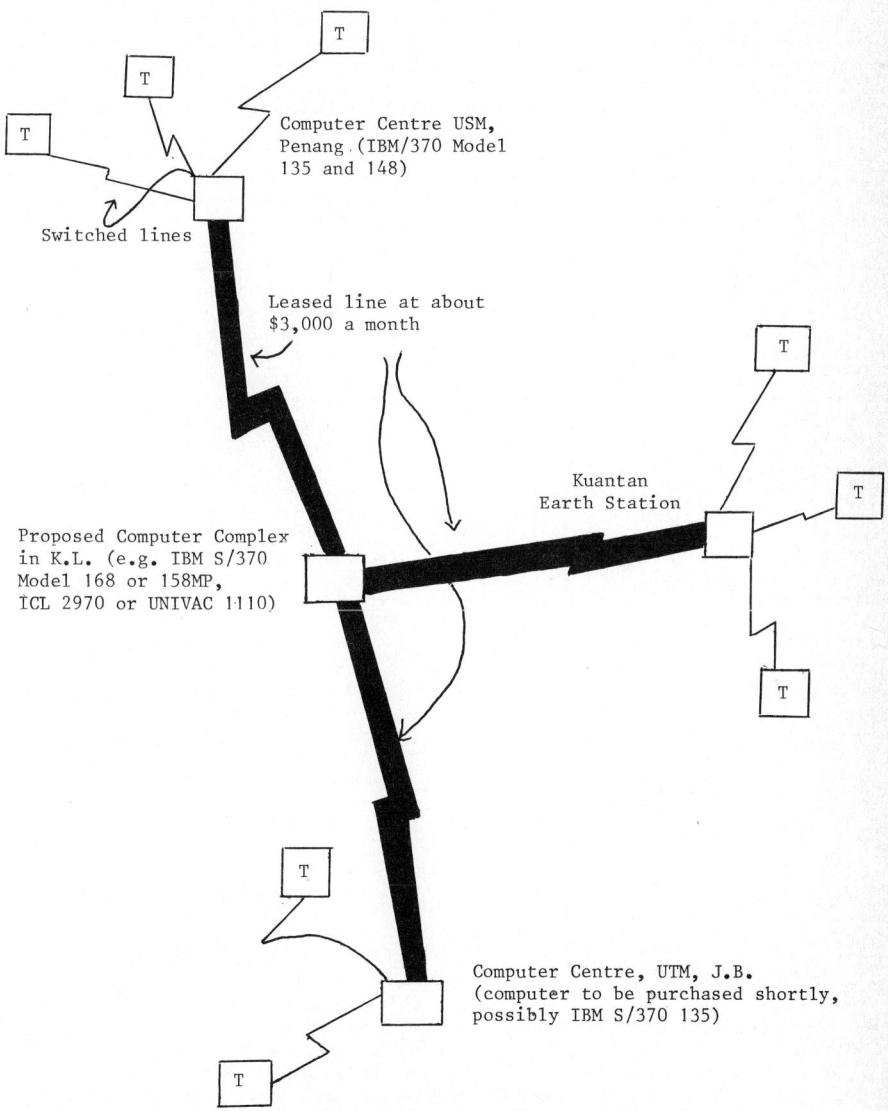

T = Terminals

The work team itself was organized into four committees, each headed by a co-ordinator: the Fieldwork Committee, the File Development Committee, the Systems Development Committee and the Geocoding Committee. Programmers, project analysts and field co-ordinators were assigned to each of those committees. In the last phase of the project the support staff has been reduced to a complement of 34 members, while at the height of the fieldwork over 1,000 field supervisors and enumerators were employed.

The costs of development of the various NIDAS files are given in table 3. Given the size of the task, it would seem that the development of the pre-pilot phase is quite cost-effective. One should note however that the table does not include the salaries of the professionals involved (except for nominal honoraria) or the cost of computer time, both of which are borne by the University as its contribution to NIDAS. Nevertheless it would appear that the financial feasibility of extending NIDAS to the whole country after the pilot phase is clearly evident.

Table 3. NIDAS expenditure: costs of file development[a]

File	Staff and salaries	Computer system	Capital equipment	Materials and other consumables	Total
Prefieldwork concepts and tests	27,600	–	–	3,668	31,268
Census Register Stage I	512,725	2,500	8,520	38,665	562,410
Stage II	306,549	1,900	7,406	59,160	375,015
Land File	352,850	2,000	–	35,708	390,558
Geocoding	87,242	5,276	158,788	67,799	319,085
Systems	437,400	131,435	50,990	1,000	620,825
Health	52,552	–	–	2,509	55,061
Office and Administration	59,518	–	2,295	3,881	65,694
TOTALS	$1,836,436	$143,111	$227,999	$212,370	$2,419,916[b]

a/ Figures are in Malaysian dollars: $US 1.00 = $M 2.22, approximately.

b/ The excess over the $M 2.2 million allocation is covered by independent contributions from special projects.

F. CONCLUSIONS; further developments

The remainder of the work on the pilot project is indicated in table 4. As indicated earlier, the winding down process is already beginning in order to meet the completion data of September 1979, with the project team concentrating on residual data cleaning, enhancement and rationalization of the data base structure, applications programming and documentation.

Table 4. Further work programme for NIDAS

TASKS	Jan. 1978–July 1979	Aug. 1979–Dec. 1979	1980	1981 Fourth Plan	1985	1986 Fifth Plan	1990
NIDAS system development							
1. Data Cleaning and loading	▮						
2. File enhancement	▮						
3. Developing alternative system structure	▮						
4. Conversion	▮						
GEOGRAPHIC information system	▮	▮					
APPLICATIONS programming							
1. Systems work	▮						
2. User workshops	▮						
3. Analysis and Documentation	▮	▮	Preparatory work for Fourth plan				
POST-pilot consultations							
1. Census 1980 (geocoded)	▮	Planning (Min. land dev.)	Preparation	Data capture and system development →			ment
2. National Land Data Bank		Consultation	Development				
3. Special data systems (education, health, etc.)							

1. NIDAS applications

In the area of applications, the project team is undertaking several exercises aimed at demonstrating the utilities and capabilities of NIDAS both for administrative as well as planning and impact evaluation. Among the applications the following are included.

(a) Social-economic indicator system

Development of socio-economic indicators has been in progress in several countries and in Malaysia within the Economic Planning Unit (EPU) of the Prime Minister's Department. However, there has been an absence of a complete data system from which the indicators can be generated. As such, NIDAS can fulfil this role by computing the indicators, possibly at regular intervals, as the data is being updated to give policy makers a periodic grasp of the socio-economic conditions in the country.

(b) Village classification

Some interest has been generated among policy makers in Malaysia on village classification. However, the exact nature of the classification procedure has yet to be discussed.

The village classification could be done on a matrix basis resembling the structure described below.

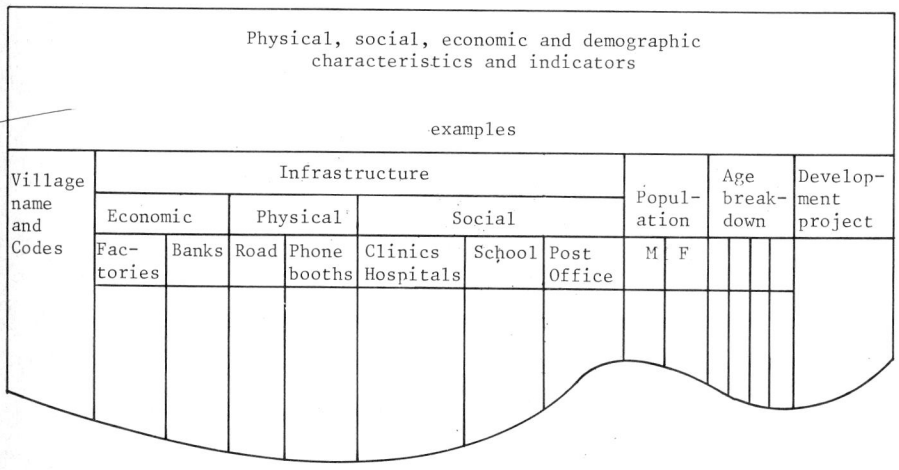

The village classification matrix

The matrix would be set up by first aggregating all the data records in the system which are not found within Urban areas, into villages. The selection of the data for each record would go by the address, and the Address Coding Guide could be used. Once records were distributed according to the various villages a set of indicators would be computed on the data and the results output in matrix form as shown in the structure above.

The Village Classification Programme is to be developed in a packaged form, that is, a tailor-made programme where the data fields, the computation operation procedure and the output structure are all pre-specified and when executed on the system at different points in time, would provide on the spot up-to-date information on the status of villages, provided of course that the system is updated periodically.

(c) District information system/district data bank

Supplementary to the village classification exercise, a district information system would be useful especially for development in the rural areas. One example is information relating to Farmers Organization Authority areas.

(d) Development impact analysis

The movement towards the assessment of the impact of development plans has been going on for several years. NIDAS will attempt to develop a development impact assessment system within the Development Project Information System (DEVPRIS) for government projects.

(e) Census update on a sampling frame

Consistent with United Nations recommendations, a complete census should be taken every 10 years as well as updating on a sample basis at more frequent intervals of say two to five years or even on a continuous basis. A satisfactory sample selection would depend on the use of a regional sampling frame which CPR will be developing within the next two years.

(f) Reassessment exercise

The NIDAS building file which resembles that of a complete Revaluation of Property Information System (REPIS) would be useful to local governments in rationalizing their assessment procedure, as well as for local planning.

(g) Planning applications

It was an original objective of NIDAS to provide basic variables useful in planning applications. One type of application would be that of a locational analysis device where several potential locations could be evaluated and simulated for a particular use and the most optimum location selected for actual construction. This would be more appropriate and less wasteful than trial-by-error judgement presently in use.

In addition, NIDAS will attempt to develop several other cases of applications, for example, the Butterworth Port Expansion Project and the Coastal Highway Developmental Project in Penang. This work will be for documentation purposes and also as a possible technical input into the planning for the Fourth Malaysia Plan, 1981-85.

2. Development and extension of operational systems

As can be seen from table 4, the decision to extend NIDAS to the rest of the country, will entail post-pilot consultations. While the decision depends on the final briefing to the National Action Council in September 1979, discussions are already being held with several agencies on the work done in the functional areas which could serve as a basis for the national extension. In fact these activities would be carried out even if the whole system is not implemented nationally. In this respect, a decision has been taken by the Statistics Department to geocode the 1980 Census. This will therefore help to provide small area information for applications by lower level authorities as well as by the central agencies, particularly the EPU, in the research work for the Fourth Plan. The Ministry of Land and Regional Development is already contemplating the development of a National Land Data System. The Committee on Computerization of Land Records, created by the Ministry in 1974, had decided to introduce an index card system in order to develop a central land record for the whole country; this proposal has since been incorporated into a fuller proposal to computerize the entire land record, keeping operations in the country. A special committee will probably be formed in the near future in order to formulate a paper to be submitted to the National Land Council for a decision on this issue.

In the meantime, Penang State has a prototype operational computerized Land Data System as a result of the NIDAS pilot study which incorporates Penang State. The State Government has in principle agreed to continue this work and to make provisions for personnel and any necessary administrative reorganization resulting from the change-over from the manual system now being followed. This is a highly complex matter and will probably involve considerable discussion over a number of years between the State authorities and the Centre for Policy Research. However, the Penang computerized Land Data System will also be used as an operating model for the other States when the extension of the Land Data Bank is made to the whole country. The problems faced by other States will be less complex than those of the land record system of Penang, which will contribute to the advancement of the Federal Ministry's Land Data Bank Project. In this regard, on the basis of the work on the Penang Land Data System, it has been estimated that data capture costs for the rest of the country (consisting of about three million lots) can be considerably reduced to about $M 3.00 per lot which is not overly costly. In terms of the actual work, it has been calculated that it will take about 450 man-years to capture the existing land data, 330 man-years for updating and about 400 man-years for the geocoding of land lots.

With regard to operating integrated data systems arising out of the NIDAS pilot project, it should also be noted that Penang State itself will have the full complement of NIDAS data files and systems features. It is therefore possible to rationalize this into a State Planning Information System for use by the State Government in its administrative and planning functions. The immediate applications of the system would be in revising the 1969 Master Plan for the State as well as undertaking research for the State's submission to the Fourth Five-Year Plan. Here also, as a result of both NIDAS and Project REPIS, the Seberang Perai local council would have an operational real estate and property information system which could be used again as a model for other local authorities to undertake a similar exercise both for local planning and administrative work as required by the recent Planning Act.

On another front, the EPU has proposed a plan for a National Resource Mapping exercise in order to update the previous land capability exercise. It would be fully automatic and use remote sensing. This again would provide a useful basis and headstart for the extension of NIDAS to the whole country.

In the area of hardware, the Electronic Data Processing Council, which is responsible for the rationalization of acquisition and planning for computer needs of the Government, including personnel and training, has been expanded and modified with considerably more muscle. It is now located within a new Automatic Data Processing Committee of the National Development Planning Council. It is understood that this Committee is now working on the possibility of evaluating the feasibility of a network for the whole country through testing of a computer link between the Kuala Lumpur and Penang installations. This is also in line with the thinking of NIDAS as indicated earlier in figure XVII.

Annex

Detailed information on the NIDAS project can be found in the following reports:

1. NIDAS/GIS - Geographic Information System:
    specifications and applications   N-MTR-1(78)

2. NIDAS/GIS: Geocoding Manual   N-MTR-2(78)

    NIDAS Aerial Reference and Data Dictionary:
    Appendix to the NIDAS application report   (N-MTR-12(78))

3. NIDAS fieldwork report   N-MTR-3(78)

4. NIDAS mid-term report   N-MTR-4(78)

5. NIDAS systems report   N-MTR-5(78)

6. NIDAS LDS: a mid-term development report   N-MTR-6(78)

7. NIDAS/B'WORTH PREPILOT: a report on a NIDAS
    prototype system   N-MTR-7(78)

8. Original proposal: development of a National
    Integrated Data System (with supplementary
    notes)   N-MTR-8(78)

9. NIDAS/health information system: fieldwork report   N-MTR-9(78)

10. EIS: development of an Environmental Information
    System   N-MTR-10(78)

11. Property Information System   N-MTR-11(78)

12. NIDAS application   N-MTR-12(78)

INFORMATION SYSTEMS IN PUBLIC ADMINISTRATION
D. Eade, J. Hodgson (editors)
North-Holland Publishing Company
© DFD, 1981

DEVELOPMENT PROBLEMS AND DATA COLLECTION REQUIREMENTS

Michael Ward*

Abstract

The paper argues for the need for statisticians to become more selective in their objective investigations of the processes of economic and social change. It suggests that methods of data collection and classification have been influenced on the one hand by an incomplete and prejudiced view about the nature of development and, on the other hand, by an unquestioned acceptance and observance of standard statistical techniques of enquiry as manifested in particular by the random sample survey and the choice of arithmetic mean averages. Like the data drawn from administrative files and registration records, the systems of coding, classification and tabulation commonly adopted in developing countries reflect the perceived dynamic relationships in society and the established political, economic and institutional structure that dominates activity. This provides little scope for investigations covering the activities of special and otherwise disadvantaged groups in the country and for enquiries into important problem areas of basic need.

*Fellow, Institute of Development Studies, Sussex University, United Kingdom of Great Britain and Northern Ireland.

A. Introduction

1. The quantification of phenomena

In principle - if not always in practice - many problems and issues are capable of being objectively assessed. A somewhat smaller proportion perhaps may be sensitive to some form of more precise numerical quantification which enables quite specific action to be taken or the arguments for and against a given proposition to be properly balanced and formulated. The principle objective of this paper is to suggest alternative methods of statistical enquiry to try and improve the measurement of observed phenomena in developing countries. This alone, however, is not sufficient because the data have to be collected in ways that, it is hoped, will help to reflect more closely the underlying reality of particular situations.

The pursuit of objectivity in analysis demands that appropriate links should be forged between some perceived reality, an assumed hypothesis and the apparent relevant explanatory theory. But past experience suggests that people's perceptions of reality are strongly influenced not only by their own experience but also by the information they already have available on hand. At the same time, however, this exposure to a particular situation and their understanding of it bears an important relation to the range and type of data that are collected. Beyond this inherent circularity in scientific enquiry, the accompanying analysis is additionally influenced by the adoption of conventional classifications and concepts which help to pre-determine (and occasionally restrict) the type of question that is asked. It will also be inevitably affected by the application of an accepted theoretical methodology. In many practical situations these traditional techniques could well prove to be, on further consideration, quite inappropriate to the precise problem under investigation.

Just as in many other areas of economic analysis there are discrepancies between theoretical concepts and their empirical measurement, so too in the field of development economics there is a gap that exists between observable problems relating to the dynamics of socio-economic change and their conventional methods of quantification. It is insufficient simply to describe what is being observed, especially if such observations are generally made from only a single viewpoint, because a priori an understanding of the various underlying real relationships is clearly necessary. Unfortunately, in the measurement of socio-economic phenomena in developing countries and in the formulation of policy, the choice of statistics is often predetermined. It tends to be conditioned both by pre-conceived notions about the basic social and economic causal relationships concerning development and also by the actual availability of data. In many situations this has not infrequently led to the use of approximate and proxy measures that have possibly imparted an unintentional distortion to conceived notions about the process of change.

The discipline of statistics is an integral - indeed an essential part of the scientific process. The main purpose of collecting and assembling data is to compile and organize information in such a way that it will lead to a better understanding of the world in which everyone lives. This implies making certain initial assumptions about the nature of reality. In such circumstances there is little possibility and scope or, in fact, need for the statistician to remain neutral. If he is to perform his various functions properly there is no way in which he can assume an impartial role. The statistician must face up to the fundamental dilemma that to be objective and relevant he must also be prepared to select and reject information.

In the past, this is a responsibility that many civil servants and politicians - and not just the statisticians themselves - have not deigned to recognize as being an inevitable and essential part of the role of the statistician. They have preferred to relegate the statistician's function to one of a processor who is destined to carry out work on behalf of (or under the instructions of) others who administer, plan and otherwise make decisions.

This paper then is also a plea for statisticians to make more conscious efforts to identify problems, select relevant and important issues and exercise greater objectivity. It applies to the practising role as well as to the accepted preconceived notions of the status and functions of statisticians. It also critically affects the theoretical assumptions and operational techniques normally adopted in statistical enquiry and analysis. The emphasis in developing countries must be on the deliberate but careful selection of problem areas, assumptions, definitions, classifications and methods of investigation - possibly sometimes necessarily eschewing the classical random approaches and standard classification procedures to highlight issues and reduce the costs of obtaining information for policy purposes.

2. Limitations to the boundary of enquiry

This paper is primarily concerned with those factors which tend to distort the perception of reality in developing countries. In drawing attention to essentially technical and practical issues, the paper must necessarily ignore certain more general philosophical questions relating to the fundamental concepts implicitly incorporated in the recognized language and vocabulary of development discussion and to the role of prior knowledge and intuitive thought in the selective process of observation. To a considerable extent, however, both broader issues lie at the root of the problem of devising suitable data series to monitor social and economic changes. Had alternative approaches not influenced by a long prior history of economic and political thought been taken, then measures to evaluate development policy might have been much more effective than they are at present.

The paper will not be concerned with other underlying ideological or political issues which, it can also be reasonably argued, are similarly significant to the debate about generating relevant data for development. Whether a developing economy can be viewed as being subject to the ravages of a primitive capitalism introduced and imposed by some external imperialist power or as a satellite at the mercy of a centrally controlled bureaucratic system, undoubtedly has a strong bearing on the choice of the type of statistics collected and produced by both the government and resident economic agents. Any compilation of statistics should be related in an ideal situation to the particular political and administrative decision-making process if the data are to be at all relevant and useful.

B. The influence imparted by the conventional wisdom of economic and statistical theory

1. Economic

From a purely practical point of view, two basic and significant factors can be identified that have led to the introduction in the past of an important element of unintentional bias into development analysis and its associated supporting statistical structure. A further undesired distortion has crept into the development of information systems for policy purposes in developing countries because of the professional acceptability of certain standard theoretical statistical techniques (and hence unacceptability of other methods of unscientific enquiry).

The first of these factors was what is now regarded as a simplistic and uni-dimensional view of the pattern and process of development, but it exerted a strong influence over the world's general understanding of events. Paradoxically, despite the growing criticism in more recent years of GDP as a measure of development achievement and progress, this view gave rise to the implicit belief that agricultural and industrial change, increased financial transfers and appropriate investment policies would provide the necessary and sufficient solution to the perceived problem of increasing economic growth and raising living standards.

Sadly, these internal remedies ignored the fact that most developing countries are continually forced to enter established world markets from a position of weakness and engage in the operations of the international economy on the basis of existing terms in which they have had no say. They are compelled by circumstances to produce and trade under conditions of operation which are predominantly disadvantageous to them. This situation of comparative disadvantage has occurred mainly because of the existing structure of ownership of the world's assets and the way the different institutional structures of production, trading and financial activities in the world economy have historically evolved since the earliest eras of modern industrialization and colonial territorial expansion. The recognition of the need in developing countries for significant structural changes, both internally and externally, calls for rather different and more extensive data requirements than those normally provided by traditional economic series relating to income, output and expenditure.

Concentration on this type of information inherently reflects an implicit assumption that there is a reasonably freely operating market situation in which the price mechanism still serves as the essential signalling system. Even with the controlled intervention of the government as an agent, prices are deemed to reflect the relative strength of different needs and the most appropriate priorities for the allocation of scarce resources. The most cursory observation quickly reveals, however, that a production system responding to such impulses has very little relevance either to the alleviation of poverty[1] or the satisfaction of basic individual and social needs of the majority of the population in a developing country.[2]

2. Statistical

The second important factor which continues to exert a strong influence over the way that data are collected, is the common and conventional - and usually unquestioned - statistical assumption that a proper, balanced understanding of economic and social problems requires the fair and equal treatment of all phenomena. This demands the collection of data using unbiassed random survey techniques. This is not simply because administrative and registration records of all types are regarded as being - for a wide

---

[1] Unless a fair and realistic redistribution policy is implemented and, equally important, is capable of being rigorously enforced.

[2] This has led some development economists - notably from Latin America - to argue that the economic system should be changed to ensure that production is basically geared not to profit but to human need.

variety of legal, practical and efficiency reasons - selective and discriminatory (as indeed they are), but because random selection methods are in some sense, "ideal".

Even if the theoretical elegance of a comprehensive random selection of the population under investigation can ever be actually achieved in practice - and this is doubtful in the evaluation of most economic and social questions - it must be recognized that this will not reflect a neutral or truly impartial choice but a deliberate selection procedure. To make a random choice and to give each sampling unit an equal change of selection not only presumes that each primary unit is identical but implies a decision to attach no special weight or importance to those of the population most in need. In many cases, these groups are also the least politically influential.

A random sampling process, in principle, will attach equal importance not only to the rich and employed but also to the poor, the illiterate, the indigent, and other undefined and unidentified disadvantaged groups in the population. For almost all relevant current official policy purposes in developing countries, this approach to the investigation of problems is probably far less appropriate than a selection procedure that, by contrast, concentrates entirely on the group for which some action has been proposed or on the area of interest for which information is required.

Furthermore, in actual practice it is often these policy focussed groups, the most disadvantaged and others at each end of the spectrum of society, who tend to be omitted or ignored in a traditional sample survey enquiry. They are excluded either deliberately on the grounds of cost or unintentionally because they have no fixed abode, no employment, or other easily identifiable activity to facilitate a contact reference point. In some cases it is the respondent who decides - for one reason or another - to exclude himself or his activities from the survey.[3]

The common (although fortunately no longer universal) acceptance in the past of these two principal assumptions governing the collection and compilation of data in developing countries has led inexorably to the generation of information frameworks and flows which have not been entirely relevant and useful to the conduct and formulation of economic and social development policy. They have contributed significantly to the introduction of unnecessarily expensive and lengthy collection procedures.

These assumptions have also given rise, in practice, to the adoption and absorption of a variety of standard coding and classification systems specifically associated with the perceived understanding of the dynamics of change.

The introduction and application of a family of related common statistical techniques, survey methodologies and standard tabulations has meant that, on many issues, only a partial illustration of the real problems of development confronting the country has been provided.

It is thus unnecessary to seek very far to find an explanation of the current situation where existing data series are considered to be relatively

---

[3] Hence the general lack of personal information concerning royalty, politicians, stars, millionaires, etc.

unhelpful in framing development policy. People's perceptions of reality have been influenced by both the information they have received and the conventional wisdom of the time. In turn, this has affected the kind of information government agencies have decided it is necessary to collect in order to identify and clarify policy issues. The net result is that official data, submitted as apparently objective, independent and neutral quantitative reports on the status of individuals, communities and other groups, have tended to a large extent to reflect the particular ideologies current at the time. Consequently, the statistics collected tend only to confirm accepted perceptions of reality and other commonly held assumptions about the way in which the world works.

It is important not to ignore the context in which statistics are collected and developed. It is also equally important not to assume that official data provide an impartial record which is in some sense independent and external to the way in which it is anticipated the information will be used. To a large extent, the origins of the present problem can be traced back to the proper desire to consolidate the great mass of data in existence. A wide range of information is generally available from surveys and administrative records and this must be condensed into salient figures that can be readily grasped. The use of summary measures that possess some semblance of meaning not only to those in authority but also those subject to that authority is now considered essential for policy. Unfortunately, because of the underlying slant of the distribution, the average estimate (the so-called representative value) often too successfully obscures the real situation and circumstances of those sections of the community most requiring and deserving of official attention. In a practical sense, much of the operational policy in developing countries should be directed towards the extreme, literally "abnormal", groups - the lowest paid, the single parent families, the aged, the super-rich, etc.

In these instances, the representative value symbolizes little and indicates nothing about basic needs. It stands only as a standard of comparison, a relative measure against which not even general progress nor the over-all success of policy can be effectively monitored.[4] But it is a shifting standard which is not independent of the type of success that is actually achieved. Such measures are also influenced by the structural changes that have occurred elsewhere in the group or in the system as a whole. A policy of poverty alleviation, for example, which attempts to bring the income of low-paid workers in a particular industry up to the national average in that sector, often tends to ignore the fact that the original target itself, the goal of the policy, was directly affected by the existence of those low wage-earners in the first place. The objective itself shifts progressively with the continual success or failure to achieve the original goal.

Other things being equal, it is quite obvious that, in cases like this where the underlying distribution is very definitely slanted, a more genuine measure would be the model estimate rather than the arithmetic mean. It would

---

4/ It should be mentioned, of course, that success (as measured by raising the average) can be simply achieved by increasing the size of the values in the upper section of the distribution, particularly in the top segment.

be the most appropriate representative value against which to assess the effectiveness of policy measures, some of which – it may be hopefully surmised – being to reduce the observed differentials between the mean and mode.[5]

Practical questions such as these, although not always very clearly evident, abound in everyday policy management. Averages, which are specifically derived (or imputed indirectly from aggregates adjusted for the recorded corresponding number of observations) are now regularly quoted and used by all walks of society, many times during the day. For the most part this springs from a genuine desire to understand and come to grips with the complexities of a particular question.

C. The nature of the development process

Although there now exists a number of separate theories that attempt to provide some appropriate explanations for the observed process and pattern of social and economic development that has occurred in the world, most can be classified essentially into two broad categories, each reflecting a particular and broadly opposing line of political thought. Not surprisingly, both can trace their origins to similar historical roots.

1. Growth and resource – base theories (the internal constraints)

The first of these so-called theories, which can be generally described as the standard, traditional Western explanation, considers the process of development to be a function of economic change. The present backward state of the third world is seen to be a reflection of the rate of industrialisation (or lack of it) and economic growth in the countries concerned. The approach was widely recognized as providing an intuitively reasonable explanation which adequately described the process of change leading up to the present status and role of the already industrially advanced nations. This was only because by default, the more wealthy constituted the few select countries for which a full historical profile was available. There was no real evidence that, in the natural order of events, other countries would follow a similar pattern of development[6] or, indeed, that it was desirable for them to do so.[7] The main ideas and underlying arguments are both neo-classical and Keynesian in their descriptive analysis of change and, in consequence, it is primarily the economic aspects – the real resource base, investment, government expenditure – that are stressed.

At its most popular level, this type of approach is epitomized by Rostow's influential stages of economic growth hypothesis[8] which co-ordinates neo-classical and Keynesian theses within a broad historical context. The theories have long conditioned the popular approach to the problem of development faced by low income countries and they have strongly influenced the character of aid flows in the past. They led, in practice, to the adoption of economic policies which implicitly or explicitly reflect on essentially Harrod-Domar formulations concerning the main determinants of the rate of

---

[5] That is, to improve the over-all distribution.

[6] To the extent that they can often be ascribed to deliberate international and domestic government policy in the past.

[7] This would pre-suppose that, in the past, development policy (which has taken on many different shades and aspects) had been particularly successful as far as the developed industrial countries were concerned.

[8] Which he himself describes as a "non-communist manifesto".

growth. These policies concentrated attention on the assumed dynamic
relationship between savings and investment. It was deduced that the lack of
growth and development arose from inadequate investment which in turn was a
reflection of the dearth of utilizable domestic savings and foreign exchange
earning opportunities.[9]

Although this macro-economic approach is essentially Keynesian in its
perception of the pattern of events, it nevertheless also implicitly
incorporates elements of neo-classical analysis relating to such important
matters as the limited factor resource base, specialization, comparative
advantage, economies of scale, etc. These concepts were all regarded as
relevant to the choice of an appropriate investment programme and the
development of suitable products and markets. (It may perhaps appear somewhat
strange in retrospect that the investment-oriented approach - in heavy base
industries - was also enshrined in early Soviet development strategy and the
general policy was to sacrifice everything to rapid industrialization.)

Structural-dependency theories: the international perspective

The alternative explanation, although having its foundations in the same
basic historical evidence, tends to emphasise the international and internal
structural imbalances that have been established both in developing countries
and in the world economy. These have arisen during the process of development,
mainly because of the differential rate of economic progress (and consequential
acquisition of power and accumulation of capital) in different parts of the
world. This has led to the concentration of economic power in specific centres
and an unbalanced international dependence.

To a certain extent this line of thought had its origins in Marxist
theories of colonialism and exploitation. But in more recent years, the theory
has been considerably developed beyond the original rather rudimentary
ideological and political level of analysis to provide a somewhat more
plausible structural and institutional explanation as to why so many countries
are at varying stages of development. Perhaps, and more importantly, it also
attempts to explain why such very varied states of progress and wide
disparities in levels of living exist within quite different developing
countries without many links occurring. The theory recognizes that different
levels of development can still persist despite efforts to raise production,
income and expenditure levels and that the process of change has to be viewed
within the context of the country's historically unavoidable involvement
in the international economy.

The marked differences in well-being and the immense inequalities of
wealth and income which occur even within developing countries are reinforced
by the existing power structure and institutional framework. This is only too
evident even to the casual observer in a low-income country. The wide
disparities between income levels, standards of living, levels of production
technology and so on, are - in the main - directly and indirectly inherited
from the already advanced industrial world whose institutional structure,

----

9/ Latterly, when investment was seen not to provide the desired stimulus
to economic progress, it was thought to be the quality or the character of the
investment that was wrong; in particular, attention began to be concentrated
on the need to improve "human capital".

philosophy and socio-economic patterns of living are transported, somewhat piecemeal over time, to the developing world.

The first line of approach focuses primarily on the purely economic and technological character of the process of change within a domestic context whereas the latter recognizes that development has also an essentially institutional as well as a social and cultural dimension and is strongly influenced by adverse international factors. This is clearly important when attempting to establish an element of national independence[10] and sovereignty within the institutional structure of the international economy and society. This structural view emphasises the lack of certain important domestic internal interrelationships which are essential prerequisites for national development. It stresses the overriding dominance of international linkages and continued foreign economic management and control. It sees these linkages (or lack of them) as giving rise to the existing social relations in production in developing countries. This structure has failed to loose the motivating forces that might be expected to bring new classes to power. The pattern of foreign investment, the terms and conditions of employment, the differences in purchasing power, the conditioned patterns of consumption, imported production technologies, the nature of education and cultural influence, etc. have all reinforced the type of change that has occurred.

Figure XVIII attempts to outline in a very simplified way the historical pattern that emerged and the sequence of events that took place involving the more significant foreign interventions as they occurred in an approximate chronological order. It has given rise to the co-existence of widely different development levels in the same country. These have served to emphasise the incomplete articulation and inter-relationship between the different and distinctly identifiable sectors of society in most low-income countries (see figure XIX). The foreign owned and controlled corporate sector provides, for the most part, relatively high wage level employment. It also uses modern capital and a sophisticated technology. The public (and state controlled) sector also tends to operate at a similar level. The local capitalist sector, that is, domestically owned business, generally operates on a much smaller scale (yet it is often more varied and full of risk-hedging options) and a wide range of manufacturing, transport, distribution and service activities. It may employ some unpaid family workers and it invariably utilizes a much lower level of technology, although this is still mainly imported. The comparatively large informal sector of mainly unregistered, unincorporated one-man and family businesses fills the essential gap left to provide processed goods to the poorer and mainly urban based sections of the community who are unable to support themselves on food produced from the land.

The dominant traditional sector, which is almost entirely rural based, employs little labour in a conventional sense and has changed only imperceptibly in character over the centuries. By far the largest number of people in the country are engaged (in the loosest sense of the term) in the activities of this sector.

10/ What most Less Developed Countries (LDCs) seek is a reduction in dependence on markets, outside technology and expertise, imports, foreign finance, etc.

Figure XVIII.

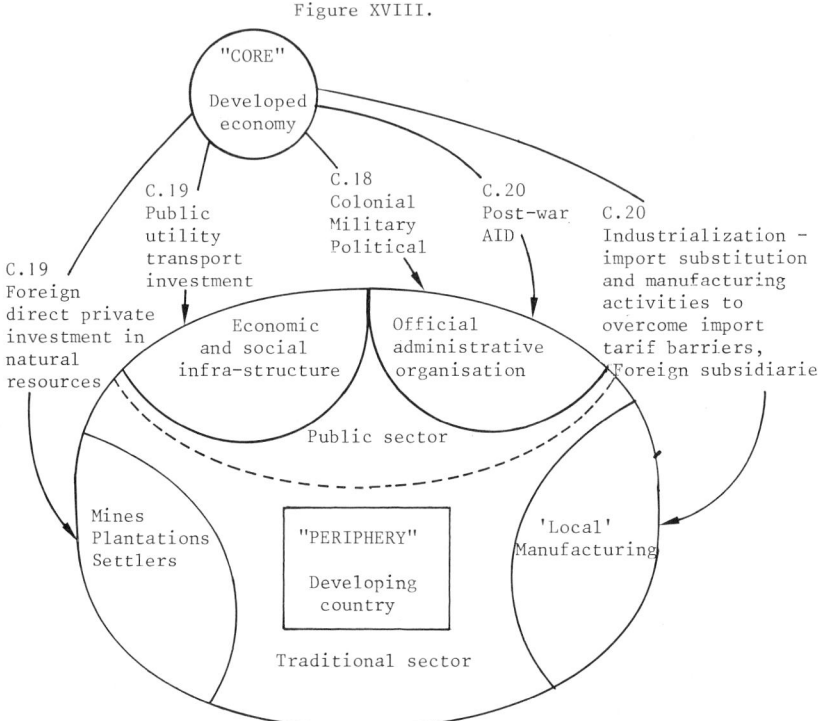

Note : Internal demand is therefore seen as a function of imported industrial
       capitalism and technology.

Figure XIX. Domestic internal linkages with overseas

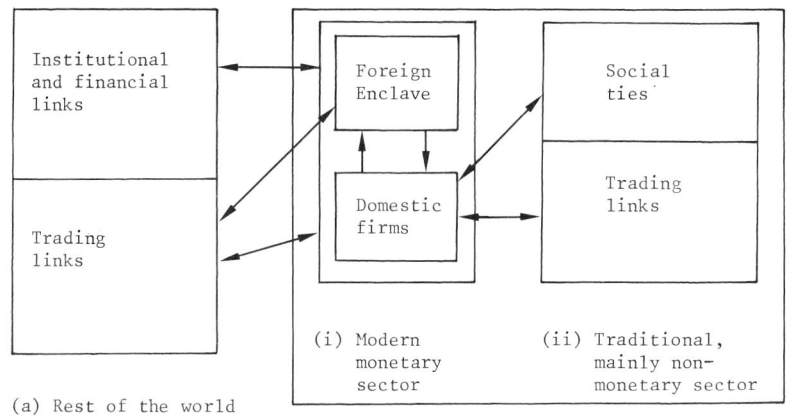

Source : Osvaldo Sunkel, "The transnational economy", Institute of Development
         Studies discussion paper, 1976.

The difference between all these sectors is principally one of technology
and production organization and clearly the more advanced enclaves have little
impact on the rest of the economy and what links that do exist are strictly
limited. There is little filtering of knowledge from the bigger firms to
the small local enterprises (which are in competition with each other) and no
trickling down of more modern processes and methods, partly because of the
lack of capital (or rather access to it) in the smaller firms and partly
because of the lack of relevant knowledge. Thus the society presents a picture
of communities still at different stages of a fairly rigidly fixed development.
There is clearly no place for a Rostowian explanation of change in such a
situation. Although the nature of the output in the end may be the same,
the various modes of production are clearly widely different in the different
enclaves of the economy.

The present place of official statistics in this scheme of events emerges
quite distinctly; it is located, if at all, in the foreign-owned and state-
controlled sectors where the techniques of problem solving are appropriate
to the type of administrative organization employed, the technology applied,
the production methods used and the nature of decisions to be taken, even
though they are not necessarily relevant to the problem itself. Statistics
are usually narrowly restricted to those specific issues thought, from the
experience of other countries, to be conventionally applicable to national
policy, for example prices, wages, production, imports, exports, etc. Until
quite recently statistics have rarely been used in the consideration of wider
problems and matters of social concern and in any fundamental analysis of the
constraints to development.

The impact of conventional statistics in their immediate area of use is
rarely significant (partly because of the absence of other essential factors,
particularly supporting administrative skills and organizational capacity) and
its effect on the rest of the economy and the population as a whole is minimal.
What needs to be explored now more thoroughly is how statistics and an
associated new and possibly more selective micro method of approach can
be used to benefit the majority of the community, rather than very limited
specific, easily identifiable and vociferous segments of it; and in what
ways statistics can improve the process of decision-making – and
consequently the conditions of existence of most people in a developing
country.

D.   The primary data collection process

This section is concerned with the various ways in which information is
gathered. It looks particularly at the random survey not, as conventionally,
by comparison with the census but with respect to the real information
required and the type of policy objectives that might be defined by developing
countries.

In the past, official statistical systems have tended to evolve from
two separate approaches; primary data collection on the one hand and secondary
source material (administrative files, etc.) on the other. Primary data are
collected with a deliberate set of objectives in mind using both comprehensive
surveys, such as censuses, and specially selected sample surveys which are
intended to be representative of the population as a whole. The sample
survey, however well designed, suffers from an important disadvantage in so
far as it is usually unable to reflect all objectives of an enquiry equally
well. Secondary statistics, on the other hand, have been generated as
automatic by-products of the administrative process although particular
information requirements may also have been added at some stage. Examples
such as the trade statistics from customs collection, births and deaths from
vital registration, and education data from school enrolment, etc. should,

in principle, (in representing regular and detailed micro data relating to
individual activities, people and transactions) provide an ideal basis of
information. But in the developing countriés of the world, many of these
secondary administrative data systems were set up by foreign colonial powers
as exercises concerned with specific and limited policy ends which were mostly
geared to their own interests and needs for control. In many cases it is
evident that these policy ends and objectives - and indeed the whole
administrative structure - were different from those that might be chosen and
pursued by the country itself at the time. Such data also suffer from the
major disadvantages of invariably being both restrictive and selective in their
scope and coverage. Registration or licensing data for example are applicable
only to those observations and events which are registered or licensed. The
process of registration is governed not only by the precise terms, conditions
and restrictions of registration but also by the willingness (and ability)
of people to register the event in question.

1. Surveys and census

Traditionally, discussion concerning the relative merits of the sample
survey as a means of collecting data have taken place only in the alternative
context of implementing a complete census to obtain comprehensive coverage of
a particular issue under investigation. There is rarely any evaluation of
whether the sample survey itself is the most useful and appropriate method
of collecting information, or more specifically, whether it might be
expected to generate data directly relevant to intended policy decisions.
In many cases, survey data merely serve as interesting descriptive background
to such decisions and the information has proved to be of limited potential
use.

Two important assumptions seem to be implied by this comparison between
the sample survey and the census approach to data collection. The first is
that the two methods of enquiry can be regarded simply as alternative means
of collecting the same information. The second is that the survey is assumed
to provide the basis for a representative cross-sectional overview of the
whole population under investigation. Neither of these assumptions is in fact
either accurate or necessary.

In the first place, it can be readily observed in practice that censuses
can only be used for collecting a certain and indeed fairly restricted type
of very basic information which is mostly of a qualitative, factual nature. The
generally more useful quantitative data can only be effectively collected by
some form of more detailed sample survey or from regularly updated
administrative records. Surveys are probably more directly and immediately
useful if they are focussed on a specific problem or target group. When they
are designed to provide a representative random selection of the whole
population and are concerned with a variety of objectives and variables they
tend to become difficult to manage efficiently and effectively.

However, attempts to build up an over-all view by producing specific
group or class averages and estimating the associated aggregates are
undoubtedly useful, especially when trying to establish a comparable and
meaningful context. They are also necessary when attempting to compile
appropriate base period data, but such general information is usually not
often needed. Apart from the special need to identify the extremes and
specific groups, which are not usually defined as the primary objectives in a
representative sample, it would seem more important to try and devise new more
limited surveys that can be more readily integrated with the existing
administrative data sources. At the same time, statistical offices should
attempt to obtain a greater degree of consistency and compatibility with
already established definitions and records.

In order to understand more fully the limitations of what may be loosely termed "the simple random sample survey" approach, it is useful first to re-examine the role of the census against the background of its historical evolution and to assess its accuracy and usefulness.

2.   The census

The earliest censuses were simply straightforward population counts. These demographic exercises were primarily associated with some form of regulatory control which, more often than not, was basically military in purpose. Later, as in the case of the Biblical tribes and then the Doomsday Book, censuses also became concerned with recording trades, asset holdings and wealth. Consequently, people's economic activities were incorporated into the enquiries. Incidentally, because most people's activities were concentrated on the land, such counts were also, by their very nature, crude agricultural censuses that identified not only the major crops grown but also the size of holdings.

Although the population census covers a wide variety of personal information, it is first and foremost a demographic exercise. Generally speaking, most modern censuses usually encompass enquiries relating to the social and economic characteristics of the population, such as level of education achieved and occupation engaged in, but they are still mainly concerned with the basic population dynamics. Agricultural censuses, and even industrial production censuses, are often misnamed because they tend to be either sample surveys or partial surveys rather than complete census inquiries. In the case of the agricultural census, and particularly the calculation of crop area and crop yield statistics to derive output estimates, the use of the classical survey methodology in developing countries (where there are wide variations in plots cultivated, crops, methods employed throughout the country and over the year) has been seriously questioned. [11]

Of all inquiries into the different aspects of human behaviour, demographic characteristics seem, on the surface, to present the least difficulties for data collection and analysis. But concepts regarded as essential to the collection of information – such as household or resident – are far from unambiguous. [12] Indeed, even those concepts most directly relevant to basic demographic measurement itself (such as live birth and age) are not always clearly defined or uniformly identifiable. Furthermore, evidence gained from a number of different countries suggests that, given similar conditions, the values obtained for the usual basic demographic variables may be significantly affected by such factors as the wording and presentation of the questions asked, the characteristics of the respondent (as well as those of the enumerator), the extent of the control and supervision of survey procedures and the nature of these procedures themselves. Only some of these factors are subject to the statistician's general control and the larger the country and survey size, the more difficult it becomes to exercise really effective supervision.

---

[11] D.J. Casley, "Problems in estimation of crop areas and crop yields", International Statistical Institute (ISI) conference paper, Warsaw, 1975.

[12] William Selzer, "Demographic data collection: a summary of experience", an Occasional Paper of the Population Council, 1973.

In practice, this means that the most reliable censuses are those where
there is only a limited range of customary and commonly acknowledged census
questions which are simple to answer because they relate mainly to individual
personal characteristics. All survey questions have to be comprehensible and
answerable by those with a relatively unsophisticated intelligence and level
of understanding. The questions must not be too long or complex and the
accuracy of the responses must to some extent be capable of being checked by
observation or related questions. The census, which is primarily concerned
with tagging and mapping ascertainable population characteristics, appears to
be an eminently suitable method for collecting and classifying information that
either changes comparatively little over time or is likely to change only in
some easily predictable and straightforward fashion. On the other hand,
concurrent checks of enumerator records and questionnaire responses using
tape recordings of the interview as actually conducted indicate that even the
simplest questions can be misunderstood (for social and cultural reasons as
well as because of the customary inadequacies in education) and thus wrongly
reported on the enumerator's register.

Censuses have the major disadvantage of being very expensive both in terms
of their absorption of real resources and their actual financial cost,
especially when there are so many other competing, and perhaps equally
important, demands on the limited resources available. Censuses are also a
lengthy process, consuming a great amount of time from the inception of the
detailed organization until the publication of the final report. The
combination of cost and, literally, years of gestation until the final results
are published means that most countries can only afford to hold full censuses
at infrequent, although preferably regular, intervals which are usually every
ten years.

The more questions that are asked, the longer the inquiry takes and the
more costly it becomes. Both the timeliness and the usefulness of a census
suffer if there are too many questions.

Many observers are critical of the value and validity of collecting
socio-economic data (such as employment condition, occupation, social status,
etc.) by means of a census.[13] These critics would argue that not only is
the socio-economic data collected inherently unreliable[14] but also that it
detracts from the worth of the basic demographic data.[15] This is because the
apparently more complicated and often newer questions on status, occupation,
etc. in developing countries require more attention, organization and
enumerator training. Less time can be devoted therefore, to obtaining good
demographic responses – not all of which are as straightforward as they
appear, for example number of confinements and/or live births applicable to a
particular woman.[15]

---

[13] J.G.C. Blacker, "A critique of the international definitions of
activity and employment status and their applicability in population censuses in
Africa and the Middle East", Centre for Population Studies, London School of
Hygiene and Tropical Medicine (paper presented to the Institute of Developmental
Studies' Seminar 69, National Accounts and Development Statistics).

[14] J.G.C. Blacker op. cit. M. Ward, "A critique of occupation censuses",
Department of Applied Economics, Cambridge University, 1965.

[15] W. Selzer, op. cit.

Furthermore, there is a suggestion that for cultural and other reasons the very questions themselves exert some degree of influence over the nature of the demographic response.

It has to be admitted that without a great deal of supplementary data it is difficult to define or make sense of any national scale information in a developing country which relates to employment status. At the same time, other pertinent demographic questions for developing countries, particularly those relating to internal and external migration patterns, may be omitted (although on this specific issue it is difficult in practice to define an effective and meaningful question which will accurately record the geographical mobility of the population).

It would be wrong, however, to assume that a census on the other hand would provide a complete and comprehensive enumeration of the most salient socio-economic characteristics in which a country is interested. Given such physical and financial restrictions, there is a clear trade-off between extending the coverage of the survey on the one hand and extending the scope of its contents on the other. To collect even more detailed information in a census would undoubtedly lead to a rapid falling-off of accuracy, as well as an extension in the already lengthy time taken to publish any meaningful results. In addition, the potential alienation of the population against any further surveys to be conducted by the Government must also be taken into account. The questions normally asked in a census are therefore limited to a descriptive character and relate to relatively easily obtainable status information. They usually refer directly to the people themselves and to certain related discernible characteristics, such as their housing conditions. Even these questions cannot always be easily ascertained and observed at the same time. A census rarely offers any scope for collecting information on many important components of every-day living standards such as health conditions or level of nutrition. Other potentially more disputable and subjectively evaluated characteristics which really affect the basic day to day living conditions of many people such as access to economic and social amenities cannot be effectively quantified in this way.

The size of a population census operation and the complexities of its associated administration organization render it difficult to extend its scope beyond what may be commonly regarded as a conventional population enquiry. Censuses are prone to very serious delays between the collection of data and the publication of the results. In the presentation of information, the quality and usefulness of the statistics collected are invariably impaired by this delay. Furthermore, the census – being an exercise concerned primarily with tagging and mapping the main demographic characteristics of the whole population – relies heavily on a standard format. This approach has been conventionally established by the tradition of previous censuses and the limited requirements of the census itself which do not permit, in practice, much variation in the context of the schedules used since a number of basic questions must always be asked. Different questionnaires cannot be employed in a census, by definition in effect, to allow for differences between particular groups or regions. Such distinctions, however, may be especially important in large countries or in those countries where there is a very heterogeneous population structure, for example Nigeria, Fiji, Malaysia, etc. A standard procedure comparing a general and uniform approach must inevitably give rise to a certain element of underlying variance and hence distortion in the results of the enquiry which will not be revealed explicitly in the data themselves.

Geographical regions, population groups and sectors identified in the census may not be relevant or meaningful to the objectives of the inquiry nor to the definitions employed in the census itself. The system of traditional economic, political, social and cultural organization is often very different in some sub-regions from those assumed for the country as a whole. More important, the local areas which house such varied groups in the population may not coincide with the regional administrative or planning area customarily used for enumeration purposes in a census.[16], [17].

3. The sample survey

A number of significant advantages are normally attributed to survey sampling (and particularly random sampling) procedures. Probably the most important is cost-saving. A sample costs less than a complete enumeration in total because it covers fewer observations.[18] It is argued that for lower over-all input cost it is possible to obtain the same type of information from either a sample or a census and it is also implicitly assumed that such knowledge can be just as equally obtained by a sample as a census. Indeed, a second declared advantage of a sample is that it is often feasible to introduce improvements into a survey without adversely affecting the end objectives or the quality of any (or all) of the information required. A third advantage is that with a sample, this information is derived with a much shorter time lag than if it had been collected by some other means. Certainly, excessive delays in the complete publication of census results impairs their relevance and usefulness. But it is beginning to become increasingly less evident that sample survey information, by comparison, is any more timely from any really practical viewpoint. It may be true that the requisite data are obtained quicker than if collected through a census but if the time lag still means that most of the results lose their current validity and relevance for policy determination, then the real value of the survey is jeopardized.

A sample survey can be most effectively and reliably operated when only one appropriate major objective is identified. In these circumstances the selection procedure can be orientated towards this aim accordingly. Delays and difficulties develop, on the other hand, when the investigation is designed to serve a number of similarly important (and occasionally unrelated) purposes at the same time. This seems particularly true in those studies where each question is inter-related or covers problem areas that are considered to be (or are in fact) inter-dependent. If the time delay was due only to the actual collection, processing and tabulation of returns, a random sample would undoubtedly produce fairly rapid results. The necessary pre-survey organization, the survey administration identifying and contacting

---

16/ M. Ward, The Role of Investment in the Development of Fiji, (Cambridge, University Press, 1971) and Urban-Rural Data Sets, (Paris, OECD, 1979).

17/ In practice, however, with the very detailed disaggregation of census units into very small enumeration areas, this problem will rarely arise since the smaller enumeration areas can always be aggregated in a different way and then combined with the data already available for the area from other sources.

18/ The average unit costs of a sample, however, are invariably higher.

respondents, the supervision of enumerators, checking of returns, however, all
introduce added time dimensions into the actual sampling and survey procedure.
The more numerous the objectives, the greater the sophistication needed in the
sample design and the more complicated the organization of the survey. In
practice, the increased sophistication often leads to less reliable results.
This is especially true at the disaggregated stratified micro group level for
which the added information is often usually desired. The greater the
consequent complexity thought necessary, the longer it takes to publish results.
Another commonly defined advantage of survey sampling is that it reduces or
restricts the irksome burdens placed on the public in general. In practice,
few respondents themselves would concur with such a statement because most
sample survey questionnaires are personally far more exacting and time-consuming
to complete - even with help - than equivalent census forms, especially when
a greater degree of detailed accuracy is demanded.

The organizers of sample surveys also frequently state that surveys are
much less demanding of manpower resources and other necessary equipment and
facilities. Whilst it may be true that, in terms of absolute numbers, sampling
operations require fewer people, in terms of educational qualifications,
necessary experience and relevant training - indeed the whole absorption of
skilled manpower - the demands are much greater. They are perhaps
disproportionately high in a developing country where a premium is placed on
skills of almost any kind, let alone those scarce ones required for the
efficient operation of a survey. The processes of recruitment and training of
survey personnel are thus often more difficult and lengthier. Furthermore,
the time needed to have such manpower available is much longer for a scientific
sample survey than for other types of enquiry. There is, however, a reduced
demand on other resources such as transport vehicles, materials and office
space.

Even the best theoretical techniques of survey sampling are limited in
their applications, especially where the variability between measures of the
basic components in the population itself is thought to be substantial. Thus,
even using the most efficient optimum method of selection, the sampling error
of the estimate may turn out to be unacceptably large, at least for certain
sub-group values. (In practice, however, this seems highly doubtful where most
official policy decisions are concerned.). What may be more important from a
practical viewpoint is that Governments may sometimes find it impossible to
identify actual changes by means of two sample surveys taken at different times
or in different places. Where the change in certain elements is likely to be
small, or slow to take effect, successive or simultaneous sample surveys are
unlikely to reveal any underlying shifts because of the difficulty of ensuring -
without substantially increasing the survey costs penalties - that the sampling
error is of a lower order of magnitude than the actual change which has
occurred.

More generally, the design of the sample, the organization of the survey
and the selection of sampling units need to be accommodated within the
financial limitations imposed by a publicly accountable budget. At the same
time they must still adhere closely to the principal objectives of the enquiry
which ideally should have the primary influence over the survey procedure
selected. Where detailed interregional and cross-sectional comparisons are
required, however, the complete enumeration of the population may be the only
feasible method of achieving the desired objectives with any acceptable degree
of reliability because, beyond a certain sample size, a census will probably
turn out to be less expensive and more efficient in the long run - provided of
course, the scope of the actual inquiry is kept reasonably simple and short.
Even then, the conventional methods of survey analysis normally adopted attempt
to consolidate sample and census data into meaningful aggregates to derive
certain generalized results and over-all averages that can be easily

comprehended and utilized. At the same time, unfortunately, these may not necessarily identify the real problems and issues involved.[19]

Where, in a given population, special problems of coverage, identification and location of units exist, special problems of enumeration and sample selection arise. What holds good with respect to normal data collection and survey exercises then no longer applies, particularly when suitable population lists are not available. This usually means that the characteristics of the units to be surveyed are basically very different. An undisclosed number will undoubtedly fall outside the practical and convenient or legal and administrative boundaries defined by government. Alternatively, the units may drop below the cut-off points evolved in preparing the basic list. The list itself may not necessarily be precisely applicable for identifying the whole group. Paradoxically, in many instances, the lower the cut-off point and the stricter the attempted regulatory control, the more indistinct and blurred the classification becomes, especially in LDCs where the routine organization and practical communications are difficult. Of course, if the classification framework is imprecisely or ambiguously defined in the first place, then the corresponding population groups will also be unsatisfactorily identified. The main problems tend to occur where all but a select minority of units generally form individually small, unorganized and uncontrollable elements of a changing population. Such units usually possess incomplete records, lack adequate knowledge and frequently have no fixed location for their different activities. All these characteristics conspire against any conventional methods to facilitate easy, economic and accurate data collection.

It is unfortunate that, to many government officials, the actual statistical procedures and detailed collection methods, per se, assume an over-riding importance as desired ends in themselves whereas they should reflect the primary objectives for collecting the relevant information and recognize the broad degree of accuracy deemed necessary for policy implementation. In the process, the practical and operational implications of adopting and implementing the usually complex technical and organizational statistical recommendations proposed are either obscured, overlooked or ignored.

Quite apart from the very real practical operational difficulties and costs of trying to organize a broadly based random survey, there are really two features of classical statistical sampling theory which make this approach less applicable to developing countries.[20] The two reasons are as follows:

---

[19] See Barry Hindess, The Use of Official Statistics in Sociology: a Critique of Positivism and Ethnomethodology (New Jersey, Humanities, 1973), for a criticism of the 1951 Census of India, for example.

[20] Together, the disproportionately higher survey costs combined with what are usually less reliable and, more particularly, less relevant results, seem to provide sound prima facie reasons for reviewing the possibilities of adopting alternative data collection procedures.

(a) To adopt a random sampling procedure and to attempt to give each sampling unit in the population an equal chance of selection, represents a specific purposeful choice. It is a decision to accord equal attention to the very rich and those in extreme poverty, to those holding fixed and liquid assets and those that do not; 21/

(b) Sampling theory attempts to generalize from the particular; to do so it has to concentrate on the calculation of key estimates – statistics – which possess the relevant theoretical characteristics to permit such calculations to be made. In most cases the key statistics are less useful and relevant to policy determination than those deliberately selected.

Perhaps, in particular, many of the approaches customarily adopted to resolve the difficulties of collecting statistics relating to households, individuals and small-scale units of different kinds are basically misdirected. Part of the problem arises from an essential misunderstanding. Many officials believe that the fundamental issue of obtaining real information can be regarded primarily as a matter of improving the existing standard statistical techniques. This means extending the scope of sample survey inquiries to increase coverage, representation, etc. while at the same time expanding or adapting the investigations and the generally accepted international recommendations on coding procedures and classifications to the special circumstances of the country. These points are regularly reflected in the official position papers and statements prepared by United Nations specialized agency secretariats and their consultants.

This can be illustrated by reference to the special problems of identification, location, coverage, contact and actual enumeration of dispersed or isolated small units which pose particular and rather fundamental statistical questions of data collection. These issues apply to a wide variety of operations peculiarly characteristic to developing countries. To take a simple matter of coding, for example; the official concern with the problems of integrating large and small scale industrial units into some standard international classification (such as the United Nations International Standard Industrial Classification of all Economic Activities (ISIC)) seems to be far less important in developing countries, at least for national purposes, than the need to devise a size-ownership (or control) taxonomy of firms. The latter would facilitate the evaluation of the role of indigenous small-scale productive units in the development of the national economy. Whether the conventional official wisdom reflects a Rostowian growth or Structuralist imbalance explanation of the universe, the underlying theory for advocating greater disaggregation of economic activities along such lines would seem, prima facie, fairly important. The practical need for such detailed data seems equally self-evident. Many solutions currently being proposed to cover in an inquiry the vast proportion of smaller economic operations in society, result from a narrowly restrictive view of conventional sampling procedures. This traditional approach, until now, has been widely adopted. But it is extremely costly in terms of the financial, physical and time resources that must necessarily be expended. Paradoxically,

---

21/ Statisticians will be quick to respond, however, by saying, "Ah yes, but haven't you heard of stratification?" This undoubtedly alleviates possibly the worst aspects of the problems encountered in conducting a totally random selection, but it tends to ignore the very real practical issue in most developing countries of having first to establish a suitable, reliable and satisfactory comprehensive frame.

perhaps, it is also likely to generate information that is biased, incomplete and internally inconsistent. On a number of practical accounts, it is not always correct (and occasionally it might be quite useless) in representing what is really taking place in the economy or society.

To substantiate these critical comments it is worth reflecting briefly on what are the essential features of many small developing countries' economic activities[22] and what, therefore, are the fundamental constraints and limitations of a standard random sampling survey approach. This is best demonstrated - in summary fashion - in the table 5. For illustrative purposes, the experience of specific countries is also referred to, the references being extracted from papers presented at a recent Economic and Social Commission for Asia and the Pacific (ESCAP) seminar dealing with sample survey problems.[23]

Evidence of earlier failures to elicit complete and accurate information from small scale units and the problems involved had previously been brought to the attention of the ESCAP secretariat,[24] but the difficulties identified appear to have been largely ignored or overlooked in the preparation of subsequent official proposals.[25]

Official statistical policies tend to be in broad general agreement with the United Nations Statistical Office's view that for most types of national socio-economic inquiry, probably the best strategy is to conduct infrequent censuses which are designed to facilitate the collection of a few key basic items of information,[26] and to follow up these large-scale studies with more frequent but smaller and much more detailed surveys using well-trained field staff. It is also suggested that some countries requiring regular trend series (and possessing the necessary administrative machinery as well as adequate resources to conduct frequent surveys) could, in addition, carry out annual sample enquiries. The basic sampling unit normally recommended for most purposes in these surveys is either the establishment or the household.[27] Investigators can then choose a basic sampling frame which either comprises a list of sampling units (with identification particulars) or a detailed map of

---

[22] Some of the basic principles apply also to social and cultural activities.

[23] Seminar on Small Scale and Household Industries, Bangkok, 11-17 July, 1978.

[24] "Problems and methods of collecting statistics of distributive trades for household and small-scale enterprises", (E/CN. 11/ASTAT/SDT/L.4), Bangkok, 26 August, 1966.

[25] Perhaps it should be added that in this earlier document, the solutions suggested to overcome the problems identified were very similar to those officially proposed later. Both sets of official recommendations have proved to be equally ineffective in practical surveys conducted in the region.

[26] Such information can usually be collected also through decennial population censuses.

[27] The problem of possible overlap between these two groups and the difficulties of identifying each group, are rarely recognized.

Table 5a. Examples of the distribution of selected key economic and social indicators

Indicator	Industrially developed countries	AFRASIA		Income group	
		Whole country	Upper 2%[a]	Upper 5%[a]	Lower 95%
GDP per head ($)	8,000	450	8,000	5,200	200
Capital per head ($)	26,000	1,000	25,000	15,000	200
Infant mortality rate	15	180	15	18	190
Life expectancy	72	48	70	68	45

a/ Usually urban residents.

Table 5b. Statistical problems associated with the informal sector

Characteristics of small-scale and household "industrial" sector	Statistical problems arising	Country evidence	ESCAP recognition of the problem	ESCAP recommendation
Unregulated activities; often unregistered firms and illegal operations	No comprehensive list of units; no sampling frame	STAT/SSHI/ CRP.4 (Iran) CRP.10 (Indonesia)	E/CN.11/ASTAT/ SDT/L.4 paras. 7-9	1. Produce comprehensive and up-to-date lists 2. Introduce or enforce legal compulsion, use Presidential/ official decrees
No fixed location, no easily identifiable address or accessible location; rented units	Difficult to contact sample respondents; low response	CRP.7 (Bangladesh), CRP.12 (Thailand)	Draft report, paras. 15-16, 34	3. Use area sampling and prepare comprehensive lists for selected areas
High rate of mobility between (a) locations and (b) activities; high rate of turnover of enterprises (high birth rate and death rate)	Unstable universe; difficulties in defining (a) industries (b) activities (c) units	CRP.3, CRP.4 CRP.6, CRP.7 CRP.12, CRP.6	Draft report para. 10	4. Gross-up on the basis of directories or population ratios 5. Survey non-respondents
Diverse and often vertically integrated processing and selling activities	(enterprises, establishments, households)	CRP.3 (India) CRP.2 (Fiji)	Draft report, paras. 21, 23	6. Improve enumerator training
Temporary/part-time/seasonal and regional variations in activities	Varying size, scatter and volatility of units; no space/time dimension or reference base	CRP.6 (Sri Lanka)		7. Introduce a system of post-evaluative checks to sift out poor survey data
Illiterate, uneducated and unskilled operators; family enterprises	Non-response, poor co-operation; lack of understanding of questionnaire	CRP.4, CRP.7	Draft report, para. 30	8. Define units and activities more precisely to avoid overlaps and produce unique classifications
No accounts, poor/inadequate records (for survey purposes)	Irrelevance of conventional terms used; missing data	CRP.6, CRP.7	SDT/L.4, paras. 8,9	9. Convince respondents of the value of the survey to encourage co-operation
Reliance on memory and individual	Low recall; national and imprecise values; high survey cost/time	CRP.4, CRP.5		10. Carry out surveys at irregular intervals 11. Conduct random surveys

area units containing reasonably relevant or related information as a possible basis for selection. Where the basic starting data are lacking, a strong preference has nearly always been expressed for a two or three-stage area sampling approach because this represents a reasonably practical solution. It is usually further proposed that those countries already utilizing an expensive and labour-intensive, continuous-round, multi-purpose household survey system as a basis for their general socio-economic inquiries, could integrate certain other household, institutional (such as schools) or industries' surveys into the same programme. Unfortunately, this might well mean that the survey activities would become unevenly distributed over the country and the survey itself unmanageable.

Even on the assumption that a comprehensive list of units can be compiled, an official recommendation to conduct a "stratified systematic sampling after rearranging units according to some important economic characteristics such as employment, income, wealth holding, workers employed or the value of fixed assets or invested capital owned" must clearly be taken with a pinch of salt. This is particularly true when the very meaning and interpretation of these terms in developing countries must remain open to considerable doubt. Furthermore, it is not easy to be convinced that such concepts are relevant.

The illogicality and inconsistency of many of these technically best statistical proposals, though difficult to fault theoretically, are quite evident from a practical viewpoint. The common scientific approach seems based on the belief that the more vague, imprecise, dispersed and logistically difficult the data collection problem, the more complex and sophisticated must be the survey procedure. But sampling units are not independent of the survey design eventually adopted and respondents are not neutral to the approach taken in any inquiry. To assume that conventional sampling procedures and accompanying official recommendations, if reasonably well followed, will, in the end, lead in practice to a random general-purpose survey that will generate valid and unbiased aggregate estimates, is often a complete delusion. Indeed, it is sometimes a gross misinterpretation to describe what transpires in practice as a random survey, in view of the rather unique theoretical and operational factors pertaining to many socio-economic situations in developing countries.

The possibility and advantages of adopting a purposive or selective case study approach using a few highly skilled surveyors and a probing, open investigation, needs to be explored and then perhaps canvassed more widely. In the past, however, such heretical proposals have been viewed with considerable suspicion - and scepticism - by practising official statisticians and their theoretical advisers. This approach is, nevertheless, much cheaper, quicker and more directly analytical than a conventional descriptive survey (since the questions can be deliberately slanted, quite informally, towards particular important objectives). It is also less likely to lead to non-sampling errors which, in many sectors and areas of inquiry in developing countries, represent the overriding practical operational problem to be overcome.

When there is some doubt about the validity of the survey results (because of perhaps a low level of response) and a follow-up survey is considered necessary, the approach usually followed, that is, to take the adjusted figures, effectively leads in the final analysis to the adoption of a selective sampling procedure and an implicit rejection of many of the original survey results. A number of developing countries, either in desperation or from default, have basically decided to resort to selective or purposive survey techniques when they have discovered that conventional sampling procedures are not effective in covering adequately the population under investigation.

This detailed case–study approach is not, of course, random and the technique
undeniably poses some problems when it is desired to aggregate estimates.
(But these are not insurmountable issues given some basic population
information.)   It might well be asked, however, whether aggregation is really
necessary and what purpose does it serve?[28/] Perhaps the main reason for
collecting so much small scale, disaggregated data is for the national accounts.
These tables are now out of fashion and regarded as being – perhaps incorrectly
– of lesser importance, but they are relevant to long-term policy strategy.
Other than for this purpose the use of over-all national aggregates for on-
going sectoral policy control and operations is limited.

Much practical work still needs to be done in this field of survey
technology. It has hardly been considered – and even less employed – in offical
national surveys. In principle, however, even at its least effective level,
a purposive case-study enquiry could hardly lead to worse results than many
other conventional survey methods given the situation and acceptable margins
of error for policy control. Long before the pre-publication data processing
stage of standard surveys, many errors and inconsistencies will have already
been ironed out, often by a variety of ad hoc, unscientific and selective
adjustment procedures. These are inevitably based mainly on personal
judgements and so they come close to being regarded as purposive.

The main point is that special problems demand special attention and
possibly different treatment from that usually adopted. Alternative survey
approaches should clearly be investigated and evaluated for their inherent
worth and not dismissed as peripheral, unsound or irrelevant. Negative comments
and statements concerning the value of selective in-depth sampling have been
made which are substantially incorrect as far as producing useful and
utilizable information is concerned. On the other hand there is rarely any
indication as to how the descriptive information obtained from a conventional
survey approach will be related to policy. The potential uses to which it is
proposed the data may be put are usually vague and open-ended.

The recent emphasis of development policies has been on specific groups,
social and economic. The need to define the inter-relationships and other
links between key sectors in the economy requires a different and clearly
selective approach. There is a desire to acquire knowledge of the
dynamics of a situation to try and discover why and how things are happening
at present. The conventional requirement to portray a numerical picture of the
past or place on record or what happened at some historical time period is much
less obvious.

4. Codes and classifications

Classification systems are normally pre-determined by the nature of the
administrative organization and survey exercise or by the type of data
themselves. More often than not, the basic structure of information reporting
follows well recognized procedures recommended by the experts and international
agencies and is formally laid down in commonly accepted international standards
and conventions. Although in practice this may be the easiest and the most
convenient way to organize the mass of usually unordered data that are
collected in any survey or regular administrative exercise, in principle this
procedure may well not always be the most relevant and correct one to adopt,

---

28/ So much of development policy is focussed on specific groups and
problem areas.

especially for internal domestic policy use.

Classification involves a consolidation of information and this is inevitably accompanied by some loss of detail. Since the data to be processed are usually too substantial and extensive to facilitate ready comprehension in their existing raw state, some summarization of the vast range of statistics is clearly both necessary and desirable; indeed it is unavoidable. But the question must then become, "What particular details can any specific enquiry afford to lose?" Such questions can only be answered effectively and appropriately in relation to the matter under investigation. It can not always be solved by reference solely to some international standard or established convention. Not infrequently, in certain situations, externally determined nomenclatures and procedures will undoubtedly prove to be the most convenient and relevant (and thus useful) ones to adopt, but statisticians must be urged never to lose sight of the real purpose and end-use for which such information has been gathered.

It is useful, perhaps, to select here a particular example to illustrate this point. The United Nations ISIC, a classification system commonly adopted in developing countries, is of very little use in helping to draw distinctions between modern and traditional modes of production because it is principally an activity based coding procedure. From a policy viewpoint, however, the mode of production or a production organization distinction may be a much more useful basis for an industrial enquiry if it is the Government's declared intention to support local domestic economic activities rather than provide protection to, say, a recently established soft drinks manufacturing industry (which, more often than not will come under direct foreign control or operate under some concessionary licence from overseas). The point is that under the existing international classification all types of firms and industrial operations get grouped under the same various components of food processing or, say, manufacture of metal products activities when it may be more desirable to identify each type separately according to its technology and organization.29/ In this particular case, the issue that has to be resolved is whether it is more significant to lose detail relating to the method of industrial operation or to the type of economic activity. This specific problem - and the fact that activities (or rather the units that engage in them) are difficult to classify uniquely and must serve several varied purposes - defies easy solution.

The importance of implementing an appropriate classification because it lies at the very foundation of subsequent analysis - cannot be over-emphasized. Whether the classification is qualitative or quantitative (or a mixture of both) it involves assigning groups with similar characteristics into distinct classes and related sub-sets. Normally, if a comprehensive and unambiguous picture of the "universe" under study is required, it should not be possible to allocate any particular unit to two different classes at the same time, nor should any unit be omitted. This principle is not always so easy to follow in practice except where the classification is both simple and exhaustive and it comprises clearly defined, mutually exclusive, categories (although in practice, in the majority of cases, it is usually necessary to incorporate a special class for "other" or "not elsewhere specified", "not reported", etc. to complete the

---

29/ And perhaps, ideally if resources permit, by category of economic activity as well.

INFORMATION SYSTEMS IN PUBLIC ADMINISTRATION
D. Eade, J. Hodgson (editors)
North-Holland Publishing Company
© *DFD, 1981*

THE ARCHITECTURE AND ORGANIZATION
OF THE STATISTICAL DATA SYSTEM

An experimental approach in the
Central Statistical Office, Budapest, Hungary

Jozsef Dörnyei*

A. Introduction: appearance of the problem

The requirements of modern Government demand increasingly sophisticated
statistical systems. In addition to the traditional services, a system is
required to give support to the decision-making activity of government and
establish the organizational, technical and methodological conditions for
planned and co-ordinated co-operation among other information systems of the
state administration.

The extension of these descriptive and analytical statistics to also cover
the field of decision-making relates to the conscious activity of the
Government to develop and transform society. Decision-making however is
becoming more and more difficult because, simultaneously with the development
of society, the interrelations are becoming more complex and the stock of
descriptive data more difficult to survey.

This has resulted in a contradiction in that, while the time necessary for
decision-making is constantly growing, the time available for decisions is
decreasing. It is only by means of the development of statistical information
supply that this contradiction can be resolved.

The development of information supply should cover both quality and the
rapidity of complying with information demand. These requirements have
logically forced the statistical services to develop a new systems approach in
relation to their stock of data which has been collected and stored with
considerable financial and intellectual investment.

The idea of developing a logical unified system of the different
statistical data and of the process of data management arose at the
Conference of European Statisticians in 1967 (paper by Svein Nordbotten).
Working groups within the framework of both the Conference and the Council for
Mutual Economic Assistance have dealt with the elaboration of the methods and
means necessary for the establishment of statistical data systems.

---

*Central Statistical Office, Budapest, Hungary

range of alternatives open). Even then, as implied in parenthesis, the
completeness of the classification depends partially on the inherent quality of
the reported data and its characteristics. But rather than simply rejecting or
consolidating such data into somewhat vague and uninteresting "other" categories,
it is worthwhile carrying out a separate analysis of this information to try to
ascertain what information has not been provided and perhaps, more important,
why it has not. If nothing else, it could lead to an improvement in the survey
process or classification system used in future surveys.

When confronted by a set of statistical tables in which different
classification procedures have been adopted, the skilled and experienced analyst
looks first at the general headings and table structure and the various
definitions and categories used before examining the data themselves. This is
because it is necessary to ascertain at the outset what the statistics are not
going to reveal. From there it is possible to discover something about the
organization of government and the process of decision making by asking oneself
the question why the data are left out. The answer, however, may simply lie
in the classification being faulty in that it could be insufficiently precise
or unambiguous. The definitions and categories used must obviously be clear
enough to enable both coders and respondents to classify each unit in the same,
common objective fashion. The larger and more sophisticated and complex a
classification, the more unmanageable it becomes and the more difficult it is to
ensure that not only are all entities coded consistently but also that users
will be able to recognize and understand the information, again in the same way.
The most common practical problem confronting statisticians is that reality
does not conform to basic and consistent rules and many objects of enquiry
possess only certain features in common but otherwise contain no other clear
degree of homogeneity, especially over time.[30]/

The classification systems so far discussed have referred to situations
where the data collection process has either not yet been implemented or has
only just been completed. The proposals relate to fixed categories which, for
the most part, are predetermined (and precoded) because they are intimately
connected with the actual tabulation process which in itself is a reflection of
the objective of the enquiry. Qualitative and quantitative characteristics are
cross-classified with each other to test the inherent reasonableness of any
preconceived hypothesis that perhaps attempts to link certain attributes with
others or to specific values of a given variable. Sometimes the outcome is
inconclusive or empty. In addition, the range and number of possibilities
for disaggregation and dissection is·limited by the essential two-dimensional
nature of the tabulation. This is especially pertinent if it is also intended
to analyse the same characteristics concerned over a given time period.

Prima facie, it would seem fairly sensible, therefore, to try and process
the data on the basis of the actual results obtained and, in some instances,
to pre-select a much wider range of identifiable characteristics that will form
the basis of a defined group. Such cluster analysis techniques have been
widely adopted in the natural sciences, particularly in zoology, botany and
astronomy. They have contributed to the formulation of typologies and
taxonomies and have helped to identify (as well as define) new species and
groups. In the social sciences – except in research studies – the use of
such techniques is still fairly uncommon, although with the flexible and wide

---

30/ Renaud Decoster, Classifications, Plan/LS/2.1, General Course,
Statistical Institute for Asia and the Pacific, Tokyo, 1977.

ranging approach they offer, there are sound arguments for encouraging their
adoption in selected situations. The quality of data analysis would be
improved and the most important necessary detail (which is now defined by the
inherent characteristics of the data themselves) would become a centre of
focus and be more clearly identified. This should prove to be a particularly
useful advantage in problem oriented policy.

The system is robust because the basic criteria used to define the groups
also establish parameters for the classification of successive units into
similar categories. This is not meant to imply, however, that different
classifications can not be made for different uses, but it should ensure that
the sets of characteristics adopted are quite explicit. The data analysis
process itself generates information that automatically indicates between
which variables the closest relationships exist and it also reflects the nature
and strength of those relationships.

5. Comprehension and compulsion in data collection

In the design of official forms and survey schedules, the general ease of
comprehension of the questionnaire by respondents is of prime importance. This
implies the need to understand not only the actual questions themselves and
their accompanying instructions but also the main objectives of the exercise.
Despite the constant stress placed on this matter, administrative forms – and
in some cases even enumeration schedules issued by official statistical agencies
– continually fall far short of the desired simplicity. Government forms
throughout the world invariably employ uncommon terminology and legalistic
jargon which sometimes even the data processors themselves do not fully
understand. Since much of this information has to be collected as part of some
regulatory control imposed by administrative statute, it is hardly surprising
(although still nonetheless unforgiveable) that the instructions to respondents
are infused with legal phraseology and authoritarian command which inevitably
contains some accompanying explicit warning or hinted implicit threat of
punitive action for failure to respond. Such a framework for information
collection – even without any formal specific powers to enforce a response – is
not conducive to the generation of relevant, accurate and useful data.[31]
In these circumstances, the actual incorporation of statutory powers to
exercise control and compel response may be almost entirely inappropriate. The
fault lies primarily with the information gathering agency. Adding a legal
requirement enforcing the population to respond often only serves to ensure that
the data collected – especially the extra data that would not otherwise have
been absorbed – will be internally inconsistent and unreliable.

This situation applies even to populations which are reasonably literate
and numerate and where both the level of education and methods of communication
are fairly well advanced. In many developing countries, unfortunately, these
desirable conditions do not prevail and still less trust can be placed on
administrative data and survey results.

It is also sadly true that – for a wide variety of well-known reasons –
voluntary surveys tend to generate selective, biased and unsatisfactory data
(although each individual piece of information may well be good in itself).

31/ A formal enquiry already prejudices responses.

Relying on a suitably persuasive convering letter of assurance from a senior
member of the Government – such as the Minister or even the President himself –
may, paradoxically, implant the kiss of death on the results of a survey and
undermine the inherent validity of any independent fact-finding exercise.

6. The acceptable margin of error?

The important issue again is, By what standard are such demands being
compared? Can adequate information (for policy purposes) dealing with special,
specific disadvantaged or privileged groups be obtained more quickly and cheaply
by means other than a random (of some sorts) survey or a complete or partial
census? The situation in most LDCs seems to be one where the conditions seem to
be, if not ideal, then particularly favourable to the conduct of well designed
and properly focussed selective purposive surveys. The margins of error
associated with any survey – if, in fact, they are ever taken into account in
the practical formulation of decisions – are generally irrelevant when the time
factor (real or political) is urgent and it is only the normal two-way decision
that is really crucial, that is, whether to proceed or not.

In terms of sheer numbers, any form of sampling does reduce the need for
personnel but it does not, at the same time, ease the burden of recruiting the
appropriately educated and motivated personnel normally required to conduct a
survey efficiently and effectively. Indeed, if the intention is to carry out an
in-depth purposive study (particularly if it is informally conducted and
relatively unstructured – except for its ultimate objectives) there will be a
need for even more highly qualified and experienced enumerators and social
scientists than at present. The greater practical relevance of the results,
however, should be weighed against the possible unknown sampling and survey
errors. But excessive time delays in publishing results and the generally
descriptive (as opposed to analytical) content of the reports of more
conventional sample surveys limit their real usefulness. The more analytical
and explanatory the information that investigators are able to glean from sample
surveys or complete enumerations, the greater the likelihood of errors arising
in the data collection process itself (that is, in the enumeration, collation
and compilation of data) and the higher the chance there will be only a partial
coverage of the population. Both under-coverage and incompleteness in a
census enquiry are bound to affect the validity of subsequent surveys which use
the census information as a basis for sample selection. Even with ideal frame
conditions it is hardly truthful to state – as is so often done officially –
that the accuracy of the results of a scientifically based sample survey enquiry
can be predetermined at the planning stage with a reasonable (that is,
acceptable) degree of precision. Survey errors are not independent of the
nature of the enquiry nor the state and complexity of the investigation and
its organization. While in a theoretical milieu the sampling errors can be
calculated in advance, the non-sampling errors can not and the over-all survey
results may be highly questionable, particularly for sub-groups and sectors.
This will apply especially to those areas of concern in which many social
scientists will have the greatest interest (that is, those groups where, for a
variety of well-known reasons, many of them statistical, there is a dearth of
relevant, adequate and useful information).

In these circumstances it seems pointless to state (quite as categorically
as most statisticians are prepared to do) that a sample can be devised which
will yield results of a specified precision at minimum cost or, alternatively,
to provide the maximum precision at some given cost. Public expenditure
budgetary appraisals relating to survey cost estimates rarely query the general
costing of the survey not its precise nature since these are essentially
regarded as purely technical issues and on such questions the budget's
administrators usually accept they are not really competent to intervene. The
administrators will normally be much more concerned with whether the whole

exercise itself is really necessary or not and, if so, with questions as to
how it is going to be funded and by whom.

In many LDCs the expected sample errors involved in any enquiry will be
large and hence the costs of undertaking a scientific survey will be high.
With relatively large non-sampling errors also to contend with, a fixed size
and an upper budgetary limit may be imposed at a level which, say, in an
agricultural crop yield or food consumption survey, leads to the adoption of
a smaller scale or more restricted coverage survey which produces aggregate
and per caput estimates that are not meaningful or useful because of the
associated wide margins of error possibly involved (especially, say, in
projecting total output). In principle, there is no means of checking the
reliability of the results unless a complete count is undertaken at the same
time covering a similar problem area and group of respondents, although this
would obviously undermine the inherent value and previously described virtues
of carrying out a survey in the first place.

All sample surveys, whether random or not, are inadequate if the
information desired is required - as in census and registration procedures -
from all units in the population concerned. Such data collection exercises
invariably demand the implementation of supporting and enabling legislative
action or regulation. But this statutory enforcement in itself will, in turn,
have both a direct and indirect effect not only on the respondents themselves
but also on the quality of their responses. Any survey which is accompanied
by an official form, stencilled letter and reference to authority is likely to
have, at best, an intimidating and, at worst, antagonistic effect on respondents
in developing countries. The printed form or questionnaire and pencil are
symbols of authority, bureaucracy and officialdom.[32] This feeling is frequently
reinforced by the nature, number and probing character of questions and the
complexity or length of questions actually asked. Selecting certain respondents
to answer particular or additional questions may also raise difficulties of a
legal or political nature especially when groups appear to be discriminated by
race, wealth holding or income status. Reaction to a survey depends as much
on the general public interest in the objectives of the enquiry as on
respondent's particular attitudes to the questions posed.

It seems fairly clear from evidence that already exists in developing
countries relating to internal disparaties in living standards, production
technology, agricultural holdings and practices, etc. that new data series
must identify and quantify the structural imbalances and institutional
differences that persist. This implies a greater concentration of attention
than has been the case in the past on the distributional characteristics and
discontinuities in significant socio-economic variables.

In particular, attention must be redirected towards the common elements
and components comprising the extreme ends of such distributions. Whilst the
derivation of appropriate measures of central tendency and their associated
aggregates must remain an important integral part of any statistical analysis,

---

32/ See for example Lea Jellenik, "A survey of street traders in Jakarta",
Institute of Development Studies research paper.

it is necessary to stress that measures relating to institutional and household operations, physical asset holdings, liquid wealth income flows, etc. must more adequately reflect the dispersion of the distribution of such variables.

This can be done in two complementary ways; by selecting more appropriate descriptive measures of dispersion which may possess rather limited analytical properties (and which therefore will also impose somewhat severe restrictions on the relevance and use of sample survey techniques) and by deciding to concentrate the focus of any enquiry on specific target groups and objectives rather than on the whole population.

It was in 1970 that systematic activity on systems development was begun in the Hungarian Central Statistical Office. This work has resulted in the establishment of various data bases and data catalogues since 1974; the planning of a unified and integrated data system was launched in 1977.

B. Architecture of the Statistical Data System (SDS)

The SDS incorporates the totality of the data collected, processed and stored in the statistical system and data documentation and management methodology.

Disregarding the form of presentation and the techniques of processing, all data constitute an integral part of the SDS; thus the concept of the Statistical Data System is not a direct function of the computer application.

In view of its content, the SDS appears in a specific form in each phase of the statistical working process in the following order:

(a) Data collection;

(b) Data processing and storing; and

(c) Analysis and dissemination.

The content of the SDS forms the raw material of the statistical work at the same time as serving as a basis for present and future statistical analyses and information.

When statistical data are integrated into a unified system one finds that in the course of development it is not the differences but rather the similarities which receive greater emphasis and the trend of development is towards integration rather than separation, a distinct advantage.

In this concept, by logical cross-reference the horizontal/sectoral (for example industrial statistical) and the vertical/by subject (for example labour statistical) data collections, processing and information become supplementary to one another.

A unified interpretation of the content and data components of the SDS implies:

(a) Definition;

(b) Identification; and

(c) Description.

The totality of these elements comprise Statistical Data Documentation. Statistical Data Documentation includes:

(a) The lists and definitions of the statistical concepts;

(b) The descriptions of statistical nomenclatures and general classification systems;

(c) The registers of data collections;

(d) Catalogues of indicators and nomenclatures;

(e) The documentation of data bases and data archives;

(f) The content catalogues of publications; and

(g) The data management methodology of the Data System.

Physical preservation of the content of the SDS is made in Statistical Data Files. This physical storing – depending on the individual phases of statistical working process – is possible in three ways:

(a) By different data carriers (questionnaires, magnetic tape);

(b) In different forms (basic, processed); and

(c) By different methods (storing, archiving, data bases).

Consequently, Statistical Data Files, from the point of view of the technics of management and preservation, may be broken down into the following four groups:

(a) Data files based on questionnaires;

(b) Files stored in a traditional way in machine readable form on magnetic tape;

(c) Data bases; and

(d) Files preserved in and retrievable from publications (for example data compendia).

The SDS therefore has two sub-systems belonging to one logical unit;

(a) Statistical Data Documentation; and

(b) Statistical Data Files.

Both are indispensible and conditional upon one another. The architecture and organizational interrelations of the SDS are shown in figure XX.

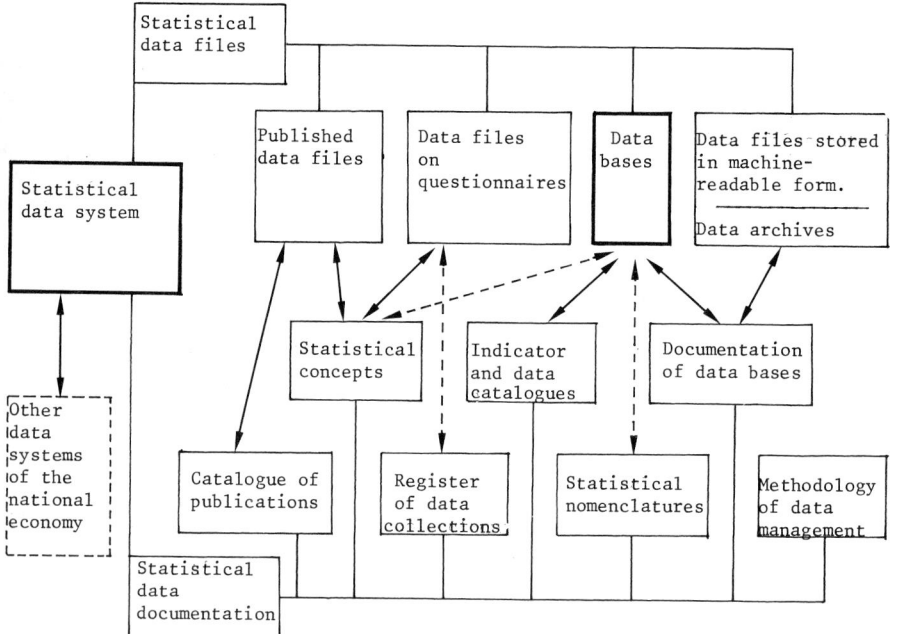

Figure XX.

C. Aspects of development of Statistical Data
Documentation

In the development of Statistical Data Documentation, systematization of statistical concepts should be regarded as a starting point. By concept (in general), the notional form is implied, which is derived from the major characteristics or peculiarities of the individual phenomena which differentiate them from all other phenomena.

All concepts have content and coverage. The content comprises the totality of the essential criteria and characteristics; the coverage is the scope of phenomena to which the given concept refers. The concepts may be classified into groups by some type of criteria, as for example by identical reference scope, and, on the basis of the logical interconnexions of the groups of concepts, a system of concepts may be developed. For the unified interpretation of the concepts it is expedient to give a definition of the content of non-trivial concepts.

The observations of statistics cover the phenomena of the real world; therefore, a considerable number of concepts used in statistics are identical to those which are valid for everyday life.

Among the concepts used in statistics however are the following:

(a) Those which relate to a criterion of the phenomena used or are interpreted by statistics only (for example finished production); or

(b) Those to which the discipline of Statistics is adding specific content or interpretation (for example workers).

These concepts are called statistical concepts.

From statistical concepts - by logical consideration - a system of statistical concepts can be built up. This system should, in its structure, reflect the architecture of the SDS, since the statistical concepts refer to its components, that is, to the data.

The content of the non-ambiguous statistical concepts, as with other concepts, should be defined. It is desirable for the conceptual definitions, as in the case of the concepts, to be composed of systematized groups for the sake of ensuring transparency and eventual publication for official use (dictionaries of statistical concepts).

For the purpose of increasing the usability of this type of definition/ collection of concepts, it is advisable to select from among the concepts applied in statistics:

(a) The general criteria of classification; and

(b) The lists of the components of the reference scope.

From these concepts it is advisable to develop nomenclatures and to publish them separately.

In the above outline there was a requirement for statistical concepts to be interpreted from several aspects. However, for a statistical concept to be interpreted and identified from several points of view, it is necessary to attach to them appropriate identifying signs (code numbers). These code numbers facilitate reference to the given concept in another part of the Data System. For ensuring many-sided identification it is necessary for the identifying code-number system of concepts to reflect the internal structure of the Data System.

The objective of the compilation of the dictionaries of statistical concepts is to unify the content and definition of the concepts. The content however is transformed in time; consequently, it is not sufficient to define the concepts but also fix the initial point of time of the validity of the unified content of the concept and to make a retrospective collection of the variants in time of the content of the concept (since no unification can be carried out retrospectively and, with the existing data, the definitions of concept should also be preserved).

Further utilization of Statistical Data Documentation can reveal:

(a) Whether data collections identical with or similar to the given data demand have been carried out, and where and in what form the required data are available (to eliminate repeated data collections); or

(b) Whether there are plans for data collections of the same or similar content (to avoid parallel data collections).

Finally, access by all authorized organs to data collected by any one organ within the statistical system must be ensured. These requirements can be met by the Register of Data Collections by Content, in the elaboration of which the determination of the degree of detail of the registrations needs methodological consideration. In other words, the degree of scale and detail of a register is directly related to the measure of its compliance with the requirements outlined above; at the same time, it is more labour-intensive to develop and continuously up-date.

In the organization of the administration of the register it is expedient:

(a) To utilize the methods of computerized automatic indexing and registering;

(b) To consider the stock of concepts of the system of statistical concepts in the description of the content and search words; and

(c) To use codes of data register which fit the code system and serve the purpose of identifying the concepts.

It is a requirement of the Register of Data Collections that it cover all data collections; therefore, it is not expected that in the near future it would be detailed by indicator. At the same time, in the case of data stored in data bases, there is no point in storage if the user can not retrieve from the data bases the indicators demanded. This latter requirement can be met by the so called Indicator Catalogues and Catalogues of Nomenclatures.

The Indicator Catalogues and the Catalogues of Nomenclature should together be suitable for facilitating user access to the stored and available data, even at a basic level. It is an essential requirement in this case;

(a) That the catalogues of the indicator descriptions should use the concepts adopted for the system of statistical concepts;

(b) That the descriptions should correspond to the aspects and approaches of statisticians and, at the same time, should reflect the data structure of computerized storage; and

(c) That the catalogues should contain direct cross-references, to both the dictionaries of concepts and the register of data collections.

The indicator Catalogues and Catalogues of Nomenclature are compiled mainly for users, yet at the same time they serve as a bridge between the statistician-users and the computing experts managing the data.

The documentation of the data bases and data archives is prepared mainly for the computing experts. The objective is to ensure the functioning of the data bases and data archives and to lay down the internal, technical considerations of the architecture, etc. However, for both types of documentation it is necessary in this instance to first include the references relating to the Indicator Catalogues and Catalogues of Nomenclature.

The Statistical Data Files, as may be seen from the architecture of the SDS, are stored not only on questionnaires or technical data carriers but also in publications. At present, however, there are no methods and means available for registering the content of the publications and facilitating the retrieval of the published data.

For the solution of this problem the method used for the Register of Data Collections should be applied; computerized registering and retrieving could also be utilized. By these means a systematically up-dated and republished Catalogue of Publications could be developed, registering not only the publications but also, by a sufficiently detailed processing and grouping of the content of the publications, serving as a useful means for users to meet their data demands.

Several problems of methodology common to each component of the SDS demand solution. As methodological material does not lend itself to classical methods of statistical analyses, it would seem to be expedient therefore, for the sake of differentiation, to place the material relevant to our subject-matter under the Methodology of Data Management.

This Methodology of Data Management would contain:

(a) The procedures of compilation, editing of the individual parts of the Data Documentation (for example the Dictionaries of Concepts, the Register of Data Collections, the Indicator Catalogues and the Catalogues of Nomenclature, etc.);

(b) The regulations in connexion with the management and up-dating of the Data Documentation;

(c) The regulation of the entitlement to have access to the data; and

(d) Organizational regulations relating to Data Management.

The collection and organized storage of this methodological material forms part of the Data Documentation; without it, the efficient and regular operation of the system would not be realized.

D. Aspects of development of Statistical Data Files

Statistical Data Files form another subsystem of the SDS. In theory, all data which enter the statistical information system, which will be processed and stored and/or in some form (for example in a publication) disseminated, belong to this subsystem.

The first large group within this subsystem consists of Data Files on Questionnaires, that is, data which are preserved in original form for a few years after the completion of processing.

In these files the following points should be defined:

(a)   The requirement to qualify for lasting preservation;

(b)   The sphere of authority and regulations of the qualification;

(c)   The storing place of the preserved files and the organ responsible for the storage; and

(d)   The central register of the stored and retrievable files on questionnaires.

Statistical Data Files require organized application of microcopying (microfilming) techniques to preserve documents of specific importance and archival worth. Copying should follow current methods and the Microfilm Collection regarded as a part of the Statistical Data Files. When determining the sphere of responsibility and functioning of the Microfilm Collection, the fact that not only questionnaires but also working tables for processing are microcopied should be taken into consideration. Management and registration should be reflected in the system as a whole according to subject-matter.

Data files corrected for computerized processing, are stored on magnetic tapes beyond the occasionally stipulated preservation time. The Magnetic Tapes Store is responsible for the placement and protection of data files preserved on magnetic tapes; the Computerized Registration System of Magnetic Tapes registers the magnetic tapes preserved in the given time. This system should cover not only the physical appearance and identification of the tapes but also the registering of their content (file-register).

Of especial importance are data files stored traditionally and for a limited time, that is, Data Archives on Magnetic Tape which comprise data files preserved under particular security (in 2 copies) and for a period of time stipulated by regulation. Access is possible only by a predetermined indirect procedure.

Computerized registers of the files of the Data Archives are prepared and, in this case, the register by content is of greater importance.

The Statistical Data Base Systems also form part of the Statistical Data Files. Files are considered to be data bases given that:

(a)   The methodology of their collections has been appropriately stabilized;

(b)   The importance of their content dictates that they should be managed as items of high priority from the point of view of preservation and access;

(c)   Their special importance precludes processing planned in advance; consequently, of secondary and ad hoc character, stored in special structures and by specific techniques with computers; and,

(d)   Their descriptions of content are the specific catalogues of indicators and data and their documentation is made by the documentation system of data bases.

The Statistical Data Base Systems, conforming to the structure of the SDS, may be developed in relation to the sectoral data systems (for example I-STAR, - Data Base System of Industrial Statistics). They can also be elaborated functionally by subject-matter (for example B-STAR, - Investments Statistical Data Base System). The order and methods of the development of data bases are determined within the frame of the function of Statistical Data Management.

As a result of processing of considerable volume, the official statistical publications comprise data stocks of great value; these data should be incorporated as part of the Statistical Data Files. It is for this reason that a Collection of Publications should be constituted which, in concordance with the Catalogue of Publications, would ensure the possibility of retrieval of materials in the reference subject.

E. The function of Statistical Data Management

In the statistical offices it was found that there was not any comprehensive function which could have complied with the task of operating the SDS or within which all activities relating to the Data System could have been integrated. Therefore, it will be necessary to develop a specific function, Statistical Data Management, in order to meet the demands outlined above.

This function would consist of:

(a) Statistical Data Co-ordination, responsible for the maintenance, up-dating and development of subject-matter and content of the Statistical Data System. These tasks comprise:

(i) Relations with data collections and dissemination;

(ii) Qualification of the preservation of data files;

(iii) Conceptual determination of the entitlement for access to the data files;

(iv) Co-ordination of data exchanges with other organs;

(v) Management and up-dating of Statistical Data Documentation (in certain respects by convoking widescale co-operation); and

(vi) The register and management of data files stored on questionnaires and in publications.

(b) Statistical File Management, consisting of:

(i) The Microfilm Collection together with its current operation;

(ii) The Magnetic Tapes Store and the Data Archive on Magnetic Tapes, the register of magnetic tapes (including archives), as well as the register by content of files preserved on magnetic tapes;

(iii) The Maintenance and up-dating of data bases;

(iv) Ensuring the access to data bases and the physical protection of the content of data bases;

(v) Editing, management and up-dating of the Indicator Catalogues and of the Catalogues of Data relating to the Data Bases;

(vi)   The official collection of publications, the Collection of
       Publications and ensuring the retrieval of publications.

The logical (not structural) interrelations of Statistical Data Management
are shown in figure XXI and the relation between SDS and Statistical Data
Management is illustrated in figure XXII.

Figure XXI

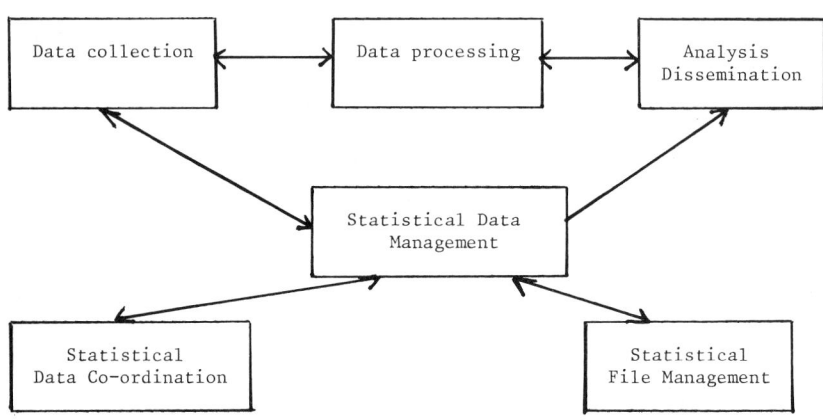

ŗigure XXII

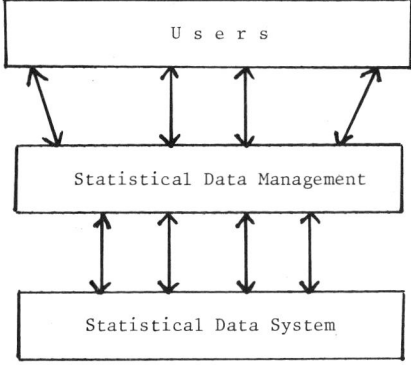

F.   Realization of the SDS

In some parts of the Data System certain aspects of development are carried out in parallel, in a co-ordinated way. As a part of Data Documentation, 12 volumes have been published of Dictionaries of Statistical Concepts, 6 volumes of Statistical Nomenclatures and 2 volumes of Indicator Catalogues of statistical data bases. The documentation of statistical data bases was adopted as the standard for internal use. The national catalogue of the content of the statistical data collection has been published in several editions in the form of KWIC-Index.

The automatic register of content of the magnetic tapes has been developed as a subsystem of Statistical Data Files, and as many as 5 data bases are already functioning within the statistical system.

As an organizational frame of Statistical Data Management, Statistical File Management began functioning as an independent organizational unit in 1977 and Statistical Data Co-ordination in 1978. The former is basically computer oriented and the latter is designed for complying with statistical demands.

The total realization of the SDS will take several more years. The use of existing components of the system indicates, however, that it is already suitable in its present form for improving the conditions and circumstances of statistical information supply.

INFORMATION SYSTEMS IN PUBLIC ADMINISTRATION
D. Eade, J. Hodgson (editors)
North-Holland Publishing Company
© *DFD, 1981*

USER'S ASPECTS OF THE INTEGRATED STATISTICAL
INFORMATION SYSTEM DEVELOPMENT

Peter Lieskovský*

Abstract

Improvement of automated information systems and prospects for their
integration come to the forefront of interest of those who develop nationwide
information systems. One such system in Czechoslovakia, developed within the
area of socio-economic information, is called the Statistical Information
System (SIS).

In an endeavour to clear up discrepancies between the designers and users
of information systems, possible fields and tools are searched which would allow
active participation and co-operation of users in the process of development
and design. The paper illustrates one of these fields, namely, that of data
base construction and use, within which the design of a user-oriented subsystem
of the SIS was attempted.

A. Introduction

The approach to designing an integrated automated Statistical Information
System (SIS) is characterized by a functional view of the system. If we study
the SIS structure from this standpoint we can only identify two groups of
differing yet conditional activities:

(a) The first deals with data collection and preparation, and
preparation, and the generation of data pools which have the same structure
as the reporting units;

(b) The second transform primary data into specially organized files and
evaluates this data by statistical analysis and balance methods. It includes
user-oriented processes at a qualitatively higher level.

This functional division of the SIS is reflected in two subsystems:

(a) The source-oriented subsystem,

(b) The user-oriented subsystem.

This paper discusses problems of the user-oriented subsystem (UOS).

Methodology of the UOS design can be divided into the following steps:

---

*Computing Research Centre, Bratislava, Czechoslovakia

(a) Delimitation of the subsystem and of its main functions;

(b) Analysis of the functions and their decomposition into lower-level components;

(c) Determination and assignment of sources, procedures and activities needed for relevant functions execution;

(d) Aggregation of partial functions into logical entities from which functional units of the proposed system (modules) are created;

(e) Construction of the UOS functional model which is the basis for:

> (i) Working out the UOS function, design and programme specifications;
>
> (ii) Designing the UOS and testing its functional units;
>
> (iii) Experimental verification of a sample of selected data.

B. Strategy of designing the user-oriented subsystem

For choosing and determining a general strategy for the construction of the functional model, certain basic matters were taken into account. It was necessary to recognize a division of tasks in that the SIS project reaches into three problem areas. For the research level it means a division of work among three research teams closely co-operating with each other. The following areas are concerned:

(a) Source area of the SIS, first of all in the relation between the SIS and the ISO (information system of organization);

(b) User area of the SIS which is oriented mostly to system-user interface, having in mind rational forms of data base generation and utilization;

(c) Development of an information metasystem that will serve successively for recognition, operation, designing and management purposes of the SIS.

Basic links among the above project components are illustrated in figure XXIII.

Main functions of the source-oriented subsystem (SOS) are data acquisition, primary processing (checking, correcting, etc.) and storing of corrected data in the form of conventional files.

The aim of the UOS is to organize and store data acquired from the SOS or from other sources and to produce information from it. Its main functions are thereby determined, namely, those of storage of data that has passed primary processing, and of information presentation.

In fulfilment of the above functions attention will be paid mainly to the following problem areas:

(a) Relations between the SIS and users;

(b) Relations between the UOS and SOS;

(c) Creation of user data bases that are modelled on various data base kinds and types.

Figure XXIII.

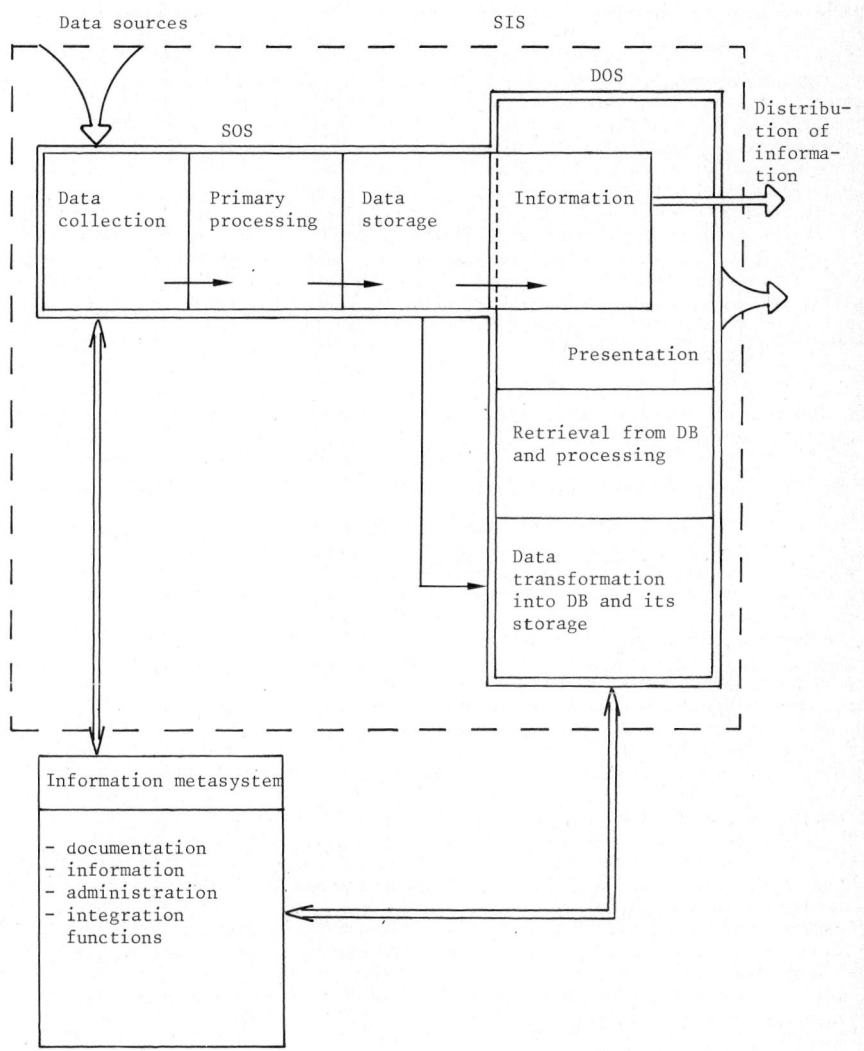

In the individual problem areas, the following elements of rationalization will be projected into the solution:

(a)   In the area of SIS-to-user relations, the link between the UOS and the SIS environment is provided by the function of information generation and presentation.   In view of the fact that the information presentation function is a primary one for the UOS, it appears profitable that the methodological and technological aspects of information presentation be solved for both subsystems within the UOS framework.   While the presentation of information from the source-oriented data pool (SDP) will generally be characterized by regular publication with standard content, the UOS will accomplish its presentation from the user data pool (UDP), in the form of shapable outputs according to foreseen and unforeseen user requests.

(b)   Relations between the UOS and SOS will be realized in form of data acquisition from the SDP.   Problems related to data acquisition are common for both prototype subsystems; their solution will facilitate internal integration of the SIS itself.   Content and scope of the acquired data will be determined by needs of meeting tasks of the UOS, while frequency and data acquisition schedule will depend on the mandatory terms of reporting duties from the SIS environment as well as on the time necessary for assembling and verifying the data.

The necessary prerequisite for the communication between the UOS and SOS is an information metasystem.   Its task is to provide information, as far as possible in automated form, on the SDP needed for the UOS data bases physical creation and updating.

(c)   Generation of user data bases is another aspect of the UOS activity. It is based upon the user's active role in the process of data base (DB) development.   This activity rests essentially on an idea that proved to be of key significance in the course of elaboration of the basic concept of this subsystem; namely, that from the aspect of time, the DB should be generated only after formulation of the user requirement.   At the same time, the actual content of the DB should be created during the process of DB generation, that is, during the "dialogue" between the user requirement and data pool capabilities (upon which the DB is created).   The approach we have put forward permits implementation of systems within the UOS that on the technological level will provide for DB generation, updating, retrieval and output; while for the UOS, machinery will be created that will enable the user to define the actual content of the DB.   This, in its final form, will be the result of the confrontation of the SDP capabilities with the user requirement.

It follows from the analysis of the process of statistical information generation that the system can meet these requirements in different ways.   If there is relevant data stored in the DB and adequate software exists, the requirement can be satisfied by information distribution function.   If the necessary data is not available in the DB, the system is to be provided with functions that will enable flexible acquisition, editing and processing of such data, its storing into the DB in proper structure and being made accessible to users at the time of retrieval and output query.

From these outlines of user requirements, two basic functions can be derived and developed within the UOS:

(a)   Generation of data bases ensuing from user requirements which have been accepted by the system after previous analysis;

(b)   Presentation of information to the user in the form requested and in different ways.

C. Design of a functional model of the user-oriented subsystem

In order that the subsystem can fulfil the requested duties as outlined above, new functions, tools, products and procedures for enabling new modes of the subsystem operation need to be considered in its design. An inevitable prerequisite for the UOS development and operation is the implementation and utilization of a number of recommendations of co-operating teams that have been incorporated into this project, as well as of research groups taking part in development of the SOFIS.

Besides the above-mentioned SDP and information metasystem consisting of a set of description catalogues, the following features are concerned:

(a) Implementation of a dialogue language through which communication with description catalogues will be assured;

(b) A semantic analyzer of user requirement to assess feasibility for DB generation (meaning the function of analysis and evaluation). In case of a negative answer the dialogue language rejects the user requirement or diverts the user to other options;

(c) A function of data retrieval from the SDP and data analysis and transformation into a format suitable for storing into the UDP; this function will also be active in complementing meta-information on the DB that is to be developed;

(d) A DB management system that, by means of standard functions, will provide conversion of files into the DB system and monitor their updating, retrieval and output;

(e) A UDP (in fact the target product of data bases generation); besides DB it will also include external files sequentially organized on magnetic tape;

(f) A set of catalogues consisting of the UDP catalogue, software catalogue and unsatisfied user requirements catalogue;

(g) A register of statistical information users   an important UOS component. It will have several uses, among them:

(i) Users registration;

(ii) Checking authorized use of the system;

(iii) DB access checking (data protection and security);

(iv) Background for users évaluation (based on statistical data and other characteristics);

(v) Background for new inquiries, statistical data collection, etc. in concurrence with the unsatisfied user requirements catalogue.

These features, in addition to the required functions, are basic components of the UOS. Within particular stages of the DB development or utilization, looser or closer links among system components can be defined according to the functions they support.

In this process, one system component acts as the carrier, while other components, which co-operate in supporting a particular function, act in a

back-up capacity. These components, in accordance with the proposed method of
development of the UOS functional model, may be grouped into logical entities
that form functional units - the system modules:

    (a)   Module of user requirement analysis and evaluation;

    (b)   Module of data retrieval, analysis and storing;

    (c)   Catalogue of the UDP;

    (d)   Catalogue of system products;

    (e)   Catalogue of unsatisfied user requests;

    (f)   Register of users of statistical information.

Arrangement of the above units with their mutual links schema is shown in
figure XXIV. The diagram represents the functional model of the proposed UOS.
To discriminate between the DB development and utilization processes, full and
dot-and-dashed arrows were used. The dot-and-dashed line illustrates
integrity of description of the information metasystem and the source-oriented
subsystem. Around the UOS core, which is marked by thick line, there is a
shaded belt which envelopes a set of all possible system products that are
relevant for the UDP files and data base creation, updating and use. For the
sake of lucidity, functions and activities linking the units which form the
subsystem core are marked by a limited number of lines even if in some cases
a multiple-transmission "communication channel" may be concerned.

D.   The functional model of the user-oriented subsystem

    Activities of the proposed functional model will be explained by
describing the main tasks of the UOS, namely:

    (a)   DB generation according to user requirement;

    (b)   Information presentation to the user (operation of built-up data
bases).

    With regard to the succession of operations, the DB development stage will
be dealt with first.

E.   Formulation of the requirement

    The initial step necessary to activate the operation and functions of the
UOS is a statement of user requirements.

    DB generation is based upon catalogues of indicators and reports that
appear in the form of publications. (Later, gathering of information through
dialogue with relevant catalogues of the information metasystem may also be
considered). With regard to current statistical practice, which rests on
automated processing of statistical reports, the possibility arises of
demarcating DB content by means of mandatory parameters that are based on:

    (a)   Unambiguous identification of reports and indicators or their mutual
combination;

    (b)   Statement of the time necessary for the DB creation.

In addition, optional parameters contained in the requirement (reporting
units to be covered by the data base, price standards in which the source files

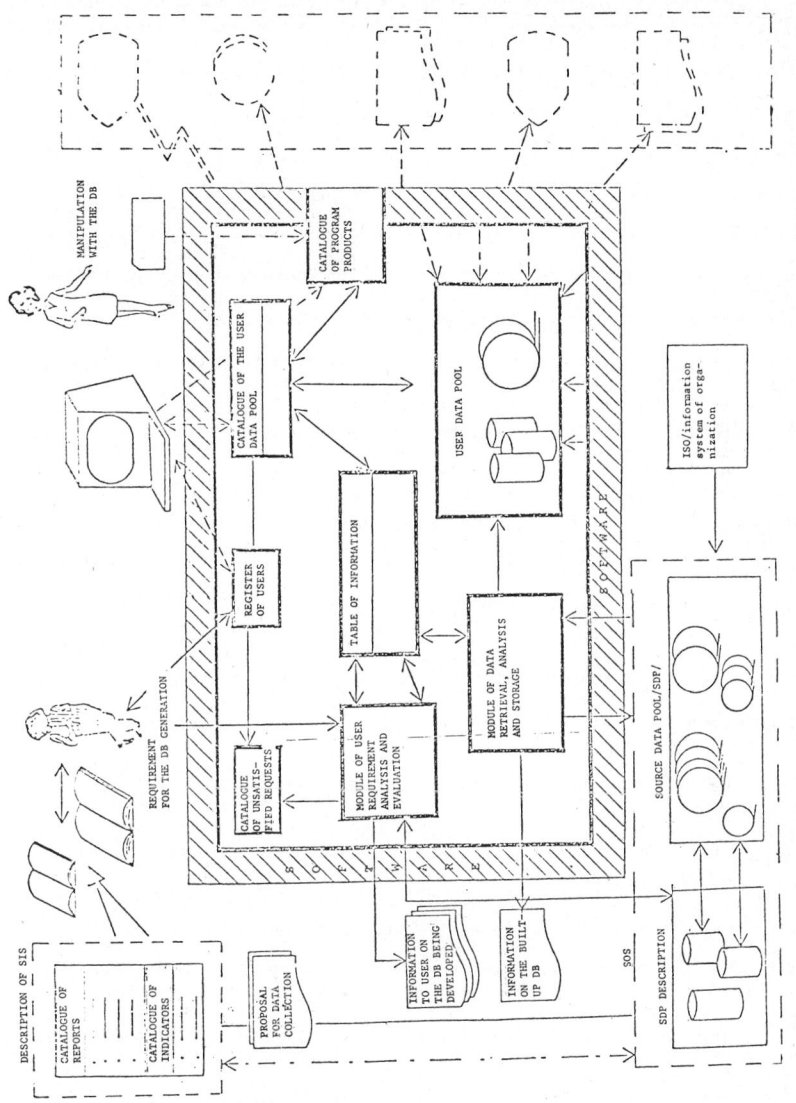

Figure XXIV. UOS Functional Model

are quoted and stored, aspects of eventual file aggregation, etc.) should be considered.

F. Analysis of the requirement

Before semantic analysis of the requirement formulated by the user is taken up by the system, it checks user authorization for access. Acceptance of the user's requirement will be conditional on his presence in the UOS users' register and his observance of relevant communication language syntax.

The analysis itself consists of several steps:

(a) With regard to the fact that statistical indicators will be a chief item of the DB generated when the requirement is formulated by an identification number of the report, its composition into indicators is assumed;

(b) It should be ascertained whether the required SIS indicators are available in the SDP; and

(c) Whether the indicator (reports) will be available in time according to schedule of DB generation.

Unless each condition is fulfilled, further system activities are broken off. The user will be informed of the result and the corresponding diagnostics; the requirement itself will be recorded in the unsatisfied requirements catalogue.

G. Modes of meeting user requirement

In the proposed system, possible alternative methods of the execution of user requirement are considered, with regard to different situations. This is, in fact, rationalization of the DB generation process motivated by several aspects, one of which relates to the creation of a DB previously developed (time and cost aspect).

H. A test against the user data pool catalogue

Before starting the preparatory phase of DB generation (including construction and evaluation of the table of information), a list of all items (indicators) of the required DB should be tested against descriptions of all actual UDP data bases and files in the UDP catalogue. Again, various possibilities may occur. If the required data is contained in an existing DB, the system executes its evaluation, notifies the user of the result, records information on the DB in the relevant record of the UOS users register and provides information on software for manipulation with the existing DB.

If the requirement cannot be met by the existing data pool, generation of a new DB should be initiated.

I. The process for generation of a new data base

The process of development of a new DB can be divided into a preparatory phase and a generation phase. The preparatory phase is aimed at the creation of a table of information (which concerns gathering and processing of metadata), and its evaluation.

The table of information (internal) is in fact a register of metadata. It is composed of logical elements with fixed position. These elements contain information acquired from catalogues, indicators, reports, source data files, processing characteristics of operational data strings (data files prepared for conversion into the DB system), data bases and, eventually, other information relevant to management of the subsystem itself.

J. Creation of the information table

The content of the information table may be created either successively (information is acquired by means of relevant SDP catalogues) or in a single step (if data is added from the UDP catalogue and provided that the content of the DB required by the user is a subset of an existing DB).

K. Evaluation of the information table

Evaluation of the information table represents the second phase in the preparatory process of the DB generation. It results in information on the possibilities of development of the required DB by comparison of:

(a) Indicators, from their reporting level aspects;

(b) Range and structure of classification data;

(c) Reporting unit sets, etc.

Actually, it is a confrontation between user conception and SDP capabilities. The user will receive the information in the form of an analytic report. By evaluation of the user request, the first part of the process of DB creation concerning work with metadata is concluded. In the sequence of activities it represents the first checkpoint of the system's operation. Further development of the system can be influenced by the user's decision:

(a) If he agrees to the required data base capabilities, the system starts its generation;

(b) If he disagrees strictly, his requirement is recorded as an unsatisfied one;

(c) If he agrees with reservations, he may modify his requirement and the cycle is repeated.

L. The data base generation phase

The following steps form the phase of data base generation:

(a) Access to the SDP is carried out on the basis of information on data storage structure in the SDP that is contained in the table of information;

(b) Retrieval of required data and construction of operational data strings (files);

(c) Analysis of processing properties of the acquired data strings from the viewpoint of the efficiency of their storage in the DB with regard to data implemented in the system;

(d) Conversion of files within the UDP under selected DB type; it may be preceded by editing of the format of operational data strings;

(e) Supplementing the information table with processing properties of the built-up DB (eventually of operational data strings);

(f) Transmission of relevant information from the table of information into the UDP catalogue;

(g) Linking the built-up DB with corresponding software to enable its operation and utilization on the level of meta-information in the UDP catalogue;

(h) Recording the fact of DB generation into the user's record in the UOS register of users;

(i) Providing the user with printed information on the built-up DB and its software.

The system allows for the existence of external sequentially-organized files in the UDP; in case of a requirement to generate such a file, the process will be similar. Nevertheless, availability of adequate software is assumed in order to provide updating, retrieval and output of these data files. An alternative solution would allow the user to render his own application programs with corresponding instructions for use, which would be stored in the UOS routines library.

M. Manipulation of the user data pool built-up data bases

Manipulation of the UDP built-up data bases will involve the following aspects:

(a) Gathering of information on UDP capabilities;

(b) Techniques of utilization of relevant software - mostly of output record generators, application programs or libraries of standard statistical routines. This aspect has a bearing upon the gathering of meta-information for the purpose of subsequent acquisition of statistical information. A conversational mode of operation between the UDP catalogue and the OUS software catalogue is assumed.

In accepting a requirement for work with a concrete DB, the UOS users register will be employed in following additional directions:

(a) Besides the authorization of use of the system it will be utilized to control authorization of access to data bases or their parts (data protection, security and integrity questions);

(b) To control DB handling (data retrieval, updating, editing, conversion);

(c) To check authorization to acquire and use output information.

Provided the access matters have been found in order, the user proceeds himself or through an application programmer to formulate his requirement on DB retrieval and output. The requirement activates the systems programs and functions which ensure

(a) Sorting of files;

(b) Access to files for retrieval, computation and format editing purposes;

(c) Output of the system in the selected form.

This concerns not only printed output by standard report generators but other possibilities of information presentation, as for example display forms, graphic output forms, standard data provision on magnetic tape, etc. With regard to the open character of the system, its capabilities to provide information by these other methods will, among other things, depend on software created within the SOFIS framework that is to be implemented in the user-oriented subsystem.

N. Conclusion

By creating the UOS functional model, definition pre-project stage of the proposed system has been concluded. Currently, the efforts of the research team are concentrated on drafting a basic organizational and technological solution. Works on the verification of capabilities of available program products and of their functions were started in form of joint tests of the SOFIS program modules. Results of these tests will give an answer to general strategy of the design both at the technological organizational and program levels. At the same time, the set of products which are to be created and edited at the software level will be determined. This will become on of the prospective tasks of the research team for the next stages of work.

INFORMATION SYSTEMS IN PUBLIC ADMINISTRATION
D. Eade, J. Hodgson (editors)
North-Holland Publishing Company
© DFD, 1981

THE FUTURE OF PACKAGES

A.S. Douglas*

A. Introduction

It is a commonly observed fact that few package programs are usually popular with users. Numerous reasons are given for this. There is, for example the n.i.h. (not invented here) syndrome – which undoubtedly operates against acceptance of any program not conceived of and written by the local team, if it exists – but does not explain the relative lack of success of packages with those who have no local team. In those cases the reluctance is usually explained by "lack of documentation", "lack of reliable support" or some other similar comment. It is very seldom attributed to bad package design or lack of marketing technique on the part of the seller, although these are much more likely to be the reasons.

In point of fact, the most successful packages have been those written by computer people for computer people. Out of 32 packages on the 1977 Datamation honour roll,[1] all but 5 are in this category. Of those 5, 3 are financial – ALLTAX, FCS, and Software 1040, and the other 2, SAS and SPSS are for the analysis of statistical data. It could be said that, if operating systems designers were better trained, the 27 would be unnecessary – or, equally, that if we paid as much attention to the needs of our customers as we do to the needs of programmers, there would be many more than 5 customer-oriented packages on the honour roll.

Of course, it is arguable that the Datamation survey underestimates the number of successful packages provided to users by software products companies. And there are significant omissions from their list, such as:

(a) Proprietary linear programming packages – mostly derived from LP 90/94, such as MPS 360, Umpire, the various Bonner and Moore codes, the Haverlee codes, Apex and so on;[2]

---

* Professor, London School of Economics, United Kingdom of Great Britain and Northern Ireland.

[1] "The honour roll of packages for 1977", Datamation, June 1977.

[2] See for example A.H. Land and S. Powell, Fortran Codes for Mathematical Programming: Linear, Quadratic & Discrete (New York, John Wiley & Sons, 1973), and A.H. Land and S. Powell, "Computer codes for problems of integer programming", Annals of Discrete Mathematics (Amsterdam, North-Holland).

(b) A fair number of engineering packages for project control (PERT and its derivations)[3] and for finite element analysis;[4] together with

(c) A number of statistical and mathematical support packages, such as BIMED,[5] the NAG library[6] and so forth, which are freely available and widely used - at least in the Universities.

However, it is probably true that packages are seen more as tools for programmers, offering advantages in machine time used or in convenience to the programmer, than as the clothing around a computer which makes it usable by the relatively uninitiated.

B. Development problems

The would-be package developer faces a number of problems. Firstly, he needs to understand how the package will be used. Unless he is an engineer, it is unlikely that he will make a success of an engineering package, for example, because he will not otherwise understand the problems of the user. This probably accounts for why so many of those packages deemed successful are written for programmers to use, since it may be supposed that the developer understands his own needs and can see the practical value of what he is designing.

Equally, the designer must understand good software engineering practice.[7] His package must be easily maintainable and capable of modification. It must be well documented for user, operator and maintenance staff. These are matters not usually attended to by the amateur, in the form of, say, an engineer who has "learnt to program".

3/ See for example A. Battersby, Network Analysis for Planning and Scheduling (London, Macmillan, 1967).

4/ K. Robinson, "Survey of finite element software: a consumer's guide to availability, cost and scope", the POLYMODEL 2 Conference, Teeside Polytechnic, 23 May 1979 (in press). For further information see Finite Element News, published monthly by Robinson & Associates, Horton Road, Woodlands, Wimborne, Dorset BH21 6NB, United Kingdom.

5/ W.J. Dixon, ed., BMD-P Biomedical Computer Program (Berkeley, University of California Press, 1977).

6/ Contact the NAG Library Service, Numerical Algorithms Group Ltd., 7 Banbury Road, Oxford OX2 6NN, United Kingdom.

7/ See for example M. Jackson, Principles of Program Design (Academic Press), and E. Yourdon, Techniques of Program Structure and Design (Englewood Cliffs, New Jersey, Prentice-Hall, 1975).

The developer will normally have only limited funds available to develop his package. Indeed many packages offered for sale are really only adaptions of work commissioned by users from the firm concerned, which has often invested little itself. There are, of course, good commercial reasons why little should be spent within a software house on packages. The record of such investment is not good - less than 15 per cent of the packages reviewed by Datamation appear on the Honour Roll, and it is far from clear that all these have cleared the expenses of development, or will do so over their life, let alone produce a satisfactory return to the developer.

It is significant that, so far, no firm dealing solely in packages has emerged, even in the United States of America. Undoubtedly this is in part due to the lack of protection afforded to the developer by either patent or copyright law. Such protection as is available is given by a combination of secrecy and contract law. For this reason there is a reluctance to reveal the workings of a package to potential customers - which must obviously inhibit sales - and leads to the supply of a "black box" of relocatable binary code, which is unmaintainable and unmodifiable except by the creator, and thus less acceptable to the user, particularly if he is sophisticated enough to be able to carry out such operations himself.

It must be said at this point, however, that the writer is not whole-heartedly in favour of strengthening protection for a variety of reasons, not least among which is his general aversion to monopolies. Nevertheless, the present situation obviously contributes to the problems confronting the package developer by discouraging investment and making sales more difficult to obtain.

C. Portability

A developer can expect the maximum return on his package by making it usable on a wide variety of machines. It is a feature of programmers packages, of course, that they tend to make better use of a particular machine class than those of the manufacturers. Clearly, portability in such cases is, at most, confined to movement between machines of the same family, and thus the number of machines sold represent a limit to the market available. It is not surprising therefore that most successful packages are written for IBM machinery.

Very few packages can in fact be transferred from machine to machine. This is not only because of the usual obstructions to portability such as incompatible implementations of languages (even when standardized like ANSI, FORTRAN or COBOL) but also because the resulting programs can readily become so inefficient as to be unsaleable, due to making the necessary allowances to ensure portability. Thus it is more usual to rewrite the package for another machine, using the same logic, and of course one would seriously consider the use of a cross-compiler to assist this process.

D. Accessibility and response

There is no doubt that the use of packages has been inhibited by their relative inaccessibility. In order to use them, elaborate manuals must be prepared and read. It is common experience that the manuals are incomplete and sometimes difficult to follow, if not unreadable, since background knowledge is assumed which is not possessed by the reader. It becomes necessary for the user to assimilate a great deal of computer knowledge which is largely irrelevant to the task he is trying to perform. The barrier raised is often more formidable than that of the user learning FORTRAN and doing it himself - which contributes to the natural n.i.h. factor.

The introduction of rapid response using terminals on-line to a computer obviates a good deal of this difficulty. The manual is replaced by a questionnaire-type approach at the VDU. Of course there is no reason that manuals should not be written in this way - a form of programmed learning - but this is usually considered too elaborate and costly. Naturally the computer program has to be more elaborate in order to pursue this approach, but the effort put into this is no greater and often more amenable to the programmer than that put into the construction of a manual.

Undoubtedly, package solutions are more saleable over on-line terminals, since the user will not be confronted by massive tomes covering every eventuality and will often never have to delve into those recesses of the program which cover unusual circumstances.

E. The influence of advancing technology

The writer has long since given up trying to decide whether we are now in the 4th or 5th generation of computers - if indeed such a classification was ever anything more than a salesman's gimmick. What is clear is that since 1950 there has been a steady reduction in the cost of circuitry, with certain quantum jumps occurring with the introduction of transistors and integrated circuitry on chips. It appears that physics can carry this further forward, and that even comparatively complex circuits will become throw-away items if manufactured in sufficient quantity - as it seems very likely will be the case.

It has long been established that one of the implications of advancing technology is that money spent on computing equipment now can buy not just more power (however it is measured) than yesterday, but disproportionately more. While not everyone agrees with "Grosch's Law",[8] partly because the increase in power per dollar is not easily measurable and partly because it has been seen to be modified by the growth in importance of peripherals, the costs of which do not depend on circuitry, nevertheless it is still true qualitatively and may be expected to remain so as regards the central processor unit and main store (see table 5 and figures XXV and XXVI at end of paper).

However, a number of problems have been successively highlighted which were previously obscured by the dominance of central processor costs. There has already been reference to the question of peripherals. While circuitry costs have come down steadily, this has not been quite so true of drums, disks and tapes, although the introduction of floppy disks and cassettes as replacements has already changed matters somewhat. Moreover, the costs of such things as paper tape and card input/output devices and printers have not reduced at anything like the same rate as circuitry. For reduction in cost in the areas of input and output we have tended to look to new devices or towards a new method of use, for example, over terminals, which tend to reduce input/output costs by reducing the cost of expendables such as paper, tape or cards rather than capital costs. Recent evaluations at the University of

---

8/ See A. Ralston and C.L. Meek, eds., Encyclopaedia of Computer Science (New York, Petrocelli/Charter, 1976)

Waterloo, for example, show that in a teaching environment the savings on expendables by using a scheme such as WIDJET rather that WATFOR will pay for the terminals in less than two years.9/

The inclusion of peripherals in total system cost means that Grosch's square law must be considerably modified. The central processor, to which it certainly applies, is now less than 10 per cent of the total cost. It is clear that a square law does not apply to peripherals, where the reduction in cost appears to have been geometric (see table 5) using a factor of $2\frac{1}{2}$ to 3. Over-all, the increase in power per dollar has tended more towards that which is appropriate to peripheral reductions – say to the power of 1.3 to 1.5.

F. Limits to growth

As installations have enlarged in response to the economies of scale indicated above, so factors have emerged to limit their growth. Firstly a large installation necessarily presents a problem in resource scheduling. The more balanced the load between large and small jobs, those with deadlines and those without, and those with varying response requirements, the more complex this task has become. The result has been a growth in the cost of software construction and in the need for provision within the installation of house-keeping software. The former is a one-time cost, of course, and has only a minor effect on the cost of individual machines, provided these are manufactured in quantity. But the latter is a cost per machine and has tended to rise steadily with machine size and complexity, thus severely limiting gains due to scale. It has also provided a fruitful market for packages improving on the manufacturer's method of solving the resource problem.

The position has been further affected by the question of catchment for data and programs. Economies of scale have tended towards the formation of larger and larger central complexes. In order to load this machinery, access to it must be provided over a larger and larger geographical area. This has been done by data collection services by van, post and remote job entry over dedicated telephone lines of varying speeds. This communication complex has now grown to be a significant part of the cost of a major installation.

Currently, its cost is only indirectly affected by the cost of circuitry, (see table 5), although it is to be hoped that in due course lowered costs in this area will be reflected in tariffs. The handling of the computer/communications interface is proving another fruitful area for package builders. Not every programming group can afford to specialize in this technology, any more than it can in operating systems, and is therefore willing to buy from others considered more expert, despite the n.i.h factor.

It must be clear, therefore, that for the average user, economies of scale are becoming less and less realizable, whereas costs of smaller units continue to reduce, since these are most affected by changes in circuitry cost.

9/ For further information on the WIDJET system, refer to J.W. Graham, University of Waterloo, Canada (the cost information is a private communication).

This forms the basis of the questions now being asked as to whether a group of
co-operating small units can be made to do the work of a single larger unit
more cheaply or at the same cost with greater user satisfaction - the questions
regarding "distributed computing" treated by Jim Emery at Toronto[10] and on which
research is being pursued at the London School of Economics by, for example
Bob Davenport.[11] It goes without saying that such a move will stimulate the
package market towards providing suitable new solutions to old problems.

G. The way forward: Word processing

Apart from the possibility of distributing the work of main frames,
free-standing units in the office equipment field are becoming both cheaper
and more powerful. The application of electronics to the typing process has
produced a range of upgraded typewriters, the most powerful of which has
considerable computer capacity. These word processors,[12] consisting of a
keyboard, VDU and printer attached to computing equipment, are primarily
designed to facilitate the editing of text and to simplify the work of the
typist. The computing equipment can readily be built up with additional
storage to form a powerful unit. Most suppliers now provide accounting
packages to run on this equipment. It may also be attached as an intelligent
terminal to a mainframe or interconnected with other similar equipment to
form a cluster, some of the logic of the system thus being shared and the costs
per terminal reduced.

The provision for programs for this equipment is at present relatively
laborious, since high level language facilities are not usually provided by the
manufacturers, storage space being too limited. However, the development of
suitable packages is a potential market of considerable magnitude. Moreover,
as the users are not sufficiently qualified or supported by qualified groups,
there is resistance to a package approach. Indeed, it would probably be the
preferred route for most of them to take provided the package suppliers could
guarantee support for maintenance and development of their products.

H. The way forward: dedicated machinery within networks

As the cost of hardware continues to decrease, the advantages of
dedicating specific equipment to specific tasks will continue to increase.
Every computer becomes a dedicated machine (or several such machines) by
allocating some or all of its resources to a program. Allocation by an
operating system introduces considerable overhead. This is reduced by
separating the functioning of programs between machines. It may also be
reduced by changing the machine architecture, and this is further discussed
below.

10/ J.C. Emery, "The economics of distributed computing", IFIP 77
Proceedings (Amsterdam, North-Holland, 1977)

11/ R.A. Davenport, "Distributed processing systems", Infotech State of
the Art Report, 1978, and R.A. Davenport, "Distributed database technology - a
survey", Computer Networks, 1978.

12/ See for example Online Word Processing Conference (Uxbridge, United
Kingdom, Online Ltd.), and A.S. Douglas, Document Reproduction, Infotech State
of the Art Report on Man/Machine Communications (Infotech International Ltd.).

This forms the basis of the questions now being asked as to whether a group of co-operating small units can be made to do the work of a single larger unit more cheaply or at the same cost with greater user satisfaction - the questions regarding "distributed computing" treated by Jim Emery at Toronto[10] and on which research is being pursued at the School by, for example Bob Davenport.[11] It goes without saying that such a move will stimulate the package market towards providing suitable new solutions to old problems.

G. The way forward: Word processing

Apart from the possibility of distributing the work of main frames, free-standing units in the office equipment field are becoming both cheaper and more powerful. The application of electronics to the typing process has produced a range of upgraded typewriters, the most powerful of which has considerable computer capacity. These word processors,[12] consisting of a keyboard, VDU and printer attached to computing equipment, are primarily designed to facilitate the editing of text and to simplify the work of the typist. The computing equipment can readily be built up with additional storage to form a powerful unit. Most suppliers now provide accounting packages to run on this equipment. It may also be attached as an intelligent terminal to a mainframe or interconnected with other similar equipment to form a cluster, some of the logic of the system thus being shared and the costs per terminal reduced.

The provision for programs for this equipment is at present relatively laborious, since high level language facilities are not usually provided by the manufacturers, storage space being too limited. However, the development of suitable packages is a potential market of considerable magnitude. Moreover, as the users are not sufficiently qualified or supported by qualified groups, there is resistance to a package approach. Indeed, it would probably be the preferred route for most of them to take provided the package suppliers could guarantee support for maintenance and development of their products.

H. The way forward: dedicated machinery within networks

As the cost of hardware continues to decrease, the advantages of dedicating specific equipment to specific tasks will continue to increase. Every computer becomes a dedicated machine (or several such machines) by allocating some or all of its resources to a program. Allocation by an operating system introduces considerable overhead. This is reduced by separating the functioning of programs between machines. It may also be reduced by changing the machine architecture, and this is further discussed below.

10/ J.C. Emery, "The economics of distributed computing", IFIP 77 Proceedings (Amsterdam, North-Holland, 1977)

11/ R.A. Davenport, "Distributed processing systems", Infotech State of the Art Report, 1978, and R.A. Davenport, "Distributed database technology - a survey", Computer Networks, 1978.

12/ See for example Online Word Processing Conference (Uxbridge, United Kingdom, Online Ltd.), and A.S. Douglas, Document Reproduction, Infotech State of the Art Report on Man/Machine Communications (Infotech International Ltd.).

The separation of tasks within a machine complex in order to proceed
simultaneously is not new, especially as between the central processor and the
peripheral equipment. The trend towards giving the peripherals greater
autonomy has existed for a considerable time, and has been facilitated by
ever-cheapening logic. The lengthening of connexions between units to include
telephone, telex or satellite links introduces nothing new in principle.
However, the interfaces are dictated by considerations other than those solely
related to computer technology. Programs have had to be written to deal with
those interfaces. Due to machine architecture limitations and to the rigidity
of existing communications system, is has proved convenient to introduce
specialized machines to effect a satisfactory interface. This has shown the
way in which more significant devolution of activities may well proceed.

The ARPA network[13]/is based on the principle that access to specific
machinery from a remote terminal can be organized among a group of several
interconnected processors and is a demonstration of one way in which this may
be done. The local machinery and the communications system are, in a sense,
"transparent" to the user, who is able to use one particular program on one
particular machine from his remote location. The only limitations are those
common to many terminal systems, namely, that large amounts of print-out
cannot be transmitted directly and files are retained locally at the
installation used and are similarly limited as regards transmission. Systems
with similar characteristics exist elsewhere, the London University Metronet
system being a typical example.[14]/ The ALOHA system based on the computer at
the University of Hawaii[15]/ uses a satellite to broadcast to its remote users
and permits access over the satellite from one at a time, but in a packet-
switched mode, so that the appearance of multi-access working is maintained
to the user. In each of these cases, packages constructed for one machine can
be accessed from elsewhere in the network. Thus if one of the machines in the
network has a package of special virtue in the eyes of the user, he can,
admittedly with some minor penalty in convenience, gain access to it. In so
far as one machine in a network is specially suited to a particular task, it
is possible to assign it to dealing with that task alone, although this has not
yet been carried to its logical conclusion in the design of networks.

The packages for which this approach would seem most suited are those
large programs which require powerful machinery to be effective. Examples are
packages for mathematical programming, for finite element analysis and for
economic modelling. While these are found in Universities, they are also used

---

13/ F. Heart, "The ARPA network", R.L. Grimsdale and F.F. Kuo, eds.,
Communications Networks (Leiden, Netherlands, Noordhoff, 1975).

14/ For information on Metronet, write to the Director, University of
London Computer Centre, 20 Guildford Street, London. WC2, United Kingdom.

15/ For information on the ALOHA network, write to Professor N.
Abrahamson, Computer Science Department, University of Hawaii, 2424 Maile Way,
Honolulu Hawaii 96822. For information on the economics of such networks, see
M. Joseph and F.C. Kohli, eds., SEARCC 76: Proceedings of the First South East
Asia Regional Computer Conference, Singapore, 6-9 September 1976 (Amsterdam,
North-Holland, 1977), paper by N. Abrahamson.

major problem for the package designer will remain that of deciding exactly what he has to package to meet the requirements of a wide enough range of customers to make the investment worthwhile. In view of the increasing cost of personnel in the software industry, any move to increase their effective productivity by the investment of capital is likely to be more and more welcome, and this trend could be accelerated by increased protection for the products, which may result from the technological changes foreseen.

The possibility is foreseen in the longer term of some swing back from the distributed approach envisaged above towards access through a telecommunications network to packages mounted on machines particularly favourable to their efficient working, but the extent to which this occurs will depend on tariff reductions in telecommunications being given.

If the 1950s were the decade of the pioneers, the 1960s of commercial exploiters and the 1970s of the software specialists, perhaps the 1980s will be the decade of the package developers.

Table 5. Memory costs chronologically

		1955	1960	1965	1970	1975	1980	1985
Flip-flops	$/Unit	102	53.6	34.1	12.8	2.04	(0.5)[a/]	(0.01)[a/]
Mainstore	$/Kbits	966	25.3	81.8	21.4	3	(0.6)	(0.1)
Disc system	$/Kbyte	8	3	1	0.38	0.1	(0.03)	(0.01)
Magnetic tape	$/IMB	10.0	4.42	1.36	0.47	0.14	(0.05)	(0.05)[a/]
Data tariffs	cents/ Mbit/sec.							
	min.		0.08	0.05	0.07	0.07	-	(0.05)[b/]
	max.		7.00	8.22	3.4	3.4	--	(2.0)[b/]

Source : Montgomery Phister, Jr., Data Processing Technology and Economics (Santa Monica, California, Santa Monica Publishing Co., 1976).

a/, b/ These figures are projections based on the trends exhibited. Those marked a/ are approximately consistent with the figures given in Computers in the 80s by Rein Turn (Columbia University Press, 1974). Those marked b/ take no account of likely improvements in technology, such as packet switching and satellite systems. For costs relating to the latter see, for example, the article by N. Abrahamson, in the Proceedings of SEARCC 76, edited by David and published by North Holland (15).

commercially. In most cases they are run on bureau services, the originators also providing consulting services in connexion with their use. An extension to these services is clearly most likely within the bureau networks which are already developing internationally - Boeing Computer Services, for example.

I. The way forward: dedicated package systems

Another way in which the free-standing machine can be developed is towards a hardware/software system which is itself a package. To some extent, this is already the direction taken by word processing systems. Moreover, much interactive teaching is now done on machines dedicated to the task and equipped with suitable packages, such as WIDJET[16/] for the PDP11/70. Similar moves are taking place with small business systems. In such cases the characteristics of the program package are of course of much more importance than those of the hardware. Some software houses rather than the traditional hardware firms have already started to market such systems, while the latter are tending more and more to become involved in the provision of user-oriented packages. This trend may be expected to continue.

A logical development from this would be to build the hardware in such a way as to facilitate the running of packages and to have these themselves in a hardware form - as ROMS, PROMS or E-PROMS - the analogy being with tape-playing high fidelity equipment having plug-in facilities for programs. Machines with pluggable microprograms already exist, so that this is not perhaps the major step it might seem.

This has merit from the point of view of the package designer, in that the result can probably be more thoroughly protected. It is likely that patent law, rather than copyright, could be invoked successfully, and investment might not then be such a hazardous business. By analogy with other industries where patents are enforced, it is likely that the major marketing outlets would tend to benefit at the expense of the designer.

J. Conclusion

It seems clear that as hardware costs fall, but software costs do not, the balances are changing towards the promotion of package approaches to problems. This can lead either towards greater specialization of hardware, culminating in a hardware/software package being sold as the solution to a specific task or towards adaptation of hardware towards a more ready acceptance of packages, probably on ROMs. In all probability both these directions will be pursued simultaneously for different applications. The

---

16/ See footnote 9.

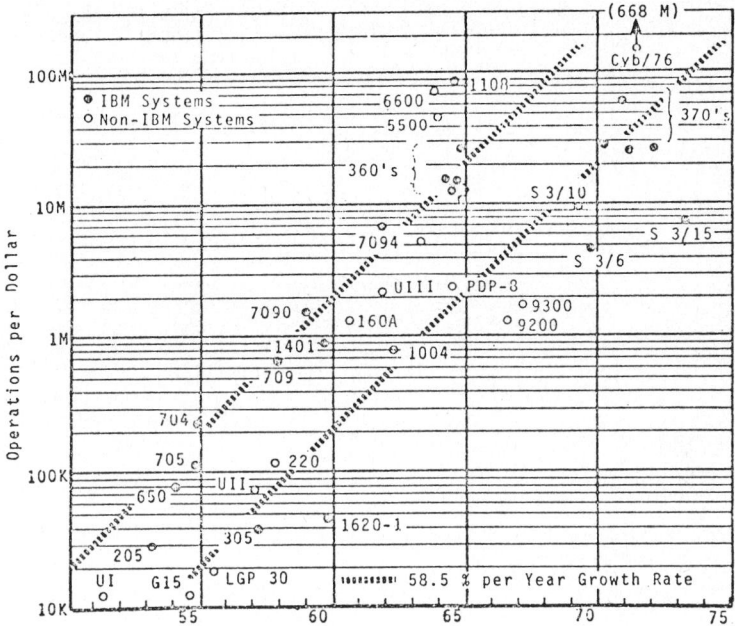

Figure XXV. Evolution of processor performance (operations per
            dollar)

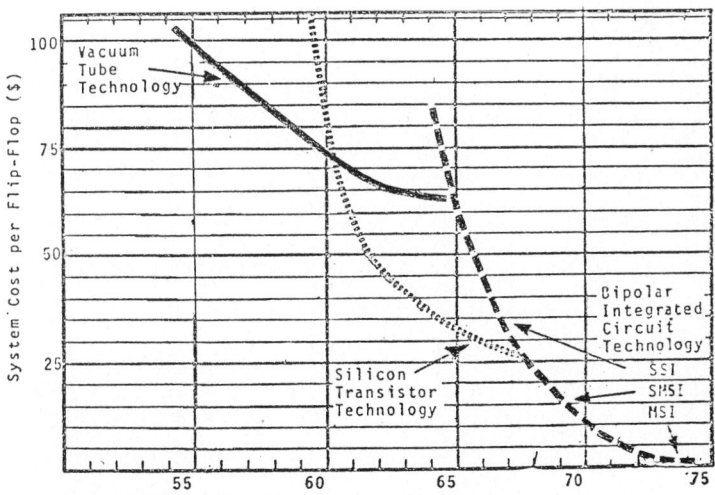

Figure XXVI. Evolution of the cost of a flip-flop in different technologies

INFORMATION SYSTEMS IN PUBLIC ADMINISTRATION
D. Eade, J. Hodgson (editors)
North-Holland Publishing Company
© *DFD, 1981*

REFLECTIONS ON PUBLIC SERVICE AND DEVELOPMENT

John E. Fobes *

I was invited to talk this afternoon about my reflections on thirty-eight years of life married to public service, both national and international, a period which, not incidentally, corresponds to a marriage with Mrs. Fobes.

Reflections, as you know, are constantly changing. Even as I talk, I find that my reflections over that public service are shifting, somewhat like the weather in the mountains outside our windows today. In fact, what I offer is in large measure stimulated by what we heard yesterday and today, and for that I thank you.

My remarks are in three parts. First, I need to say something about personal history and experience. Second, I will try a little analysis, not as rigorous as most of you insist upon, certainly not as rigorous as that reflected by Michael Ward in the last hour. Third, I will offer some concluding observations relevant to the Seminar.

As to history and changing reflections thereon, I am reminded of the story of the boss in the office who was dictating to a stenographer. At the conclusion of the dictation, the boss said to the secretary, "Now read that back to me. Sometimes I get new ideas from your version". This leads to two questions: How can we adapt that story in the light of the new electronics office and word processing machines now advertised by IBM and others? Are we likely to lose the benefit of the reading of oral dictation, of other similar exchanges and of the learning from such processes?

First, personal history. I studied political science and international relations, thinking to become a professor, but promptly was forced to be an administrator. A first exposure to public administration came just before military service. At the end of World War II, and after helping with the establishment of the United Nations Secretariat, a post in the U.S. Bureau of the Budget gave me the privilege of knowing some of the grand figures who had developed and applied the modern "science" of public administration and business management, beginning in the 1930's.

---

*previously Deputy Director General, UNESCO, Duke University and University of North Carolina, U.S.A.

During the Marshall Plan and again when I was in India, where I was Deputy Director of the American aid mission, I became conscious that "they" in Europe, in India and in other parts of the world, desirous of more rapid development, were asking questions about it. "We" including those involved in administering "aid", as it was called, were not answering those questions in a satisfactory manner. We were unable even to explain the emergence and fitting out of the models by which our nations had achieved such a high degree and pace of development. I took a special course in economic development at that time, but it only made me more conscious of an inability to answer questions. We were offering programs and solutions in our own image, but, although I felt some satisfaction in being a good administrator, I had some unease about the rationale and applicability of our programs. You will remember that, roughly in the period 1958 to 1962, many planning commissions were created. The "boys from Harvard" and elsewhere went out into the world, pressed the utility of such institutions for rapid mobilization of resources and were eager to suggest development models.

I do not recall, however, that they asked many questions about supporting information systems. They complained about the inadequacy of statistics, but they did not really question and seek to improve the information base in the way you are doing today.

I had the good fortune in the period beginning about 1960 to meet or to read the writings of persons – some of them with truly great minds – who were formulating questions about the way in which information and models had been structured and who had visions about alternative futures. These consciousness-opening contacts with a wide variety of people began when I was in India and accelerated after 1964 thanks to my work in Unesco. Much questioning and ideas came from young anti-colonialists who lived in both worlds, the industrialized, privileged sector and the other, emerging world. In addition, individuals like Buckminster Fuller, artists, peace researchers, mystics and some futurists often were more stimulating than the economists, exceptions made for Kenneth Boulding and John Kenneth Galbraith.

At the end of the 1960's, to continue this personal history, I participated in the preparation of the so-called Jackson Report for the UN Development Program and was on the periphery of the Pearson Report to the World Bank. These marked an important stage in the evolution of modern development thinking. But both represented only partial answers to the growing resentment in the world against domination, against acceptance of a particular economic development model, and against the failure of the northern/western industrialized world to listen.

The Jackson Report was an attempt to introduce greater efficiency into the international development program and development assistance generally. The section of the Report dealing with improved information systems and their importance was salutary and immediately cited by the government officials and diplomats. At times, however, it seemed that they were merely catering to national sentiment which was ready to place blame on the UN system for many world problems, claiming that its management information practices were weak.

Little basic change in the development system emerged as a result of these reports. They now appear as attempts to placate the developing world which was asking for more assistance, on the one hand, and, on the other, the leaders and administrators in capitals of the Western world who thought that more efficiency was the remedy to what was obviously a failure of the First UN Development Decade.

The reactions in the "other world" to both the Jackson and Pearson Reports could have been predicted from positions taken as long as before as the Bandung Conference in 1955 or the first UNCTAD meeting in 1964, among many conferences. These reactions reflect a curious combination of thinking by those raising profound questions about development models, by others who only partially sensed that the guidance of existing models was not as effective and relevant as it appeared to be, as well as by the elites in developing countries who saw a chance to gain more power. These latter joined the growing resentment and espoused the new international economic order and now the new international information order. It seems to me, however, that these elites do not seek a basic change in the system, but merely a shift in the power to themselves, while retaining much of the existing framework. There are exceptions to this, of course; I offer the observation as a reminder to question the usual rhetoric about new orders.

Early in the 1970's, I concluded that development as we were describing it was "dead". This was a very unpopular view in many circles. Also that much of technical assistance was lacking in vitality, that is, particular forms of external intervention. The way in which we viewed problems and described and constructed projects reflected the economics and hierarchy of an industrial model which should not be applied to all development. Earlier this afternoon, reporting for his group, Warren Crowther expressed these same doubts. Even "accountability", a principle adopted by the UN Development Program and applied by SIDA, U.S. AID and other bilateral aid agencies was an expression of an industrial model which needed adaptation if there was to be genuine partnership. I also felt that the practice of annual authorizations for and the expectation of quick results from development assistance simply helped to kill the utility of international co-operation.

This led to the feeling that some principles and structures of public administration and management were ineffective and that a new approach and rationale was needed. Those of us who were practitioners were uncomfortable in the business, but did not have the answers. At that moment, the concept of informatics appeared to offer a fresh way of looking at organization and methods. It seemed to embody an attitude of mind, a spirit which was integrative, that asked difficult questions, that saw the information process all the way from beginning to end, including dissemination, accepting information and its processing as a form of energy in the management of human affairs, as a way of planning and operating societies. The English speaking world is reluctant to adopt the world "informatics" - witness a recent authoritative report in the U.K. concerning micro-electronics - and insists on speaking of information and communication technology. I find that to be a fragmented approach, interested mainly in the manipulation of technology rather than in selective economic and social growth, in cultural development and in humankind as the means and the goal of all such development.

So much for the description of personal history and changes in attitudes. That leads to a little analysis and a few conclusions. How all pervasive, sometimes blatant, sometimes subtle, is the industrial model that we have applied to almost everything in life today! Important as it is for many aspects of society, we must admit, nevertheless, that we have structured almost all aspects of our lives according to that model. By this, I mean specialization, first of all, which leads to fragmentation, and organization according to hierarchy, which puts the emphasis on management of that specialization and fragmentation, which has given rise to an all-pervasive bureaucracy whether in private or public sectors, productive or public service enterprises. What is more, technology services that hierarchy of management and bureaucracy in ways which enhance central control. And now we must add "finance" because the financiers feel that they must exercise as much control as possible and secure maximum benefits from the industrial system, using information as the tool. Management and finance in fact have accepted the ethic and aim of technology: indefinite growth.

That's all that technology has as its motivation in most cases.

What may be worse, in my view, is that science, its content, its method and
its research orientations, has all but sold itself to technology, therefore to
serving the industrial model. We are beginning to question this now, and in some
places to take science and technology apart. The relationship can be very productive, but it may need to be dissected and looked at again in the context of
different cultures.

If that is true - this all pervasive nature of the industrial model in our
lives - how profound is the cleavage, how profound is the change, the adjustment,
which is necessary to understand, to modify and to apply selectively that model.
For a long time, I thought that it was sufficient to accelerate the necessary
process of transformation by working within and adapting management and public
administration so that they could facilitate the search for alternatives,
including alternative ways of re-ordering information and thereby making it
possible to adapt social structures and procedures. But that does not seem to
me to be enough for getting somewhere else from where we are now. I also
thought, as noted earlier, that informatics would force the asking of questions
in a way that would open up the alternatives. Yet the fact that it helps to
deal with a growing volume of data and information has dazzled us, and we have
been mainly interested in the functions and services of the computer and
computer-related technology. Ironically, it seems to me, informatics, at least
temporarily, has tended to reinforce the concepts and rules of the old model,
although it should be challenging them.

Now, to conclusions. First, I offer observations on three points which seem
relevant to your current discussions. It seems to me that we may need new
mediators as information systems are improved and expanded - new question-posers,
systems analysts of a new type or higher degree. I have in mind mediators who
can interpret social policy aims, to look at cultures and what it is that people
really want to preserve and to ask ethical questions relevant to informatics.
At one point in history, at least in my country, public service commissions were
established to exercise surveillance over the generation and transmission of
two forms of energy, electricity and gas. Is there a place for a public service
commission to oversee the ordering, storage, manipulation and transmission of
another form of energy, that is, information?

The second observation relates to communications. We have not yet talked
much about this subject, about the melding of electronics, computers and the
new technology of communications. We will. Crowther, dealing with the particular
situation in Bolivia, concluded that it was desirable to keep the media, that is,
the mass media, in particular, radio, out of the picture when trying to make
reforms in information systems. I doubt, however, we can keep this separation
long; we have a responsibility to see our roles with information systems within
the total new information society. One of the key questions which is assuming
greater importance - apart from the equitable and balanced flow of information
around the world - is access to information of all types and through all media.
One of the concepts which is going to catch fire in connection with next year's
report from the Unesco International Commission on the Problems of Communications
is that of "the right to communicate" - the right to speak, to be heard, the
right to decide when you don't want to listen, the right of access to information
in all of its forms and to participate in the way in which it is delivered or
made available to you.

The third observation deals with diversity and decentralization. We hear
much of the need to put order into our records as the volume of information
expands and to make them more complete and comprehensive. Also about the need
to improve access to those records, to be able to test, compare and display them
against information from all sources, including those external to a country.

This urging is usually in the context of improved central planning. Here I wave a flag of danger. The aim of such improvements in informatics, it seems to me, should be to <u>allow</u> development to happen, to encourage and facilitate self-reliance at all levels, not simply to make central planning more complete and neat.

In one group presentation today, reference was made to the ability of communities to have the information they need to solve as many problems as possible locally. The danger is that while we are saying that we agree with that, that we want to encourage and preserve diversity, we will in fact work in the opposite direction. Informatics carries the seeds of technocracy, tends to support elitism and can be source of alienation. Those in public administration must guard against this, must work for public understanding and participation. One of the ways to fight against remoteness, the impersonal, the cold quantification, reductionism, is through decentralization of information systems.

Although the new information and communication technology makes it possible to handle a great many more units than in the past, it tends to push us towards greater centralization, whereas I feel that we should on the contrary observe the principle of economy: do as much as possible "close to the workface". Thanks to Dr. Price for this phrase. It reminds me of a law of public administration discovered by one of those modern pioneers referred to earlier. It is the law of the specific gravity of decision-making: the more ponderous a decision, the lower it will be made in the hierarchy; only the light weight decisions rise to the top.

You will be talking later about the availability of low cost micro-processors which could be widely dispersed. They can be used, of course, to assert greater central control for standardized reporting and dependence. On the other hand, such processors can also be used to facilitate the decentralization to which I refer. Solutions can be devised at the lowest possible levels close to real problems if we make it possible for communities to define their problems and needs and then to organize information to fit that diagnosis, using links to central data banks when necessary.

I conclude with suggestions about attitudes we could usefully adopt and reflections about "commonalities". First, what attitude should we adopt toward the transnational actors who are active in informatics? I will leave the corporations to others and deal with the intergovernmental organizations which I know. The weaknesses of the UN and its Specialized Agencies, especially Unesco, are apparent to you, but I ask that you remember the important role they have to play in arranging agreement on international policies. They are providing a framework within which co-operation is fostered, exchanges can take place and support can be made available to other transnational actors, especially the non-governmental organizations which mobilize voluntary energies such as Data for Development, the convenor of this seminar. I think that we should be willing to see an increased number of such informal, non-official associations because there is so much to be done, so great a need for exchange. These words are addressed not only to you here but to the governments in Unesco.

What about attitudes toward the bureaucrats in the UN system and in the national governments? I think that we need friends inside the official hierarchies (and even in the transnational corporations). We will have to be selective; many are caught up in the self-serving nets of bureaucracy. Happily there remain those within public administration who are sensitive to what is happening and can be helpful.

A final suggestion concerns the posture of advisers, as many of you are, to national political and social leaders. How can we best provide advice of a technical and professional nature and help such leaders to be more responsive, more responsible and more anticipatory in respect to the dynamics of informatics?

How can persons concerned with information systems help decision makers to face
the issues of priorities we have been discussing, presenting them with options
and avoiding the tendency toward enlargement of central bureaucracies and rigid
technocratic solutions?

It wasn't long ago, perhaps 30 years, that public administrations worked
reasonably well. I think that was because they allowed enough deviants and
diversity in the systems. Moreover, partly because life then was simpler,
administrators were more willing to admit re-ordering of information and adjustments among systems. There were enough highly motivated general practitioners,
including those who were adept in advising political leaders, so that change was
possible, adequate change for each particular situation. Now the complexity and
the pace of change is greater and we lack the senior civil servant, the permanent
undersecretary, in a relationship of trust to the political leader. Perhaps we
shall find ways to re-introduce this flexible generalist and mediator.

My final remarks are reflections of a philosophical nature. At a recent
international meeting, we were talking about the capacity for learning about
global issues so that humankind could adapt to the challenges of today and
tomorrow. It was natural to begin talking about energy, environment, water and
other commonly recognized global issues, including those involved in the North/
South dialogue. But we finally turned out attention to what could be called
common concerns of all humankind, found in all cultures to some degree and on
which cross-cultural exchange of learning experiences would be useful. I feel
that the seven global concerns or commonalities thus identified can provide
guidance to the development of information systems and their interrelationships.

The first concern on the minds of people everywhere is how to deconcentrate
to some degree the centralized industrial model and discard the unnecessary
hierarchy which has grown up with that model? The aim: communities on a human
scale. The second, related, concern is how to have the autonomy and the greater
self-reliance now demanded while still accepting that human kind is moving
toward integration/solidarity at all levels? A third common concern, related
to the first two, is how to balance and combine stability and change - stability
for the sake of the coherence and cohesion of cultures and change because the
world *problematique* demands it.

A fourth concern of many societies involves the re-conception and re-
definition of authority and power. I believe that this must be done with the
help of qualities sometimes identified as feminine which we have tended to
exclude from traditional views of authority, if for no other reason than the
changing status and role of women in development. Changes in the concept of
power result in part from and will have influence on information flows.

The fifth concern is how to plan and live with mixes of technology that
might seem disorderly and troublesome. Yet I believe that we must increasingly
be able to live with the most sophisticated technology on the one hand and the
most simple and rudimentary on the other, both within and among societies.

A sixth concern of humanity is how to increase willingness and courage to
deal with the global *problematique*, that is, a tremendous tangle of world issues
no one of which can be tackled without its effects on the others. People are
afraid to do so now, lack visions of the future or have little hope of making
significant inroads on those issues. Our need is to prepare to deal with new
and unexpected situations, to accept consequences, to have options ready.
Geoffrey Vickers speaks of the need for the "responsible individual" as a
replacement for the "autonomous individual" of industrialized society who is
content to remain in his specialized slot, a fragment in a system.

The final common concern: how to balance the scientific and problem-solving approaches, so important to us, with a myth-making, myth-preserving and myth re-discovering attitude. The wholeness of life has been reduced or blurred by our fascination with a scientific and technological approach.

It will be well to keep in mind these concerns, these commonalities, as we develop strategies and policies for informatics, as we develop the ways in which the information energy resource will be managed for the welfare of mankind. I feel that we should remind ourselves with great humility and with some humour - both of which happily have been present at this seminar - that we are discussing today's representations of only a part of life. Important as they are and much in need of improvement, the information systems on our agenda do not portray all of our lives and potentials. It is terribly important that we help in the re-ordering and availability of such partial systems. But each of us should also contribute to the capacity of our societies to understand the wholeness of our cultures and to learn about their world environment. While rationalizing the handling of data and information, do not lose sensitivity to myths and the need for a great deal of intuitive, sensitive imaging of the future.

PART TWO
WORKING GROUP PAPERS

INFORMATION SYSTEMS IN PUBLIC ADMINISTRATION
D. Eade, J. Hodgson (editors)
North-Holland Publishing Company
© *DFD, 1981*

HUMAN FACTORS NEEDS FOR DEVELOPMENT
PLANNING AND MANAGEMENT

John Beresford*

A. Review of the structure of an information system and types of human factors data pertinent to its construction

Before examining human factors data needs, it is useful to review what is meant by the concept of an information system. In Data and Development, published by Data for Development, a simple model of an information processing system shown (see figure I). The operating environment consists of everything that is believed must change to carry forward development.

Figure I. The structure of an information processing system a/

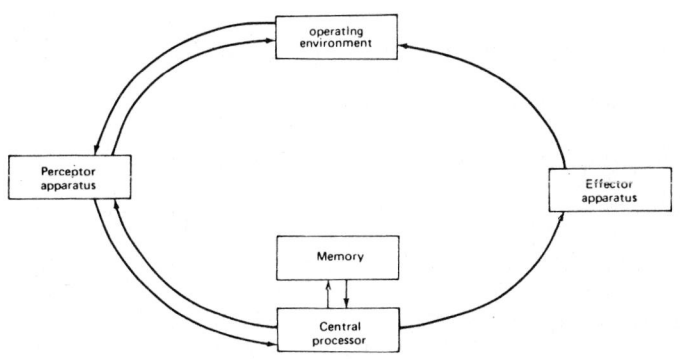

(Adapted from Bager and others in Data and Development (Marseille, Data for Development International Association, 1979)

---

*Data Use and Access Laboratories, Arlington, Va., U.S.A.

a/ See E.S.J. Dunn, Social Information Processing and Statistical Systems -
Change and Reform. (London, John Wiley and Sons, 1974), pp. 32-33.

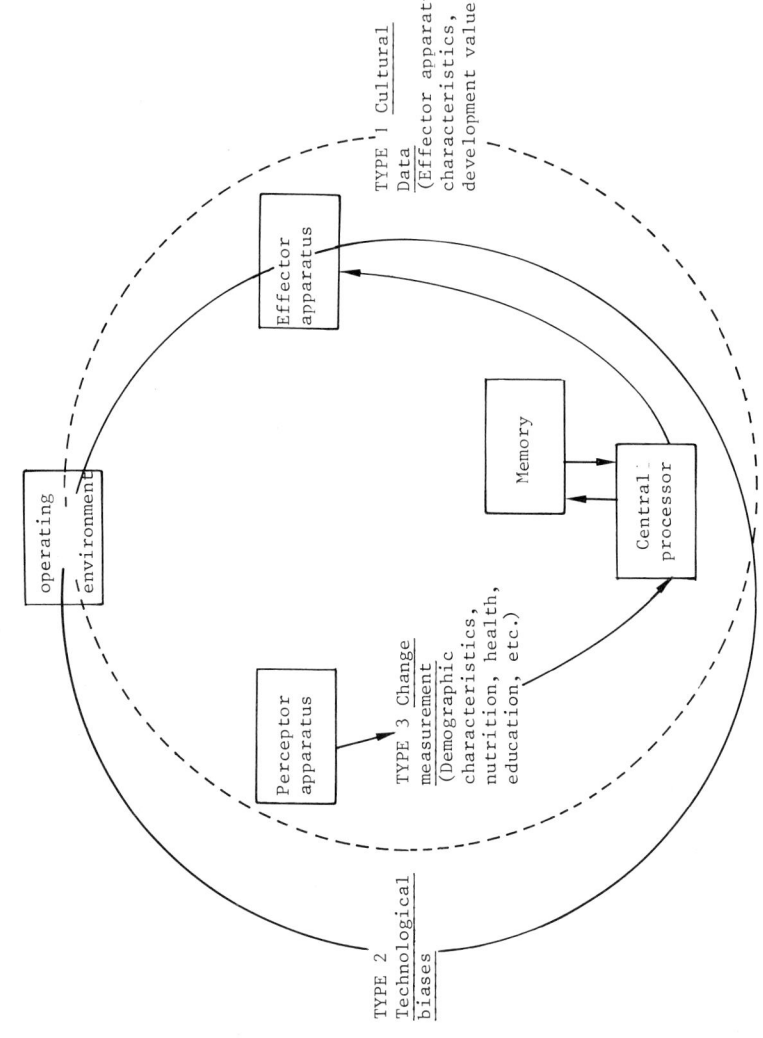

Figure II. Relation to three types of human factors data to the structure of an information processing system

The perceptor apparatus consists of all the mechanisms for receiving information or signals from the operating environment. In the development context, this apparatus might include censuses, surveys, or other methods of collecting information. The apparatus selects only certain predetermined signals. These are transformed into symbols or data which are transmitted to the central processor. The arrow from the perceptor apparatus back to the operating environment indicates that the apparatus itself may affect the operating environment or the signals, or both.

The central processor interprets and evaluates signals with the help of the memory. The central processor represents the "intelligence" of a system. The central processor of a fully mechanized information system, such as a thermostat which switches on a heating or cooling device when the ambient temperature crosses a threshold, could consist of a set of mechanically executed rules for interpreting, evaluating, and sending signals to the effector apparatus. The thermostat interprets a change in a measuring device as a signal indicating a change in ambient temperature in the operating environment. It evaluates the change in relation to the threshold. If necessary, it sends a signal which turns a switch to start or stop the heating or cooling process. Systems with humans do the same thing as mechanized systems. The human systems have statistical, planning and management agencies to interpret and evaluate signals from the perceptor apparatus and to send signals to the effector apparatus. Human systems are less precise and more complex than mechanical systems, of course. We compare signals that we are receiving with previous signals that we have determined to be important. We subject these signals to standard analytic processes and we convert them to measures of performance of the operating environment. We compare the signals received with norms and goals of organizations we serve. Finally, we perform operations on the data which are designed to suggest policy actions for our organizations. The suggested actions are then transmitted to the effector apparatus, which presumably has some power to act to try to change the operating environment.

Meanwhile, the memory stores, retrieves, and rearranges symbols. Its work is not analytic, as such. It may be perceived, in the short-run, as part of a machine, such as a computer. It may be thought of, in the long-run, as a file system or a warehouse or library of previous observations.

In social information processing systems, the effector apparatus is managed by and consists of people with sufficient power to control people and things in the operating environment. In the development context, this would be represented by our political, governmental, business, religious, educational and other leaders. In figure II there is a symbolic presentation of three types of human factors data in a social information processing system. Each type is discussed below.

1. Type 1: Cultural human factors data

The culture of a society is a source of human factors data which may define the human information processing systems presently in existence. The effector apparatus consists of those who are recognized by persons in their culture to have power. The characteristics of the operating environment are also defined by the culture. In the same way, the other features of the information processing system are affected by the culture.

Development implies change. The purpose of development at the societal level is to establish new ways of adapting to the environment. The environment includes other societies. Human institutions and culture are products of successful past adaptations to the environment. Cultures and institutions, by their nature, conserve successful adaptations of the past and resist changes in these adaptations. One may use information about cultural traits and norms to estimate probable obstacles to change and to determine if there are ways to

enhance the possibility of success for proposed changes. Cultural data
represent one form of human factors data needed for development planning and
management.

2. Type 2: Technological bias human factors data (unconsious prejudice)

A second kind of human factors data needed for development planning and
management is data about technological biases. Technological biases are the
norms, mores and folkways of a scientific culture. The scientific culture is
international in scope. Its members are educated to place a high value on
industrial technology, material wealth, and domination of the environment by
man. Technological biases appear as "standard procedures" for measuring all of
the quantitative and qualitative factors concerned with human activity. Where
science and technology are in control of information systems, then the systems
produce measurements related to industrial technology material wealth and
domination of the environment. For example, per capita gross national product
(GNP) is often used as a comparative measure between nations. Assuming GNP
can be measured the same way, with the same accuracy and the same meaning for
all nations, the question remains: why is this measure relevant to all national
development plans?

Scientists and engineers base measuring systems on the accumulation of
knowledge accepted by the scientific culture. It is useful to examine their
biases in economic and social measurements associated with human factors data.
These biases consist of things which the technologists accept as standard, but
for which there is no empirical evidence that the standard exists. The bias
is sometimes evidenced in the assertion that a highly technical instrument is
required for accurate measurement or monitoring of some aspect of development.
For example, a computer may be represented as essential for taking an accurate
census. We all know there is no necessary relationship between a computer and a
census, any more than there is between a hoe and basket of corn. How humans use
the tool determines the result.

Technological biases tend to emphasize scientific or technical activity at
the expense of time spent analyzing or understanding broader human purposes and
needs. However, a careful scientist is constantly questioning his or her
biases. To be successful in development work, we are called on to look carefully
at human factors that produce technological biases in our information.
Development means changing the culture and for this one needs data on the
culture as well as on the resources in order to monitor change. But before
change is evaluated we can benefit by carefully examining biases in the existing
and proposed technology of measurement to see how the observational procedures
can affect or distort the reality which is being observed.

3. Type 3: Change measurement human factors data

The third kind of human factors data concerns factors which can be used to
measure change. In our information system model, the human factors produce
signals to be monitored by the perceptor apparatus and to be changed by the
effector apparatus. The human factors data depend on and are affected by the
culture of a society and its technological biases. That is the point of figure
II. For example, even if the culture of a society placed a high value on an
increase in the love of humans for one another and a continuing improvement in
the sense of well being for all humans, it seems unlikely that the norms and
mores of scientists and technologists who are trained under the influence of
industrial technology would permit setting up a system to process the type of
information that could be used to increase love and a sense of well being.
However, there is no reason why an information system to measure love and a
sense of well being could not be set up.

Planning and management implies that conditions which exist today will not exist tommorow. To change conditions by rational means requires use of a culturally acceptable measurement or test. There are many kinds of measurements applicable to food production, natural resources, industry, and other areas. Certain measurements specifically assess the quantity, characteristics, and distribution of human populations. These are human factors change measurements which are the subject of this working group. It is difficult to love if one is starving. Regardless of cultural data and technological biases, human factors change measurements are likely to focus on human needs most of us would regard as basic and of high priority. These are food, health and productive capability and opportunity for its use.

B. Cultural data in relation to change measurement data

Planning and management is part of a broad social process. Many people will be involved in making decisions based on the suggested actions of those of us who work in the central processor. The effector apparatus of a society is not necessarily well organized or in complete control of its power. The people who have power have differing capabilities for using change measurement data and differing reasons for using the data. Some may not use such data or even know they exist. The skills of powerful persons in the effector apparatus vary. Their political and personal tactics vary. These variations result from the position of each person in their culture and also from the influences of the culture on each person. Before the human factors change measurement data needed for development planning and management can be assessed, knowledge of the culture in which the system will operate must be taken into account. This can be a very complex process. Certain obvious cultural human factors which should be considered are listed below.

1. Characteristics of the audience for change measurement data (especially persons in the effector apparatus)

(a) Age, sex, marital status, parental status, career history, education, training, ethnic background, urban/rural origins, and other potentially relevant demographic characteristics of persons in the effector apparatus who are to respond to change measurement data;

(b) Spheres of influence and control of each member of the effector apparatus and each member's position in the power structure of the society;

(c) Ability to comprehend change measurement data among members of the effector apparatus;

(d) Forms of delivery of change measurement data preferred by members in the effector apparatus;

(e) Probability that change measurement data will be accepted as legitimate indicators;

(f) Professed values and probable career objectives of members of the effector apparatus.

2. Culture-wide development values that bear on change measurement data

(a) Goals and purposes of development planning for a society (for example, to meet basic human needs and improve the quality of life; provide increasing opportunities for a better life; provide more equitable distribution of income and wealth; raise the level of employment; improve facilities and provision of education, health services, housing and nutrition; reduce sectoral, regional and social disparities);

(b) Values in the culture that support or are contrary to goals and/or purposes of development planning;

(c) Strength of values which inhibit development; measurement of this strength and assessment of possibilities for change.

To illustrate the importance of culture-wide values in determining development objectives and the types of change measurement data useful in development programmes, take an easily measured demographic characteristic: sex. There are a great many ways in which the people in the effector apparatus could use data on men and women, depending on the society's cultural values. For example, an information system might focus on data illustrating changes in the status of women who are involved in development programmes. Basic human needs are met at the traditional level, at home (food, shelter, clothing) and at the community level (education, community health care, water systems). Women are integral and central to meeting these needs at both levels.

Basic cultural data on women's activities must be evaluated before meaningful measurement of change in their status can be made. For example, it would be useful to understand the society's customs and norms relating to family organization, marriage and fertility, as well as its civil laws or religious customs which control women's involvement in such activities as marriage, schooling, migration, and labour force participation. These values may be significant in supporting or inhibiting development efforts on behalf of women.

In summary, there are two kinds of cultural human factors data. Firstly, data on a culture's definition of a subject (in this case the role of women) would be assembled to determine the impact on development goals. Desired changes would be identified. Change measurement data would then be specified for the information system.

Secondly, cultural data on the capability and willingness of members of the effector apparatus would be assembled before taking action on the information system. These data would determine their willingness and ability to understand and use the change measurements and would predict their comprehension of the role of women in development and their willingness to accept change in women's roles in their culture.

The cultural data assembled by the planner will be useful in selecting change measurement data bearing on human factors or other factors noted in figure II (industry, etc.). There will be differences of opinion as to which data ought to be included in an information system for development planning and management and differences as to how the information system should be developed. If these differences have a cultural basis, an object lesson in the importance of culture-wide human factors data will result.

C. Technological biases in relation to change measurement data

Human factors data on technological biases are most difficult to assemble because the technologists find it difficult to recognize their own biases. It may be said, for example, that they will seek out cultural biases by identifying key values. A procedure for identifying values is then selected. Possible procedures include an analysis of a country's law, an analysis of religious documents, a survey of the behaviour of the population, a content analysis of popular literature and entertainment, a compilation of folk wisdom, etc. Each of these procedures have weaknesses and strengths; the selection of one in preference to another reflects a bias. The bias cannot be avoided, but it can be recognized and its impact on the information system assessed. Much the same can be said of every measurement symbol attached to a signal from the operating environment, of every central processor tool and procedure and all other technical components of an information system. Care should be taken with any assertions.

D. Human factors data for change measurement

I have noted that data are created from signals obtained from the operating environment. The signals are usually selected by information technologists. These signals are not random noise emitted by human activity. They are abstractions of reality which represent something that it is believed can be measured and changed, and which is related to the goals of the culture. The measures are the signposts selected for the road to development chosen by national policy. The values of a culture or of the people in control of the information system effector apparatus will determine the human factors data chosen.

Many people believe that there are serious problems ahead for all nations because of their dependence on the use of non-renewable resources and their rate of population growth. All nations will be affected because the world will become an increasingly unstable and dangerous place in which to live when the population has increased from four billion to six billion in the next twenty years or so. People in all countries will then be poorer than they are now. Organizations most concerned with the international aspects of national development are the United Nations, the foundations, and the national government agencies which extend aid to the poorest of the nations. These bodies presently seek to direct their development programmes to basic human needs. As was shown earlier, it is obvious that the meaning of basic human needs is affected by the cultures of the people preparing the definition. Several examples drawn from a United States Agency for International Development (USAID) Policy Paper have direct implications for human factors data needs.

"The emphasis of basic human needs-oriented development strategies must ... necessarily be on increasing the productive base of developing country economics. But the way in which this is to be accomplished is crucial; it must involve some combination of:

"-- expanded access by the self-employed poor to productive resources (such as land, water, credit, and the improved techniques, tools and materials that go with them);

"-- increased investment and production in sectors and techniques which make greater use in labour surplus situations of abundant unskilled labour relative to scarce factors of production; and

"-- expanded basic services of health, nutrition, family planning, and education which improve over time the productive capacity and employment potential of the poor.

"Moreover, the expansion of productive employment can only come about from increased investment in and production of both basic needs ... related and other goods and services -- for both domestic consumption and, for many countries, export. Accelerated investment and economic growth are thus essential prerequisites for the achievement of basic needs objectives." [1]

---

[1] United States Agency for International Development, A Strategy for a More Effective Bilateral Development Assistance Program: An AID Policy Paper (Washington, D.C., March 1978), p. 11.

Data could be developed to measure access to resources, increased investment and expanded basic services. The AID paper suggests, however, that the human factors measures which the central processor sends to the effector apparatus need not directly measure economic activities:

> "It is possible ... to give some indication of the steps involved
> and the problems encountered in some recent attempts to provide
> more precise quantitative estimates of aid requirements to meet
> basic human needs objectives. The first step in any such attempt
> is to set objectives targets for basic human needs. One approach
> is to frame these objectives in terms of the status or well-being
> of individuals. Target values for some indicators of well-being
> have been suggested by the 1976 Club of Rome report (entitled
> Reshaping the International Order -- or the 'R10 Report') as
> goals toward which all countries might strive by the year 2000:
> life expectancy at birth of 65 years of more (compared with a
> current average of 71 years for countries with 1974 per capita
> GNP above $2000; 55 years for countries with 1974 per capita GNP
> below $2000 and 48 years for countries with 1974 per capita GNP
> below $300); an infant mortality rate of 50 per thousand births
> or less (compared with current averaged for the country groupings
> defined above of 21, 101 and 134 per thousand, respectively);
> a birth rate of 25 per thousand population or less (compared with
> current averages as defined above of 17, 35 and 40 per thousand,
> respectively); and a literacy rate of at least 75% (compared
> with current average as defined above of 97%, 39% and 33%,
> respectively).*

> (*Jan Tinbergen, co-ordinator, Reshaping the International Order:
> A Report to the Club of Rome, (New York, E.P. Dutton and Co., 1976),
> p. 130. Comparative figures from John W. Sewell and the staff of
> the Overseas Development Council, The United States and World
> Development: Agenda 1977 (New York, Praeger, 1977), table A-1,
> p. 157)."2/

The AID document from which these quotes were taken emphasizes that their proposed approach is distinguished from present practice: (a) by organizing aid programmes in terms of common basic needs rather than sectors (for example, agriculture, health, etc.); and (b) by linking the aid "to the accomplishment of measureable basic human need objectives." 3/

The human factors data which the working groups identify as needed to measure change and which could be obtained by available measuring procedures, will probably be drawn from these broad topics:

(a) Basic demographic characteristics of age, sex, living arrangements, marital status, fertility and migratory status;

2/ Ibid., pp. 18-19.

3/ Ibid., p. 32.

(b)   Education and training;

(c)   Social welfare requirements;

(d)   Food and nutrition;

(e)   Housing;

(f)   Health and medical services;

(g)   Labour force status and occupational skills;

(h)   Special characteristics significant to political social development (religion, ethnic status).

In selecting the needed data, the following particular data needs for specific stages of development programmes could be considered:

(a)   Planning stage;

(b)   Operational and/or administrative stage;

(c)   Evaluation and measurement of change stage;

(d)   Data to measure changes in values.

These four kinds of data needs can be considered for each specific development objective.

Finally, when the working sessions on human factors consider information systems, the group members will then be concerned with all the topics implied in figure II. The specific measuring procedures will probably be limited to censuses, surveys, administrative record data programs, and indirect or remote sensing. Although there are legitimate questions to be raised about information system tools (computers, remote sensing devices, questionnaire forms, software, etc.) the more difficult and critical issues revolve around the culture within which and in the service of which the information system operates.

Finally, figures III and IV give projections of the future and comparisons with respect to children and population change and educating the world's children. There are implications in these figures for the fundamental and crucial role of women in development which should not be ignored.

Figure III.   Children and population change

Increase in Numbers of Children Under 15: 1950-2000

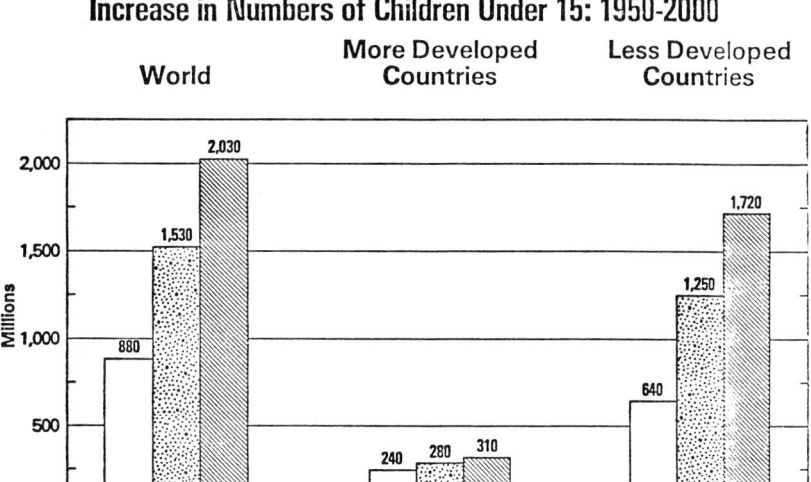

Proportion of Population Under 15: 1979

Source : United Nations Population Division, WP 55

Figure IV. Educating the world's children

School Enrollment in 10 Selected Countries: 1975

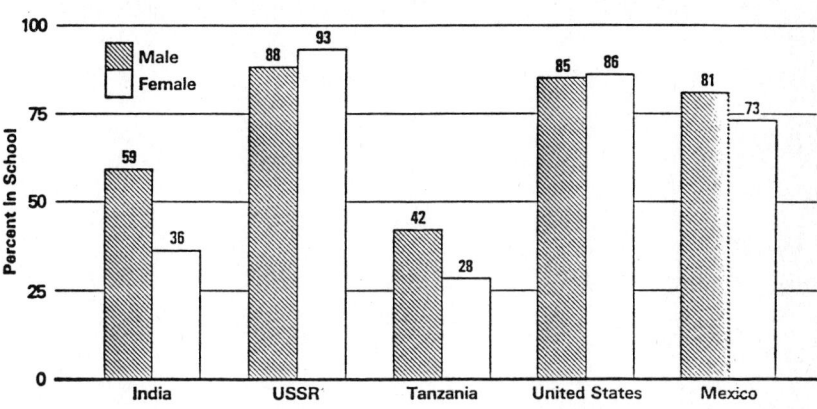

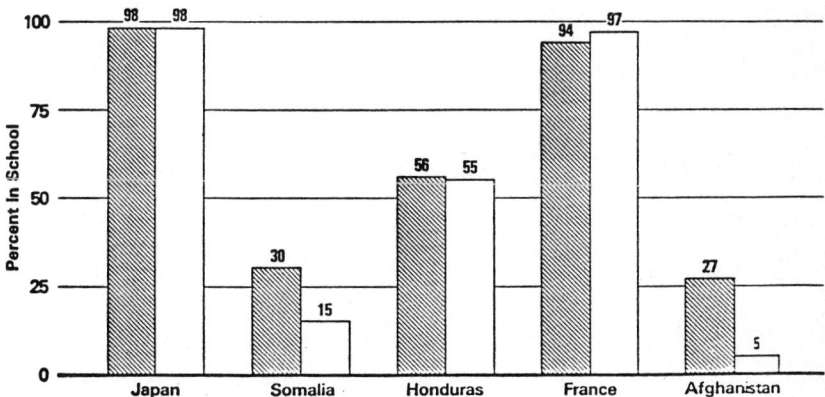

Percent of Children 6-18 Years Old in School

Source : UNESCO Yearbook, 1976

INFORMATION SYSTEMS IN PUBLIC ADMINISTRATION
D. Eade, J. Hodgson (editors)
North-Holland Publishing Company
DFD, 1981

INTEGRATED SOCIAL DATA SYSTEMS: THE ROLE OF HOUSEHOLD
CENSUSES AND SURVEYS AS SOURCES OF SOCIAL, DEMOGRAPHIC
AND MANPOWER DATA IN BRITAIN

Catherine Hakim*

Abstract

Recent developments in household census and survey work that represent
progress towards an integrated social data system are described. Continuous
surveys on the population and its characteristics provide the primary sources of
data that serve developmental functions. However, the feasibility and
desirability of using standard entity concepts (for example standard definitions
and classifications) for making connexions between datasets is questioned; the
resulting constraints on the application of different conceptualizations of
problems or issues (the entity problem) is particularly limiting on the
developmental mode of social information processing. The use of sampling as an
alternative technique for making connexions between datasets is explored.

A. Introduction: integrated social data systems

Social, demographic and manpower data have been collected in Britain, as
elsewhere, for a long time, and with increasing precision and detail. This
paper seeks to describe some recent developments in household census and survey
work that represent progress towards an integrated social data system. It also
discusses some of the problems encountered and reviews the benefits in terms of
the applications – current and potential – for social policy, planning and
research. Social data are defined in their broadest sense, to encompass
demographic, health, housing, education and manpower data as well as the more
recent additions of leisure data, distribution accounts and time accounts.

The concept of integrated social data systems is based largely on
Richard Stone's work for the United Nations on a System of Social and
Demographic Statistics, (SSDS). The purpose of SSDS is "to show what data
are desirable on human beings, both individually and in groups, and on
the institutions with which they are connected and how these data should be
organized in order to provide an information system which will be useful for
description, analysis and policy making in the different fields of social

---

* Research and Planning Division, Department of Employment,
United Kingdom.

life." 1/ The integration of disparate datasets into a cohesive system requires that connexions be made between the parts. Common definitions and classifications across datasets are of course crucial here, as well as consistency in the identification of entities, the specification of time, and areas. 2/

Similar problems in data integration have been identified in the Data For Development (DFD) concept of the government data network. Data integration requires common concepts and definitions, common sets of entities to be observed, and common periods or points in time for observation. It is also suggested that models for explanation, prediction or evaluation be similarly standardized, as for example in macro-economic growth models or population growth models. 3/ The benefits and advantages of standardized modelling techniques may be open to question. However, SSDS represents an innovative and practicable model of an integrated social data system.

Techniques for making connexions between datasets are clearly central to the development of social information systems, but have so far received relatively little attention. To some extent the techniques required will be determined by the nature of the data sources: if these are extensively linked at the data collection level there will be fewer problems of conceptual (or logical) linkage of discrete datasets. However there are some issues of data integration that will still remain and these should perhaps not be seen purely as problems to which there is technical solution. These issues are examined further in the final section.

The focus on British data sources and datasets is perhaps pertinent. In discussing potential sources of data for SSDS, particular reference was made to British data collections – notably the continuous household surveys and longitudinal studies that are carried out by, or on behalf of, government departments. 4/ A number of other less well-known developments will also be outlined.

The focus is on recurrent multiple-use data on the population and its characteristics – that is, household censuses and surveys and datasets derived from or linked to them. These can be regarded as the primary sources of data that serve developmental functions, in contrast to administrative sources of data that in the main are usually designed to serve performance activities. Information processing can operate in two modes: the performance mode, which involves routine adaptations within the operating environment that are already provided for, that is, the routine decisions typical of an administrative context; and the developmental mode, which involves adaptation to a changing environment, decisions which lead to change

---

1/ United Nations, Department of Economic and Social Affairs, Statistical Office, Towards a System of Social and Demographic Statistics, Studies in Methods, Series F, No. 18 (ST/ESA/STST/SER.F/18, New York, 1975), p. 3.

2/ Ibid., p. 20.

3/ Data For Development (Marseille, Data For Development International Association, 1978) pp. 118-119.

4/ United Nations, op. cit.

in the frame of reference and conceptual structure. 5/, 6/ Furthermore,
household census and survey data have tended to be the most important sources
for social reports. 7/, 8/

B. Household censuses and surveys: recent developments

The population census is traditionally regarded as a demographic database;
but the modern census can more appropriately be regarded as the most important
single source of social, demographic and manpower information on the population.
Relatively infrequent censuses are now complemented by household surveys that
are, like the census, multipurpose in design and applications, but are carried
out at more frequent intervals - annually or biennially. Thus the boundary
between the census as headcount and the social survey has become eroded.

The range of topics on which information is collected in the census now
goes well beyond a simple headcount, to include data on employment, living
standards, income (in some countries), education, and other topics. Where the
population and housing censuses are carried out as a single exercise, or are
subsequently linked, there is the advantage of a richer combined data source,
and in some countries the census of agriculture is also linked to the census.
The basic census topics can be regarded as those recommended by international
organizations, notably the United Nations, but also the Statistical Office of
the European Economic Community (EEC) and other regional organizations. These
basic topics include demographic data such as sex, age, marital status,
country of birth and/or citizenship; economic data such as type of economic
activity, occupation, industry, employment status and place of work; educational
attainment; data on the characteristics of households and families such as
relationships, type of family, number of economically active members and housing
tenure status; and data on housing such as location of the housing unit, number
of rooms, available facilities, type of heating, type of building, period of
construction and multi-occupancy. Additional topics for the census are even
more wide-ranging: duration of residence; place of previous residence; farm
or non-farm residence; year of immigration into the country, place of birth
(for native-born); national or ethnic group; language; religion; fertility of
women; main source of livelihood; hours worked (of those in employment);
income; duration of employment; secondary occupation; number of persons

---

5/ E.S. Dunn, Social Information Processing and Statistical Systems:
Change and Reform (London, John Wiley and Sons, 1974), pp. 32-33.

6/ Data for Development, op. cit., p. 13.

7/ E.J. Thompson, "Social trends: the development of an annual report for
the United Kingdom", International Social Science Journal, vol. 30, No. 3,
pp. 653-659.

8/ United Nations, European Social Development Programme, Social Reports:
Their Contribution to Integrated Development Planning, results of a Seminar held
at Saint-Pierre, Aosta Valley, Italy, 20-30 April, 1976 (New York, 1976).

employed (by an employer); the journey to work; school attendance; location of
school or other educational establishment attended; educational qualifications;
literacy; type of institutional or communal establishment in which a person
lives; dependency relationships; rent paid for accommodation; ownership of
durable consumer goods; area of floor space in housing unit; cooking facilities;
type of sewage disposal system; type of energy used for heating; availability of
telephone; number of floors in building; and availability of a lift. In some
countries, the census has also been used on occasion to collect information on
an even broader range of social topics, for example, holidays taken, child care
services used, place of parents' birth, race, car ownership, value of personal
property, physical disabilities and number of marriages.

This extensive list of topics covered by the census, on a standard or
occasional basis, indicates clearly that the modern census has been extended
into a general purpose survey of socio-economic conditions. Since the census
is most commonly compulsory, this has led in recent years to some public concern
over the alleged invasion of privacy represented by such a broad based survey
of citizens' levels of living and life styles. This has resulted in attempts
by Governments to place limits on the number and type of questions that can be
included in a census. In some countries, response to certain parts of the
census form has been made voluntary rather than compulsory. Yet another
reaction has been to allocate the additional questions to follow-up surveys
after the main census, that is, voluntary sample surveys for which the census
serves as a sampling frame. Finally, a fourth solution adopted by census
offices has been to limit the additional questions to a sample of census forms —
in some cases the various additional questions are allocated to different census
forms, so that no single household is required to answer all of them. In sum,
census offices have had to develop new approaches to the design of the census
in order that additional social information may be collected without placing
an excessive reporting burden on the public. As a result, the boundary
between a census, in which all questions are addressed to the whole population,
and a sample survey, in which information is collected only from a
representative sample of the population, has become blurred.

The increasing overlap between censuses and social surveys is highlighted
by the use of sampling in census work. A census enumeration is in principle
universal; in practice, censuses are sometimes taken on a sample basis. In
Britain for example, the quinquennial census taken in 1966 was a Ten per cent
sample census. But censuses conducted wholly on a sample basis are still
relatively rare, whereas the use of sampling as an integral part of decennial
censuses is well established. Information on certain additional topics is
sometimes collected from specified samples of the population, usually between
5 and 25 per cent, in Britain 10 per cent. The additional sample census
questions may be allocated to a separate questionnaire or even to a separate
second stage of the census operation. Thus to some extent the principal
distinguishing characteristic between a sample census exercise that follows
the main 100 per cent enumeration and a follow-up survey to the census is that
the former shares the compulsory character of the census while the latter is
voluntary.

While the differences between census data and survey data are less sharply
defined, important differences remain. Censuses are normally compulsory, while
response to surveys is usually voluntary. Censuses are typically restricted to
factual questions to which there is a single truthful reply, although there can
be some ambiguity in defining economic activity, for example, or in describing
an occupation. Surveys often include questions on attitudes and opinions, or
seek information on motives, reasons and intentions. In general, more
detailed and more personal information can be obtained through a voluntary
survey than can be collected through a compulsory census, as census questions
must be acceptable to the majority of the population. Thus the two types of

data source are both complementary and alternative. $\underline{9}/$, $\underline{10}/$

Goldstone has argued that two of the key elements in improving social data in developing countries is the more widespread use of sampling techniques in data collections, and the establishment of a continuing household survey capacity as a complement to the census. "In most developing countries, household sample surveys are the only practicable way of obtaining up-to-date national data on social conditions and trends, access to needed services, and the impact of policies to reduce the poverty in which the vast majority lives. Moreover, if suitably designed and implemented, household surveys can be an important instrument for the integration of social statistics." $\underline{11}/$ This approach has already been implemented in some countries. $\underline{12}/$

In Britain there are four major continuous household surveys: the Family Expenditure Survey (FES), the National Food Survey (NFS), the General Household Survey (GHS) and the Labour Force Survey (LFS). (See note No. 1). Other national surveys are regularly carried out as part of the EEC programme of data collections.

The FES has run continually since 1957 and each year seeks interviews with about 11,000 private households in Great Britain. The main content of the survey is household income and expenditure, and the main purpose is to provide up-to-date weights for the Retail Price Index and to provide a monitor of the income distributional effects of changes in taxation and social assistance regulations.

The NFS has run since 1940 and currently each year seeks interviews with around 15,000 housewives. The main content of the survey is the purchase of food and the data are used mainly to calculate expenditure on food for national accounts purposes, dietary studies, and to monitor the elasticities of demand for use in forecasting demand for different foodstuffs.

The GHS has run since 1971 and has a set sample of about 15,000 households per year. This is the most truly multi-purpose of the national

---

9/ C. Hakim, "The population census and its by-products: data bases for research", International Social Science Journal, vol. 31, No. 2 (1979).

10/ S. Rokkan, "National primary socio-economic data structures: Norway", International Social Science Journal, vol. 30, No. 3 (1978), pp. 621-652.

11/ L. Goldstone, "Improving social statistics in developing countries" International Social Science Journal, vol. 29, No. 4 (1977), pp. 756-771.

12/ P. Singh, "Towards a social perspective: a statistical appraisal", Kenya Statistical Digest, vol. 13, No. 3 (1975), pp. 5-9.

surveys, with no dominant subject theme. The main topics covered are
demography, housing, employment, education and health and income, but a great
variety of subsidiary topics are also included either on an ad hoc or regular
basis. The GHS includes attitudinal questions (for example on job satisfaction,
pay, hours worked) and thus permits studies of the relationship between
behaviour or physical circumstances and attitudes, and more generally the
contribution of objective and subjective factors to the quality of life. The
option of including variable additional topics in the GHS, and the wide range
of basic topics against which additional topics can be cross-tabulated, make
it a very flexible source of ad hoc data at the national (and regional) level.

The biennial LFS has been conducted in the spring of 1973, 1975, 1977 and
1979, as one of the United Kingdom commitments to the statistical programme of
the EEC. Interviews are sought with a sample of 0.5 per cent of all households
throughout the United Kingdom, some 105,000 households in total. The LFS is a
multi-purpose source for labour force data, with some core sections providing
time series, and additional sections on particular aspects of the labour force
that vary between surveys.

There are a number of other surveys in the EEC series that provide data on
a reasonably comparable basis for all member countries. The EEC survey on
Consumer Attitudes and Buying Intentions has been carried out in Britain in
January, May and October each year since May 1974. There have so far been two
rounds of the Social Indicators Survey for the EEC Statistical Office.
The first, focusing on housing and health, was conducted in June/July
1977 in Britain ; the second, on the quality of working life, was
carried out in September 1978. These national surveys differ from
most other regular official surveys in collecting attitudinal data
as well as factual data on the characteristics of households.

All of these surveys retain a relatively fixed subject matter, while the
samples change over time. Another type of continuous survey is based on a fixed
sample followed up over time. There are two longitudinal studies of this type
in Britain, the Douglas longitudinal study and the National Children's Bureau
longitudinal study. The first follows the progress of some 5,000 people born
in March 1946 through childhood and adult life. The second is based on a
larger sample of 17,000 people born in 1958, who are re-interviewed at
particular stages of the life cycle.

A rather different type of continuous survey is the national Longitudinal
Survey (LS) carried out by the Office of Population Censuses and Surveys. This
covers a one per cent sample of the population identified at the 1971 Census as
usually resident in England and Wales, updated with a one per cent sample of
those recorded as being born in, or migrating to, England and Wales after 1971.
The data included in the study consists of census information (from the 1971
Census and, in due course, future censuses) and other information routinely
collected when vital events occurring at different stages of the lives of
people in the LS sample are recorded - for example births of children, death of
a spouse, cancer registration, emigration, internal migration and death. The
LS (one per cent) can be used for studies of fertility, mortality or
occupational mobility over the life cycle, and related personal and household
characteristics.

The LS (one per cent) illustrates one method of data integration, namely the
merging of information relating to the same individuals from different sources
to create a new and more complex data base.

Another approach is to use the population census as a source of data on the
characteristics of both respondents and non-respondents to the continuous surveys

outlined above. This has been done for both the GHS and FES, in order to study differential non-response to these surveys in 1971.

A third approach is to use household censuses and surveys as sampling frames for ad hoc surveys. Such follow-up surveys may use the census/survey purely as a source of a sampling frame for a study that is otherwise quite separate, or information from the two data collections may be merged. For example, the 1971 Census was supplemented by two follow-up surveys, one on income, the other on qualified manpower, and information from survey respondents was merged with census information on each sample. Similarly, the GHS, the FES and the LFS are used from time to time as sampling frames for supplementary surveys, either of the population as a whole or, more commonly, particular sub-groups in the population. The use of continuous surveys as a source of sampling frames for follow-up surveys is particularly advantageous for surveys of relatively small and geographically scattered sub-groups in the population.

A fourth approach to data integration is the use of common or compatible concepts, definitions and classifications - for example, of economic activity, unemployment or the household. However, standard definitions and classifications are not always feasible and advantageous for all data collections.

A fifth approach to data integration is the development and application of a national socio-economic classification of small areas. The 1971 Census small area statistics provided the basis for three social area analysis classifications, of local authorities, wards and census enumeration districts. The three area typologies facilitate data integration in two ways. They can be used as area sampling frames for surveys, and can also be used in the presentation of survey results at sub-national level. Data from other sources (such as local or national surveys or local authority administrative records) can be linked to census data at the level of the social area typology, and thus multi-source datasets at the sub-national level can be created.

In summary there is a high degree of integration between the social, demographic and manpower datasets derived from household censuses and surveys. The connexions between datasets take various forms. There is increasing overlap between the subject content of censuses and other continuous surveys, so that continuous surveys can offer both complementary and alternative sources to the census. The use of the census and surveys as a source of samples for follow-up surveys and the creation of datasets based on file merging makes the census a core database, to which surveys can be linked, either conceptually, logically, or physically.

While these inter-related data sources fall short of what would ideally be required by the proposed SSDS - the absence of time budget studies being most notable - they go a long way towards it. Collectively they provide the basis for a wider range of applications than administrative sources offer, frequently for studies that could not have been envisaged or planned for in advance. It is not possible to review all the policy, planning and research applications here, but they include fields as disparate as health, demography, social policy, education and manpower.

C. Issues in data integration

Nevertheless, important problems in the development of integrated information systems on the population remain. Among them, one that has so far received relatively little attention: the feasibility and desirabiity of standardized definitions and classifications or, more broadly, what Dunn has termed the entity problem. [13]

---

[13] E.S. Dunn, op. cit., p. 141.

All social data consist of representations of entities, of the states, activities and processes that describe them. Data may refer to single entities (such as a specific individual, household or enterprise) or to aggregate classes (such as socio-economic groups, types of industry). The problem is that entity concepts are subject to a reification bias. Adaptive social behaviour and developmental decision making require flexible entity concepts in order to perceive changing realities or to reconceptualize the phenomena observed. [14/]

One of the proposed solutions to the problem of integrating social data systems is the use of standardized definitions and classifications which would allow logical connexions to be made between systems. But this solution entails a further problem; standard definitions and classifications constrict and constrain the representation of the states and processes of entities, so that none of the data sources permit the entities to be differently conceived. For example, there have been attempts to develop a single standard occupational classification for use in all multi-purpose and some more specialized data collections. One of the major conceptual problems encountered was the difficulty of reconciling an occupational classification designed primarily for economic and manpower studies with an occupational classification designed primarily as the basis for social classifications (such as social class or socio-economic group). Similarly it is difficult to develop a truly multi-purpose classification of household composition that would fully account for all the characteristics of household members (such as age, sex, employment status, kinship, dependency) that may be required for different data applications.

The entity problem is not necessarily resolved when microdata are available, although microdata generally offer greater flexibility in data analysis. There is a tendency to think of the human respondent as the most "micro" of all "micro" building blocks. But much social data is necessarily hierarchical in nature. The characteristics and attributes of entities are more than simple aggregates of the subentities; the representation of social systems requires the description of behavioural and structural characteristics which transcend those of their human components. For example, the characteristics of an enterprise cannot be completely described by aggregating information on its human components. Similarly, a household cannot be completely described by adding up all that is known about individual members of the household. Thus, proposals that there should be universal standard identifiers for people, and greater use of microdata to make connexions between data systems, do not resolve the entity problem. In many cases the choice of the conceptual level, or entity level, is crucial to the framing of a problem or issue. For example, poverty may be studied at the level of the individual, the family, the household, or even on an area basis. Each approach implies not only different entity concepts but also different descriptive data on the states, activities and processes to be observed. Similarly social class (or social stratification) can be conceptualized at the level of the individual, the household, or on an area basis. More generally, economic activity and all

---

14/   E.S. Dunn, op. cit., pp. 71. 143.

related topics can be conceptualized at the level of the individual (most
commonly in economic and manpower studies) or at the level of the family or
household (most commonly in social policy research). The entity problem is thus
not only a matter of changing definitions, classifications, identifiers,
and descriptors in response to, and to appropriately reflect, changing social
realities (with the related problem of discontinuities in time series), but also
a problem of not excluding the option of different conceptualizations of social
reality at a given point in time. The problem is particularly germane to
multiple-use data systems and to the developmental mode of information
processing, but also to data derived from administrative sources that are even
more tied to current policies, activities and conceptual frameworks (see note
No. 2).

Dunn has proposed a number of approaches towards an integrated data system
that rely to a much greater extent on sampling than on standardized
classifications as a means of making data linkages possible while avoiding some
of the pitfalls of the entity problem. The most important of these is the
development of master sampling - the development and utilization of a set of
master samples drawn from a master statistical frame which includes identical
or overlapping (that is, rotating) panels of respondents. Sample records could
be linked with a complete file (such as that offered by the census) or a master
statistical frame so long as the sample file is a subset of the complete file,
and provided they both possess standard unit identifiers. This approach allows
data linkages to be made without being tied to a particular set of entity
concepts. 15/

One example of master sampling in Britain is the use of the census as a
sampling frame for a number of follow-up surveys. Whether the survey data
are merged with census information or not, this approach permits surveys to be
linked to the census, or set in a national context, while the conceptual
framework of the survey (that is, the entity concepts utilised) may well be
different from that of the census. Similar exercises can be conducted with
follow-up surveys to national household surveys, such as the continuous surveys
noted above.

Dunn suggests that an established base of recurrent multiple-purpose data
is one of the first requirements of an integrated set of data systems. There
should also be a capability for generating more specialised nonrecurrent data,
and for linking these data and more specialised data from other sources with the
data elements in the recurrent data base. This approach is evidenced, we suggest,
in the established set of continuous surveys, the option of follow-up surveys to
the continuous surveys, and the development of the Longitudinal Study in
Britain. Thus many of the desired characteristics of an integrated set of
social data systems have already been built into recent developments in
household census and survey sources in Britain. However the master sampling
approach is not explicitly used, for example, to link the various recurrent
data. More generally, there have been no attempts - with the exception of the
Longitudinal Study - to use master sampling to generate longitudinal data.
Master sampling may be more explicitly used in the future. For example some
consideration has been given to supplementing recurrent data with a one per
cent annual national continuous household survey.

15/ E.S. Dunn, op. cit., p. 148.

The national socio-economic area classifications represent a somewhat unique solution to the entity problem as regards the definitions and classifications of areas at the sub-national level. At the very small area level, the socio-economic classifications of wards and Enumeration Districts offer a flexible alternative to areas defined by administrative criteria; flexible in that the relative size, level of detail, and topic specificity of area typologies can be modified to suit the particular problem, policy issue or research topic in question. The area classifications are thus particularly useful in developmental research and policy-formulation.

D.   Conclusions

Recent discussions of the need for, the potential benefits, and possible approaches towards the integration of social data systems have tended to focus on the technical and methodological aspects of the topic. It is argued that substantive aspects of social data systems need further thought, and that the entity problem may represent a far greater problem than has so far been recognised. Recurrent demographic, social and manpower data have a wide range of overlapping applications, but the overlaps are not always such as to allow a single set of entity concepts to be utilized. Standard definitions and classifications may actually constrain or prohibit the developmental mode of information processing. In this context, the linkage of social datasets through sampling, or through master sampling, may well merit further consideration.

Notes

1. There are several types of continuous survey. In some cases the sample changes (in whole or in part) but the subject matter is fixed to some extent, although additional variable topics may be included from time to time. In other cases the same remains the same and is followed up at intervals over a period of time. Continuous surveys include those that are time-specific (such as the census) as well as those in which interviews are spread out over the year in order to provide annual and quarterly data. Continuous surveys are thus one type of what Dunn refers to as "recurrent multiple-use records". 16/ (Dunn, 1974: 149).

2. To some extent the problems encountered in attempts to analyse the same datasets from differing ideological stances can also be seen as an example of the entity problem. See for example the discussions of the various concepts of social class, unemployment, wealth and poverty in Irvine, Miles and Evans. 17/

16/   E.S. Dunn, op. cit., p. 149.

17/   J. Irvine, I. Miles and J. Evans, Demystifying Social Statistics (London, Pluto Press, 1979).

This article originally appeared in 'Social Science Information Studies' Butterworths, 1980.

INFORMATION SYSTEMS IN PUBLIC ADMINISTRATION
D. Eade, J. Hodgson (editors)
North-Holland Publishing Company
© *DFD, 1981*

FINAL REPORT OF WORKING GROUP 1*

A. The human factors domain

Social, cultural and political factors pervade and influence entire information systems and the development process, as outlined in figure II of the paper by John Beresford (page 148). These factors vary a great deal between areas. Therefore we cannot make general statements on how to collect or apply data on social, cultural and political influences in information systems. We can state that such factors must be taken into account, as elaborated in Data and Development.

Human factors can also be considered for the goals, measurements, and data flows in a topic information system. The two alternative models of the development process outlined in the paper by Michael Ward (section C of his paper) were considered to have somewhat different implications for data sources, information needs and approaches to data analysis. The "growth and resource-based" models of development suggested that human resources were to be treated primarily as inputs to the development process with the focus on the demand for and supply and geographical distribution of manpower. The "structural dependency" model suggested that human factors should be treated primarily as results of the development process, with the focus on the (re)distribution of income and wealth, access to goods and services, equality of opportunity in the educational system and labour market, and access to the decision-making (or political) system. It also suggested greater emphasis on analysis of data in terms of the socio-economic structure and under priviledged sub-groups in the population rather than on a collectivity of individuals, and greater emphasis on focussed studies rather than national surveys.

---

* Participants: S. Arzoo, Bangladesh, J. Brackett, U.S.A., J. Beresford, (English moderator), U.S.A., K. Clark, Thailand, M.J. Evers (Spanish rapporteur), U.S.A., E. Eviota, Philippines, V. Gonzales, Peru, C. Hakim, (English-French Rapporteur, Great Britain, A. Hernandez, Panama, J. Kekovole, Kenya, L. Martides, Cyprus, S. Poedjastoeti, Indonesia, D. Pomerance, U.S.A., V. Rodriguez, Costa Rica, M. Sicron, Israel, K. Tshibambe (French moderator) Zaire.

In practice, elements of both approaches might underlie much developmental decision making and combinations of both types of data would be desirable and likely.

It was agreed that in at least nine, and perhaps most developing countries, both models and approaches would require essentially similar types of information and data on basic needs and well-being as follows:

(a)   Nutritional levels and water supply;

(b)   Shelter and housing;

(c)   Health;

(d)   Education;

(e)   Employment (participation in formal and informal labour markets);

(f)   Law, order and peace.

B.   Developmental goals and problems

The Group considered developmental goals and problems for the society as a whole. Problems of particular interest to the group were:

(a)   Rapid population growth and the need to control such growth;

(b)   The imbalance between the geographical distribution of the population and manpower needs, and the need to promote a better fit between the regional labour supply and demand; the lack of information on internal migration;

(c)   Inequalities between individuals and social groups, and the need to promote equality of opportunity;

(d)   Legal inequalities and non-enforcement of administrative procedures for status recognition (especially if

(e)   Lack of procedures for establishing priorities and allocating resources.

C.   Information system problems

In relation to development goals, a number of information system problems were identified:

(a)   The entity problem (the identification of relevant concepts, operational definitions and classifications of units of count such as families, households, communities, their activities and characteristics);

(b)   Data inadequacies as reflected in coverage of population subgroups (the non-traceable sectors), timeliness, lack of comparability between data sources;

(c)   Government (or national) priorities as reflected in resource allocation decisions;

(d)   The failure to manage information as a resource, resulting in duplication of effort, poor data dissemination systems and little linkage of

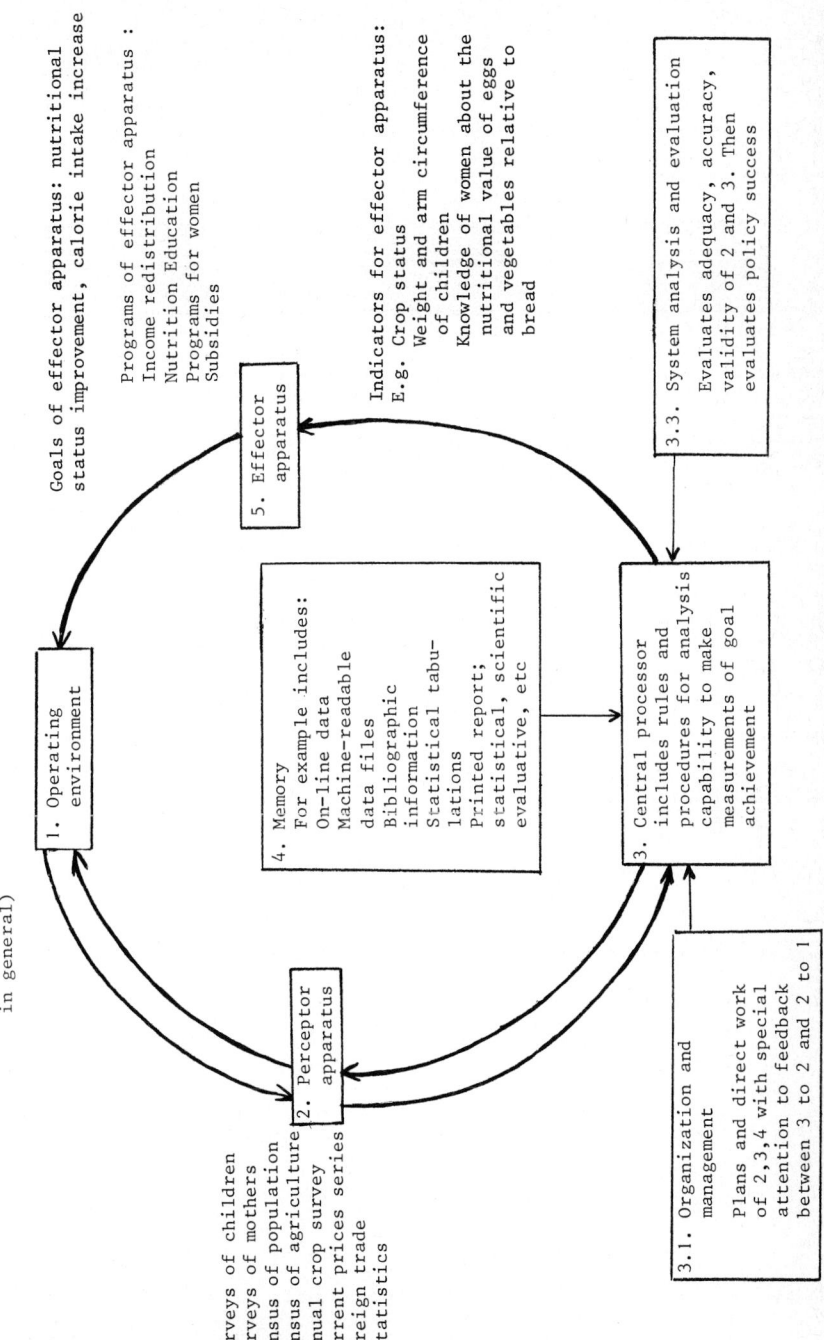

Figure V. Conceptual framework of an information system (Nutrition case details are not in boxes ; boxes are the information system in general)

data sources where this is feasible in principle;

(e) The inapplicability of certain data collection or data analysis techniques to situations in developing countries;

(f) Social and cultural barriers to the populations' adoption of "respondent" behaviour during field work/data collection, and lack of experience with the respondent role.

D. Information needs in relation to goals and data sources

A case-study approach was used to consider the relationship between goals, information needs and information sources. The example used concerned nutritional levels. Tables 1 and 2 outline these relationships. Figure V differentiates long-term goals that are monitored by socio-economic indicators derived from repeated or continuous data collections (administrative, censuses and surveys, etc.), and short-term goals determined by specific policies that are evaluated using a wide range of data sources. The types of information and the range of possible data sources in relation to nutrition are outlined in table 2. Ideally each country should have a datalogue, listing all available sources of data. More detailed indexes to particular types of data would also be desirable.

E. Definition of audiences and appropriate methods of presentation of information

The audiences for an information system on human factors were identified as:

(a) Decision makers;

(b) Analytic users and researchers including academics and international agencies;

(c) Opinion leaders and motivators within the community;

(d) The general public and the communications media.

Methods and formats for the presentation of results and reports include:

(a) Machine-readable formats (magnetic tape, punched cards or tape);

(b) Statistical tables in publications;

(c) Computer printouts of tables;

(d) Graphs and diagrams;

(e) Textual summaries and reports;

(f) Maps and cartographic presentations of data (including computer produced maps);

(g) Microfiche, microfilm;

(h) On-line data retrieval and data display via terminals.

The latter is usually limited to persons and organizations that are heavy users of particular data sources; it is particularly appropriate for access to time series that are updated regularly (for example, on a monthly basis). It is also

Table 1:   The relationship between goals, information needs and sources

Goals	Information needs	Information sources
Improve nutritional level	(a) Social indicators to monitor improvement, e.g.	(a) Surveys of children at home in schools
(a) Identify extent of problem, e.g. % under nourished	Arm circumference)% Weight)below standard Height)on each etc.)indicators	
(b) Identify causes, e.g. Nutrition ignorance Poverty Poor local crops etc.	(b) Policy implementation evaluation, e.g. Knowledge of nutritional value of food Income redistribution, food subsidies etc. Subsidies fertilizers, better quality seeds, etc.	(b) Survey of mothers' information on nutrition Knowledge + access + use of subs-foods from households or mothers Continuous surveys of crops, prices, land, Administrative sources Farmers use of services

Table 2. Sources of information and data (nutrition)

Types of data	Lab. experiments	Census	Remote sensing	Surveys	Regis-tration	Adminis-trative	Derived data
Age distribution		X		X	X	(X)	X
Geographic distribution		X	X	X	X	(X)	
Standard and analytic frame-work sheet Food balance	X						
Mortality Morbidity	X			X	X	X	
Pre and post natal care					X		
Food prices				X			X
Disability				X			
Body measurement	X			X	X	X	X
Family income		X		X		X	X

likely to be increasingly important in future years.

In addition, many actors and organizations are involved in the data dissemination network, for example:

(a) The media;
(b) Libraries;
(c) The educational system;
(d) Organized labour;
(e) Research institutions and publications.

F. Application of the nutrition case to the general concept of an information system

The general concept of an information system is presented in figure I of Beresford's paper. It was applied to the nutrition case outlined in figure V.

Points to note

The system is directed by the goals determined by the effector apparatus, consisting of people with the power to introduce and apply policies to change the operating environment to achieve goals.

The central processor is able to evaluate goal achievement when it has evaluated positively the adequacy, accuracy and validity of the measures it produces.

Therefore, the central processor is able to modify the information system and provide evaluation to the effector apparatus to modify policies and/or goals.

G. Related issues

Available data may sometimes be misused, misinterpreted, or not used at all due to poor information about the full range of existing data sources and their potential applications. Training and education for data users should help guard against the misuse of data and encourage the fullest exploitation of available data.

In some cases organizations with vested interests in particular models of the development process and of appropriate policies might seek to suppress or censor valid analyses of available data. Procedures to prevent the suppression and censorship of information are desirable.

The protection of privacy – both of individuals and of groups – has been the subject of discussion and reports in developed countries. Similar reviews of the situation and policies in developing countries are desirable.

H. Recommendations for Data For Development

1. It is recommended that working groups be created on a number of topics and that they co-ordinate their activities with those of the United Nations regional commissions. Working Groups might be initiated by particular countries, requesting assistance on any of the topics listed below. There would be advantages in comparative studies of specific topics in more than one country.

Administrative records

Administrative records provide a relatively under-used source of data. They are increasingly being put into machine-readable formats, thus

facilitating access to such files for statistical purposes. Among the
records that could be more fully used:

(a)   School records;
(b)   Health records;
(c)   Social security records;
(d)   Unemployment records;
(e)   Police and crime records;
(f)   Records of religious institutions.

Case studies of particular types of administrative records and of specific
countries could provide a better knowledge of:

(a)   What administrative files are available;
(b)   Potential for and limitations on use;
(c)   Procedures and methods of use;
(d)   Costs;
(e)   How improvements to the records would increase their utility both as
basic documents and as sources for statistical data.

Registers

Population registers, registration of vital events (births, marriages,
deaths), and civil registers could be the subject of this working group.
Among the problems identified for further work:

(a)   Problems of coverage and reliability, and possible solutions to these;
(b)   Feasibility and potential value of linkages between registers, or
between registers and other sources (for example, housing or property).

Human factors

This working group could carry out a case study of an information system
with reference to women and children as part of the government data
network. Two relevant examples are the Information Network on Population
and Family Planning of Indonesia and the Maternal and Child Health
System of Kenya. Other population subgroups, such as the elderly or the
disadvantaged, could be investigated.

Organization and management of data agencies

The organization and management functions of agencies responsible for data
collection, analysis, storage and dissemination could be reviewed. Among
the topics for consideration:

(a)   The role of training in developed countries;
(b)   The roles of those who work in areas 2, 3, 4 and 5 as identified in
figure V;
(c)   Data dissemination;
(d)   Linkage to the government data network.

I.   Other recommendations

6. More pilot projects should be launched. There should also be
evaluations of DFD pilot projects and of other projects concerned with any
aspect of the government data network. Seminars should be held at the start of
each pilot project to inform participants, other interested organizations and
the general public (via the media) of the aims of the project and of DFD
activities.

7. DFD should organize an international seminar on techniques and procedures for data dissemination, on approaches to and methods of data analysis, and on the problems of misuse or non-use of available data.

8. DFD should try to obtain appropriate funding to prepare and offer a service to create bibliographies oriented to user-specified topics. The service could be based on a DFD master bibliography, suitably indexed by keywords.

9. There should be summaries in English, French and Spanish of all major DFD documents, as an aid to their wider dissemination. For each country in which DFD conducts a project, translations should be made into the major local language of all project-related documents.

INFORMATION SYSTEMS IN PUBLIC ADMINISTRATION
D. Eade, J. Hodgson (editors)
North-Holland Publishing Company
© DFD, 1981

FINAL REPORT OF WORKING GROUP 2*

A. Introduction and background

To a growing extent, today's economies are coming to run on knowledge and information which needs to be taken into account in socio-economic decision making at all levels of government administration. To be useful to decision makers, information must be relevant, of acceptable quality, provided on time and in the proper form of presentation. And in order to properly develop the agricultural sector and its related populations, knowledge and information are essential.

The Working Group recognized that data are not information and that an information system in agriculture and food includes not only the production of data together with the analysis and interpretation of these data in some purposeful policy decision or problem solution context, but also the reliance on documented scientific and technical information which could be used to postulate - in the absence or together with real world - measurements to arrive at logical conclusions which in turn contribute to the decision making process. A description of an agricultural information system relying on the two approaches for decision making is outlined in figure VI.

A degree of arbitrariness in defining the scope of the Working Group's efforts and consequently of the present paper was unavoidable. Despite frequent contacts and co-ordination with chairmen and members of other working groups, some duplication is unavoidable particularly with the Human Factor, Environment and Traditional Sector working groups. In fact an agriculture and food information system could not disregard such important concerns as the population within farm or non-farm and their quality of life; for in least developed countries (LDCs), farm populations represent close to 80 per cent of the population. The Group views this overlap positively for it illustrates the importance of an integrated sectorial approach to development and to the development of information systems.

The relationships between different universes for which information is necessary in an agriculture and food information system are represented in figure VII (for clarity, the flows of scientific and technical information are not included).

---

* Participants: K. Henderson, H. Herr, M. Nor-Ghani, J. Pines (rapporteur), A. Terjanian (Chairman)

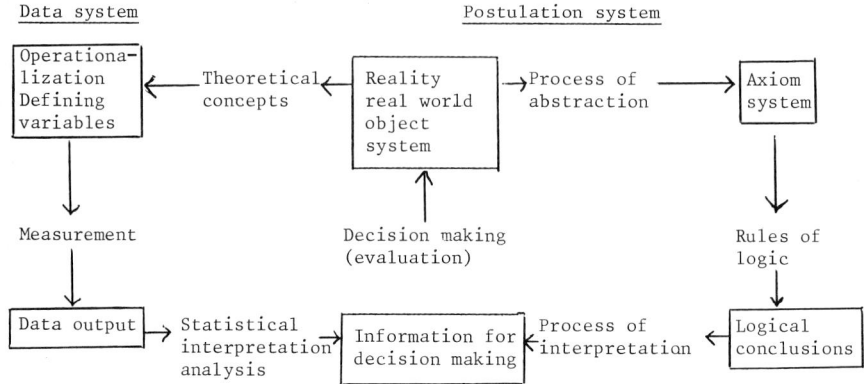

Figure VI. The complimentary nature of data-based and postulation-based
          decision making in an agricultural information system

(Adapted from R.M. Thrall, C.M. Coombs and R.L. Davis,
Decision Processes (New York, John Wiley & Sons, 1954)

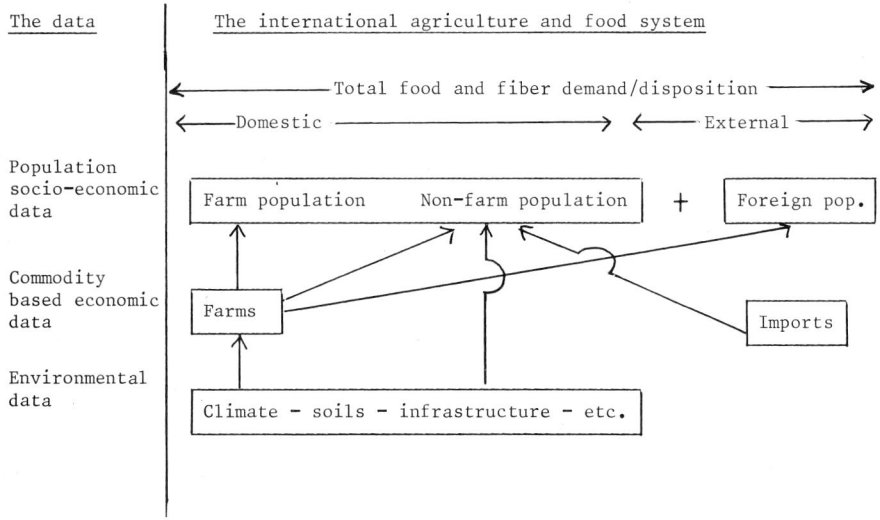

Figure VII: The agriculture and food information system (excluding STI)

Even though the above scheme reflects international concerns for information, the Group concerned itself with agricultural and rural development problems related to national development objectives. Particular emphasis was given to examples and problems emanating from countries represented on the Working Group, namely Canada, Kenya, Malaysia and the United Kingdom.

When necessary, distinction was made between problems related to developed countries and problems related to the LDCs especially as it concerns the adoption of new technologies. The Group notes however that problems to which similar solutions could apply are common and that exchange of information on approaches and solutions could benefit both developing and developed countries. The Group also notes that in some cases the rapid adoption and assimilation of new technology (leap-frogging) can better be achieved in areas where outdated technology has not been implanted through heavy, yet unamortized investments but that it often requires the existence of some basic infrastructure (for example, electricity).

The Group spent some time identifying and discussing areas of concern for agriculture and food policy (which invariably include super sectoral goals) which are summarized in the matrix in annex I. From this point, the Group identified the types of relevant information that are essential for the formulation of the national, regional and local policies. Examples of these are also reported in the matrix, for the Group did not consider it practical to list in detail in this report all commodities for which information was needed, nor all the different types of socio-economic or environmental variables or scientific technical information necessary for the development process. In general, the Group's efforts were concentrated on presenting an analytical framework illustrated by matrices and other diagrams.

Specific conclusions and recommendations are covered in sections D and E. Most of these, even though examined by the Group from an agricultural and food sector angle and based on specific examples from the same sector, do not seem to be sector specific and could generally be applicable in other integrated sectors. This further indicates the advisability of an integrated approach to the development of intersectorial information systems. It must be noted however that sector-specific subject-matter knowledge and the understanding of sectorial problems are important for the detailed implementation and running of sector-related data and information.

B. Information problems related to agricultural concerns

1. Main development planning issues

The relationship of food and agriculture data systems to development planning has been influenced heavily by the resource-growth orientation within which they have developed. This orientation has produced considerable information about macro-economic variables, such as national and world production and prices, about meterological and scientific-technical information useful to commercial and export agriculture, and about processing and marketing of agricultural commodities. However, typical food and agriculture data systems currently provide far less information about subsistence farming, cultural patterns related to agriculture and rural life, or the nutritional and quality of life status of rural people. The Working Group is satisfied though, in general, of the existence of data relevant for various aspects of agricultural development. This is shown in the matrix in annex I. The matrix is a useful tool for exploring the adequacy of available agricultural data.

As agricultural policy concerns in developing countries increasingly include the full range of consumption, rural development and well-being issues,

the inadequacies of current data systems become more apparent. The main
developmental planning issues that can be served through agricultural data
systems require that those systems go beyond typical production-oriented and
commercial data to include information useful for assessing the impact of
production and related policies on the distribution of development benefits and
on the quality of rural life. A reorientation of agricultural information
systems to be more responsive to the requirements and needs of planners and
decision makers, for whom agricultural policies are integral to (and inseparable
from) rural development decisions, is critical to the future usefulness of such
systems. This reorientation is completely consistent with continued production
of the well-established market-oriented agricultural data that remain essential
for all countries.

2. Short-term decision making issues

Short-term agricultural decision making needs are inadequately met because
agricultural information, though collected in adequate quantities, is frequently
of poor quality, made available with excessive delays, and presented in
quantities and ways that reduce its value to users. Improvement of quality,
speed and extent of dissemination and forms of presentation is critical to more
effective response of agricultural data systems to short-term decision making
requirements. The tailoring of information delivery to the specific needs and
time constraints of each level of decision making requires explicit attention.

3. Planning and management issues

Planning and management of development suffer from overcentralization of
agricultural data systems. Information becomes available too late to be useful
and, at decentralized local planning levels, may never arrive. Increased
integration of agricultural and rural development policies requires more
decentralized, community-oriented planning and management. This implies more
rapid feed-back of information or short-circuiting of feedback mechanisms by
retaining information at local levels, as it is simultaneously communicated to
central agencies. Rural development planning also requires that agricultural
and related information be community-specific. Agricultural data systems are
still far from responding to these new planning and management concerns.

The inadequacies of data flow for rural development needs are illustrated
by the matrix in annex II, which emphasizes the disparities between requirements
and availability at decentralized levels.

Improved contribution of agricultural information systems to economic and
social development depends on both (a) orientation of collection practices to
encompass data needed to integrate agricultural and rural development policies,
and (b) reorganization and modification of information systems to improve
availability and quality of required information, both macro-economic and
micro-rural.

4. Process related issues

The different types of data required for agricultural development can be
collected, processed, analysed, synthesized and disseminated by a variety of
organizations and at different levels. The Group has found that every
different organization could be involved in the process of developing and
running an information system for agriculture and food. This creates a variety
of options with a number of implications for each. The uncertainties involved
in these options are set out in annex III.

6. Institutional and organizational problems

The compartmentalization of the public bureaucracy into ministries and departments has necessarily led each one of them to be concerned only with specific aspects of development. As such, their data and informational need is also confined to specific areas of interest such as land development, transport and communication; health, agriculture, education, public works, welfare services, etc. What is often not realized is that for effective planning and decision making in their specific area of concern, data and information from other aspects of development is also useful and sometimes crucial. Thus, planning for agricultural development will require data from many areas of concern as illustrated in figure VIII.

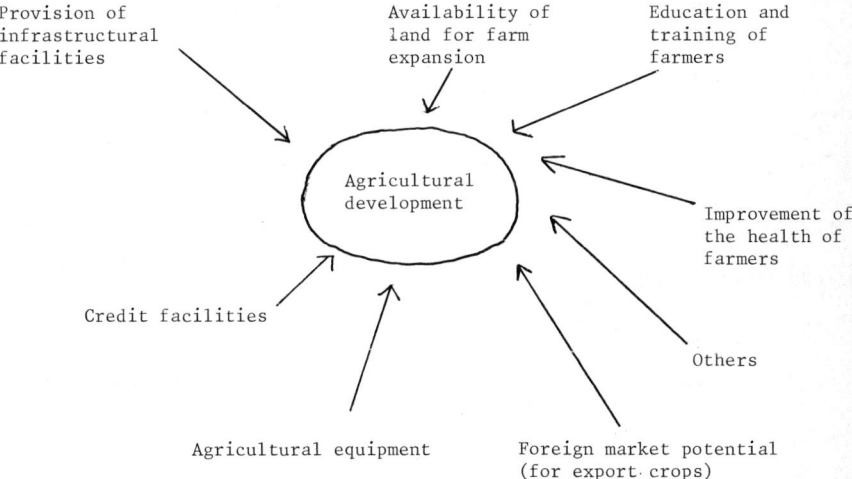

Figure VIII. Necessity for an intersectoral approach to agricultural development

The availability of such data as generated for example by a central bureau of statistics or other relevant agencies, the awareness of such availabilities, the readiness to acquire and utilize the data, and the capacity to integrate all the data, will determine the quality of development plans and decision making made by the ministry/department of agriculture. All interministerial or interdepartmental barriers such as parochialistic tendencies, jealousy over a domain of authority, personal conflict or misunderstanding between high-ranking officials, over-enthusiasm over the secrecy of a programme and plan of action, etc. will interfere with the free flow of data and information between ministries or departments. It will further impede any move towards a meaningful integration of the data base with those of the other ministries and departments and promote further conflict and disagreement over issues where a set of data differ from those acquired by other agencies.

Aside from organizational barriers prevailing between ministries and
departments with a resultant lack of lateral communication and meaningful data
exchange and co-ordination in the acquisition of data, a vertical lack of
communication can also prevail within a single organization. This is
especially true of large ministries or departments whose structure and
authority are likely to be widespread, reaching into the remotest areas of a
country. The geographical spread of an agricultural hierarchy, for example,
causes difficulties in communication, not only between various levels of
supervision but also between various strata of national, state, local and
village administration. Thus, all forms of political, administrative,
legislative and even socio-cultural differences will be encountered. These
differences can impede a free flow of data and information between the
administrative centre and its periphery as illustrated in figure IX.

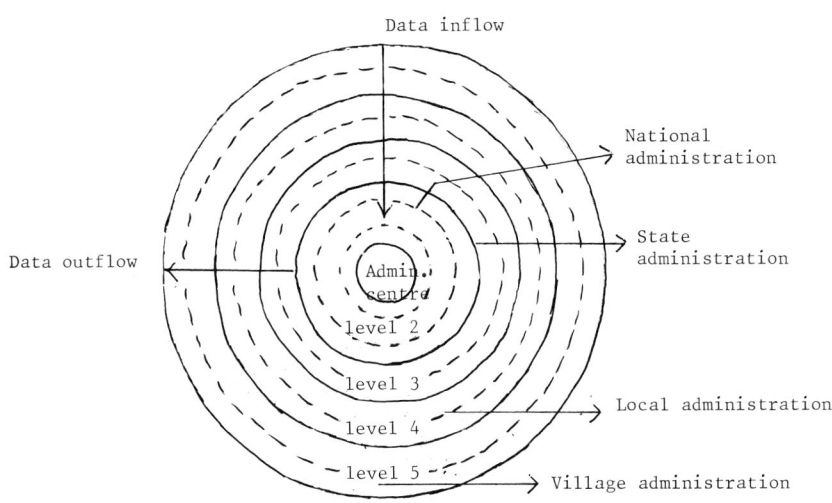

-- -- -- -- -- -- Hierarchical level in agricultural administration

_____ Levels of national, state, local, and village administration

Figure IX. Overlaps in the hierarchiacal and geopolitical levels
of administration which can impede communication and data flow

In view of the lateral and vertical barriers to communication and data flow, the question of what and how much data will ultimately reach farmers at the village level becomes very crucial. Information inadequacy and distortion may occur at various administrative levels resulting in a lack of guidance, confusion, and the wrong "signals" being received by the farmers in terms of what crops to grow, how much, what assistance and subsidies can be expected, what marketing facilities will be provided, etc. Hence the need to review the inadequacy, timeliness and reliability of data and information that flows through the agricultural hierarchy and finally reaches the farmers.

D. Reorientation of the agricultural data system to meet rural development needs

The proposed rural information system functions from the principle that detailed information is unnecessarily maintained at the central government level. Detailed information is generally required only at the lowest level where micro-decisions are made. The matrix provided in annex III illustrates the tool used to arrive at this conclusion. An objective of the rural information system therefore is to keep detailed data at the local level while passing only aggregate information up to the central government. In addition, data on the rural condition will be maintained by the district level statistical or planning officer. The function of the central government will be to maintain a village level master file and to integrate this file with census and other centrally collected data through cross-file standardization of identifiers. Information integrated by the central government will then be passed down through the province or district to the village level.

A village level master file is used to classify and focus the national level distribution of development resources. The village level master file can also be used centrally to monitor population growth, differential growth, market price data availability of public facilities, rural health conditions and other conditions as determined by the development of locally collected data.

The proposed information system is comprised of augmented administrative record keeping at the local level coupled with systems of national sampling. The detailed illustration which follows is based on a Kenyan example.

1. Elements of an improved record keeping system at the sub-location level:

(a) The local sub-chief will be instructed in the use of standardized forms for the collection of local level data. These data may consist of the following items presented at regular intervals to a representative of the provincial statistical office (PSO):

Number of plots
Number of dwelling units
Number of commercial structures
Number of persons
Vital statistics
Number of vehicles owned by village residents
Market price information
Local criminal activity (incidents)
Number of school rooms
Number of students
Number of health clinics (visitor)
Number of family planning clinics (visitor)
Marriages
Disease occurance

Government roads (meters)
Crop production estimate, etc.

(b) The data collected by the local sub-chief will be vetted by the
PSO representative in random spot checks. Items for instruction will include
what the sub-chief should monitor including the following:

New households
Unworkable government facilities
Market prices for a sample collection of goods
Stocks of commodities on hand in local stores
Serious crop disease
Illness
Defining criminal activity
How to aggregate the data for submission
Birth and death registration

2. Village level data assembled from administrative records at the local
level will be maintained by the PSO or district level statistical officer (DSO)
for purposes of district level planning. Aggregate data will be forwarded to
the central bureau of statistics (CBS) who will maintain a village level
master file (VLMF). The VLMF will, after initial construction, be updated by
regular periodic amendments. In addition to aggregate data passed upward,
the VLMF will contain village level data extracted from the 1979 Census of
population file. Efforts will be directed toward augmenting the VLMF with
additional data from government administrative files through standardization of
geographic identification.

3. Information added to the VLMF by the CBS will be forwarded downwards
to the PSO or DSO to augment local planning information. Field verification
of this data can be undertaken. An objective of the system will be to
monitor the village level universes of households, plots, commercial
establishments and public facilities so that these can be used as bases for
estimations of socio-economic conditions.

4. A national sampling frame for rural development:

(a) The national survey sampling frame, such as NISSP in Kenya, will be
integrated with the village level administrative record system so that village
level estimators of socio-economic conditions can be made through sector
estimates (based on household or holding-size for example);

(b) Village level social indicators based on the national survey will be
prepared by the PSO with guidance and review from the CBS. Province, district
and village level indicators will be maintained by the PSO for local planning
purposes. Data suitable for village level considerations will be disseminated.

5. Appropriate information technology for rural development:

(a) The constraints to high information technology in the rural area are
severe. Electricity and other energy and communication resources are scarce
or non-existent. Giving high priority to this development when other needs are
more severe involves appropriate technology;

(b) Two areas for technical improvement are:

(i) The improvement of record keeping at the local level through
     training in proper indexing and storage and the consistent
     supply of record keeping material;

(ii)   The development of a village level information or operation room
       containing accessible (manually) village level information. The
       latter suggestion implies the organization of village level
       administration to carry out an information role;

(c)   In the framework of severe constraints to high technology, the use
of local level terminals (micro-processors) could serve multipurpose functions.
A terminal might serve as a training device for the local secondary school,
a receiver and sender of electronic mail, a communicable disease alarm to the
central government, or a village record keeping and retrieval device.

E. Proposals for research by Data For Development (DFD)

Any international programme of research and co-operation in the food and
agricultural sector cannot be restricted to that sector alone. Typically, in
most developing countries a large majority of the population live in rural
areas and are probably engaged in subsistence farming and related activities
(cattle raising, fishing, coconut gathering, etc.). An information programme
in this sector would need to be expanded into a rural development programme
embracing the traditional sector, including local handicrafts. This is in line
with current trends of international organizations, many donor countries, and of
developing countries themselves where rural development is now seen as a special
field of study, research and assistance.

Among the organizations concerned with this are the Food and Agriculture
Organization of the United Nations (FAO) and the United Nations Development
Programme (UNDP), particularly through their regional offices; on
employment aspects, the International Labour Organization (ILO), the
World Health Organization (WHO) and the United Nations Children's Fund
(UNICEF) also have an interest through nutrition problems, which are most acute
in rural areas.

In addition, many research organizations throughout the world, both in the
developed and third world countries, such as the International Rice Research
Institute and the United Kingdom Tropical Products Institute, are concerned
with specific crops, different types of crops or special problems of storage,
pest control, etc. Some organizations are already linked through parent
bodies or through special groups such as the Australian Mineral Industrial
Research Association (AMIRA).

DFD is already engaged in pilot studies of national government data
networks, which must inevitably include the food and agriculture sector, and
proposes to enhance this programme. Information problems appear to exist
among the various organizations and institutions mentioned above. This is
known to cause problems at a national level also, since unco-ordinated advice
and assistance can be received by developing countries from these different
sources; internal information problems are further exacerbated because of
single direct links between the international bodies and their national
equivalents, whether these be ministries or departments or lower level bodies
(veterinary services, local research stations, etc.). Based on this, the
Working Group proposes the following considerations:

1. A study of international information systems for rural development

A useful project for DFD would involve a study of the information
activities of the various organizations mentioned and their impact on national
governments. The study could be carried out at two separate but interlinked
levels. The first would establish which organizations and research
institutions operate in the rural development sector and what information
problems there are between them. The second could be an investigation, possibly

on a regional basis, of the information problem within developing countries in
relation to external entities. This could be a special component of existing
and proposed DFD pilot projects or a separate project, possibly extended to
cover all external sources of information (that is, not only in the rural
development sector). If the second over-all approach is used, then a regionally
organized activity for this level of the project may be advisable since some of
the organizations are orientated, wholly or mainly, towards particular areas of
the world, either because of the distribution of the particular commodities,
animals, etc. with which they are concerned or because the rural situation varies
throughout the world, for example AMIRA.

2. A study of vertical information flows with countries

A completely different area of research arises from the problem raised in
section B, that information should be tailored to the specific needs and time
constraints of each separate level of decision making. Although this problem
is common to all vertical information flows, it is particularly acute in the
rural development sector because of the length and attenuation of the chain.

It is suggested therefore that DFD might undertake a pilot project, in a
suitable country where there are multiple levels of decision making, to
ascertain the minimum content and detail of the information in the rural
development sector which must flow in both directions, up and down the ladder of
decision making, and whether transmission can thereby be facilitated and speeded
up and the content made more useful to the recipients.

Obviously, at the top of the chain the maximum content and range of
information is required, but only in the minimum necessary detail. The latter
restriction is necessary to prevent decision makers at this level and those who
collect and analyse the information for them from being overwhelmed by detail,
thereby delaying delivery. Conversely, at the lowest levels the maximum detail
is required and the content and range of information reduced to the minimum
necessary to reach meaningful decisions. Bombardment with unnecessary
information at this relatively unsophisticated level can cause confusion and
delay implementation.

What is not clear is by what means and to what extent detail can be
reduced without affecting content; and conversely, how detail can be
progressively increased and content reduced. It could be that data should be
aggregated, analysed, and a copy retained for local use at each level; but
this may not necessarily speed up transmission to higher levels while making
local data available quickly at lower levels. Also, some data required by the
lower levels may not have originated at those levels.

Appropriate technology may well be relevant to this research proposal
and likely advances should be taken into account.

3. A Study on the integration of national sampling with a local system of administrative records

An area of research related to the previous proposal has been raised in
section D, 4(a). It consists in determining how a national sampling scheme can
effectively and efficiently be related to a village based system of
administrative record collection, such as proposed by this Working Group.

F.   General comments

The Group received a very positive impression of the Chamrousse Seminar and hopes to participate two years from now in a follow-up DFD seminar.

The organization of the seminar from the physical point of view, that is isolated location and small working group (in this Group's case) is felt to be ideal and very conducive to valuable significant achievements being reached and promotes appropriate levels of interaction, given the short time for contact. It is essential however that flexibility for modifying the programme and the time allocated to plenary and group sessions is indispensable to overcome any unforeseen delays or requirements.

The Group felt that it would be desirable in any future conference that participants in working groups be given more time to agree on working plans in advance and that the tasks of preparing adequate and current documentation be equally divided.

The Group found particularly attractive the format of this international gathering where individual experts could exchange personal opinions without being hampered or constrained by organizational or political considerations. Such a format ensures that so-called "radical" proposals or solutions are given due consideration and are not blocked or replaced by compromise.

The Group expresses deep appreciation to the staff of the Seminar for their warm welcome and efficient support and to the DFD Programme Committee for its excellent organization.

Annex I

One of the ways by which data requirements in the agricultural sector can be identified is by focussing on the areas of information need, and the levels at which such information should be obtained. This may be done through a matrix as in the following table. Some types of data required at various levels are given as examples.

Table 3. Areas of concern and levels of data requirement for agricultural development

Levels of data requirement / Areas of concern	International	National	Sub-national (local)	Village
Commodity demand and supply	World demand and supply to plan export and import; Export potential of major commodity producers, etc.	National consumption requirements; Export capacity import substitution requirements; Optimal agricultural mix, etc.	Local needs and supply; Inter-regional commodity exchange, etc.	Village production capacity and potential
Marketing and pricing	World price fluctuation and forecast; International terms of trade, etc.	Local market price; Price control and stock pile subsidies, etc.	Implementation of price control; Local incentives; Marketing facilities logistics	Actual price offered to farmers; Marketing facilities, etc.
Factor inputs	Supply of agricultural equipment; Technology transfer, etc.	Land capability classification; Production or import of equipments, fertilizer, insecticide, etc.	Land distribution and utilization	Supply of inputs; Credit availability, etc.
Government and institutional factors	Foreign aid commodity supply agreements, etc.	National agricultural policy and goals; Employment, migration, etc.	Local needs and priorities, etc.	Crop preference; Consumption pattern, etc.
Environmental factors, etc.	Atmostpheric and ocean pollution and artificial modifications	Health, education, nutrition policies; Forest, water, use of pesticides, etc.	Settlements and housing; Pollution, etc.	Housing, villages and farms, environment, etc.

Annex II

While the availability of data in various areas of concern pertaining to agricultural development and the levels at which the data should be generated can be evaluated through figure VI, current flow and utilization of data between users at many administrative levels should also be considered. Availability of data does not necessarily equate with affective utilization at various levels. The flow of data in terms of collection (inflow) and utilization (outflow) can be examined through a matrix as in table 4. Some examples of the problems involved are given for illustrative purposes.

Table 4. Identification of problems in data flows

Levels of data Requirement / Levels of Utilization	International	National	Sub-national (local)	Village
Central agencies (bureau of statistics, planning units, etc.	Nature of contact plus subscriptions to International Organizations	Co-ordination between central agencies	Little or no contact	No contact
Ministries	Contact in specific areas of concern only	Specific areas only	Specific areas only	No contact
Departments	Little or no contact	Specific areas only	Specific areas only	Some contact in specific areas
Local administration	No contact	Some contact	Constant contact	Adequate contact
Village administration	No contact	Little contact	Some contact	Constant contact

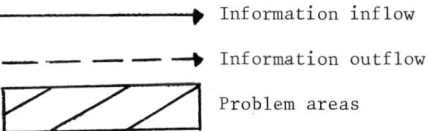

——————————▶ Information inflow

— — — — —▶ Information outflow

▨▨▨▨ Problem areas

<u>Annex III</u>

Data for development in general and agricultural development in particular
must satisfy various needs related to planning, administration, decision making,
public information, etc. However, for the purpose of highlighting the current
emphasis on development efforts, these needs can also be categorized in terms
of (a) the need for economic development, (b) politico-social development and
(c) evaluation of progress in human well-being. The first category, which
emphasizes the need for growth resource data, is usually quite adequately
satisfied. It is in the latter two categories that a dearth of data often
exists because conventional censuses and surveys do not usually cater for its
collection, such data being considered as subjective and difficult to manage.
The problems of data collection, processing, analysis, synthesis and
dissemination in the three categories are highlighted in table 5.

Table 5. Types of database and responsibilities for collection, processing,
          analysis, synthesis and dissemination

Process / Types of data	Collection	Processing	Analysis	Synthesis	Dissemination
Growth Resource data	Central bureaux of statistics (CBS)		Can CBS undertake meaningful analysis for various users?	Who synthesizes data and information for decision making?	CBS? Various agencies? How?
Politico-social	CBS, other agencies or political bureaux?	?	?	?	?
Human well-being	CBS or other agencies? · At national or community and village level	Computerized? Manual?	At macro or micro level? By whom?	For whom and by whom?	How?

INFORMATION SYSTEMS IN PUBLIC ADMINISTRATION
D. Eade, J. Hodgson (editors)
North-Holland Publishing Company
© *DFD, 1981*

CONCEPTUAL FRAMEWORKS FOR NATURAL
RESOURCE INFORMATION SYSTEMS

Tony Friend*

A. Introduction

In the past few years we have witnessed a dramatic shift in the underlying paradigm of how man relates to his endowment of natural resources. It is perhaps fair to say that the prevailing viewpoint of the 1950s was to consider resources as merely potential generators of economic growth, which in partnership with technology, led to the road of abundance for all. At that time, natural resource information systems would undoubtedly have been viewed as an adjunct to economic data, limited essentially to cataloguing and mapping resources for the purpose of accelerating economic growth. This somewhat narrow perspective may still be viable in third world countries where there is a paucity of data on available resources.

By the 1970s however, an almost apocalyptic image has been evoked whereupon natural resources are not only considered limiting factors to economic growth, but of vital importance to the quality of life, if not mankind's very survival. The corollary is that the wasteful past habits of resource use would inevitably lead mankind down the road to penury and that to avoid this eventuality would require the development of new attitudes or ethics of conservation and protection and careful management of potentially scarce resources.

It is hoped that the following notes and diagrams contribute to the discussions on the nature of the "new paradigm" and the characteristics and properties of data systems required to support it.

To start with, the following questions may be examined:

To whom is the natural resource information system addressed? Here we may wish to explore different levels of data needs, ranging from detailed data required for specific programmes or projects to highly generalized data for strategic planning purposes, national assessments, and public information.

To what extent should the system be integrated with social-economic statistics? This question focuses on the interface of human activities and natural resources and considers the key question of whether natural resources can

---

* Visiting Fellow, Science Policy Research Unit, University of Sussex, United Kingdom.

be defined outside its socio-economic context.

What kind of models should be employed for the development of the conceptual
   framework of a natural resource data base? Here we can examine an
   equilibrium approach exemplified by a system of material-energy balances,
   or consider an alternative (although complementary) dialectical model
   based on historic processes of human activity, their pressures on
   resources, their resulting human (and natural) responses, and the
   consequential "new synthesis".

What are the suitable concepts, definitions, and classification systems for
   natural resource accounting? Of particular interest are the use of
   ecological principles and to what extent they can be satisfactorily applied.
   Other areas that can be examined are concepts of environmental space,
   carrying capacity, common accounting units, for example energy
   classification of production and consumption processes, measures of
   stock and flow of natural resources, etc.

How can the relevant properties and characteristics required for policy
   decisions be built into the system? Here we may discuss the data concerns
   of three fundamental policy actions: those directed at conservation and
   protection of natural resources; those concerned with long-term
   modification of human behaviour, that is changes of production-consumption
   processes; and those of more short-term duration directed at ameliorating
   adverse conditions such as environmental clean-up.

What kind of natural resource data base is relevant for strategic planning and
   development of third world countries? The point of focus is the generally
   weak state of resource data and the choice of priorities for development;
   for example, the need for an integrated data base of resource inventories
   and resource mapping should be emphasized. Furthermore, considerations
   can be given to "inexpensive methods" for obtaining data, for example,
   remote sensing techniques.

What techniques can be employed in the collection, compilation, integration and
   dissemination of natural resource data? Here it might be worthwhile to
   assess the potential of remote sensing techniques for the collection of
   resource data, the application of geo-code system of co-ordinate or grid
   identifiers to statistical records, the transformation (digitization) of
   mapped data into computerized data files, the potential of merging microdata sets from other fields - demography, agriculture, industry, etc.

Who should be responsible for the development of a natural resource information
   system? Should the agencies concerned with natural resources be
   responsible for their particular domain with an outside body, perhaps a
   statistical office, acting as a co-ordinating and integrating agent, or
   would a single agency provide a more consistent framework for the system?

B. The concept of entropic processes and natural resource information systems

   Natural resource data are first and foremost physical measures of the
"availability" of, and "access" to, the earth's stock (store) and flow of low
entropy. The concept of entropy is, in essence, a rigorous definition of
environmental degradation based upon the second law of thermodynamics. In
"The Entropy Law and the Economic Process" by Georgescu-Roegen the idea of
entropy is introduced as follows:

   "The common fact that heat always flows by itself from the hotter
   to the colder body, never in reverse, came to be generalised by

the Entropy Law ... All it says is that entropy of the universe
(or of an isolated structure) increases constantly ... We may
say instead that in the universe there is a continuous and
irrevocable qualitative degradation of free energy into bound
energy. Nowadays, however, one is more likely to come across the
modern interpretation of this degradation as a continuous turning
of order into disorder." [1]

Economic activity may be generalized as a local reversal of the entropic
process, albeit at the cost of accelerating the rate of growth of entropy in the
universe as a whole - manifested, for example, by the generation of waste
residuals, environmental degradation, and run-down of the stock of low entropy,
that is, natural resources. In the long run, even "economic processes" cannot
escape the entropy law and it is just as valid to conclude, therefore, that
economic activity is the physical transformation of low into high entropic
materials (that is, into waste). However, before we become too alarmed by this
prospect, we may give some consideration to the connexion of purpose and value
of economic activity and the entropic process. Georgescu-Roegen expressed this
link as follows:

"Since the economic process materially consists of a transformation
of low entropy into high entropy, i.e. into waste, and since the
transformation is irrevocable, natural resources must necessarily
represent one part of the notion of economic value. And because
the economic process is not automatic, but willed, the services
of all agents, human or material, also belong to the same facet
of that notion. For the other facet we should note that it would
be utterly absurd to think that the economic process exists only
for producing waste. The irrefutable conclusion is that the true
product of that process is an immaterial flux, the enjoyment of
life. This flux constitutes the second facet of economic value.
Labor, through its drudgery, only tends to diminish the intensity
of this flux, just as a higher rate of consumption tends to
increase it.

And paradoxical though it may seem, it is the Entropy Law, a law
of elementary matter, that leaves us no choice but to recognise
the role of cultural tradition in the economic process. The
dissipation of energy, as the law proclaims, goes on automatically
everywhere. This is precisely why the entropy reversal as seen
in every line of production bears the indelible hallmark of
purposive activity. And the way this activity is planned and
performed certainly depends upon the cultural matrix of society
in question. There is no other way to account for the intriguing
difference between some developed nations endowed with poor
environment; on the one hand, and some underdeveloped ones
surrounded by an abundance of natural riches. The exosomatic
evolution works its way through the cultural tradition, not only
through technological knowledge." [2]

---

[1] Nicholas Georgescu-Roegen, The Entropy Law and the Economic Process,
(Boston, Harvard University Press, 1971).

[2] Ibid., p. 19.

1. Some entropic definitions and concepts

Production (of tangible commodities) is the process of transformation of matter from a lower to a higher state of organization, that is, decreasing entropy. Energy and material inputs are a necessary but not sufficient condition of this process. All biological growth and maintenance processes are in principle production, requiring energy and material inputs. Man-made production can be distinguished from the latter by the application of outside "intelligence" (that is, knowledge, skills, technology) in the transformation process. Production of "biologically based" commodities is a mixture of natural and man-controlled processes.

In traditional economics, production is often classified into primary, secondary and tertiary activity.

Primary production is the extraction process of "environmental commodities" from the "stock" (non-renewable resources) and from the "flow" (renewable resources) of low entropy.

Secondary production is the complex (industrial) physiochemical processes of producing low entropy goods by refining, combining, shaping and assembly of "environmental commodities" into "economic commodities".

Tertiary production is the process of organizing non-tangible "products" required in the process of production-consumption. This includes the organization of knowledge (information), transportation and distribution. From an entropic standpoint these activities are, like energy, through-puts (that is, not directly embodied in materials) and this is therefore a quasi consumption phenomenon. In effect, tertiary production is an important part of "intermediate consumption", the other part being the service flow from capital stock, and human resources (that is, labour).

Consumption is the process of transformation of matter and energy from a higher to a lower state of organization, that is, increasing entropy. We can further distinguish intermediate from final consumption as follows.

Intermediate consumption is the "through-put" of matter and energy required as agents of the production process, the flow of services obtained from capital stock (that is, machinery and equipment, buildings, transportation, etc.), the flow of services from the "labour stock", and the institutional services such as banking, insurance, business services, etc. It should be noted that all the above "services" are in effect "through-puts", which can be viewed as an "entropic flow" through the transformation processes, and although an integral part of the process, are in themselves not an embodied component of the commodity being produced. The material-energy through-puts become in effect "waste residuals" of the production process. Labour stock provides two distinguishable flows, those of energy (manual labour), and those of intelligence; both however are obtained from the "low entropy stock" of human resources.

Final consumption is the "through-put" of matter and energy required as agents for the "enjoyment of life". We observe that the difference between intermediate and final consumption is that of "purpose" rather than its material form. Thus, it is quite possible, from an entropy-environmental perspective, to consider a large part of what is traditionally classified as consumption activity as production and/or intermediate consumption. For example, the process of preparing a meal is, by the above definitions, clearly "production" - regardless of whether it is produced commercially or in the home. Similarly, the process of daily maintenance of the home is an "intermediate consumption" - unless by some happy chance it is a joyous end in itself. It should be noted

that the Lancastrian approach to consumer theory is not too dissimilar, to the
extent that it distinguishes "goods" and their "characteristics" and recombines
them to form new consumer goods, such as a meal made up of nutritional
characteristics and ambiance of presentation – in contrast to a simple
aggregation of the individual items that went into it.

Accumulation of man-made stock is the process by which man creates a
"stock" of low entropy. It is, however, merely a special case of the
production-consumption process where additions to capital stock and its
maintenance in a quasi-steady-state are associated with the reversal of the
entropic process (production) and the process of "using-up" (reduction of waste)
is associated with increasing entropy (consumption). It should be noted that
the interposition of a time dimension in the production-consumption process
characterizes the difference between current production and capital formation.
Stock therefore is a time relative concept, where for example current
production that is carried forward to the next period is in effect a stock
transfer (of wealth) to future periods. But by the same token, current
productions (and consumption) benefit from the past accumulation of man-made
stock. To account for this we must make explicit recognition of the "flow of
services" obtained from past activity. Depreciation rates have been the
traditional form of accounting for this phenomenon, yet from both theoretical
and practical grounds this method has been highly unsatisfactory since it is
related to the original investment value of the stock and is only remotely
connected with the quality of the flow of services obtained. A more satisfactory
approach would be to measure the physical capacity of the stock to produce the
desired "services".

Waste residuals are high entropy by-products of the production consumption
process. The levels of entropy of these products are too high to be efficient
(in an economic sense) and become in effect the unusable state of matter and
energy. It should be noted that waste is often a relative state in terms of
price, technology or social attitudes. Thus wastes can shift from "unusable"
to "usable" by any change in the above factors.

Pollutants are a derivative of waste residuals (although not all wastes
are pollutants). These can be viewed as elements that degrade the quality of
natural life support systems and/or stress the natural functioning of
biological species (including man). In a sense they interfere with order and
stability, and may accelerate disorder in natural systems. Similarly, acoustic
energy (noise) and aesthetic pollution are elements contributing to disorder.

Recycling material is an activity that retards the entropic process. There
may be exceptions to this rule, when for example the energy and/or material
consumption for recycling is greater than when obtained directly from its
environmental source.

Non-renewable resources are a stock of low entropy, accumulated by
historical production processes of nature.

Renewable resources are essentially a flow of low entropy created by the
continuous production process of nature – the action of solar radiation,
photosynthesis, geophysical forces, etc.

New methods of measuring final output, productivity and efficiency can be
developed from entropy-environmental concepts. For example, an efficiency
objective of economic activity could be to obtain final consumption at the least
cost of entropy. Thus, the ratio of materials-energy inputs to final output
could be viewed as a measure of productivity.

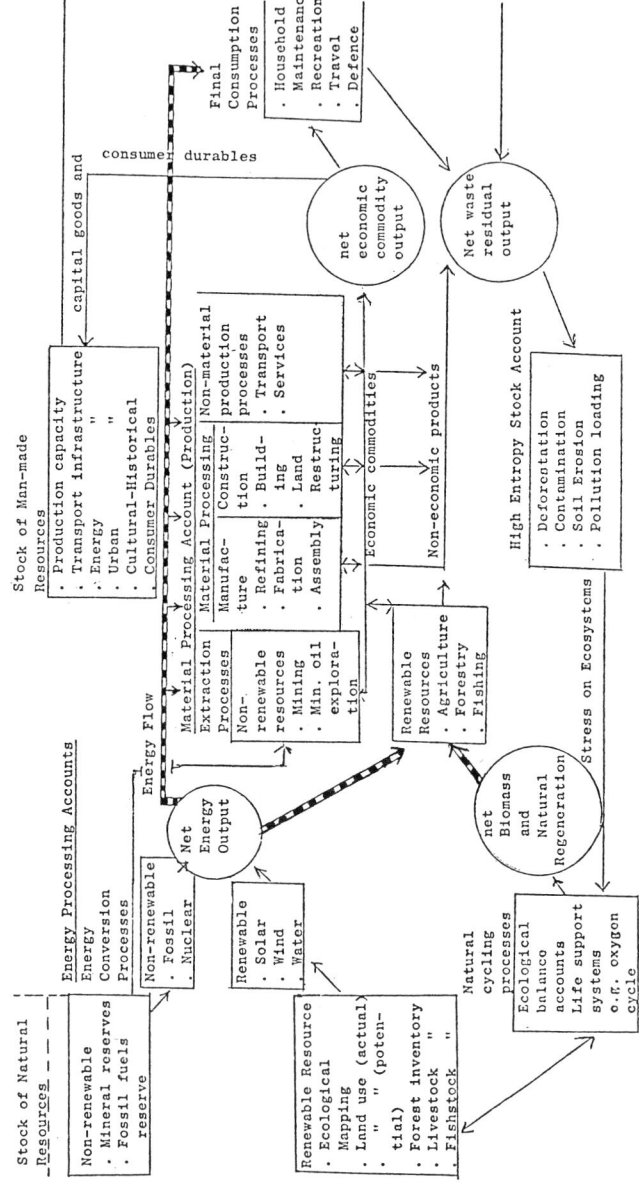

Figure X. An accounting framework for a material-energy balance statistical system

C. Equilibrium model: material-energy balance

Scarcity of environmental commodities has stimulated interest in developing new methods for accounting for the physical flow of material and energy through transformation processes of economic activity. The underlying physical laws of the conservation of matter and energy provide the conceptual basis for these kinds of accounts and the experience in input-output models provide the technical basis for their construction. The practical work requires the compilation of a set of stock-flow accounts where the levels of activity (processes) are dependent on the available stock of low entropy (see figure X). The core tables are those that depict material-energy inputs in transformation processes. These would include: (a) processes of extraction of materials and energy from nature's stock of low entropy (primary production and energy conversion processes); (b) the transformation of materials into economic commodities (secondary production); (c) the material-energy inputs in the processes of non-tangible products, such as transportation, business and consumer services, etc. (tertiary production); (d) the material-energy inputs of (final) consumption processes; and finally (e) a set of accounts describing the resulting waste residuals generated by the above activities (material and thermal waste returned to the environment). In addition to these basic tables, other supplementary accounts could be set up to describe recycling processes, or balance of trade accounts (that is, transboundary inflow and outflow of low entropy).

1. Low entropy stock accounts (natural resources)

These accounts focus on the measurement of natural (and man-made) stocks of low entropy. Stock and flow are essentially time relative concepts and there are no inherent properties that can distinguish them outside of the conventions employed in the accounting frame. However, in a broad sense we can recognize stock as a "store of natural resources" in which the absolute amount may never be precisely measured, but for practical purposes it may be sufficient merely to keep track of additions to, subtractions from, and steady state conditions of them. These accounts can be broadly divided into non-renewable resources (where additions to is new knowledge rather than real accumulation) and renewable resources. The latter type of accounts are particularly difficult from a methodological standpoint. This stems from the wide range of qualitative properties of renewable resources, and quite different measures will of course be obtained dependent on which properties one chooses to emphasize or equally, suppress. Forest inventories for example have been measured by "cubic meters of the merchandisable timber" - this approach would however be anathema to an ecologist.

Interest in the area is growing and recent initiatives in ecological mapping, land use surveys and wildlife inventories, as well as the potential of remote sensing techniques, bodes well for rapid development in this complex domain.

2. High entropy accounts (environmental quality)

This mirror image of the low entropy stock could presumably be defined and possibly classified by levels of degradation along the lines of "pollution loads" in water bodies, areas of deforestation, soil erosion, etc. However, the mere classification of areas and levels of environmental degradation does not satisfy the stringent equilibrium relationships defined in the material-energy balance framework. The move should be towards more complex concepts that can deal with human activity and natural cycles of renewable resources (for example, oxygen cycles), rates of regeneration (for example, sustainable yields in forestry), carrying capacity (for example, population - technology loads on the natural environment), and human pressures on ecosystem (for example, measures of resilience, stability and recoverability of natural systems).

Quite clearly, high entropy conditions are in a sense the qualitative dimension of the low entropy stocks and are the measure of their degradation (decumulation).

D. Dialectical model: stress-response system

This approach emphasizes historical trends where the dynamic forces are modelled on dialectical processes as opposed, for example, to those of equilibrium. The critical parameters of the system are statistical measures of environmental stress resulting from human activity, their synogestic relationship with nature (for example, combination of human activity and background environmental factors such as climate), and the complementary statistical measures of environmental response derived from observations (for example, monitoring records) of environmental change. And since environmental responses in turn stress human activity, conditions for dialectical processes are inherent in the continuous adjustments and adaptation of man to his environment, and vice versa.

Although at conceptual level the framework attempts to provide a coherent picture of real world activity, in practice severe constraints are imposed by the nature and limitations of statistical data. In the first place, scientific knowledge of environmental change, in particular in the sensitive area of ecological transformations, is insufficiently developed to identify with any degree of certainty stochastic relationships between stress and response. Nevertheless, considering that decisions are made daily on assumed cause and effect relationships, it would seem reasonable to organize the data from which these decisions are based in a more coherent fashion, even if this implies something of a chicken and egg argument.

The starting point is to identify the major activities that can be said to accelerate the rate of entropy in the biosphere. The framework identifies essentially eight entropic processes, of which six originate from human activity and two are largely outside human control, that is, geo-physical forces of nature and population dynamics. It should be noted that assigning the complex human interaction into these categories must of necessity be somewhat arbitrary; nevertheless, they are distinguishable in the different type of environmental stresses and responses produced and can be further related to major economic production and consumption functions. The 40 modules depicted in table 6 should be considered as suggested guidelines for organization purposes. During the process of compilation, the framework would be modified and adapted to take into account special interests and needs, the very real absence of data and the inevitable restraints on resources.

1. Some concepts and definitions of STRESS

The following definitions and concepts correspond to the row and column headings of table 6.

Activity accounts provide the background data on essentially the global activity of humans and nature which can be said to be a major contributor to the process of environmental transformation. They are in a sense the independent variables of the system of which stress-response indicators can be considered as derivatives. These accounts are largely made up of time series records of new activity (flow data) measured as gross output of production and material-energy consumption (broadly defined) and where possible further sub-divided into coherent environmental regions. However, other global activity should complement these records including that of changes in the geographical distributions of population, over-all land use charge, rates of depletion of non-renewable

Table 6. Structural framework for the stress-response environmental statistical system (STRESS)

Activity Category	Activity Statistics	Stress Indicators	Response Indicators	Collective and individual response	Inventory of stock
I Generation of waste residuals	Production and consumption of economic commodities	Pollution loadings in environmental media	Measures of the state of the environment	Actions to reduce pollution loadings	Pollution abatement and recycling capacity
II Permanent environment restructuring	Construction activity and land use change	Location of construction activity and land use change	Ecosystem transformation	Actions to protect and conserve environmental assets	Accumulates stock of man-made structures Area of protected environments
III Harvesting activity	Production from renewable resources	Exploitation and technological stresses	Sustainable yields Quality of renewable sources	Actions to control technology and establish harvest quotes	Stock of renewable resources
IV Extraction of non-renewable resource	Rates of depletion	Rate of substitution Exploration activity	Environmental impact of substitutes and exploration	Conservation measures	Stock of non-renewable resources
V Environmental	Production, disposition, and disposal of potentially hazardous substances	Leakage of P.H.S. in environment Application of P.H.S.	Level of contaminants in the environment	Action to control the use of P.H.S.	Stock of P.H.S.
VI Energy	Production, use and distribution	Thermal loadings noise (acoustic energy); Energy infrastructure	Impact of energy related activity	Energy conservation	Energy infrastructure and networks
VII Natural activity	Climate, geographical events	Floods, droughts, earthquakes, tidal waves	Change in harvest productivity, loss of productive lands	Expenditure incurred to protect against extreme natural events	Mapping of climates and bio-physical regions
VIII Population	Population change on temporal and spatial planes	Population in relation to carrying capacity	Disease and diminution of quality of life	Control of population growth and habitat.	Census of population

resources, etc. These data are characteristically macro-statistics obtained from industry and household surveys, population censuses, land use mapping, meteorological records, and a variety of estimates of resource use. They provide in essence the background description or reference point for the subsequent stress-response indicators.

Inventory accounts are the complementary stock information of the flow (activity) account. The basic dimensions of environmental stock are physical quantity, spatial distribution, and to some limited extent, economic value. The latter is an important attribute to many measures of physical quantities - the most obvious case is the reserves of certain kinds of non-renewable resources in which economic viability is an integral component of the calculation. However, in many other areas the pure physical measures independent of the economic validity factors are of little analytical or policy interest, for example, production capacity. It should be noted that the statistical measures of stock are generally crude in comparison to flow data - often requiring special qualifications of the best available estimate given within a wide range of error. Moreover, much of the environmental stock data is in fact a spatial mapping of resources which of course can be digitized to obtain quantative statistical aggregates but may, on the other hand remain in its more unfamiliar form of cartographic maps (that is, spatial display of statistics).   Indeed there is great potential in producing statistical data from cartographic maps and remote sensing photographs and this area of statistics is probably one of the most underdeveloped.

Stress indicators are essentially statistics which describe what might be called the stress dimension of the activity accounts. Stress can be defined as the elements that place pressure on, and contribute to the breakdown of, the natural and man-made environment. These indicators would be constructed from monitoring records (for example, emissions), special surveys on stress factors (for example, solid waste disposal), administrative records (for example, leakage of hazardous substances), and in practice, from further detailing of the global activity data, that is, more specific in terms of location, estimates of "externalities" based on gross output estimates.

Response indicators are statistics that describe the observed effects of stress upon natural (and man-made) environments and perform the function of critical indicators for the assessment of the state of the environment. These are further categorized as direct response - essentially measures of the condition of environmental media (habitat) - indirect response - which measure the condition of living species, including the health of man. The statistics are obtained directly from monitoring records of water and air quality, surveys of soil quality, wildlife species, human health, etc., and special programmes to assess the state of the environment, including that of ecosystem health. Other response indicators can be obtained indirectly by calculating specific parameters of environmental quality based upon concepts of sustainable yield, carrying capacity and resource depletion rates, etc.

Collective and individual responses can be described in broad terms as man's reaction to environmental change. These can be further distinguished by actions of Governments (collective), individuals as members of households, individuals as legal entities, that is, enterprises, and group actions, that is, public pressure groups. These statistics relate to the measurement of actions to improve the ambient quality of the environment or to establish preventive or protective measures. A large part of these statistics are expenditures of Governments and industry for the purpose of pollution abatement or conservation measures (protection of nature). However, part of the response is in the form of legislative action and statistics could be compiled on, for example, the effect of environmental restraints on economic exploitation (for example, on balance of payments), or areas covered by protective legislation (for example, on landscape preservation or rehabilitation).

2. Activities

(a) Generation of waste residuals is an integral part of all activities
which utilize materials and/or energy. The framework focuses on the
measurement of the waste output of industrial and household activity as a source
of environmental stress. It should be noted that not all wastes are pollutants,
nor for that matter do all pollutants originate from waste disposal; moreover,
pollution abatement does not reduce the quality of wastes (except in the case
of recycling), but rather changes the form.

(b) Permanent environmental restructuring activities are associated with a
class of stressors that result from a permanent transformation of the ·
environment, in particular, the adaption (restructuring) of natural ecologies.
The environmental impact assessment of major construction projects, the
expansion of urbanization, the growth of transport networks, the expansion of
agriculture, drainage of wetlands and reforestation, are the major focuses of
this group of statistics. It should be noted that an important countervailing
response to these stresses is the conservation and protection policies for
highly-valued natural areas and landscapes and the designation of national
parks.

(c) Harvesting activity is the class of environmental stress originating
from man's ever-increasing demand for food, fibre and wood. Stresses occur
when the exploitation of these resources is greater than their carrying capacity
measured by their natural rate of regeneration. Indeed, the externalities due
to the application of new technologies, introduction of hybrid species, the
economic (or market) pressures that change the scale and nature of harvesting
activities need also to be captured by appropriate statistics. There is
increasing interest in this field as a result of the world-wide need to improve
food production.

(d) Depletion of non-renewable resources results in a set of stresses
which are in essence potential rather than actual. This is because they are
concerned with the rate of extraction in terms of known (or anticipated) supply.
Conceptual basis of a stress measure of this class is the impact on the
environment of exploiting increasingly low-grade sources, or of alternative
actions required to substitute the exhausted supply. This is reflected directly
in terms of the additional energy and infrastructure required to exploit
increasingly low-grade deposits, the exploration costs of finding alternative
supplies, the effect of recycling activity and the impact of synthetic
substitutes. It should be noted that stress by the activity of extraction
(mining) is included in categories I and II of table 6.

(e) Environmental contamination resulting from human activity stands out
as one of the most damaging and long-term issues. The major concerns are the
pathogenic, carcinogenic and mutagenic properties of many toxins and the
apparent growth of these potentially hazardous substances both in quantative
and qualitative terms. This class of stresses have had explicit recognition
in various national and international efforts to control their production, use
and dispersion in the environment. The statistics in this area are the macro
data on production and use and the micro-data on environmental leakages, spills,
aerial application (for example, pesticides) and the environmental response in
its direct form, that is, concentration in environmental media, and indirect
form, that is, concentration in living matter, human health, etc.

(f) Energy production and consumption are the sources of a large number of
stressors on the environment. Of major concern today are the environmental
impacts of the different techniques for organizing energy in a usable form

(production), the environmental impact of energy networks and exploration and development of fossil fuel extraction in ecologically sensitive areas, for example, the sea bed and the arctic. On the consumption side are the potential environmental stresses of the expansion of high-energy technology, of which the most pervasive is the use of the private automobile. On the whole, statistics on energy are well developed and in some respects the framework merely suggests a form of organizing these data for assessing the state of the environment.

(g) <u>Natural activity</u> stressors are essentially the deterministic forces of the state of the environment whereby all life in its myriad forms must adapt. Meteorological records are fundamental descriptors of the state of the environment and thus form a background variable in the assessment. Of major concern are the impacts of extreme conditions (those that are far above or below the normal range). Thus, of interest are statistics which show the influence of climate on additional fuel consumption due to a particularly severe winter, or the loss of crops due to prolonged drought. Another concern would be long-term trends in change of climate.

(h) <u>Population dynamics</u> are influenced both by natural activity and human activity. In its broadest aspect this includes, in the spatial context, expansion and contraction of the population's habitats, and, in the temporal context, the growth and decline of natural population. Statistics in this area, when dealing with human population, are available from censuses and vital statistics. The framework suggests new dimensions in demography for the purpose of environmental assessment. For other species, detailed statistical documentation is not readily available. Nevertheless, there is an increasing interest in this field, and the development of ecological mapping promises a potential methodology for keeping records of natural populations and their habitats.

INFORMATION SYSTEMS IN PUBLIC ADMINISTRATION
D. Eade, J. Hodgson (editors)
North-Holland Publishing Company
© *DFD, 1981*

FINAL REPORT OF WORKING GROUP 3*

A. Introduction

The Group adopted a broad environmental view of resources as opposed to a traditional economic view of resources as potential generators of economic growth. Natural resources should not be defined outside their socio-economic context. The concept must be extended to include the human modification or adaptation of the environment.

The Group decided to regard the subject from a developing country's point of view which required the identification of the distinct features that differentiate developing countries' data needs from those of industrial countries.

B. The problem

Given the present level of technology and what may reasonably be expected to evolve over the next decades, and given the prevailing view that materials consumption is the way to a better life, the facts indicate that:

(a) Materials throughput will double, and then double again, over the next 30 or 40 years;

(b) The quality of ores and other natural resources will decline and rapidly available sources will be exhausted;

(c) Only by increased use of energy per unit of output and per capita will intensity of materials throughput be maintained;

---

* Participants: C. Arvas, Sweden ; G. Coiner, USA ; L. Diaz Zuloago, Venezuela ; A. Friend (Moderator), Canada ; A. Laihonen, Finland ; S. Lydersen, Norway.

Figure XI. Relationship between economic, social, and environmental
goals and utilization of natural resources

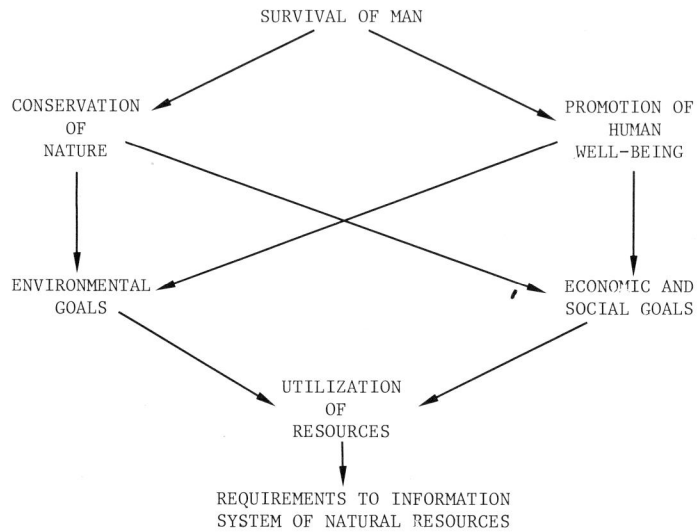

Figure XII. Connexions between economic, social and environmental
planning and information

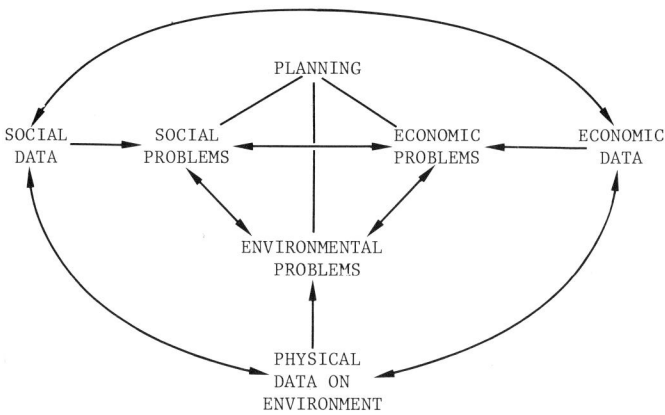

Table 7. Resource management

Biomes	Problems
SUB ARCTIC ARTIC	o MINING o SLOW VEGETATION RECOVERY
CONIFEROUS/DECIDUOUS FORESTS	o URBAN (INFRASTRUCTURE) CONVERSION o AGRICULTURAL TECHNOLOGICAL IMPACTS
+ ARID/SEMI-ARID GRASSLAND/ DESERTS	o DESERTIFICATION o WATER SUPPLY o RESOURCE DEPLETION (OIL)
+ TROPICAL FORESTS GRASSLAND SAVANA	o DEFORESTATION o AGRICULTURAL TECHNOLOGY o CONVERSION IMPACTS o MINING

+ Biome concentrated in developing countries

Figure XIII. Overlapping of economic, social and environmental
            domains

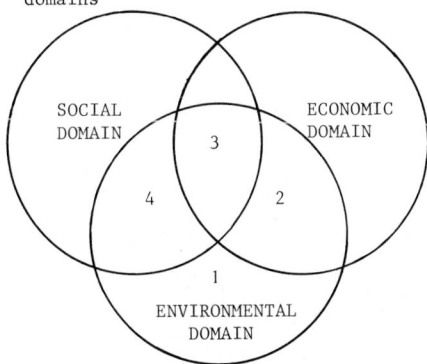

Examples of information specifications in the environmental domain

1. Natural resource inventories; ecological mapping; indicators of environmental
   quality

2. Output of primary industry, that is mining, agriculture, forestry and
   fishing; economic cost of pollution abatement; estimates of proven reserves
   of non-renewable resources

3. Environmental quality of human settlements; health of the population;
   access to resources by social group

4. Synthesis of social-economic environmental factors, for example, natural
   resources in relationship to "basic human needs", "ecodevelopment", "alternative technology"

(d) The environmental stress per unit of production will increase correspondingly;

(e) Biological and other renewable resources may be exploited at rates which exceed their renewal;

(f) Use and transformation of raw materials and energy will increase disturbances in ecological and environmental balances.

Development of developing countries depends upon the availability of resources. They must be managed properly, and an essential element is their regular monitoring of availability, use and quality.

Management and information problems concerning the environment and natural resources are in the programmes of the United Nations and regional organizations such as the European Economic Community (EEC) and the Organization for Economic Co-operation and Development (OECD). For example: OECD has focussed on state-of-the-environment reporting; EEC has studied a common framework and classification system for environmental statistics.

The Group adopted figure XI as the underlying premise for the need for natural resource data. This demonstrates that there is a strong relationship between economic, social and environmental goals on the one hand and the management of natural resources on the other. The figure also illustrates the relationship between the conservation and utilization of natural resources.

Until recently, planning and development only took account of economic and social problems. Today it is realized that environmental aspects of development must be taken into account and considered in relation to both economic and social problems (see figure XII). Of course this is easier said than done, since goals may be in conflict. In particular, economic and environmental goals often seem difficult to harmonize. Social and environmental goals on the other hand often support each other.

Data needs for economic and social planning and development are well defined and to a greater or lesser extent available through statistical and administrative information systems. This is not the situation in the case of the environmental component of the planning system. Of course there is some overlapping between the data requirements for economic, social and environmental planning, as figure XIII illustrates. However, an environmental dimension needs to be added to traditional data gathering.

In developing countries there is usually a national planning system which produces a national development plan. A consequence of the Group's basic premise is that environmental management should be regarded as part of the national planning system. The Group examined the Venezualan planning and environmental management model (see annex I) for the purpose of focussing on the data needs of a developing country.

The ecosystems which constitute the natural environments of earth are susceptible to modification by human activity. Each environment is modified differently as human activity extracts the requirements of human settlement from nature (table 7). It should be noted that in relation to the development of environmental information systems the geographic location of the developing countries is heavily concentrated in arid and semi-arid and humid tropical regions of the planet. The biomes will determine the nature of the physical data requirements and the nature of human impacts within each country. This in turn will influence the data needs of the environmental information systems which would support the planning process. Table 7 illustrates the biome/problem relationship.

C. USER NEEDS AND INFORMATION REQUIREMENTS

The Group considered user needs and requirements from the hierarchical decision-making structure of Governments, the information needs of the public, and the particular requirements of the research establishment (see figure XIV). The Group saw a potential conflict between the articulated demand of government agencies and those of high level decision making (that is, political and strategic planning). These latter required a few critical indicators to describe environmental conditions whereas the former sought detailed data to implement and evaluate policy. Although in principle a well structured framework with hierarchical classification structure could satisfy both levels of decision making, it was feared that the process of organizing data may, by default, fail to recognize the higher level needs. The Group emphasized that priority should be given to data development that could serve the public desire to have knowledge of the critical trends. An underlying premise is that a well-informed public could have a greater influence on strategic planning decisions than would be generated by the government establishment.

The Group finally concluded that the most urgent requirement was for data needs for strategic development planning. This was because at that level, socio-economic decisions were being made that had long-term impacts on the environment and due to the lack of appropriate environmental data these decisions were being made in default of environmental considerations.

1. Environmental data for development

The needs for real world data for development planning are prescribed by the information needs related to the main developmental decisions of government. These can be structured with respect to the types of activities which affect the environment. Broadly speaking, there are three types of activities which need to be monitored:

(a) Permanent environmental restructuring activities;

(b) Harvesting activity;

(c) Depletion of non-renewable resources.

Permanent environmental restructuring activities are associated with a class of sources of environmental stress that result from a permanent transformation (restructuring) of natural ecosystems. The environmental impact assessment of major construction projects, the expansion of urbanization and the growth of transport networks are the major focusses of this group of data. Nevertheless, other kinds of permanent environmental restructuring should also be included such as the expansion of agriculture, drainage of wetlands and reforestation.

Harvesting activity is the class of sources of environmental stress originating from man's ever increasing demand for food, fibre and wood; stresses occur when the exploitation of these resources is greater than their carrying capacity measured by their natural rate of regeneration.

Depletion of non-renewable resources is a function of rate of extraction and known or anticipated supply. Conceptual basis of a stressor measure of this class is the impact on the environment of exploiting increasingly low-grade sources, or of alternative actions required to substitute the exhausted supply. This is reflected directly in terms of the additional energy and infrastructure required to exploit increasingly low-grade deposits, the exploration costs of finding alternative supplies, the effect of recycling activity and the impact of synthetic substitutes.

Figure XIV. Users and uses of environmental information

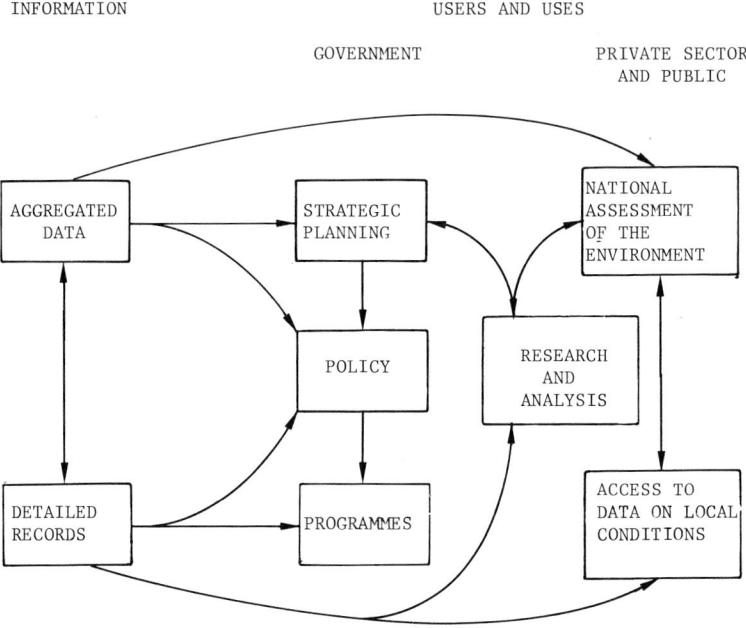

INFORMATION   USERS AND USES

                     GOVERNMENT   PRIVATE SECTOR
                                              AND PUBLIC

Figure XV. Norwegian resource accounting system

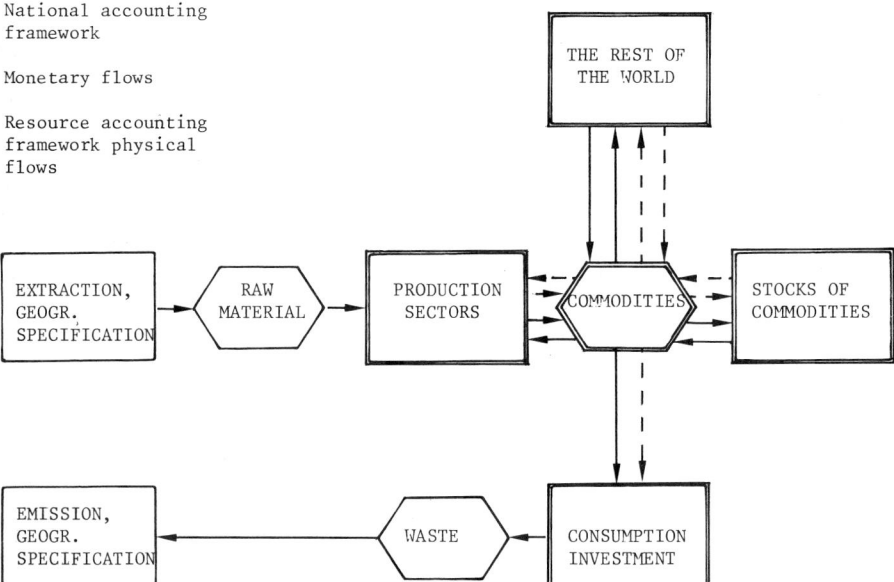

National accounting
framework

Monetary flows

Resource accounting
framework physical
flows

2. Minimum data set

The high costs of collecting environmental data make it desirable to try to define the minimum set of data which meets requirements. These are of course influenced by socio-economic goals and local conditions.

The broad-based concept of natural resource data adopted by the Group implies the need to define not only the physical data characteristics but also the relevant socio-economic parameters. Moreover, to the extent possible, the data specifications would be adaptations from existing data collection and compilation. Table 8 provides an example of how the environmental dimension can be drawn from a socio-economic data base; similarly, data such as estimates of proven mineral reserves and inventories of forest or land use already collected by resource agencies could be organized as an integral part of the minimum data set. Nevertheless, even when all existing sources are drawn into the system, there would be the inevitable data gaps which will require new surveys to fill them. However, the Group felt that a great deal could be gained by merely modifying the existing data base from an environmental perspective.

One important method is that of spatial referencing of existing statistics through geocoding techniques. This allows flexibility in reorganizing data in different geographical units such as coherent ecological regions. Moreover it allows observation of flows between geographical regions, such as migration of people.

D. Approaches to natural resource data

The Group deliberated on the efficacy of approaching the problem of natural resources information systems from either a preconceptualized model or from a more pragmatic approach. It was generally agreed that, at least in principle, the deductive method was probably more efficient in identifying the data parameters and moreover could function as a heuristic device for understanding the basic relationship of man and his environment. Nevertheless, the group also recognized that from the point of view of administrators, more ad-hoc methods such as the Government Data Network approach may have greater appeal. Firstly because it is based on existing data structure as defined by administrative responsibilities and procedures, and secondly, it requires less effort in implementation. The Group felt however that this approach might completely fail to produce the kind of data required for strategic development planning. On the other hand, experience in the development of structural framework is limited. The Group examined the following models as possible methods for organizing natural resources data.

A material-energy balance approach which accounts for natural resource stocks and flows was examined. The Norwegian experience was considered in this context and the Group was particularly impressed by its harmonization with national accounts. However it saw as a problem the requirement for sophisticated data bases, in particular those of input-output accounts.
Even though the construction of a complete material-energy balance model might not be feasable in developing countries, it could nevertheless be usefully applied at a sectorial level. The Group thought it was worthwhile to study the feasability and desirability of material-energy balances (see figure XV).

A second model examined was the stress-response statistical system currently being developed in Canada. This approach emphasizes historical trends where the dynamic forces are modelled on dialectical processes, as opposed for example to equilibrium. The parameters of the system are statistical measures of environmental stress resulting from human activity and complementary measures of environmental response obtained from monitoring records of environmental change. And since environmental conditions in turn effect the well being of

Table 8. Environmentally relevant statistical series from the demographic and socio-economic data base

Data base	Data series	Environmental dimension	Data base	Data series	Environmental dimension
Census (population)	Growth, distribution, migration	Rural-urban, river basin, biome	Forestry	Land use	Area and type of forests
				Stock	Volume of timber; Heavy machinery stock
Health statistics	Mortality rates	Sickness and death rates from diseases where exposure to stressful environment is considered a key factor. Reported incidence of contaminant poisoning e.g. insecticide spraying, food poisoning.		Input-output	Quantity of wood cut
	Morbidity rates			Forestry	Inputs - energy, pesticides, etc. Regeneration rates, loss due to forest fires, disease and cut-over
Housing statistics (Census and surveys)	Individuals	Crowding index. Facilities per household. Shift in dwelling type	Fishing	Stock	Estimates of available by type of fish; Number and types of fishing vessel
	Dwelling type			Input-output	Fish catch; Fuel consumption; Cost per unit output
Household surveys	Income and expenditure surveys	Environmentally directed expenditure - travel, recreation. Ownership of high environment impact goods - cars, 2nd homes, motorised recreation equipment	Transport	Stock	Network of transport system; Stock of equipment
	Asset surveys			Input-output	Movement of goods and people; Fuel consumption
Special surveys	Ad-hoc surveys	Perception and attitudinal surveys regarding environment. Recreational use of natural resources. Travel habits, commuting and holiday	Trade Statistics	Imports and Exports	Imports of hazardous substances; Imports of energy e.g. fuels, electricity
National accounts	Production and expenditure	Aggregate estimates of "externalities"		Exports	Exports of energy; Exports of goods from high environmental impact industries; Sales of hazardous substances, e.g.
Manufacturing statistics	Inputs and outputs	Production of hazardous substances. Inputs of chemicals, fuels; electricity; expenditure on pollution abatement equipment; process type; recycling activity; water inflow-outflow		Wholesale and Retail	fertilisers, pesticides, chemicals; Sales of high environment impact goods, e.g. cars, detergents
Mining	Inputs, Outputs	Same as above	Service statistics	Input-output	Fuels for heating, e.g. office buildings; Waste disposal services
Agriculture (Census and surveys)	Land use	Area used for crops, livestock, wood lots, orchards, etc. Area irrigated, improved, fertilised, etc.	Government statistics	Expenditure	Environmental management; Water purification and waste treatment facilities
	Stock	Number and type of livestock, machinery		Facilities	Waste treatment facilities by type, e.g. primary, secondary, tertiary; Government monitoring facilities for air and water
	Input-output	Production of food, fibres, etc. Inputs - fuel, electricity, fertilisers, pesticides, etc.			

Table 9. Structural framework for the stress-response environmental Statistical System (S-RESS), type of statistics

Activity	Measures to reduce environmental stress			Policy response	Conservation measures
	A (preventive actions)	B (curative actions)			C (conservation actions)
	Stressors measures	Stress measures	Environmental response measures	Collective and individual response	Inventory of stock measures
I. Generation of waste residuals	Production and consumption	Pollution loadings	Monitoring of environmental quality	Abatement expenditures and process change	Capacity to abate pollution and recycling capacity
II. Permanent environmental restructuring	Construction and land use change	Construction and land use change at local level	Ecosystem transformation	Protection and conservation of environmental assets	Accumulated stock of man-made structures Protected areas
III. Harvesting activity	Production from renewable resources	Over-production and technological stresses	Sustainable yield response	Control of technology and establishment of quota systems	Stock of renewable resources
IV. Extraction of non-renewable resources	Production and consumption and alternative substitutes	Same as I and II.	Same as I and II	Conservation measure	Stock of non-renewable resources
V. Production and consumption of potentially hazardous substances	Production, disposition and disposal	Application of potentially hazardous substances and leakage	Level of contaminants in the environment	Restrictions and control of use of potentially hazardous substances	Stock of potentially hazardous substances
VI. Production and consumption of energy	Production and use	Development of supporting infrastructure. Noise generations	Thermal pollution, (noise) nuisance	Energy conservation	Stock of energy resources. Capacity of energy production
VII. Natural activity	Meteorological records and geo-physical events	Variation of climate and geo-physical events beyond normal range	Drought, flood, earthquakes and long-term biome damage	Socio-economic response to natural activity	Mapping of climate and ecological zones
VIII. Population dynamics (human and other biological species)	Population change on temporal and spatial dimensions	Population in relation to carrying capacity	"Over use" of natural resources. Increase in mortality and morbidity	Control of population size and habitat expansion	Population count

Source: Towards a comprehensive framework for environmental statistics: a stress-response approach (Ottawa, Statistics Canada, 1979), Cat. No. 11-510.

Figure XVI. Interrelationships between mapping,
modeling and monitoring

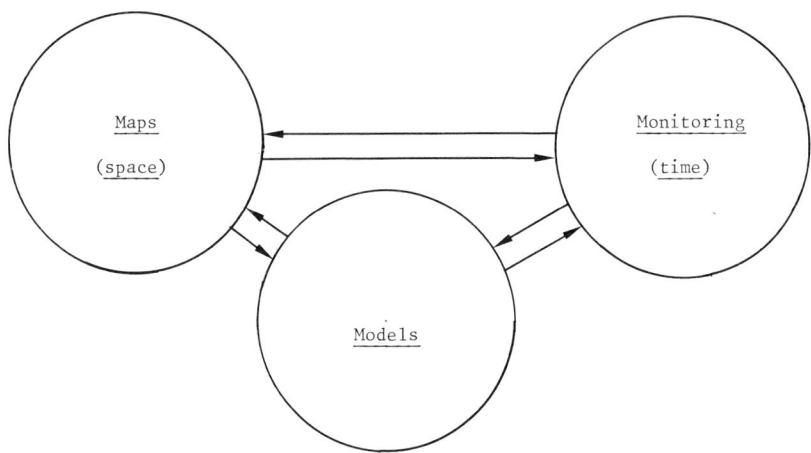

(a) Mapping affects modeling by setting the boundary conditions for the model,
   i.e. identifying the physical system to which the model pertains and the
   degree of openness of the system.

(b) Models affect geographical mapping by establishing the conceptual framework
   for defining a system of interest and identifying the key characteristics of
   the system whose spatial configuration is likely to be important in understanding the system.

(c) Mapping affects monitoring by defining the region in which monitoring occurs
   and, as a result of the scale of mapping, suggests sampling programs and
   techniques for monitoring.

(d) Monitoring affects mapping by providing the technical bases for mapping. For
   example, remote sensing might permit certain mapping configurations, but not
   others due to the technical limitations of current decoding

(e) Monitoring affects modeling by providing the information base upon which
   models are validated and subsequently modified. Also monitoring provides the
   possible sources of data for testing models and thus may influence the choice
   of parameters used in models.

(f) Modeling affects monitoring by indicating the key parameters for which data
   should be gathered, if possible, and the importance of spatial and temporal
   considerations in designing the monitoring system.

Figure XVII. GDN approach as a framework

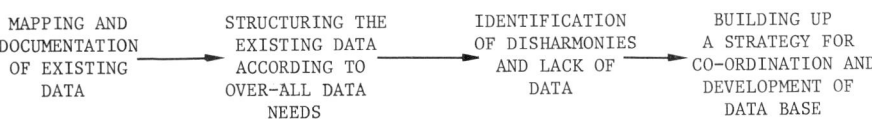

| MAPPING AND DOCUMENTATION OF EXISTING DATA | STRUCTURING THE EXISTING DATA ACCORDING TO OVER-ALL DATA NEEDS | IDENTIFICATION OF DISHARMONIES AND LACK OF DATA | BUILDING UP A STRATEGY FOR CO-ORDINATION AND DEVELOPMENT OF DATA BASE |

man, there is an inherent circularity of the adaptation of man to his environment (see table 9). The Group considered this approach useful in ordering the complex data on the environment in a form that was significant for observation of environmental trends – in particular since these data can be classified into coherent environmental regions.

The third approach considered by the Group was referred to as the "M3 approach" (that is, Model $\longrightarrow$ Monitoring $\longrightarrow$ Mapping). The structural characteristic is that of mapping of ecosystems and monitoring of key indicators of ecological health in respect to a conceptual model of ecosystem transformation (see figure XVI). It is recognized that this particular perspective is an effective method for introducing the critical ecological perspective to natural resource management.

A fourth approach considered was the pragmatic Government Data Network approach of Data for Development. The merits of this method is its highly efficient means for administrative data systems. The major caveat was, as mentioned above, its lack of model to describe man and environment interaction (see figure XVII).

The Group considered that all approaches could in turn be complementary, or parts of each separate approach could be adapted into a new system of natural resource data for development.

E. Proposal for action by Data for Development (DFD)

The Group felt that the area of information systems for management of natural resources was of fundamental importance for development in all countries in the world. DFD activities need to be strengthened in this field and it is suggested that a work programme for DFD should be defined.

It was not possible for the Group to specify such a work programme but it was envisaged that it would include a variety of pilot projects, workshops, seminars and case studies. The Group would recommend however that a seminar be convened shortly. One important objective of that seminar would be to work out a proposal for a working programme. The seminar could be labelled as:

"Information Systems for Natural Resource Management in Development"

One important objective for the seminar as well as for the work programme would be to draw attention to the relation between the economic use of natural resources on one hand and environmental effects on the other. Three main topics for the seminar were suggested.

1. Alternative conceptual frameworks for the information systems

In order to structure and organize data in such a way that the data bases may be used as input to all different aspects of natural resource management, a common conceptual framework is needed. Examples of such frameworks are "stress-response", "resource-accounting" and "monitoring". The "Government data network" approach taken by DFD in its present pilot projects can be considered as one strategy for the primary data collection.

2. New technologies and methodology

New technologies and methodologies for data collection and storage should be examined i.e. remote sensing, geocoding, ecoregions, climate, non-renewable resources, renewable resources, etc.

3. Definition of minimal datasets for planning decisions

A very important question is to try to define the minimal data sets required for the central strategic decisions in the area of management of natural resources. In this connection it could prove practical to pick a number of typical decision-making situations and discuss the minimal data-sets required for planning and analysis.

Annex I

Planning and environment in Venezuela

National development planning in Venezuela and the co-ordination of efforts in that field is the responsibility of the Central Office for Planning and Co-ordination (CORDIPLAN), which is an office at ministry level. There is also a Central Office for Statistics and Informatics and a Central Office for Budgeting. The five-year national plans are built by the following from nine sectors of development:

1. Agriculture

2. Energy

3. Transportation

4. Housing

5. Education

6. Recreation

7. Industry

8. Health

9. Public security

Each sector of development is headed by the ministry which participates the most in it, and the planning committee for each sector is composed of the planning group of each ministry involved in that sector of development. The central offices are also part of all the committees.

The Ministry of Environment participates in almost all the sectors.

For the building of sectorial plans, information is required from the ministries that participate in the sector. Such information comes at different levels of aggregation.

The Ministry of Environment groups its activities into 15 basic programmes, each one receiving support from the 4 operative units of the Ministry (see figure XXII). The Ministry is represented locally through its regional offices, each one with the same structure found at the central level.

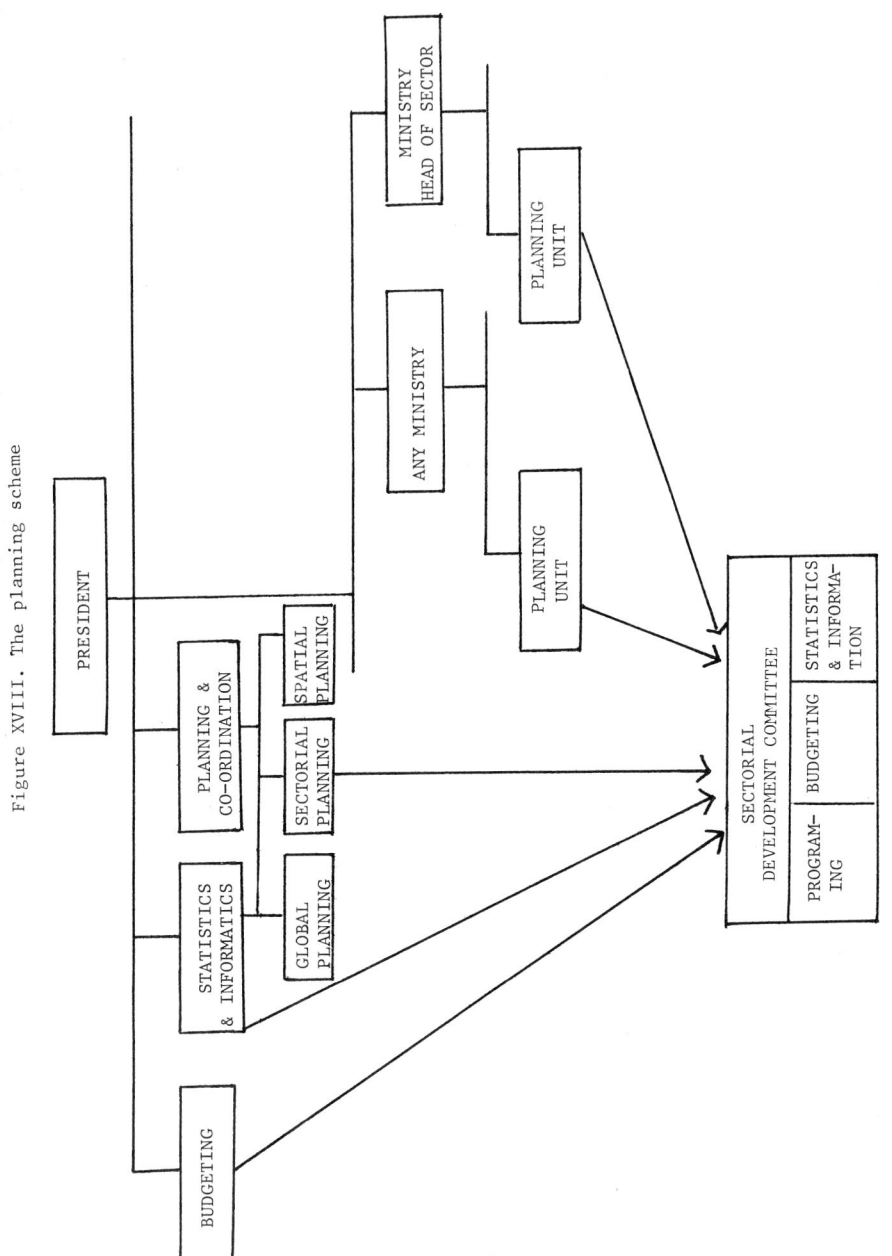

Figure XVIII. The planning scheme

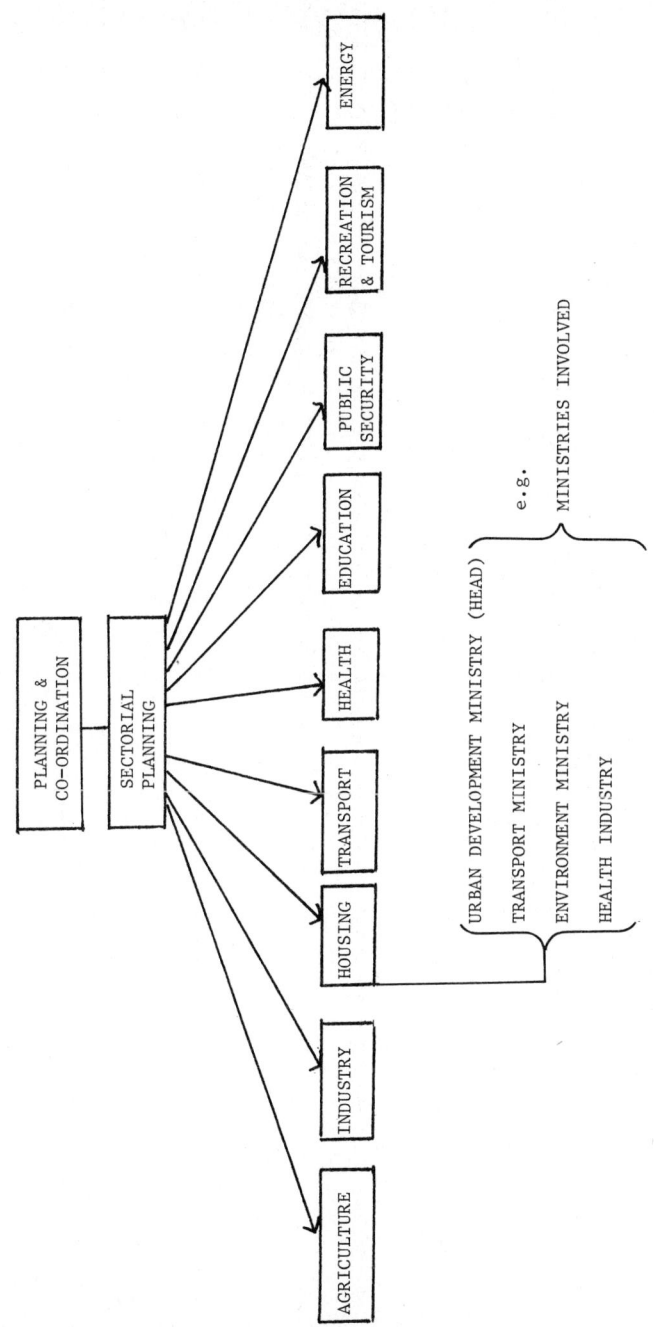

Figure XIX. Sectors for planning

Figure XX. Process of decision making for the plan

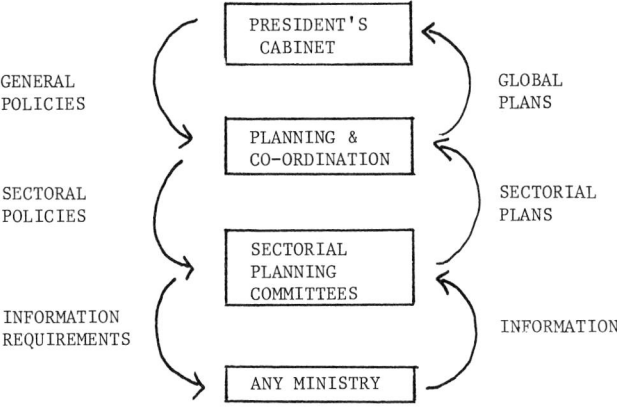

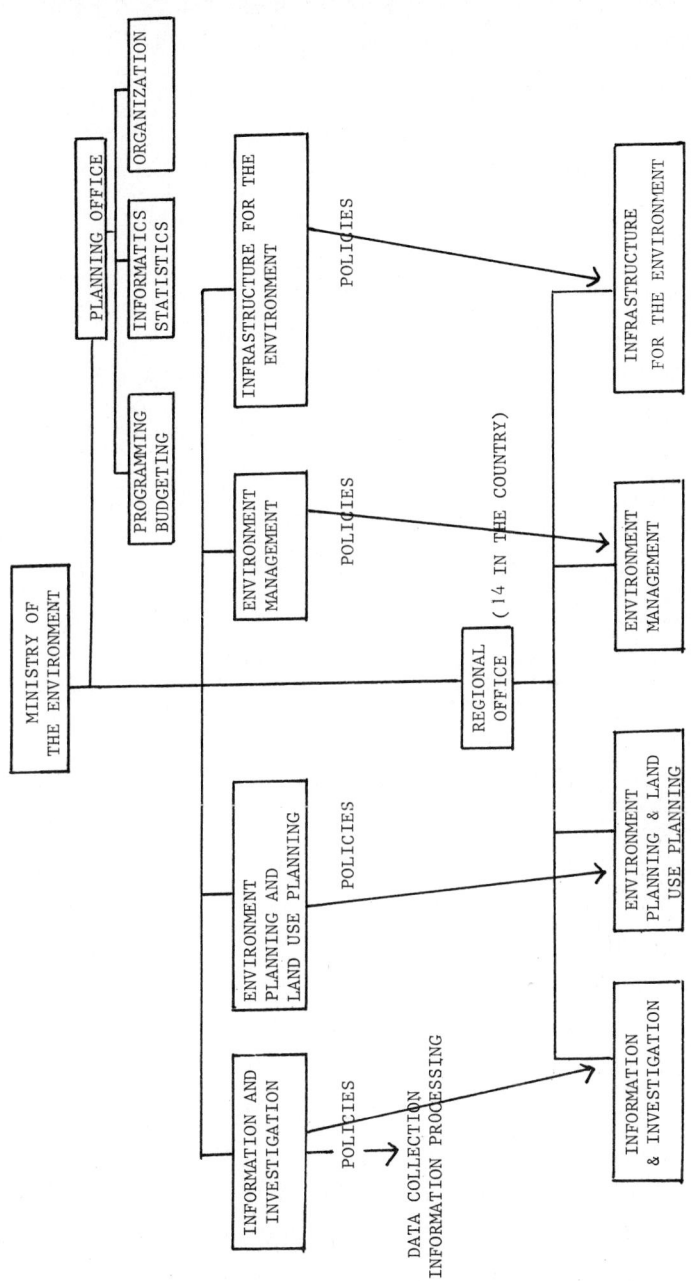

Figure XXI. Organization of the Ministry of the Environment

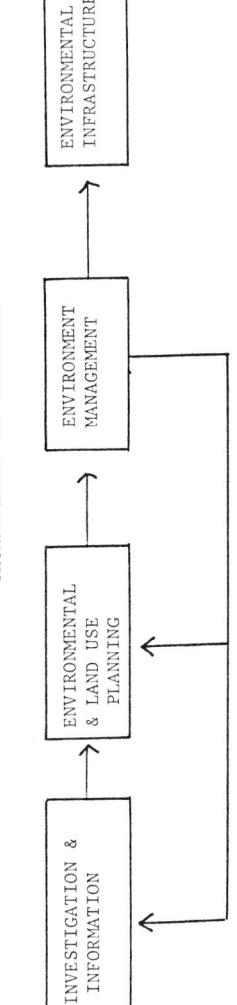

Figure XXII. Ministry of Environment

ORGANIZATION BY FUNCTIONS

Basic Programmes

1. LAND USE PLANNING
2. WATER POLLUTION CONTROL
3. ATMOSPHERIC CONTAMINATION CONTROL
4. WASTE CONTROL (SOIL CONTAMINATION)
5. FOREST AND WILD LIFE MANAGEMENT AND CONSERVATION
6. FOREST FIRE CONTROL
7. INTEGRAL WATER RESOURCES ADMINISTRATION
8. FLOOD CONTROL AND LAND RECOVERY
9. BASINS MANAGEMENT AND CONTROL
10. NATIONAL PARKS
11. REGIONAL WATER SUPPLY SYSTEMS
12. ENVIRONMENTAL EDUCATION
13. PROFESSIONAL DEVELOPMENT IN ENVIRONMENTAL ACTIVITIES
14. LEGAL SUPPORT DEVELOPMENT

ENVIRONMENTAL INFRASTRUCTURE

ENVIRONMENT MANAGEMENT

ENVIRONMENTAL & LAND USE PLANNING

INVESTIGATION & INFORMATION

Annex II

The Norwegian system of natural resource accounting

Introduction

The concept of resource accounting was introduced by the Norwegian Resource Committee in 1968. The Committee's second report in 1971 suggested that Parliament should be given regular reports on the state and use of natural resources. The Committee also proposed establishment of a Ministry of Natural Resources. In the early 1970s however, environmental issues such as pollution, nature conservation, etc. were felt to be more important. During 1972, the Ministry of Environment was established and early in 1974 was expanded by the establishment of a resource department and given the responsibility of preparing an annual report (resource accounts) reviewing the quantities, qualities and consumption of natural resources, as well as proposals regarding future use of these resources (resource budgeting). The methodological work on resource accounting started in 1975 and the results were reported in 1977 to the Ministry of Environment and later to Parliament.

The Parliamentary report recommended that pilot studies be initiated on selected resources. The Ministry subsequently wanted resource accounts to be developed on energy, land and fish. The Central Bureau of Statistics of Norway was to be responsible for both the pilot studies and the further methodological development of resource accounts. This work started in 1978, and the final decision on resource accounting and budgeting will be made by Parliament late in 1980 on the basis of results from the pilot studies.

The working group in the Central Bureau of Statistics at present numbers nine professionals (geographers, statisticians, economists, planners and biologists) and four full-time assistants. Including part-time assistants and students, approximately 20 persons are taking part in the work. The costs will be about 2 million NKr, which corresponds to approximately $400,000 a year.

The first accounts on energy have been published for the year 1976. During 1979, accounts for 1977 and 1978 will be presented as well. Preliminary accounts for land will be presented early in 1980, whereas resource accounts for fish will not be presented until late 1980.

Methods and techniques to be used in resource budgeting are to be developed. A working group consisting of members from the Central Bureau of Statistics, the Ministry of Finance, the Ministry of Environment and the Ministry of Oil and Energy are preparing a report regarding energy budgeting. The main purpose of such budgeting will be to co-ordinate and synchronize economic planning and development of new energy systems, such as hydroelectric power plants.

A major problem in the development of resource accounting will be to develop an integrated system where the linkages between the different resources and their utilization can be analyzed. In order to achieve this, the System of Resource Accounts (SRA) ought to be compatible with the Norwegian System of National Accounts which is based on the United Nation's System of National Accounts (SNA). In addition such aspects as pollution and environmental impact must be taken into account.

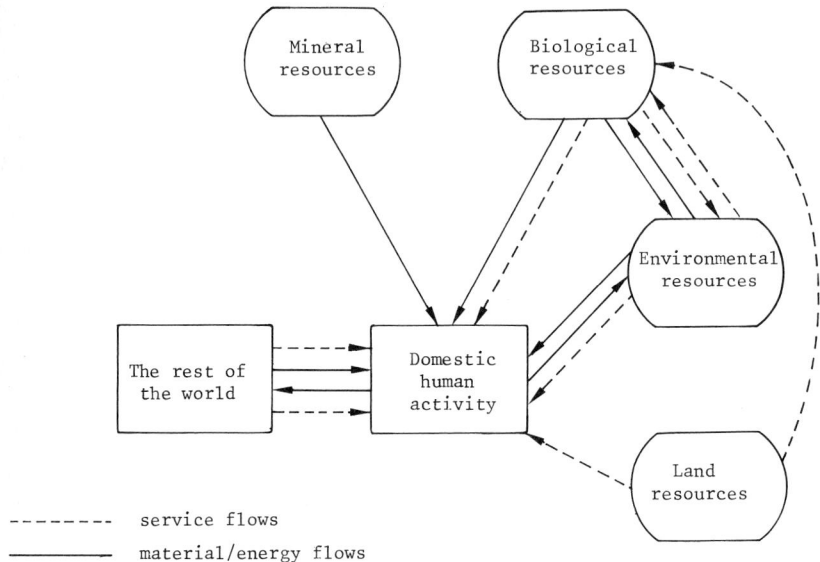

-------- service flows
———————— material/energy flows

Figure XXIII. Flow chart of the System of Resource Accounts

In figure XXIII some of the main flows between the stock concepts of the
resource accounts are presented. Some flows are omitted in the chart, for
example, exploring in order to discover new mineral reserves and revaluate
estimates on known reserves, and buying, selling and developing land.

Only the market flows of human activity are represented in the national
accounts, almost all other flows are omitted. In addition, the stock accounting
is fragmentary, omitting all accounting of natural resource stocks. This is
however no reason for rejecting the SNA as a starting point of an accounting
system for resource accounting. On the contrary, the SNA is the basis for the
SRA which should adapt to all standardizations of the SNA whenever possible.

In the following, the data of the kind given in the national accounts are
called "macro data", to be distinguished from "geo information", which is
information with either geographical co-ordinates or having another detailed
geographical specification attached to it. Macro data are usually given on a
national level with some sort of sector specification, while geo information
primarily has a geographical specification.

Table 10 presents the accounting system interpreted as an input-output
system. The purpose of the figure is to give the information content and
specification of the most inputs and outputs. On the diagonal, measures of
state or activity level of each part of the system are given.

Source \ Destination	Human activity	Environmental resources	Biological resources	Land resources	Mineral resources
Human activity	Production and consumption levels	Emission of waste products		Changes in land use	Prospecting
Environmental resources	Productive services and conditions for life	Indicators of environmental quality	Conditions for life		
Biological resources	Food and raw materials		Annual yield		
Land resources	Productive and recreative services		Space for life	Land use	
Mineral resources	Raw materials				Known reserves of minerals

Table 10. Interaction between the main parts of the Resource Accounts

Table 11. Economical reserves of energy resources

	Coal	Crude oil	Natural gas	Hydro power [a]
	10^6 t	10^6 t	10^9 Sm^3	TWh
Economical, undeveloped reserves, Jan. 1st, 1976	14	595	411	71,2
Revaluation	−	−151	−76	−1,6
Discoveries	−	60	42	.
Reserves developed in 1976	−	−	−	−0,4
Economical, undeveloped reserves, Dec. 31st, 1976	14	504	504	69,2
Developed reserves (developed hydro power), Jan. 1st, 1976	9,1	108	129	81,2
Revaluation	1,2	11	−9	0,2
Reserves developed in 1976	−	−	−	0,4
Extraction	−0,5	−14	0	.
Losses in extraction	−0,1	−	−	.
Developed reserves (developed hydro power), Dec. 31st, 1976	9,7	105	120	81,8
Energy equivalent of water in reservoirs, Jan. 1st, 1976			TWH	40,6
Mean production potential [b]			81,5	
Deviation from the mean			−9,6	
Useful inflow				71,9
Gross production of electricity				−82,0
Energy equivalent of water in reservoirs, Dec. 31st, 1976				30,5

a/ Mean production (potential) of a year.

b/ Mean production potential in 1976 is calculated as an average of the production potential of Jan. 1st, and the production potential of Dec. 31st.

Table 12. Energy use outside the energy sectors, 1976 (Norway)

Industry / ISIC	Coal	Coke	Gaso-lines	Petro-leum	Light fuel oil diesel etc.	Heavy Fuel oil	Elect-ricity
	1000 t	1000 t	1000 t	1000 t	1000 t	1000 t	1000 t
Total							
Production sectors, enterprises	349	1 201	1 534	830	3 514	11 141	67 082
1 Agriculture, forestry and fishing ...	–	–	20	13	448	34	707
11 Agriculture	–	–	11	1	150	34	707
12 Forestry	–	–	4	–	12	–	–
13 Fishing	–	–	5	12	286	–	–
2 Mining	7	–	1	2	40	48	876
23 Metal ore mining	7	–	–	2	20	47	743
29 Other mining	–	–	1	–	20	1	133
3 Manufacturing	325	1 171	242	6	462	1 459	37 093
31 Manufacture of provisions	–	–	8	1	113	252	1 445
32 Manufacture of textiles, leather and leather products	–	–	1	1	16	15	294
33 Manufacture of wood products	–	–	3	1	30	23	540
341 Wood-processing	–	–	–	1	32	415	4 109
342 Printing, publishing etc.	–	–	2	1	10	1	216
351 Manufacture of industrial chemicals	13	125	212	–	18	222	5 125
352, 354 355, 356 Manufacture of chemical products and products of mineral, oil coal, rubber, and plastic	81	63	3	–	45	27	617
3692 Manufacture of cement and lime ...	–	2	–	–	6	288	352
36+ 3692 Manufacture of other mineral products	1	34	1	–	33	67	384
37101 Manufacture of iron and steel	–	293	4	–	14	6	2 144
37102 Manufacture of Ferro-alloys	225	463	–	–	3	4	6 141
37103 Iron and steel fouding	3	5	–	–	8	2	246
37201 Manufacture of primary aluminium .	1	160	–	1	18	30	11 606
37202 Manufacture of other metals	–	24	–	–	2	69	1 752
37203 Rolling and founding, non-ferrous 37204 metals	–	–	–	–	3	–	118
38,39 Manufacture of workshop products, other manufacturing industries ...	–	2	7	–	109	39	2 006
5 Construction	–	–	16	1	175	2	709
6 Wholesale and retail trade, restaurants and hotels	–	–	203	26	285	9	2 382
61,62 Whole and retail trade	–	–	203	20	241	9	2 058
63 Operation of hotels and restaurants	–	–	–	6	44	–	324
7 Transport, storage and communication	–	–	56	440	1 192	9 561	760
7111, 7122 Rail transport etc.	–	–	–	–	17	–	554
71121 Scheduled bus transport	–	–	2	–	69	–	–
7113 Taxi and other unscheduled bus transport	–	–	16	–	17	–	–
7114, 7116 Other transport by road	–	–	–	–	161	–	–
7121 Ocean transport	–	–	–	–	500	9 500	–
7122 Coastal and inland water transport	–	–	–	–	412	61	–
713 Air transport	–	–	3	483	–	–	–
7123, 719 Services allied to transport .	–	–	7	–	–	–	–
72 Communication	–	–	28	2	16	–	206
8 Financing, insurance, real estate and business services	–	–	37	4	32	1	606
81, 82 Bank and insurance	–	–	10	2	14	–	230
83 Real estate and business services	–	–	27	2	18	1	376
9 Other services	–	–	45	4	52	–	1 147
Production, sectors, public services ...	–	–	100	28	346	11	4 003
91 Public administration	–	–	–	5	32	–	449
931, 932 Educational and researching services	–	–	–	16	112	–	1 760
933, 934 Health and veterinary services, social care, etc.	–	–	–	7	65	1	1 061
Other sectors in public administration	–	–	100	–	137	10	733
Households	17	30	814	306	482	16	18 799

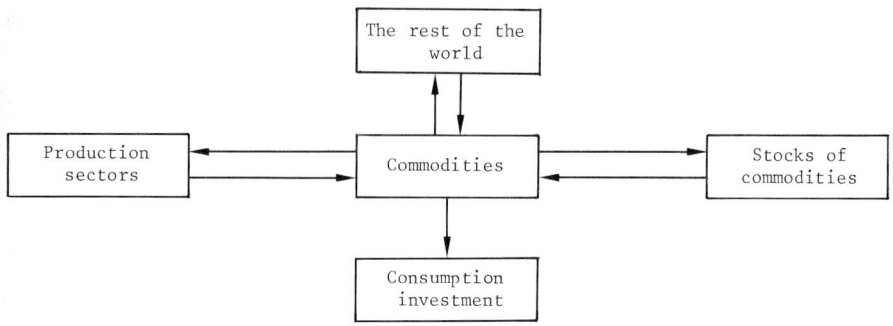

Figure XXIV. Commodity flows in the SNA

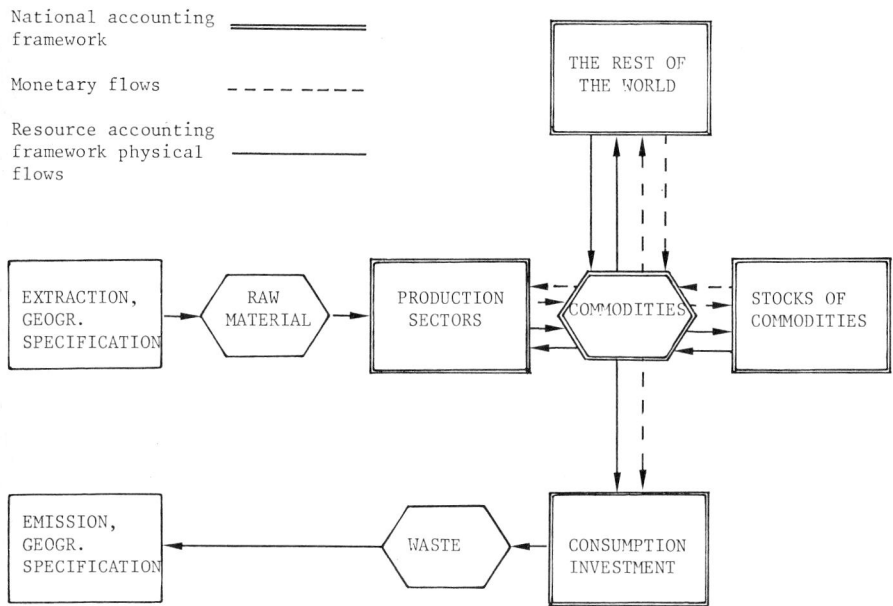

Figure XXV. Extended National Accounts

Note : 1. For a number of important resource commodities there will be a parellel
          accounting of monetary flows in the national accounts and of physical
          flows in the resource accounts.

       2. Extraction is linked to production through physically measured raw
          materials balances which equal extraction of each raw material distri-
          buted among geographical areas with extraction specified in terms of
          production sectors.

       3. Emission is linked to production through physically measured waste
          balances which equal emission of each waste product distributed among
          geographical areas with ditto specified in terms of production sectors
          (including private households).

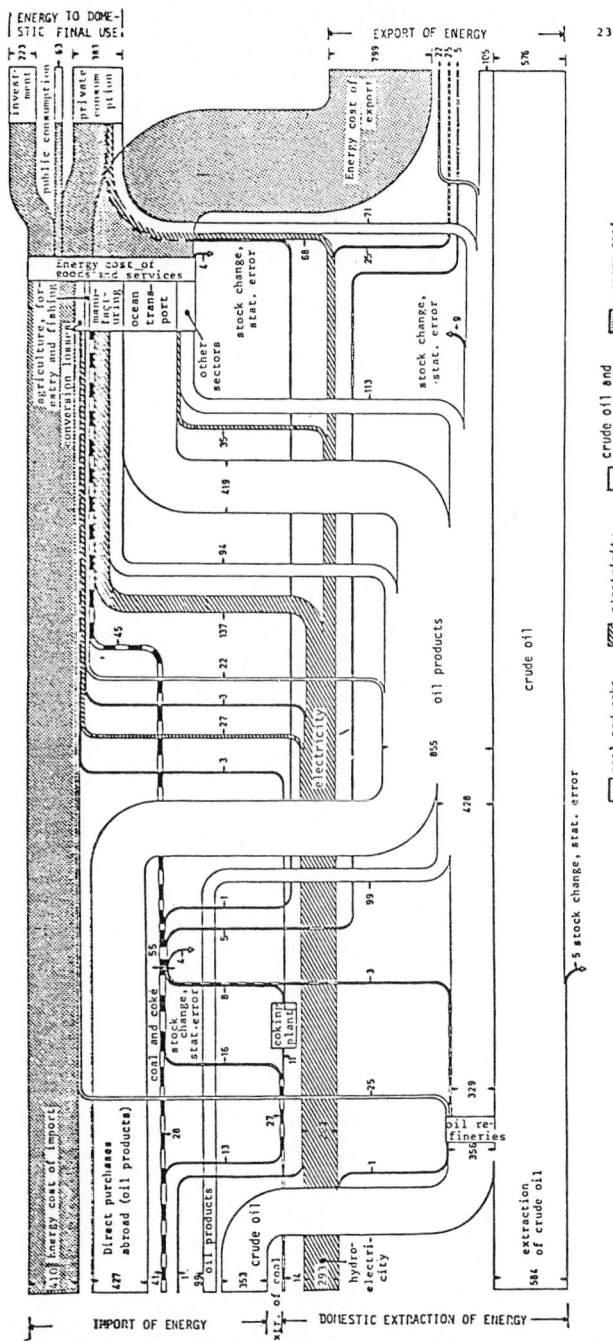

Figure XXVI. Energy flows in Norway, 1978.

Resource budgeting: general remarks

In Norway the short-term economic plans (up to four years) are called
national budgets, corresponding to the National Accounts. "Plan" has been used
for both local physical plans and national four-year economic plans. The
four-year economic plans are more verbal than the annual national budgets, but
still closely linked to the accounts.

We have chosen the term "resource budget" instead of "resource plan" or
"resource programme", and one reason for this is to stress the strong link to
the accounts. Further, the resource budgets must contain a flexible programme
for legislation, taxation, and other instruments to be used in the resource
policy (strategic planning).

The macro part of the resource accounts gives a direct and strong link
between macro-economic development and resource parameters: extraction of
natural resources and waste disposal. Therefore, macro-economic budgets
and resource budgets must be based on the same set of assumptions concerning
the economic development. In Norway, macro-economic models (MODIS and MSG)
are being used to set up the macro-economic budgets. By using these models,
this co-ordination can be taken care of.

As with economic budgeting, resource budgeting will have two aspects:

(a) An institutional/political side;

(b) A methodological/technical/analytical side.

There exists an economic planning routine in the central administration and
in the first years to come, resource budgets probably will be implemented through
a step-by-step integration into the economic planning process.

This institutional/political side of resource budgeting is the
responsibility of the Ministry of Environment, whereas development of technical
apparatus is the responsibility of the Unit for Resource Accounting. On the
macro side, only slight revisions of the economic model apparatus will be
required to cover the immediate needs. Planning on the geo resources,
especially land resources, is at present mainly a local and regional concern.
National planning is fragmentary (sectoral) and the model support is weak.
There is practically no formal connexion between macro-economic planning routine
and physical planning routine (in our terminology: the geo aspect of resource
budgeting). It is probably possible to use regionalized macro-economic models
as a starting point for budgeting of geo resources.

INFORMATION SYSTEMS IN PUBLIC ADMINISTRATION
D. Eade, J. Hodgson (editors)
North-Holland Publishing Company
© *DFD, 1981*

A DATA BASE APPROACH
FOR MAINTAINING A REGISTRY OF ESTABLISHMENTS

David B. Gottlieb*

Abstract

The United States Bureau of Labour Statistics (BLS) has adopted a data base approach for the management of name, address and characteristics information for over four million United States establishments. The Bureau's solution, called the Universe Maintenance System, provides efficient and cost-effective support to an establishment universe base for industry and area oriented BLS surveys.

In the past, States provided unemployment insurance tapes annually to the BLS. These tapes replaced the previous year's data. Field corrections made to establishment address or other data could not be shared across surveys and could not be brought forward at year's end. The new direct access system provides modular capabilities for annual update, ad hoc maintenance or entry of corrections and the extraction of subsections of the universe for survey sampling. The latter is facilitated by a user-oriented query language.

A. Introduction

As a major federal statistical institute, the Bureau of Labour Statistics, launches dozens of surveys of the living and working conditions of the average rank-and-file worker in the United States. The study of these events is accomplished at the least cost, in most instances, by selecting a sample of the cases to be looked at. For most of the post-war years, the Bureau has relied on magnetic tapes as the medium to record and store the information on the nearly five million establishments that constitute the universe of industrial, commercial, government and non-profit establishments in the United States.

Several years ago the Bureau undertook a project to improve its ability to manage this huge file of establishment based information. The work had its roots in a comprehensive systems redesign programme conducted by the Bureau during the mid-1970s. At that time, several dozen of the computer systems that process price, wage, employment and similar survey data, were reworked to take advantage of new technology.

---

*Bureau of Labor Statistics, U.S. Department of Labor

Historically, a registry or universe file of United States establishments was assembled once a year, primarily from the administrative records of the 50 states. The records are created as a consequence of an Unemployment Insurance Programme. Although supported by federal funds, the unemployment system is administered by state agencies and most establishments are required by law to report to their state authorities. As a result, about 80 reels of tape containing name, address and employment characteristics information for about four million establishments covered by the Programme were the primary source for selecting sample cases for participation in BLS surveys. These 80 tapes were replaced entirely each year by more current copies from the 50 states as the method of updating the file.

In this connexion, an establishment is generally defined as a single physical location where workers engage in one, or predominantly one type of activity.

While the majority of establishment information is obtained from state unemployment registers, lists of establishments that are not included are obtained to supplement the BLS data base. Such cases include governmental enterprises and offices, non-profit institutions, hospitals, and so forth.

B. Deficiencies of the old approach

A review of this system pointed out several serious shortcomings. For many nation-wide surveys, all 80 tape reels of the data base had to be searched.

Maintenance of the tape data base was impossible. In order to make corrections to any establishment entry, an entire tape was passed, the individual record located, corrected, and the entire tape copied. Because the data base had a life of one year, and the correction process was costly and cumbersome, few if any corrections were made. To overcome the operational problems caused by this annual replacement of the file, an approach was needed that would permit correction of data and retention of the corrected data for subsequent years.

Another area for improvement involved cost. The computer cost for selecting samples was usually insensitive to the number of eligible candidates. Another goal, therefore, was to make the cost of picking sample cases roughly proportionate to the number of eligible establishments. That is, to somehow identify and partition that portion of the universe from which cases would be drawn.

C. Constraints

The constraints facing systems development in general can be categorized as resources (staff, time, budget) and operating environment (hardware, software, standards, philosophical approach) and, of course, the functional requirements that must be met to do the job. It is of interest to note that both the approach and the requirements exhibited remarkable stability during the development life cycle.

The early replacement of an IBM 7074 computer made possible an interim conversion of the old tape-oriented system to an IBM 360 machine. This was a relatively inexpensive measure and served as a stopgap. But it did nothing to enhance functionality. On the positive side, the time constraint for the present project was diminished. The project proceeded at a pace determined by resource availability and the scope of essential requirements.

During the three year development period, the hardware environment improved from a relatively slow 360/65 with little direct access storage available to users, to an IBM 370/163 multiprocessor facility and, more recently, an IBM 3033.

Consistent with the Bureau's approach to computing which favours generalized software, the goal of the project was to produce a generalized registry system. The TOTAL data base management system, purchased from a company called CINCOM, had been employed successfully as a central feature in the redesign of about 16 of the Bureau's systems. It became a prime candidate for use in this project. The tools and techniques used in the analysis, design and implementation of the system, which came to be known as the Universe Maintenance System (UMS), included structured analysis and design, HIPO, and structured PL/1 code.

Two cost objectives influenced the design of the UMS. The first, already referred to, was to make survey sample selection cost proportionate to size. The second placed an upper limit on the total cost to update and maintain the data base. These were two new functions. In addition, there was the need to partition the full file into sub-universes for sample selections. The later function was not new.

D. Overview of the UMS

Figure XXVII shows an overview of the UMS. It is a repository, that is, a data base of establishment information and a set of tools to update, correct and maintain, and extract establishment information to support Bureau survey needs. The three basic functions of the UMS are: (a) update, to insert annually establishment information from state-supplied unemployment insurance files and other primary establishment data sources; (b) maintenance, to improve establishment information based on the findings of surveys that take place during the year between updates; and (c) selection, to extract establishment information for one or a group of surveys.

The update function has been used to store the first set of 80 reels of establishment information supplied by the 50 states. As these tapes are processed each year to update the data base, the establishment records are matched with those already in the data base. Establishments which no longer exist will be removed, and those which were created during the year will be added. Data from other sources will also be processed through the UMS update function in a similar fashion.

Figure XXVIII depicts the update processing flow. Update source data are converted to a standard format, certain fields are encoded for storage efficiency, and the file is sorted to improve processing efficiency. Maintenance changes that have accumulated are introduced into the data base from the deferred maintenance file as the first stage of the update process. Controls are provided to assure that apparent establishment births and deaths, produced by non-matches, are legitimate.

The maintenance function improves and enhances establishment information in the data base. In general, new or enhanced establishment information is obtained during the survey process when the respondent is approached for data. This information might consist of a better or preferred address (multiple addresses are permitted), a different industrial classification or employment size, or might consist of an indicator to show that an establishment participated in a particular survey.

In any event, the maintenance function provides the capability for ensuring that the data base contains the most up-to-date information on establishments. A corollary is that once entered, this information is available, should the establishment subsequently appear in another survey universe. Provision has been made to retain information obtained through the survey process when the full

D.B. Gottlieb

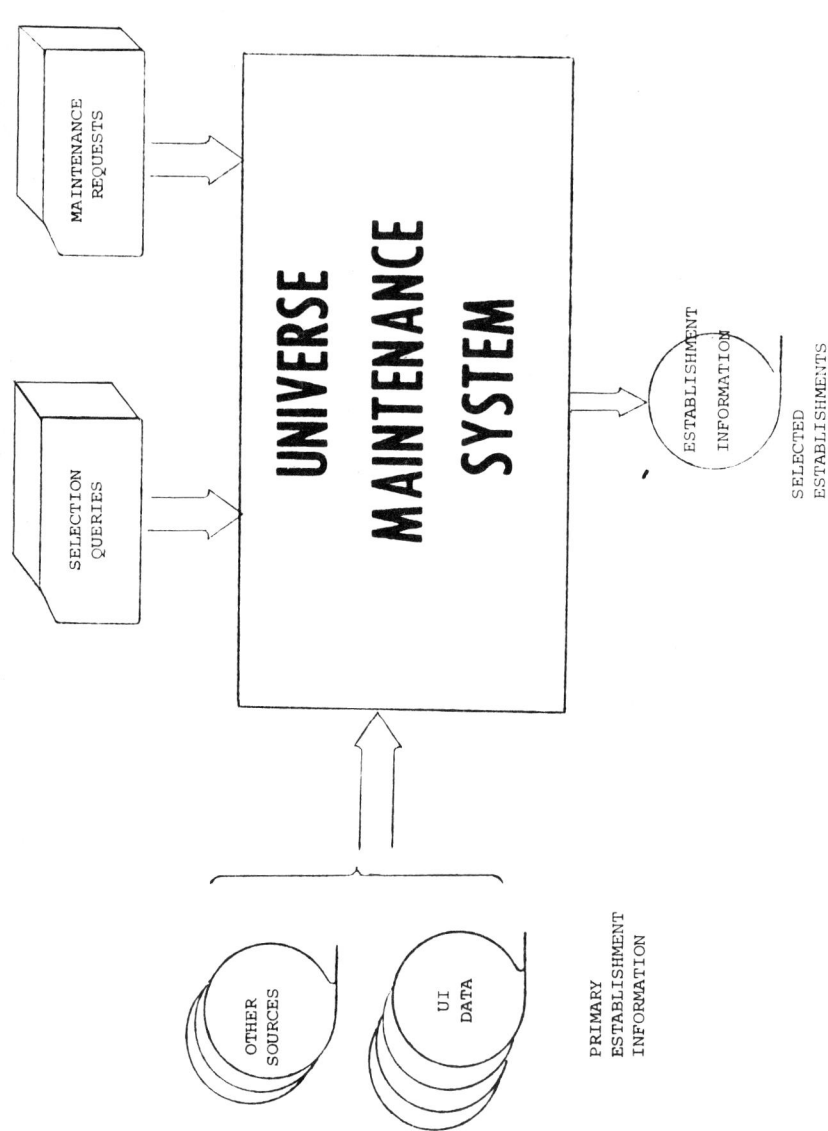

Figure XXVII.

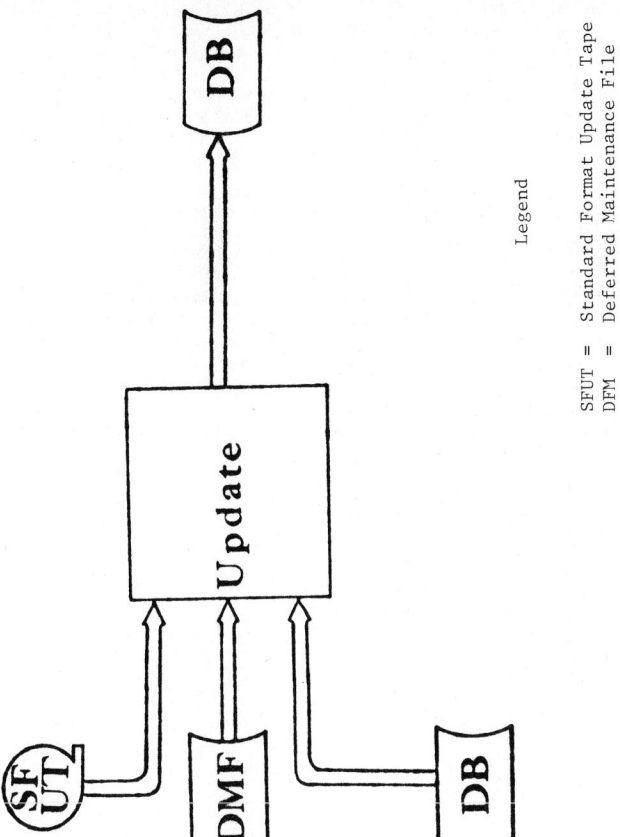

Legend

SFUT = Standard Format Update Tape
DFM = Deferred Maintenance File
DB   = Database

Figure XXVIII. Update flow

file is updated with the tapes from 50 states.

Through maintenance, any information about an establishment may be
expanded, changed, added or deleted from the data base. The maintenance process
may be initiated upon demand – a likely occurance if mass changes were desired –
or may be deferred. The deferred mode of maintenance, the normal process,
screens and holds information until another system function is performed, thus
minimizing operating costs. In either mode the effective result is the same.
Maintenance is always done prior to updating or extracting information.

The flow of maintenance processing is illustrated in figure XXIX. The
general categories of maintenance are: adding or deleting establishments;
changing establishment characteristic information; or adding or deleting
establishment name and address. The first two categories would usually occur
after the manual resolution of exceptions flagged during the update process.
Otherwise, maintenance information would be generated as a by-product of the
survey operations process. At the users option, maintenance information is fed
directly into the data base or held for later processing.

A third UMS function is selecting, the primary process used to extract
establishment information from the data base. With a defined set of
establishment characteristics (geographic, industry, size, ownership, etc.) the
selection function will partition a portion of the data base including the
detailed information for establishments which satisfy the selection criteria.
This portion is then extracted for subsequent use.

The selection process consists of three subfunctions shown in figure XXX:
(a) selection, where criteria are defined and information about the
characteristics of establishments is extracted for the defined subuniverse;
(b) sampling, where statistical criteria are applied to the extracted
establishments to produce a survey sample; and (c) name/address resolution,
where the name and address information is associated with the final set of
selected establishments. Sampling is actually done outside of the basic UMS
and, to increase efficiency, name and address are held in a separate space in
the data base where they are called upon only when needed.

As with update, the first step of selection processing consists of the
entry of maintenance changes into the data base, if these had been deferred.
The complete data base or a subuniverse generated by a previous selection is
the target for a selection query. The query, consisting of parameters used to
select a subset of establishments, is constructed by the user and may be stored
for future modification and use. The selected partition is then made
available to the sampling programs outside of the UMS. The final stage of
selection is the retrieval and association of name and address information for
those establishments that have been designated survey candidates. The
reassembled information for the survey sample is contained in the
Establishment Specific Information File.

While not attempting to elaborate in great detail, several features of
selection are worthy of mention. The design criterion of cost proportionate
to the number of establishments has been achieved through design of the data
base and the selection process. By storing name and address information apart
from establishment characteristics information, space saving and processing
efficiencies have been accomplished. Name and address undergo compression
techniques before storage and are retrieved and expanded only when needed.
A free-form English query language has been provided as the user interface
to the selection process. Through the query language the user selects options,
specifies input files (the data base or a previously extracted subset),
specifies up to twenty sets of selection criteria consisting of geographic
areas, industries, sizes, sources, and owners, and may optionally specify a

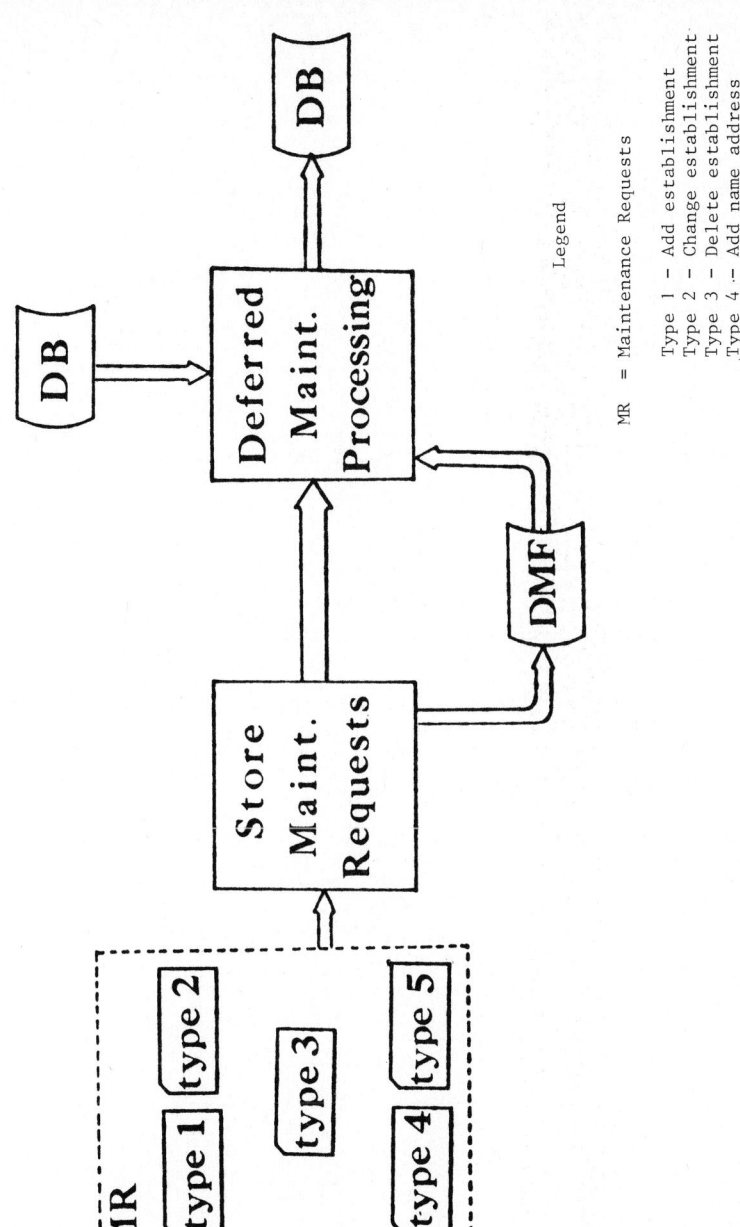

Legend

MR = Maintenance Requests

    Type 1 – Add establishment
    Type 2 – Change establishment
    Type 3 – Delete establishment
    Type 4 – Add name address
    Type 5 – Delete name address
DMF = Deferred Maintenance File
DB = Database

Figure XXIX. Maintenance flow

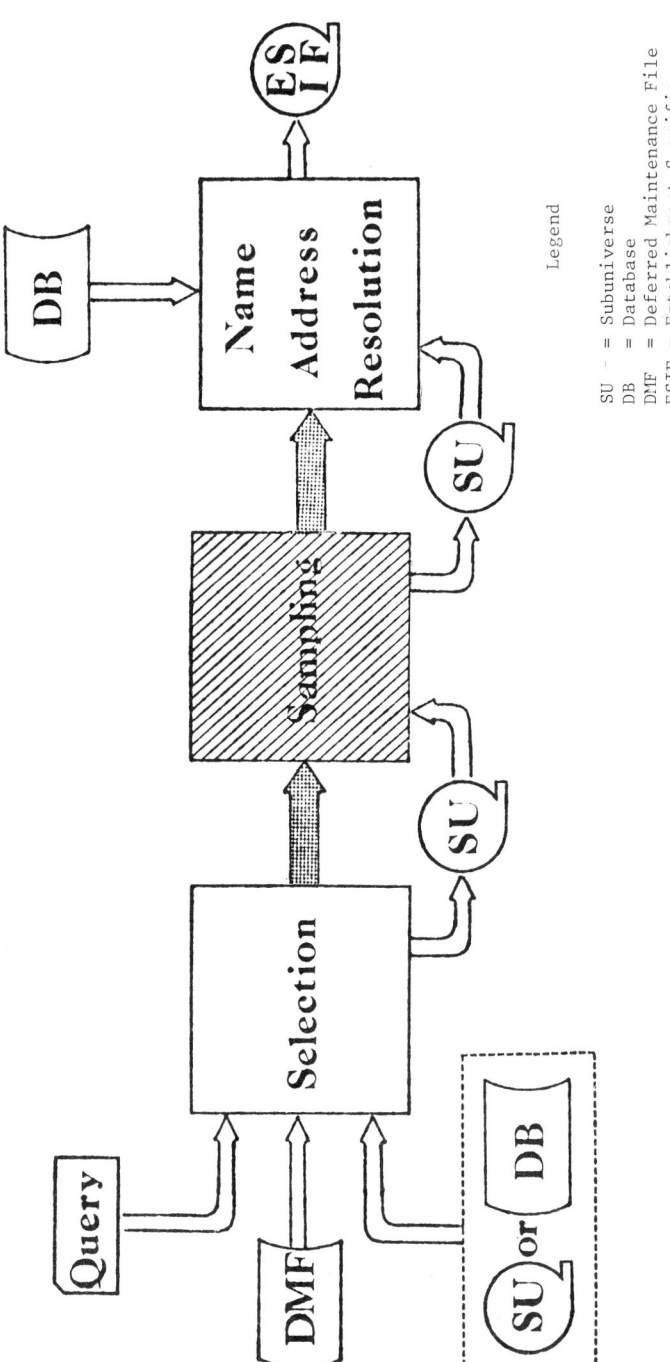

Figure XXX. Selection flow

sort sequence of the extracted subuniverse file.

E. The UMS data base

The most challenging problem encountered in the project was the design
of the data base. It was necessary to provide economical storage and access for
a volatile file containing about five million entries. It was obvious that
magnetic tape, while economical for storage, would permit neither the required
maintenance nor efficient access to varying cross-sections of the file.

Given the Bureau's commitment to data base technology coupled with the
availability of the TOTAL data base management system, the decision was made to
use that tool to solve the problem. This was not an easy process but, in the
end, a fortunate marriage had occurred.

The data base structure that emerged permits updating to occur in the
same way the incoming data are provided, that is, according to state. It also
divides establishments according to the number of employees, which is related
to the likelihood of their appearing in a subuniverse, and separates name and
address information from characteristics information. The name and address
(up to nine names and addresses are permitted per establishment) are compressed
by a process that removes blanks, changes various notations to standard
abbreviations, and, if necessary, performs a bit conversion and, finally,
truncation. Physical space requirements, permitting reasonable growth, cause
the data base to reside on eleven disk packs, each able to contain at least
100 million characters.

Benchmarking was used well into the project to assess the reasonableness of
the design. Preliminary cost projections indicated a serious problem with the
approach which, if not resolved, would have made the UMS prohibitively costly
to operate. With the use of program analyzers such as STROBE, the difficulties
were pinpointed and resolved. The initial loading of the new data base has
been accomplished at a cost of about $US 6,000, compared to an estimate of
$US 400,000 on the first approach. The reduction was made in successive stages,
numbering perhaps a half dozen, before we were satisfied. A worst case cost of
less than $US 3,000 is estimated for extraction of the entire file. The
system is now undergoing operational validation.

F. Conclusion

Looking forward, the Bureau is preparing to make operational a capability
for a centralized establishment registry that will make possible the
incorporation of Standard Industrial Classification and address changes, permit
multiple addresses, (for example, for mail, personal visit, other contacts),
establish relationships between parent and subordinate establishments, and
record survey participation. It is anticipated that over time, operation of
the new system will reduce duplicative efforts involving rediscovery of the
correct information on a survey by survey basis, will likely minimize the need
for redundant files at various operating levels, and may provide some
assistance in maintaining respondent co-operation and goodwill.

INFORMATION SYSTEMS IN PUBLIC ADMINISTRATION
D. Eade, J. Hodgson (editors)
North-Holland Publishing Company
© *DFD, 1981*

LABSTAT:
A DATA BASE AND INFORMATION SYSTEM FOR NATIONAL STATISTICS

Rudolph C. Mendelssohn*

A. Background

In a typical month, the Bureau of Labour Statistics (BLS) issues about 16 press releases. They give basic economic news to the Nation on employment and unemployment, consumer and producer prices, employment cost, and productivity. In addition, the Bureau publishes a wide range of other Statistical information on current national issues. Over the last year, BLS published over 1,600 pages of statistics and analysis in news releases alone.

These data must be made readily and promptly available by the fastest and most accessible means. The notion is not accepted that the job ends once a popular current figure has been compiled, a press release issued, or a journal issued to our readers. The data must be managed, once they are compiled, so that they remain a viable historical record of events that have touched and shaped the economic life of the rank-and-file worker.

It is fair to say that the United States has been a leader among Nations in collecting and disseminating statistics, based on the speed, range, and volume of data collected about current affairs. But the way in which data have been held, once collected and disseminated, has been less admirable - not enough thought was given to the preservation, storage, and recovery of the masses of numerical information compiled by the Federal Government about the social and economic life of its citizens, and that of its business and commercial enterprises.

This situation dates back at least to the 1950s when the electronic computer was put to work to compile statistics. At that time, the production of Federal statistics began to increase markedly. By the mid-1960s, figures were gathering in every corner of the Federal establishment and they had clearly become unmanageable. It was evident to those in the Federal statistical system at that time that good housekeeping practices had to be set up.

Staff responsible for Federal statistical policy in the Office of the President sought guidance and help. The Social Science Research Council, a private group, had already proposed that a Federal centre be set up to house and give access to the nation's stock of statistics. Edgar Dunn of Resources for the Future, a private agency, was asked to review the proposal. The BLS

---

* Bureau of Labor Statistics, U.S. Department of Labor

having already constructed an information system to store and retrieve the masses of data that it compiled, was asked to assist by taking an inventory of the stock of statistics held by Federal agencies. The Dunn report, issued in December 1965, recommended that the Federal Government support a unified computer-based facility, founded on orderly housekeeping practices, for the storage and retrieval of statistics. [1]

Although Federal statisticians had long been zealots in the protection of confidential data, the notion of a unified data bank triggered grave public concern about the invasion of privacy. The idea was popularly seen as a Federal intelligence system with a dossier on each citizen. As a result, it provoked close scrutiny by Congress.

The popular fears raised by the proposal were not without grounds. The inventory of Federal holdings which the BLS prepared for the Dunn report showed over 20,000 reels of magnetic tape available at that time. Almost half of these held data about individuals. Over 2,000 reels were Social Security files with information about most of the United States population. Together with 5,000 Internal Revenue Service tapes with personal tax records and 1,500 Census reels also holding data about persons, these files were seen as tools to create dossiers. In testimony before Congress, computer scientists spoke on the jeopardy to personal privacy if computers were used to keep track of everyone. [2]

The deep public reaction prompted the Government to abort the move to set up a National Data Centre. But the baby was thrown out with the bath. Although no one intended to keep the public away from data that was public, efforts to make them readily accessible through computers ceased. The data thus submerged included an ample supply of printed information and a larger volume of public statistics too massive to publish. [3], [4]

Today, despite revolutionary advances in the use of computers elsewhere in the Federal Government and in the private sector, easy access to most public data using modern technology is still not possible - they remain widely scattered among a dozen or more Federal statistical agencies. In some cases they are offered on reels of tape or even punched cards, but each agency has its own standards and techniques for sharing data.

The BLS approach to public access

During the 1970s, efforts to install good housekeeping practices for data storage and retrieval continued at BLS as an integral part of a massive programme to upgrade the Bureau's approach to the use of computers. The effort was prompted by a Department of Labor switch to large-scale machines in the early 1970s. The BLS had been using a second-generation IBM 7074 computer during the decade beginning in the early 1960s. Rather than simply transfer

---

[1] Edgar S. Dunn, Jr., "A review of proposals for a national data center", _Statistical Evaluation Report No. 6_, December 1965 (Washington, Office of the President).

[2] Carl Kaysen, "Data banks and dossiers". _The Public Interest_, No. 7 (Spring 1967), pp. 52-60.

[3] Joseph W. Duncan and William Shelton, _Revolution in U.S. Federal Statistics, 1926-76_, (Washington, D.C., Government Printing Office, 1978).

[4] E. Glaser, D. Rosenblatt and M.R. Wood "Design of a federal statistical data center", _The American Statistician_, vol. 21 (February 1967), pp. 12-20.

out-dated production systems, part and parcel, to the new large-scale third-generation IBM computers, a longer, perhaps more costly, but in the end more efficient and productive approach, was decided upon.

A six-year plan was developed. [5/] In it, each of about twenty computer systems that manufacture the BLS statistical products, such as the Consumer Price Index, the Employment and Earnings data, and our wage data, was completely reworked. This approach allowed BLS to take advantage of the advanced capabilities of the much more powerful hardware. Equally important, the Bureau's computer scientists made a special effort to apply the most advanced and sophisticated software techniques available. Underlying the sweeping redesign plan that emerged, there was a central theme: the systems that produce the Bureau's ongoing, recurring monthly statistical products must be rebuilt so that their statistical products fall into a general data pool, accessible to all according to rules for authorized access.

By early 1977, transfer of work to the larger machines was nearly complete. In March 1977, the first steps were taken to pull the production systems together so that the fundamental principle by which they were designed would automatically lead to the formation of the common data pool. In addition, new tools that would allow our economists, demographers, statisticians, and other social scientists to manipulate and analyze the data were moved into position. By October 1977, the machinery binding the production systems, the data base, and the user tools was in place. At that time, direct on-line access through computer terminals to the new combined data base and information system was given to Bureau staff, including those in the eight regional offices across the country. This comprehensive system was named LABSTAT (for LABor STATistics).

B.   Judging a social science information system

What are the requirements for an information system for economists, survey statisticians, demographers, and other social scientists? Before describing LABSTAT in detail, some criteria should be set forth by which successes and failures can be judged. The following are paramount:

(a) The data to be retrieved, processed and displayed must be an organized store for ready availability;

(b) The data must be well described with regard to such matters as sample coverage, definitional concepts and sampling error;

(c) There should be conditions which insure that the files are kept current as new data are generated and corrections to stored data are indicated;

(d) The system must be placed in the hands of users and minimize the time between search and retrieval.

5/   Rudolph C. Mendelssohn, "Data processing at BLS", Report No. 471 (1976), (United States Department of Labor, Bureau of Labor Statistics).

How does the BLS LABSTAT system stand up to these criteria?

C. Data availability

In judging the response to the first criteria namely, data availability - one finds a mixed bag. Some things have been done well, others poorly.

The product of the surveys is mostly time series. They include important measures of the nation's economic well-being, such as the Consumer Price Index, the Producer Price Index, and the unemployment figures. There are about 144,000 series comprising more than 15 million observations of economic events. Most of the series are monthly data and are for the post-Second World War years; some, however, go back to the First World War. All of these data are "public".

The principal time-series files and their numbers are as follows:

Labour force	33,000
Nationwide data on industry employment, hours, and earnings	3,500
State and area industry employment, hours, and earnings	20,700
Industry labour turnover	1,250
Consumer Price Index	8,600
Producer Price Index	4,100
Industry-sector price index	900
Industry employment and wages covered by unemployment insurance laws	42,500
Unemployment and labour force State and Area	27,300
Imports	700
Miscellaneous	2,200
Total	144,750

Thus, the record for making a large quantity of macro time-series data available is good.

Cross-sectional data that is, information referring only to one time period, are also compiled by BLS. The scope of cross-sectional files is less easily measured. One way might be to count the number of cells; for example, there are nearly a million in a file that shows number and per cent of employees by industry and occupation for 1970 and 1974. Several Leontief-type input/output matrices of the United States economy are stored, each holding comparable numbers of data items.

In contrast to the record for time series, the record for making cross-sectional data available through LABSTAT is poor. Satisfactory solutions to this difficult and challenging task have not yet been found and one continues to rely on past approaches.

D. Data and file descriptions

The BLS, through its publications, provides a wide range of descriptive information (meta data) about the characteristics of its data files. Meta data, such as geographic, industrial, and occupation coverage are published in Bureau journals along with comprehensive definitions of specific variables and information on sampling error. However, little meta data is available in machine-readable form. This hampers analysts. Their work would be substantially enhanced if machine-readable catalogues were available to assist them.

For example, the only machine-readable meta data connected with LABSTAT is a directory listing each of the 144,000 time series by name and code. Locating the exact names and codes used by the system means laborious search through computer printout. Plans for computer-aided search of this meta data are being developed. The immediate goal is to allow the users to browse through an index of attributes, aided by the system, to narrow their focus and thereby arrive at a better understanding of analytical needs. Another step is to provide English synonyms for names and codes so that the system can accept less than exact description and prompt the user for more information when the synonyms fail. Ultimately, textual definitions and allied information, such as sampling error, would be included to augment computer assistance for the user. 6/

E. Keeping LABSTAT data current and correct

How is such a huge collection of key statistics kept in order? It was found that the best way was to have the data pool involved in current affairs. Here is the broad sequence of events that lead to a current monthly figure for any one of the Bureau's major products.

Over a quarter of a million reports come to BLS each month from scientifically selected samples of factories, offices, shops, governmental agencies, and similar establishments (as well as households) throughout the country. Separate computer systems for each statistical survey shape these reports into summary (macro) data. The resulting data on current employment and unemployment, hours and earnings and consumer prices, for example, are then poured into LABSTAT as the last step in the production process. Corrections and modifications to earlier figures are made at the same time. Current and selected data about the past are then retrieved by prepacked programs to form tables for reproduction in press releases and various Bureau periodicals and bulletins. These tables typically include the two preceding months and previous year, as well as current figures.

Major Bureau book publications that regularly print all of the assembled series for a subject area, such as employment, hours, and earnings, rely heavily on the accuracy of the LABSTAT pool. Thus, the interaction between current

---

6/ I.P. Fellegi, "A functional analysis of an ideal statistical system", Statistical Services in Ten Years Time, a report of a Seminar of the Chief Statisticians, Conference of European Statisticians, Economic Commission for Europe, (Washington, D.C., March 1977).

production and the files of· historical data in LABSTAT offers a direct
connexion between production and publication, without which the data base
would not be properly maintained and the files of historical data would
deteriorate.

F. The system as a common research tool

The data base is used as a tool for economic research and statistical
analysis in the following way. Most Bureau data processing is done on
computers belonging to the National Institutes of Health (NIH). 7/
Bureau staff communicate with the NIH computers through an array of keyboard
terminals. Most terminals give hard copy, but one in four display messages and
results on CRT-type terminals. There are about 200 of these slow-speed
terminals, strategically placed about the BLS headquarters building, and
available to about 800 users, some of whom have exclusive use of their
equipment for ease of access while others share in pooled arrangements.

To augment the slow keyboard terminals, six remote job entry terminals
handle large-volume input and output tasks. Magnetic tape and punched cards
provide mass input, and fast 1,100 line-per-minute printers generate listings
and display results.

The BLS computer workload makes heavy use of immediately available on-line
storage during 1,500 low-speed terminal sessions every day, about 15 sessions
averaging almost four hours per day for each of the BLS terminals. These
figures reflect a typical research environment, one which has readily accessible
data from on-line storage for rapid assessment with prompt return of results
through conveniently available terminals.

G. Data accessibility

Central to making BLS data accessible is a data base management system to
process all of the Bureau's data elements (figure XXXI). The data base
manager called TOTAL was selected, rather than working out the Bureau's own.
This software allows direct access for production and also allows researchers
to get to the data they want.

To aid in understanding the selection of the TOTAL data base manager, it
may be helpful to know something of the background against which the choice was
made.

An efficient method of storing and subsequently retrieving parts or all of
144,000 time series in an on-line environment was needed. Through ten-year's
experience with a second-generation, tape-oriented information system it was
found that there were benefits in storing time series data in a standard format.
The systems in existence at that time (the early seventies) were evaluated:
TOTAL, and the IBM Information Management System (IMS). During the evaluation
it was found that TOTAL would perform as advertised. Specifically, the use of

---

7/   Rudolph C. Mendelssohn and Henry J. Juenemann, "An innovation for
federal agencies: computer sharing", Government Data Systems, vol. 6, No. 5
(September-October 1977), pp. 14-19.

TOTAL (a) smoothed the updating workload by making it cost-effective to run in
a "semi-continuous" rather than batch mode; (b) offered the opportunity of
revising data records without affecting existing programs which processed those
data; (c) promoted more comprehensive documentation of data elements; and
(d) would facilitate the use of generalized systems. Also, it was discovered
that TOTAL was relatively easy to use.

Evaluation of IMS revealed that it was a much more powerful tool than
needed and, therefore, for the Bureau's purposes, operated slowly and required
greater amounts of main memory. It was also found that a substantial commitment
of systems programming resources would be required to install and maintain
the system. In comparison with TOTAL, IMS was judged to be more difficult for
the systems staff to use for the strictly statistical purposes in mind.

The prime uses of the data base manager approach is in the storage of
summary time series. A two-level standard format has been developed in which
the master or highest level record contains the series key or descriptor and
related information, such as beginning and end dates, continuity breaks, and
date of last update. The subordinate or lower-level record contains data for
12 months and an annual average, status codes describing such attributes as
availability and footnoting, and codes describing rounding and decimal
configurations.

H. Data base codebook and dictionary: data documentation

Personnel and computers have common problems when processing data: all
need to know what is available, which data are to be processed, where they are
located, and how to get them. Whether one is a computer programmer or a
research analyst, the variables intended for use must be identified and somehow
a path mapped to locations in various storage media where the data are stored
to locate data that the programs must extract and process.

The BLS goal is to provide a comprehensive Codebook and a Dictionary, which
personnel and machine can read for this information. For researchers, there is
a Dictionary which names what is in the data base. For the programmer, there is
a Codebook with technical data needed for describing the data formats and
locations. Together, the Codebook and Dictionary form a data documentation
system (figure XXXI).

Enhancement of the Dictionary has superseded work on the Codebook for
several reasons. Dictionaries are most helpful when there are numerous
inquiries by persons unfamiliar with the data base. This is not the case in
BLS where the same people tend to manage and analyze data bases over a long
period of time. In addition, much of the information that would be stored in
a Dictionary is already available, although published in fragmented sources.
For most surveys, there exist system and program documentation, a separate
statement of the statistical methods used, and a separate document giving lists
of data codes and titles.

Work on the Codebook began some years ago, at the same time that work on
one of the generalized systems which required a Codebook. The Codebook contains
for each data element its name, length, and position occupied in the record.
For elements which are viewed as controlling processing (for example, industry),
a Codebook entry describes permissible values and titles associated with each.
For elements which are viewed as contributing to computations or display, the
format of each is described.

Unlike other codebook applications, the BLS Codebook does not provide data
definitions for application programs. Instead, it is intended for use by the
generalized systems which BLS is developing. Thus, the Codebook is used each

time a researcher or other user employs a generalized system (for example, cross-tabulation) as a substitute for an application program. It is hoped that in the long run some application programs might find a way to tap the Codebook to get their data definitions.

Preparation of the Codebooks is not restricted to one unit in BLS. Thus, Codebooks have been prepared by researchers, by staff responsible for creating and maintaining data files, and by the systems staff which designed the Codebook processor. Once created, however, Codebooks are maintained in object form and automatically updated by the Codebook processor based on changes submitted by users.

I. The second ring: levels of accessibility security

The process of compiling summary statistics for publication generates, along with this public information, data that must be withheld and yet be accessible to authorized users within the Bureau. To insure security the BLS data base has been surrounded with a ring of protective software which recognizes three types of accessibility to the core (figure XXXI): The first is to data that are published. These are available to anyone in BLS and the public. The second allows for access by BLS employees to data that are not published. They include summary figures that contribute to published information but are not statistically reliable on their own account. Usually, these figures are accessible only to the professional staff that is responsible for the figures. A third level of accessibility is offered to analysts who wish to keep their tentative summary results private during the time of their research.

J. The third ring: modular, general-purpose statistical processing programs

In progressing to advanced computers some years ago, it was found that common functions were shared among many Bureau survey systems and that it was possible to identify these rather easily. Identification of like functions resulted in generalized software to replace ad hoc programming. The third ring holds general-purpose programs that are tailored to the unique needs of large-scale, statistical data processing. As a result, users can retrieve and process time-series data stored in LABSTAT by a variety of computer systems which provide generalized tabulation and statistical analysis facilities.

K. Retrieval tools

Two retrieval methods are available. One, known as Macro Data Language (MDL), is intended for use primarily at the low-speed, keyboard terminals. It interacts in a conversational mode with the on-line LABSTAT data. The MDL offers the ability to retrieve and display data in tabular form and perform simple statistical operations, such as moving averages and indexes.

The second LABSTAT retrieval method, known as Tailored Retrieval and Information Management (TRIM), offers the ability to retrieve volume data in batch mode and prepare it for input to systems and programs which perform complex statistical operations. Using TRIM, one is able to format input for a wide range of systems and programs, such as regression analysis, seasonal adjustment, and comprehensive statistical operations, including the users own tailored programs.

L. Table Producing Language

LABSTAT's powerful table generating facility, Table Producing Language
(TPL), is a computer system designed to select, restructure, and display data. [8]
The system was designed primarily to reduce the need for special computer
programs that produce cross tabulations of micro data. However, TPL can be used
to prepare a wide range of tables from LABSTAT macro data.

Using the TPL language, one is able to control table stubs and columns,
contents, order, titles, spacing and format. TPL also offers the ability to
calculate and display the results of simple computations, such as sums, ratios
and over-the-month changes. An adjunct, called Print Control Language (PCL),
allows users to format tables according to Bureau publication standards and
drive electronic photo-composers so that printed tables appear to be typeset
without the cost of that approach.

M. Charting

The Bureau has acquired a generalized time-series charting system called
DISSPLA. Use of the system requires some programming knowledge. To simplify
use, it has been embedded in a very high-level language in the same way that
cross-tabulation routines are at the core of the TPL. The enhanced system
allows users to produce time-series charts, editorially suitable for publication.

A wide choice of features is available. Users can produce charts with
time axes of varying physical and time period lengths. The periods may be
annual, semi-annual, quarterly, monthly, or weekly. Solid, dashed, or dotted
vertical and horizontal grid lines may be shown. Up to eight vertical axes
may be shown with automatic generation of length and location when desired.
However, explicit length and location are permissible. For each vertical axis,
up to eight data lines are allowed, as well as a variety of line types, such
as dashed, dotted and dot-dash.

Alphabetic information may be placed freely at various locations. There
may be titles and headnotes at the top; interior data line labels, at tic
marks, and alphabetic information as footnotes and source notes at the bottom.
Users can specify the character size of any line, as well as choose between
bold or light font. Multiple charts may be run at one time. Special
features such as automatic shading to indicate the span of business cycles
between peak and trough are available.

These and many other choices are designed to permit the user to have
control over the appearance of the chart so that it can be photographed for
photo-offset printing without further editing.

---

[8] Rudolph C. Mendelssohn, "Development and uses of table producing
language", Report No. 515 (1978), (United States Department of Labor, Bureau
of Labor Statistics).

N.   Statistical and econometric routines

Several multipurpose statistical analysis systems may be used in conjunction with LABSTAT. Among these are the Statistical Analysis System (SAS) and the Statistical Package for the Social Sciences (SPSS). They are typical of those found in universities and research environments and include: (a) a broad library of statistical operations; (b) a user-oriented language not heavily encumbered by computer science practices or terminology; and (c) the ability to reformat and restructure data files. Typically, these systems' statistical libraries include procedures for the following operations: analysis of variance, correlation and regression analysis, and factor and scale analysis. Several single-purpose statistical programs are available. Included among these programs are routines for seasonal adjustment of time series, and regression analysis.

Each of the foregoing systems and programs for charting, tabulation and analysis has its own special retrieval and transfer requirements for the arrangement of data that it will accept. In the past, the user employed TRIM to retrieve and format data for electronic transfer. However, most of these systems are now bound directly to the data base in a way that eliminates the extra TRIM step. Users need not be concerned with retrieval or formatting as the system does this work automatically.

O.   Analytical use

A recent project shows how LABSTAT may be used. The Bureau was called upon to provide an analysis of steel price movements in support of policy recommendations to the President of the United States. A simple model covering 28 years of annual data was constructed for steel price changes using wholesale price indexes for coal, iron ore, scrap iron and steel, and steel mill products. Two series from the employment statistics program - the number of steel workers and the average hours they worked each week - were also used. Total man-hours worked by all steel workers combined were computed by multiplying employment by average weekly hours to serve as a proxy for level of production. Then, over-the-year changes were computed for the proxy and the wholesale price indexes. Finally, the changes covering yearly data for the past 28 years were put through one of the regression analysis programs.

The entire process of model building, data retrieval, and computation was complete in less than a day. While the model was of necessity somewhat crude, the fortuitous presence of LABSTAT at that particular moment improved the quality of the Bureau's analysis. Bureau economists were able to derive and analyze the historical relationships between input costs and price, and the relationships between price and the level of production.

Regular requirements for erasing distortions due to seasonal change from literally thousands of time series each year are met by recovering the data and processing them through the seasonal-adjustment program attached to the system, and storing the historical seasonally-adjusted data for further use by analysts. Naturally, the seasonal factors developed in this process are used to adjust the current data as they are generated in each succeeding month.

P.   Summary

How did LABSTAT come about? What lies behind the tools that are used to get work done? In effect, BLS systems designers have coupled two maturing computer technologies. The first of these is the idea of exploiting "problem-oriented languages". These are the tools for which the user need only specify "what is to be done" and not "how to do it". In the latter case, users must understand how the computer works so that they can instruct it, step by step, exactly how to solve the problem.

With problem-oriented languages, on the other hand, little or no knowledge of how computers work is required. Users can solve problems in the context of their own sciences rather than having to step into the computer science as well. For example, to a cross-tabulation system that already knows how to construct tables, the user need only describe the variables to be tabulated and the form of the resulting table display. This approach allows Bureau social scientists to use the everyday common BLS nomenclature to describe their work. In short, this approach has reduced a burden, speeded work, and increased the BLS capacity to respond.

The second technology exploited in constructing LABSTAT is that of data base management (DBM). Unlike the problem-oriented tools, the role of the DBM (TOTAL) is entirely unknown to users. It is the heart of the system. Not much is said about it because it supervises, accepts, organizes and delivers data automatically without the user ever being aware of it. TOTAL, and therefore LABSTAT, puts users in immediate touch with their data, as opposed to the time required to search spinning reels of magnetic tape.

Timely and efficient data retrieval are supported by storing and relating data from diverse sources in a uniform way. Retrieval of small pieces of data is possible without the need to look through the whole data base. This approach allows the application to deal only with relevant data, thereby insulating it from the total size of the data base. Thus, the retrieval of 100 time series has the same cost in a data base of 100,000 series as it does in a data base of 1,000 series. The data base manager approach also allows any number of users having any mix of jobs, whether in the batch or conversational mode, to access data without interfering with each other. .

Q.   Conclusion

It seems that more national Governments will soon seek to bring order to the way they stock their statistical data. Canada already has a powerful system called CANSIM, which together with the BLS LABSTAT system may offer some helpful guidelines as well as warnings and danger marks to others who might wish to move in the same direction.

If data are to stay fresh and alive, the system controlling them must play a part in current affairs. It will accept the newest statistic, not to file away but to be used in meeting current needs for tables and analysis for the press and current periodicals. When the system participates in current events in this fashion, there will be institutional pressures to keep its data files current and correct so that an historical perspective is also possible.

Most Governments conduct their statistical affairs, I understand, through a central statistical agency, and for these a single national base may be entirely natural. On the other hand, in countries such as the United States where statistical data gathering is decentralized among a dozen or more agencies, some other pattern may have to be worked out. Perhaps each agency could install a data base system according to central government standards and requirements.

Figure XXXI.

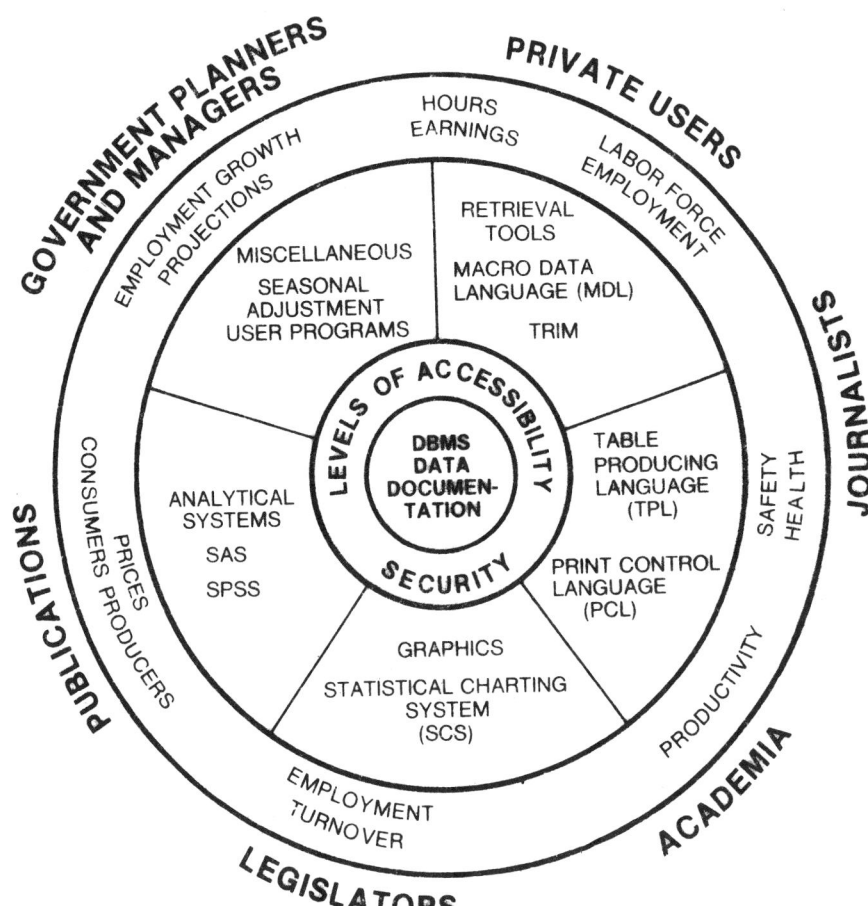

INFORMATION SYSTEMS IN PUBLIC ADMINISTRATION
D. Eade, J. Hodgson (editors)
North-Holland Publishing Company
© *DFD, 1981*

UNE EXPERIENCE DE SYSTEME D'INFORMATION SUR LES ENTREPRISES:
LA MISE EN PLACE DU NOUVEAU PLAN COMPTABLE ET L'EXPLOITATION
DES DECLARATIONS STATISTIQUES ET FISCALES AU CAMEROUN

G. Osbert*

Avant-propos

Cette note est constituée de l'étude d'une expérience concrète à laquelle l'auteur a participé d'avril 1975 à avril 1979 en tant que chef de projet informatique concernant l'exploitation des déclarations statistiques et fiscales à des fins de comptabilité.

Cette étude a été menée à deux niveaux:

(a) Etude descriptive des réalisations effectuées par une équipe constituée de comptables, de statisticiens et d'informaticiens, dans le cadre d'un projet inter-administratif d'exploitation des déclarations d'entreprises.

(b) Etude des potentialités qui étaient celles du projet au départ, notamment en matière de système d'information et en deça desquelles les réalisations effectives se situent très nettement.

Ce deuxième niveau ne consiste pas en une critique du travail effectué, ni encore moins à dégager les responsabilités respectives de ceux qui y ont participé, mais a pour objet d'éclairer cet écart inévitable entre les objectifs souvent théoriques (d'un projet) et les réalisations pratiques inhérentes à toute entreprise humaine.

Ce problème prend une acuité toute particulière dans les pays en développement, caractérisés par un système administratif jeune et ouvert, ce qui favorise naturellement les expériences les plus ambitieuses et entraine inévitablement certaines déconvenues.

L'expérience décrite dans les pages qui suivent est celle du Cameroun et reste indubitablement positive. Il était important, à notre sens, d'en tirer le maximum d'enseignements.

Introduction: Contexte et plan de l'étude

La notion de système d'information inter-administratif sur les entreprises est apparue au Cameroun dès la fin de 1972 à l'occasion de la mise

---

*Institut National de la Statistique et des Etudes Economiques, France

en place du nouveau plan comptable général des entreprises (à l'époque, plan comptable OCAM) et a été concrétisée par l'élaboration de la "Déclaration statistique et fiscale" (DSF), document unique à remplir à la fin de chaque exercice budgétaire par les entreprises industrielles et commerciales opérant sur le territoire camerounais, et conçu pour répondre aux besoins d'information en provenance des entreprises et des différentes administrations du pays.

Notons, en effet, et ceci était clairement explicité par les auteurs du plan OCAM, que l'opération de normalisation des comptabilités revêt un double aspect: d'une part, le nouveau plan comptable constitue un outil de gestion meilleur pour les entreprises, et d'autre part, il est le centre d'un système de traitement de l'information économique et financier sur le secteur moderne de l'économie, destiné à la gestion de l'Etat.

C'est ainsi que parallèlement à l'importante campagne de sensibilisation menée auprès des entreprises afin de promouvoir le nouveau plan comptable, une réflexion a été conduite en collaboration avec les principales administrations concernées (Administration économique, fiscale, institutions financières) afin de concevoir le support de l'information puis son exploitation dans le cadre de ce deuxième aspect.

L'ensemble de ces travaux a débouché sur l'élaboration d'un projet inter-administratif de traitement des DSF que nous décrirons dans la première partie de cette note, après avoir présenté succinctement le contenu et les implications du nouveau plan comptable adopté.

Dans la deuxième partie, nous étudierons les étapes parcourues et les réalisations effectives à ce jour. Comme nous le verrons, elles se situent soit en deçà, soit à côté des objectifs primitivement fixés. Analyser les causes de cet état de fait et dégager les principaux problèmes qui se sont posés lors de la mise en pratique des idées de départ du projet, constituera le contenu de la troisième partie.

Première partie: un projet prometteur

Nous décrirons dans cette partie les deux volets successifs du projet, à savoir:

– d'abord l'implantation chez les entreprises du nouveau plan comptable de l'OCAM, en mettant en valeur le langage commun qu'il permet de créer entre ces dernières et les administrations concernées, notamment l'administration économique;

– ensuite, la collaboration inter-administrative centrée autour de l'élaboration d'un système d'information sur les entreprises.

A. Le nouveau plan comptable: contenu et implications

Que le lecteur se rassure, nous n'entrerons pas ici dans une étude des techniques comptables, mais nous nous bornerons à souligner les aspects originaux qui font du plan comptable OCAM un langage commun entre les entreprises et les administrations à qui elles ont à faire, et grâce auxquelles l'information recueillie est digne d'un traitement élaboré.

En effet, en plus d'une modernisation des pratiques comptables qui s'avéraient plus que nécessaire (le plan comptable en vigueur au Cameroun s'inspirait directement du plan comptable francais de 1957!), le plan comptable OCAM apporte trois perfectionnements majeurs:

- l'utilisation systématique des nomenclatures

- l'analyse de l'exploitation en marges successives

- une nouvelle conception pour la présentation des mouvements patrimoniaux dont nous allons rapidement mesurer les implications en ce qui concerne l'aspect "système d'information" du projet.

1. Utilisation systématique des nomenclatures

(Nomenclature des biens et services, des immobilisations, des opérations financières, des frais de personnel ...), a pour avantage fondamental de permettre la ventilation des postes comptables caractéristiques, dans un détail nettement plus fin que celui de la comptabilité générale, et ce afin de préparer, dès l'organisation comptable, les rubriques standards sur lesquelles l'administration posera ses questions.

On voit donc apparaître la possibilité d'un échange d'informations au niveau le plus fin, mais en plus, et ceci résulte de l'utilisation de la nomenclature des biens et services, on peut déjà pressentir les exploitations futures nécessaires non seulement aux statisticiens mais à l'industrie elle-même dans le cadre par exemple de l'analyse sectorielle de ses inputs et outputs.

2. L'analyse de l'exploitation en marges successives permet, dans le même sens, de créer le cadre d'analyse commun sans lequel la communication n'est pas possible et ce au niveau même de la structure des comptes. C'est ainsi que pour la première fois en comptabilité privée apparaît la notion de valeur ajoutée, si chère aux économistes: le langage commun est créé!

3. La nouvelle présentation des comptes patrimoniaux va également dans le sens d'une conception véritablement économique des flux de patrimoine (distinction des flux internes et externes à l'enterprise) et de plus se rapproche du système utilisé par la comptabilitié publique.

En débouchant naturellement vers la construction du tableau de financement, elle permet le passage continu entre l'analyse du comptable d'entreprise et celle du comptable national dans les comptes d'affectation de capital et financiers.

On mesure par l'étude de ces trois exemples le progrès effectué pour l'échange entre l'administration économique et les entreprises, ainsi que les potentialités de l'information ainsi élaborée.

Il s'agit maintenant de les concrétiser en étudiant le deuxième volet du projet portant sur la collaboration entre les différentes administrations concernées et l'élaboration d'un système général d'information sur les entreprises.

B. Le projet de "Centrale d'information sur les entreprises"

Ce projet comprenait deux étapes que nous décrirons successivement:

1 - : l'unification du système de collecte de l'information sur les entreprises, devant déboucher sur la constitution d'une base de données inter-administratives;

2 - : la définition du système de gestion de cette future base de données. Remarquons qu'au niveau de cette seconde étape, l'option informatique est explicite, ce qui conférait au projet un atout supplémentaire puisqu'il est connu que l'automatisation est le meilleur prétexte à la réorganisation des

circuits.

1. L'unification de la collecte de l'information en provenance des
enterprises suppose un effort à deux niveaux:

a) la création d'un système unique d'immatriculation des entreprises pour
toute l'administration. Au Cameroun, ceci a consisté à créer le SCIFE (Service
Central d'Immatriculation et du Fichier des Entreprises) qui avait pour
objectif d'affecter un numéro d'immatriculation à chaque entreprise et à chacun
de ses établissements, d'établir un répertoire général des entreprises non
forfaitaires et de réaliser le passage entre l'ancienne et la nouvelle
immatriculation.

b) l'établissement d'un document unique de collecte de l'information
issue des entreprises, baptisé "Déclaration Statistique et Fiscale (DSF)" à
remplir par l'entreprise à la fin de chaque exercise fiscal à partir des données
fournies par la comptabilité conformément au cadre défini par le nouveau plan
comptable et à l'aide des différentes nomenclatures présentées plus haut.

Cette information informatisable devait permettre la constitution de la
base des données inter-administratives sur les entreprises.

2. La définition du système de gestion de la base de données

On entend par système de gestion l'ensemble des fichiers ou répertoires
administratifs disponibles ainsi que les programmes de traitement nécessaires
aux différentes exploitations de ces fichiers.

Définir le système de gestion consiste donc à faire l'inventaire de
l'information dont on dispose, parallèlement à l'analyse des résultats demandés
par les différents partenaires du système. Le nombre et la structure des
fichiers, ainsi que leurs critères d'accès d'une part, les traitements ou
chaines de programmes à élaborer d'autre part, découlent de cette double analyse.
La Centrale d'information sur les entreprises prévoyait ainsi deux étapes dans
le traitement des DSF:

a) le traitement commun réalisé au niveau d'un organe de contrôle composé
de comptables, fiscalistes et statisticiens et constitué du contrôle des
déclarations et de l'élaboration de la base de données sur les entreprises
(ensemble de fichiers interconnectés).

b) les traitements spécifiques répondant à chacun des besoins exprimés
au moment de l'analyse: ces traitements se distinguaient suivant deux types:

- Traitements systématiques annuels pour les partenaires privilégiés du
système: administration fiscale, administration économique et entreprises. Il
s'agit dans ce dernier cas de la Centrale des bilans, véritable banque de
données comptables et financières, mises à la disposition des entreprises et de
leurs organismes professionnels. Notons à ce sujet qu'il était important de
prévoir à titre incitatif une contrepartie offerte par l'administration au très
important effort fourni par les entreprises pour la rédaction de leur
déclaration.

- Traitements à la demande pour les partenaires associés au système tel la
Banque Centrale pour laquelle il était prévu l'édition d'un dossier de
financement par entreprise comportant son tableau de financement ainsi que
l'évolution de ses principaux ratios financiers.

Deuxieme partie: Les étapes parcourues et les réalisations

Nous venons de présenter de façon détaillée le contenu du projet au départ. Il s'agit maintenant d'en étudier la mise en oeuvre par un rapide historique mettant en évidence les étapes successivement parcourues puis par l'étude des réalisations effectivement menées à bien.

A. Les étapes parcourues: historique du projet

Janvier 1970: le conseil des chefs d'Etat des pays de l'OCAM adopte à Yaoundé le nouveau plan comptable des entreprises.

Juillet 1972: le nouveau plan comptable est implanté parmi les entreprises industrielles opérant au Cameroun, après un remarquable travail d'animation réalisé par le Secrétariat Permanent du plan comptable dépendant de la Direction de la Statistique.

Juillet 1973: création du SCIFE (Service Central de l'Immatriculation des Entreprises et du Fichier des Entreprises) dépendant de la Direction de la Statistique.

Octobre 1973: élaboration de la première version de la DSF et des nomenclatures permettant aux entreprises assujetties d'y répondre. Cette première version n'est pas destinée à être informatisée.

Octobre 1974: décret rendant obligatoire l'utilisation du nouveau plan comptable à toutes les entreprises non forfaitaires implantées au Cameroun et mise en oeuvre de la version informatisable de la DSF.

Novembre 1974: début des travaux d'informatisation de la DSF dans le cadre de l'élaboration de la Centrale des Bilans.

Juillet 1975: début des travaux informatiques concernant l'exploitation des annexes statistiques à des fins de comptabilité nationale.

Octobre 1975: mise en oeuvre de la 3ème version de la DSF après modification des principales imperfections détectées. Cette version est conçue pour rester intangible jusqu'en 1980.

Juillet 1976: sortie des premiers résultats par la chaine statistique concernant les déclarations des 370 plus grandes entreprises ayant répondu en 1973/74. Elaboration du TES du secteur moderne pour cette année.

Octobre 1976: sortie de la première Centrale des Bilans pour les 750 entreprises ayant répondu pour l'exercice 1973/74.

Novembre 1976: reprise complète des chaines statistiques compte tenu des nouveaux besoins exprimés par la Direction de la Statistique et de la nouvelle forme de la DSF.

Avril 1977: élaboration des comptes provisoires pour 1974/75.

September 1977: élaboration des comptes de secteur pour 1974/75.

Décembre 1977: élaboration des comptes de produits pour 1974/75.

Février 1978: élaboration des comptes provisoires pour 1975/76.

Juin 1978: élaboration des comptes de secteur pour 1975/76; mise en chantier d'une nouvelle chaine pour doubler le volume de ces comptes de secteurs afin de répondre aux besoins du Service des Statistiques Industrielles.

Novembre 1978: sortie des nouveaux comptes de secteurs pour 1975/76.

Décembre 1978: élaboration des comptes provisoires pour 1976/77.

Janvier 1979: Sortie des comptes provisoires pour 1977/78.

Mars 1979: Sortie des comptes de secteurs, des comptes de produits et du TES 1976/77.

Cette énumération un peu fastidieuse a néanmoins le mérite de donner au lecteur attentif la mesure des efforts accomplis et surtout de permettre une comparaison entre les délais de réalisations de chacun des objectifs du projet. Nous reviendrons dans la troisième partie sur l'appréciation de ces performances. Il convient d'abord, afin de donner de ce projet le maximum d'informations, de décrire rapidement le contenu des principales réalisations à ce jour opérationnelles.

B. Les réalisations

1. L'informatisation des Déclarations Statistiques et Fiscales

La DSF sous sa forme actuelle se présente comme un ensemble de 32 feuillets codifiables et est mise chaque année à la disposition des entreprises dans les inspections des impôts.

Elle doit être fournie en trois exemplaires, les deux premiers étant destinés aux besoins spécifiques des services opérationnels (impôts et services régionaux de la Statistique), le troisième étant après un rapide contrôle visuel de sa qualité, centralisé à Yaoundé où il est enregistré à l'atelier de Saisie de la Direction des Impôts puis transmis à la Direction Centrale de l'Informatique pour être traité.

Deux expériences de nature très différente ont été menées à la Direction de l'Informatique en matière d'exploitation automatisée des DSF, un troisième projet concernant l'exploitation fiscale des DSF n'a pu aboutir par manque de moyens et actuellement cette exploitation est effectuée manuellement par les Impôts.

2. Les traitements informatiques

a) La Centrale des Bilans: mise en chantier à la fin de l'année 1974, la chaine "Centrale des Bilans" n'exploite que les six premiers feuillets de la DSF ainsi que les données de référence et de structure fournies par le répertoire des entreprises.

Elle a pour but d'établir d'abord par entreprise, puis par secteur d'activité, quatre principaux tableaux comptables ou financiers:

1. le tableau de financement et des variations de fonds de roulement

2. le tableau des soldes caractéristiques de gestion

3. le tableau des bilans comparés

4. le tableau des ratios de gestion.

Ces quatre résultats à vocation plus comptable qu'économique intéressent surtout le monde industriel et financier auquel il procure un outil de gestion précieux ainsi que la possibilité d'analyse comparative des secteurs entre eux. Sur le plan informatique, cette chaine est opérationnelle depuis Septembre 1976. Cependant le caractère extrêmement strict des contrôles qu'elle implique (ces contrôles sont effectués au franc près et une entreprise ne peut être traitée qu'au moment où toutes les erreurs détectées ont été corrigées) ne va pas sans poser de graves problèmes quant au délai d'élaboration des résultats.

b) L'exploitation statistique à des fins de comptabilité nationale

Les premiers travaux informatiques ont débuté en Juillet 1975 et avaient pour objet le traitement des annexes statistiques de façon à compléter l'exploitation de la Centrale des Bilans par l'établissement des tableaux Emploi-ressource par produit puis d'un TES par branche pour le secteur moderne de l'économie.

A partir de Novembre 1976, les programmes ont été intégralement remaniés pour trois principales raisons:

- le changement de présentation de la DSF intervenu en Juillet 1975 comportait de nombreuses modifications portant sur les annexes statistiques;

- la Direction de la Statistique exprimait le besoin d'avoir des comptes de secteurs plus détaillés que ceux produits par la Centrale des Bilans;

- l'intégration entre les deux chaines de traitement s'avérait impossible compte tenu de la grande disparité tant en ce qui concerne les contrôles effectués que les délais d'élaboration des résultats. La nouvelle conception a consisté à entreprendre le dépouillement statistique de la totalité de la déclaration, et a débouché sur l'élaboration de cinq chaines de traitement:

1. la chaine "fiche synthétique d'entreprise" comme sa dénomination le laisse présager, traite une vingtaine de données par entreprise, reportées manuellement de la DSF sur une fiche spéciale, dont l'exploitation très rapide permet de disposer de données essentielles à la construction des comptes provisoires.

2. la chaine "Contrôle et Edition des DSF"

3. la chaine "Comptes de Secteur"

4. la chaine "Comptes de produits"

5. la chaine "analyse économique" et TES

Ces cinq chaines de traitement sont actuellement utilisées de facon courante par les statisticiens pour l'élaboration des comptes économiques du secteur moderne.

Troisieme partie: Essai d'analyse de l'évolution du projet

Nous ne reviendrons plus ici sur la première partie du projet, de la mise en place du plan comptable jusqu'à l'élaboration de la DSF qui peut être considérée comme une grande réussite, le Cameroun étant à cet égard en avance de plusieurs années sur les autres pays de l'ex-OCAM. Cependant, comme on peut aisément s'en rendre compte en comparant les deux schémas de la page suivante la deuxième partie du projet qui concernait la réalisation d'un système d'informations interadministratif sur les entreprises ne peut pas être considérée comme ayant été pleinement menée à bien.

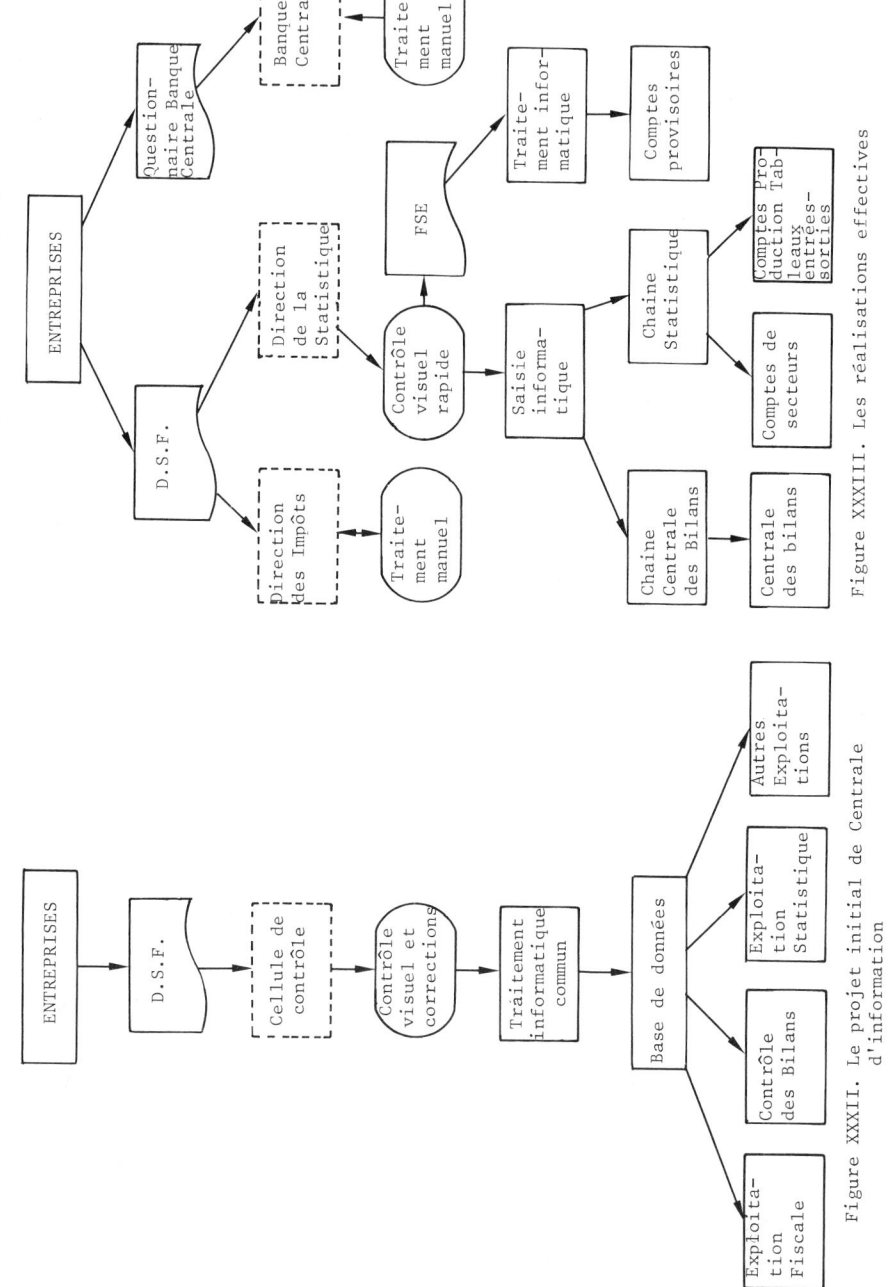

SCHEMA GENERAL DES TRAITEMENTS DES DECLARATIONS STATISTIQUES ET FISCALES (DSF)

Figure XXXIII. Les réalisations effectives

Figure XXXII. Le projet initial de Centrale d'information

Pour parler en terme de système d'information, l'objectif était, du moins dans l'esprit des auteurs du projet, de réaliser un système d'information mixte (administratif et statistique) qui soit un système d'offre (partagé entre plusieurs administrations).

La réalité telle qu'elle se présente aujourd'hui en fait un système presque exclusivement statistique, fonctionellement orienté vers la comptabilité nationale!

Rechercher quelles sont les explications d'une telle évolution est le but de cette troisième partie où nous essaierons d'abord d'envisager les raisons liées aux aspects généraux du projet (esprit, organisation, définition du contenu) pour passer dans un deuxième temps à l'analyse des problèmes plus techniques qui se sont posés lors du passage aux réalisations, notamment l'étude très instructive des causes de la non intégration des deux sous-projets ayant pu alourdir: la Centrale des Bilans et l'explosion statistique des DSF à des fins de comptabilité nationale.

A. Les aspects généraux

Malgré leur caractère très imbriqué, nous distinguerons parmi les raisons d'ordre général du semi-échec du système d'information interadministratif sur les entreprises, trois niveaux d'analyse:

1. l'animation et l'esprit du projet

2. les problèmes d'organisation ou la coordination du projet

3. les traitements à mettre en oeuvre ou la définition du contenu du projet

1. l'esprit du projet: nous regrouperons dans ce paragraphe tous les aspects liés à la finalité du projet ainsi qu'à l'animation des différents acteurs qui y participent. Il convient de remarquer d'abord qu'il s'agissait d'un projet très vaste tant par son contenu (un nouveau plan comptable + un système d'information à créer), que par le nombre des acteurs qu'il concernait, et qui nécessitait donc la mise en oeuvre de moyens très importants pendant une durée considérable (il a fallu plus de cinq années pour passer de la décision d'implantation du plan comptable à l'utilisation courante de ses résultats par l'administration).

De plus, si toute la première partie du projet (plan comptable + DSF) a pu réussir c'est que d'une part sa finalité était clairement définie (recueillir une meilleure information de la part des entreprises), et que d'autre part, des textes législatifs officialisaient cet objectif et en réglementaient la réalisation.

Dès qu'il s'est agi de passer à l'exploitation de cette information, et surtout de préciser la collaboration entre les différentes administrations concernées, le problème des motivations s'est nettement posé: un phénomène de lassitude est apparue et l'objectif insuffisamment précis de "système d'information pour le développement" n'a pas suffit à accroître la participation des principaux acteurs.

Plus clairement, les différentes administrations concernées n'ont pas réalisé le lien qui existait entre l'amélioration du système d'information en général avec leur activité propre; fait révélateur, les quelques textes ou comptes rendus de réunion sur ce sujet restent très généraux et le passage entre potentialités et réalisations concrètes n'est jamais analysé de facon précise!

2. La coordination du projet

Il avait été préconisé la création d'un organe central, le Conseil National de la Comptabilité, ayant pour objet précisément d'effectuer la coordination des différentes actions concourant au projet.

Au Cameroun, cet objectif a été dévolu au Secrétariat Permanent du Plan Comptable (SPPC) rattaché à la Direction de la Statistique du Ministère du Plan. Cependant le SPPC s'est limité presque exclusivement aux relations avec les entreprises et n'a eu qu'un rôle consultatif auprès des autres administrations.

En conséquence et très rapidement, les relations traditionnelles liant les administrations ont prévalu et ce qui est plus grave, celles qui les liaient aux entreprises également. Il en a résulté une détérioration des délais de réponse à la DSF, les entreprises conservant par ailleurs leur habitude de déclarations différenciées suivant l'administration destinataire (Impôt, Statistique ou Banque Centrale).

Si le projet a pu cependant aboutir à des résultats, c'est en grande partie grâce à l'apparition d'un nouvel acteur, la Direction Centrale de l'Informatique (rattachée au Cameroun à la Présidence de la République) qui a pris en charge le traitement général de l'information issue des DSF.

3. La définition du contenu du projet

Il est ainsi apparu un clivage entre les administrations concernées par le projet les partageant entre acteurs passifs et actifs.

- Deux acteurs passifs, la Direction des Impôts et celle de la Statistique pour lesquelles le projet se limitait à un changement de document, qu'elles se sont d'ailleurs mis l'une et l'autre à dépouiller manuellement.

- Un acteur actif, la Direction de l'Informatique qui s'est employée à définir les traitements à automatiser, et à mettre en oeuvre l'organisation nécessaire pour y parvenir.

Trois sous-projets ont ainsi été mis en oeuvre:

- le traitement des tableaux fiscaux pour le compte de la Direction des Impôts.

- la Centrale des bilans à la fois pour les organismes financiers et les entreprises elles-mêmes.

- L'exploitation statistique pour la comptabilité nationale.

Le premier de ces projets a du être abandonné faute de moyens et de personnel qualifié en matière fiscale à la DCIT.

Quant aux deux derniers projets, ils ont pu se développer l'un et l'autre, mais après une tentative d'intégration, ont rapidement divergé pour aboutir à des exploitations séparées.

Ce sont les causes de cette divergence, que nous nous proposons maintenant d'analyser.

B. Les aspects techniques

1. L'objet de la réflexion

Nous entendons par aspects techniques, les problèmes spécifiques que l'on rencontre lors de l'élaboration puis de la mise en oeuvre des traitements prévus par le projet.

Ils sont de par le moment toujours tardif où ils apparaissent difficilement maitrisables et s'il est très difficile de les prévoir, il faut du moins savoir qu'ils sont quelque soit le projet, toujours présents et résultent des aspects généraux situés en amont des traitements qu'ils concernent.

Pour ce qui est de notre sujet, les principales causes des graves difficultés rencontrées se situent à trois niveaux:

1. la mauvaise qualité du répertoire SCIFE et le problème général de la non exhaustivité des réponses à la DSF.

2. le fort taux d'erreur par déclaration lié au volume et à la complexité de celle-ci ce qui pose le problème de la correction des erreurs détectées par le contrôle informatique.

3. la détérioration des délais de réponse puis d'acheminement des documents, ce qui vient limiter la valeur des résultats produits trop tard.

Face à de tels problèmes, il était inévitable que les deux sous-projets de traitements de l'information issue des DSF, divergent au niveau des solutions à adopter. Il est à cet égard intéressant de noter qu'alors que les deux projets étaient somme toute similaires et en tout cas complémentaires la divergence fut totale et peut se résumer par la formule: des traitements différents, sur des populations différentes, pour des objectifs différents!

2. Etude de la divergence

a) des objectifs différents :

La Centrale des Bilans, rappelons le, avait pour objectif la sortie de résultats élaborés au niveau même de l'entreprise, destinés à être utilisés par un large public.

Pour des raisons liées principalement à la volonté de raccourcir les délais, les tableaux produits par les cinq chaines de l'exploitation statistique des DSF sont constitués de résultats valables seulement au niveau du secteur ou de la branche d'activité, dont la présentation brute ne permet une utilisation que par des techniciens de la statistique.

Face à un produit fini, qui constitue un tout indissociable, élaboré une fois pour toutes, nous avons une multitude de sorties intermédiaires s'échelonnant dans le temps et dont la qualité et le degré d'élaboration sont évolutifs.

b) sur des populations différentes

Pour la Centrale des Bilans, chaque entreprise, grande ou petite, est une finalité dans la mesure où sa déclaration est présente.

Or d'une part, comme nous l'avons vu, il n'a pas été possible d'atteindre l'exhaustivité des entreprises assujetties et d'autre part, l'expérience a prouvé que plus une entreprise était petite, plus la qualité de sa déclaration

laissait à désirer. Face à une telle situation, l'exploitation statistique a
considéré les réponses à la DSF comme celles d'une enquête auprès des
entreprises dont on a tiré un échantillon représentatif, stratifié suivant la
taille, les plus petites ne faisant l'objet que d'un dépouillement restreint.

c) ... et donc des traitements différents:

Il a résulté des divergences énoncées dans les deux paragraphes précédents
des traitements de nature très différente:

- pour la Centrale des Bilans, la présentation comptable des résultats a
nécessité l'établissement d'un contrôle au franc près, toute déclaration ne
pouvant être validée, c'est-à-dire admise dans le fichier des résultats qu'au
moment où toutes ses imperfections auront été corrigées.

D'autre part, le nombre des entreprises à traiter devait être le plus
important possible, quelle qu'en soit la taille et enfin, l'aspect fini des
états de sortie autorisait l'utilisation de procédures presqu'entièrement
automatique.

A l'opposé, les procédures utilisées par les chaînes d'exploitation
statistique se caractérisent par des possibilités d'intervention manuelle à
tous les niveaux, les contrôles n'étant jamais bloquants et appliqués sur
les données exprimées en milliers de FCFA, avec un taux d'erreur variable suivant
l'importance des grandeurs et la nature des résultats à produire.

Les deux chaînes sont actuellement exploitées parallèlement à partir de
fichiers différents et suivant des circuits différenciés.

Le degré trop strict des contrôles nécessité par la Centrale des Bilans,
la complexité des corrections qu'ils supposent, au niveau comptable, et surtout
le nombre très important des déclarations à recycler (près de 90% des
réponses) a entraîné l'accumulation de retard, l'exercice 1975/76 n'étant à ce
jour pas encore traité complètement.

L'aspect très pragmatique de l'exploitation statistique fait qu'elle est
actuellement à jour, les déclarations du dernier exercice étant traitées au fur
et à mesure de leur arrivée.

Il reste maintenant aux comptables nationaux la tâche d'exploiter la très
riche information produite, qui est en définitive la preuve de la réussite
globale du projet.

Conclusion

Il n'est pas dans notre intention de tirer de cette expérience très marquée
par son contexte des conclusions générales, d'autant plus que le sujet qui nous
intéresse ici, à savoir les systèmes d'informations, n'était pas l'objectif
déclaré du projet présenté.

Cependant il nous parait fondamental de souligner qu'en matière de projet
interadministratif, aucun système ne peut être considéré comme une fin ce qui
impose aux animateurs de projet de ce type la très importante préoccupation des
motivations respectives de chacun des partenaires.

Cette préoccupation doit exister tout au long de la réalisation du projet
ce qui suppose que chaque utilisateur final des résultats soit associé de très
près à l'élaboration des traitements.

En effet, c'est l'utilisateur de l'information qui la connait en général le mieux et c'est en suivant l'élaboration de chacun des traitements qu'il sera en mesure de préciser si nécessaire ses besoins.

De plus, les travaux d'élaboration impliqués par ce genre de projet, surtout s'ils sont menés informatiquement sont longs et il s'agit de résoudre le problème de la période intérimaire.

Enfin, et ce point fut également négligé au Cameroun, tout projet nécessite une phase d'expérimentation par laquelle l'utilisateur futur puisse avoir un aperçu concret des résultats qu'il pourra obtenir.

Bibliographie

Notes du Gradia:

Juillet 1972: plan comptable de l'OCAM et système de traitement statistique des entreprises

Juin 1973: Comptabilité Nationale et gestion quantitative de l'état dans les pays en voie de développement

Juin 1974: Aspect information économique du plan comptable OCAM

Brochure DCIT (Yaoundé 1977)

P. Richard: la centrale d'information sur les entreprises et la centrale des Bilans

Stateco Mars 1979

G. Osbert: le nouveau plan comptable des entreprises et l'informatisation des comptes nationaux au Cameroun.

INFORMATION SYSTEMS IN PUBLIC ADMINISTRATION
D. Eade, J. Hodgson (editors)
North-Holland Publishing Company
© *DFD, 1981*

FINAL REPORT OF WORKING GROUP 4*

The Group had some difficulty in structuring and harmonizing its members' ideas on industrial information systems and in defining its work programme. This may be explained by the complexity and importance of the information concerned, illustrated by:

(a) The great variety of activities concerned;

(b) The diversity and importance of the information;

(c) The difficulty of dissociating the industry sector from the other sectors as far as information is concerned.

A. An information system on the industrial sector: generalities

The following principle ideas were put forward:

(a) In a developing country context the system should permit planners to orient industrial development towards the increased well-being of the population, for example:

(i) By increasing distributed income;

(ii) By the development of employment through a judicious division of production between the factors labour and capital;

(iii) By the production of goods and services which meet the real needs of the country;

(b) An important factor in the openness of developing economies is that a large part of the companies operating in developing countries are controlled

---

* Participants : R. Mendelssohn (Moderator), U.S.A. ; G. Osbert (Rapporteur). France ; C. Sarino, Philippines ; J-M. Treille, France.

by foreign managers and foreign capital.

In this context it is important that the information system enables these companies to have a better knowledge of the realities of their host country in order to genuinely implicate them in the development process.

We are thus led to consider two distinct aspects of the information system:

(a) The information system on companies, permitting the Government to make informed planning decisions; and

(b) The information system for companies which provides, in addition, an excellent means of encouraging those companies to see themselves as part of the local development effort.

The second type of system covers a wider field than the first, including both economic data (local and international), and a large amount of specific information, notably scientific and technological. The design and implementation of such systems is currently the subject of research in the industrialized countries.

B. Work plan

Another aspect of the Group's work was the working out of a classification of information by source and by subject (sub-system). Eight classes of information were chosen:

1. Basic economic (more exactly, macroeconomic) information

2. Market information

3. Information on production

4. Financial, accounting information

5. Information on the legal and regulatory system

6. Scientific and technological information

7. Other specific information.

Each class is defined according to its content, sources, and the main problems or special features of the collection, treatment, storage or use of information.

1. Basic macroeconomic information

This first class of information takes in all the classic economic data, from demographic data to money supply statistics, including all the major national accounts aggregates. Information of this kind is available for all countries though, naturally, with differing degrees of refinement.

The principle sources are:

(a) The national statistical office;

(b) The statistical services of international organizations

Among the secondary sources mention should be made of regional organizations

The problems of information management in this area concern the co-ordination of standards and definitions between the different sources, and timeliness.

2. Market information

This includes data on:

(a) Internal and external trade;

(b) Prices (production costs, wholesale, retail);

(c) International market trends (primary products);

(d) Competition.

In addition to the sources given above for class 1, such information may be drawn from:

(a) National and international budget offices;

(b) Customs statistics;

(c) Specialized reviews.

The major problem of this area is timeliness.

3. Information on production

This information comprises:

(a) The geographical situation of industries and raw materials;

(b) Productive capacities and the degree of amortization of capital;

(c) Stock levels by category of goods;

(d) Studies of production costs and productivity by sector;

(e) Relationships with the craft sector via sub-contracting (study of the respective shares of added value).

The main sources of this information are companies' statistical and tax declarations.

The establishment of this information – in particular of sectoral input-output tables – demands sophisticated statistical methods.

4. Financial and accounting information

This information has a dual aim: to enable the administration to monitor the viability of individual companies and sectors, and to give companies the means of comparing their performance against others in their sector.

Specific sources of this information are, among others:

(a) Balance sheets published by central banks;

(b) Sectoral studies undertaken by public or private organizations (the latter tend to be very expensive).

The main problem in this area is the reliability of the information. Companies continue to regard such information as confidential.

5. Information on the legal and regulatory system

This concerns:

(a) The different legal statutes of companies;

(b) Investment regulations;

(c) Customs duties, etc.

The necessity for guides on the application of the existing legislation to the regulation of companies is becoming increasingly apparent, both for established enterprises and for new investors.

This information must be clearly presented and illustrated with concrete quantified examples to serve as a guide to the application of the rules and to check that they are respected. Small and medium-sized companies, who do not themselves have the means to undertake such studies, are principally concerned here.

The only source for this information is the administration responsible for industry.

6. Scientific and technical information

This mainly concerns knowledge of technical processes and their development in different application areas:

(a) Patents and industrial property rights;

(b) Technology transfer.

Sources are rare in this domain too, companies being reluctant to share their technological expertise. However, sources include:

(a) Private commercial data bases (notably in the United States of America);

(b) National research centres for the development of processes adapted to the utilization of local raw materials in goods for the domestic market.

7. Other specific information

This information is mainly documentary and drawn from newspapers and press agencies. It should be computerized if it is not to be lost.

C. Conclusions

With this seven-part classification of industry-relevant information in mind and noting that information may be available within the country or from foreign sources, the comments and specific proposals of the Group on the problems of industrial information systems are set out below.

1. General comments

It is by using information that its importance can be measured, its imperfections noted and methods for its improvement proposed. This leads to two observations:

(a) The existence of important external sources of information must be made known to the different economic agents and its use organized. This could become a factor of emulation for the development of national information systems;

(b) The development of information systems is an evolutionary process and, in the view of the Group, a dialectic one.

Thus, as we have seen, the actors concerned are both providers and users of information (though these roles are, of course, played by different actors for "information on" and "information for") and the improvements necessary can be determined by each actor by comparing information supply with information needs (for decision making). An inventory of newly-defined needs thus established will determine the actions to be taken by information suppliers.

These considerations led the Group to formulate the nine specific proposals which follow. They should be understood as recommendations to Data for Development and, by that association, to other international organizations concerned with these kinds of problems.

2. Specific proposals

1. It is necessary that guides to the information available or becoming available around the world, and data base catalogues be established; in other words, to set up an "information system on information".

2. In general, automated information systems and the main data banks are available only in the industrialized countries. While it is true that access to them is not restricted, it would nevertheless be desirable that information centres be established in other parts of the world (Africa, Asia, for example), regularly supplied with tapes from existing sources, thus favouring local use of these sources.

3. It should be noted that although detailed information exists on many subjects areas, the means of access, and therefore the usage, are adapted to the needs of the industrialized countries establishing the information. It is thus desirable that the documentation of these sources be improved and their domain enlarged to cover subjects more specifically linked to development problems.

4. Concerning more technical information and conjunctural information (state of markets, new technologies, etc.) it is desirable to make available to developing countries a list of up-to-date studies and findings and to establish rules for their distribution based on an international code of conduct.

5. In addition to such quantitative information, information on methodologies or software could be collected (by DFD for example), and descriptions and objective evaluations of their advantages and drawbacks circulated.

6. As far as external information is concerned, co-ordination among international organizations would enable this information to be elaborated, evaluated and synthesized, thus protecting national systems from suffocation

under masses of information and allowing them to develop unhindered by the creation of multiple centres of interest.

7. Concerning the development of national information systems, it is recommended that very large systems be avoided in favour of multiple smaller systems adapted to the needs of each class of economic agent.

8. For the construction of such systems, it is recommended that a study be made of iterative methods of step-by-step improvement, involving the collaboration of the various "user-providers" concerned.

9. Finally, turning again to the companies themselves, information on the behaviour of multinational corporations of all sizes should be collected, and studies undertaken leading to the definition of a code of conduct for these corporations.

Although these remarks reflect the content of the Group's discussions, not all of them would be supported by all Group members. The Group agreed, however, that the principal ideas that emerged should be given wider circulation.

INFORMATION SYSTEMS IN PUBLIC ADMINISTRATION
D. Eade, J. Hodgson (editors)
North-Holland Publishing Company
© DFD, 1981

TOWARDS IMPROVED UTILIZATION OF PUBLIC ADMINISTRATION
INFORMATION FOR INTERNATIONAL DEVELOPMENT

Elizabeth K. Miller and Marie Velardi*

Abstract

This paper attempts to describe various types of information systems and
services now available for those who are engaged in international development
in the field of public administration. Included in the paper are (a) a
definition of users of public administration information and identification of
types of information utilized; (b) a summary of means available to access public
administration data – primarily soft data often contained in both published
and unpublished literature – with special emphasis on the needs of those who
are in developing countries; and (c) description of trends and possible
improvements to the current practices.

A. Introduction

In recent years, the traditional role of public administrators has
undergone rapid change as governmental processes are becoming more and more
complex. At the same time various sophisticated information and knowledge
gathering and processing systems and services are becoming available to them at
an affordable price. The availability of advanced information processing
technology has also improved the capacity of public administrators to make
decisions more effectively, as they are able to make choices based on the full
range of options possible in a given problem solving situation. Systems such
as "integrated financial management systems" which provide comparative or
specific data dealing with cross organizational financial information covering
all agencies of a city, and "personnel profile systems" which provide individual,
aggregate or comparative data on employees on city payroll, can be made readily
available to a city manager utilizing modern data processing technology at a
relatively modest cost.

With the advent of mini and micro computers, costs of electronic data
processing equipment are being reduced at a rapid rate making it possible to
utilize automation in the areas which have not been considered cost effective
in the past. At the same time, as costs of human resources and accompanying
overhead costs seem to rise continuously, it has become more prudent to
minimize the use of human resources. Thus the "paperless office" is beginning
to be considered seriously as a means of replacing expensive, manually
maintained files with low maintenance computerized files.

* Information Systems Unit, Department of International Economic and
Social Affairs, United Nations.

However, since legislative processes of·most Governments still require
generation of "paper work", mainly in forms of reports and documents, it is still
mandatory to have some sort of document referencing system which provides access
to information contained in printed pages. The availability of inexpensive
electronic data processing equipment and efficient software packages useful for
obtaining ready access to a collection of materials makes it relatively easy
today to bring improvement to the way decision makers and researchers in the
field of public administration utilize information. What is needed now is the
initiative on the part of administrators and decision makers to include the
adoption of advanced information processing technology and techniques in their
future plans so that the way information is utilized will be enhanced in the
immediate future. In order to facilitate those who are in a position to take
necessary steps to bring in new technology and techniques, the present paper
attempts to describe the parameters of the users' information needs and
identify some of the ways and means for adopting changes.

B. Users of public administration information and types of information utilized by them

There are roughly four different groups of users of public administration
information. They are:

1. Politicians who require:

(a) Information about their constituents;

(b) Analytical information on politically sensitive issues;

(c) Information about the Government they are entrusted to serve, that
is, budget, legislation, etc.;

(d) Information concerning political, economic and social trends of the
country they serve and the global implication of these trends;

2. Public administrators, for example, city managers, agency heads, etc.
who require:

(a) Financial information of the Government and agency they manage;

(b) Programme information of the Government and agency they manage;

(c) Laws and regulations and other legislative information;

(d) Information about the constituency they serve;

(e) Management information of the agencies and Government they
administrate; and

(f) Information on management practices, theory and techniques;

3. Public servants and bureaucrats who need:

(a) Information on methodology and techniques dealing with their areas
of responsibility;

(b) Laws and regulations and legislative information concerning the areas
they manage;

(c) Statistics concerning the programmes they administer; and

4.   Students and scholars of public administration who require:

(a)   Historical information on public administration;

(b)   Information on theory and methodology of public administration;

(c)   Case studies;

(d)   Survey data;

(e)   Laws, regulations and legislative information;

(f)   Manuals and textbooks and other instructional materials;

(g)   Research techniques and methodology;

(h)   Organizational management and related information; and

(i)   Information on economic theory and practice as they relate to public administration.

C.   Systems and services providing support to users of public administration
                                    information

Within individual Governments, the following types of services are usually available to provide access to information-in-print on public administration:

(a)   Libraries and archives of government agencies;

(b)   Research and analysis groups or centres, that is, congressional research services, municipal reference centres, etc.;

(c)   Information clearing houses.

Outside the Government, various information collection, dissemination activities are conducted by:

(a)   Councils of Governments, public administrators' leagues, public interest groups, each providing libraries, information clearing house service, publications, indexing and current awareness services to their members;

(b)   University and research institutions, each with libraries, publication services, information clearing houses, data collection and analysis services;

(c)   Profit and non-profit information services.

A cursory survey of how information contained in printed pages is accessed today in the field of public administration reveals the fact that most governmental organizations are still depending on traditional municipal library or archival systems by which information contained in paper copies is filed away in shelves or file cabinets.   Access to these printed pages is obtained through a referencing system, manual or mechanized.

Archives or libraries in public administration are of three major types;

1.   Special administrative libraries created for the purpose of serving the agencies to which they are attached;

2.   Libraries or archives which serve academic institutions in public

administration; and

    3. Archives and libraries which serve Governments as national archives or parliamentary libraries.

    On the whole, these depositories use predominantly manual referencing systems rather than computerized systems. Typically, services offered include current awareness services (publication of acquisitions lists, routing of periodicals, distribution of contents pages); document referencing systems (preparation of specialized bibliographies, locating documents for special requests, making indexes to holdings available for users); special subject files; and the publication of indexes and abstract journals. For example, the India Institute of Public Administration issues <u>Documentation in Public Administration</u>, a widely read abstracts periodical, and the United States Office of Management and Budget compiles and distributes <u>Public Management Sources</u>.

    Information analysis centres, supported by a group of subject experts and information processing experts, collect literature in a well-defined field, organize and store it for retrieval, and produce critical reviews, data compilations, correlations and codifications, as well as other materials which make intellectual contributions to new knowledge. For example, the Global Information and Early Warning System on Food and Agriculture (GIEWS), a system created by the Food and Agriculture Organization of the United Nations (FAO) utilizes reports from field officers and Governments in monitoring the world food supply and demand conditions on a continuous basis, and to identify areas where food shortages are imminent. This system also distributes the Food <u>Outlook Report</u>, a periodic reassessment of future food supply and demand based on changing economic factors. [1] Another example is the Congressional Research Services of the United States Government which not only provides extensive research support services to the United States Congress, but is also responsible for the establishment and maintenance of computerized files on the current status of legislation.

    Many clearing houses also serve as central agencies for the exchange and interchange of information including documentation in specific subject areas. Although the collection is not normally made directly available to the users, they perform many of the same services provided by libraries. For example, the United Nations European Social Development Programme, which has operated a bibliographic clearing house since 1965, provides information searches on request, question/answer services, advisory services, and publishes and disseminates circulars, newsletters, and reports on welfare research and regional meetings. [2]

    There are a number of so called documentation centres specializing in providing information useful to those in the field of public administration. The term documentation centre is often synonymous with library or clearing-

---

    [1] Inter-Organization Board for Information Systems, <u>Directory of United Nations Information Systems and Services</u> (Geneva, 1978), p. 87.

    [2] <u>Ibid</u>., p. 41-42.

house, but can also have broader implications. Generally, it refers to a centralized unit that collects, records, and disseminates documentation from diverse sources, and acts as an information repository. A documentation centre is often the co-ordinating bibliographic control centre for a network of information services. On the international level, the Computerized Documentation System of the United Nations Educational, Scientific and Cultural Organization (UNESCO) provides bibliographic control of documents and publications of UNESCO and its affiliated institutions, facilitates access to specialized files of information, and acts as a demonstration and training centre for the application of advanced computerized techniques in information storage and retrieval. 3/ At the regional level, Informatech France-Quebec, provides services in Quebec as a centralized agency for the dissemination of automated documentation in urban management and planning, as well as environment and related fields. Informatech also co-ordinates 13 other documentation centres in Africa, Europe, Eastern Europe, Latin America, and the Middle East. 4/

Automated document referencing systems are, for the most part, citation retrieval systems, although a few full-text searching and retrieval systems can be found within the realm of public administration (for example, JURIS, a system used by the United States Department of Justice). In addition to automated document referencing and retrieval systems, several other types of systems used in public administration are:

(a) Administrative management systems used for budgeting, accounting, procurement, contracts and grants management, and agency or bureau-wide administration;

(b) Programme and/or project management systems concerned with the management of agency resources and functions;

(c) Agency and/or bureau-wide analytical planning and forecasting systems, models for forecasting, simulation and decision making. 5/

The most salient distinction between these systems, which are often referred to as data banks, and the document referencing systems is that the former are mainly numeric systems. Other essential differences are;

(a) Document referencing systems are often not designed exclusively for management purposes. Very often they are established as a service to a variety of user groups. Many document retrieval systems of the governmental agencies

---

3/ Ibid., p. 87-88

4/ Ministry of State for Urban Affairs, Directory of Canadian Urban Information Sources 1977 (Ottawa, 1977), p. 135-136

5/ United States Comptroller General, Federal Information Sources and Systems: A Directory (Washington, D.C., 1977), p. 635

are available to the general public through direct access via agencies
themselves. They are also accessed through services provided by commercial
vendors on a subscription basis as bibliographic citations are often not
classified information even when the documents themselves might be restricted;

(b) Document referencing systems are often archival in nature, that is
they contain static information since information is very rarely purged, and
they normally contain a much larger store of permanent information than other
types of information systems. Data banks, on the other hand, purge old
information and add new information on a continuous basis;

(c) Document referencing systems perform relatively little processing on
the information they contain. Information is only reformatted when generating
variant outputs, such as special indexes or publications. Data banks tabulate
and reformat numerical data on a continuous basis;

(d) Document referencing systems contain secondary information, rather
than primary information. The purpose of a bibliographic citation is to guide
the user to primary information contained within a document. Data banks utilize
primary data extracted directly from records, reports, forms, statistical
compendia, and other internal and external sources.

Computerized document referencing systems for technical and development
information pertaining to local, regional, national and international needs
are available both as in-house services and commercial products throughout
Western Europe and the United States. These include urban management
documentation files serving particular metropolitan areas and regions, such as
IFMIS in New York City and ACOMPLIS in London. Numerous data bases originally
produced as in-house services by the United States Government (NASA, NTIS,
MEDLARS, AGRICOLA), by for-profit and non-profit organizations, and
international organizations (LABORDOC produced by the International Labour
Organisation and ASFA by FAO/UNESCO), have been made available on both
continents through on-line suppliers such as Lockheed and Systems Development
Corporation, the European Space Agency's Information Retrieval Service in
Frascati, Italy, and BLAISE, an on-line service supplied by the British Library.
The European audience is expected to increase when the Euronet Direct
Information Access Network for Europe (DIANE), a new international
telecommunications network, becomes operational later this year.

D. Problems encountered by the documentation centres and their document
referencing systems

Traditionally, the usefulness of libraries and documentation centres in
the governmental decision-making process has not been fully recognized. These
services are generally assigned low priorities in funding, often placed among
general housekeeping units of agencies along with general services, or
otherwise excluded from the policy decision arm of organizations. This is
partly due to the fact that the techniques and tools currently in use to
support conventional manual retrieval systems, such as card catalogue files,
have not been able to satisfy the requirements of their users in locating
information efficiently and effectively. Constraints on the accessibility of
material has also contributed to user resistance against traditional services,
since much of the literature pertinent to the needs of users of public
administration information remains unpublished in the usual sense because of
lack of centralized monitoring and publishing programmes in most Governments.
Moreover, even the advent of computerized document referencing systems had not
been able to reverse fully attitudes stemming from repeated disappointments
users have experienced with traditional services.

Labin observes that documentation centres that utilize computerized systems "are still not used by more than 10% of their potential customers, and the lists of bibliographical references they supply in reply to a question ... always contain 50% noise and 50% 'miss'". 6/ This deficiency stems from the fact that by indexing documents with keywords and thesaurus descriptors it is never possible to satisfactorily identify and retrieve all the subjects covered in any given document. Additionally, many of the concepts in scientific, technical and development literature used for public administration are still in the process of being formulated and the topics themselves are not clearly or consistently defined.

Poor administration of available resources, facilities and services also poses serious difficulties. Even where document referencing systems for public administration proliferate, there often exists a lack of co-operation and co-ordination between institutions and systems serving the same patronage. The result is a costly and time-consuming duplication of effort in the acquisition and processing of materials, in indexing, abstracting, publication and reference services, and an equally wasteful duplication of methods, techniques and technology.

Apart from these internal shortcomings, which are certainly not insurmountable, there exists among users of public administration information in general a failure to appreciate the value of non-statistical information, or to realize that such information could be systematically collected, organized and disseminated. In recent years, the attention focussed on the development of numeric data bases and the manipulation of statistics has overshadowed the value of qualitative information and the systems designed to access it. However, very little effort has been made to date to seek out methods of co-ordinating these two types of services so that users will not overlook relevant sources of information.

E. Public administration in developing countries and use and availability of public administration information

In most countries, and particularly in developing countries, the last 20 years have seen a rapid growth in activities in public administration, including research and development and international co-operation. Accompanying these activities is an equally rapid growth in internally and externally produced literature relating to economic and social development. However, generally speaking, the lack of dependable national information infrastructures and well-defined information policies perpetuates inadequate control and management as well as underutilization of useful information generated for or by Governments.

National Governments, quasi and semi-governmental agencies, which are not only primary sources but also primary users of technical and development

---

6/ Edouard Labin, "Information analysis and data banks", Second European Congress in Information Systems and Networks, 27-30 May 1975, ed. by the Commission of the European Communities (Munich, 1976), p. 125.

information, suffer in many cases from a lack of co-ordination of their own
internal information and communications systems. Intra-agency document
referencing systems, often of the most rudimentary sort, falter due to
fractionalization or overlap of subject interests, careless management of
restricted or confidential information and a general lack of availability of
information outside of the generating department of authority. Additionally,
ineffective government publications policies, and non-existent or unenforceable
depository laws have hampered the flow of internally generated information in
many countries.

The primary responsibility for acquisition, processing, management and
dissemination of public administration information has been assumed largely by
libraries affiliated with institutions devoted to the training of civil servants
and/or research in public administration (including university libraries),
professional institutions, and national libraries and archives. The role of the
latter group in serving the needs of the users of information in public
administration is a vital one as they often serve as depositories of official
public records, government documents, legislation, foreign documents, and
documents produced by or for international organizations. The importance of
services provided by these libraries and archives is beginning to be recognized
in recent years by authorities in some Governments. Jordan and Uganda, for
example, have sought expert advice from the Public Administration and Finance
Division of the United Nations in reorganizing or improving their existing
institutions.

Another example of the growing awareness by Governments of the importance
of strengthening their ability to make full use of information they generate
can be seen in a recent undertaking by the African Training and Research Centre
in Administration for Development (CAFRAD). In recognition of the potential
national libraries and archives have in serving as focal points for an
integrated network for information dealing with public administration and
economic and social development, a project was proposed by CAFRAD to establish
a document referencing system in public administration. This document
referencing system, christened the African Integrated Network of Administrative
Information (AINAI), would engage existing national libraries, archives and
documentation centres to co-ordinate and mobilize local libraries and
information services within their respective countries in order to supply a
regional clearing house, based at CAFRAD, with input into its data base. The
institutions that are members of the network would also serve as national
distribution centres for AINAI output products in the form of printed
publications and magnetic tapes. 7/

However, the problems faced by most national libraries and archives and
other institutions dealing with the management and dissemination of public
administration information will continue to plague its users until a number of
basic obstacles for progress are eliminated. One of the most urgent is the

---

7/ M. El Hadi, "The African Integrated Network of Administration
Information - AINAI: a conceptual project proposal", African administrative
studies, No. 18 (Dec. 1977), p. 135-143.

paucity of professionally trained librarians, documentalists and information scientists. Too few institutions are providing adequate training to a sufficient number of students in this field. The resulting lack of rigorous documentation programmes to encourage the development of sophisticated methods and procedures is reflected in the scarcity of adequate classification systems, thesauri, and other tools essential for providing ready access to information contained in printed materials dealing with public administration.

It has also been observed that most countries, and particularly developing countries with limited experience in producing information, have not yet instituted mechanisms for identifying their own information needs in the area of economic and social development or for acquiring or disseminating this information. 8/ However, some initiatives have been undertaken in recent years to mount a comprehensive effort to provide improved utilization and exchange of information in public administration. For example, with support from the International Development Research Centre (IDRC) of Canada, the Latin American Centre for Economic and Social Documentation (CLADES) of the United Nations Economic Commission for Latin America conducted an inventory of socio-economic information in the libraries and documentation centres of 26 Latin American countries in preparation for the establishment of the Development Science Information System (DEVSIS). Yet, additional efforts to enable Governments to know their current capabilities for making efficient use of their knowledge resources and to identify the gaps that are preventing them from having the information essential for better management of their countries are still urgently needed.

Another obstacle facing improved handling of public administration information in developing countries is the attitude of administrators themselves towards soft data. As discussed earlier, the value of qualitative information for decision making is not as apparent to users as the value of statistics or numbers. Since the primary users of document referencing systems are scholars, students and researchers, and not those who are in the position of influencing the quality of information services in their countries, inadequate national policies and programmes to improve access to information in print continue to remain unnoticed.

This neglect for the adequate document referencing systems in public administration becomes more acutely felt when one realizes that new technology capable of bringing immediate improvement to the still elementary state of the art in this field is available, and, in particular, that extensive application of computers has already been made in handling other types of information for public administration. On the other hand, although studies have been made to determine the feasibility of creating document referencing systems in support of international development, much more needs to be accomplished in terms of their actual implementation. This might be due partly to the lack of support by Governments, coupled with the shortage of seasoned documentation systems specialists in developing countries. But also, when financial and technological resources are limited, as they are in developing countries, priority will naturally be given to processing those types of data that have always been considered more useful.

8/ M. Osei-Bonso, "The contribution of organized information to national development: the roles and values of libraries", Greenhill Journal of Administration, vol. 2, No. 1 (April-June 1975), p. 93.

F. Identification of areas in which international organizations can
    contribute to improving access to public administration information

Without much effort one can recognize the existence of a need to improve
the capacity of most Governments to utilize efficiently both soft and hard data
relevant to public administration. There are a number of areas in which
international organizations can make meaningful contributions so that sharing
and improved utilization of knowledge useful for international development in
the field of public administration might be more aggressively encouraged.

Scarcity of public funds to be used for improved utilization of public
administration information, apparently of low priority to public officials,
adds weight to the challenge of international organizations in concentrating
their effort to achieve maximum results with a minimum amount of resources.
The first and foremost in this regard is   well co-ordinated information system
and services related activities of the international organizations, so that
limited resources are well used in all essential areas without unnecessary
duplication of effort. The strengthened and enlarged mandate of the
Inter-Organization Board for Information Systems (IOB) should be helpful in
maximizing the collective resources allocated for information systems and
services by the international organizations and their member states.

IOB, in co-operation with the UNESCO/UNISIST programme, should be able to
provide the basic tools of co-ordination by maintaining inventories of information systems related activities including information about the hardware and
software in use, in addition to being the impartial source of knowledge on
information processing technology and methods.

Among the tasks which might be undertaken by an international organization
such as the United Nations to promote the sharing of experience and knowledge
in public administration, is an assessment of the present capabilities of each
Government to efficiently utilize information in print. The result of such an
assessment would be an inventory or a directory of information sources and
resources in public administration. Such an information gathering task has
already been undertaken in part by some of the regional commissions and
international organizations in their attempt to identify existing capabilities
and the areas that are in need of improvement. As a result, a mechanism
necessary for gathering updated information has already been installed in some
regions and sectors. With a modest initiative on the part of a leading
organization in public information, an information referral system for the
existing sources and resources of public administration information could be
created and maintained. Further, since enough working models for such a system
are in existence, for example UNEP/INFOTERRA and UNDP/INRES, the main effort
can be concentrated on the collection of accurate and up-to-date information and
on the wide utilization of information based on the system.

The DEVSIS feasibility study, as well as studies conducted for SPINES and
DARE by UNESCO, have yielded enough information about the appropriate
methodology and technique in the collection and processing of information useful
for development in the field of public administration and related areas. These
studies showed that international exchange of information must be based on the
well-established national information infrastructures which act as the basis
for all activities necessary for international co-operation in information
sharing. The General Information Programme of UNESCO provides for a number of
important elements in this regard. Working closely with member states, issues
regarding national information policies, training of information science
professionals, guidelines for information systems, and mechanisms for
interconnecting relevant information systems are being addressed by UNESCO
with a view towards the establishment and strengthening of national
infrastructures for information systems. A modest collaborative effort by a

substantive office responsible for the sector in public administration should
facilitate progress in these areas.

Additionally, the tasks essential for the economic exchange of information
at the global level, such as application of common indexing terms through the
use of a multi-lingual thesaurus, establishment of common format for exchange of
machine-readable bibliographic information, and adoption of international
standards for codified information, may also be undertaken by UNESCO in
collaboration with an international organization responsible for the sector in
public administration.

Another area which warrants serious consideration is the application of
micrographics to documentation which is helpful in cutting the cost of document
distribution and storage. Some of the regional collaborative efforts which
included establishment and operation of regional depositories and literature-on-
microfilm distribution centres that are temporarily inoperative due to shortage
of funds should be reactivated and brought into the over-all plan of future
information sharing efforts.

Creation and support by international organizations of regional and global
information networks which link relevant information sources for public
administration might also be considered as a possible means of information
sharing efforts. By its very nature, a network often serves a catalytic role
in strengthening local information infrastructures, without which a network
cannot be established. A consortium of documentation centres linked by a
network also provides an ideal forum for sharing of information processing
techniques, facilities and software, which contribute towards economical use of
limited resources. In this connexion, the important role which can be assumed
by the regional economic commissions variously as network co-ordinating centre,
regional depository, and training centre, must not be overlooked.

International organizations responsible for the public administration
sector could also make significant contribution towards improved utilization of
information by initiating programmes which encourages effective use of
information available for planning and decision making. Those who are in the
position to bring about necessary changes will recognize the importance of
establishing policies and providing a means for making the wealth of knowledge
contained in printed material readily accessible to them, when they see that
successful results are consistently achieved through full use of available
information.

INFORMATION SYSTEMS IN PUBLIC ADMINISTRATION
D. Eade, J. Hodgson (editors)
North-Holland Publishing Company
© *DFD, 1981*

SUBJECT BIBLIOGRAPHIES OF MORE INDUSTRIALIZED COUNTRIES
AND PROBLEMS FOR THEIR USE, ESPECIALLY IN DEVELOPING COUNTRIES

Warren Crowther*

Abstract

The activites in public administration of defining issues and problems, of
studies and of decision making, lead logically to the search for plausible
models, working hypotheses and variables in a great variety of information
sources, and for data related to the variables in studies in which local
conditions are approximated. Systematic retrieval using periodical subject
bibliographies (indexes, abstracts, serial bibliographies) can be a very
important method of obtaining the needed information, although it does not always
justify the added effort and the costs of creating such a system, as opposed to
a system of direct access. In developing and more industrialized countries
there are many problems for manual searching using subject bibliographies. In
developing countries especially, there are many difficulties in organizing
for the effective use of subject bibliographies. Also, the construction of such
bibliographies does not always address the special characteristics of manual
searching (as opposed to searching on computerized data bases). Concrete
suggestions are made to deal with these problems.

---oo0oo---

Periodical subject bibliographies (indexes, abstracts, serial
bibliographies) and data bases are important working tools for public
administration. They can be efficient instruments to expand the range of the
information used in decision making and studies in public administration, and to
assure greater possibilities that this information will be the most pertinent of
that which is available for such needs. They also permit a wider and more
cumulative knowledge of the methods, products and results of the work in public
administration.

As shown in figure XXXIV, public administration is both source and user of
information, and systematic retrieval using subject bibliographies or data

* Resident Adviser, Bolivian National Development Information System and
Fund (SYFNID) and Project Official, International Development Research Council,
Canada.

The author is grateful to Ana S. de Gutierrez and Hugo Loaiza for comments
on an earlier draft.

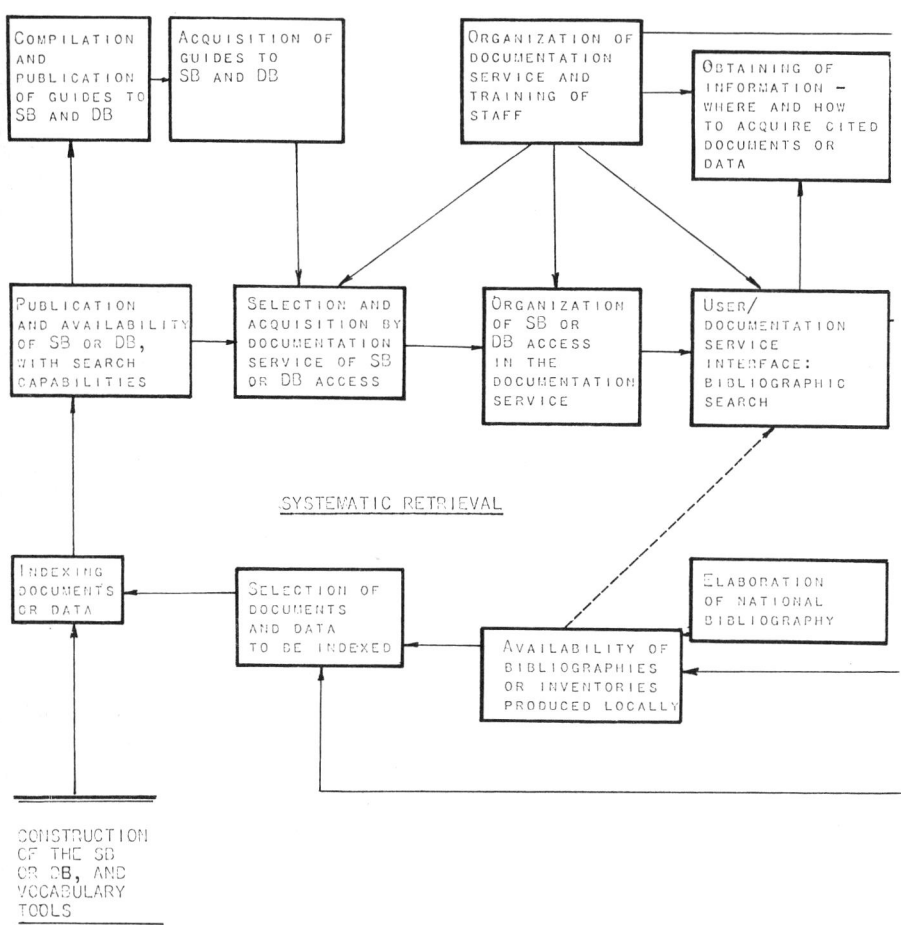

SYSTEMATIC RETRIEVAL

Figure XXXIV. The subject bibliography as a working tool of public administration,

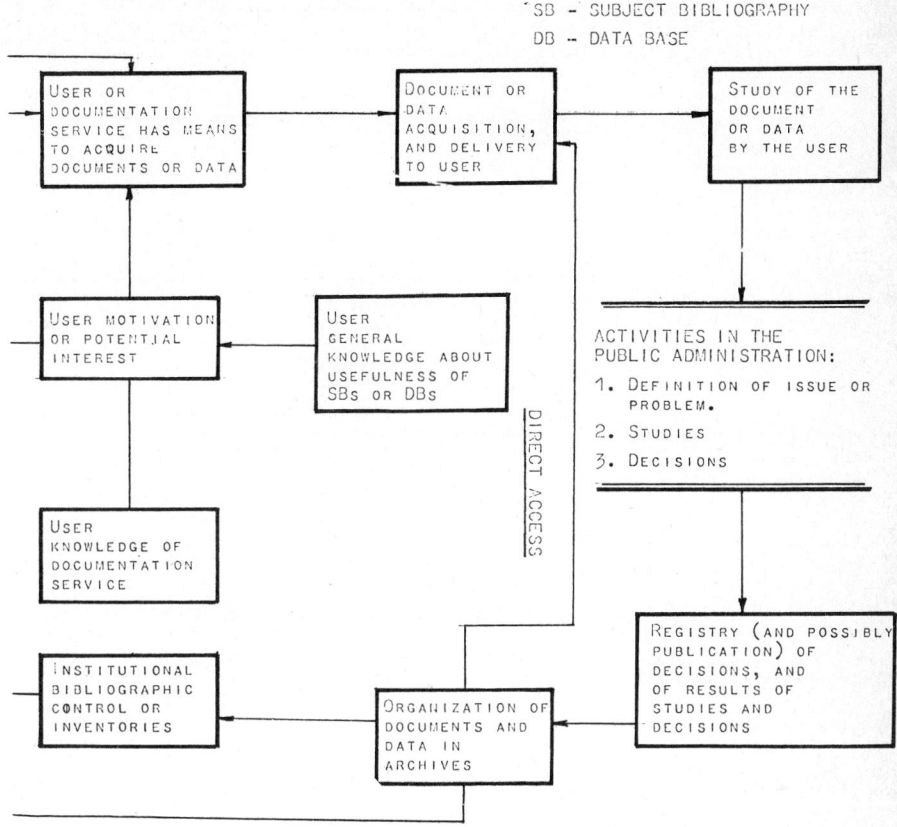

public administration as a source/user of information.

bases is meant to help assure greater discrimination of a broader set of information than would be the case with more direct access to that information. The same figure also shows that systematic retrieval presumes the organization of many separate actions or elements.

In practice, there are many impediments to a satisfactory encounter between the subject bibliography and the potential source/user of this information, to the application or utilization of the information, and to the application or utilization of the information by the user. Many factors intervene in what is selected for indexing, the attributes of documents or data which are indexed, what is available for searching, what is selected among what is available, and the possibilities of obtaining the documents or data that are desired. The usefulness for public administration of a hardcopy subject bibliography (as well as for a computerized data base) requires careful design, programming and support of these elements and activities. Otherwise, the public administration is likely to achieve a better cost-effective solution for its information needs by concentrating its attention solely on better organization of direct access channels. 1/

The uses of subject bibliographies are varied. Collison finds that 3/5 of abstracts users search for information directly pertinent to work at hand, 2/5 intend to keep up to date in their field, 2/5 intend to keep up to date in related or fringe fields, and 1/5 use the abstracts for retrospective reference. 2/ The retrospective searches could be rather exhaustive in terms of the parameters of the users' interests, or quite superficial, or intended to help in formulating and refining questions for on-line searches or mailed requests to computerized data bases (that is, an interactive stage prior to making the data base connexion). The subject bibliographies can be used to gather data directly from synopses or statistical summaries, for refining concepts for specific projects or decisions, for training in searching and for bibliometric studies. Their major use in developing countries, other than the uses cited by Collison, is likely to be acquisition decisions regarding books and reprints.

The users in public administration need this reference information for the

---

1/ Usually much can be done to improve direct access channels by better organization of local archives for browsing, by more intensive correspondence directly with sources of information or by a more efficient dissemination of information which is generated in or arrives at the interested institutions. Direct access offers not only a cost advantage but also the advantage of unexpected discoveries of useful data not in conformity with the user's intellectual predispositions which data tend to orient the user's more systematic bibliographic search.

2/ The sum is greater than one (1), given multiple answers by many users. Robert Collison, Abstracts and Abstracting Services, 1971.

definition of issues and problems, for studies and for decisions related to
projects or ongoing administrative activities. In a responsible society, the
definition of issues and problems to be considered would originate among the
people who are or will be most affected by that definition; at the same time,
recognition would be given to the interdependence of all nations' actions,
and the issues and problems chosen for attention by other societies would be
studied and taken into account.

The studies and decisions of public administration can benefit from three
kinds of information: suggestions of variables, and hypotheses for interrelating
these variables, which could be pertinent to the problem at hand; models which
integrate the hypotheses into a coherent set; and the most reliable and/or
pertinent data available on the variables. The administrators and technicians
would ideally be open to suggestions of possibly pertinent variables, hypotheses
and models from a wide variety of information sources; and would give greatest
weight to reliable data on the variables pertaining to environmental and
institutional conditions which are the same or similar to those of the problem
being studied or which can be achieved realistically by economic, social or
political change.

Therefore, the subject bibliography is especially useful if it facilitates
access to a wide variety of sources of conceptual information (variables,
hypotheses, models) or if it helps to discriminate in order to choose the
most relevant documents and data on each variable prior to acquiring them.
There is also the general contribution which subject bibliographies can make
to the transfer of technology (in information form) or technological
co-operation, and to bibliographical control of the intellectual production of
each country.

In this paper, attention is given to those problems which the author
considers critical, especially from the point of view of the information source/
user of the subject bibliographies produced in the developed countries or
international organizations. While many of the problems cited in this paper
directly affect information sources/users in the more industrialized countries,
and the solutions proposed would certainly benefit them, the primary concern
here is the special situation of the developing countries' sources/users, and in
particular those of Latin America. One special circumstance is the relatively
heavier reliance on published reference materials, as compared to the use of
on-line connexions to computerized data bases. Because of the normally long
delays involved, access by mail to computerized data bases will be considered
a special case.

Using figure XXXIV as a guide, the following analysis will consider the
problems for using the subject bibliography, beginning with the situation of
potential users in developing countries, the problems of organizing adequate
documentation services and the limited access to the primary documentation
or data which are desired or needed in those countries. The solution to these
problems mostly rests on the developing countries themselves, with the help
of international organizations. Next is a brief analysis of the means by which
the developing countries may become informed about and acquire subject
bibliographies. Following this is a critical examination of the subject
bibliographies themselves and the indexing vocabularies for them leading to
suggestions of techniques and devices to facilitate manual searching (annex IV),
most of which depend on initiatives by those who construct subject indexes.
Finally, the problem of obtaining better coverage of the developing countries'
own intellectual production is mentioned.

A. Potential users and non-users

Administrators in the public sector of the more industrialized countries are part of a larger clientele of documentation services. The university, business and industrial research and administrative organizations in those countries are very closely interrelated in activities of scientific and technological development. Based on this mutual interest, they support elaborate systems of documentation and reinforce norms of status and job advancement based on personal utilization of and contributions to these systems.

In the lesser developed countries it is common for administrators and technicians of public programmes to lament the lack of an adequate information infrastructure for the decisions which they need to make. The need is immediate, and the person who takes a strong interest in the problem often lacks the patience or the continuity in the same post to set up a working solution, or he finds that he is very alone in the priority he gives to this problem.

In these countries, the size of the literate, higher educated and even professional populations is at most a very rough indicator of the potential source/user population of a systematic retrieval system. According to a study in one Latin American country, a small group of people, mostly within the professional strata, makes repeated use of existing systems or relies on personal subscriptions, while most of this group's professional colleagues, and the students preparing for the profession, lack any contact at all with subject bibliographies. The tradition is strong to consider oneself "educated" when the university degree is obtained and to rely on colleagues (due to convenience) or institutional superiors (due to the obligation of working conditions) as information sources. 3/

Education of the professionals in the use of subject bibliographies and journals would be an obvious answer, implying the need for simple propoganda and instructional materials (this will be discussed later). However, it is difficult to obtain an audience where most of the professionals express satisfaction with the type (but not the quantity or accessibility) of the information sources on which they rely already. A more effective solution might

---

3/ The studies of the National Development Information System (SYFNID) of Bolivia have concluded that 98 per cent of the medical doctors and health administrators, planners and researchers based in La Paz read or are acquainted with a wide variety of medical journals (with a rather low concentration of titles), but only 1/3 even make occasional use of subject bibliographies (almost all of this group using Index Medicus) and 1/5 make use of the National Documentation Centre's reference and document acquisition services connected through Brazil's Regional Medical Library to MEDLINE. Of a sample population of 40 geologists, only 1 regularly and 9 occasionally consult international subject bibliographies. It is an extremely rare school teacher, among 50,000 in the country, that even knows about subject bibliographies or professional journals. In these fields, the most regular users of these materials are the small groups of researchers. Other professionals tend to rely on information generated in their own institutions, much of which (except in education) is labelled "confidential". SYFNID, "La geologia en Bolivia frente a la problematica de la informacion. Resultados de un estodio y propuestas de acciones a ser tomadas", February 1979. The studies on the remaining sectors will be finalized during the year.

be to educate university students in the use of reference sources. 4/

There are groups of more active users, for example in larger developing countries, with concentrated groups of specialized researchers in "centres of excellence"; sophisticated documentation centres are maintained with substantial budgets for acquisitions and are strongly supported by their users. Also, one investigation concludes that Latin Americans who have studied in the United States tend to read technical literature, especially of that country, more extensively than their United States counterparts. Ninety per cent of the respondents reported regular exposure to technical publications and 59 per cent had read a technical publication the day before being interviewed. 5/

Fortunately, with some encouragement from governmental agencies, university faculty and student leaders and international organization representatives and experts, the small core group of persons in the developing countries who do recognize the importance of systematic retrieval and are users of subject bibliographies or journals can be convinced to co-operate in elaborating and implementing an over-all plan to broaden the reach of documentation services in their field. The challenge is great, but certainly not impossible, and this activity is a most important candidate for attention from the international organizations interested in fostering scientific and technological development in the developing countries.

There are some very positive examples of this. The AGRINTER system in agriculture in Latin America, with regional-wide inputs into its subject bibliographies, elaborates materials and trains documentalists in user education. The industrial information centres of several countries of the region, following a pattern and leadership role set by INFOTEC of Mexico, send bibliographical information to industrialists to encourage their use of various documentation services. The Latin American Population Documentation (DOCPAL) system also uses an information dissemination system to attract the interest of potential users in technical documentation. Although it is more expensive than demand-induced development of documentation systems, the tactic of these systems in creating broader user interest on the basis of supply may be much more viable, given the user situation described above. Special attention should be given to upgrading information inputs in the professional education programmes in the universities. Another tactic would be for the international organizations to support actions on this problem by those regional professional organizations which in some fields in Latin America have become increasingly stronger. The international organization would adopt a supportive role similar to that of

---

4/ The Bolivian study cited above concludes that 60 per cent of the medical students would not be inclined to develop this capability, unless strongly pushed by their professors (who generally are not regular users themselves of subject bibliographies). A huge restriction is the deficiency in language instruction at the university.

5/ Paul Deutschmann, Hurber Ellingsworth and John McNelly, Communication and Social Change in Latin America: Introducing New Technology, 1968.

the Office of Science Information Service of the National Science Foundation of
the United States. Unfortunately, information exchange at the regional level and
improvement of access to subject bibliographies in general have been rather
marginal issues in the professional organizations up to now.

B. The information impasse

The following interrelated conditions were discovered recently in a
developing country, collectively implying the existence of an information impasse
at the point where documentation services should be provided:

(a) A study of the viability of a public entity to facilitate acquisition
of bibliographic materials in the country (by making foreign exchange easier by
eliminating red-tape in the approval and accounting procedures, by consolidating
requests to reduce duplications and negotiate discounts, by reducing the costs of
using chains of brokers or buyers, etc.) concluded that the project was not
justified since too few institutions could be counted on to purchase materials on
a regular basis. Budgets for bibliographic acquisition are susceptible to large
fluctuations or are used for other unanticipated expenditures, even in the
largest universities, corporations and public sector institutions. The
agricultural sector fares best: The National Documentation Centre subscribes to
22 subject bibliographies of this sector, the Agricultural Ministry Library to
13, the largest experimental station to 6 and the largest university department
of agronomy to 1;

(b) A very small proportion of the working librarians know how or attempt
to buy a book or order a journal from abroad. Where the institution has a
budget for buying bibliographical material, these are more often used, if at all,
by individual officials and not by the library;

(c) The small amount of training which has been offered (in the Library
school and in a basic audio-visual course for librarians) to librarians or
library students on acquisition has been over simplified with regard to
purchasing procedures, and gives cursory treatment to the other means of
obtaining materials and developing collections (exchange of publications,
donations, deposits of publications of the sponsoring institutions or other
organizations, requiring officials to deposit the conference and seminar papers
they receive, etc.). Although almost all the libraries in the country depend
on these latter methods of acquisition, they do not have systematic procedures
to exploit these methods;

(d) In the all too few cases where the librarians seek to purchase books
or subscriptions, they deal with local booksellers who are unreliable and charge
very high commissions, or go through a tremendous amount of red tape in
obtaining approval of the foreign exchange and the purchase itself. A one-year
delay is common;

(e) There is no real continuity of subscriptions. Typically, when
librarians change, which they do often, the new librarian is disinterested or
lacks the knowledge of or influence on budgeting and money disbursement
in the institution to continue the subscriptions;

(f) The lack of continuity in previous acquisitions and the high cost of
starting up an adequate collection development, make collection development based
on internal financing seem utopian;

(g) Funds are obtained sporadically from some international agencies and
large-scale purchases are made; or a private collection is donated, resulting in
the existence of incomplete and expensive collections. On occasion, the library
or documentation centre which receives this material is ill-equipped to process

or adequately service the collection. Nonetheless, these collections are jealously guarded and it is up to the user to circulate among libraries and make a personal survey of the availability of editions of the bibliography or journal which interest him;

(h) The user must often learn himself how to find and use subject bibliographies because the low-paid and poorly-trained library staff tend to concentrate on other types of materials which are in greater demand and easier to handle (for example, reprints of class notes for students, texts). Expensive reference works go unused at times because the staff does not understand searching procedures;

(i) The inventory of available national statistics is very incomplete and very few librarians are interested in helping the user find such material.

This somber picture is common in many, but not all, developing countries. One Latin American country has over 30 complete sets of Chemical Abstracts. A neighbouring country does not have a single complete set.

To break the information impasse, sporadic actions to fill gaps must give way to a determined programme of educating public officials, training librarians, motivating potential users and channelling funds where they are most effective. It is unfortunate that when there is a critical need for such institutional development in the information field, some Latin American Governments are reducing the budgets and importance of the national documentation systems which are in charge of training and development of documentation services. Administrators interested in this problem, instead of taking individual initiatives which are likely to be short-lived, would do better to strongly support their national documentation systems in trying to implement effective long-term programmes.

C. The road to frustration

Not only can published subject bibliographies be very expensive, but they can lead the user in the developing country into a series of frustrations. Documentation centres in developing countries are sometimes purchasing the bibliographies instead of journals or other primary materials. The user has access to information about what he cannot obtain. An abstract on occasion can serve as a useful substitute for the original document, but a title is seldom useful in itself.

To obtain the primary document, the user needs to know where the document is and the procedures for acquiring it. Union serial catalogues, data inventories, data base catalogues and complementary directories (such as CASSI for the Chemical Abstracts Service) are important for indicating the location of the document. Unfortunately, these are often lacking in developing countries.

An even more serious problem is arranging transfer or loan of the documents across national boundaries, among cities in a single country or even within an urban area where there is no tradition of inter-library loans.

The ordering of copies of documents, using deposit accounts and coupon systems, is a growing practice in developing countries. However, while there are ways to reduce the time delays in obtaining documents in these systems, to satisfy the needs of general or of well-planned research activities, these systems are not adequate to meet the immediate requirements of administrative decision making. This is an area that justifies serious experiment and innovation.

D. Guides to subject bibliographies

The information centres of developing countries need to evaluate existing subject bibliographical systems, networks, services and publications, for the purpose of determining which subject bibliographies to acquire for national information users or in which data bases it is more cost-effective to participate. There is one great obstacle to such an evaluation: the guides to subject bibliographies are generally very poor for these purposes. Although there are marked differences among guides in their coverage and in the aspects of each bibliography which are described, it is a very rare guide that offers more orientation than a simple checklist. 6/ Their authors seem to presume that the user will have ready access to copies of the subject bibliographies in order to determine their over-all usefulness.

As a result, the developing countries are very dependent on a hit-and-miss system of salesmen, brochures, consultants, international experts and other sources of partial information. The exaggerated chasm which separates commercial systems and international organizations, so that the relative advantages and disadvantages of their respective services are not easily ascertained, adds to this confusion. 7/

What would an adequate guide say about subject bibliographies? Annex II lists the most important information which is required. 8/ Most of this information, which is necessary to evaluate a priori the usefulness of subject bibliographies, can be gathered and reported quite easily. The most difficult information to obtain is with regard to search efficiency, which requires some direct experimentation with the subject bibliographies or the interviewing of users. In this regard, a number of studies already exist on coverage of journals and duplication among subject bibliographies; the results of these studies could

---

6/ Walford refers to a similar criticism, that annotations in guides "are predictable and tell the reader nothing beyond what he or she has already gleaned from the title and sub-title" of the reference material being described. A.J. Walford, "Compiling the 'Guide to Reference Material'", Journal of Librarianship, vol. 10, No. 2 (April 1978), pp. 88-96. See also Carl White, "How to avoid duplicated information", RQ, Winter 1970, tables 1 and 2. Note that White's table 2, although only comparing 8 kinds of information about journals supplied by 13 guides, demonstrates that most guides lack even the most elementary information. More recent guides generally have not improved in this. Better than most in this regard, in the field of public administration, is Antony Simpson, Guide to Library Research in Public Administration, 1976. An unusual guide in giving details on searching strategy and elements of the subject bibliographies is Marda Woodbury, a Guide to Sources of Educational Information, 1976. In part, because of the lack of adequate guides, the most valuable study for a Latin American librarian who has the opportunity to travel abroad is that of reference materials.

7/ As an example of this chasm, note the lack of reference to international organization data bases in Hilary Burton, "Multi-data base searching in agriculture", Special Libraries, vol. 69, No. 7 (July 1978), pp. 244-249. Reference courses in United States library schools often treat international sources very superficially.

8/ A much smaller list of suggestions in this regard is found in Christopher Needham and Esther Herman, The Study of Subject Bibliography with Special Reference to the Social Sciences, 1970.

be cited in the guides. 9/ However, a cautionary note is in order given that
this duplication is relative. Although there is duplication of subject and
journal coverage (or other document) apparently similar subject bibliographies
can differ considerably with regard to the access vocabulary to the references.
The adequacy of each vocabulary for the documentation service and its users must
be evaluated. Institutions in developing countries usually cannot afford
large-scale indiscriminate acquisitions of subject bibliographies. Nor are there
adequate instructional materials to aid this selection.

Ideally, there would be greater availability of audio-visual packages or
guides for documentation centres and libraries which would aid them in the
selection process, and from which instructional materials for users could be
separated. Present packages deal with only one or a few subject bibliographies
and do not offer a clear-cut vision of comparative advantages of the different
subject bibliographies.

E. Offers of subject bibliographies to documentation services

Documentation centres in developing and more industrialized countries alike
receive printed announcements, reviews, commercial salesmen and representatives
or experts from international organizations, all of which are sources of
information on the availability of subject bibliographies. What is offered?

In some cases the published bibliography is offered at a discount price to
developing countries or a sample edition will be given to the documentation
centre or library, often in recognition of the fact that, because of the
communication distances, the users in the developing countries will not take
advantage of the whole set of services which the publisher offers. In some
cases, the publishers simply refuse to allow institutions in developing
countries to make blanket purchases of services.

In 1971 Parkins and Kennedy predicted that special publications as
derivations from large computerized data bases would become more important and
that there would be a gradual decline in the growth rate of the massive
secondary journals. 10/ Unfortunately, this has not appeared to have taken
place, at least in South America; the publishers distribute their regular
publications and have not shown much interest in spin-offs geared to regional

---

9/ Particularly interesting is the methodology used by John Martyn and
Margaret Slater, "Tests on abstract journals", Journal of Documentation,
vol. 20, No. 4 (December 1964), pp. 212-235. A more common approach is that of
Thelma Freides, "Bibliographic gaps in the social science literature", Special
Libraries, vol. 67, No. 2 (February 1976), pp. 68-75.

10/ Phyllis V. Parkins and H.E. Kennedy, "Secondary information
services", Annual Review of Information Science and Technology, vol. 6,
(1971), pp. 247-275.

interest.

F. Effectiveness of subject bibliographies as searching tools

Although some subject bibliographies are oriented to specific purposes
such as searching on citations, "browsing", or SDI, this alone hardly explains
the wide variations of efficiency among the rest of them as searching tools.
This relative efficiency could be analyzed in retrieval studies of published
bibliographies, in comparisons of the existence of searching aides and in
comparisons of manual and on-line searching.

The author does not know of recent studies by independent analysis rating
only published subject bibliographies in terms of ease of search. 11/
In his 1977 social science reference class in the Graduate School of Library and
Information Studies, University of California, Berkeley, a rating was made by
several students of major subject bibliographies, each student choosing a
different search question. In each case study, the ratings for different subject
bibliographies were quite varied. The author's own ratings are given in annex
III.

The techniques and devices which are and can be used to facilitate manual
searching are many, as indicated in annex IV. Most of these techniques and
devices are practiced or at least considered in the sophisticated construction
of thesauri. Some scholars have made favourable and critical commentaries
regarding the incorporation of such techniques and devices in selected subject
bibliographies, but without a systematic study of their relative
effectiveness. 12/

Elchesen alludes to the differences in ease of subject retrieval through
subject bibliographies, when comparing the relative efficiency of using on-line
searching (with off-line printing) over manual searching. His study, which
controls for different search topics or information sources and for factors
which are incomparable between the two modes of searching, concludes that there
is a general uniformity of differences between manual and on-line searching
with regard to search time (on-line advantage), labour costs (on-line advantage),
costs of acquisition of the information and of reproduction (manual advantage,
although his formula for calculating information costs for manual searching is

---

11/ Of 40 pertinent citations by Elchesen of studies of the effectiveness
of on-line and manual searching, 11 deal with both types of searching and 29
deal only with on-line searching. Dennis R. Elchesen, "Cost-effectiveness
comparison of manual and on-line retrospective bibliographic searching", Journal
of the American Society for Information Science, vol. 28, No. 2 (March 1978),
pp. 56-66.

12/ Collison, Abstracts and Abstracting Services, pp. 41-50. Also
Robert Collison, "Current American trends in indexing", The Indexer, vol. 8,
No. 1 (April 1972), pp. 20-22. K.G.B. Bakewell, "Indexing methods used by
some abstracting and indexing services", The Indexer, vol. 10, No. 1 (April
1976), pp. 3-8. Barbara Hale, The Subject Bibliography of the Social Sciences
and Humanities, 1970, chaps. 6 and 7. Thelma Freides, Literature and
Bibliography of the Social Sciences, 1973, chaps. 7-9.

most debatable), precision ratios (manual advantage) and total turnaround time
(manual advantage). However, "the search tools available for the hard copy
and machine-readable versions of many information sources differ considerably in
terms of subject control, ease of use and intercompatiblity'." Large variations
were observed among the published information sources regarding total costs of
searching, number of citations per search, recall ratio and "perhaps the single
most important cost-effectiveness measure: cost per relevant citation retrieved."
13/ Caballero also affirms that the unit price to the user (subscription price
divided by number of references) varies markedly among published indexes. 14/
Lantz concludes that a higher "degree to which the structure of the indexing
language reflects the subject of the query" and the lack of abstracts or
summaries result in cost-effective superiority of a subject bibliography, in
comparison to its computerized reference counterpart. 15/

G. The tendency to automation

    While the upward tendencies of publishing costs (and thus subscription
prices) and the downward tendencies of computer processing, CRT terminal and
telecommunication costs mean that on-line searching will generally enjoy ever
greater cost advantages in the more industrialized countries, there are certain
conditions in developing countries which must be weighted in making such cost
comparisons. These conditions could include: lower searcher skill and labour
costs; higher costs of acquisitions and transmission of information (due to the
longer distances which are often involved); less intensity of use (and thus
delays in connexion) of the on-line connexion; improvised physical layouts
for terminals; a less reliable communication system within the country; less
familiarity by computer personnel with retrieval software; language difficulties
in using vocabulary tools and interactive capabilities; differences in
interpretations of retrieval vocabulary terms (meaning user time taken in sorting
out these differences in his mind); more delays in complete turn-around time;
and other specific circumstances. When all these factors are added, they could
demonstrate that on a cost-effectiveness basis, the relative advantages of
manual searching would predominate in places further removed from world
communication centres. Factors which could favour automation include a high
grade of development of the communication system, of investment in the
hardware system and of experience with data bases, 16/ or on the contrary, a
strong underdevelopment of basic reference collections (meaning that the

---

    13/ The fact that the CIS data base searches were much more costly in the
initial experiment than the manual CIS searches, perhaps has to do not only
with "searcher inexperience and data base complexity", as Elchesen reports, but
also to the CIS published indexes being very well constructed to facilitate
manual search. See annex III in this paper, Elchesen, "Cost-effectiveness
comparison...".

    14/ F. de A. Caballero, "Aspectos de la economicidad y comercializacion
de las bases de las bases de datos", Revista Espanola de Documentacion
Cientifica, vol. 1, No. 3 (1978), pp. 249-250.

    15/ Brian Lantz, "Manual versus computerized retrospective reference
retrieval in an academic library", Journal of Librarianship, vol. 10, No. 2
(April 1978), pp. 119-130.

    16/ Which is the case in Mexico. Myla K. Goldman, "Technical information
services in Mexico", Special Libraries, vol. 69, No. 9 (September 1978),
pp. 355-360.

initial investment in published works would have to be very
high). 17/

The likelihood and cost advantage of continued long-term reliance on hard
copy reference materials in developing regions needs to be generally recognized
by the publishers of such materials and by scholars on the subject. There are
various points of view, justifying more systematic studies and experiments on
whether published subject bibliographies are being relegated to accessories or
supplements to the use of computerized systems, or, on the contrary, publishers
and data base organizers are still tied to old ways (suitable for published
subject bibliographies) and not really exploiting the advantage of newer
technologies.

One argument refers to a low level of attention being paid to the
techniques and devices which could be tested and adopted to facilitate manual
searching in subject indexes (see annex IV). Also, some hard copy bibliographies,
especially in the social sciences, appear to have become spin-offs from the
computerized data base and the manual searcher is forced to simulate computer
operations of post-combination (post-co-ordination). A symptom of this is
overloading of descriptors in the indexes with so many cross-references
(identifiers) that the manual searcher is discouraged from having to look up so
many references. Another symptom of this is the use of factored terms with such
a broad meaning that they must be combined (or co-ordinated) with one or more
additional descriptors in order to be useful for searching. Examples of these
problems are given in annex III, and in the author's experience, several of these
subject bibliographies actually have become more difficult for manual searchers
in recent years.

A different argument, based on the experience with other subject
bibliographies and data bases, is that the design of the indexes in the data
bases is patterned too much on the published version and the retrieval
capabilities for data bases are unnecessarily restricted. The common complaint
then is that there has been insufficient discrimination by many system designers
between a structure of indexes appropriate for manual searching.

This topic is related to that of standardization which in general is
important for documentation centres in developing countries, the personnel of
which are ill-prepared for different search procedures with each subject
bibliography. While standardization of data elements for bibliographic
reference identification numbers and other elements is most laudable, it is
important to take into account the particular searching characteristics of
using printed services and of using computer-stored data bases.

17/ Two case studies of this in the United States are: Jane Beaumont,
"Providing an in-depth information service", Special Libraries, vol. 69, No. 8,
(August 1978), p. 289; Jean Martin, "Computer-based literature searching",
Special Libraries, vol. 69, No. 1 (January 1978), p. 2.

H. The vocabulary problem

A common complaint about subject bibliographies and data bases originating in the more industrialized countries and international organizations, is the lack of adequate attention to indexing vocabularies by designers of these systems. Some alarm is expressed about subject bibliographies which have no controlled vocabulary at all. The developing countries in particular would seem to have contradictory claims. On the one hand, the documentation services find bibliographical searching to be most cumbersome, because of the lack of standardization of vocabularies. Thus the users' requests have to be interpreted separately for each subject bibliography. On the other hand, there are claims for greater recognition of regional cultural and language differences. Several years ago, the Transport Division of the United Nations Economic Commission for Latin America considered regional transport planners' points of view regarding the most urgent and critical problems of that sector in the region. Although much had been written on these problems, the major sectorial documentation systems of the more industrialized countries had no appropriate or even reasonably adequate entry terms for searching on many of the problems. Also, the public administration uses of subject bibliographies, set out earlier in this article, each require special vocabulary development; a more flexible construction, perhaps, for the selection of concepts (models, hypotheses, variables); and a facet approach when specifying parameters for data on the variables.

A related claim is that traditionally the influence of developing country users and information specialists on vocabulary construction and maintenance has been quite weak. However, this situation is changing; the Latin American Centre for Economic and Social Documentation (CLADES) has taken a leadership role in consolidating Latin American points of view for the modification of the OECD Macrothesaurus, which is perhaps the most utilized thesaurus in the region. 18/ Also, during the last decade, many specialized thesauri and other vocabularies and codes have been developed with considerable innovation in Latin America; these products could be studied by the indexing services abroad as clues to regional points of view on appropriate vocabularies. 19/ More attention should

---

18/ Organization of Economic Co-operation and Development (OECD) and International Development Research Centre (IDRC), "Acta resumida", Macrothesaurus meeting, Paris, 5-7 October 1977.

19/ An inventory of such classification developments in the region is now being undertaken by the Argentine Centre for Scientific and Technological Information (CAICYT/CONICET), for the Iberoamerican Conference on Scientific and Technological Information and Documentation (Reuniber).

be paid to research on multi-lingual thesauri and switching mechanisms. The
latter can be of many types: (a) new vocabularies, as source or cumulative
thesauri, as a broad ordering of terms or for shallow indexing; (b) designation
of a host vocabulary or immediate lexicon (which could be the UDC, for example);
(c) free text searching on existing controlled vocabularies; (d) development
of an adjunct thesaurus; (e) a synonym or conversion table. [20]/ While
increasing their participation in the construction and maintenance of indexing
vocabularies, the institutions of the developing countries must realize that the
different objectives which are pursued in this endeavour are in fact
contradictory, and compromises must be made. However, this is a lame excuse
for the limited attention paid by some indexing services to the vocabulary
problem, or for the construction of vocabularies which do not meet any of the
criteria set out in annex IV. [21]/

I. Indexing of the developing countries' material

There is a surge of bibliographic control activity in developing countries,
even to the point of duplication of activity and a serious lack of co-ordination.
CLADES has made an inventory of such activity in the social sciences in Latin
America and a more general survey of indexing activities in the region is being
carried out by FID/CLA (Latin American Committee of the International Federation
of Documentation). Unfortunately for public administration, among the documents
which lack bibliographic control are the very ones (for example, unedited
documents) which are of particular importance to administrators. Sometimes
heroic efforts are required to sustain this bibliographic control activity.
One South American abstracting effort covering Latin American economic journals
was maintained for 10 years, although with a very small edition and not well-
known outside the country in which it was published, only to be curtailed for
some time due to the lack of paper. Several countries have concentrated on
their national bibliographies, with very uneven results. [22]/

Despite the problems involved with regional and national efforts, it would
be regretful if initiatives originating in the more industrialized countries
did not take these efforts into account, encourage them to continue and to

---

[20]/ These alternatives are discussed in R.T. Niehoff, "Development of an
integrated energy vocabulary and the possibilities for on-line subject
switching", Journal of the American Society for Information Science, vol. 26,
No. 1 (January 1976), pp. 3-17; and Dagoberto Soergel, Indexing Languages and
Thesauri: Construction and Maintenance, 1974.

[21]/ Win (Warren) Crowther, "Estructura y flexibilidad en los sistemas de
clasificacion de documentacion: una propuesta para America Latina", 2o
Congreso Regional sobre Documentacion y 11a. Reunion FID/CLA, (1972), pp. 17-20.

[22]/ Simeon B. Aje, "National libraries in developing countries", Advances
in librarianship, vol. 7, (1977), pp. 106-143.

standardize, help them become more co-ordinated and extend their coverage and seek ways to link them to international indexing activities.

A problem for developing countries interested in outside linkages is the lack of co-ordination and the implicit competition between commercial producers of subject bibliographies and international organizations. Commercial publishers seem to operate on the assumption that information is like any other raw material on the international market, whereby the developing country exports information for processing and can buy back the finished product. The publisher selects the information and enjoys a large part of the value added. He pays a royalty to the source, although will often argue that information he wishes to acquire should be a free-flowing commodity. 23/ International organizations seem to say that the developing country should process, deliver and get back the information on a cost basis, and should control the selection of what is indexed. 24/ An in-between position is that of the universities and professional organizations that publish subject bibliographies and that are often mainly concerned with satisfying their most immediate users and in minimizing their financial losses. 25/

From the point of view within the developing countries, the general policy issues include the following:

(a) How to get a better coverage of national intellectual production;

(b) Who collects and analyzes the information and submits it to the bibliographic publication or data base?

(c) What international indexing exists on the subjects of interest, and what are the terms of participation in those systems?

(d) National requirements for a national bibliography and specialized indexing;

(e) Compatibility of these national requirements with the norms of the international bibliographic efforts;

23/ A case study of the terms of incorporation of an indexing service into a commercial data base is John Newton, "World agricultural information service", Special Libraries, vol. 69, No. 7, (July 1978), pp. 250-254.

24/ John Woolston, "The importance of international information systems for building national capabilities", International Forum on Information and Documentation, vol. 2, No. 2, (1977), pp. 16-21.

25/ Herbert S. White and Bernard Fry, "Economic interaction between special libraries and publishers of scholary and research journals: results of an NSF study", Special Libraries, vol. 68, No. 3 (March 1977), pp. 16-21.

(f)   Controls for confidentiality and other safeguards needed in the national interest;

(g)   Who retains the value added for processing the materials?

(h)   Conservation of and access to the primary documents themselves;

(i)   Who manages the system?

Whichever system processes the developing country's materials, if any are interested and organized to do so, the country faces a difficult negotiation process of accommodating both national interests and the interests of the parties linked to the bibliographical system, network or service. The public administration of the country, to satisfy its own information requirements as well as the country's in general, needs to play an active role in defining positions on each of the issues.

J. Conclusion

With regard to each of the activities or elements of systematic information retrieval (figure XXXIV), much needs to be done to improve the utility of subject bibliographies. Although the problems affect all users of such reference materials, users in developing countries are especially affected. This paper has made a series of recommendations, some of which could be implemented on the initiative of the users of this information, particularly in the public administration, and some by the indexing service. A key mediating role could be played by interested international organizations.

Annex I

The arrangement of indexes in subject bibliographies

All the data elements about a document or set of data (for example, regarding a research project), its subject matter content or its statistical data, which are included in a subject bibliography are consolidated in the primary index (analogous to the data base "data map", "data model" or "conceptual model"). The data elements (analogous to "attributes") can be: (a) bibliographical data elements, (b) types of subject matter (for example, facets) or (c) statistical indicators. The specific values indicated for each document or data set (analogous to an "entity") which is represented or entered in the primary index, are: (a) bibliographical data if related to bibliographical data elements, (b) descriptors or keywords if related to subject matter, (c) statistical values if related to statistical indicators, (d) a number which is assigned to the document or data entries in a correlative or random manner, and/or (e) a significant code which combines this number with one of the other types of values. Any of these types of values is an identifier (for example, title of document, UDC, ISBN, significant code, name of subject of an interview, correlative number) if each value in the data element is unique to a document or data entry. Each document or data entry, and the complete set of values for it (for example, full bibliographic description) in the primary index is identified by at least one identifier. The information on the documents or data sets is ordered vertically in the primary index by an alphabetical, classificatory or numerical arrangement of determined identifiers. An inverted index is ordered vertically by an alphabetical, classificatory or numerical arrangement of the values (that is, key values) of one or more selected data elements. These values are each followed by an identifier (from the primary index) for each of the documents or data sets which is correctly described or the content of which is adequately described by the key value. While inverted indexes usually are limited to an ordering of key values and their corresponding identifiers, additional information is sometimes included after each identifier. This additional information consists of other values (or descriptors) about the document or data entry which is identified. In this way, an expanded inverted index is constructed with inclusion of data elements from the primary index, in addition to the data element(s) with key values and identifiers (pointers) to the entries in the primary index. A subject index is an index in which the key values (if it is an inverted index) or identifier (if it is a primary index) used to order the entries, are descriptors (key descriptors) or significant codes which are coded for descriptors. Examples of subject indexes are those based on geographical names, commodities, transport modes, academic disciplines, etc. Not all the key descriptors in an inverted subject index are necessarily followed by corresponding identifiers. The descriptors followed by identifiers (and thus used for cross-referencing to the primary index) are primary terms (P.T.), chosen as the "best" representation of a set of closely related descriptors. In the inverted index, the key descriptors not chosen as primary terms are followed by pointers to the related primary term in the index. In searching on an inverted subject index, the user begins with a descriptor of interest to him or her. By means of a thesaurus, or in the inverted index itself, the user is led from the descriptor to a preferred term and notes the identifiers which correspond to that term. These identifiers identify the document or data entries in the primary index for which the descriptor is relevant. The user may choose to combine (or co-ordinate) two or more preferred terms, selecting only the common identifiers among these terms. If an identifier is thus chosen, and that significance does not coincide with the user's interests, the user may choose to ignore it. Once he has selected identifiers of interest, he passes to the primary index to see the full entry of the document or data sets identified by the selected identifiers. If the document or data set entry in the primary index has an annotated or sentence-form representation of the content of the document or

Figure XXXV. Indexes in subject bibliographies

Inverted index

KEY DESCRIPTORS		IDENTIFIERS
P.T. A	–	(1) (20)
P.T. C	–	(1) (20)
P.T. F	–	(1) (5)
M	–	A (20)
	–	BOOK M C

Primary index

IDENTIFIERS		DESCRIPTORS AND OTHER VALUES
(1)	–	THESIS A C F
(5)	–	REPORT F
– BOOK M C		

Expanded inverted index

KEY DESCRIPTORS	IDENTIFIERS AND OTHER VALUES
A	–(1) THESIS, C, F (20) BOOK, M, C
C	–(1) THESIS, A, F (20) BOOK M
F	–(1) THESIS, A, C (5) REPORT
M	– A

Note : Several of the terms in this explanation here are based on analogies to terms commonly used to describe data base structures or in thesaurus construction. This is considered preferable to the inventing of a special vocabulary to describe the arrangement of subject bibliographies.

data set, that entry is an abstract.

Figure XXXV is a representation of the interrelationship between indexes used in bibliographic searching.

Annex II

Information necessary to evaluate subject bibliographies

The following information about each subject bibliography would be included in the guide. (The meaning assigned to key terms used here is given in annex I):

1. The subject matter on which the subject bibliography tends to specialize. In most cases, this can be a lot more specific than what the title indicates, or than the name of a discipline and/or sector of economic activity. The relationship of the selection of topics in the subject bibliography to a position (in agreement or disagreement) regarding the subject's current "paradigm" could be stated; a/

2. Use of techniques and devices to facilitate manual searching through the subject indexes (see annex IV);

3. Measures of, or user commentaries on searching effectiveness using the subject bibliography;

4. Information on how and from whom to purchase or request the subject bibliography;

5. Organization of the references in the primary-index(es) of the subject bibliography, and exploration if such an ordering of references is conducive to scanning or browsing;

6. The data element used for ordering references in each primary and inverted index. Thus, the identifier for ordering references in the primary index(es) is specified, and examples are given of the key descriptors which are used in each of the inverted subject indexes. The limits (maximum and minimum) of specificity of these descriptors is defined;

7. The information included for each reference in the subject bibliography, in the primary index(es) and in each inverted index. Preferably an example is given in the ·guide of typical entries in the primary and inverted indexes;

8. What primary and secondary sources are indexed, and if this demonstrates a tendency to favour "core" literature, non-conformist literature or other literature;

9. The types of documents which are cited in the subject bibliography;

---

a/ "Paradigm" is used in the Kuhnian sense (Thomas Kuhn, The Structure of Scientific Revolutions, 1970).

(a) Types of documents in terms of objective (theses, pamphlets, reports on research underway, translations, conference reports, etc.); (b) Types of documents in terms of form (microfilm, record, disk, photocopy, book volume, etc.);

    10. Extent of duplication of coverage with other subject bibliographies;

    11. Access by a computerized data base;

    12. Access to the documents or data cited in the subject bibliography.

Annex III

The ratings given in table 13 are admittedly impressionistic and not really measured. They primarily reflect the need for and difficulties in post-combination (or post-co-ordination) of terms using the subject indexes in searching on a variety of social science topics. An inverted subject index is considered to facilitate searching, especially if it has an uncomplicated classificatory structure, if there are "see also" and "see" cross-references among descriptors in the index, if the index is expanded to include more information (titles or additional descriptors) than the key descriptor and the corresponding identifiers, if there is no problem of overloading of too many references (identifiers) on each key descriptor, if broad highly factored terms are avoided and if there is word-ending or homonym control. The meaning of the terms used here is indicated in annex I.

Table 13. Subject indexes of major subject bibliographies:

	Alphabetical or classified	Inverted index-expansion and cross-references			
		"See also" to other descriptors in index	Expansion with other descriptors for each reference	Expansion with other title or keywords in title	"See" to other descriptors in index
PSYCH. ABSTRACTS Monthly	A	yes	——————————— no ———————————		yes
Biannual	A	yes	yes	no	yes
SOCIO. ABSTRACTS and LLBA	A	————————————————————— no —————————————————————			
IBSS	A	no	one or two terms only	no	no
HIST. ABSTRACTS and AMER. HIST. & LIFE	A	yes	- up to 5 keywords in alpha. order -		yes
BOOK REVIEW DIGEST	A	no	——————————— yes ———————————		yes
POPULATION INDEX	C	"See also" to other references	Annotation and title given		"See" to other references
POVERTY & HUMAN RESOURCES	A	no	——————————— yes ———————————		no
IBZ (Germany)	A	"See also" to other descriptors with relevant references	no	yes	yes, to descriptors in other languages
J. OF ECON. LITER.	C	no	no	yes	no
UNIVERSAL. REF. SYSTEM	C	yes	yes	no	yes
NTIS GOV'T REPORTS	A	no	no	yes	no
CIS/INDEX	A	yes	——————————— yes ———————————		yes
INTERNATL. LABOUR Doc.	A	no, need to use thesaurus	no	yes	no, need to use thesaurus

a/ Unless otherwise stated, the bibliographies being compared are not
   accumulations, which may have merited different ratings.

b/ Scale from 10 (post-co-ordination in manual search is relatively easy) to 1
   (greatest difficulty).

efficiency of search a/

Uniterm with overload	Specificity		Broad undefined terms	Word ending and homonym control	Controlled vocabulary or based on titles	Rating of searching ease
	compounded terms, less overload					
-	yes		-	yes	cont.	8 c/
-	yes, with overload		-	yes	cont.	7 c/
yes	-		yes	term endings	Title influenced	1 c/
-	yes		yes	no	cont.	2 c/
yes no overload due to chains	-		-	no		5 c/
-	yes		yes	no	both	4
-	yes		— defined by classification —			5
-	yes		yes	homonyms	both	5
-	yes with overload		yes	no	cont.	2 d/
-	yes		— defined by classification —			5 c/
yes	-		— defined by classification —			3/7 e/
-	yes		-	no	largely title influenced	3 c/
-	yes		-	yes	cont.	10 c/
yes	-		yes	no	cont.	2

c/ Search can also be made directly to the classified primary index of the biblio-graphy, requiring scanning, by users familiar and comfortable with the subject-heading classification. The primary index lends well to browsing by such users.

d/ Rating could be higher when index to subject headings available for most recent years.

e/ Access rating is much higher for users with practice in faceted approach.

Annex IV

Techniques and devices to facilitate manual searching through subject indexes

Note to annex IV: It is beyond the scope of this paper to enter into a
detailed explanation of each of the techniques or devices cited here. The
terms: primary index, identifier, inverted index, expanded inverted index,
descriptor and preferred term, are defined in annex I. The concepts of semantic
factoring, mutual exclusivity of meaning, pre-combined (pre-co-ordinated) and
post-combined (post co-ordinated) terms, specificity of terms, links, roles,
relator codes, PRECIS role operators, thesaurus construction elements, feature
or uniterm cards, and random clumping (L'Unite System) are described in
Alan Gilchrist, The Thesaurus in Retrieval, 1971. Also see Dagobert Soergel,
Indexing Languages and Thesauri: Construction and Maintenance, 1974; and
F.W. Lancaster, Vocabulary Control for Information Retrieval, 1972.

A.   In construction of the subject indexes

Vocabulary construction-choice of terms

1. Semantic factoring and control for mutual exclusivity of meaning
(perhaps with scope notes where necessary) for clarity of the significance of
concepts.

2. After the semantic factoring of terms, the vocabulary can be expanded
and concept distinctions clarified by adding pre-combined (pre-co-ordinated)
terms, parenthetical qualifiers for homonyms, and parenthetical qualifiers or
compound terms for terms with very broad meanings (for example, administration,
planning, region).

3. Consistency in the range of (maximum and minimum) specificity of the
terms included for any facet. For example, there would not be much more
specific terms for one subsector of industrial products than for another,
unless there was a sound justification for such discrimination.

4. Choice of levels or ranges of specificity so that there is not
over-loading of (too many) references (identifiers) on any key descriptor.

Expanded inverted indexes

5. Add the other pertinent descriptors for each reference in the inverted
index, along with the identifier (see example of expanded inverted index in
figure XXXV, annex I).

6. Add other pertinent descriptors for each reference (identifier) as
suggested in A5, but only those which form a meaningful "link" in the document
being described.

7. Insert between the complementary descriptors listed after each
identifier a relator code (for example, Perrault relators) or PRECIS role
operators.

8. After each identifier, print the title of the document.

Cross-references and codes

9. Use significant rather than merely correlative coding for the
identifiers. .In this way, more is known about the content of a document when
it is identified in an inverted index, than otherwise would be the case, before

making cross-reference to the full bibliographic reference in the primary index. The UDC or Dewey/Cutter combination could be used for this purpose.

10. Make cross-reference to near-synonyms, acronyms and spelling variants (see, see also) in the primary and/or inverted indexes.

Display of indexes

11. Construct separate indexes for each of the most important facets (space, time, products, institutions, etc.). It is useful to separate (and clarify the difference) between bibliographical description and content description here. For example, the same descriptors could be used to indicate when or where a publication was published, or to indicate the period of time and geographical space considered in the content of the document.

12. The construction of separate inverted indexes for different "roles"; but this could complicate the searching for most users.

13. The grouping of common morphemes, near-synonyms, acronyms and spelling variations together as one term. That is, after a preferred term in an inverted index, these other related terms would be placed.

14. All descriptors in an inverted index are placed in classified instead of alphabetic order or the index is accompanied by a graphic display (mapping) of the relationships between the descriptors.

15. Rather than the usual display of descriptors followed by identifiers in the inverted index, the index could be published in the form of feature or uniterm cards. Naturally, this technique could not be used together with significant coding for the identifiers (A. 9 above).

B. Rules for indexing each document

(beyond what would be required by the techniques and devices incorporated in the construction of the subject indexes)

1. Use separate identifiers (or subcodes) for different sections of each article or document being analyzed, based on "links".

2. If the title has significant terms not included in the controlled vocabulary, these terms are incorporated into the corresponding inverted index(es) in that issue of the subject bibliography.

3. The descriptors are weighted, and only in the case of the weighted descriptors is the reference (identifier) cited alongside of the same key descriptor in the inverted index.

4. The descriptors are included in the abstract, but are given special prominence, such as done by the International Labour Organisation and the institutions participating in DEVSIS indexing.

5. Each reference in the primary index includes all the descriptors for that reference.

`C. Searching techniques

1. Leading questions are compiled to lead the user in using the inverted indexes easily.

2. Post-combination (post-co-ordination) of terms is carried out by the "random clumping" (the L'Unite System) of the descriptors in the inverted indexes. This technique could be combined with that of A.15 above, whereby each feature or uniterm card has the identifier for a group of descriptors.

Objectives for an adequate indexing vocabulary

The indexing vocabulary:

1. Facilitates communication and interface between the documentalist or data analyst and the user who will search for the documents or data;

2. Facilitates communication among languages, terminologies and disciplines, among persons whose subject matter interest may coincide on occasion;

3. Is appropriate for the level of analytical capacity of the persons, equipment and software and for the amount of resources which will be available for analysis and processing;

4. Is constructed so that the user feels comfortable with the terminology, and participates in the construction and maintenance of the vocabulary. The users/sources should be able to visualize the relationship between the vocabulary and their own experiences and concepts;

5. Facilitates access to specialized terminologies;

6. Lends well to efficient retrieval of relevant and useful information;

7. Specifies ties to other vocabularies on the subject matter. In particular, is compatible with (or has switching to) existing vocabularies of major international organizations and documentation services, taking advantage of the indexing work done elsewhere, offering an efficient access to the data bases developed in such organizations and services and sharing responsibilities for vocabulary maintenance;

8. Keeps the quantity and complexity or ambiguity of terms to be maintained at a reasonable level;

9. Lends well to interaction or browsing by the user with regard to the data base.

INFORMATION SYSTEMS IN PUBLIC ADMINISTRATION
D. Eade, J. Hodgson (editors)
North-Holland Publishing Company
© *DFD, 1981*

INFORMATIQUE: UNE DIMENSION HUMAINE?

Alain Lédérer*

Nul ne niera que l'informatique, vue sous son aspect technologique, a fait des pas de géant durant ces dix dernières années. Parallèlement, l'abaissement spectaculaire des coûts a mis ce moyen, autrefois réservé à une élite, à la portée des plus petites cellules socio-économiques, et même à la portée de l'individu.

De plus en plus, l'informatique envahit notre vie, ce qui conduit les mass-média à revenir périodiquement sur l'influence de ces moyens. Et en général, ce n'est pas pour en dire du bien.

Qui, en effet, n'a jamais constaté "d'erreur de l'ordinateur" dans les nombreux documents imprimés qu'il reçoit?

Si nous nous contentons de la réaction de l'homme de la rue et des média, nous constatons que l'informatique est en général plutôt reconnue utile, mais qu'elle est aussi génératrice de nuisances, ou plus exactement de possibilités de nuisance.

Ce simple fait est, en ce qui me concerne, un pur constat d'échec.

Ces réactions ne sont pas sans rappeler les grandes colères populaires de la révolution industrielle. Pour l'homme de la rue, G. Orwel, auteur de "1984" n'a pas écrit un simple roman d'anticipation. Et en matière d'informatique, l'homme de la rue est aussi le directeur, le PDG, le dirigeant qui va devoir, dans son entreprise, choisir SON informatique. Pour ce faire, il devra s'adresser à des "spécialistes", vendeurs d'une part, informaticiens d'autre part. Si nous ne pouvons reprocher au vendeur de chercher à placer ses produits, nous pouvons nous demander quel sera l'impact du, ou des, informaticiens choisis pour le projet final.

Ayant eu de nombreux contacts avec des informaticiens d'expérience et de pays variés, j'ai toujours été étonné de constater que nombre d'entre eux

---

* International Standards Organization, Switzerland

conçoivent encore l'informatique comme elle l'était dans les années 60.

Ce qui me pousse a conclure que si la technologie à fait de réels progrès, il n'en est pas de même des hommes.

La centralisation, nécessaire compte tenu des moyens de l'époque, a créé une tour d'ivoire où l'être humain n'a que peu de place.

Et comme l'être humain a peur de l'inconnu, il craint les ordinateurs. Par ailleurs, s'il n'est que géné de devoir de temps en temps faire réviser sa voiture, et donc de s'en passer momentanément, il lui paraît intolérable de devoir se plier aux exigences de ce qu'il ne considère pas encore comme un simple outil de travail. De même, il accorde une grande importance à la somme des petites erreurs de programmation qu'il constate au fil des ans.

Tout ceci ne contribue pas à créer une relation harmonieuse entre l'homme et l'outil.

C'est donc à nous, informaticiens, de faire le premier pas. De changer périodiquement nos concepts. De nous tenir à l'écoute permanente de l'utilisateur. De lui fournir une aide réelle, un conseil, plutôt que de simplement jouer le rôle de traducteur langage humain - langage machine.

Dans tous les cas, il est essentiel pour la réussite d'un projet qu'une information claire soit effectuée, non seulement envers les personnes directement concernées, mais pour l'ensemble du personnel.

De même, les machines doivent être définies en fonction de la facilité d'utilisation par le non-informaticien, et là programmation toujours pensée dans ce but.

C'est donc l'homme qui fait la machine, et toute la différence entre le supportable et l'inacceptable.

Le dilemme de chaque chef d'entreprise lors de la mise en place d'un service informatique est:

Qui sera le futur chef du service?

Qui est cet homme, et comment le choisir?

Pour plagier un slogan célèbre, cela peut se résumer par: "l'imagination au pouvoir". C'est en effet pour moi le premier critère de sélection, car si la technique peut s'apprendre, l'imagination est innée, et elle seule peut donner toute sa dimension aux moyens mis en oeuvre.

La seconde qualité est d'avoir une bonne mémoire, de préférence du type associative ou photographique. Dans le cas précis de l'informatique, il ne s'agit pas de connaître par coeur l'ensemble des manuels, mais de se souvenir dans quel manuel se trouve la réponse à une question donnée.

La troisième qualité est d'être méthodique et organisé, et par conséquent logique.

La somme de ces qualités, alliée à une bonne expérience pratique, est très certainement une base saine. Le chef de service saura alors choisir des collaborateurs efficaces, en général plus spécialisés que lui en fonction des tâches à accomplir.

La première qualité citée implique également une vaste curiosité, et par conséquent, la personne concernée se tiendra au courant de l'avance logistique et technologique.

Ce qui nous conduit à examiner, en concurrence, les moyens techniques à notre disposition.

Nous connaissons d'une part les concepts traditionnels, ou en temps partagé, caractérisés par une importante centralisation et d'autre part, le concept de "l'informatique distribuée conversationelle".

Je suis un fervent supporter du second. La condition essentielle de "l'humanisation" de la machine, de la compréhension des problèmes complexes qu'elle pose, repose sur son utilisation.

Dans une organisation hautement centralisée, l'humain est enfermé à l'intérieur d'une cage de contraintes, dues tant à la machine qu'aux programmes et aux autres utilisateurs. Toutes choses qu'il ne peut pas maîtriser de façon supportable.

Au contraire, "l'informatique distribuée conversationelle" repose sur des petites unités autonomes, essentiellement constituées de non-informaticiens qui sont directement responsables de leurs travaux.

Les écrans sont particulièrement utiles dans ce cas, et les machines modernes permettent à l'utilisateur d'organiser son travail à sa guise, sans se soucier (dans la majorité des cas) de ce que les autres utilisateurs font.

Ce concept a plusieurs avantages majeurs, principalement pour les entreprises, collectivités et administrations n'ayant aucune expérience en ce domaine.

En effet, ces ordinateurs sont pour la plupart d'un type (appelé mini-ordinateur) permettant leur installation dans des bureaux normaux. Ils ne nécessitent qu'un minimum de personnel spécialisé, de l'ordre de quatre personnes. La puissance de traitement de ces ordinateurs est égale à celle des gros systèmes pour un prix nettement inférieur.

Et surtout, ils permettent une introduction extrémement progressive de l'informatique dans l'entreprise, accompagnée d'une information motivant le personnel non spécialisé qui influencera directement les résultats par son travail à l'écran, et corrigera automatiquement ses propres erreurs grâce au mode conversationnel.

Pour le dirigeant, le PDG ou le responsable de la mise en oeuvre des moyens automatisés, le faible investissement de départ permet en tout état de cause un retour en arrière aux méthodes manuelles s'il s'avère que les résultats ne sont pas satisfaisants, ce qui est pratiquement impossible avec un système conventionnel centralisé.

L'ensemble de ces caractéristiques font du concept de "l'informatique distribuée conversationelle" un outil de choix pour les projets inclus dans l'activité de Données pour le Développement.

Elles correspondent également aux critères d'efficacité et d'éducation généralement recherchés par les pays concernés. Par ailleurs, elles contribuent largement, à moyen terme, à l'information directe de l'homme de la rue, et à l'humanisation de la technique qui en découle.

L'expérience prouve que ce concept tend à se généraliser, et il est certain que cette tendance s'accentue rapidement. Pour terminer, chacun devrait se souvenir que l'homme et la technique ne sont rien si l'organisation

les entourant est défaillante. Bien des entreprises ont eu à supporter les
conséquences de l'oubli de cet axiome, trop souvent négligé par les
informaticiens eux-mêmes.

L'accès a l'informatique technologique repose donc sur des concepts
rapprochant les moyens techniques modernes de l'homme, qui permettent
d'établir une relation de confiance garantissant de bien meilleurs résultats
à long terme.

INFORMATION SYSTEMS IN PUBLIC ADMINISTRATION
D. Eade, J. Hodgson (editors)
North-Holland Publishing Company
© *DFD, 1981*

FINAL REPORT OF WORKING GROUP 5*

A. Introduction

Group 5 was established to consider management and development issues as they relate to technological information systems. In this context the Group defined technological information systems as including all non-numeric systems.

This report is based on the deliberations of the Group and contains its major conclusions. It contains a definition of the Group's understanding of what is meant by "development", some underlying assumptions and several specific recommendations concerning priority action to be undertaken by DFD. In the preparation of this document, the Group has drawn extensively from the material contained in its working papers. As a first major conclusion of its work, the Group considered that the historical differentiation which has existed between numeric (particularly statistical information systems) and non-numeric information (such as bibliographic information systems) is no longer valid. The rapid development which has taken place in computer and communications technology coupled with the significant cost reductions now make it possible to consider significantly increasing the level of integration of numeric and non-numeric information systems in order to provide faster and more complete response to user information needs.

B. The meaning of development

The Group agreed that in the context of the problems which are currently being faced in developing countries, there are three essential elements associated with the present concept of development, namely:

---

*Participants : L. Basave Aguirre, Mexico ; J.C. Cohen, France ; W. Crowther (rapporteur), U.S.A. ; V. Jorssen, Canada ; J. Kennerley (Chairman), Canada ; H. Zuleta Garcia, Venezuela.

(a) The need to provide for continuity and effectiveness;

(b) The ability to change system boundaries; and

(c) The need to strengthen national and community problem solving capabilities.

The problem of continuity was raised in the context of the situation encountered in many developing countries in which there is a very high degree of mobility of senior public servants and decision makers. This occurs for a number of reasons: because of the scarcity of qualified persons and the need to promote public servants to fill new positions; because of the drain of qualified staff into corporations in the private sector; and because of changes in Governments. The frequent changes of senior decision makers in the public sector has had and continues to have serious consequences for information systems development programmes in developing countries and not infrequently, this has considerably reduced the effectiveness of national and international efforts in this field.

The Group suggested the following simplified formula to describe the conditions under which significant changes and/or information systems development programmes are most likely to be successful:

Ideally $X < Y < Z$

where X = the amount of time necessary to implement a significant change/information systems programme

Y = the amount of time permitted by the system of rotation of decision makers

Z = the inertia factor, where by the decision maker places more emphasis/importance on his or her role as an organization member or system defender than as a change agent

In other words, and under ideal conditions, significant changes can be effected when the time required to make the change is less than the time permitted by the system of rotation of decision makers (that is, government election cycles) and less than the time it takes for a decision maker to lose interest in making the change.

The second important element associated with development relates to the need to be able to expand system boundaries. Our lives are determined to a large extent by the system(s) in which we live, the cultural, social, economic and political environment; organizations objectives and procedures; scientific and technological paradigms, professional competence and prerogatives; technological packages and definitions of problems. These, especially in well-established societies, tend to build in inflexibilities and adversely affect society's ability to innovate and change. Yet the modern concept of development requires that society has the ability to continuously adapt, change and expand its horizons.

The Group considered that information systems have tended to be developed in order to describe the present (stable) conditions prescribed by existing "systems" - for example statistical systems - and to satisfy historical data needs. Far more emphasis however needs to be placed on the development of flexible information systems capable of meeting changing needs and expanding horizons.

The third important element addresses the need to build up and strengthen indigenous problem solving capabilities, particularly in developing countries.

In this context, the Group considered that a very large part of national information systems efforts and international assistance, including DFD's activities, has been directed towards developing high level scientific technological and socio-economic information systems (networks) and that not nearly enough effort has been directed towards making information more readily accessible usable by end-users.

This phenomena can be depicted as in the information flow suggested in figure XXXVI. In the information flow, the Group recognized two problems. Firstly, in the absence of a well structured national information network (particularly within the community of problem solvers), and of reliable information concerning national activities and information sources, too much reliance is placed on drawing from external information sources. Secondly, discontinuities/static in the information flow typically exist in the absorption of data from the community of problem solvers into national systems.- point A in the figure - and in the absorption of data as derived from national systems by problem solvers - point B in the figure.

Figure XXXVI. Problems in information flow to end users
(aimed at building up national problem solving capabilities)

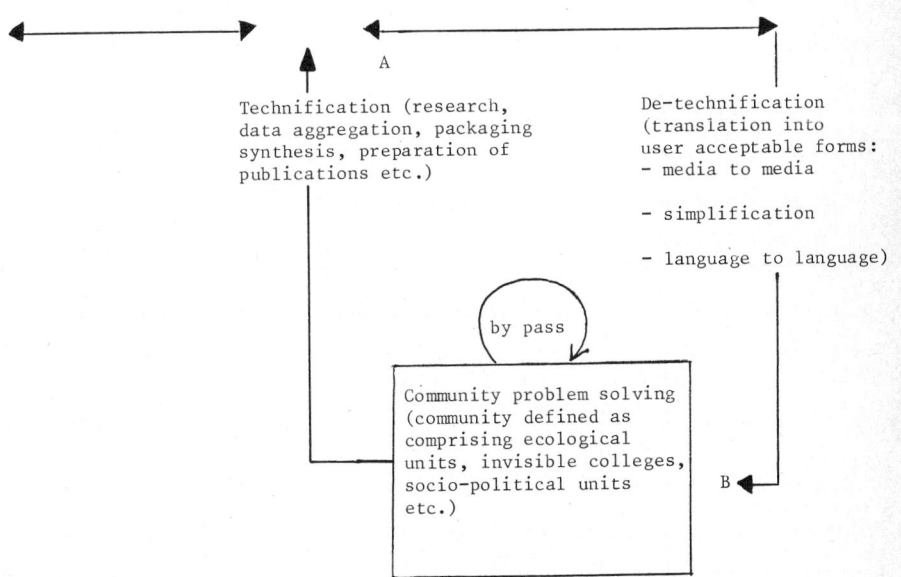

International/regional information systems and networks

National scientific, technological and socio-economic information systems and networks

A

Technification (research, data aggregation, packaging synthesis, preparation of publications etc.)

De-technification (translation into user acceptable forms:
- media to media

- simplification

- language to language)

by pass

Community problem solving (community defined as comprising ecological units, invisible colleges, socio-political units etc.)

B

C. Information systems development design parameters

Although the Group recognized the existence of a large number of information systems development design parameters, time permitted consideration of only two, namely the concepts of

(a) Decentralization versus centralization; and

(b) Information priorities and needs.

Considerable stress was placed by the Group on the concept of decentralization versus centralization in information systems design. In this context, the Group identified a number of advantages associated with decentralized systems. These included:

(a) An opportunity for information sources to become more closely identified with information processing activities, resulting in an incentive for those involved in data collection to generate accurate data - increased reliability;

(b) An opportunity to distribute data collection costs; and

(c) An opportunity for those involved in data collection to ensure better control over confidentiality of the data.

The Group recognized, however, that decentralization also implied the need for considerable emphasis to be placed on standardization in respect of classification procedures as well as a need for close adherence to data collection schedules.

Concerning information needs/priorities, the Group considered that these evolved or could be identified in a number of ways and that the final selection of priorities frequently resulted from the dynamic interplay/interaction of needs as identified by:

(a) National goals;

(b) Basic needs (individual users);

(c) Deficiencies and constraints;

(d) Availability of technologies, technological packages and alternative solutions.

The interaction/interplay just referred to is depicted in figure XXXVII.

Figure XXXVII. Factors influencing the selection of information priorities

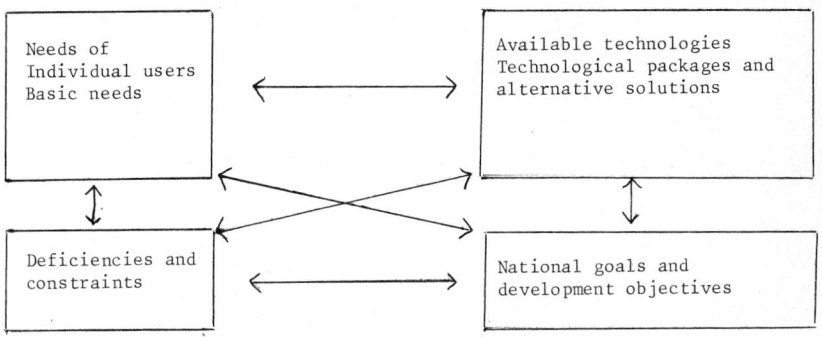

D. Underlying assumptions

In order to set the framework for the Group's consideration of some of
the major problems and issues which are being experienced in respect of
technological information systems and the reasons for many of these, the
following underlying assumptions were identified:

(a) The information needs of managers, officials, engineers and
researchers in the public and private sector, particularly their needs as
related to development planning and decision making, are highly diffuse. This
is reflected in part by the information contained in table 14;

(b) Historically, users of information have tended to place far more and
perhaps undue emphasis on the value of quantitative information over qualitative
information;

(c) With the advent of advanced information processing and communications
technology, there is a strong tendency to "individualize" information systems;

(d) With the tremendous mass of data and documents being produced (and the
tendency to move towards "an information society" particularly in developed
countries) there is going to be a need for greater selectivity in the information
being collected and stored. This in turn calls for the development of carefully
derived criteria governing the selection of data and its accessibilities. These
criteria need to be institutionalized to curtail individual interventions which
limit access to documents/data;

(e) Given the technological developments which are taking place, it is
unnecessary to continue to use non-numerical data versus numerical data, as the
basis for discriminating input, processing systems and output; and

(f) There is a generalized cycle of documents/data handling, summarized in
table 15 which is applicable to both quantitative and qualitative information.
The similarity of basic functions for handling all types of information is
obscured by the terminological difference among the different specializations of
information.

Table 14.   Information requirements of decision making
for development

ACTIVITIES

TYPES OF INFORMATION	Issue Definition	Planning	Decision making	Imple-mentation	Control	Eval-uation
Expressions of community positions	A	B	A	B	A	A/I
Political, economic and social trends	A	A	–	I	–	I
Laws and regulations	–	B	A/I	B	A	–
Alternative Technologies	B	A	A	B/I	–	I
Historical information	–	B	B	–	–	I
Methodology of work	–	A	A	A	A	A
Economic and social theory	A	A	B	–	–	B
International environment	A	A	A	B	B	A/I
Suggestions as to models, hypotheses and variables	–	A	A	–	A	A/I
Indications for variables	–	A/I	A	–	A	A
Values for the indicators, based on case studies, survey data, etc. of resources and performances	–	A	A	A	A/I	A/I

A = Very important type of information for the activity

B = Important type of information for the activity

I = Activity generates this type of information

Table 15. The secondary information source as a working tool of public administration: public administration as a source/user of information

I. Organization and processing of secondary sources for "co-ordination"	II. Organization information services	III. User situation and activities	IV. Handling of primary sources and of simple secondary sources
Compilation and publication of guides to SB and DB	Obtaining of documentation service and training of staff	User or documentation service has means to acquire documents or data	Selection of documents and data to be indexed
Acquisition of guides to SB and DB	Obtaining of information on where and how to acquire cited documents on data	Document or data acquisition and delivery to user	Availability of bibliographies or inventories produced locally
Publication and availability of SB and DB, with search capabilities	Organization of SB or DB access in the documentation service	User motivation or potential interest	Elaboration of national bibliography
		User general knowledge about usefulness of SBs or DBs	Institutional bibliographic control or inventories
Selection and acquisition by documentation service of SB or DB access		Study of the document on data by the user	Organization of documents and data in archives
			Registry (and possible publication) of decisions, and of results of studies and decisions

ACTIVITIES IN THE ADMINISTRATION : 1. Definition of issue on problem ; 2. Studies ; 3. Decisions. User knowledge of documentation service.

Note : Each of the steps indicated here of the "direct access" and "systematic retrieval" (with co-ordination of terms) approaches to organizing the information products and meeting the information needs of public administration, involves a complicated design and implementation process. If any of these steps is not duly taken into account, the entire effort is subject to breakdown (that is, the pertinent part of the available primary information does not arrive to the public administration opportunely).

E. Areas for consideration

Based on the foregoing assumptions and an appraisal of the present
situation, especially in developing countries, the following list of key problems
and recommendations for action was drawn up. This list is only meant as a
summary statement, based on the documents submitted to this Working Group and
the discussions of the Group. The recommendations are grouped under "general"
and "specific" considerations for the development of national integrated
information infrastructure, organized along the general lines indicated in
table 15.

1. General considerations

(a) Bring economics into information science

DFD has, as part of its ongoing activities, set out a very useful set of
distinctions and definitions of concepts. However, little effort has been
devoted to assessing the cost/effectiveness of the concepts. Within the
framework of its pilot projects and other activities relating to integrated
information systems approaches, DFD could usefully undertake some work on this
subject. This work could be carried out by economists who are DFD members.

(b) National information policies

Historically, generally speaking the absence of a dependable national
information infrastructure and well-defined information policies, particularly
in developing countries, has tended to result in inadequate control and
management as well as under-utilization of useful information generated for or
by Governments.

National Governments, quasi and semi-governmental agencies, which are not
only primary sources but also primary users of technological and development
information, suffer in many cases from a lack of co-ordination of their own
internal information and communications systems. Intra-agency document
referencing systems, often of the most rudimentary sort, falter due to
fractionalization or overlap of subject interests, careless management of
restricted or confidential information, and a general lack of information outside
of the generating department or authority. Additionally, in many countries
ineffective government publications policies and non-existent or unenforceable
depository laws have hampered the flow of internally generated information.

The design of an information policy should be a continuous effort, not a
one-shot project. It thus requires an institutional mechanism, preferably a
national institute or body responsible for information policies, to assure
continuous research, development, training, experimentation and evaluation.

In this context, the present work of UNESCO/UNISIST on national
information systems is particularly important. It should also be focused to
take developing countries experience into account, and aimed at developing
suggestions for the solution of certain key policy issues.

(c) Training of information scientists

A major handicap in the design and implementation of integrated
information systems is the overspecialization in the training and institutional-
ization of the information professions: archivology, communication, documentation, library, science, statistics, computation, etc.

Solution of multidisciplinary information systems problems that require
knowledge from a variety of specializations can only occur when there is a good

foundation and sound terminological and conceptual integration among the information sciences.

To overcome this handicap, there is an urgent need _inter-alia_ to develop:

    (i)   A glossary, in various languages, of the equivalent terms used by the various specialties to describe analogous functions; and

    (ii) Courses and workshops which bring together all the information specialties in order to study concepts of information science, design and implementation of information systems, information policies and data collections. Universities should be encouraged to incorporate such courses in a joint curriculum for information related departments.

A DFD special interest group or working group should be established to work up the glossary (together with the corresponding ASIS commission), and DFD members with experience in this field should be asked to assist in teaching courses, giving workshops and preparing national teachers for these courses and workshops in this field.

(d)   Extending information services to the general population

Historically, there has tended to be a considerable degree of elitism in the elaboration of technological information systems in developing countries. These systems promote a "technification" of the observations and research on technological and social experience as well as in the exchange of information among the technicians and to some extent a "detechnification" of the function for popular consumption (see figure XXXVI). This is a costly process and often distorts the reporting and dissemination process. To solve this problem, means should be sought which permit a by-passing of the "eliticism" process in order to facilitate more direct access to information by problem solvers at the community level. This is an important area of research which might possibly be undertaken by UNESCO.

(e)   Identification of information needs/requirements/priorities

Priorities regarding information developments can be established according to any of the following criteria:

    (i)   Basic needs of the population;

    (ii) Stated national goals;

    (iii) Deficiencies and constraints: needs minus resources, taking into account available solutions;

    (iv) Information system qualities which are lacking; and

    (v) Packaged (technological) solutions.

It is the last-named of these criteria which seems to be most influential in the developing countries. A methodology needs to be elaborated to help in the determination of priorities among information projects at the national level. This would be a logical follow-up activity to DFD's work on data and development.

(f) Conceptual approach to the setting up of national networks of information systems

The advent of modern information handling, communication and retrieval technologies and methods now make it possible to achieve a greater degree of integration. Traditionally, the latter have stressed retrieval capabilities. However, historically, this has not been the case for statistical information systems which have only recently begun to emphasize this aspect as a result of the rapid growth and diversity of user requirements.

From the user's point of view, more and more synthesis should take place among information systems to this end and a more integrated approach should be considered to better meet individual user needs.

DFD can contribute to conceptualization of this approach, taking into account the advanced technological possibilities which are evolving, by producing realistic estimates of a need to refocus priorities in such a way as to satisfy the real information requirements of users, especially in LDCs.

2. Specific considerations

User situation and activities

(a) Support activities in systematic information gathering, analysis and dissemination by professional organizations in developing regions and countries in any fields related to development

In many developing countries, the professional infrastructure is very weak and the information collection and dissemination processes are almost non existent. In an effort to improve this situation, international organizations should provide support to national and regional organizations. This could take much the same form as the service of the Office of Science Information Service of the National Science Foundation of the United States. Unfortunately, however, information exchange at the regional level in the developing world and improvement of access to secondary services in general have been rather marginal issues in the professional organizations up to the present time, and those organizations will need to be encouraged to enter more actively into this field. Publicity concerning the availability from DFD members to professional organizations on this subject could stir interest in this subject. This is an ideal subject for inclusion in the DFD pilot projects.

(b) Methodology to identify core user groups, and to use them to promote wider user motivation and knowledge of information systems

Fortunately, with some encouragement from governmental agencies, universities and international organizations, the small core group of persons in the developing countries who recognize the importance of systematic retrieval and who are relatively sophisticated users of information, can be convinced to co-operate in elaborating and implementing an over-all plan to broaden the reach of documentation and statistical services in this field. The challenge is great, but certainly not impossible, and this activity is a most important candidate for attention from the international organizations interested in fostering scientific and technological development in the developing countries. The elaboration of a suitable methodology for this might be undertaken by the International Federation for Documentation (FID) or a comparable organization. Particular attention also needs to be given to promoting awareness of the value of non-numerical information within the framework of integrated systems.

(c) Full use of pertinent information for national planning and administration

      International organizations interested in the public administration sector of the developing countries could make a significant contribution towards improving the utilization of information by initiating programmes which encourage effective use of information available for planning and decision making. Decision makers, when they see that successful results are consistently achieved through optimum use of available information, will soon recognize the importance of establishing policies and providing means for making the wealth of knowledge contained in printed materials readily accessible.

      Professionals, university students and other potential users need courses on research, planning and decision making methods as well as the use of information for such purposes. Universities should be encouraged to include such courses as part of their regular academic and extension programmes.

(d) Experimentation and evaluation of the supply-inducement strategy for the implementation of information systems

      Libraries have traditionally set up collections for rather unspecified future consultation by users, with the expectation that the users will be interested and motivated to make use of the collections. More recently, there have been comparatively sophisticated versions of this attempt to induce the use of systems by setting up an offer of pertinent information. The AGRINTER system in agriculture in Latin America, with regional-wide inputs into its subject bibliographies, elaborates materials and trains documentalists in user education. The industrial information centres of several countries following INFOTEC of Mexico, send bibliographical information to industrialists in each of these countries to foster their use of various documentation services. The Latin American Population Documentation (DOCPAL) system also uses an information dissemination system to induce interest of potential users in technical documentation. Although it is more expensive than demand-induced development of documentation systems, the tactic of these systems in creating broader user interest on the basis of supply may be much more viable, given the user situation which exists in many developing countries.

      Research on this strategy and a systematic comparison with demand-inducement strategies would be very useful, particularly for developing countries having relatively unsophisticated information users.

User-system interface/information services

(e) User-related audio-visual materials on information sources and training for those providing information services

      Ideally, there should be far more audio-visual packages or guides for documentation centres and libraries for use in helping to select information sources and organizing user oriented information services, and from which instructional materials for the education of users could be separated. Present packages tend to deal with only one or a few information sources and services and do not offer precise information concerning the comparative advantages provided by acquisition possibilities in the full range of information services which could or should be provided.

      International organizations should be encouraged to finance or prepare the materials which can then be reproduced and distributed broadly among developing countries.

      DFD members could be registered, for teaching the courses on information services.

(f) Feasibility studies of information retrieval and reference systems

Given the upward tendencies of publishing costs (and thus subscription prices) and the downward tendencies in computer processing, CRT terminal and telecommunication costs, on-line searching can be expected to enjoy ever greater cost advantages in the more industrialized countries. However, a similar situation may not be applicable in developing countries in which other factors may outweigh cost considerations. These conditions could include lower searcher skill and labour costs, higher costs of acquisition and transmission of information (due to the longer distances which are often involved), less intensity of use (and thus delays in connexion) of the on-line connexion, improvised physical layouts for terminals, a less reliable communication system within the country, less familiarity by computer personnel with retrieval software, language difficulties in using vocabulary tools and interactive capabilities, differences in interpretations of retrieval vocabulary terms (meaning user time taken in sorting out these differences in his mind), more delays in complete turn-around time, and other specific circumstances. When these kinds of factors are taken into account they could demonstrate that intensive cost-effectiveness and use of manual searching techniques could be more advantageous than automated techniques, particularly in remote areas. Factors which could favour automation include a high grade of development of the communication system, of investment in the hardware system and of experience with data bases, or on the contrary, a strong underdevelopment of basic reference collections (meaning that the initial investment in published works would have to be very high).

There is an urgent need for DFD to carry out studies relating to:

(i)   The trade-offs to be considered in developing countries, or in more isolated or remote areas, in choosing manual or automated storage and access to documentation and data sets; and

(ii) The choice of manual, semi-automatic, mini-computer and intelligent terminal retrieval systems, which permit later technological upgrading of the system at least cost.

(g) "Humanized" systems

System builders have tended in the past to apply a technological connotation to the solution of complex problems in developing countries, many of which cut across many cultures and different kinds of fields of technology. To be able to pursue the concept of providing systems which meet user needs, the participation of non-information specialists in the design phase of systems is needed. These specialists for example would have expertise in the fields of sociology and economics.

It is therefore recommended that DFD:

(i)   Create a special interest group to study the involvement and interface of end users in the development of computer systems;

(ii) Sponsor or co-sponsor short seminars in co-operation with other international organizations on this subject for developing countries.

(h) Mechanisms for documentation/data acquisition for the user beyond what is immediately accessible in a local collection

Use of published subject bibliographies and data reference systems can be frustrating for users in developing countries. Many documentation centres in developing countries are purchasing expensive bibliographies instead of journals or other primary materials. Furthermore because of financial and physical space constraints, collections are highly inadequate. Thus it is not common to find that users in developing countries only have access to information on documents which are not available. An abstract on occasion can serve as a useful substitute for the original document, but a title is seldom useful in itself.

To obtain primary documents, users need to know where these are, and the procedures for acquiring them. Union serial catalogues, data inventories, data base catalogues and complementary directories (such as CASSI for the Chemical Abstracts Service) are important for indicating the location of documents and data. Unfortunately these are often lacking in developing countries.

An even more serious problem is arranging transfers or loans of the primary documents or data across national boundaries, among cities in a single country or even within an urban area where there is no tradition of inter-library loans.

The ordering of copies of documents, using deposit accounts and coupon systems, is a growing practice in developing countries. However, while there are ways to reduce the time delays in obtaining documents in these systems to satisfy the needs of general or of well planned research activities, these systems are not adequate to meet the immediate requirements of administrative decision making.

This is an area that justifies serious experimenting and innovation, perhaps most logically under the sponsorship of UNESCO.

Organization and processing of secondary sources

(i) Guides and inventories of information sources

Information centres in developing countries need to evaluate existing bibliographical systems, networks, services and publications, for the purpose of determining which secondary sources to acquire or access for national information users. There is one great obstacle to such a determination: the guides to secondary sources are generally very poor for these purposes. Although there are marked differences among guides in their coverage and in the aspects of each bibliography which is described, it is a very rare guide that offers more orientation than a simple checklist.

As a result, developing countries tend to be very dependent on a hit-and-miss system of salesmen, brochures, consultants, international experts and other sources of partial information. The exaggerated chasm which separates commercial systems and international organizations, so that the relative advantages and disadvantages of their respective services are not easily ascertained, adds to this confusion.

There is a great need for criteria to be set out for editors of such guides to assure that the guides are useful for reference and acquisition in developing countries. At the very least, such guides should incorporate references to the information products of the developing countries.

(j) Inventories of institutional information sources

There is a great need in developing countries for the preparation of a complete national inventory of national directories of information sources and resources in public administration. Such an information gathering task has already been undertaken in part by some of the regional commissions and

international organizations in their attempt to identify existing capabilities
and the areas that are in need of improvement. As a result, a mechanism
necessary for gathering updated information has already been installed in some
regions and sectors.

The country or regional inventories would separate out data for
international reference, ideally using the UNEP/INFOTERRA framework as a basis
for the design of the national and regional inventories, and using INFOTERRA
as the vehicle for sharing. All countries should be encouraged to associate
with the INFOTERRA system, and to request UNEP assistance in preparing
national variations of the data collection formats in tune with national
needs.

Offer of secondary sources

(k) Feasibility of preparing custom-tailored subject and bulletins for developing regions

During the early 1970s, it was predicted that special publications as
derivations from large computerized data bases would become more important,
and that there would be a gradual decline in the growth rate of the massive
secondary reference sources. Unfortunately, this has not been the case.
In fact publishers have tended to continue to market their regular publications
and have not shown much interest in preparing special purpose publications
geared to regional interest. The alternative for the developing country user
is to develop an individual search of SDI which is also a very expensive
solution.

As a result, developing country users have in many cases been forced to
rely on receiving secondary sources with overly broad subject matter coverage
and with reference to only a portion of the information on the subject matter
which is of real interest to them.

While there has been some innovation in the design of secondary
reference output (for example, citation indexes, industrial information
bulletins, statistical reports), there really has been little experimenting and
elaboration of ways and means of helping users in developing countries to
identify relevant information sources.

IFIP should encourage the study of regionally focussed outputs, as a
possible compromise between the more generalized secondary information
publication (too costly because of the volume of material included) and SDI
or retrieval products (too costly because they are customized for each
individual user).

Preparation of secondary sources - subject bibliographies, data bases, etc.

(1) Criteria (techniques and devices) for the construction of manual and automatic searching aides

The likelihood and cost advantage of long-term reliance on hardcopy
reference materials in developing regions needs to be generally recognized by
the publishers of such materials and by scholars on the subject. There are
various points of view, justifying more systematic studies and experiments
on whether published secondary reference sources are being relegated to
accessories or supplements to the use of computerized systems, or on the
contrary if publishers and data base organizers are still tied to old ways.
There is more difference than is usually recognized between the techniques
and linguistic devices which facilitate manual searching and those which are

appropriate for computer-aided searching. The former especially should be studied systematically, and their effectiveness ascertained in experiments. This perhaps could be recommended to FID.

(m) Criteria for indexing vocabularies

The lack of rigorous documentation programmes to encourage the development of sophisticated methods and procedures is reflected in the scarcity of adequate classification systems, thesauri, and other tools essential for providing ready access to information contained in printed materials dealing with public administration.

A common complaint about subject bibliographies and data bases which originate in more industrialized countries and international organizations, is the lack of adequate attention by designers of these systems to indexing vocabularies. Some alarm is expressed about reference systems which have no controlled vocabulary at all. Developing countries in particular would seem to have contradictory claims. On the one hand, users of documentation services in these countries find bibliographical searching to be most cumbersome due to the absence of standardized vocabularies resulting in users' requests having to be interpreted separately for each subject bibliography. On the other hand, there are claims for greater recognition of regional, cultural and language differences.

To meet these conflicting needs, more attention needs to be given to:

(i)   Research on multi-lingual thesauri and switching mechanisms. The latter can be many types: (a) new vocabularies, as source or cumulative thesauri, as a broad ordering of terms or for shallow indexing; (b) designation of a host vocabulary or immediate lexicon (which could be the UDC, for example); (c) free text searching on existing controlled vocabularies; (d) development of an adjunct thesaurus; and (e) a synonym or conversion table; and

(ii) The development of simple guides to help developing countries in the selection, adaptation or construction of indexing vocabularies and in participating in international activities.

These tasks logically could be undertaken by UNESCO and FID.

(n) Formats and vocabulary control for combined inputs of documentation descriptors or keywords, and statistics

In those countries where numeric and non-numeric information needs can be rationalized and reasonably predetermined, as with MIS statistical flows and controlled vocabulary documentation systems, information users should be able to receive or retrieve the combination of numerical and bibliographical information that best suits their needs, without having to make separate searches. Some of the most urgently required applications in developing countries (for example, project control systems) make use of such combined inputs. There has been little work, however, in the design of indexing systems for such purposes.

(o) Training in indexing

Sophisticated technology for the user/system interface cannot fully compensate for poor indexing and preparation of the system input. There is a serious shortage in developing countries of persons who can apply a controlled list of descriptors, keywords or statistical indicators to the analysis of a data or document set, in order to facilitate efficient retrieval of SDI. In networks, each group of indexers tend to use the same vocabulary differently, which considerably weakens the usefulness of such controlled vocabularies.

There is an urgent need to register those DFD members who can provide aid training assistance and advice and to inform concerned personnel in developing countries how they can obtain this help.

Secondary sources and international activities

(p) Guidelines for constructive participation of developing countries in outside information linkage

A problem for developing countries interested in outside linkages is the lack of co-ordination and the implicit competition between commercial producers of subject bibliographies and international organizations. Commerical publishers seem to operate on the assumption that information is like any other raw material on the international market, whereby the developing country exports information for processing and can buy back the finished product. The publisher selects the information and enjoys a large part of the value added. He pays a royalty to the source, although will often argue that information he wishes to acquire should be a free-flowing commodity. International organizations seem to say that the developing country should process, deliver and get back the information on a cost basis, and should control the selection of what is indexed. An in between position is that of universities and professional organizations that publish subject bibliographies, and that are mainly concerned with satisfying their most immediate users and with minimizing costs.

In the light of the above considerations, developing countries need the following:

(i)   Guidelines for determining the relative advantages and disadvantages (cost-effectiveness) of participation in the different types of secondary reference networks. These guidelines could, for instance, include model questionnaires that the developing country could submit to each proponent of such a network, in order to ascertain the condition and costs for constructive participation; and

(ii) Guidelines on how to integrate or standardize the interfacing between international networks and the information requirements of users at the national level.

Unless these guidelines are co-ordinated in such a way as to ensure optimum use of limited resources, the developing countries will continue to be placed at a competitive disadvantage in negotiating for and using the information systems and services of international organizations. The strengthened and enlarged mandate of the United Nations Inter-Organizational Board for Information Systems (IOB) should be helpful in helping to optimize the collective resources allocated for information systems and services in the United Nations system.

The DEVSIS feasibility study, as well as studies conducted for SPINES and DARE by UNESCO, have yielded enough information about the appropriate methodologies and techniques which can be used to process information useful for development in the field of public administration and related areas. The results of these studies indicate that the international exchange of information must be based on well-established national information infra-structures which can act as the basis for all activities necessary for international co-operation in information sharing.

Co-operative international initiatives by organizations such as UNESCO, IOB, DFD and FID are urgently needed on these all important tasks.

(q) Organization of regional networks

Creation and support by international organizations of regional and global information networks which link relevant information sources for public administration might also be considered as a possible means of information sharing efforts. By its very nature, a network often serves a catalytic role in strengthening local information structures without which a network cannot be established. A consortium of documentation centres linked by a network also provides an ideal forum for sharing of information processing techniques, facilities and software, which contribute towards economical use of limited resources. In this connexion the important role which can be assumed by the United Nations regional commissions as potential focal points for the development of regional networks, regional depositories and training centres must not be overlooked.

Primary sources

(r) Documentation selection and acquisition policies for information collections of developing countries

Information units in developing countries, particularly those having severely deficient collections, seldom make use of the wide variety of methods which can be used to obtain materials and develop their collections (exchange of publications, donations, purchases, deposits of publications of the sponsoring institutions or other organizations, requiring functionaries to deposit the conference and seminar papers they receive, etc.).

Although, it is recognized that problems exist in most developing countries (for example, exchange controls, restrictions by the Controller General on transfers, tight budgets) which inhibit and affect the way in which these acquisition methods can be applied, nonetheless, ways do exist such as those just referred to which enable the building up of collections. As a result, there is a serious need for a systematic treatment of such methods in the developing country context.

A related aspect of acquisition policies is the selection of materials. Document-handling or data-handling and storage are becoming increasingly more expensive, and the indiscriminate collection and indexing of material on a "whatever arrives gets processed" basis is becoming less and less justified. Selectivity of input is even more necessary if the criteria of relevance and cost effectiveness is used to replace the arbitrary delimitation of information systems according to numerical or non-numerical information.

The introduction of reprography and micrography can make the handling of large quantities of information more manageable, but these are costly processes and the amount of indexing of the material is not reduced. A major obstacle to attempts to set out criteria for selecting material is the inescapable problem of objectivity in the process and methodology used in the selection of documentary material and acquisition policies. In this context, there needs to be some serious theoretical and practical attention to this perhaps most crucial of all aspects of information-handling.

This could merit consideration by a DFD special interest group.

(s) Institutionalized criteria of confidentiality

In practice the selection of the most pertinent primary sources for

information collections will frequently be constrained for reasons of
confidentiality or because of vested interests - that is unless institutional
criteria of confidentiality are adopted as substitutes for the personal and
arbitrary criteria which prevail. Many duplications exist in R and D projects
as well as other frequently costly activities due to the fact that there has
been restricted access to documents even for public servants working in the
same sector.

F. Areas for priority action by DFD

In the light of the considerations and suggestions referred to in the
previous section of this report, the Group suggests that DFD give consideration
to undertaking the following:

1. General

(a) Undertake studies to draw up the cost-effectiveness implications
associated with development of integrated information systems (as referred
to in E. 1. (a) above).

(b) Establish a special interest working group to develop a glossary
of information systems: in related terms, in various languages, of the
equivalent terms used by the various specialists which are analogous (as
referred to in IV. A. 3. (a) above).

(c) Make available DFD members to assist in the teaching the courses
or workshops (as referred to in E. 1. (c) (i) above).

(d) Undertake studies with a view to developing methodology for use by
national governments as to how to determine priorities among national
information projects (as referred to in E. 1. (e) above).

(e) Assist in, and contribute to conceptualizing integrated information
systems approaches, in line with the technological possibilities which are
evolving, with the realities of limited resources and a need to refocus
priorities especially in the developing countries, and with the user's real
information requirements (as referred to in E. 1. (f) above).

(f) Joint work with other international organizations on "guidelines for
network linkages" (as referred to in E. 2. (p) above).

2. Specific

(a) Encourage support in systematic information gathering, analysis
and dissemination by professional organizations in developing countries
(possibly also have a pilot project in this area) (as referred to in
E. 2. (a) above)

(b) Undertake the elaboration of a suitable methodology to identify core
user groups as well as on how these can be used to increase the user base
(as referred to in E. 2. (k) above).

(c) Register DFD members having experience in the audio visual training
field as well as indexing training programmes and who can make their experience
available to assist in the teaching of general courses on the information
sciences information systems and services in developing countries;

(d) Undertake studies and/or establish DFD interest groups relating to:

(i) Analysing the trade-offs to be considered in developing countries

or in more isolated sections of all countries, in choosing manual
or automated storage and access to documentation and data sets;

(ii)   The choice of manual, semi-automatic, mini-computer and intelligent
terminal retrieval systems, which permit later technological
upgrading of the system at low cost (as referred to in E. 2. (f)
above);

(iii)   Acquisition selection criteria and methodologies;

(iv)   Institutional criteria of confidentiality: see reference E. 2. (s)
above;

(e)   Establish a standing group to study the involvement and interface of
end users in the development of computer systems and the sponsorship and
co-sponsorship of such seminars in co-operation with other international
organizations on this subject for developing countries.

INFORMATION SYSTEMS IN PUBLIC ADMINISTRATION
D. Eade, J. Hodgson (editors)
North-Holland Publishing Company
© DFD, 1981

URBAN PLANNING IN DEVELOPING COUNTRIES:
SOME COMMENTS ON THE ORIGINS OF DATA NEEDS

Marcos Rodrigues*

Abstract

The paper raises some topics for discussion on informal aspects of urban
planning data needs and information systems in developing countries. The
legitimacy of data needs is considered vis-a-vis the objective development
process and within a broader context of methodologies for urban analysis.
Similar considerations are put forward in relation to the methodologies for
information systems.

This paper aims at stimulating the discussion of some informal aspects of
data needs for urban planning in developing countries and the information
systems that are intended to supply those needs. It cannot be claimed that the
treatment of the topics covered is exhaustive but hopefully they reflect a
common phenomenon. Although the situations to be discussed refer to urban
planning in Brazil, they seem to be relevant to a wider range of cases.

A major aspect of data needs is their legitimacy vis-a-vis the
development process. For the purpose of this examination this process is
assumed to involve the following groups:

(a) Municiple government;

(b) Heads of planning agencies (appointed by municipal government);

(c) Experts of planning agencies;

(d) National consultants;

(e) Foreign consultants;

(f) Municipal administration.

The situations for consideration are those related to the fact that these

_____

* Institute for Technological Research, Sao Paulo, Brazil.

groups do not necessarily share the same common motivation and do not always
work harmoniously. Some of these motivations are extraneous to the planning
process and thus generate data needs that cannot be envisaged or understood
within the process. Attempts at developing planning information systems very
frequently go astray because they are based on only partial appreciation of
what is going on, for example, information system developers are not told the
full story, sometimes because the full story is not known and sometimes because
it cannot be told. The drama contains some rather well-known acts involving
the protagonists listed above.

Municipal government (MG), for political or less noble reasons, presses
the heads of planning agencies (HPAs) for a particular course of action.
Since HPAs are appointed to office by MG, it is not rare for them to surrender
to MG authority. These projects or studies do not usually fit into the routine
and the data is needed for the justification of a decision already made; data
usually end up justifying impressive quantitative shields. This sort of
phenomenon occurs with subjects such as the provision of health centres, schools,
bus lines, etc.

Heads of planning agencies promote a particular programme of political
prestige which is frequently divorced from other aspects of governmental
administration. These enterprises are based much more on the charisma
of HPAs than on reality; they are ephemeral though very demanding in terms of
data and other resources as a whole. Examples of these phenomena are special
land taxation studies, comprehensive planning models, etc. As a fashion they
wear out with time. Conventional post-mortem dissections suggest lack of
funding, backwardness of remaining administration, etc; very rarely is the
conclusion reached that the enterprise was ill-conceived, that is, that it was
inadequate to the real situation. The shelves are full of "incomprehended"
studies.

It must be accepted that experts of planning agencies (EPAs), as with any
other human beings, are subject to temptation. The temptations of more
concern are those related to the use of modern and sophisticated methodologies
out of context. What sirens lure EPAs to sophistication? Training abroad,
foreign consultants, technical journals, etc. Quite understandably,
professional ambition blurs criticism, the career ladder is climbed with
professional expertise (sophistication!) and not with simple down-to-earth
enterprises. Adaptation may be seen as a lowering of standards and
simplification as a lack of alternatives. To all this is contributed the fact
that projects involving modern sophisticated methodologies are easier to sell
to the upper grades of the hierarchy (HPAs, MG). On this subject, Alonso
(1971) points out that:

"Planners in developing countries often bewail the lack of some
data and the low quality of what data is available. It is
often thought that if only the data were available the elaborate
mathematical planning models developed in the economically
advanced countries might be applied. Foreign experts in these
techniques are often consulted, and young national planners aspire
to master what they regard as scientific sophistication. This is
a fundamental error because the poverty of data is an intrinsic
condition of underdevelopment, not a happenstance. Rich and
frequent data is the by-product of the organization of an
advanced economy." [1]

---

[1] W. Alonso, "Planning and the spatial organization of the metropolis in
the developing countries", Working paper 153, Institute of Urban and Regional
Development, University of California, Berkeley, 1971.

National consultants employ a significant part of the expertise available
and are involved in most of the great enterprises such as mass transportation
studies. Being involved in this way they keep the pressure on MG so as to
ensure the stability of their slice of the planning cake. Tenders are won with
technical proposals, curricula, prices and prestige; this stimulates sophistication, usually implying association with foreign experts in the most demanding
enterprises.

An inspection of these aspects suggests innumerable situations in which
combined interests lead to sophisticated data needs. There is nothing
intrinsically bad with sophisticated data needs provided one does not forget
the basic needs and has resources to supply both. Unfortunately this is not
the case and elaborate methodologies prevail and require sophisticated data
while sacrificing the basic.

However, one should not unintentionally seed xenophoby but consider the
phenomena within a broader context of methodologies for urban analysis. One
assumes the methodologies in use to be inappropriate and this may be because
the world methodologies are inappropriate, because an inappropriate subset is
available to the country, because an inappropriate selection is made, or for
some combination of these reasons. The latter alternative is most probable
although it is not known how to apportion inappropriateness to the various
sources.

World methodologies comprehend those from the developed and the
developing countries and therefore it is possible that there exists a subset
that is appropriate to a particular developing country. Nevertheless the subset
available seems to be inadequate, possibly because it has mostly permeated down
from developed countries. These methodologies arise in a context of income,
organization and technical development that is quite different from that
prevailing in developing countries, and thus arises its potential
inappropriateness.

It is upon this subset that selection mechanisms will act and determine
the methodologies to be incorporated. The selection mechanisms were
illustrated by the situations just described, and it is suggested that they
are biased towards inappropriate sophistication. Since the methodological
approach adopted determines the data needs, not surprisingly one finds cities in
a dispossessed situation striving for data of a Scandinavian sophistication.
This is the case of Sao Paulo where, of the estimated 1,300,000 buildings, only
60 per cent are connected to water mains, 40 per cent to the sewerage network,
10 per cent to the gas network and, of an estimated total length of 11,700km
of roads, 7,000km are unpaved. 2/ This situation has to be dealt with on an

---

2/ I. Fang, "Informacao para o planejamento metropolita no", Simposio
de Informacoes para o Planejamento, IBP, Gramado, RS, 1977.

annual budget of £63 per capita as compared with the average figure of £260 per
capita in the United Kingdom. 3/ Notwithstanding this situation, the
municipality frequently gets involved in rather elaborate modelling. Data for
these applications are gathered, surveyed and/or "prepared" through convoluted
procedures. Concomitantly, information on some basic aspects such as
infrastructure may be disregarded.

Discussion of data needs thus seems to require a closer scrutiny of the
methodologies that generate them. This would include the study of ways of
improving the communication between developing countries so as to generate a
more pertinent set of "available methodologies". In addition, there is scope
for speeding up the maturing of "selection mechanisms" by means of professional
training and funding of research, as adequate to the local situation.
Admittedly, these are measures heavily dependent on an over-all political and
administrative maturing which is the indispensible basis for legitimate
development planning.

The information systems that are going to supply those needs should now be
considered. The conceptual model of the choice of methodologies for urban
analysis can also be used in relation to the choice of methodologies for
information systems. Similarly, temptation to use sophisticated methodologies
comes into play and computer manufacturers play a significant role in this.

A review of activities with regard to the development of planning
information systems in Brazil suggests that:

(a) In general, information is badly kept. The lack of delegated
responsibilities, unreliable maps, incomplete and duplicate thematic coverage,
inability to agree on standards, all combine to erode the utility of information
systems;

(b) Public sector resources are limited so the systems envisaged should be
cheap and simple;

(c) Any implementation will present professional and technical problems
given the existing levels of expertise;

(d) There is an urgent requirement for planning information and the major
data sources lie in administrative files. 4/

3/ Prefeitura municipal de Sao Paulo (1977). Orcamento e Finan cas,
Sao Paulo (Table 4-5, cmnd. 7049).

4/ M. Rodrigues, "Urban information systems in Brazil: summary of
activities", Working paper No. 14, SORSA, Stockholm, 1978.

In this context, the planning administrative approach to information systems 5/ is the most likely to succeed in a developing country like Brazil. It is more suited to the kind of development in which the gradual learning by the user provides the lines for further development and it has the sort of flexibility that does not exist to the same extent in the other approaches. There is thus scope for the integration of data originating from administration, surveys and censuses. The framework of spatial reference to be adopted plays an important role in this integration and in the over-all definition of the capabilities of the system envisaged.

In Brazil, two distinct types of locational attribute can be identified in the existing files. There are those based upon the property and those using data referenced to the zone. The former group are referenced either by address or by block. 6/ The files referenced in these ways are listed in table 16.

Type of reference	Information
Address	Surveys Economic activity School enrolment Infrastructure Property
Block	Property Land use Infrastructure
Zone	Population and other census data Land values Land use restrictions Surveys

Table 16. Locational referencing in Brazil

5/ J. Willis, "A strategy for developing computerized information systems for local government: the end of the mega-system", LUBFS Conference Proceedings No. 1 (London, MPT Construction, 1974).

6/ In Brazil, in general, property files have a locational attribute that is a hierarchical code taking the form ZZBBPPDD, where:

ZZ - identifies the administrative (or fiscal) zone;
BB - identifies the block within the zone;
PP - identifies the property within the block;
DD - identifies the sub-division within the property.

The two types of framework currently in use in developed countries that provide for the spatial location of properties and their subsequent aggregation (point and segment referencing) have certain shortcomings in developing countries such as Brazil. This is because they:

(a) Presuppose reliable maps and property addresses;

(b) Are expensive to implement in the pertaining social context;

(c) Are over-sophisticated and imply unused capacity.

The interrelationships between costs, sophistication and quality of the information base can be represented as shown in table 17. It seems that this sort of interrelationship is usually overlooked and information system developers usually end up attempting to rectify a situation (quality of the information base) that is, to a considerable extent, out of their control.

Sophistication of the framework	Quality of information base	Implementation costs
HIGH	BAD	VERY HIGH
	GOOD	HIGH
LOW	BAD	MEDIUM
	GOOD	LOW

Table 17.   Determinants of the decision for a framework of spatial reference and their interrelationship

Thus there seems to be a case for information system design to start from very broad contextual considerations, gradually moving towards the more specific aspects and culminating in that particular sector of the planning process it is going to serve.

In conclusion, despite the problematic situations discussed above and the somewhat disheartening impression they may give, these are essentially dynamic and still admit of positive reappraisal and concrete improvement.

INFORMATION SYSTEMS IN PUBLIC ADMINISTRATION
D. Eade, J. Hodgson (editors)
North-Holland Publishing Company
© *DFD, 1981*

CONTROLLING THE TOWN EXTENSION WITH THE USE
OF INFORMATICS SYSTEMS

Michal Ziebinski*

Abstract

This paper presents the application of the FORUM informatics system for planning, controlling and co-ordinating works connected with the extension of towns and large town agglomerations. In many countries recently huge state or municipal funds have been allotted for town extensions. Hence, adequate organization, planning and controlling of the implementation of a large number of building engineering works becomes of essential importance. The presented method and FORUM informatics system render detailed control of the implementation of many building projects in a relatively simple and inexpensive manner possible. The FORUM system has been applied, among others, for controlling housing engineering in the Warsaw agglomeration area.

A. Introduction

In many countries, both developed and developing, enormous funds have recently been alloted for extending large towns and town agglomerations. In many cases state and municipal funds serve for financing not only public service building engineering - schools, hospitals, public office buildings, etc. - and infrastructure - roads, streets, sewage disposal systems, water supply systems, gas supply systems, etc. - but also a large part of housing engineering.

Owing to the extensive scope of the investment undertaking and great financial means involved, correct planning, co-ordination, control and financial settlement of such investment undertakings becomes of paramount importance. Incorrect control of such huge and complicated municipal investments may result in inadequate use of the financial means and even serious losses. Owing to the wide scope of such investments, very often comprising several hundred or even a few thousand separate buildings, the application of modern organization methods based on informatics systems is indispensable.

This paper presents a method of planning and control for implementing large groups of municipal building engineering projects. The method is based on

_____

* Electronic Data Processing Centre, POLIMEX-CEKOP, Poland.

the use of the FORUM informatics system which defines planning and controlling
the implementation of the investment in both material and financial respects.
Both the method and the FORUM informatics system have already been tested in
the course of application by a great number of design offices and building
engineering enterprises in Poland. The most extensive use of the FORUM
system was its application for the management of housing and relevant
engineering in Warsaw. The system was used for planning, construction progress
control and financial settlement of several hundred of buildings, with
detailed control of over 5000 items.

A distinctive feature of the FORUM system, in comparison with other systems
used for planning and controlling investment undertakings (that is, PERT), is
its simplicity. This feature allows for its wide application, requiring no
preparatory work, no highly qualified informatics staff and no high
exploitation costs.

B. Scope of investment activities comprised by the FORUM system

The FORUM system can be used for controlling the whole investment cycle
starting from preparation of design documentation and concluding with the
financial settlement. The scope of activity of the FORUM system is shown in
figure XXXVIII. The particular stages of the investment activity shown in the
figure can be divided into the following four groups:

Group 1. Regional planning of towns and housing estates (panel 1),
constituting the first stage of preparatory work (not included in the system);

Group 2. Preparation of the investment process of a building, housing
estate or a residential quarter consists of three stages (panels 2, 3 and 4).
It comprises preparation of technical documentation, formal, legal and technical
preparation of the building site and preparation of the external (town)
infrastructure for a given building or a group of buildings. The
incorporation into the system of the last stage (representing an investment
process all by itself) depends on the local conditions of financing and
implementation of the investment and can be approached as preparatory work or
part of the main investment process;

Group 3. This group contains the basic investment process (panels 5, 6 and
9) which for organizational reasons is divided into the following three stages:

(a) Constructing the internal infrastructure of the housing estage,
     earth works (excavations, levelling) and execution of foundations
     (the so-called raw condition);

(b) Building or erection up to the raw condition;

(c) Installation and finishing works of the building as well as the final
     finishing work of the green areas.

Depending on needs, the above division can be changed;

Group 4. Technical tests of the installation, technical control and
acceptance of the building and financial settlements conclude the whole
investment process.

C. Description of the FORUM-74 system

The FORUM-74 system serves for controlling the implementation of the contracts concluded for the execution of building and assembly works. The scope of the system includes the whole investment cycle beginning from working out an offer for the execution of works, elaboration of design documentation and preparing the building site and concluding with complete finishing and financial settlement of all the works specified in particular contracts. The main functions of the system are as follows:

(a) Detailed recording of all contracts for working out of documentation and execution of construction and assembly works;

(b) Detailed monitoring of all formal activities connected with preparation and signing of particular contracts and with their modification and clearance;

(c) Working out of work schedules in any selected planning period (ex. month, quarter, year, etc.);

(d) Detailed monitoring of the progress of work and signalling any incorrectness related to the time limits;

(e) Detailed monitoring and balancing of particular contracts as well as finding deviations from the contract stipulations regarding clearance.

Depending on the accepted organization system on particular building sites, their monitoring can be effected based on one, two or scores of contracts. Under each contract, up to 99 contract items constituting separate stages of work can be monitored. Each contract and each item of the contract have an eight-character classification mark enabling classification of particular elements of the contract. This has a crucial significance for investment control on the central scale as it allows proper comparison and analyses to be made within the classification groups of:

(a) Contractors;

(b) Types of work;

(c) Regions;

(d) Character of investment, etc.

The FORUM-74 system fulfils the above mentioned functions based on 34 printouts prepared in four thematic groups:

(a) Recording printouts;

(b) Planning printouts;

(c) Monitoring printouts;

(d) Accounting printouts.

Each of these printouts can be emmitted for any date interval or for any arrangement of a classification mark. This gives a wide range of possibilities in proper selection and aggregation of data, depending on requirements.

Hence the FORUM-74 system is a universal tool in the field of investment control and clearance. It allows, among other things, a systematic trace of the execution of material tasks ·(in case of delays they are automatically aggregated) as well as a systematic trace and balance of the costs.

In spite of the wide range of tasks covered by the FORUM-74 system, it is relatively simple and easy to operate, both by staff supervising the particular building site and by management at the central level.   The printouts of the system are utilized by the investment planning and preparatory staff, the investment supervisory and executive staff and the financial and accountancy staff.   The system can be operated with the use of the ODRA series 1300 and RIAD-32 computers of Polish manufacturer, the ICL series 1900 and 2903 computers of English manufacture and the IBM 360 and 370 computers of American manufacture.   The flow of information in the system is shown in figure XXXIX. The data can be fed into the system in the form of perforated cards, cassettes with magnetic tapes or directly from screen monitors.

D.   Description of the group of FORUM systems

The first FORUM system was prepared in 1974, hence its designation FORUM-74. The high success it enjoyed in many design offices and building enterprises (over 60 applications) formed the basis of a group of systems by further development, extension and modification.   Currently there are four FORUM systems designated 74, 75, 76 and 77:

FORUM-74.   The first and most simple of the group with the highest possible number of applications, described in C above;

FORUM-75.   A subsequent but completely new system with increased application possibilities.   The FORUM-75 system includes:

(a)   An increased number of items in a single contract (from 100 to 1000);

(b)   Each item divided into 32 sub-items;

(c)   The introduction of whole groups of printouts into planning, useful for large building enterprises and design offices;

(d)   An extended range of data introduced into the system;

(e)   An increased number of printouts (from 34 to 44);

FORUM-76.   An extended and modified version of the FORUM-75 system as a transitory system between FORUM-74 system and the last in the group FORUM-77 system, the main changes in comparison with the FORUM-74 system being:

(a)   The introduction of a number of synthetic planning and accountancy printouts;

(b)   A changed scheme of input data; and

FORUM-77.   The last version of a completely new system combining the experience and conclusions gained over several years exploitation of the earlier systems.   The FORUM-77 system is at present used in the Warsaw Development Consortium (WADECO) Consulting Office.

E.   Application of the FORUM-74 system

The most extensive use of the FORUM-74 system was its application for controlling the housing engineering implemented by the Housing Co-operative. Considering that co-operative housing constitutes about 80 per cent of the total housing in Warsaw, it can be said that the system was applied for controlling the extension of the whole town, as apart from residential buildings, the FORUM-74 system also included schools, nursery schools, shops, etc.

The system was fed with information from the contracts concluded between the Capital Management of Co-operative Investments and particular contractors, totalling about 20 large building complex works and enterprises. In the first stage of exploitation about 500 contracts containing about 5000 items were introduced.

Each contract or contract item was classified according to the classification features of the following structure:

Contractor (enterprise, design office)

Investor (housing co-operative)

Inspector supervising the building site

Undertaking (large housing estate)

Task (small housing estate, part of a large housing estate)

Type of building engineering (residential, service, roads)

Building technology (large block, monolith, traditional)

Type of order (investment, documentation, supervision)

In this way printouts were obtained and they presented:

Monthly, quarterly or annual plans of completion of the buildings in respect of the whole town

Current financial progress of the tasks executed by a selected contractor, or in respect of a selected group of buildings

Lists of delayed buildings

Lists of shops scheduled for exploitation in a given month or quarter

Lists of buildings already finished for co-operative A

Buildings scheduled for starting in a given month

Lists of delayed technical documentation

Lists of delays in commissioning the sites

Plans of receipt of documentation in a given month or quarter

Lists of agreements scheduled for conclusion with enterprises in a given period of time

The basic printouts were prepared according to the agreed time-table and arrangements (enterprise, type of building, etc.) and for defined time intervals (monthly, quarterly, yearly, and accumulatively). The system was processed every two weeks. After each processing, the printouts were analysed and in written form submitted to the Head Management of the Capital Management of Co-operative Investments (CMCI).

The application of the system to CMCI brought a number of advantages of an organizational nature. According to the statement of the management of CMCI, the FORUM-74 system considerably improved and accelerated the settling of official matters (signing the agreements, financial settlements, etc.), rendered possible the taking of direct steps in case of delays and improved the whole recording, planning and accountancy systems. A pictorial diagram of the application of the FORUM-74 system in the CMCI is shown in figure XL.

F. Application possibilities of the FORUM systems and application advantages

As already mentioned in this paper, the FORUM systems can be used for controlling the investment processes in municipal building engineering on the following scales:

(a) National;

(b) Regional or town agglomerations;

(c) Town;

(d) Housing estates or residential quarters.

Thanks to the simple structure, service and method of preparing the information fed into the FORUM system, the system can be used in practically all countries of the world. It should be emphasized that the system is particularly suitable in countries which do not have a large number of highly qualified informatics staff or computers. A pictorial diagram of the application possibilities of the system and its application advantages are shown in figure XLI.

Bibliography

Ziebinski M. Application of the FORUM-74 system for improving the management of design offices. Informatics no. 7-8: 1-6, 1975.

Gestion de projets pour les bureaux d'études et les entreprises de construction. Convention Informatique. Les applications par secteur (Paris) 101-110, 1975.

Anwendung des Systems FORUM-74/2 zur Leitung eines Projektierungsburges. Translation of a lecture delivered during the Information Days of the Polish Peoples' Republic in Berlin, 26-28 November 1974. Duplicated by the Bauakademie der DDR, Berlin. 34p.

FORUM-74 - a system of the control of the implementation of contracts and orders as well as task planning, INFOGRYF-76. Directory on duplication systems (Szczecin-Kołobrezeg), pt. III: 179, 1976.

FORUM-75, a system of the management of a design office and construction and assembly enterprise, INFOGRYF-76. Directory on duplication systems (Szczecin-Kołobrezeg), pt. III: 179, 1976.

Better organization - more dwellings. Co-operative houses no. 5, 1976.

Figure XXXVIII. Scope of investment activities covered by the FORUM system

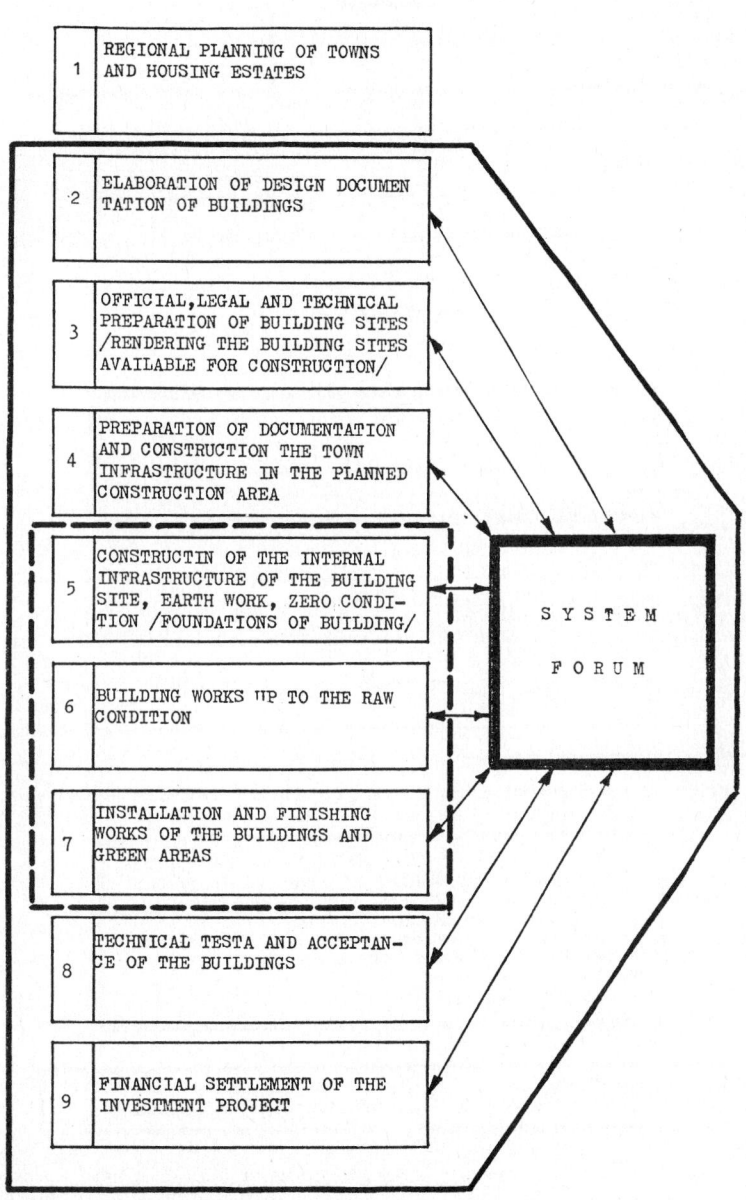

Figure XXXIX. Information flow in the FORUM-74 system

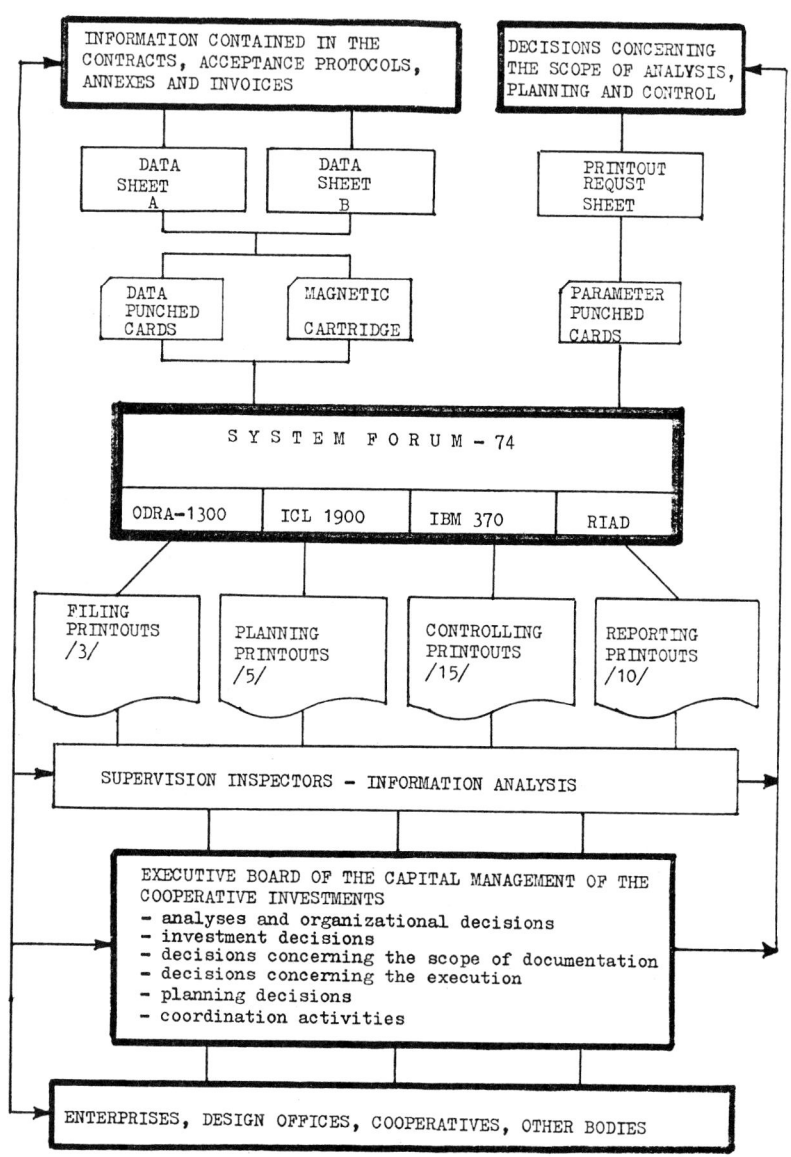

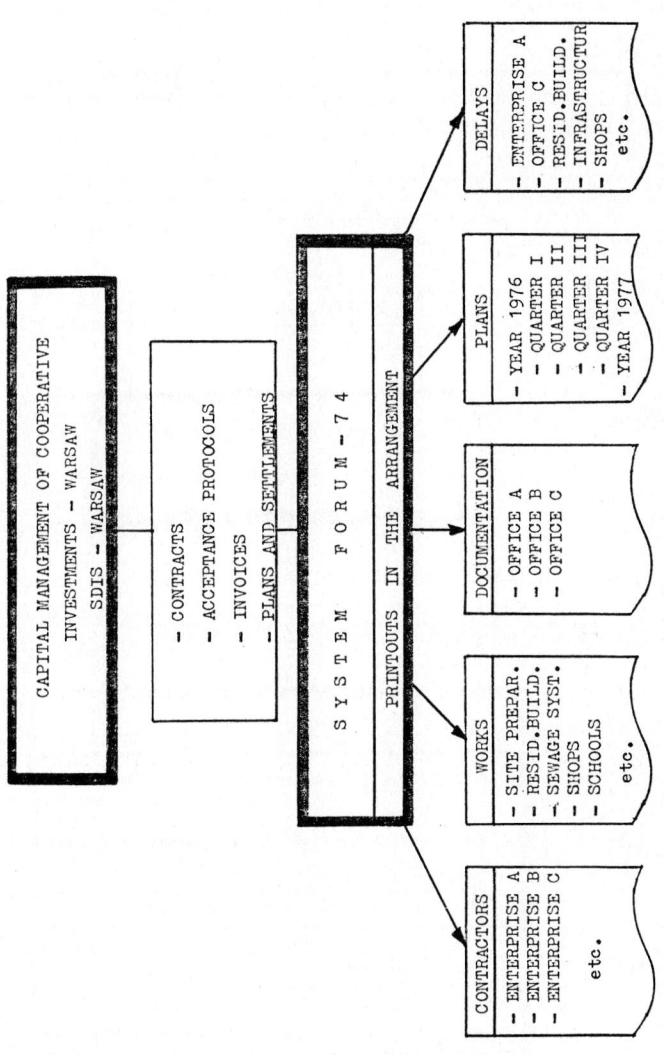

Figure XL. Application of the FORUM system in the planning and controlling the Warsaw Housing Engineering

Figure XLI. Application possibilities and advantages of the FORUM systems

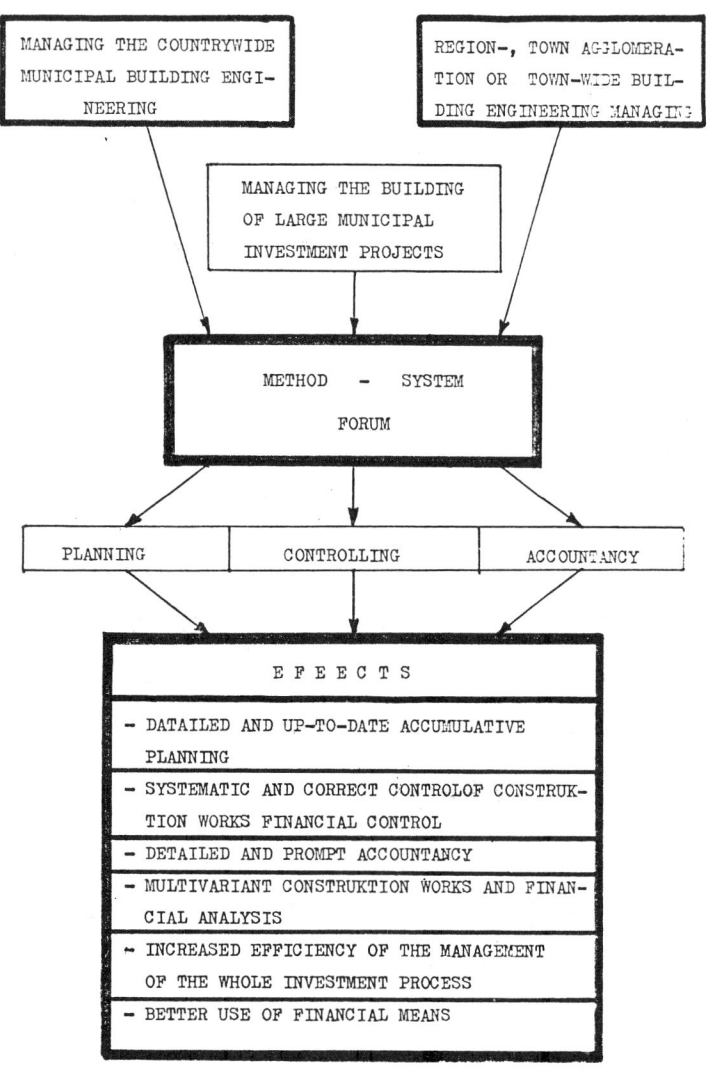

INFORMATION SYSTEMS IN PUBLIC ADMINISTRATION
D. Eade, J. Hodgson (editors)
North-Holland Publishing Company
© *DFD, 1981*

URBAN DATA MANAGEMENT IN BOGOTA

Harry Koppel*

Abstract

Bogota, the capital city of Colombia, with about one-fifth of the country's 25 million inhabitants, faces the problems of high urbanization rates common to many Latin American cities. The collection and processing of data on municipal aspects (for example, cadastral, public utilities, population, transportation, urbanization) has been generally achieved through the efforts of various local government agencies and through the elaboration of large scale studies on the city. Each one of these developments followed its own methodology and a particular definition of the information problem.

The same information and/or information on the same elements was collected several times by different agencies using varied formats and definitions of data. This resulted in duplicate unco-ordinated efforts which generated large amounts of unrelated information on the same subject. An example of this situation is the number of different codes which serve to identify land parcels.

Some integration in the information was obtained when different agencies had to share the same data (for example, cadastral data) thus interrelating their filing systems. Another integration factor was the creation of a municipal data processing centre which forced local government agencies to use the same type of hardware.

The time has come to establish a municipal information policy. By means of the application of this policy or plan all municipal agencies must co-ordinate their efforts in the collection and processing of data and in the distribution of information which represents municipal elements.

---

* Head, Electronic Data Processing Department, Institute for Urban Development, Bogota, Colombia.

A. Introduction

In this paper a brief description of the city will be given, including aspects of its administration and the use of data processing. This setting is shown to describe the environment where future information systems for government use will be placed.

B. Background

1. Setting

Bogota faces today, as many other Latin American Cities, the problems created by large urbanization rates. Its population of approximately 5 million grows at a rate of about 6 per cent each year.   Out of 25 million inhabitants in the country, two-thirds live on the Andes Cordilleras. These mountain ranges cross the country from south to north. Bogota is located in the mountainous area occupying part of a plateau (50 x 20 kms.) at 2,600 meters above sea level.

The city constitutes a special administrative sub-division called the "Special District" as opposed to the other regional political divisions in the country, known as departments. The executive head of the Municipality is the Mayor who has under him a number of administrative bodies such as secretariats, institutes, departments and municipal enterprises. The legislative body is the City Council which is elected by popular vote every two years.

2. Use of data processing

The first establishment to use mechanized forms of data processing was the Electric Power Company in 1935, when its accounting was carried out with the use of tabulating machines. New methods and procedures were chosen in several of the municipal establishments as new machines were brought into use. Finally, in 1966 the City Central administration recognised that high costs were being paid by many of its subordinated agencies for processing data at their own computer centres (as was the case for public utilities) and at service bureaus. At that time, another important fact was that larger computers had a lower cost per production unit when compared to the smaller and less sophisticated machines then in use. Such circumstances prevailed when a new municipal enterprise was created under the name of Computing Services.

The objectives of this enterprise were the creation of a computing centre to serve the whole municipal administration and provision of professional support to those establishments that could not have their own electronic data processing (EDP) departments. This idea worked initially and all processing was centralized at the two IBM-360 computers purchased by Computing Services.

Integration in the use of the machines came about without any formalization in the use of information. Nevertheless, there was some conformity in that data forms containing certain information elements were shared between departments.

As time passed the equipment used at Computing Services also became obsolete. Financial and legal difficulties made a change of equipment proposed in 1972 impossible and the company became unable to satisfy the processing demands generated by all municipal agencies. Therefore two additional computers had to be utilized outside of the original framework of the centralized service, to be used by the public utilities and health services. Annex I gives a general view of the different establishments existing in the administration and their use of automated information systems.

The use of data processing has usually started with the same sort of application, for example in payroll, accounting, budgeting and materials administration. Public utilities have billing systems that account for a significant percentage of computer time. Each administrative subdivision that uses EDP usually has an application characteristic of the service given. Several kinds of taxes are also invoiced automatically, for instance land, industry and commerce taxes and a special kind of contribution that is charged to owners of land parcels neighbouring new urban development works.

The base to charge land taxes is the cadastral system and within this system files are kept with basic data on urban parcels. This system is perhaps the one that is more widely used by separate agencies at the municipality. Apart from the cadastral application, no other EDP application is shared by different agencies, either in data or procedures. Work has been duplicated creating the same kind of applications at different establishments in spite of many similarities in the organizations that could have permitted the use of only one process or one class of data. These information systems have been developed independently, mainly due to a lack of a municipal policy on application development.

C. Present situation

As it was acknowledged a few years ago, large expenditures in EDP were discovered and the un-co-ordinated use of hardware was the rule. Today there are also signs of uneasiness in the use of informatics. However, the solution tends towards the use of distributed systems, contrary to the idea of a centralized equipment that was proposed over a decade ago. The trends in the development of computing equipment that each time offer greater capacity at relative lower costs, have induced different municipal agencies to seriously consider the alternative of having their own computers which would have capabilities which in the past were only available at the central machine. The configuration now considered is one where separate agencies can have their own machines as long as there is a certain compatibility, especially for back-up purposes and data and program sharing. These computers, however, would be branched to a host computer at Computer Services and would serve as an integration and communications centre (see figures XLII and XLIII for a possible configuration).

A more fundamental step is to be taken to establish a policy for the integration of information resulting from different sources, which differs significantly from the plans of a decade ago which attempted only to achieve a more efficient use of machines. This new policy will certainly be conducive to a better administered city. Large amounts of data are processed daily for operational (transactional) systems at the municipal agencies. This information, properly selected and probably complemented with information from other sources, will be most helpful for the town administration.

It is rather difficult and inefficient to serve a town with "blind eyes" without knowing the relevant facts of its administration - as has happened in Bogota - and will continue to happen as long as a municipal information policy is missing. The city has grown too large to co-ordinate all information flows without such policy. Up to now, each time a new project is launched (for example, in transportation, master plans for health), it must include the form in which information is going to be collected and analysed. The intention is to create a centre of information where information already collected can be distributed - whether it has been obtained in an automated or manual form.

356   H. Koppel

Figure XLII. Computers in use in two years

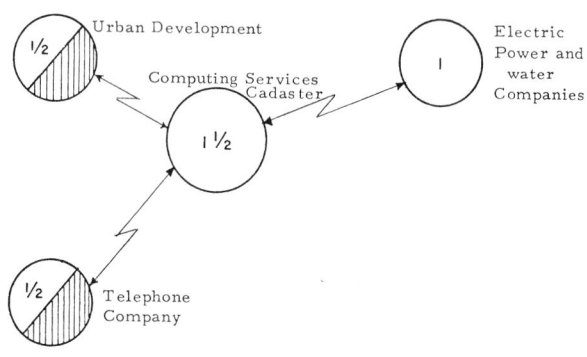

Figure XLIII. Computers in use in four years

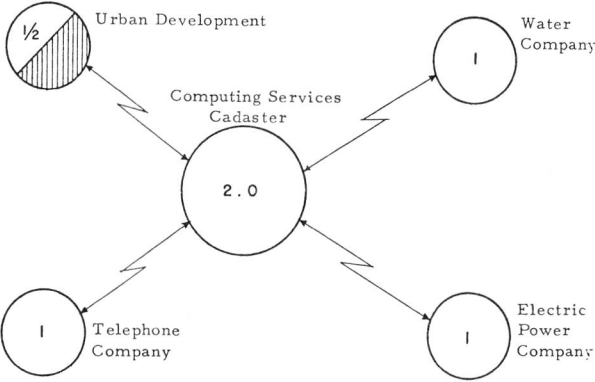

Note to figures XLII and XLIII. A reference computer of rating I should contain
the following features : Data base management system, Teleprocessing, Interactive
systems, Virtual memory, One megabyte principal memory, 1200 megbytes D.A.,
Intelligent terminals, Two high speed printers, Diskette input, Optica
character reader, Four magnetic tape units, 25 local CRT terminals.

D. Meeting the future

1. Information policy

The first step towards the accomplishment of the new objectives was to set up a committee of representatives of the main municipal agencies, generally those responsible for informatics in each agency. The Informatics Committee will establish city information policy covering integration of information flow. It will also give guidelines to follow in the development of what has been called the Special District Information System (SIDE). The Committee should take care of the inter-communication between systems at local government and other levels. Within information policy, norms will be given for the specification and acquisition of computer and related equipment. In addition, an integrated use of informatics will be obtained through standardization of object definitions, data formats and certain information processes. Each Agency will have its own responsibility with respect to data collection, processing and distribution. The Committee will supervise and enforce its norms. The Committee will establish and maintain a liaison between local government and other bodies such as universities, international organizations and agencies at regional and national levels.

A harmonious systems development will result from the application of the information policy. Every new development should aim at the same common goals. Such integration will enhance the co-ordination and co-operation between agencies, resulting on a more efficient performance of interdepartmental actions.

2. The Municipal Information System

The following paragraphs describe some aspects of the Municipal Information System (MIS), especially with regard to what is called here the external administration of the city, that is, the administration of city elements different from the local government as such. Although the information requirements for the internal administration of the local government are not referred to, they should also be regulated by the norms of an information policy.

The basic objective of the MIS is to represent those aspects of the city that are relevant to municipal administration. The main objectives of municipal administration (to satisfy in the most efficient way a number of citizens' needs) must be reflected in the structure of the information system. It should serve the administration's role of resource reallocator. Resources are obtained (for example, from taxes) and transformed into services that satisfy citizens' needs. In this way the information system should dynamically represent resources available and ways of transforming them into services for citizens and for community requirements.

The basic structure initially chosen for the MIS has been the cadastral system. There are several reasons for this selection, among them the following:

(a) Through an extension of the cadastral system it is possible to represent town elements with reference to their spatial characteristics. For instance, service distribution and demand are quantified according to their geographical coverage;

(b) The cadastral system already exists to a certain extent and it is one of the few systems that is widely used by separate municipal agencies;

(c) The cadastral system covers the whole city and if related to a spatial co-ordinate system gives a static reference to dynamic elements.

One way to start building the system, besides the establishment of an information policy, would be to bring the cadastral system to a higher standard in order to be able to charge and collect land taxes more efficiently. In this form the system is made, in money terms, rentable with its first step and would start generating resources for the city and possibly provide finances for the MIS project. Such an action may be seen as the application of the "quick and dirty" methods mentioned on one of DFD's newsletters. Further developments would add other relevant data around the concept of the parcel and would include information about people who carry on activities in or around those parcels, spatial co-ordinates, etc.

Another step taken has been the standardization of the postal address code for all agencies. Postal addresses for urban land parcels in Colombia are based on a grid system that gives the approximate spatial location of the parcel. This sort of address system is very helpful when data is treated from a geographical point of view. However, it was not coded in a computer readable form in the same way at different agencies, making the interrelation of data from parcels impossible.

E.   Conclusion

The Municipal Information System concept is slowly spreading and it is possible to envisage its future application at other large communities in the country. The attention of the National Planning Department to these developments will be especially important. If the integration of the use of information that is expected within the municipalities is also going to be found between the municipalities, the MIS would constitute an excellent base for a national data network. Integration of the MIS within the municipalities could feed regional information systems which in turn could feed a national information system. This idea may seem futuristic; nevertheless it could be advantageous to set these objectives now that the MIS is being developed. From another point of view it would seem that local governments are much closer to most sources of relevant information than higher government levels.

Annex

CITY ADMINISTRATION

CITY COUNCIL   CITY COMPTROLLER

MAYOR

SECRETARIES	INSTITUTES & DEPARTMENTS	MUNICIPAL ENTERPRISES
Government	* Urban Development	* Water & Sewage
+ Education	* Traffic	* Electricity
* Public Health	Communal Activities	Urban Development
* Public Works	* Social Security	* Computing Services
+ Finance	+ Planning	+ Transport

* Have their own EDP departments

+ EDP management provided by Computing Services

MAIN AUTOMATED INFORMATION SYSTEMS

Personnel	Accounting & Budgeting
Stock administration	Cadastral
Land, commerce & industry taxes	Public utilities
Transport, models	Road building
Health administration	Traffic

INFORMATION SYSTEMS IN PUBLIC ADMINISTRATION
D. Eade, J. Hodgson (editors)
North-Holland Publishing Company
© DFD, 1981

ELABORATION D'UN SYSTEME D'INFORMATION REGIONAL
ASPECTS TECHNIQUES, POLITIQUES ET ECONOMIQUES

Bernard Guesnier[*]

Le développement régional et urbain est la manifestation de l'inter-dépendance entre le sous-système d'économie industrielle et le sous-système spatial; deux niveaux d'intervention de gestion et de planification et, par conséquent, deux niveaux d'analyse des phénomènes économiques et sociaux peuvent être utilement distingués: le niveau national impliquant une analyse interrégionale et le niveau régional impliquant une analyse intrarégionale. La référence à la théorie systémique étant posée, l'Unité Systémique Région, sous-système hiérarchiquement dépendant du Système Nation est définie comme un ensemble d'agents et d'éléments interreliés en vue d'une finalité de développement: la taille de l'Unité Systémique n'est, certes, pas complètement indifférente, il importe seulement que la Région présente une certaine unité, et qu'elle soit structurée et au moins partiellement maîtrisée et contrôlée par une Entité Responsable.

Les besoins d'information de cette entité responsable, nés de la gestion et de la programmation du développement de l'Unité Région ne semblent pas pouvoir être satisfaits à partir d'un Système d'Information National dont le principe repose sur la production d'informations et de variables agrégées, utiles notamment pour des comparaisons des performances interrégionales, alors que l'analyse intra régionale exige une désagrégation des données très fine pour saisir l'interaction entre les agents et les éléments du système, qui se manifeste parfois ponctuellement.

L'élaboration d'un Système d'Information spécifique pour cette Unité Systémique apparaît donc pleinement justifiée: c'est incontestablement l'instrument privilégié pour une véritable aide à la décision de l'Entité Responsable de l'Unité Systémique car c'est le seul moyen d'obtenir simultanément et de manière cohérente un tableau de Bord, des simulations et prévisions et des calculs de décision vraiment adaptés. Il est cependant nécessaire de préserver une articulation et une possibilité d'intégration du Système d'Information local avec le système d'information national et plus généralement avec celui de tous les systèmes englobant, hiérarchiquement, l'Unité Systémique.

L'objet de cette communication est d'exposer les fondements de l'élaboration de Systèmes d'information pour le développement régional et urbain, les principaux obstacles rencontrés dans la construction et quelques éléments de solution en prenant pour exemple une expérience actuellement en cours dans la Région Poitou-Charentes.

---

*Institut d'Economie Régionale, Poitiers, France

Le Système d'Information Régional pour cette région, commencé depuis une dizaine d'années, couvre plusieurs aspects de l'évolution économique et sociale, appréhendée, quantifiée et mesurée à partir de sources d'information administratives, publiques et privées. Les problèmes rencontrés par cette réalisation ont révélé l'interpénétration entre les dimensions techniques, économiques et politiques: les solutions retenues, actuellement, ne présentent pas un caractère général et définitif, mais elles ont l'avantage de souligner l'importance des améliorations à envisager et de déjà constituer quelques éléments méthodologiques assez aisément transposables (le S.I.R. intègre des fichiers d'employeurs, d'artisans, d'entreprises, d'équipements publics, de communes, etc...).

Le fondement du S.I.R. est la mémorisation de données fines, c'est-à-dire de mesures d'attributs relatifs à des entités très désagrégées: certes, les principes théoriques et techniques de fusion et d'intégration de l'information ne soulèvent pas de difficultés majeures, mais leur mise en oeuvre sur des données issues de sources administratives implique des choix et l'élaboration d'algorithmes spécifiques de création et de mise à jour de fichiers.

Les problèmes liés à la définition des entités, à la définition des attributs (nomenclatures, critères de regroupement et choix des variables), et aussi aux modes de mesure ont des conséquences au niveau de l'utilisation pour la planification. Il en est ainsi, par exemple, lorsque l'on veut couvrir exhaustivement un champ d'observation, une population économique à partir de sources administratives hétérogènes. Le problème déjà difficile à résoudre en coupe instantanée, est encore plus crucial en évolution chronologique: la définition des entités de base ainsi que la définition des attributs peut varier au cours du temps; les techniques d'enquête et les modes de mesure des données peuvent être changés. L'expérience du S.I.R. Poitou-Charentes, couvrant, sur certains points, seize années montre la richesse et les potentialités des sources administratives et permet d'en souligner les limites.

Une fois mis en place, le S.I.R. constitue, techniquement, un instrument puissant de gestion, d'aide à la décision et de planification du développement: créé progressivement depuis dix ans, il permet de fournir maintenant quelques indicateurs d'un tableau de bord accepté et apprécié par les Responsables régionaux. Bien que techniquement au point, le S.I.R. n'est pas considéré encore comme un outil d'aide à la décision.

Pourtant, l'expérience suggère que la mise en relation des sources et des systèmes d'information de l'Administration permet d'abaisser les coûts de création de l'information pour des variables de base comme les variables démographiques et l'emploi intégrés nécessairement dans toute décision de planification: toute extension par intégration de données issues d'autres sources économise, bien sûr, une nouvelle collecte spécifique.

Le problème prédominant qui apparaît alors est bien le problème politique lié au statut de l'Unité Systémique Région et à la place donnée au Système d'Information Régional: la solution, semble-t-il, passe par un choix politique de structure organisationnelle susceptible de faciliter la coordination entre les systèmes d'information des différentes administrations et de renforcer la communication entre les décideurs et la cohérence entre les décisions.

Toutes ces considérations seront reprises dans les deux points suivants qui vont tenter de montrer que la génération souvent volontaire d'information destinée à compléter des données spontanément apparues dans la vie des administrations n'atteindra une pleine efficacité que dans la mesure où elle sera la conséquence d'un plan politique et économique d'information conçu par l'Unité Systèmique considérée et pour le(s) système(s) hiérarchiquement supérieur(s).

la gestion des relations entre l'administration et ses ressortissants (les entités). En dehors des problèmes de stabilité de la définition des caractéristiques,
il y a aussi à tenir compte du fait que les codifications universelles ne sont
pas toujours validées empêchant une intégration entre des fichiers d'entités
différentes. Il en est ainsi de la localisation communale qui est cependant encore
facile à rectifier. Le problème le plus difficile actuellement rencontré est celui
du code Activité Principale Exercée (A.P.E.) qui est souvent modifié (avec un certain arbitraire) de telle sorte que la même entité entreprise peut se trouver avec
des codes d'activité variable d'une administration à l'autre. Il ne suffit pas de
standardiser, il faut aussi coordonner les actions de génération des informations
et de diffusion.

    L'examen de la gamme des caractéristiques et attributs suggère deux types
de question : d'abord il y a un risque de non suivi systématique par une source
administrative de toutes les caractéristiques disponibles à un moment donné pour
des raisons propres à cette administration (coût élevé, besoin disparu : sans
doute, dans ce cas pourrait-on imaginer une concertation entre les différentes
administrations et les utilisateurs, mais est-ce possible sans certaines réformes
profondes). En second lieu, il peut se poser un problème d'extension de la gamme
par accès à d'autres sources : le caractère confidentiel exigeant que des règles
de communication et d'utilisation des données individuelles soient établies.

    c) les mesures : si les modes de mesure des attributs changent au cours du
temps le suivi chronologique risque d'être perturbé, entraînant la nécessité de
procéder à des raccordements. Ainsi, le passage de la nomenclature 1959 des activités à la Nomenclature des Activités et des Produits a créé des ruptures assez
gênantes pour l'analyse de l'évolution.

    Une autre difficulté résulte du fait que la même caractéristique est parfois
mesurée d'une manière différente d'une administration à l'autre : ce qui fait dire
souvent que les incohérences en question enlèvent toute valeur à l'utilisation de
telles sources. Cet inconvénient est limité car la multiplication du nombre d'observateurs placés à des noeuds d'interdépendance différents de l'Unité Systémique
nous paraît, au contraire, receler une richesse d'analyse.

    Malgré les inconvénients affectant les entités, les attributs et les mesures,
le S.I.R. constitué en Poitou-Charentes a permis certaines analyses du développement régional que nous allons maintenant présenter.

B. Les applications du S.I.R.

    Le S.I.R. en Poitou-Charentes a été créé pour répondre aux besoins de l'ana-
lyse préalable à l'élaboration de la planification du développeemnt régional.
L'objectif était double : faire l'analyse rétrospective de l'évolution de l'économie de la région et élaborer des projections, ces applications répondant encore
à un besoin, mais il semble que l'Unité Régionale et ses responsables n'éprouvent
pas la nécessité de passer à une étape ultérieure de calcul économique.

1. Le tableau de Bord Economique Régional

    Outil d'analyse rétrospective le Tableau de Bord est un instrument de sur-
veillance et de contrôle : l'exploitation du S.I.R. permet de suivre les indicateurs au niveau régional, mais aussi pour tout découpage interne à la région. La
mémorisation d'informations relatives à des entités fines permet de représenter
pour une classe d'entités l'évolution des effectifs d'entités et de pondérations
de ces entités suivant certains critères, codes relatifs aux entités ou classes
de valeurs des attributs, et il est également possible d'étudier le processus de
passage de la population des entités de caractéristique à caractéristique (localisation, activité, taille, etc..). Un fichier d'employeurs comportant quelques
indications telles que l'activité, la localisation et les effectifs de salariés
constitue dans cette optique une excellente base d'analyse du redéploiement indus-

triel.

L'intégration de ce fichier avec un fichier communal disposant de nombreuses
données caractéristiques de l'environnement a permis d'appréhender l'impact de
l'évolution de l'activité industrielle sur le développement régional et la répar-
tition dans l'espace de la population, du chômage, des logements, de l'artisanat,
etc. Nous avons bien là une manière de saisir et quantifier les interrelations
entre sous-système économique industriel et sous-système région constitutifs de
l'Unité Systémique Régionale.

D'autres applications révélatrices de changements dans la structure de l'économie de la région et des tendances des principales grandeurs ont été effectuées
pour différents organismes responsables, ou pour les Instances Régionales : le
Tableau de Bord Economique de la Région Poitou-Charentes ayant été édité en quatre
volumes pour le compte de l'Etablissement Public Régional.

2. Les projections et prévisions

Si le nombre des analyses rétrospectives réalisées à partir du S.I.R. est
important, il n'en est pas tout à fait de même pour les études prospectives qui
ont été plus fréquemment demandées pour des secteurs restreints ou pour des variables très générales (démographie). Aucune projection d'un ensemble cohérent d'indicateurs n'a été demandée par l'Etablissement Public Régional : nous sommes encore loin d'élaborer des simulations pour l'Entité responsable de l'Unité Systémique Région à partir d'hypothèses d'évolution ou d'action formulées par des re-
présentants de cette entité responsable.

Il est clair que le Système d'Information Régional n'a pas pour le moment
été sollicité comme il aurait dû l'être, ni reçu toute l'attention souhaitable.

Ces constatations expliquent sans doute que bien peu d'efforts ont encore
été réellement lancés pour que les conditions d'intégration des informations dis-
persées soient effectivement réunies. Nous l'avons vu, il ne s'agit pas de rendre
communes les nomenclatures ou les codifications, mais de faire en sorte que chaque
organisme valide son information, c'est-à-dire contrôle la vraisemblance, la cohérence interne et externe des valeurs des informations qu'il détient sur chaque
entité. Cela paraît être la condition nécessaire de tout progrès dans ce domaine
de l'analyse du développement à partir de sous produits de la gestion administrative. Que la génération, au niveau individuel de chaque entité de l'information
issue des catégories universelles, soit mieux organisée, constitue la base obligée
de toute communication entre responsables, de tout véritable dialogue sans lequel
il serait vain de concevoir un développement régional. La technique d'élaboration
de S.I.R. est au point, la solution des problèmes dépend du rôle effectivement
reconnu aux puissants moyens de traitements informatiques et de l'organisation des
pouvoirs : c'est un choix politique.

II. Coût et valeur du S.I.R. pour l'unité régionale

Nous avons montré que les problèmes techniques n'étaient pas solubles sans
une intervention de volonté politique susceptible de donner un statut à la région
et par conséquent un rôle au S.I.R. En effet, le pouvoir effectivement attribué
à l'Unité Régionale, donne au S.I.R. sa signification et sa portée et, par conséquent, justifie la mise en place des règles permettant de constituer un S.I.R.
en utilisant massivement et en rentabilisant par conséquent les nombreuses informations déjà collectées et exploitées par de nombreuses administrations. L'expérience française actuelle fait apparaître un certain degré de décentralisation
même si le poids représenté par le budget des Etablissements Publics Régionaux
demeure modeste : il semble que la France pourrait aller plus loin dans ce sens
au moment où l'on souhaite promouvoir des formes de développement "par le bas",
c'est pourquoi nous allons tenter de faire ressortir l'intérêt économique et poli-

tique d'une mise en concordance des informations relatives aux problèmes économiques et sociaux.

A. Minimisation des coûts et maximisation des résultats

Tirer un maximum d'informations d'un stock de données, sous condition de mettre en place quelques règles de "bonne gestion" des systèmes administratifs, minimiser consécutivement les coûts de collecte, de validation, de mémorisation et d'exploitation des données nécessaires à la préparation des projets de développement et à leur suivi, apparaissent comme les deux arguments de base d'une prise de considération politique de l'opportunité de construire des systèmes d'information régionaux.

1. Complexité du système et processus décisionnel

Le nombre de décideurs intervenant dans le développement économique régional, la diversité de leur compétence, les interférences nombreuses entre les différentes décisions imposent de plus en plus que chaque domaine d'intervention ne soit plus considéré comme un isolat : agriculture, industrie, commerce, artisanat, équipement public, etc.. sont trop longtemps restés sans liaison. Le caractère systémique de l'interdépendance entre activité économique et environnement suggère que chaque décideur puisse appréhender non seulement l'évolution des variables qui sont de son ressort, mais également l'impact de ses choix sur l'ensemble du développement, ainsi que l'effet possible sur son domaine propre des autres décisions.

L'Entité Régionale a incontestablement un rôle de synthèse à jouer dans la coordination des nombreuses décisions affectant l'aménagement du territoire et le développement économique : il est bien clair que ce rôle ne sera efficace que s'il existe un système d'information satisfaisant, la valeur d'un S.I.R. apparaît ainsi sous l'angle de l'opportunité de sa mise en place qui dépend de choix politiques. Cependant, avant d'aborder ce point, nous voulons encore montrer l'intérêt pratique d'une meilleure coordination.

2. Diversité des observateurs : un maximum d'information pour un coût minimum

Le système économique et social est de plus en plus différentié, les fonctions et les relations d'interdépendance sont de plus en plus complexes, aussi il parait vain d'imaginer qu'un organisme central puisse, dans le futur, concevoir et mettre en place le système d'information susceptible de satisfaire tous les besoins. Même au niveau régional, il faut bien reconnaître que l'entité responsable de la gestion et du développement régional ne peut provoquer la collecte de toutes les données nécessaires.

La diversité actuelle des observateurs d'un même système régional grâce à la multiplicité des administrations collectant des informations éventuellement redondantes mais certainement complémentaires, est un avantage considérable. Aucun technocrate ne peut s'affirmer capable d'exhiber la liste complète des variables qui sont vraiment nécessaires à l'étude du développement, et encore moins de définir parfaitement les modes de mesure des attributs et des caractéristiques. On conçoit qu'il est bien préférable de laisser chaque administration responsable de la collecte des données nécessaires à ses besoins propres mais qu'un effort d'unification des possibilités d'intégrer toutes les informations en un système unique est absolument nécessaire. L'avantage est double, non seulement on économise les coûts d'une collecte autonome, mais en plus on rend cohérents entre eux les différents systèmes d'information relevant de chaque administration : la coordination des décisions devrait y gagner grâce à la communication facilitée des informations.

Par ailleurs, le maintien de plusieurs observateurs constitue aussi, selon nous, un avantage, non pas seulement comme moyen de contrôle réciproque des informations mais surtout comme moyen de révéler des changements et des évolutions qu'un indicateur trop synthétique risque de masquer.

Enfin, il faut souligner que mobiliser cette masse d'informations pour analyser le développement ne signifie pas une centralisation physique de toutes les données, mais bien plutôt la possibilité permanente d'une intégration partielle ou totale suivant les besoins : ce qui signifie surtout que les inconvénients et les obstacles rencontrés dans l'exemplbe développé ci-dessus devront être levés.

Ces considérations de coût et de valeur d'un système d'information n'ont d'autre but que de donner une justification à une solution politique qui ne dépend, bien sûr, ni de l'économiste, ni de l'informaticien chargé techniquement de créer le système d'information.

B. Statut de l'Unité Systémique Région et rôle du S.I.R.

La création d'un S.I.R. et son utilisation sont liées incontestablement au degré d'intégration interne du système Région et aux relations hiérarchiques que la Région entretient avec le Système Nation et les sous-systèmes dépendants. Le choix politique actuel donne une place relativement importante à la Région, mais il ne semble pas que toutes les conséquences en aient été tirées dans la constitution des systèmes d'information des régions. Au contraire on assisterait même à un certain renforcement de la centralisation des informations, au grand dommage de la connaissance locale : les exploitations centrales de données non validées près de leur source procurent aux responsables régionaux et locaux des surprises de toute sorte, qui évidemment n'influencent pas beaucoup les utilisateurs macro-économiques.

Les objectifs nouveaux de développement économique s'appuyant sur des initiatives locales, concernant des P.M.I. ou des micro-régions, on mesure les difficultés que vont rencontrer les responsables régionaux en l'absence d'une information suffisamment fine. Il est évident que la responsabilité confiée effectivement aux régions en matière de développement exige une meilleure définition politique des rôles respectifs des différents rouages. "Donner et retenir ne vaut" dit l'adage : on ne peut concevoir un accroissement des compétences sans la mise en place corrélative des mesures concernant le système d'information. Il s'agit d'abord et surtout de créer les conditions d'une validation des informations le plus près possible de la source, c'est nécessaire si l'on veut pouvoir intégrer les données issues des diverses sources, améliorer la connaissance et fournir consécutivement des informations cohérentes à chaque administration et responsable.

Conclusion

L'élaboration plurielle des décisions participant au développement régional et la complexité du système économique et social invitent à résoudre en priorité les problèmes de communication des informations entre les différents décideurs et par conséquent les problèmes d'intégration des informations administratives. L'Unité Systémique Région reposant sur l'interdépendance de nombreux agents et activités, nous proposons une mémorisation des données pour des entités fines : il en résulte que le coût de constitution du S.I.R. doit être minimisé. Sa valeur d'utilisation pour la connaissance, la programmation et le contrôle du développement économique dépend des efforts qui seront faits sur le plan technique à la suite des choix politiques.

Bibliographie

La liste des références ci-dessous est limitée aux aspects méthodologiques et aux principales applications du S.I.R. créé pour étudier l'économie du Poitou-Charentes.

DEBORD J.
- Economie d'une ressource naturelle. Analyse et gestion d'un système eau locale. Thèse de Doctorat ès Sciences Economiques 1976.

GUESNIER B.
- Le Système d'Information Régional. Construction et utilisation d'un S.I.R. dans la Région Poitou-Charentes. Colloque de l'ASRDLF. Aix-en-Provence. Cahiers d'Economie Politique d'Aix en-Provence du 7 fév. 1979.

- Le Système d'Information Régional (Informatique et Gestion n° 94, mars 1978).

- Unité Systèmique et ressources naturelles de l'environnement. Le Système d'Information : outil de connaissance, instrument d'intervention. Mondes en Développement : Externalités et Déveoppement (II) n° 24 - 1978.

GUESNIER B. & LAVALLEE J.
- Algorithme de constitution de fichiers cinématisés. Article paru dans la "Revue Française d'Automatique, Informatique, Recherche Opérationnelle" de janv. 1973, publié par l'AFCET.

- Algorithme de constitution de fichiers cinématisés - 1972.

LAVALLEE J. & Ch.
- Exploitations et simulations de la démographie d'un secteur industriel. Analyse et programmation. (1977).

- le Système d'Information Régional. Choix et techniques de présentation cartographique. 1979.

LAVALLEE J.
- Une économie de l'information économique ? (ATP-CNRS sur l'information économique) 1977.

MARCHAIS J.L.
- Le Tableau de Bord du secteur des Métiers. 1977.

- Les créations et disparitions d'entreprises industrielles. Incidence sur l'évolution de l'emploi salarié en Poitou-Charentes. 78

AIMELAFILLE N.
- Sensibilité de la main-d'oeuvre féminine aux changements structurels et conjoncturels dans le cadre de la région Poitou-Charentes. Contrat DGRST - Action Programme : Travail féminin 1978.

MOREAU L.
- Propositions pour un système intégré de gestion des collectivités locales. Traitement d'une application aux problèmes de financement. Thèse de Doctorat de Sciences Economiques. 1975

BROUARD A.
- la Démographie et l'Emploi de Poitou-Charentes

en 1976 et 1981. La Région serait-elle devenue
attractive ? - 1975

DURAND G.   - Le Système éducatif dans la Région Poitou-
                               Charentes. Prévision des flux de sortie des
                               différentes filières. Calcul des besoins
                               d'équipements scolaires. Etude des conditions
                               d'insertion des jeunes dans la vie active. 1976

Collectif I.E.R.   - Le Tableau de Bord Economique de la Région
                               Poitou-Charentes. Les indicateurs régionaux
                               après exploitation du Système d'information
                               Régional. - Juin, septembre, décembre 1978, et
                               mars 1979.

INFORMATION SYSTEMS IN PUBLIC ADMINISTRATION
D. Eade, J. Hodgson (editors)
North-Holland Publishing Company
© *DFD, 1981*

FINAL REPORT OF WORKING GROUP 6*

A. Introduction

The mandate of Group 6 was to discuss the major issues involved in
developing information systems for urban and regional development. The short
period of time available however forced the Group to narrow its discussion
mainly to the urban level. The fact that most experts of the Group were urban
oriented contributed to this decision. The report structure does not reflect
the evolution of discussions but the framework within which issues were
approached. As such, it is comprehensive though it is not exhaustive in its
coverage of relevant issues. The conclusions reached reflect the Group's
major concerns throughout the meeting and are thus the product of thorough
discussion.

B. Basic differences between developed and developing countries

Developing countries differ from advanced industrially developed countries
in two fundamental respects:

(a) Their level of achievement in terms of both economic progress and
individual (as well as community) social welfare;

(b) Their potential for achieving more acceptable levels of both wealth
and welfare for the vast majority of the population.

These differences are manifested in developing countries in:

---

*Participants : R. Beca, Chile ; A.A. Eigbefoh, Nigeria ; B. Guesnier,
France ; H. Koppel, Columbia ; A. Léderer, France ; P. Pezant, France ;
M. Rodrigues (Chairman), Brazil ; J.P. Sabatier, France ; K. Salih, Malaysia ;
O. Salomonsson, Sweden ; J. Schafer, Federal Germany ; O. Touré, Ivory Coast ;
M. Ward, United Kingdom ; M. Ziebinski, Poland.

(a) The continued existence of a significant proportion of the population
in a state of absolute poverty without adequate food or shelter and in an
unsatisfactory condition of health;

(b) The rigid persistence of wide disparities in income and wealth
between different population groups;

(c) The failure of the state machinery – for a variety of reasons (and
despite, in certain notable cases, the best of intentions) – to provide a
satisfactory social wage to help redress this imbalance. This arises from the
inability of the government organization to facilitate the transfer of existing
resources within the economy to supply more public goods and services to those
most in need (and thereby both reduce the degree of absolute poverty and narrow
the growing gap between the rich and the poor within the country);

(d) The lack of opportunity for individual advancement within the
established economic, social and institutional structure as it directly affects
people's access to employment, education, housing, etc., amenities and services.

They are unfortunately reflected in the marked differences in a wide
variety of economic and social indicators such as income per head, calorie
and protein intake, infant mortality rates, life expectancy, literacy levels,
morbidity rates, etc; notably between developed and developing countries but,
even more important, within developing countries as between different social
groups.

The basic reasons for the co-existence of these apparently disjoint groups
have been extensively discussed in the literature and they need not be detailed
and developed here. Suffice to say, however, that in the long term,
fundamental changes can only be brought about by a restructuring of the present
institutional framework of the international market combined with a shift in
the basis of trading relations and the existing control of industrial and
financial operations in the world economy. Only then will the essential
environment for an improvement in the status and well-being of individuals
in developing countries be established.

Two other important internal factors combine and contribute to aggravate
the problems of increasing the welfare of the community in developing countries:

(a) The lack of adequate human capital, that is, the number of people
sufficiently trained and appropriately qualified to raise and maintain the
level of economic activity;

(b) The lack of relevant capital assets to develop fully the available
natural resources.

(These two factors also impinge directly on the nature and quality of the
existing information system).

In practice, the combined effect of all these factors has been to limit
the scope, impact and power of Governments to implement and plan desired social
and economic development policies. Consequently, the outreach of the State
and the adequacy of the actual coverage of its operations are severely
constrained in practice. By force of circumstances or unintentional default –
difficulties relating to the identification, location and precise determination
of problem areas – those in the community most demanding of the Government's
attention and in need of its assistance and support (the poor, sick, weak,
illiterate, homeless, etc.) are largely ignored. They do not fall within the
conventional boundaries of regular and routine observation and information
collection.

At the same time, because of the maldistribution of income and wealth and political power and the differential access to legal expertise, public amenities and information (that is, provincial and municipal), the central and local government organizations cannot raise sufficient funding through traditional tax structures and the related tax base to bring about the various changes desired.

These same endogenous "deficiency" factors are nevertheless exogenous to the more specific problems to be resolved in urban situations. In particular, the structure of the administrative organization and the limited outreach of the supporting technical framework - telecommunications network, transportation system, level of technology and supply channels for technical equipment (the dependence on external sources for expertise and physical capital) - reinforce the identified difficulties.

The nature of the national planning system and the unavoidable need for developing countries to depend for project implementation on outside agencies for funding (for which the Government has to exercise acceptable standards of stewardship, define plan priorities and demonstrate proper accountability and financial control) leads to a greater centralization of real administrative and financial power within the central government. Municipal authorities not only have to compete with other departments and organizations of the State in the general allocation of official funds but they must also become increasingly dependent on the central government for continued approval of programmes and the provision of regular supplies of finance and other real resources to implement their urban policies.

In the following sections it is suggested that although the identified problems and even the planning methods may be very different, the apparatus for collecting appropriate data relating to them is essentially the same (although the actual data collection methods themselves may be quite different). Once these methods have been defined what should be common is the process whereby relevant and real information is produced from the actual data acquired. What is not clear is whether because of the essential differences between developing and developed countries, there is any scope for the adoption, with appropriate adaptation and improvement, of already available techniques employed in both the capture and subsequent analysis of data.

C. Differences between urban and regional phenomena

The Urban level of analysis can be regarded as a subsystem of the national economy: it belongs to the network and framework relating to the "armature urbaine", of population agglomerations in identifiable geographical locations. The interdependance between the rural phenomena and urban phenomena must be considered both in relation to short-term management decision-making issues (dealing with commuting, transport, power, etc.) and to more fundamental developmental planning issues (environmental structure, public investment, equipment acquisition, etc.). The interaction between the two quite distinct features of agricultural economic factors and scattered small business on the one hand and urban growth factors (the attraction of towns, employment, wages) on the other, is controlled and regulated by many factors at different local, regional and national levels, for example, corporate enterprises, government departments, etc.

The planning or decision-making information demands from these factors is different. It depends to some extent on the degree of decentralization of planning and the dispersion of decision making. The methodologies of information supply must take these differences into account. Planners' information needs differ when dealing with identifiable urban and regional problems and also the relations between these systems. If the information system devised is specific to each level and/or sector there is a risk the identification and evaluation of the interrelations between them becomes impossible to define.

The entities as areas, points or lines must be integrated with various keys. Moreover the control of the factors in these different zones including both the geographical entities and also the relations between the activities of other entities (persons, enterprises, etc.) must be considered.

The information given to actors at local, regional and national level must include relevant information on all the customary (economic, demographic, etc.) variables, extended in scope and coverage to incorporate the different nature, content, significance, scope, time, range and aggregation levels of the data concerned.

The rural and urban data available are also quite different, so the formalization of interdependance requires integration of relations between actors at each level and a capacity to solve problems of information semantics and relevance for each level of decision. For instance, it is necessary to distinguish firstly information needed for decision making and indicators necessary to monitor the evolution of urban-regional interaction; and secondly, information needed for each hierarchical level.

In the following sections, the report concentrates especially on the urban management-planning-development problem, partly because it is easier to identify (in that the Group had insufficient time to elaborate all the regional issues) and partly because the primary intention of the Group was to try and identify a general methodology and its associated superimposed theory for implementing an integrated urban information system. In this respect, there was an attempt to regard the urban area as an entity within a more general environmental and regional context.

D. Characteristics of the prevailing urban situation in the least developed
                                countries

Urban areas in developing countries contain a number of distinguishing socio-economic features that separate the nature of their problems from those in developed countries:

(a) The structure of cities in the least developed countries (LDCs), particularly the principal centres such as the capital region or the main city (as distinct from that found in more advanced countries) is basically dualistic. It consists of a modern/formal/organized sector and a so-called informal sector. Although there is some controversy as to the precise nature of the relationships between these sectors, it is apparent that the city structure reflects the wider structural features of a dependency development process;

(b) The size of the urban informal sector in general appears to be increasing, if not relatively, then at least in absolute terms. Its persistence can be both demographically explained (viz., higher than average rates of urban population growth reflecting not only the natural increase of population but also a pronounced rural-urban migration, which is inadequately absorbed into the modern sector), and in terms of conservation tendancies in the economic development of the LDCs cities;

This dual structure is reflected in a basic inequality in the provision of amenities and access to urban services and functions in such areas as housing, employment, transportation and other essential public facilities (water supply, sanitation, health, etc.). In the urban sector, these observable disparities may coincide with reasonably well-defined ecological areas such as slums and squatter housing, with self-employment and small-scale individual enterprises. These often tend to occur at the interstices of the modern sector areas, with poor environmental neighbourhood conditions coexisting and contrasting with the opulence of a modern sector that is increasingly imitative of the cities of industrially advanced nations;

Urban areas and authorities in LDCs have, in addition, a number of administrative and structural characteristics that limit their ability to cope with the observable problems in a satisfactory way;

(a) Urban budgets are small, in relation to the problems arising from the growing pressure to provide basic needs, employment opportunities, social services, etc. in LDCs cities. In per capita terms, the amount available for spending ranges from 0.5 per cent to 25 per cent of the levels current for the urban areas of developed countries. Furthermore, the limited resources available are invariably allocated in a way which biases expenditure towards modern sector development, rather than to the acute formal sector needs;

(b) The whole urban administrative structure also appears to be biased more towards the needs of the modern sector because of the type of services it provides: for example, improvements in existing urban water supply or transportation facilities by renewing pipes or replacing old buses have an impact only on those in the community who already benefit from them.

The combination of these two general factors has important implications for identifying data needs and information system design in urban areas in developing countries as follows:

(a) If priority is to be given to the development of the informal sector in LDC cities, then the data collection procedures and the information systems designed for those urban areas should take into account the particular needs of this sector, whilst not ignoring the existing requirements of the already organized urban centre;

(b) Administrative data should be made available for both sectors in terms of water supply, housing conditions, transportation structure, licensing of businesses, etc;

(c) There is a need to take extra-urban processes into account. For example, data is needed on rates of migration and rates of absorption and their impact on urban organization;

(d) It is necessary to accommodate any information system development within co-ordinated over-all government data networks at the local level in terms of compatible manual or computer files and their techniques including the non-traceable elements in the informal sector;

(e) The data for the informal sector should not be treated individually, but in an integrated fashion and interrelated with the problem area and the services provided by the administration;

(f) At present, official data/statistics operations tend to focus solely on the modern sector, rather than on the urban informal sector which constitutes the main part. Administrative records also miss out on these sectors many of which comprise unregistered and often illegal operations;

(g) The planning of the provision of public goods and services, for example, parks, should take into account the alternative uses that may be made of the amenities provided as well as their indirect impact on different social groups;

(h) Data collection particularly for the essentially non-traceable informal sector is expensive and, unfortunately, the tax base for municipal revenue collection is normally very narrow. The subvention of special funds from the central government may be necessary to ensure the information is obtained.

E. General administrative information needs

Administrative information is not an aim in itself, it is essentially one of the elements that contribute to the operation of public services. The intention of these services is to provide certain goods and facilities by means of a certain number of resources.

The goods and services produced and also the resources available depend on the type of society concerned. But in general, regional and municipal governments are responsible for:

(a) Managing the services of health, education, culture, sport, etc.;

(b) Developing and maintaining utilities connected to these services ;

(c) Undertaking various public works such as school building, road construction and maintenance, etc.

The production of these services implies the payment of public servants, and at different levels and for various purposes, the use of external enterprises. The authority dispenses funds collected from taxes raised directly at the local level or indirectly obtained via subventions from the central government from its own tax revenues.

Local administrations are characterized on the one hand by the interrelations between themselves and, on the other, by their connexions with the central administration. The operations of local administrations and the central administration and its associated agencies lead each organization in different ways to an involvement with the following entities:

(a) Land and agricultural production;

(b) People and housing;

(c) Enterprises and "artisans" and industrial products;

(d) Utilities;

(e) Transactions in goods, services;

(f) Incomes.

For example, an agency or authority concerned with trading will try to ascertain the characteristics of its enterprises and the value of exchanges within itself and with the exterior.

The establishment, development and organization of administrative documentation has at first to follow certain essential efficiency rules:

(a) The format of base data (traditional files and computerized files) and the organization of data (file structure, standardization of data) must be directly related to the available techniques;

(b) The various interconnexions between local administrations and with the central administration that can be represented in the form of a network

(the use of common identifiers, data exchanges, physical connexion, etc.)
should be directly connected to available techniques;

(c) Adaptations, improvements and modifications introduced into this
documentation to facilitate smoother administrative operations will have to
take into account the established unity and harmony of the existing
organization and documentation. This existing unity will at the same time act
as a constraint to change and development;

(d) The differences between administrative information and that required
for planning are numerous. Administrative information has to satisfy
well-defined efficiency and accountability criteria: in an administrative
process, the judgement of reality is severe, precise and rapid because it is
related to the short-term requirement to fulfil routine, regular, well-defined
functions and commitments.

Choice and priorities appear to be very dependent on the nature of the
administrative units in question and are connected to the available techniques.
Actual project choices have to be made in practice according to the identified
cost/benefit ratios and efforts made to reduce costs. For example, when a
new file is created, allowance is not, in general, made for data not useful
for the responsible administration. When data useful for other purposes
are registered, the costs of operation have to be seriously estimated because
they may often be higher than the obtained results.

The development of a highly integrated data system implies the existence
of agencies responsible for their proper operation and not only of a
temporary co-ordination; but this often leads to centralized administrative
organizations, or implies the institution of a co-ordinating body within a
single assigned agency that is responsible for the operation and maintenance
of the whole system (see DFD reports). The organization of a co-ordinated
data network must nevertheless avoid creating useless processings that
increase the final costs for results of limited use and doubtful validity.

F. Administrative information provision

The various agencies of local government have to collect and process data
for their day-to-day operations. There are three main ways by which these
agencies get their data:

(a) The citizen provides the information directly. In this case there
is a personal application for a service (for example, the installation of
power supply or a telephone line). A standard pro-forma provided by the
authority is used to obtain the necessary information;

(b) The citizen must also be informed as to how to supply certain other
data;

(c) The administration has to look for the information.

In this case there is no direct citizen need or personal wish to provide the
information. The administration can proceed in two ways:

(a) Extracting the information from existing data and records of
administrative procedures. These data "files" may be held with a different
agency from that which requires it. (The land tax collecting agency gathers
its information from existing cadastral files);

(b) Creating a procedure to get the information. When the information
does not exist the administration has to initiate a special survey to provide

the relevant data.

Some of the considerations that must be taken into account when adopting a methodology for the provision of administrative data are:

(a) That a number of municipal agencies and departments will work on, or influence, the same urban elements. There is a need in those cases for some co-ordination of their activities which should be reflected in their information systems;

(b) Avoidance of duplicated effort when collecting information that is used by several departments. It is convenient to assign the data gathering task to only one agency even if this means extra-work to collect some additional information (for example, not for its internal use but to be utilised by another agency).

It is also important to consider some functional aspects of data collection, especially with regard to inter-departmental data sharing. Function data are collected for two purposes:

(a) Data used in statutory regulation or control (for example, land and property registration);

(b) Data collected for internal agency tasks (land use factors, etc.).

The accuracy required for these two types of information when applied to the same objects is usually different. Generally greater accuracy is required for data used in regard to legal procedures. This means that if information is to be shared, the agency responsible for its acquisition should be the one tha' ha's the greatest accuracy demands. Therefore, functional priorities of data should give the basic guidelines for co-ordination and integration on informational aspects.

Another consideration is the collection and updating of information. Most city administrations, especially in the developing countries, lack facilities for collecting data and for updating such data. As most data required for administrative decision making are of a socio-economic nature. There is a need for regular updating of such information before they become obsolete. There is a tendency to underestimate the efforts required for data collection and updating.

Some data are automatically updated in the operational system (for example, when paying regular bills) but the data are updated only periodically and for the latter a satisfactory prior sampling frame (for example, a population file or geocoding system) is necessary on which to base a relevant survey.

Usually city administrators become apathetic in collecting data which they do not urgently require. Efforts should be made to gather information on various aspects of a city's operations which would be required in the future or by another municipal department.

Information exists in most urban economics only in the formal sector. While appreciating the difficulties associated with the collection of data from the informal sectors, there is a need to bring such elements into the general framework of information gathering in the cities. It is only when they are introduced and incorporated into the existing framework that urban data can be regarded as complete and comprehensive.

In the process of gathering and processing information, there is a tendency among city administrators to purchase or acquire data processing

Table 18. Data needs for urban planning

Stage of the planning programme process [a]	Exogenous	Data from urban information systems [b]: Population	Social	Economic	Topography soil	Land use	Land property	Land value	Infrastructure characteristics	Infrastructure conditions	Utilities	Level of service in facilities	Environment, natural res.	Income	Financial
I. LONG RANGE STRATEGY (25-35)															
Aims at:															
Determining a long range strategy for the city															
Preserving future choices mainly by reservation of land for infrastructure, utilities, facilities		L	L	L	L	M	M	M	L		L		L		
Inputs from other levels:															
National and regional goals for economic and social development	X														
National special policy including an urban framework	X														
II. LONG RANGE PLANNING (10-20 years)															
Aims at:															
Establishing a Mast Plan including:															
Population perspectives		M	L	L	M	M	M	M	M		L	M	L	L	L
Land use maps															
Location and main normative characteristics for the basic infrastructures and utilities					M	M									
Objectives for levels of services															
Inputs from other levels:															
National locational policy for economic activities	X														
National forecasts and/or objectives for:															
Demographic growth including urban growth	X														
GNP per capita + income distribution	X														
Production per sectors	X														
III. PROGRAMMING (3-12 years)															
Aims at:															
Undertaking actions to reach objectives in a co-ordinated way for the different sectors including: Education, Health, Security, Housing, Transportation, Utilities, Environment		M	M	M	H	H	H	H	H	M	H	M	H	M	M
Inputs from other levels:															
Funds availability from national/regional budgets	X														
External financial and technical assistance	X														

[a] The time-scale is usually sectorally related and therefore may overlap.

[b] Level of accuracy: L = low; M = medium; H = high; X = as required.

hardware and software for prestige purposes. Sometimes no consideration is
given to the suitability of the equipment or the ability of the users. This
results in an inability to utilize the equipment effectively.

G. Planning information needs

There is an obvious relation between the planning methodology to be used
by a city and the availability of the data required to support the methodology.
Nevertheless the data availability is not an absolute constraint for the
planner. An improved planning process putting more demand on the urban
information system will normally result in an improvement of this system.
Moreover, if most of the data required by the city planner is to be provided by
this system, important inputs to the planning process will remain endogenous
and out of the control of the city decision makers. Another fact is the
planner's tendency to underestimate and even ignore those sectors for which no
reliable data are available, for example, the "untraceable" or "informal"
sectors.

A correspondence between the planning stages and data needs is shown in
table 18. It should be noted that data accuracy is not the same for the
different stages: as a rule, the longer the time range, the lower the
required accuracy.

1. Long range strategy determination

As data required for this purpose are generally neither numerous nor
precise, the existing non-availability of the information at the city level
is rarely a stumbling-block.

The problems are rather with inputs from national and regional levels.
In many countries, there is no well-defined long-term spatial policy which
would allow cities to foresee their future in the national context. The lack
or the insufficiency of long term perspectives is also due to the overwhelming
nature of present problems of rapidly growing urban communities.

Nonetheless, a long-term approach is no less necessary in developing
countries. On the contrary, because it is extremely costly not to reserve and
identify a long time ahead those resources that will be needed in the future
for the realization of basic infrastructures or utilities, proper provision must
be made for them in both physical and financial terms.

2. Long range planning

City managers have become increasingly conscious of the necessity to
prepare a long-term framework for their development; sometimes under pressure
from the state money-lender. Unfortunately, master plans have serious
shortcomings. For quite a few cities, probably for a majority of them in the
developing world, these master plans are established with external assistance.
Designing such plans usually requires huge quantities of data. If they are not
readily available, costly surveys must be undertaken to collect them.

Often there is an excellent opportunity to start with the implementation of
an integrated data base, but it is rarely accomplished because the team
responsible for the completion of the master plan is normally under heavy time
pressure and has no direct interest in such undertaking.

This is more than a missed opportunity because the very utility of a master
plan is directly related to the establishment of an adequate monitoring
evaluation information system. If not updated, a master plan soon becomes an
irrelevant document, misleading, being the source of costly mistakes. An

updating is relatively cheap and easy only if the basic data are readily
available.

3. Programming

In many cities now, public services (electricity, water supply, sewerage,
highways, etc.) are conscious of the need for a close co-ordination of their
programs. This situation favours the realization of an urban data network
(UDN). But it is not sufficient to get it realized. Municipalities have still
to make a dedicated effort in this direction. However, the existence of a local
UDN is not always a sufficient tool for program co-ordination. In certain urban
areas, a central authority is the rule and there is a strong need for an
interconnexion of the UDN, the various communities in the area, or even better
for an integrated information system covering the whole area and rural
surroundings as well.

As can be noted from table 18 - which does not claim to be exhaustive -
data needed for city planning are many, and various levels of accuracy may be
required. These data can be provided by quite different sources spread
throughout numerous organizations. Therefore, building an information system
is a complex task which requires much expertise even if the most sophisticated
techniques are not involved.

H. Planning information supply

Once the information needs have been assessed, the planning of information
supply can be derived from different data sources such as:

(a) Existing files, administrative or census data;

(b) New administrative files;

(c) Special data collection activities, censuses or surveys, field
inventories, etc.

Depending on the over-all demand for quality, adequacy, precision in the
planning information, and the existing data background, various levels of
accuracy requirements can be recognized in the planning methods as well as in
the data acquisition methods. These demands vary from city to city and even
between sectors and also over time. It is important to notice that the lowest
level of accuracy chosen for the data content will influence the use of
methodologies in the planning information processing.

Urban planners are currently in a situation where they are forced to use
existing available information. Planning methods in their design naturally
reflect existing data availability rather than what the current planning
situations require.

The introduction of an UDN concept should, in co-ordination with the
urban administration and management needs, improve the situation of the urban
planners. The improvements of the data background situations, which will give
more adequate planning information, will also provide a new framework for
methodological development.

1.   The nature of planning information

Planning information is used in the planning process. The provision of adequate planning information naturally requires a thorough knowledge of the planning process and how the information serves its different operations.

This fact has unfortunately been so far very neglected in urban and regional information system design. Whereas normally a great deal of effort is spent on the question of data needs, that is what data are needed, very little if any consideration is given to the problems of how the data will be used.

The belief that if only the right kind of data are provided, the planning information problems will be solved, is false. Unfortunately, many information systems are still designed from this principle. Therefore too many planning information systems exist that, though they have a reasonable data content, have very few users.

The planner has no use for data. He needs information. The processes that produce adequate information from the existing data are therefore critical. These processes do however often require certain conditions to be fulfilled with regard to data standards and structures. If the information processing tools are not provided, the data bases will not be used.

There is also a need for a methodological framework in which the information can be further processed, evaluated and presented. This also requires specific processes without which the use of the system will be limited.

2.   Planning information analysis

The planning process in itself is too complex to be analysed as a whole. It is therefore necessary to break down the normal planning behaviour in various sectors into smaller components or operations. One such operation in health planning for example, would be to forecast future population growth in order to determine future needs. One can however immediately recognize that this operation is not unique to health planning, but is common to most planning sectors. This is so for most planning operations. It would therefore be possible to make a general classification of planning operations with regard to their nature.

Most statistical systems and even most existing information systems can only provide information about a current situation which is described in a static way (that is, the characters and geographical distribution of objects and their aggregates) but will not give information about their interaction (generally called functional description). If the information system is to be used for support during the whole planning process, it will be necessary to ensure that the needs of data processing and information analysis are taken into consideration in the design of the system.

It will therefore be necessary to make an analysis of the normal requirements that the operations in the planning process will have on data standards and structures for methodological processing. If, for example, there is a need to determine hospital areas, aggregation of certain population data must be achieved with a processing technique that allows the accumulation of   aggregates at the same time as their spatial distribution (allocations techniques) is defined. This normally requires a spatial referencing method which gives a topological file structure (a topological file structure is the spatial interrelationship between the basic geographical entities described).

In order to be able to carry out adequate data processing to obtain
relevant planning information, an analysis of the needs for basic data
processing modules (methodological) should be made. Such a processing module
should preferably be general (it should be applicable regardless of the data
content; for example a spatial aggregation module should operate on various
kinds of data such as population, employment figures, land values, etc.).

Parallel to these analyses, the analysis of data needs for the various
planning methods (see Section F) that are likely to be used should be carried
out.

It should now be possible to consider what data acquisition methods should
be used. It is here necessary to take into consideration the data structure
requirements that have been derived from the analysis of the planning process
operations and the set of processing modules that have been considered. This
will tell us not only what data should be collected, but also how and with what
degree of quality and precision. It is of course necessary to use as much
as possible of already existing data, especially from administrative files.
This will often require conversion and reformatting.

Parallel to the analysis of data acquisition methods, an analysis of the
methods of symbol referencing to be used should be carried out. It is often
necessary to compromise between the requirements set up from the methodological
analysis above and the practical circumstances such as suitable geographical
referencing objects already existing in administrative files, cost factors,
etc.

3. Data and file organization

With the background material from the previous analysis as a basis, the
design of data organization and file structures can now take place for the part
of the UDN that will serve the information needs of the planning process. The
existing file structures and the limitations already accepted for data standards
and structures (logical integration) will influence the design.

Design and development of data acquisition methods, updating procedures,
conversion methods, etc. can take place.

The data collection and file conversion and the planning data bases can be
established. This will probably be done successively and for various data
types at different times. It can also be assumed that if different urban
agencies are responsible for the contents of the data bases, updating will take
place at different points of time. This requires that the timeliness between
various data types must be considered.

4. Applications

Development or acquisition of the methodological modules with which the
data in the data bases will be processed into information will create the
software with which the user can operate the data. It is necessary to educate
the users so that they are aware of the different potentials of information
processing within the UDN. It must however be recognized that the composition of
different kinds of information to apply a specific planning method, its
interpretation, etc., must be left to the planner. The planning information
system part of the UDN will only provide the user with information processing
and information analysis tools.

The use of the UDN for planning purposes should preferably be facilitated
by some kind of planning oriented user language which will enable the planners
to use the system themselves without any deeper knowledge of EDP.

An important part of the mechanisms with which UDN supplies planning information is the way the user feedback from the planning process can be used for the continuous improvement of the system.

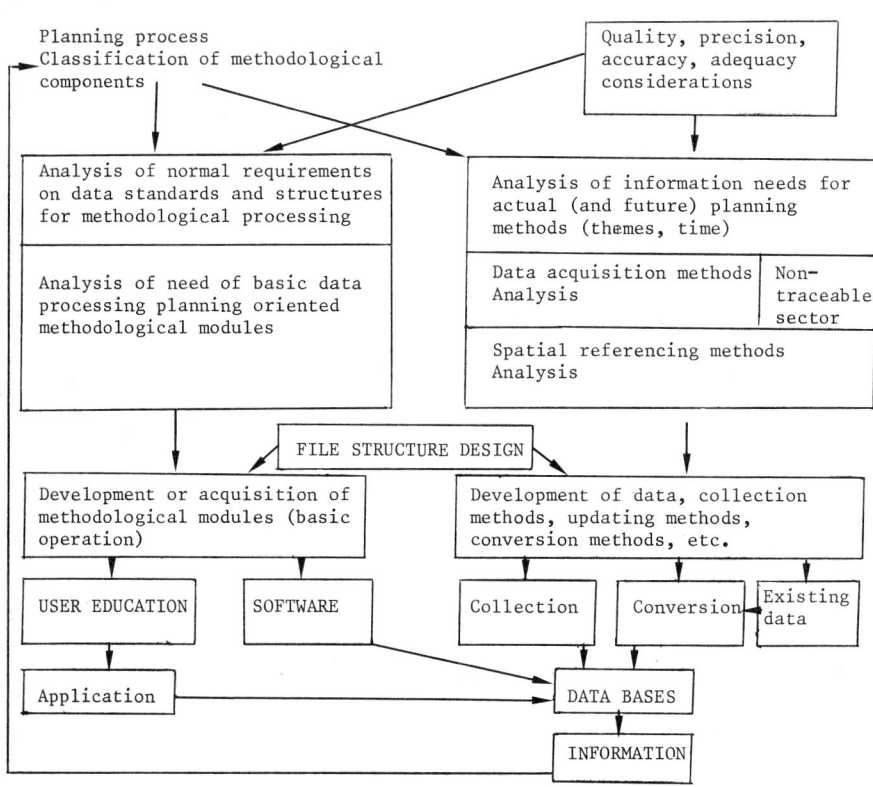

Figure XLIV. Flow-chart for the design and implementation of an urban information system

I. Conclusions

There are substantial differences between developed countries and LDCs
in terms of the requirements for problem solving and planning. In view of
the structural dependency of LDCs on the advanced countries problems of the
urban environment in the LDCs not only differ in magnitude but, in the more
important cases, they also differ in nature. This is exemplified by the
existence and persistence of a large, and largely ignored, informal sector in
most urban areas in the LDCs. In addition, problems of rural and urban
development are highly related.

The solution of these problems and the planning for development demands
data for both administration, management and planning. It is suggested that
existing data files do not take due account of the informal sector. In
addition, the co-ordination of data files plays an important role in the
avoidance of misallocation of resources or duplication of data files, and allows
a more comprehensive approach to urban problems. In this regard, the
non-traceable sector coincides with that area of concern that is characterized
by very distinctly different social and economic problems.

Though there is an interdependency between the existing information base
and the methodologies for urban analysis to be used, there must be a careful
choice of methodologies for they have direct and serious implications on the
additional data needs. This may imply problems that transcend direct
solutions, for they are intrinsic of least developed countries. This can be
represented as follows:

SOPHISTICATION OF METHODOLOGIES	QUALITY OF THE INFORMATION BASE	COSTS
HIGH	BAD	VERY HIGH
	GOOD	HIGH
LOW	BAD	MEDIUM
	GOOD	LOW

Due to differences between developed countries and LDCs there may be some
scope for adaptation of existing techniques in both the capture and analysis of
data.

Some of the conclusions and discussions referred to in sections E, F, G and
H related to the general situation in which practical case study evidence has not
been directly alluded. To explore the issues in greater depth needs the direction
of attention to more specific problem areas, through case studies, in particular
urban areas. Any evaluation of these case studies should take into account the
cost and benefits of the operations that may be recommended as a consequence.

<u>Caveats</u>

In developed as in developing countries, the introduction of computer techniques in regional and urban management and planning processes should only be done after serious studies on which the major aspects to be considered are the efficiency of the administration and the socio-economic environment.

At regional and urban levels, the concept of a data network is a very complex one for it has to consider not only the inter-urban administration relations but also the relations existing between these urban administrations and central administrations. In addition, it should take into consideration the technology available, the time factor and the investments required.

J. Recommendations to DFD

DFD should support and organize specific case studies to:

(a) Identify the problems and limitations of implementing and operating urban information systems in least developed countries;

(b) Evaluate the methodology that has been discussed in the Group report ; and

(c) Identify those urban problems and corresponding information needs which lead to the development and implementation of urban information systems.

DFD should continue to complete anthologies of experience on urban information systems in developing countries in order to facilitate and promote the exchange of information and experience between urban practitioners in developing countries.

The Group suggests that case studies should, as far as possible, be conducted in different regions of the world so that they can be evaluated for their relevance to the area and other areas as far as transference of appropriate methodologies and technologies is concerned.

The Group felt that there is no need for DFD to conduct new projects until the results of evaluation of current case studies are made available. These evaluations may be conducted by regional working groups over a period of a year or so.

On the basis of these evaluations, DFD should conduct seminars at the regional or international level in order to discuss and outline further work programmes in urban and regional information systems in ddveloping countries.

INFORMATION SYSTEMS IN PUBLIC ADMINISTRATION
D. Eade, J. Hodgson (editors)
North-Holland Publishing Company
© *DFD, 1981*

INFORMATION SYSTEMS IN THE TRADITIONAL SECTOR

Sam Suharto*

A. Introduction

In most developing countries, the economy is normally composed of two almost equally important institutions, the organized and the unorganized institutions. The organized institutions include the large industries, trading companies, transportation companies, hotels, tourist bureaus, banks, etc. These are the established business organizations either private, semi-government or government enterprises. The unorganized institutions are those which are normally engaged in very small and simple activities of a traditional nature, employing mostly unpaid family workers. They constitute the informal or traditional sector.

In the early stages of development, a country's economy is normally characterized by a large majority of the population being engaged in the traditional sector. When the economic condition improves, an increasing number will be employed in the organized or more modern sector emerging in the country. Those who are engaged in the traditional sector are the poor who mostly live in the rural areas. They have low education or are uneducated and have low technological skill. The main objective of their activities is to fulfil the basic daily human requirement for the members of their households.

The emergence of the modern sector will help the traditional sector but can also have a negative impact on its development and therefore on a large part of the population. The development planners, in setting development policy, play the most important role in keeping the balance between the two sectors. The trend in most developing countries appears to be towards a concentration on the improvement of the lowest income group of the population rather than emphasis only on the increase of the gross national product. It is therefore very important that sufficient information on this sector should be made available in addition to that of the modern sector.

Unfortunately, in most developing countries the statistical data concerning the traditional sector are not easily available compared with that of the modern sector. Although this varies from country to country, some of the reasons are:

---

* Central Bureau of Statistics, Jakarta, Indonesia

(a)   The number is very large;

(b)   The definitions have not been well established;

(c)   No registration or directory is available;

(d)   No records on any information are kept;

(e)   Very low levels of education;

(f)   Very rapid changes in activities (for example, due to seasonality).

The difficulty in obtaining information is also caused by the wide range of many different activities where the traditional sector is involved, such as agriculture, trade, manufacturing, services, transportation etc. Each activity requires its own type of information system.

B.   The information required

Although for the purpose of development planning and policy the type of information required from the traditional sector may be different from one country to another, some common basic information may be identified:

(a)   Firstly, it is important to know the extent of this sector in relation to the total economy. That is, the total number of traditional sectors in each economic sector, by the smallest regional level possible;

(b)   Secondly, the distribution of various important characteristics, again in each economic sector and by region. These characteristics may include:

(i)   Production by type, volume and value of the products or total output;

(ii)   Information on the starting capital or the size of the enterprise;

(iii)   Labour employed, paid or unpaid;

(iv)   Cost of production;

(v)   Time and hours of operation;

(vi)   Added value of the enterprise;

(vii)   Marketing of the product;

(viii)   Credit facilities required, etc.;

(c)   Thirdly, the information on the socio-economic characteristics of the owner and the members of his household, such as education, income, health, housing, etc.

Such information should be available as frequently as possible. However, due to the complexities of the data collection, it would be ideal if such information could be made available annually. In some countries certain information may be required more frequently than once a year, for example every 3, 4 or 6 months (for example, concerning food crop production in the case of Indonesia).

The type of information for various levels of management and planning needs to be determined for each sector. Some developing countries have launched various development programmes for the traditional sector which include credit facilities, taxes and import duties exemption, export promotion, domestic marketing assistance, maintenance of raw material supplies, price control policy, etc. The impact of the development programme needs to be monitored periodically so that improvement of policy can always be made.

C.   Current situation

It is believed that very few satisfactory information systems have so far been implemented in developing countries. The systems currently available generally carry out ad hoc or partial activities in order to meet the immediate needs of the planners or policy makers. In order to generate development programmes in the traditional sector, it is necessary to interrelate many variables and to show their inter-linking effect. It is therefore essential that the information systems of various economic activities be developed into an integrated information system. The known means of data collection may be categorized into three sources which are censuses, sample surveys and administrative reports.

1.   Censuses

Census results are very useful in providing universal as well as individual unit information. A census also has limitations, in particular when the total sector under study, be it population, agriculture or industry, is very large. In developing countries, censuses for traditional sectors may be grouped into two parts: an agricultural census, which includes traditional sectors in agriculture; and a non agricultural economic census. Data collected through censuses are limited to basic characteristics due to the size of such an operation and the need to maintain the quality of the data. Censuses, however, can provide information for the construction of sampling frames and for further development of the system; they can also provide estimates in very limited geographical areas such as villages. Therefore, periodic census operations may prove to be very valuable benchmark operations of information in traditional sectors.

2.   Sample surveys

In addition to decennial or quinquennial census operations, during intervening years many countries carry out sample surveys with the aim of collecting information from part of the universe. The sample is selected in such a manner that it will represent the characteristics of the universe.

Since the information unit is much smaller in sample surveys than in censuses, the interviewers are usually better qualified and better trained in data collection. Therefore, through sample surveys the data collected can be much more detailed and of a higher quality than that collected through censuses. The major difficulties in carrying out sample surveys in traditional sectors concern standard definitions and the availability of sampling frames. Sample surveys also suffer from the limitation of producing estimates for smaller geographical areas. Combined with data collected from other sources however, sample surveys can be a very valuable source of information.

3.   Administrative reports

The reports resulting from administrative recording, if very carefully designed and implemented, can become the best source of information in the traditional sector. Periodic reports from the lowest level of administrative

units hierarchically upward to the information processing centre can produce
very efficient systems. The data can be organized systematically, stored and
retrieved for the purposes of management decisions or development planning.
Many Governments have made a great deal of effort to improve their
administrative systems in order to generate periodic information. However,
there is also evidence that some of this effort fails because of the routine
nature of the reporting activities and that the completeness and consistency
of the reports can deteriorate unless strict continuous measures are
established.

    All the three sources should be employed complementarily; no one source
can generate all the required information; integration of the system requires
very careful study and systems design.

D.   Improvement of the system

    Taking into account the methods of data collection in the traditional
sector just described and the need for development planning and policy making,
it is necessary to assess the possible improvements that could be made to
the systems currently in use in the developing countries. Since the
development of the traditional sector cannot proceed independently from that
of other sectors, it will be necessary that the information systems in this
sector be interlinked with the information of other sectors, in areas such as
energy, agriculture, finance, etc. Therefore there is a need to design
integrated national information systems with the traditional sector as one of
the subsystems. With the rapid development in computer and telecommunications
technology, such integrated systems are possible but would require the
commitment of a great many government agencies, possibly a significant
determining factor to their success.

    In Indonesia an attempt has been made on a small scale to set up regional
data base systems with villages as the unit of information. All types of
information from all sectors are reported through administrative channels
to the information processing centre, the traditional sector activities being
one of the data sources. In Jakarta a large data file is being created to
enable easy retrieval and manipulation of the data. Continuous improvement of
the system is being carried out.

INFORMATION SYSTEMS IN PUBLIC ADMINISTRATION
D. Eade, J. Hodgson (editors)
North-Holland Publishing Company
© DFD, 1981

THE TRADITIONAL SECTOR AND THE SMALL FARMER: AN EVALUATION

S.M. Shah*

The small farmer is a major constituant of the traditional sector in agriculture in a number of developing countries. He forms the most important "informal sector" in the rural areas. The fundamental unit of decision making in farming is the operational unit (as distinct from the ownership holding). Consequently, the several programmes initiated by the Government are focused on the size of farming units in several countries.

Following the directives from the Food and Agricultural Organizations of the United Nations (FAO) for a world census of agriculture, the Government of India carried out an Agricultural Census from 1970-1971, the results of which were published in 1975. This Census brought out the magnitude of the problem of small and marginal farmers. The operational holding was defined as all land which was wholly or partly used for agricultural production and was operated as one technical unit by one person alone or with others without regard to title, legal status, size or location. The holder or the operator was the person who assumed the responsibility of decision maker for the management of the holding.

According to this Census, there are 70.5 million operational holdings in Indian agriculture operating over an aggregate area of 162 million hectares. The total area of holdings under agricultural operations constitutes 49.4 per cent of the total geographical area of the country.

One half of the total operational holdings in India (35.7 million out of 70.5 million) are of a size less than one hectare of land (see table 19). These marginal and submarginal holdings together operate over an area of 14.5 million hectares which constitutes only 9 per cent of the total area of land operated in Indian agriculture. The average size of an operational holding in this category is 0.41 hectares, of which the irrigated component is only 0.12 hectares. The average size of an operational holding in the country as a whole, taking the size of all holdings together, is 2.30 hectares of land. Of the total of 70.5 million operational holdings, there are about 12 million wholly irrigated holdings, 17 million holdings with part of their areas under irrigation and 41 million wholly unirrigated holdings in the country (see table 20).

* Joint Secretary, Planning Commission, New Delhi, India.

Table 19.   Number and area of operational holdings according to size - all India
(Area in thousand ha; No. in thousands)

Sl. No.	Size class (ha)	Total holdings	
		No.	Area
1	2	3	4
1.	Below 0.5	23,178	5,446
2.	0.5-1.0	12,504	9,099
3.	1.0-2.0	13,432	19,282
4.	2.0-3.0	6,722	16,353
5.	3.0-4.0	3,959	13,646
6.	4.0-5.0	2,684	11,929
7.	5.0-10.0	5,248	36,305
8.	10.0-20.0	2,135	28,521
9.	20.0-30.0	401	9,344
10.	30.0-40.0	120	4,178
11.	40.0-50.0	45	2,050
12.	50.0 and above	65	5,971
	Total	70,493	162,124

Source: Agricultural Census, 1970/1971.

The traditional sector and the small farmer 393

Table 20. Distribution of holdings according to irrigation status
(Area in thousand ha; No. in thousands)

Sl. No.	Size Class (Ha)	Total holdings		Wholly irrigated holdings		Wholly unirrigated holdings		Partly irrigated holdings		
		No.	Area	No.	Area	No.	Area	No.	Total area	Irrigated area
1	2	3	4	5	6	7	8	9	10	11
1.	Below 0.5	23,178	5,446	6,273	1,360	13,660	2,713	3,031	752	390
2.	0.5-1.0	12,504	9,099	2,497	1,692	7,145	4,614	2,776	1,877	945
3.	1.0-2.0	13,432	19,282	1,919	2,453	7,731	9,743	3,719	4,805	2,275
4.	2.0-3.0	6,722	16,353	749	1,634	3,816	8,066	2,130	4,650	2,071
5.	3.0-4.0	3,959	13,646	368	1,132	2,241	6,663	1,342	1,101	1,743
6.	4.0-5.0	2,684	11,929	211	831	1,522	5,743	947	3,667	1,458
7.	5.0-10.0	5,248	36,305	327	1,902	2,962	17,122	1,953	11,660	4,096
8.	10.0-20.0	2,135	28,521	78	822	1,230	13,314	824	9,309	2,589
9.	20.0-30.0	401	9,344	9	148	239	4,192	153	2,887	671
10.	30.0-40.0	120	4,178	2	48	75	1,830	43	1,112	249
11.	40.0-50.0	45	2,050	1	22	30	879	15	488	109
12.	50.0 and above	65	5,971	1	101	46	2,527	17	959	234
	Total	70,493	1,62,124	12,145	40,697	77,406	77,406	16,950	46,267	16,830

Source: Agricultural Census, 1970/1971.

Table 21. Distribution of holdings according to tenancy status – all India
(Area in ha; No. in thousands)

S.No.	Size class (ha)	Total holdings		Wholly owned and self operated holdings		Partly owned and partly rented holdings		Holdings wholly taken on rent	
		No.	Area	No.	Area	No.	Area	No.	Area
(1)	(2)	(3)	(4)	(5)	(6)	(7)	(8)	(9)	(10)
1.	Below 0.5	23,178	5,446	21,448	4,988	355	110	1,096	260
2.	0.5 - 1.0	12,504	9,099	11,389	8,737	449	340	608	427
3.	1.0 - 2.0	13,432	19,282	12,169	17,411	662	966	570	771
4.	2.0 - 3.0	6,722	16,353	6,099	14,812	375	915	241	551
5.	3.0 - 4.0	3,959	13,646	3,619	12,444	229	793	111	360
6.	4.0 - 5.0	2,684	11,929	2,461	10,913	158	703	66	274
7.	5.0 - 10.0	5,248	36,305	4,811	33,233	332	2,314	107	678
8.	10.0 - 20.0	2,135	28,521	1,949	25,988	155	2,105	32	389
9.	20.0 - 30.0	401	9,344	364	8,479	32	767	4	88
10.	30.0 - 40.0	120	4,178	110	3,818	9	319	1	36
11.	40.0 - 50.0	45	2,050	42	1,885	3	144	1	19
12.	50.0 and above	65	5,971	61	5,491	4	375	1	97
	Total	70,493	162,124	64,522	147,699	2,763	9,851	2,838	3,950

Source: Report on the Agricultural Census, 1970/1971.

Small and semi-medium holdings (1.0 to 4.0 hectares) numbering 24 million constitute a little over one third of the total operational holdings in the country and operate over an area of 49 million hectares, accounting for 30 per cent of the total area of operational holdings. The average size of an operational holding in this category is 2.04 hectares of the land, with an irrigated component of 0.47 hectares.

Medium size holdings (4.0 to 10.0 ha) numbering 8 million form 11 per cent of the total operational holdings in the country and operate over an area of 48 million hectares constituting another 30 per cent of the total area under operational holding. The average size of a holding in this category is 6.08 hectares of which the irrigated component is 1.05 hectares.

Holdings with a size of 10 hectares and above number 2.8 million constituting only 4 per cent of the total number of operational holdings. However, these holdings add to a total area of 50 million hectares accounting for over 30 per cent of the land under operational holding in the country. The average size of a holding in this category is 18.10 hectares of land, but the irrigated component is 1.80 hectares.

The small farmer is the core of Indian peasantry and represents the most important segment of the rural society. His mere numbers alone compel our attention for, unless the small farmer is made into a viable "economic cultivator", no amount of reform in the rural society can solve the basic malady of the poverty of a large number of small and marginal farmers and landless agricultural labourers.

In theory it is possible to increase agricultural production by concentrating on efforts to encourage "progressive (large) farmers" by providing them with a package of services. But in doing so, the gap between the large and small farmer widens. Personal incomes drift apart instead of converging. This is socially undesirable. Furthermore, what worth is economic development if the large mass of the populace are not the participants in the entire process. Such a system accentuates rather than reduces poverty. If in the process people are deprived of employment and earnings, an incongruous situation develops of a rising GNP coupled with a growing number of people below the poverty level. The naked truth comes to light if disaggregation is taken with respect to different areas and different size groups of holdings.

A strategy of economic development is therefore proposed in which the small farmer assumes a central place in the entire process of economic development. It has been proved beyond doubt that the small farmer in the traditional sector is capable of adopting modern methods of agricultural production and of raising agricultural productivity, the key to success or failure being acquired resources or assets. It has been the experience in India that those who have assets (land, for example) easily derive benefits from several government programmes. Those without assets (marginal farmer, agricultural labourer, etc.) are left to struggle for their existence. They cannot become members of credit institutions (including co-operatives) and since all programmes are routed through such institutions, this assetless group becomes ineligible for assistance.

The question of devising ways and means of making the benefits of economic development available to small cultivators and under-privileged sections of the rural community engaged the attention of the Government of India and the National Planning Commission. In the Fourth Five Year Plan, 1969-1974, a sum of RS1,030 million was allocated specifically to assist the potentially viable small farmers, marginal farmers and agricultural labourers. These programmes provided for setting up Small Farmers Development (SFD) and Marginal Farmers and Agricultural Labourers (MFAL) agencies in certain selected

districts (lower administrative units) in the country. A sum of RS15 million
was allocated for each SFD agency and RS10 million for each MFAL agency.

The functions of each SFD agency were to: (a) identify the eligible small
farmers in its area; (b) investigate and identify their problems; (c) formulate
programmes incorporating suitable measures to deal with the problems; and
(d) devise ways and means for implementing the programmes. The major
responsibilities of the SFD agencies were to help small farmers by organizing
and arranging services (including customs service and machines and implements)
and supplies (for example improved seeds, fertilizers, pesticides, etc.) at the
proper time, arrange for irrigation in the area from the most practicable source,
provide assistance in securing loans from co-operative and commercial banks as
well as from other credit institutions and arrange facilities for storage,
transportation, processing and marketing of produce.

However, a small farm may not yield enough income for a minimum level of
living and the agencies were also expected to exploit the possibilities of
augmenting the income of small farmer by animal husbandry activities (for
example dairying, poultry farming, etc.) and even agro-based industries.

The role of the MFAL agencies was to be that of a catalyst in promoting
economic interest mainly through generation of fruitful employment. These
agencies major responsibilities were to: (a) identify eligible marginal
farmers and agricultural labourers to be covered by the project; (b)
investigate their problem; (c) formulate economic programmes for providing
gainful employment; (d) promote rural industries; (e) evolve adequate
institutional, financial and administrative arrangements for implementing
various programmes; (f) promote the creation of common facilities for
production, processing, storage and marketing of products; and (g) evaluate
the programme from time to time.

The responsibilities of the MFAL agencies were greater, for it was
necessary for them to establish new institutional arrangements and organize
common facilities. In special cases, they could organize labour contract
agencies, undertake construction of small and minor irrigation works (for
example, wells, renovation of tanks) or other intensive rural work for the
benefit of the participants during the off-season, establish common facilities
and undertake processing and marketing of products till proper organizations
were established for that purpose.

The SFD/MFAL projects were sanctioned in 1970/1971. The Planning
Commission considered it desirable that the projects be monitored so that
any impediments to their efficient execution could be removed. The Programme
Evaluation Organization of the Planning Commission was asked in 1972/1973 to
evaluate the projects. Only those projects that had been in operation for
two years were selected for evaluation. The main objectives were as follows:

(a) To study the nature and contents of the programmes for small farmers,
marginal farmers and agricultural labourers;

(b) To study the organizational and operational aspects of the
implementation of the programmes;

(c) To assess the impact of the programmes on small farmers, marginal
farmers and agricultural labourers in relation to any increase in their income
and the availability of more employment opportunities.

Twenty one out of a total of 45 SFD projects and 13 out of a total of 32 MFAL
projects were taken up for evaluation. Details of their location in various
States in India are given in table 22.

Table 22. SFD and MFAL projects selected for evaluation

Sl. No.	State	Total N° of projects in June 1973		N° of projects completing two or more years on 30 June 1973		Name of the projects selected for the study	
		SFD	MFAL	SFD	MFAL	SFD	MFAL
1.	2.	3.	4.	5.	6.	7.	8.
1.	Andhra Pradesh	3	2	3	2	1. Nalgonda	1. Visakhapatnam
2.	Assam	2	2	2	2	2. Goalpara	2. Kamrup
3.	Bihar	3	2	3	2	3. Purnes	3. Shahabad
4.	Gujarat	3	2	3	2	4. Surat	4. Bulser
5.	Haryana	2	2	2	2	5. Gurgaon	5. Bhiwani
6.	Himachal Pradesh	1	1	1	1	6. Sirmur	–
7.	Jammu & Kashmir	2	2	2	2	7. Anantnag	–
8.	Kerala	2	2	2	–	8. Quilon	–
						9. Cannonore	–
9.	Madhya Pradesh	3	2	3	2	10. Chhindwara	6. Raisen-Sehore
10.	Maharashtra	3	2	3	2	11. Bilaspur	
						12. Bhandara	7. Ratnagiri-
						13. Thana-Nasik	Satare
11.	Manipur	–	1	–	–	–	–
12.	Meghalaya	–	2	–	–		
13.	Mysore (Karnataka)	3	2	3	2	14. Mysore	8. Tumkur
14.	Nagaland	1	1	–	–	–	–
15.	Orissa	3	2	3	2	15. Ganjam	9. Cuttack
16.	Punjab	2	2	2	–	16. Sangrur Patiala	–
17.	Rajasthan	3	2	3	2	17. Alwar	10. Bhilwara
18.	Tamil Nadu	3	2	3	2	18. Madurai	11. Salem
19.	Tripura	–	1	–	–	–	–
20.	Uttar Pradesh	4	2	4	2	19. Rae Bareli	12. Ballia
						20. Badaun	
21.	West Bengal	3	2	3	2	21. West Dinajpur	13. Bankura
22.	Delhi	–	1	–	1	–	–
23.	Goa	–	1	–	1	–	–
24.	Pondicherry	–	1	–	1	–	–
	Total	46	41	45	32	21	13

A total of 8 villages in each SFD project and 10 in each of the MFAL
and composite projects (that is, both SFD and MFAL) were selected from a list
of villages that had benefitted from any of the programmes. A complete list of
persons who had benefitted from the various programmes was also drawn up and
from each village 12 "beneficiaries" were selected. From each agency, 12
"non-beneficiaries" and 4 primary co-operatives were also selected to assess
their roles and difficulties. The period of investigation was May 1974 to
April 1975 and resulted in the following figures:

	SFD	MFAL	Total
Projects	21	13	34
Villages	172	124	296
Beneficiaries	1464	1333	2797
Non-beneficiaries	252	143	395
Co-operative societies	82	47	129

There were 13 major findings.

1. The size of the projects, both in terms of population and area, varied
    considerably. The total population of the target groups ranged from
    41,000 to 131,000 among the SFD agencies and from 33,000 to 370,000
    among MFAL agencies. The total geographical area of projects ranged
    from 740 sq. km to 17,400 sq. km. Inclusion of very large areas
    impeded efficient execution of the programmes.

2. The progress of identification of beneficiaries was slow in most
    of the areas. Lack of up-to-date land records was a major
    difficulty in proving titles on land for eligibility of loans.

3. The identification of agricultural labour households was poor;
    in three project areas this group was not identified at all.
    In nearly one-fifth of MFAL agencies, not more than 5 per cent
    of total agricultural labourers in the area had been identified.

4. Strengthening of the agricultural extension staff was visualized
    along with the distribution of benefits under the programmes.
    Yet in nearly 71 per cent of project areas, no action had been
    taken in this regard. Since the extension staff are the main
    means through which benefits can be extended and their
    utilization supervised, it is necessary that they be suitably
    strengthened in all project areas.

5. Administrative arrangements to supervise the programmes were
    inadequate - late appointment of SFD agency project officers,
    delays in appointment of assisting staff, frequent transfers and
    inactivity of the state level Co-ordination and Review Committee.
    The programmes did not provide a forum for discussing the
    achievements and difficulties of project officers. There was also
    the general absence of awareness of programme benefits among the

target groups.

6. It is significant and heartening to note that in 57 per cent of SFD agencies and 38 per cent of MFAL agencies, more than one-half of the identified families had been brought within the co-operative fold, providing them with a launching pad for available production credit.

7. Despite handicaps, co-operative loans increased two-fold during 1971/1972. The share of commercial banks also increased from nearly 3 per cent to 10 per cent.

8. Of the total loans advanced during 1970/1974, nearly 58 per cent were short-term (one year), 19 per cent medium-term (one to three years) and 23 per cent long-term (over three years). Short-term loans were for seasonal production inputs such as irrigation, fertilizer, seeds, etc. Medium-term loans increased 27 times, mainly for the purchase of irrigation pump equipment. Long-term loans increased by only 4 times which is indicative of problems encountered in the extension of credit for effecting permanent improvements.

9. Agricultural labourers have been totally neglected in the matter of extension of credit. Their share of total loans advanced was only 1 per cent.

10. The performance in respect of supply of current agricultural inputs to small farmers was encouraging. This is corroborated by the availability of sizeable loans for short-term credit needs referred to above. Nearly 42 per cent of SFD agencies could attain 75 per cent of the targets and another 37 per cent between 51 and 75 per cent of the targets in respect of supply of agricultural inputs.

11. Bringing small farmers within the fold of the co-operative credit structure was largely successful in that 95 per cent of the credit requirements for inputs in all projects taken together were met by the co-operative credit societies.

12. The main elements of programmes that succeeded with small farmers were: minor irrigation – one out of every eight benefitted; demonstration projects on farms; and supply of milch cattle. Minor irrigation schemes have helped farmers to produce more than one crop and to adopt the use of high yielding crop varieties. This has led to the generation of substantial additional income avenues for the small farmer.

13. Rural works programmes were taken up in all MFAL agencies, but very few projects generated additional income because the average number of days of employment of participants in the programme was 10 per year in MFAL agencies and 18 in SFD agencies. Employment on road works and in the sinking of wells were the main elements in the rural works programme.

The above evaluation indicates that small farmers in the traditional sector could make significant progress if proper institutional and infrastructure facilities were provided and if additional income streams were provided to small operators, enabling them to diversify their enterprises and earn additional income through supplementary occupations such as dairy farming or employment on rural public works. Experience in

Maharashtra has shown that as 60 per cent of casual daily wage labour on rural works was female. The utilization of female labour to supplement family earnings has great employment potential.

INFORMATION SYSTEMS IN PUBLIC ADMINISTRATION
D. Eade, J. Hodgson (editors)
North-Holland Publishing Company
© *DFD, 1981*

RURAL DEVELOPMENT: THE ANTYODAYA APPROACH

S.M. Shah*

A. A definition of rural development

"Rural Development is a process aimed at improving the well-being
of people living outside the urbanized areas. These non-
urbanized areas, however, are not a separate entity but are part
of a far flung system of spatial and economic linkages. Rural
development, therefore, takes into account the forward and
backward linkages between the rural and the urban areas." [1]

Gandhiji said that rural life must be touched "at all points".

G. Hirsh says that "Rural development involves change, change in the
physical, in the economic and in the social environment." [2]

Uma Lele (World Bank, 1975) defines rural development as "improving
living standards of the mass of low-income population residing in rural areas
and making the process of their development self-sustaining". The heart of the
problem of rural development thus lies in creating conditions for full
employment, higher wages and rising production.

B. Rural animation

Furthermore, rural development also implies changing rural attitudes,
by improving the social environment in which both men and institutions work.
This is called animation. It is an attempt to penetrate the closed circle of
village society. The essence of animation is that the peasant must not be
alienated from the traditional society and his society must not consider him
the outsider. [3] Animation approaches the community rather than the
individual. Animation works through the local power structure, not against it.
Through animation we can make great progress in building roads, constructing
small irrigation works and setting up co-operative dairies, for example The
Amul co-operative dairy is the finest example of animation.

----

* Joint Secretary, Planning Commission, New Delhi, India.

[1] (S.M. Shah, Rural Development, Planning and Reforms (New Delhi,
1978).

[2] G. Hirsh, Incentives for Rural Development (1963).

[3] David Hapgood, Rural Animation in Senegal (1964).

C. Crucial elements

The Food and Agricultural Organization (FAO) of the United Nations
mentions the following five elements as crucial to rural development:

1. The object of rural development is to improve the quality of
    life for rural people.

2. Rural development must be a comprehensive development
    programme.

3. The rural poor, especially the small farmers and landless
    labourers who have hitherto often been ignored, must be
    integrated into the development process and into the
    economic life of rural areas. Full participation implies
    accompanying agrarian and social reforms.

4. All the activities of government and other agencies
    concerned in the development process require co-ordination
    for maximum effort.

5. The institutional and physical infrastructure (roads,
    co-operatives, credit, input supply, irrigation, school
    health care) provides a framework of rural development. 4/

D. Access to the poor

A great majority of people in rural areas are poor. The World
Conference on Agrarian Reform and Rural Development, meeting in Rome in July
1979, says "destitutes" (that is absolute poor) constitute 800 million. It
states further, "The great majority of these rural people have not shared
equally or at all in the fruits of progress". A more equitable access to
land, water and other agricultural resources is a prerequisite of an agrarian
reform and rural development strategy.

E. The Antyodaya approach: the poorest of the poor upliftment

The Janata Party (India) in the manifesto of 1977, committed itself to a programme of Antyodaya or emancipation of the "last man" of Gandhiji's description.
Gandhiji asked us to "recall the face of the poorest and the weakest" in all steps
that we contemplate undertaking. The Estimates Committee of the Parliament (India),

----

4/ The Food and Agricultural Organization (FAO) of the United Nations,
Review and Analysis of Agrarian Reform and Rural Development in Developing
Countries (March, 1979)

in their thirty-fourth report (April, 1979), mentioned that the Antyodaya
Programme is a national programme. In recognizing the evaluation undertaken
by the Programme Evaluation Organization of the Planning Commission in respect
of the State of Rajasthan in March 1979, the Estimates Committee has also
desired that the Programme Evaluation Organization should undertake continuous
and concurrent evaluation of the Antyodaya Programme in all the States in
India. The Antyodaya Programme is the subject matter of mass media (see
Kurukshetra, May 18 1979). On May 29 1979, a newsreel feature on Delhi
Doordarshan focussed on the working of Antyodaya in Rajasthan. The Prime
Minister, Mr. Morarji Desai, a staunch follower of Mahatma Ghandi and
Chairman of the Navjivan Trust, Ahmedabad, custodian of Gandhiji's writings,
praised the Antyodaya approach to the upliftment of the rural poor and showed
satisfaction in its working. During his visit to village Dajar, 15 km from
Jaipur, State capital of Rajasthan, President Sanjiva Reddy commented in
February 1978 that he had not come across "such a welfare scheme during the
last 30 years" and reflected that "if implemented with determination, it would
be a remarkable achievement." The programme attracted the President of the
World Bank, Mr. McNamara, during his visit to India in 1979.

Following the lead given by Rajasthan, several other States also took up
the Antyodaya approach to the upliftment of the poorest of the poor in our
rural areas. Programmes were initiated with inauguration by Chief Ministers
as a part of the Gandhi Jayanti Celebrations on 2 October 1978. Officially,
the Programme has been taken up in Bihar, Himachal Pradesh, Rajasthan
(second phase), Gujarat, Manipur, and Uttar Pradesh. But press reports
indicate that the States of Tamil Nadu, Orissa, Madhya Pradesh and Haryana have
also taken up the Programme. It is now in operation in one form or another in
ten states.

It appears that the term "Antyodaya" was coined by Mahatma Gandhi during
his activities at Sabarmati Ashram, Ahmedabad. Whether he meant the Harijans
(Achhut) and their social upliftment (Uday) is under examination. Whatever
it may be, the disaggregation of data relating to rural poverty, as revealed
in the Reserve Bank of India's "All India Debt and Investment Survey, 1971/1972",
gives the following description of the identity of the rural poor:

"This poor class of rural households includes cultivators who are
only part-time farmers, as their land base is too small to make
a living therefrom. They are mainly wage-earners as their major
source of income is from farm and non-farm employment...Similarly,
artisans or village craftsmen like weavers, blacksmiths, potters,
carpenters, brick layers, et cetera, providing some traditional
goods for limited local market, are also covered in this
category." 5/ The essential question is that the rural poor

5/ See V.K.R.V. Rao, Capital (12 April 1979).

should share both in (a) rural per capita product and (b) rural
per capita consumption.

The operation of the Antyodaya Programme in various States is
set out below.

1. Gujarat

The Chief Minister of Gujarat declared recently that the Government of
Gujarat, in April 1979, had introduced the Antyodaya Programme in every
taluka (cluster of villages) in the State. A large number of districts in
Gujarat are covered either under Central or State sector schemes. The
identified Antyodaya families would be given preference in all social security
measures and other economic programmes. Assistance of voluntary workers
was sought in implementation of the Programme.

2. Madhya Pradesh

In Madhya Pradesh, the Antyodaya Programme was initiated on 21 January
1979 with the distribution of "pattas", that is land deeds, to 350 tribal
families in the Bastar district. Each tribal family will be given 5 to 10
acres of land under the Programme. Not only are the land deeds to be given
to the tribal families but also the actual possession of the land. Revenue
records would be corrected accordingly. The Programme envisages benefitting
a total of 150,000 families in 70,863 villages in Madhya Pradesh. It is
not clear whether the Programme is intended to be confined to tribal blocks
only.

3. Haryana

The Antyodaya Programme in Haryana has been prepared on the basis of
a master plan worked out by the Haryana Agricultural University, Hissar.
A resource inventory has been prepared based on "malady-remedy" data in
respect of 90 out of a total of 6731 villages to be covered under the
Antyodaya Pilot Project. The scheme forms part of the Integrated Rural
Development Project. The first phase will cover selected NES blocks of the
87 Community Development Blocks in the State. The total number of villages
in the State is 7,064. Under the University survey, 65 per cent of the
rural households comprising small and marginal farmers and landless labourers
were found to be living below the poverty line. The level of employment per
worker in the Antyodaya area comes to about 190 days a year. Gainful
employment for women is 104 days as against 257 days for men. A Harijan
woman gets work for hardly more than 75 days in a year. A total of 5,500
rural artisans are identified in the Antyodaya area which is also covered
under the Small Farmers Development Agency/Drought Prone Area Programme projects.
Nearly 70 per cent of Antyodaya villages need to be provided with potable
water.

4.   Tamil Nadu

In Tamil Nadu in the south, the Antyodaya scheme was taken up on
2 October, 1978 as a part of the Integrated Rural Development Programme. Five
to ten families in each of the 161 blocks in which the rural development
programme is being implemented (out of a total of 374 blocks in the State)
will be assisted to become self-employed in skills suited to them. The
intention is to help artisans such as barbers and carpenters with implements
and tools. Apart from agriculture, animal husbandry and fisheries, farm
forestry and rural industries based on locally available material will be
encouraged. The entire programme is likely to cost Rs200 million.

5.   Himachal Pradesh

In Hamachal Pradesh, a hill State in the north, the programme was launched
on 2 October, 1978. To begin with, 19,068 of the poorest families (from a
total of 18,929 villages) were identified for the granting of a number of
social security measures. Soil conservation and animal husbandry are other
programmes envisaged. For the purchase of drought cattle, a 50 per cent loan/
50 per cent subsidy is proposed. Harijans over the age of 60 are given old
age pensions of Rs50 per month. Certain families have been assisted in setting
up retail shops. A package deal has been given to Antyodaya families including
land development assistance, free education, free medical aid, free legal
aid and cheaper lands. Voluntary and youth organizations are associated with
the Antyodaya Programme. More than 53 per cent of the population lives below
the poverty line. Far flung villages present yet another problem in the
delivery of services. All efforts are directed for ameliorating the economic
conditions of the poorest section of the society and to ensure that the
benefits under this Programme permeate to the poorest, irrespective of caste,
creed, religion or even domicile. A grouping of five families per 1,000 of
the population is followed. This cluster approach is an important innovation.
The poorest identified families are approached by government machinery right
at their door step. Selection of those to receive assistance is made in open
meetings of the Gram Sabhas, the village assemblies. First priority is given
to those families who have no property or are landless, have no source of
income and do not have adequate means of livelihood. Second priority is
accorded to those families who have movable property but their means do not
provide them adequate income for their livelihood. An economic survey of
selected families has revealed that a bare minimum of subsistence of Rs66 per
month per capita at 1976/1977 prices is required as against the existing per
capita income of Rs18 per month. This indicates in quantitative terms the
"poverty gap".

The survey further revealed that as against loans totalling Rs671.6 million
advanced by the State, the Antyodaya families received only Rs300,000 over the
entire Plan period 1951-1977. Not a single person was in government service.
School attendance in the 6-14 year age bracket was 39 per cent in respect
of Antyodaya children as compared to 98.1 per cent of children attending
school in the State as a whole. Out of a total of 19,860 hectares of surplus
land, 348 hectares have been distributed to those identified as Antyodaya
families.

Of all Antyodaya families, 50 per cent have 5 or more members in their
households. Of identified Antyodaya families, 57 per cent belong to
scheduled castes and 4 per cent to scheduled tribes. By January 1979 the old
age pension was given to 4,341 families, 2,476 were granted nauter land,
3,277 were given housing subsidies, 2,696 were helped with animal husbandry
and 1,590 were given tools and equipment. Employment was provided to 816
families by 678 land development and 374 small-scale and household industries.

Out of 19,000 families, 16,000 have already been given benefits, the rest
will be given benefits by end of March 1979. A total of Rs3 million in loans
and Rs7.9 million in subsidies was given by January 1979. An evaluation study
is being undertaken to measure the impact of the benefits given. All
documents executed by Antyodaya families are exempt from stamp duty. Five
seats in each Industrial Training Institute are reserved for Antyodaya families.

The Programme will continue in the same manner in the 1978-1983 Five Year
Plan, by which time 100,000 families (72.5 per cent of the population) will
benefit. The annual expenditure on the Programme is estimated at Rs105.9
million including Rs44 million of institutional finance. Rs10.8 million are
likely to be available out of Small Farmers Development Agency (SFDA) and
IRD blocks. From the State Plan allocation, agriculture will provide Rs3.5
million, animal husbandry Rs4 million, horticulture Rs1.5 million and village
and small industry Rs2.5 million for the 1978-1983 Five Year Plan. Rural works
in off season will be provided. There is a proposal to create an Antyodaya
Corporation to raise institutional finance by standing guarantee for providing
margin money for the poorest of the poor.

6. Orissa

Orissa has the largest number of people below the poverty line - 85 per
cent according to the State Economics Bureau. A total of 279 Community
Development blocks out of a total of 314 blocks in the State are covered under
special development agencies. In each of those blocks, 20 per cent of the
villages will be covered under the Antyodaya Programme in the current year and
by the end of the 1978-1983 Five Year Plan, all the villages will be covered.

The initial identification is drawn up by the Village Level Worker and the
list is finalized by the Gram Panchayat and is subject to the approval of the
villagers in their open meeting. Appropriate methods for Antyodaya families
are also suggested by the Gram Panchayat. Families are given identity cards.
Activities include self employment and subsidiary occupations such as dairy
farming, sheep breeding and village and cottage industries. The Programme
is allied with the Integrated Rural Development Programme (IRD).

7. Uttar Pradesh

Uttar Pradesh launched Antyodaya on 2 October, 1978 with a view to
providing a means of livelihood to the poorest of the poor families in each
village within a definite time frame. The main focus of the Programme has
been on five of the poorest families of each village whose annual income does
not exceed Rs2,000 per annum and who possess less than 0.404 hectares of
irrigated agricultural land. The Programme aims to help remove the existing
disparities. It is an important component of the Area Development and Rural
Development Programme. The main steps envisaged are:

(a) To select five Antyodaya families in each village;

(b) To prepare assistance schemes for implementation; and

(c) To evaluate the levels achieved and to remove difficulties.

A Block Development Officer is made fully responsible for tne selection
of the beneficiaries under the following criteria:

(a) Families with no land or animals or any source of income;

(b) Similar families with one or two members as labourers but having an
annual income below Rs2,000;

(c) Families possessing below 0.404 hectares of irrigated agricultural land, or animals, but whose living standards are still below the poverty line.

These families are called to the village assembly where suitable programmes are specified. The Block Development Officer will process loan/ subsidy applications, ensure full utilization of the Programme and report once a fortnight to the District Planning Officer. Loans are repayable in 8 years, carry concessionary interest at 4 per cent and a limit of Rs5,000. Assistance includes supply of milch cattle, goats, sheep and poultry; other activities include fishing, pig farming and manufacture of pneumatic tyres, carts, rickshaws, handlooms, oil ghani, horse driven carts, hand driven thelas, baskets, shoes, other cottage industries and minor irrigation, etc.

By 31 December, 1978, a total of 570,000 Antyodaya families were recorded – the largest number in any state so far. Of these only 232,000 were selected for assistance but only 40,000 could be provided assistance up to March 1979. Of these, only 16,000 belonged to scheduled castes/tribes. Assistance of Rs90 million (against Rs150 million) was provided in addition to the share of commercial banks which came to Rs20 million. The Department of Panchayat Raj is the co-ordinating agency.

8. Bihar

Bihar introduced Antyodaya on 15 August, 1978 by the preparation of a list of the five poorest of the poor families in each village. Organizing the village assembly was the responsibility of the Mukhiya, the elected village leader. Two proformae on income and wealth were prescribed. Families who had neither property nor any means of production and whose annual income did not exceed Rs1,200 were to be listed first, then those whose incomes ranged from Rs1,200 to Rs1,800, and lastly, those who owned some land or property but whose per capita income was below Rs55. The occupations suggested were: dairy farming, sheep and goat rearing, poultry and pig farming, carpentry, blacksmithing, soap manufacturing, pottery, papad and vadi, cycle repairing, atta chakki, tailoring and basket making. Each selected family is issued an identity card. The responsibility of completing all formalities for loan applications etc. is assumed by the Block Development Officer not the Antyodaya family. All loans are sanctioned at a differential interest rate of 4 per cent with a ceiling of Rs5,000. Loans are not given in cash but paid by the bank to the seller of the article. Fortnightly progress reports are submitted by the District Magistrate. The Block Development Officer maintains a village-wide register of Antyodaya families indicating the loans and articles given. The estimated number of Antyodaya families from 31 districts is 337,000, of which 183,000 families had been identified; 40,461 loan applications had been sanctioned by March, 1979.

9. Rajasthan

In Rajasthan, the Antyodaya Programme was announced by the State Government in September 1977 during presentation of the State's first budget and was launched on 2 October, 1977. The Programme envisaged identification of five of the poorest families from amongst those below the poverty line in each of the 30,000 villages of the State. The process of identification formed part and parcel of the state-wide revenue campaign with the Revenue and Panchayati Raj Officers camped in the villages for that purpose. The criteria for identification of Antyodaya families, as prescribed by the State Government, were as follows:

(a) Families under severe destitution having no economic assets and no member in the 15-59 year age group capable of economic activity;

(b)   Families having no economic assets but having one or more persons
capable of economic activity, where annual family earnings do not exceed
Rs1,200;

(c)   Families with some assets whose annual income is below Rs1,800 per
annum;

(d)   Remaining families having some land and assets but who are below the
poverty line, that is, below the per capita consumption level of Rs55 per
month.

One unique feature prescribed was that the identification of Antyodaya
families was done at a meeting of the Gram Sabha.   The Block Development
Officer, the Tehsildar and Members of village Panchayats were responsible for
the final selection and MPs, MLAs and the District Collector or his nominee
were also actively associated in this process.   Physical presence of the
prospective Antyodaya families was ensured.   The decision of the Gram Sabha
in respect of the selection of families would be final since it was based on
the consensus of the village people.

As against a target of 160,000, 160,516 families were identified during
the first round of the Programme, October 1977.   The second round of
identification started from 2 October, 1978 and was anticipated to benefit
140,000 families.

Each identified and eligible family was to be provided with the economic
assistance of his choice.   For this purpose, the Gram Sabha or members of
the village Panchayat would discuss with the identified families their needs
and possible ways and means to achieve a reasonable income level.   The economic
benefit schemes devised by the Government for this purpose encompass land
allotment, agriculture and land development, minor irrigation, milch cattle
rearing, sheep/goat units, poultry farming, village and cottage industries
(for example, tailoring, basket making, niwar, mat and churi (bangle) making
and petty shop keeping), wage employment and old age pensions.   The choice
of the programme for the economic upliftment of these families was based on
the preferences of the identified families, the present status of the village
economy, the availability of resources, etc.

During the first round of the Programme, up to 31 January 1979, a total of
155,293 identified families were assisted.   Of these, 23,949 (17.13 per cent)
were covered under old age pensions, 42,666 (30.52 per cent) under land
allotment, 5,926 (4.24 per cent) under wage employment, 60,012 (42.92 per
cent) under loan assistance for different economic benefits as explained in
last paragraph, and the remaining 7,262 (5.19 per cent) under other schemes.

F. Conclusion

The following points emerge from the material presented.

1.   Rural Development is a part and parcel of the entire process of
economic development.   It is not only development of rural areas, but
development of linkages between all human settlements of different sizes,
whether rural or urban, and bestowing the functions or facilities that are
absent but warranted.

2.   Since a large majority of the population in rural areas subsists
on agriculture, rural development efforts, in order to succeed, should aim
at increasing agricultural productivity and efficiency, both per land unit
and per person.

3.   In this respect, development of irrigation facilities, land reshaping and land development works are important.

4.   The aim of rural development should be to make village communities self-reliant. Hence, a village cluster approach should be adopted to make sectoral activities viable.

5.   An important aspect of economic development is to enable people to participate in the developmental process. Hence, not only should the plans for village development be prepared at the village level but they should also be executed and implemented through the institutions so created.

6.   This "bottom up" approach envisages that the people living in absolute poverty should be the first charge on the state's exchequer.

7.   The battle against poverty should be waged on two fronts. Several investigations, including the Rural Labour Enquiry of 1974/1975, have disclosed an increasing landlessness and growing proletarianism of India's rural population. Measures should be adopted to halt this process so that village areas do not have a perpetually increasing number of poor added to their lot. Simultaneously, the condition of those who are already poor should be improved and ameliorated.

8.   Because substantive cultivation in India depends on seasonal rainfall which at times is unpredictable, there is, and will remain for a long time, a need to develop supplementary occupations for farmers to give them off-season employment. This may be through rural works such as the Employment Guarantee Scheme in Maharashtra or through provision of camel carts, bullock carts, etc., as is done in Antyodaya Programme in Rajasthan.

9.   Taking into account the fact that the rural households with a per capita monthly expenditure of Rs53.5 and below is estimated at 59.3 per cent, on the basis of a National Sample Survey taken in 1960/1961, the problem of banishing rural poverty justifies a much wider approach than that adopted under the Antyodaya Programme. Statewise, this percentage ranges from 27.05 for Himachal Pradesh to as high as 73.11 per cent for Orissa.

10.   States having more than 60 per cent of rural households below the poverty line in 1973/1974 were (a) Orissa 73.11 per cent, (b) West Bengal 70.32 per cent, (c) Tamil Nadu 64.59 per cent, (d) Andhra Pradesh 64.37 per cent, (e) Madhya Pradesh 64.59 per cent, (f) Uttar Pradesh 60.49 per cent and (g) Karnataka 69.31 per cent. These states should adopt the Antyodaya approach to rural development as a matter of high priority.

11.   In the ultimate analysis, poverty can be banished only by increasing the rate of increase of personal income of the poor. Although under the Antyodaya schemes, there has been an increase in income of Rs1,000 per year per family in dairying and camel and bullock cart manufacture, etc., the rate has to be speeded up to narrow the poverty gap.

12.   In terms of both the number of persons below the poverty line and the rate at which personal incomes of all Antyodaya families should be increased, the Antyodaya Programme as envisaged at present is over ambitious.

13.   One major merit of the Antyodaya Programme is that the largest number of beneficiaries are identified on the basis of concrete economic classifications and by village assemblies, thereby helping to ensure that fair selections are made.

14. The implementation of the various programmes should be promptly and sympathetically carried out so that any small assets bestowed (for example dairy cattle) do not become liabilities (for example in the absence of fodder).

15. On a theoretical plane, the Antyodaya approach has stopped the flow of benefits to those already having some assets (for example irrigation farmers).

16. The Antyodaya approach has also recognized the theory of equal accessibility to public facilities (inputs, credit, etc.), a principle advocated by Mahatma Gandhi in India and by Lowry in Yugoslavia. This is an improvement over the GNP approach of economic growth which has bypassed the poor and the underprivileged.

17. An important prerequisite to the success of the Antyodaya approach is its linkage with area development programmes, thus recognizing both the forward and backward linkages between cattle supply, livestock feed, veterinary care and collection and sale of milk, for example.

18. An expanded and more personal role is envisaged for the extension worker who must not only teach the poor "how to do" but also "what to do".

19. The selection of Antyodaya families through village assemblies in Rajasthan, Himachal Pradesh, Orissa and Uttar Pradesh has falsified the notion held by some sociologists that Indian society is faction ridden and that no development can take place in such a caste-ridden village society.

20. The opportunities for the village assemblies to participate more directly in village affairs have been extended, thus providing the necessary power for participant democracy. These are two great intangible achievements.

21. In 1977 Robert McNamara told the Board of Governors of the World Bank that "Economic growth cannot assist the poor if it does not reach the poor." The Antyodaya model is an indigenous model inspired by Mahatma Gandhi. It has been evolved after 25 years of planning experience and the realization that national income growth by itself does not lead to a reduction in rural poverty. As stated previously, a paradoxical situation exists in that the GNP has increased but the number of rural poor, both in absolute and relative terms, has also increased.

22. The Antyodaya approach emphasises not only income transfer but assets transfer and thus the potentiality of redistribution with growth, which is consistent with the policy objective in India.

INFORMATION SYSTEMS IN PUBLIC ADMINISTRATION
D. Eade, J. Hodgson (editors)
North-Holland Publishing Company
© *DFD, 1981*

L'INFORMATION SUR LE SECTEUR TRADITIONNEL DANS LES PAYS EN DEVELOPPEMENT

M. D. Sarr *

Un des leitmotives dans les pays en développement et particulièrement dans les pays africains pour la Troisième Décennie des Nations Unies pour le Développement est la "démocratisation du processus de développement". Cette préoccupation a dominé les récentes rencontres régionales africaines notamment le colloque Organisation de l'Unité Africaine (OUA)/Commission Economique pour l'Afrique de Monrovia sur les perspectives du développement et de la croissance économique en Afrique dans l'avenir et spécialement à l'horizon 2000, le Séminaire Commission Economique pour l'Afrique (CEA)/Programme des Nations Unies pour l'Environnement d'Addis Abéba sur les différents modes de développement et styles de vie possibles pour la région africaine et la cinquième Conférence des Ministres de la CEA à Rabat où a été élaboré un projet de Stratégie de développement pour l'Afrique pour la troisième décennie de développement. Ce projet sera soumis à la prochaine conférence au sommet de l'OUA en juillet 1979 à Monrovia.

Le mot d'ordre de "démocratisation du processus de développement" recouvre en même temps un diagnostic et un projet. Le diagnostic, c'est que le développement tel qu'il a été conçu et mis en oeuvre jusqu'ici dans la plupart des pays en développement n'a été que partiel parce qu'orienté principalement vers certains domaines de l'activité socio-économique et vers certaines couches de la population. Le projet est de s'engager dans un développement global

- qui couvre tous les domaines (éducation, santé, emploi, science et technologie, agriculture, industrie, transport, communications, etc. ;

- qui vise à promouvoir toutes formes d'activités économiques et sociales et de toutes les dimensions (grandes, moyennes et petites entreprises) ;

- et qui touche toutes les couches de la population en leur procurant des emplois productifs, enrichissants pour l'Homme et rémunérateurs.

En d'autres termes, les Administrations publiques dans les pays en développement doivent s'efforcer de rompre la dichotomie ou le caractère dualiste qui existe dans la structure et le fonctionnement de leurs activités socio-économiques en intégrant davantage le secteur traditionnel, notamment au moyen d'un système d'information exhaustif.

---

*Commission Economique pour l'Afrique, Addis Abéba, Ethiopie.

Il faudrait donc dans un premier temps essayer de circonscrire le secteur dit traditionnel. Tout d'abord, le secteur traditionnel ne doit être confondu ni avec le monde rural, ni bien entendu avec l'ensemble du secteur privé. Il y a en effet dans le monde rural des activités qui non seulement utilisent un grand nombre de méthodes et techniques modernes, mais également disposent d'un système d'information interne relié à d'autres systèmes d'information nationaux et internationaux. Par ailleurs, dans les économies de type libéral, une grande partie du secteur moderne est privé. Il faut donc comprendre par secteur traditionnel l'ensemble des activités socio-économiques urbaines et rurales :

- basées essentiellement sur les technologies locales ;

- n'ayant pas ou ayant peu bénéficié des apports de la science et de la technologie modernes ;

- et échappant totalement ou partiellement à toute influence extérieure y compris dans une certaine mesure celle de l'Administration publique.

Après cette tentative de définition du secteur traditionnel et avant d'esquisser ce qui pourrait constituer une base de programme prioritaire en matière de système d'information sur ce secteur, il serait intéressant de situer l'importance de ce secteur pour le développement socio-économique des pays en développement, d'identifier ses principales difficultés et d'analyser les politiques actuelles des Administrations publiques des pays en développement en direction du milieu traditionnel notamment en matière de système d'information.

A. Le secteur traditionnel dans le développement des pays en développement

Il n'est pas besoin d'insister sur les performances des pays en développement au cours des deux premières décennies des Nations Unies pour le développement. Celles de l'Afrique sont bien connues et se résument en quelques constatations dramatiques :

- une explosion démographique accompagnée d'un nombre croissant de sous-emploi et d'une diminution progressive du ratio emploi/production du fait de la mécanisation et de l'adoption inconsidérée de méthodes d'industrialisation des pays industrialisés ;

- une diminution substantielle du taux de croissance du secteur agricole (de 2,4% dans les années 1960 à 1,9% de 1970 à 1978) avec dans certains pays une dépendance alimentaire accrue vis-à-vis de l'extérieur et plus précisément des pays industrialisés ;

- un taux de croissance du produit intérieur brut de seulement 3,8% pour les pays non exportateurs de pétrole (soit plus de 40 pays), et de 2,9% pour les pays à faible revenu (plus de 20 pays) ;

- un renforcement du type de production compartimentalisé où la production industrielle est exclusivement orientée vers les biens de consommation avec le plus souvent des industries livrées clés en mains, donc sans aucun lien avec la nécessité de développer la capacité technologique des pays africains, etc.

On peut également voir que ces pauvres performances s'accompagnent d'une marginalisation d'un nombre croissant de personnes dans les pays africains. En d'autres termes, le caractère dualiste des sociétés africaines se renforce, la part du secteur dit moderne se réduisant comme une peau de chagrin. De nos jours, le secteur dit traditionnel représente dans certains pays africains environ 90% de la population dans les pays en développement.

Dans le milieu rural, malgré les efforts déployés par les gouvernements en direction des paysans et des éleveurs, une grande masse de ces populations échappe presque totalement à toute influence administrative soit du fait de l'insuffisance des moyens mis en oeuvre, soit parce que les masses paysannes, par incompréhension des structures qui leur sont proposées, font preuve de méfiance et préfèrent continuer à vivre dans leurs économies de subsistance.

Dans les milieux urbains, la grande masse des artisans, petits entrepreneurs et petits commerçants échappe aussi presque totalement à l'Administration, du moins quant à la connaissance que celle-ci a de leur contribution au développement national. Le plus souvent l'Administration les identifie dans un but purement fiscal, pour ne pas dire répressif, (patentes et taxes diverses, cotisations aux diverses caisses de sécurité sociale et d'allocations familiales, etc.). L'Administration publique est le plus souvent incapable ou peu soucieuse de déterminer la contribution du secteur traditionnel urbain à la valeur ajoutée globale, à l'emploi, à l'investissement, etc.

Cette méconnaissance du secteur traditionnel explique en partie l'incapacité de l'Administration publique à faire face au grave problème du chômage et du sous-emploi. Des statistiques globales de l'OIT concernant les pays africains montrent que 45% de la population active est en chômage ou sous-employée. De plus, 84% des chômeurs et sous-employés sont en milieu rural. De même, la méconnaissance du secteur traditionnel empêche l'Administration d'avoir une idée précise de la distribution des revenus et donc d'avoir une action efficace dans ce domaine.

Il est clair en conséquence que le développement des pays en développement ne saurait être rapide sans la démarginalisation du milieu traditionnel. Pour ce faire, la première tâche de l'Administration publique est de mettre en place un système d'information qui lui permettrait de mieux connaître ce milieu et de l'orienter efficacement dans l'intérêt de la communauté nationale. Malgré les déclarations officielles tendant à accorder la priorité aux problèmes du milieu traditionnel, les politiques de développement restent élitistes en ce sens qu'elles se limitent à des cercles restreints sans prise en compte ni des problèmes, ni des avis de la grande majorité de la population qui se trouve dans le milieu traditionnel.

B. Les difficultés du milieu traditionnel dans les pays en développement

Le milieu traditionnel dans les pays en développement connaît un certain nombre de difficultés parmi lesquelles le manque d'éducation, le manque de qualification, l'insuffisance de son organisation, et le manque de ressources financières.

Le milieu traditionnel, contrairement au secteur moderne, se caractérise par un taux élevé d'analphabétisme. Il est difficile de mettre en oeuvre une politique sérieuse de démocratisation du processus de développement tant que la majorité de la population est analphabète, donc handicapée dans la maîtrise de la science et de la technologie et dans sa participation à l'effort national de développement. Les conséquences de ce défaut d'éducation de base et de l'inadaptation de l'ecole aux réalités nationales ont été récemment mises en évidence par le Directeur Général de l'Unesco dans son allocution à la conférence des Ministres de la CEA en mars dernier :

"- clivage de plus en plus grand de la population en catégories distinctes et polarisation sociale accrue ;

- analphabétisme croissant qui prive les masses profondes des peuples d'une part, de toute participation directe aux responsabilités modernes qui exigent la maîtrise de la langue écrite qui est celle de l'administration, d'autre part, de tout accès direct au savoir et au savoir-faire modernes pourtant indispensables à l'amélioration de la productivité du travail ;

- chômage croissant des jeunes qui au sortir de l'école, se détournent de toute activité productive qui n'est pas liée au secteur moderne souvent saturé..."

Dans la mise en place d'un système d'information sur le secteur traditionnel, les informations relatives au niveau d'éducation et de formation sont par conséquence d'une très grande importance. Elles permettraient en particulier de définir des politiques d'alphabétisation et d'éducation compatibles avec les besoins de développement et directement liées aux problèmes rencontrés par les populations dans leurs activités socio-économiques quotidiennes.

Dans bien des cas, même si l'éducation de base ne constitue plus la contrainte fondamentale, le manque de qualification rend difficile la participation efficace du secteur traditionnel à l'effort de développement. Les politiques actuelles de développement étant principalement conçues comme une implantation des industries et des techniques mises au point dans les pays industrialisés souvent pour les besoins spécifiques de ces derniers, il en résulte que le problème de la transformation technologique des pays en développement et particulièrement du secteur traditionnel a été complètement éludé. La plupart des investissements et des efforts ont été orientés vers le secteur moderne, réduisant ainsi la dimension socio-économique du développement à une petite couche de la population et à une faible proportion des agents économiques. Même les bases de données sur l'information scientifique et technologique qui existent dans les pays en développement ont été conçues exclusivement pour le secteur moderne. Elles ne contiennent aucune information relative aux technologies traditionnelles et leur système de gestion exclut totalement le secteur traditionnel. Ainsi, un système d'information sur le secteur traditionnel doit permettre d'identifier les sources de technologies locales, de les comparer aux technologies étrangères et le cas échéant de déterminer les combinaisons possibles entre technologies locales et technologies importées.

Aux difficultés d'éducation et de qualification s'ajoutent celles relatives aux problèmes d'organisation. Du fait de sa marginalisation, le secteur traditionnel est en général mal organisé, ne disposant d'aucun système d'information comptable et financier.

Enfin, le secteur traditionnel est en général tenu à l'écart des circuits financiers classiques. Même les organismes financiers créés par l'Administration pour aider les petites entreprises définissent des critères si restrictifs que la majorité de ces entreprises se trouve automatiquement exclue.

C. Le secteur traditionnel et les systèmes actuels de planification dans les pays en développement

Dans le processus d'élaboration des plans de développement économique et social, une attention insuffisante est portée sur le secteur traditionnel. En particulier, les informations relatives aux revenus distribués dans ce secteur, aux emplois créés, aux techniques utilisées, etc. sont ou fragmentaires, ou inexistantes. Plus généralement, les systèmes de planification actuellement en vigueur dans les pays en développement supposent, pour reprendre le Secrétaire exécutif de la CEA dans son allocution à la conférence des Ministres de Rabat, que les individus auxquels ils s'adressent "sont capables d'entreprendre l'exécution des sections importantes et spécifiques des plans et ne manqueront pas de s'y atteler avec enthousiasme". Il a ajouté que cette conception de la planification "passe sous silence la responsabilité des entrepreneurs en matière de choix relatifs aux types de production, aux techniques et à l'emploi, à l'emplacement des installations, à la détermination des prix, aux bénéfices et à leur utilisation, etc".

En d'autres termes, l'Administration publique, par insuffisance de micro-données parmi lesquelles celles relatives au secteur traditionnel, exprime son orientation de l'activité socio-économique à moyen et long terme en termes généraux et souvent vagues. Les planifications actuelles, en agrégeant les données socio-économiques, appauvrissent l'information et rendent difficile toute action profonde en direction du secteur traditionnel. Il est vrai que pour les pays en développement et encore plus pour les pays africains, l'information statistique reste très insuffisante, ce qui pourrait justifier l'emploi exclusif des éléments de la comptabilité nationale pour la planification. Même pour la comptabilité nationale, il y a lieu de signaler que pour beaucoup d'Etats africains, les données résultent d'estimations souvent très approximatives. C'est notamment le cas dans la plupart des 20 pays africains les moins développés. Dans tous les cas, il apparaît que la mise en place d'un système d'information comportant le plus grand nombre de micro-données relatives au secteur traditionnel constitue la condition principale pour l'application d'une méthode de planification qui favoriserait la "démocratisation du processus de développement".

Au début de la deuxième décennie des Nations Unies pour le développement, les responsables du secteur économique des pays africains, après avoir mesuré la complexité et la multiplicité des problèmes qui se posent dans le milieu rural, ont adopté le concept de "développement rural intégré" dont les objectifs se résument comme suit :

- l'accroissement du revenu par tête d'habitant dans les zones rurales au moyen d'un accroissement de la productivité grâce notamment au progrès technologique ;

- l'autosuffisance alimentaire ;

- la promotion des exportations et la réduction des importations en particulier en développant l'utilisation des technologies locales ;

- la diminution de l'exode rural en rendant la vie en milieu rural plus attractive du fait de la possibilité d'y exercer une activité productive et rémunératrice.

Jusqu'ici, malgré quelques succès enregistrés dans certains pays, le "développement rural intégré" reste encore un concept et nombreux sont les plans de développement qui continuent à le mentionner -pour mémoire si l'on peut dire-.

On peut se demander si l'une des difficultés de la mise en oeuvre du concept du "développement rural intégré" ne se trouve pas dans le manque d'information sur le milieu traditionnel rural. Il est difficile en effet de promouvoir des activités productives en monde rural sans identification et évaluation détaillées des principaux facteurs de production : les hommes, la terre, et le capital technique et techologique disponible.

Un autre concept, celui de "conception unifiée de l'analyse et de la planification" a été introduit vers 1975-1976 par le système des Nations Unies dans les pays en développement. Il s'agit d'une démarche de planification qui vise à traiter les problèmes des déséquilibres et des inégalités dans la croissance et à faire en sorte que Société et Economie se combinent harmonieusement dans le processus de développement.

Les auteurs de ce concept reconnaissent que ces objectifs existent déjà dans de nombreux plans nationaux, mais ils soulignent qu'ils sont en général mis en veilleuse au stade des réalisations concrètes. Parmi les difficultés de mise en oeuvre de la "conception unifiée de l'analyse et de la planification", les auteurs insistent sur l'insuffisance des données. Il faut en effet créer de nouveaux systèmes de recueil et de traitement des données indispensables à la planification "unifiée". Il est certain que certains types de données statistiques basées sur les méthodes économiques d'agrégat ne sont pas d'une très grande utilité dans le cadre d'une conception unifiée de l'analyse et de la planification. Il faut donc considérer que les méthodes économiques classiques sont insuffisantes pour résoudre tous les problèmes de collecte de données.

Pour appliquer avec succès une "conception unifiée de l'analyse et de la planification", il faut s'assurer en particulier que les critères d'évaluation de projets de développement (quelles que soient leurs dimensions) intègrent des aspects sociaux (emploi, revenu, environnement, adéquation aux normes et traditions sociales, etc.).

On voit qu'une des conditions préalables de l'application de la "conception unifiée de l'analyse et de la planification" est la constitution d'une base de données micro-socio économiques en plus des données macro-économiques traditionnelles.

L'application de la "conception unifiée de l'analyse et de la planification" s'appuyant sur une base de données riche en micro-données socio-économiques pourrait également favoriser la mise en oeuvre d'une stratégie de satisfaction des besoins fondamentaux à savoir : l'alimentation, le logement, l'habillement, les équipements domestiques élémentaires, l'hygiène, les adductions d'eau, les transports publics, l'enseignement, en particulier l'enseignement technologique, l'emploi, etc. En effet, au moyen d'une "conception unifiée de l'analyse et de la planification", la stratégie des besoins fondamentaux ne serait plus perçue comme une oeuvre de charité envers les couches pauvres de la population qui se trouvent en majorité dans le secteur traditionnel. Au contraire, la promotion d'activités productives et rémunératrices, créerait les revenus nécessaires à la satisfaction des besoins fondamentaux par les intéressés eux-mêmes qui, par ailleurs, participeraient pleinement à l'effort collectif de croissance économique.

D. Quelques éléments du système d'information sur le secteur traditionnel

En créant un système d'information sur le secteur traditionnel, il ne faudrait pas perdre de vue certaines actions fondamentales qu'il est nécessaire d'entreprendre dans le but de démarginaliser ce secteur.

Dans le milieu rural, il ne s'agit pas seulement de multiplier les zones d'action rurale ou les sociétés d'encadrement rural, mais il faut également favoriser la création d'entreprises industrielles, semi-industrielles et artisanales. Il faut également donner à la population rurale la capacité administrative et technique nécessaire pour assurer le fonctionnement autonome de toutes les unités économiques.

Dans le milieu urbain (secteur urbain traditionnel ou non officiel), il s'agit d'augmenter l'efficacité et la production de ce secteur, d'améliorer son organisation et de favoriser la diversification de sa production. Jusqu'ici, l'Administration publique, au moyen de la planification centrale, a cherché à résoudre le problème du secteur traditionnel urbain en créant des emplois dans les industries et services existants ou grâce à des programmes de travaux publics. La solution se trouve peut-être dans l'amélioration des activités exercées dans le secteur traditionnel urbain.

Il conviendrait donc, au cours de ce séminaire, d'examiner quelles informations sont nécessaires pour une bonne connaissance du secteur traditionnel. Les éléments ci-dessous ne font pas la distinction suivant qu'il s'agisse des activités exercées dans le monde rural ou dans les centres urbains. Suivant le cas, certains éléments sont plus importants que d'autres. De même, aucune distinction n'est faite entre informations qualitatives et données quantitatives.

Tout d'abord, il paraît essentiel que le système d'information comporte deux types de distribution des activités traditionnelles : la distribution sectorielle et la distribution régionale.

Dans la distribution sectorielle des activités traditionnelles, on s'efforcera d'identifier dans chaque secteur, le nombre d'entreprises ou d'exploitations (y compris les exploitations familiales). Cette identification doit concerner le plus grand nombre possible de secteurs :

- Agriculture, élévage et pêche :

    - agriculture d'exportation

    - agriculture d'alimentation

    - élevage

    - pêche, etc.

- Artisanat et petite industrie :

    - artisanat de production

    - artisanat de service

    - industrie de traitement de matières premières nationales

    - industries de fabrication d'outils élémentaires de production, etc.

- Transport :

    - transports routiers

    - transports fluviaux

- Commerce :

    - commerce de gros

    - commerce de détail

    - commerce de produits en majorité nationaux

    - commerce de produits importés.

La distribution régionale sera fonction de l'organisation administrative de chaque pays. On devrait toutefois s'efforcer de ventiler les activités traditionnelles suivant la plus petite unité administrative. Cette classification est, on le sait, fondamentale pour la mise en oeuvre d'une planification régionale.

En procédant à ces deux distributions, il est important de fournir les informations suivantes sur chacune des entreprises ou exploitations du secteur traditionnel :

- nombre d'emplois (salariés et non salariés) ;

- estimation de la valeur ajoutée ;

- forme de propriété (familiale, de type coopératif, propriété individuelle) ;

- type d'équipement utilisé : il est utile dans ce contexte de faire la distinction entre équipement à contenu technologique local et équipement à contenu technologique importé ;

- revenus de l'exploitation ;

- taux d'utilisation de la capacité de production ;

- niveaux de formation et de technicité des agents de l'exploitation concernée ;

- mode de gestion de l'exploitation : on s'emploiera si nécessaire à donner une description détaillée du mode de gestion ;

- liaisons avec d'autres exploitations du même secteur et d'autres secteurs ; en particulier on précisera le cas échéant les liaisons en amont et en aval ;

- mode de financement des activités de l'entreprise et de l'exploitation ;

- méthodes de commercialisation ;

- types et qualité de produits ou des services, etc...

E. Conclusion

On ne peut suffisamment insister sur le fait qu'un système d'information, tel qu'esquissé ci-dessus, doit avoir pour principal objectif de promouvoir une politique économique et sociale qui tende vers la mise en place d'un processus autonome et auto-entretenu de développement et de croissance économique. Un tel système d'information devrait permettre la définition et la mise en oeuvre de politiques adéquates en matière d'éducation, de formation professionnelle, d'acquisition technologique, de revalorisation de technologies nationales, de financement du développement, d'utilisation de bien d'équipement, donc d'importation de ces biens. Il faudrait que l'information disponible sur le secteur traditionnel permette à l'Administration publique d'aider ce secteur dans le domaine de la main d'oeuvre qualifiée, de la technologie, de la gestion et du financement. Ainsi la participation du secteur traditionnel dans le processus de développement permettrait aux pays en développement de trouver leurs modes de développement et leurs styles de vie propres.

INFORMATION SYSTEMS IN PUBLIC ADMINISTRATION
D. Eade, J. Hodgson (editors)
North-Holland Publishing Company
© *DFD, 1981*

FINAL REPORT OF WORKING GROUP 7*

A. Introduction

In developing countries it is recognized that the traditional/informal sector represents about 80 per cent of the total population while its share of total income is 20 per cent. This places in focus the importance of the traditional sector vis-a-vis the whole economy.

Up to recent years the accepted measure of progress of the economy was the growth rate which was heavily dependant on the growth rate of the modern sector which was the catalyst. As a result, the statistical reporting system was also geared to make available comprehensive data in this sector. Today, however, such indicators as quality of life, income redistribution, availability of basic needs, etc. provide a more realistic and acceptable measurement of progress. With regard to measurement of growth in this manner, it is obvious that the statistical reporting system has failed to develop measures which could be used to construct this type of indicator. The statistical reporting system is also heavily biased towards global and aggragated estimates which are not useful for measurement of growth in the traditional sector.

At the outset, it was felt that a clear idea of what is meant by the traditional sector should be formulated. From the perspective of Data for Development, this sector may be defined in two dimensions, viz. the socio-economic dimension and the informational dimension. In the socio-economic dimension the traditional/informal sector is that sector which uses traditional methods of production, is relatively unorganized, and whose

---

* Participants: S. Suharto (Chairman)
                     D.P. Guneratne (rapporteur)
                     M.D. Sarr (rapporteur)
                     Y. Franchet
                     P. Dumas
                     G. Louvet
                     S. Shah

contribution to the national product is not well assessed. In the
informational dimension the traditional/informal sector includes that part of
the economy whose transactions are mainly non-traceable (that is, not
recorded and accounted for in administrative records).

In this report an attempt has been made to identify the basic issues of
development in the traditional sector and the information needed in this
sector. Next, a survey is made of the instruments presently available for the
collection of information in this sector; the current status of the
information systems is reviewed and finally some observations are made with
regard to feasible solutions as well as some recommendations for future action
in the context of the activities of the Data for Development International
Association.

B.   Identification of development issues

The basic development issue is to integrate the traditional sector more
fully into the development process. The implications of this are:

(a) To increase the share of this sector in the national product; and

(b) To increase its share in the benefits of the development process.

These two implications involve in concrete terms a simultaneous attack in
three fields:

1. An increase in the level of production of this sector through
    expansion of employment opportunities, by providing supplementary
    occupations and by promoting the creation of small enterprises
    as well as improving access to basic production inputs, for
    example credit, technology, extension services, tools and
    equipment;

2. The provision of basic needs such as adequate levels of nutrition,
    health, housing, education, access to public facilities, for example
    transport, water supply, etc.; and,

3. Ensuring an adequate level of income.

C.   Information required

With regard to production, the following types of information are of
great importance:

(a) Information on the extent of the traditional sector in various
spheres of the economy, for example agriculture, household industries, trade,
transport and other services. This information should include, in particular,
the total number of units by sectors and regions and the population numbers
engaged in these units;

(b) Information on production by sectors and region which should include
type of product, mode of production, volume and value of production, kind and
quantity of energy used, type of production inputs, raw materials, etc. and
seasonality of production;

(c) Information on existing equipment, on credit facilities, skills and
marketing facilities;

(d) Information on labour force characteristics such as seasonality and
hours of work, composition of labour force (employment, status, sex, age, etc.),

productivity and wages.

With regard to the second goal, that is provision of basic needs, the vital information elements are:

(a) Level of education by region;

(b) Food and quality of nutrition and health by region;

(c) Housing conditions; and

(d) Access to public facilities, for example market centres, transport, etc.

With regard to the provision of an adequate level of income, the basic information should include:

(a) National and regional income distributions;

(b) Level of income in relation to households and individuals; and

(c) Composition of income, expenditure and savings.

All this information is needed both in the form of aggregatable information obtained from censuses, administrative records and surveys as well as non-aggregatable information obtained mainly from case studies and monographs.

D. Instruments available for data collection

The available instruments for the collection of required information may be classified under five headings as follows.

1. Censuses

Although they serve as useful master frames and also enable estimates to be made for small areas, the undermentioned problems are inherent in this type of data collection. Firstly, due to the complexity of the operation, detailed information cannot be collected. Secondly, censuses are very costly and results are obtainable only after much delay. Thirdly, the information rapidly becomes obsolete due to the fluidity of the traditional sector, and finally, there is always the problem of lack of adequate definitions and classifications.

2. Surveys

Although by using surveys it is possible to obtain more information frequently, this method is subject to a number of deficiencies such as paucity of sampling frames, non-sampling errors often being larger than sampling errors, the difficulty of providing estimates for small areas (which is very important for the traditional sector) and the lack of adequate identifiers, definitions and classifications.

3. Administrative records and reports

These instruments have the advantage of being available periodically on a continuing basis and being especially suitable for small area requirements. However they are deficient in the sense that the forms are not adequately designed for statistical purposes and the administrative procedures are not satisfactorily implemented due to lack of training, control and feedback, especially in the traditional sector.

4.   Case Studies and Monographs

It is recognized that this type of instrument can provide in-depth and correlated information as well as qualitative information. Such studies can also help in census and survey planning and the adoption of appropriate classifications. However, the problems with this type of instrument are that it requires high level personnel to implement and the information produced is non-aggregatable and cannot be linked with census and survey information.

5.   Remote sensing

Although this method has the advantage of providing information speedily and economically, it cannot be used for small areas, it requires high level technology and expertise, it is still in an experimental stage and it is limited to only certain activities of the traditional sector, for example agriculture.

E.   Current status of information systems

In agriculture many of the developing countries already have fairly adequate systems of data collection for certain crops which are of importance to their economies such as paddy cultivation, corn cultivation, maize cultivation, etc. Such systems have evolved around sample surveys based on administrative records. The information is fairly accurate in areas such as the extent of the areas cultivated and harvested and the yields of the crops. However, similar information is totally lacking for other important subsidiary food crops which are just as important to their economies, for example beans, vegetables, etc. Similar deficiencies are also found in the areas of livestock production and dairy farming as well as in fisheries products. This is extremely unfortunate as these activities are very important and numerous, especially in the traditional sector. The main reason for this state of affairs is the non-availability of a suitable sampling frame to conduct crop-specific sample surveys.

The position is the same when attempting to quantify such things as the total number of the population dependent on these activities and the labour force participation in them. Information on extension services, inputs and credit facilities utilized by farmers is also not available in some countries. Seasonal migration of the labour force employed in agriculture is another important facet of agricultural activity in developing countries. There is hardly any information on the numbers moving in and out of agricultural regions during cultivation seasons.

An important deficiency in the collection of data relating to certain agricultural activities as well as other activities of the traditional sector in developing countries has been the lack of uniform definitions and classification and the difficulty of adopting suitable concepts for the conducting of sample surveys.

In the traditional sector another area of crucial importance is the cottage type industrial activity. The information here is extremely scanty and a determined effort has to be made to build up a data base for this sector. In some countries attempts have been made to identify cottage industries at the same time as the population census listing, and thereafter to conduct sample surveys. This method, though suitable immediately after the census, cannot be done on a continuous basis due to the fluidity of the cottage type of industry. Lack of data in this area has made it very difficult for Governments to service these industries with raw materials, credit facilities and marketing. Over-all project appraisal for upgrading this type of activity, especially in relation to the technology used, is another difficulty; the lack of information in this sector has made it virtually impossible to make a satisfactory assessment of the sectors contribution to the national product.

In some developing countries household trade activities form a substantial part of all activities in the traditional sector. They are also a source of supplementary income and employment. Due to the complex nature of these activities it is difficult to assess their contribution to household income. Nevertheless, it is important that some satisfactory measure should be found to make suitable estimates of their contribution. So far, the only methods generally adopted are censuses of retail trade/distribution establishments, and in some countries the registration of small traders. However, such registrations have been found to be far from satisfactory. Another aspect of this sector is the lack of information on the flows of commodities from the traditional sector. This data is very necessary to enable appropriate action to be taken to make some of these activities viable.

In the field of transport and other services in the traditional sector, there is a dearth of information. In some countries however registration of all types of vehicles used in the traditional sector could help partially to assess the extent of transport services. However, this alone is insufficient and action has to be taken to measure the extent of these activities if a suitable and reasonable estimate is to be made of their contribution to the national product.

With regard to the provision of basic needs, the spectrum of information available is not as unsatisfactory as for the levels of production. Censuses and surveys including household budget surveys carried out in many developing countries have yielded substantial information on education, nutrition, morbidity, housing conditions, etc. However, the data is periodic with long gaps between the observations. If close monitoring of the basic needs of the traditional sector is to be made, continuing sample surveys have to be carried out on a more frequent basis. Information on access to public facilities such as market centres, public transportation, health facilities, schools and mass media also have to be built up. In some developing countries this type of information is collected through village administration reports. The administration procedures prevalent in this sector however need to be strengthened.

As to the level of income of households, in the traditional sector the only generally accepted medium of collection is through household sample surveys such as family budget surveys, labour force surveys, etc. However, these surveys are sporadic and a continuous monitoring of levels of income cannot be made due to the irregularity of the information as well as the lack of standard concepts and classifications used. Measurement of income levels in the traditional sector is further complicated by the low monetarization prevalant in this sector.

F. Suggested improvements to current information systems

Having identified the instruments available for data collection in the traditional sector, it is necessary to briefly discuss in what manner the use of these instruments should be improved to build up a substantial data base.

To maintain benchmark data on the traditional sector, periodic and regular censuses of population, agriculture, industry, establishment, etc. must be carried out. They can also be used to build up suitable master frames for the conduct of sample surveys although such frames need to be updated before a survey is undertaken. However, it is essential that standard concepts and definitions should be adopted.

Another important medium of data collection in the traditional sector is the sample survey. In many instances this is the only type of instrument that can be used. Many countries have carried out specific sample surveys for assessing particular problems. Probably a more rationalistic and beneficial method of carrying out these surveys would be to adopt the integrated approach and conduct continuing multi-subject household as well as establishment sample surveys.

In the present stage of development, the greatest impact on building a suitable data base for the traditional sector will be through the improvement of administrative records. It is recognized that in many spheres of administration at the village level, large numbers of forms are being filled in to keep a tab on village activities. More use however should be made of these reporting forms to obtain sufficient basic information on such activities. A crucial deficiency in this type of reporting system is the inadequate design of the forms and the recording procedures for extraction of statistical data. Greater attention should be paid to the design of these forms through training of the administrators in the use for which the forms are designed, from the point of view of information. A very useful and effective medium that has recently found a place in developing countries is the creation of village registers containing basic village statistics. This is a medium that could be commended. Although the maintenance of such registers requires substantial and trained manpower and continuous updating, a register even with a few items of basic information would prove invaluable for decision making.

Case studies should also be carried out and monographs produced, particularly in areas where knowledge of specific activities is lacking. This type of study would enable the improvement of data collection methods such as censuses and surveys, as well as the design of administrative records. It is recognized that in the not too distant future remote sensing may play a very important part in monitoring activities in the traditional sector, especially crop cultivation. At the present stage of development not many developing countries can afford to make use of the facilities available. Nevertheless an effort should be made to keep abreast of the knowledge in this field and be aware of its capabilities.

For the process of development planning and administrative management, data is required not only individually but also as correlated information. Hence, in the collection of data care should be taken to ensure that the data can be easily integrated into an information network. There are a number of prerequisites for this:

(a) Adoption of geocoding systems. In most developing countries no attempt has so far been made to code small geographical areas uniquely. This is very important if the data collected is to be interlinked. Much emphasis must be placed on the development of suitable geocoding systems.

(b) International standard classifications. Where appropriate, the use of international standard classifications should be encouraged, however great caution must be exercised in the use of these classifications without modification, especially in the traditional sector, as there is the danger of significant information being lost because of the broader classification of international standards.

(c) Standardization of concepts and definitions. In many instances it is extremely difficult to undertake any kind of time series analysis due to the varying concepts and definitions being used in periodic data collections. This has to be avoided if the data are to be made comparable over time. This could only be done by the adoption of standard concepts and definitions. These standards should also be adopted by all agencies collecting information.

(d) <u>Use of common levels of aggregation</u>. Where information has to be aggregated, care should be taken to ensure that common levels of aggregation are adopted. Much comparable data can be lost if this is not done.

In the process of improvement of data collection and integration it should be borne in mind that maximum results can be obtained only if there is a proper understanding among data collectors of the use to which data are put. The best methods of ensuring this are to provide a feedback mechanism and to organize evaluation procedures. Finally, for the development of a data network in the traditional sector, the beneficial use of computers must always be kept in mind, especially in the development systems.

G.   Recommendations

1. It is the considered view that if the GDN idea is to be accepted, Data For Development (DFD) should organize regional and country seminars to this end for those in charge of information sources in the government sectors. It is encouraging to hear that DFD has already planned, in co-operation with the United Nations Economic and Social Commission for Asia and the Pacific (ESCAP), to hold such a regional seminar for the ESCAP countries in Bangkok, as well as one-day seminars in two countries of the region.

2. Pilot studies should be initiated on the development of the prerequisites, for example standardization of concepts, classifications, etc. for geocoding systems, necessary for the organization of an integrated government data network which will include the traditional sector. DFD experts in conjunction with country experts should undertake these studies.

3. In view of the vital part which administrative records play in the development of a data base in the traditional sector, it is necessary that DFD should undertake pilot studies in one or two developing countries to suggest ways of reorganizing those countries' administrative records and reporting systems at the lowest administrative unit so that they can be viable units in an over-all information system. Reports of such studies should be made available to all developing countries.

4. The United Nations as well as other international agencies and other funding agencies should give strong financial support to DFD for carrying out the above recommendations.

INFORMATION SYSTEMS IN PUBLIC ADMINISTRATION
D. Eade, J. Hodgson (editors)
North-Holland Publishing Company
© *DFD, 1981*

USE OF NEW COMPUTER AND COMMUNICATIONS TECHNOLOGIES
FOR INFORMATION SYSTEMS IN PUBLIC ADMINISTRATION IN
DEVELOPING COUNTRIES

(statement by the Chairman of Working Group 8, C.C. Gotlieb*)

I am not in favour of a Chairman starting his remarks with an apology, but for two reasons I find myself having to do so here. It is not that I have no views on the subject of our Group, but they are still very much in a state of flux, and it is doubtful whether I can express them even to my own satisfaction. One reason for difficulty in formulating a position is that it is less than two weeks ago, after I had already arrived in Europe, that I was asked by Mr. Salmona to be Chairman of this Group, and agreed to do so. In the meantime, I have spent one week in Vienna as Co-Chairman of a conference, and one week in Paris with Mission de l'Informatique, both of them intense activities, so there has been little time to collect my thoughts. The other reason for my hesitancy is that although I feel I am literate on the subjects of computers and communications, and I have had some experience in working with developing countries, I do not think that this latter experience is extensive enough to allow me to speak with any degree of authority.

Just so that you are aware of what that experience is, let me say that I was a principal investigator of the team from the Office for Science and Technology at the United Nations, then headed by Gresford and Barg, who produced the first report on The Application of Computer Technology for Development and a member of the team for the second report on that subject.[1] Also, for the last four years I have been one of two Canadian principals in a project funded by CIDA, the Canadian International Development Agency, intended to further computer education in Brazil. This works between two Canadians and four Brazilian Universities, and in the course of the project, which is still going on, I have made five visits to Brazil, mainly to Rio de Janeiro and the North East, and spent about four months there altogether. Finally in my capacity as Chairman of IFIPS TC-9 (the technical committee concerned with the relation of computers to society) I am working with the International Liaison Committee of IFIP to see what role IFIP or TC-9 can play, if any, in this activity of computers for development. This experience is not very continuous or extensive, but it has been enough to teach me how great are the differences between the so-called developing countries, and how careful one must be if one

---

* Professor of Computer Science, University of Toronto, Canada.

[1] United Nations publications (Sales Nos. E.71.II.A.1 and E.73.II.A.12).

thinks one can make any statement which is supposed to have general validity.

With this background I propose to state my position in the form of a series of statements. Most of the statements should really be surrounded by qualifications and caveats but I will tend to present them flatly in order to provoke controversy. I believe that I have evidence to support some of the statements, but I will not present it here, leaving this for the discussion, if challenged. In some cases I have to admit that the statements can only be taken as unconfirmed prejudices: the statements follow.

At the village level, where so much of the population of developing countries is distributed, there is very little if any room for either computer or communications technologies. Most of the effort has to go towards improving agricultural products and indigenous industry providing basic nutrition, water supplies and health facilities, and helping people cope with their local environment. This means that most development money must be spent on these vital services, so that funds expended for computers and communications should only be a few per cent of total development funds.

At the administrative and government levels there is a genuine need to have the data which will permit effective planning. At local levels this probably means that only data collecting facilities should be provided. At higher centralized levels there should be the ability to carry out data processing. But this ability should be concentrated on perhaps a dozen basic statistical services relating to population, health, finance, currency control, etc. The equipment for this should be modern, and use basic, well-tried data processing programs, adapted from other juridictions for local use.

Except for a very few countries (for example India and Brazil) which have had some decades of experience with computers, the latest and most expensive types of computer systems should not be used. This means for example that video terminals and time sharing are not needed, that management information systems and integrated data bases should be deferred, as should distributed processing and interconnexion of systems through teleprocessing. Aside from the expense, such systems are still experimental even in the western countries. Even more important, the infrastructure, particularly the communications systems, of very few developing countries is robust enough to allow these systems to work, even if serious efforts are made to introduce them.

Although most of the attention ought to be focussed on the public sector, some room ought to be left for the private sector to operate. This should be done even though the private sector is bound to be represented by multinational companies - always suspect in developing countries - and even though the multinationals are likely to introduce some high technology into their applications, of the type I have just argued against. The reason for arguing in favour of allowing a role for the private sector is that experience has shown that they do some real good in education, always a high priority, they do provide jobs good enough to attract people who have gone abroad for studies back to their native land, and they do introduce a few of the high technology components which makes it possible for the country to advance once the basic computer operations have been coped with.

Perhaps these will do as a starting point for my position. You will note that I am very conservative on the role of computer/communications, so it may be that I am betraying my trust in serving as a Chairman of this Working Group. But I am sure that there will be from you a variety of opinions, based on your own valid experiences. As these emerge I like to believe that I shall be capable of reconstructing my prejudices.

INFORMATION SYSTEMS IN PUBLIC ADMINISTRATION
D. Eade, J. Hodgson (editors)
North-Holland Publishing Company
© *DFD, 1981*

WHAT DOES DATA FOR DEVELOPMENT WANT FROM COMPUTING —
BETTER ELECTRONIC THEORY OR BETTER APPLICATION PHILOSOPHY
BASED ON THE PRIMARY ACTIVITY?

H.C. Price*

Abstract

What should be the development policy of the advanced nations for
themselves and the third world? Should there be any fundamental difference
in the application of advanced technology? Both groups of nations have an
employment problem related to the mode of application.

Historically, has our industrial development been so peaceful and
satisfactory that we can now propose it as the answer for the Third World?

The advent of the chip and the micro-circuit means back to the drawing
board for application strategy everywhere. Perhaps the correct strategy for
both groups of nations has more similarities than differences. This paper
discusses these vital socio-economic points.

A. Communication

Communication has always been an integral component of all human
relationships. The basic ingredient in the development of human relationships
has been information, craftsmanship, scientific and social interaction, etc.,
particularly in the socio-economic milieu of the day. Quite rightly, this
should be the essential objective of Data for Development. Information is also
the essential requisite for communication and control — the science of
cybernetics. Nothing in our complex society can operate efficiently and
cheaply without the skilled employment of this cybernetic function. Most of
the social, economic, religious and military disasters of the past can be
ascribed to the failure to use such a function. But which aspect of the data
do we need to develop in this manner, what information, where and how
generated? On this whole question we seem to have lost our way in recent
years, being unable to distinguish the application wood from the trees. This
situation has been made worse by the mountain of data that the computer
provides — we are in danger of becoming captives of the printout and like
Croesus of old, of being overwhelmed by the system we have designed; for

---

* Consultant physician, Department of Medicine, Charing Cross Teaching
Hospital, London, England.

having invented a new facility we appear to be unable to use it to our
benefit.

B.   Data

     Data is both the product and the servant of functional activity. We
should therefore only be concerned with the application of this functional
craft data generated direct from source. Instead we lose our way by
concentrating our attention on setting up separate data systems for
management, which originally was set up to deal with this very problem and
has failed. Management facilities have become separated from the activity of
production but were unnecessary in the precomputer age for dealing with the
mass of data manually generated from expanding industrial society. As our
servant, data is not sacrosanct, it is merely the penumbra. Whether industrial,
academic, medical or scientific, the functional data tells us how we can do the
things we consider necessary for our work or play. As a product it needs to
be employed for the benefit of all, both today and tommorow.

C.   The problem

     In all areas of life the basic communication problem that has plagued
man since the invention of the first tool has been how to control production
in order to supply the needs of society. The greatest difficulty has always
been gathering the craft or function data generated at the workface. For many
centuries the individual craftsman/owner carried out this function to a greater
or lesser extent by using his own data from his own personal workface.

     The increase in man's prosperity and his insatiable demands for ever more
goods and services led to factory production and has strained this primitive
craft workface beyond all reason. The last hundred years has seen the
tremendous growth in management services in an attempt to solve this data
transfer problem, only succeeding in interposing another system between the
workface and society. This system, having no direct knowledge of either,
merely increases the proportion of non-productive workers. Mechanization and
then automation have also attempted to control this data problem. Computers
have now entered the field with the usual fanfare of trumpets.

     But in order to plan productive forces it is essential to know exactly
what goes on at the workface, not what is reported second hand, corrupted by
repeated manual data transfer. This can only be done economically by recording
the activities carried out by the faceworker himself as he uses the craft data
necessary for his own specific task while he works. If this were possible
it would cut out all the intermediary data stages (some still manual) between
the worker and senior management which is a well known area of inadvertant
data corruption and falsification. This is the craft or functional information
pathway with the spin off necessary for a restructured management.

D.   What does the primary operator want?

     The information problem in medicine with which the author is directly
concerned should be considered at the practical level and also in terms of the
wider aspects in industrial society (which nevertheless reflects the same
basic problem).

1.   The health service

     What does the doctor want when he is presented with a patient's problem?
He wants information and the time to be able to use his skill and experience,
to interrogate, investigate, treat and follow up his patients and to have
facilities to reduce all repetitive and time-consuming information activities

to a minimum. The patient wants somebody to have time to talk with him, discuss his failing health and advise him in order to facilitate recovery.

Therefore, time, skill and experience seem to be the essence of this arrangement. Skill requires access to all the relevant data and the means to collect, collate, update and store this data in a quick, accurate, reliable and retrievable mode - the essence of cybernetics or information and control. Experience provides the power to manipulate the semantic, biological and scientific symbols and analyse the results.

Hospital management has been introduced because of the failure of the traditional medical information system. The traditional manually generated case paper to meet the needs of the doctors has become impossible to compile in modern times; it attempts to accommodate on the one side the tremendous demands for health care by a much larger and now more literate population and on the other to have knowledge of and be able to use the advances of medical science. Management is an attempt to solve this very ancient problem of providing essential data to the craftsman while at the same time extracting from him the data for subsequent use as well as for forward planning, analysis, innovation and costing.

The results to date have not been satisfactory. The doctors are still overwhelmed by the demands for health care while the essential data for clinical activity, research and planning is not available when and where it is required, in spite of a great escalation of management services; doctors therefore have less and less time or opportunity to use the new methods of medical science becoming available. Finally, computers have been introduced as a last resort in a vain attempt to solve what is incorrectly considered to be a management information problem. This has merely increased the trend today towards more specialized divisive medicine, which in itself results in prolonged patient waiting time and frustration. The result is that the doctors, partially submerged in piles of printout which they have little time or inclination to study and often containing data they do not need, protect themselves with cynical detachment.

This outline analysis, while essential for providing correct information for medical care, is also applicable to the general problems of communications outside medicine.

2. Industry

What do we want from the production worker? Goods and services of a high standard, provided where and when required and as cheaply as possible. What does the production worker want in return? Hopefully an interesting job where his skill as a craftsman can be rewarded with opportunities for advancement in his chosen craft, for facilities for innovation and invention, to be relieved of the boredom of repetition and to receive an income that will enable him to enjoy life and leisure and purchase the goods or services provided by other craftsmen.

Today none of this is granted to him because of the frenzied need for more goods and services; because of this, society and its craftsmen both get a poor deal.

E. Management or production

Because we have been beguiled by the argument that what is required is more and efficient management, computers have been introduced in order to rationalize, reorganize and even to replace management, not to enhance the production worker. Because of the supposed need to centralize and rationalize.

both management and computers have developed into things in themselves and have
tended to become more and more isolated from industrial and social reality.

Computers, though reflecting man, have received more than their fair share
of the blame for our socio-economic problems, but are useful scapegoats,
especially when endowed with the aura of scientific and technological mysticism.
For it has been said that "Computers can solve any problem, deal efficiently
and speedily with any defined function given the correct data". What a pity
we have failed so signally to define the function; thus the millenium is as
far away as ever - perhaps even further.

The failure to define the function has resulted in a policy whereby
computers are being applied to correct the manual errors generated yesterday,
when they are really needed to control the production of tomorrow, in both the
advanced countries and the Third World.

It is feared that the mistakes made in installing large main-frame units
are being perpetuated, in that Large Scale Integration and microprocessors are
now promoted as the current answer to these same communication and control
problems. If applied in the same mode as the large main-frames have been,
we shall only have advanced in order to stand still. Computer facilities must
not continue to be misapplied from the standpoint of the reality of the
socio-economic facts of life in the second half of the twentieth century. And
what is this reality? It is the productive forces and skill of the national
workforce - academic, scientific, medical and industrial - the latter being
the main producer of the GNP and enabling the others to function.

It is not just a new computer that is required to deal with man's problems,
but a new method, a new philosophy of application to exploit this cybernetic
tool. What about the job at the workface? It produces the vital functional
craft data generated by the face worker or the craftsman, however debased by
mechanization, in carrying out the essential activity of producing goods and
services for society. Main-frames cannot help here for many reasons including
the economic ones; micros can help - an error on a micro is a nuisance but
not serious; on a macro it can be economically disastrous.

F.   Is it too late to change?

How can the application philosophy be changed? It demands an
understanding of the need for a new concept vis-a-vis the direction flow of
the production data from the craft workface upwards - instead of the downward
flow of printout from the management to the workface, because in this situation
we are still employing computers as if they were another pair of hands. The
production information pathway originates at the workface, spinning off data
to vital areas; the development of management systems has tended to reverse
this direction of flow. The computer can restore this situation by becoming an
integral part of the information flow from the workface to the society it
serves.

Can computers applied cybernetically rather than as expensive desk
calculators help us in this problem, the solution of which is essential for
the rational development towards the information society of the twenty-first
century? The author has been studying the problem of communications for the last
fifteen years. A satisfactory solution in one area such as medicine could
provide a positive answer elsewhere in the economy. In medicine it is the
doctor not the manager that treats patients and spends money. The medical
record or patient case paper is the sole recipient of every action the doctor
makes and its correct compilation enables the doctor to follow the progress
of the patient and monitor the effects of his actions on the patient. It also
contains all the data required for housekeeping and hospital management. It is

therefore the basic source document, the key to medical informatics. However, to generate a reliable record is time consuming and in chronic conditions often very boring.

The many attempts to provide a computerized medical record have in the main been expensive failures because they are only of use to the dedicated computer doctors, the 1 per cent of the whole profession; the rest who have to practice routine medicine, usually outside the centres of excellence, find them unacceptable.

The medical record or patient case paper can be arbitrarily divided into two parts, (a) the preliminary function and (b) the history and the rest of the main clinical function area. Today, with time and staff being short, this history problem is often dealt with inadequately, particularly in special areas such as occupational health and follow up on discharge from specialized units. For the last six years the Department of Medicine at Charing Cross Teaching Hospital has been studying the use of a computer to interrogate patients from such special areas. This feasiblity study was satisfactory and now the technique has become routine in our follow up and occupational disease clinics. Both patients and staff approve of this method. Computers can help therefore if applied to work areas.

But this facility does not deal with the doctor's primary function. How can one achieve a recorded history from the doctor patient dialogue – the consultation itself? The answer is by using voice recognition techniques. The Department carried out its first experiment last year and obtained a 74 per cent acceptance by the computer of the patient's answers using four key words and is now commencing a combined trial using a modified microprocessor Motorola 6800 (a MICKIE), to record the doctor's dialogue – the computer will accept only the key words and commands. This is a combined trial in that it is also intended to record by tape and pen and paper and to compare the viability of each method at the end of the study. Voice input has an additional advantage in that it obviates the need for keyboard data entry, thus enabling the doctor to record effortlessly.

Perhaps the answer to the communication problem is the simultaneous transfer of function data to the computer using voice input where possible or with a microcomputer as an integral part of the control system. For example, when the millwright keys in his instructions to the lathe, a microprocessor in the control panel could enable these commands from the micrometers to be recorded and be available for innovation and invention.

What of the developing world? It has been suggested for a number of years that the developing countries need the advanced technology of the developed countries in order to advance them rapidly to the developed countries socio-economic level. Computers have been exported to developing countries in order to help in this advance but this has not been successful and many secondary problems have resulted. The Governments of the Third World should not waste their scarce financial resources on purchasing large main-frame computers with all their associated problems.

G. How did the West deal with this problem of industrial development?

The early attempts to deal with the problem of increasing production caused great trauma and social distress in Europe and the United States of America in the developing days of the Industrial Revolution. To overcome this difficulty the primitive management system inherited from mediaeval times was augmented and developed. This non-productive manual section has grown over two centuries to become today an enormous non-productive force occupied with management objectives and, for an appreciable proportion of its time, in managing itself,

a drag on production, innovation and development. There are now two industrial
objectives, one for production and one for management. These are separate
entities and often occupy separate buildings, in many instances geographically
miles apart.

H. The demise of the Industrial Society in the developed world

Having reached the end of the road in the manufacturing world we should
look back and review the means. Manual management has served its purpose
and in doing so has become one of the shackles of production and innovation.
Thus, our manufacturing society, being unable to advance, is decaying and
making way for the information society. Unfortunately a similar type of
development is being suggested for the Third World. Do they need to repeat
the mistakes of the advanced countries? In the past the answer was most
probably yes, there was no other obvious or economically viable alternative.
The developed world should have learnt by experience and appreciate that it
now has the technology to avoid the encumbrances of a top heavy
bureaucratically controlled system of production management. This experience
should be passed on to the rest of the world.

The Third World needs to develop small-scale industry to harness its
working population for productive purposes, drawing on rather than destroying
it's craft expertise and slowly and carefully bring its society into twentieth
century production without the trauma experienced by Europe and the United
States when they were similarly developing.

I. Microcomputers – do they hold the key to the future?

The silicon chip is now universal. Its invention has revolutionized
the architecture of computers and could do the same for their application.
The practical result of this miniaturization is the microcomputer which can be
placed in the hands of those at the workface who actually produce the GNP.
New ideas can be applied to production control by using a micro-based
information network at the production, not at the management level.

The misapplication of modern factory technology in the Third World has
meant that the working population, which is largely dispersed in rural areas,
is attracted to the new factories in the already overcrowded cities. This
policy has led, as in England, to a fall in food production and the diversion
of scarce capital resources for importing foodstuffs. Then there is the
additional problem of this huge mass of people accumulating in shanty towns,
with inevitable social and health problems. Left alone in their natural
environment and encouraged to improve their farming methods, most populations
can support themselves in food and basic raw materials.

Large main-frame computers are one of those products of sophisticated
modern technology being exported to the Third World to assist in
industrialization and development of management systems, without a thought
as to the socio-economic consequencies. If the industrial world cannot apply
these computers economically and usefully how can others be shown what to
do? Even here in Britain they are used either as expensive desk calculators
or in automatic control, neither of which functions could win a design prize
or claim a priority rating in the Third World. The emergent countries cannot
be expected to do better if they follow the developed countries advice or
such bad application examples. The introduction of main-frame computers
in such a mode will only waste scarce capital in paying for equipment and
maintenance and when the system goes down (as every system does at times),
there will be chaos because the old manual system has been dispersed. At best
they will produce sheets of management data for industries that hardly exist.

Many developing countries societies still use traditional methods of manufacture and food production. Developed countries should avoid exporting huge management systems to those countries to ruin their rural economy and new manufacturing industry with management that today is becoming less necessary even in the advanced countries. Developing countries need to expand and develop their existing small scale industries by using microcomputers at the workface; the spin off will help them to innovate and expand. The path of technological advancement should be taken slowly and easily through their developing era and by learning from and not repeating the errors made by the developed world.

INFORMATION SYSTEMS IN PUBLIC ADMINISTRATION
D. Eade, J. Hodgson (editors)
North-Holland Publishing Company
© *DFD, 1981*

COMPUTERS/DATA COMMUNICATIONS: AN AREA OF
TRANSFER OF TECHNOLOGY

Abubaker Mustafa*

A. Introduction

The role of the national Government of any developing country in relation
to computer technology can be divided into two major areas: the development,
direction, and control of computer technology as a national resource; and the
development, direction, and control of the use of computers within the
Government itself. Political structure will have much to say about the degree
of authority the developing country will have over the development and use of
such technology. However, regardless of the differences in authority and the
mechanics for implementation, there is an urgent need for a national policy in
introducing and effectively using computer technology in developing countries.
Already there is a wide gap between developed and developing countries in many
areas of technology and as Regal indicated, "The computer gap will become the
most serious international problem in future years, as well as the most
difficult industrial gap to cross." 1/ Solutions and attempts to narrow the
gap between developed and developing countries have been suggested by several
authors, among them Mesarovic and Pestel who recommend a model with built-in
scenarios aimed towards narrowing this gap. 2/ Computer technology may not be
appropriate for many developing countries where labour-intensive solutions are
desired and where manual or mechanical methods may be sufficient, as advocated
by Schumacher 3/ and others. De Sola Pool and others 4/ have stated that
if developing countries simply imitate the sequence of steps followed by those
who came before them in adopting new technologies, they will miss the
opportunity of rapidly closing the gap between them and the technologically

---

* National Computer Centre, Sudan.

1/ J.L. Regal, Social and International Aspects (Paris, 1972).

2/ M. Mesarovic and R. Pestel, Mankind at the Turning Point (New York,
E.P. Dutton and Co., Inc., 1974).

3/ E.F. Schumacher, Small is Beautiful (New York, Perennial Library,
1973).

4/ Friedman, De Sola Pool and Warren, Low Cost Data and Text Communication
(Cambridge, Mass., MIT, 1976).

advanced nations.

In order to help close this gap, a wide range of national policies and regulations need to be examined in the light of their impact on the use of computers and on their role in the economic and social development of a country. These include such issues as financing, export/import regulations, customs and tariff regulations, labour policies, salary structures, educational plans, standardization and national research and technical programmes. The role of the Government as a computer user concerns itself with some of these issues but in addition focuses particular attention on the selection and development of specific applications, the organization and management of computer resources and the provision of required technical systems and subsystems.

In the following sections of this paper, the major emphasis will be placed on two issues which affect the role of computers in developing countries namely computer/communication interaction and its impact in the field, and the computer's application for developing countries.

B.   Computer/communication interaction

Many developing countries are cultivating and making use of the new technologies already developed by the developed countries. What is technology? Poats defined it as "Knowledge systematically applied to practical tasks." 5/ This knowledge, he said, usually grows out of analysis and discovery through research in both the natural and local sciences. In order for this knowledge to be applied to true human needs, technology must be embodied through invention and innovation in goods and processes or techniques. Technological change has become recognized as a vital force in the progress of modern nations. Technology does, of course multiply the effective availability of usable resources, both natural and human. Quinn puts technology at the centre of development and says that "Technology is the vital growth component in each of the four traditional economic input factors: land, labour, capital and education."

Technological innovations cover many areas, one of them being communications, a very sensitive and important area in the infrastructure of a country. Within communications, data communications assumes major importance because of the new technologies embodied therein. New technologies such as computers and satellites etc. form the backbone of this technology. Gentle define data communications as "The movement of encoded information by means of electrical systems." 6/ The transmission systems include input/output devices. Communications play an important role in drawing all parts of the world closer together and data communications play an equally important role. In recent

---

5/   Rutherford M. Poats, Technology for Developing Nations (Washington, D.C., The Brookings Institution, 1972).

6/   Edgar E. Gentle, Data Communications in Business (New York, American AT & T Co., 1965).

years, as knowledge has accumulated, it has become increasingly difficult for
any one person to have access to all the information available, even in a
highly specialized field. Accordingly, the new techniques in data processing
and retrieval have added significance in man's efforts to avoid the waste
of duplicating the work of somebody else.

The merging of computers and communications technologies, the rapid pace
of technological change and the increasing use of computer/communications
services in many areas of application are causing many Governments to face
new issues where precedent is of limited help in devising appropriate policies.

The most positive features of computer/communications include: the
possibility to achieve full utilization of computer power; consolidation of
computer facilities - physical and managerial; introduction of more
sophisticated techniques; acceleration of the integration of data bases in
various government organizations for planning and control purposes; the
expansion of data collection and analysis possibilities by communicating with
different governmental units. Each of these features has strong economic
potential for developing countries.

As a result of all of this, a new era of data transmission has developed,
with a unique role. James Martin explains this role as follows:

"Data transmission will become as indispensible to city dwelling
man as his electricity supply. He will employ it in his home,
in his office, in shops, and in his car. He will use it to pay
for his goods, to teach his children, to obtain information,
transportation, stock prices, and sports. He will use it to
seek protection in the crime-infested streets. The best of
data transmission will give man more knowledge, more power,
more leisure time, he will have less mandatory travel, his job
will be more interesting. In many ways, his life will be
richer." 7/

Developing countries should grasp the opportunity to utilize and make
use of the new technologies, examples of which are the following:

(a) Computer polling systems. This computerized message switching
system which polls and switches messages among nodes, consists of a central
computer and associated dialing equipment which switches the messages and polls

---

7/   James Martin, Introduction to Teleprocessing (New Jersey,
Prentice-Hall, Inc., 1972).

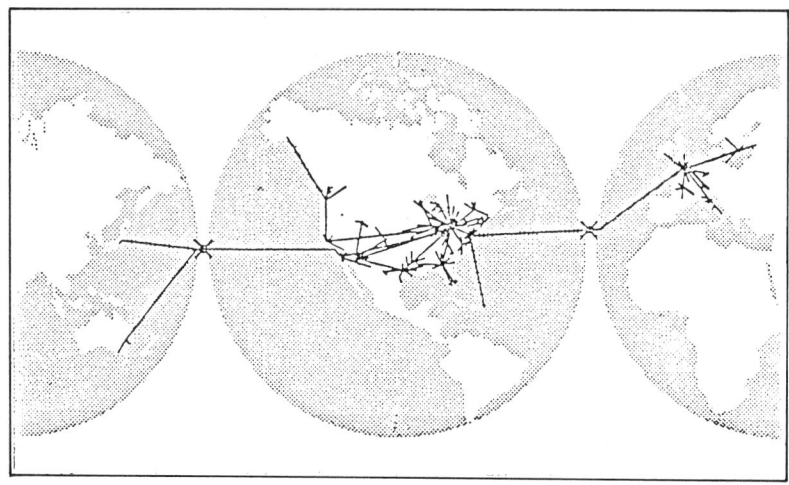

Source: General Electric

Figure XLV. General Electrics Mark III Information
Services Network

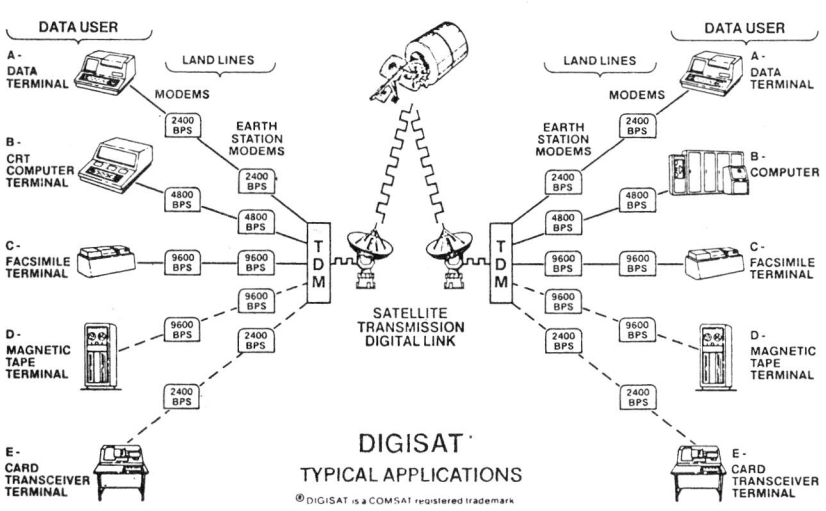

Figure XLVI.

Table 23. Geosynchronous satellites

Key No.	Satellite Name	Sponsor	Launch Year	Function
1	Meteosat	European Space Agency	1977	Meteorological
2	GEOS	European Space Agency	1976	Experimental
3	ATS-6	NASA	1974	Experimental
4	Statsionar 2	USSR	c.1976	Domestic Communications
5	MAROTS	European Space Agency	1977	Maritime & Ship Communications
6	Statsionar 9	USSR	1980	Domestic Communications
7	Skynet I	UK	1969	Military Communications
8	Skynet 2B	UK	1974	Military Communications
9	INTELSAT III F3	INTELSAT	1969	International Communications
10	Statsionar 5	USSR	1978-79	Domestic Communications
11	INTELSAT IV F5	INTELSAT	1972	International Communications
12	INTELSAT IV F1	INTELSAT	1975	International Communications
13	Future Meteorological Satellite	USSR	– a/	International Communications
14	INTELSAT II F2	INTELSAT	1967	International Communications
15	COSMOS 637	USSR	1975	Experimental
16	(Spare)	Indonesia	– a/	Domestic Communications
17	Statsionar 1 (Raduga)	USSR	1975	Domestic Communications
18	Palapa	Indonesia	1976	Domestic Communications
19	Statsionar 3	USSR	c.1976	Domestic Communications
20	Statsionar 6	USSR	1979-80	Domestic Communications
21	Molniya IS	USSR	1974	Domestic Communications
22	Statsionar T	USSR	c.1969	TV Broadcast
23	TACSAT	USAF	1969	Military Communications
24	ETS II	Japan	– a/	Experimental
25	CS	Japan	– a/	Domestic Communications
26	BS	Japan	– a/	TV Broadcast
27	GMS	Japan	– a/	Meteorological
28	Statsionar 7	USSR	1979-80	Domestic Communications
29	INTELSAT IV F8	INTELSAT	1974	International Communications
30	DCSC-II	Defense Communications Agency (U.S.)	1971 & 1973	Military Communications
31	MARISAT	COMSAT General Corp. b/	1976	Maritime & Ship Communications
32	INTELSAT IV F4	INTELSAT	1972	International Communications
33	INTELSAT II F3	INTELSAT	1967	International Communications
34	INTELSAT III F6	INTELSAT	1970	International Communications
35	TDRSS	NASA	– a/	Experimental
36	Statsionar 10	USSR	1980	Domestic Communications
37	INTELSAT III F4	INTELSAT	1969	International Communications
38	ATS-1	NASA	1966	Experimental
39	Future SMS	NASA/NOAA c/	– a/	Meteorological
40	SATCOM-B	RCA d/	1976	Domestic Communications
41	COMSTAR-B	COMSAT	1976	Domestic Communications
42	WESTAR 2	Western Union Telegraph Co.	1974	Domestic Communications
43	SBS-A	Satellite Business Systems	1979	Domestic Communications
44	SATCOM 1	RCA d/	1975	Domestic Communications
45	COMSTAR-A	COMSAT	1976	Domestic Communications
46	CTS	US/Canada	1976	Experimental
47	SMS 2	NASA/NOAA c/	1975	Meteorological
48	ANIK-1	TELESAT Canada	1972	Domestic Communications
49	SBS-B	Satellite Business Systems	1979	Domestic Communications
50	ANIK-2	TELESAT Canada	1973	Domestic Communications
51	ATS-5	NASA	1969	Experimental
52	ANIK-3	TELESAT	1975	Domestic Communications
53	WESTAR 1	Western Union Telegraph Co.	1974	Domestic Communications
54	NSS-A	National Satellite Systems	– a/	Domestic Communications
55	SATCOM-C	RCA d/	– a/	Domestic Communications
56	COMSTAR-C	COMSAT General Corp.	– a/	Domestic Communications
57	NSS-B	National Satellite Systems c/	– a/	Domestic Communications
58	INTELSAT III F2	INTELSAT	1968	International Communications
59	SMS-1	NASA/NOAA c/	1974	Meteorological
60	GOES-1	NASA/NOAA c/	1975	Meteorological

Table 23. (Continued)

Key No.	Satellite Name	Sponsor	Launch Year	Function
61	APS-3	NASA	1967	Experimental
62	FLTSATCOM	US Navy	- a/	Military Communications
63	INTELSAT 1 F1	INTELSAT	1965	International Communications
64	TDRSS	NASA	- a/	Experimental
65	AEROSAT	·· g/	- a/	Aeronautical Communications
66	INTELSAT II F4	INTELSAT	1967	International Communications
67	INTELSAT IV F7	INTELSAT	1973	International Communications
68	INTELSAT IV-A F2	INTELSAT	1976	International Communications
69	COSMOS 775	USSR	1975	?
70	Statsionar	USSR	1980	Domestic Communications
71	INTELSAT IV F3	INTELSAT	1971	Interntional Communications
72	FLTSATCOM	US Navy	- a/	Military Communications
73	INTELSAT IV-A F1	INTELSAT	1975	International Communications
74	INTELSAT IV F2	INTELSAT	1971	International Communications
75	NATO-2	NATO	1971	Military Communications
76	NATO-3	NATO	1976	Military Communications
77	SIRIO	Italy	1977	Experimental
78	AEROSAT	- g/	- a/	Aeronautical Communications
79	MARISAT	COMSAT General Corporation	1976	Maritime & Ship Communications
80	Statsionar 4	USSR	1978-79	Domestic Communications
81	DCSC-II	Defense Communications	1971 & 1973	Military Communications
82	Symphonie I	France & West Germany	1974	Experimental
83	Symphonie 2	France & West Germany	1975	Experimental
84	OTS	European Space Agency	c.1977	Domestic Communications
85	(TV Broadcast)	West Germany	- a/	TV Broadcast
X1	SYNCOM-2	NASA	1963	Experimental
X2	SYNCOM-3	NASA	1964	Experimental
-	NATO-1	NATO	1970	Military Communications
-	TELESAT F-4	TELESAT Canada	1978	Domestic Communications
-	ECS	Japan	- a/	Experimental Communications
-	DSCS III (2)	Defense Communications Agency (U.S.)	- a/	Military Communications
-	INTELSAT V	INTELSAT	c.1979	International Communications

a/ Undetermined
b/ Leader of the consortium
c/ NOAA is the National Oceanographic and Atmospheric Administration
d/ RCA is RCA Corporation and subsidiaries
e/ National Sateliite Systems is a subsidiary of Hughes Aircraft
f/ Intital location
g/ This consortium consists of the European Space Agency, COMSAT General Corporation, and Canada

Source : Extracted from a table in MORGAN, W.L., "Satellite Utilization of the Geosynchronous Orbit", COMSAT Technical Review, Vol. 6, No. 1, Spring 1976, pp. 195-205.

the network, plus several nodes equipped with terminals. Such a system is
capable of being used internationally. A cost-benefit analysis will show that
computer systems are far cheaper than any other teletype circuit.

     (b) <u>Time-sharing networks</u>. There are now a number of computer time-
sharing networks that operate internationally. The largest is General
Electric's MARK III (figure XLV). This type of system is economic when
operated internationally because of the time zone differences which keep the
computer busy most of the time. One of the characteristics of a time-sharing
system is the "mail-box" facility through which the user can address messages
directly to another user.

     Another version which employs a new concept is the packet switching
network. Examples are the ARPA and TELNET networks in the United States of
America, RCP in France, EPSS and NPL in England, and EIN (European Information
Network), an international experimental venture involving nine European
countries.

     (c) <u>Satellites</u>. "A significant contribution of satellites is that they
make the costs of communication relatively insensitive to the distance
covered." 4/

     Satellites have a power capability whether they are utilized for
communications, military, meteorological, or experimental purposes. Several
organizations such as COMSAT, RCA, NASA, A T & T, and INTELSAT are involved
in the satellite communications business. Some countries such as France,
Indonesia, Japan and the USSR have their own systems. Table 23 gives an
indication of the extensiveness of the satellite industry (see also figure
XLVI).

     Computers and communications complement each other: computers control
the immense communications switching centres and assist in managing the
enormous capacity of new transmission links into usable channels; communications
in return make available the power of computers and the information in data
banks to millions of users in remote locations. The result is an interactive
system. Cybernetically interactive systems are governed by the principles
of self-regulation and self-organization, and the behaviour of their systems -
from Beer's point of view - is governed by their dynamic structure. This
means the systems are interrelated and must include feedback loops. The
greatest danger in an interactive system, as Beer demonstrates, is not the
paucity of information but rather the problem of properly organized
information, 8/ which leads to the issue of better organizing and selecting of
applications which fit within the process of new technologies adaptable to the
developing countries.

    8/ Stafford Beer, <u>Platform for Change</u> (London, John Wiley and Sons,
1975).

C. Application

Computer technology is recognized as having significant potential in the acceleration of the economic and social development of the developing countries. This can serve as an important tool in numerous functional activities of the core of the development process. Those activities represent certain kinds of useful applications which in the developing countries, vary according to the level of development achieved in any particular country. However, in most developing countries computers are being used predominantly for business-oriented processing which includes payroll, accounting, inventory control, banking, communications, and other utilities. As additional computers are introduced and training and education begin to provide expanding skill, computer applications are extended to other areas such as science, engineering, information management, industry and education.

Within the economic development and the establishment of a programme of responsive computer support, a further role is indicated. A United Nations report describes this role as follows:

> "Computers and computer technology have played a central role in the growth of modern economics by providing an essential bridge between the accumulated body of formal theory on the one hand, and the growing availability of large data bases, on the other. The result of this crucial bridging function has been the growth of modern econometrics and more recently, an increasing application of economics to the formulation and testing of alternative policies and programmes for dealing with social and economic problems."

Different types of models (computerized) have been used extensively by economists engaged in analyzing and planning economic growth and other areas of interest. A discussion in the areas of government services may lead to the definition of certain kinds of application which can be categorized into the following:

1. Applications dealing with people

(a) Civil service personnel register for maintenance of administrative records, payroll, and payment supervision;

(b) Population registration where there is easy access to a central register for all government departments by means of telecommunications;

(c) Migrant control and other special systems such as passport control, foreigners domiciled, etc. can be kept on a current basis by an outline information network;

(d) Taxation of income, sales and land taxes are automated and utilize telecommunications systems in some countries;

(e) Special security and welfare programmes are often complex but automation and on-line or batch up-dating and payment plans are becoming feasible;

(f) Employment: registering those available for work and the jobs available; matching individuals with vacancies via computer and using communications to set up local contacts;

(g) Law enforcement: registers of crimes, criminals and criminal histories connected with automobile registers and drivers, narcotics control, etc.

2. Applications concerning goods and institutions

(a) Enterprises: various registers of businesses, investments, bankruptcies, and pollution data;

(b) Trade and tariffs relating to the monitoring and control of imports and exports;

(c) Road register: handling traffic control, highway maintenance and construction;

· (d) Weather prediction: computer/communications surveillance of weather patterns from which national predictions are made.

3. Applications concerning goods related to people.

(a) Car registration, insurance, licenses;

(b) Land register;

(c) Telephone customer billing.

4. General information systems

(a) Statistics: providing statistical registers to local governments, universities, and other approved users;

(b) Economic information systems: for national and urban development which includes collection procedures, analysis and retrieval;

(c) Political information systems: relating to voter registration and election statistics.

Besides the above mentioned categories, advanced applications can be applied and adapted to specific environments as for example:

(a) Computer-based teleconferencing. This is an interesting combination of audio-visual preception with the aid of central computer programming and storage. The operations can be interactive, both in real time and with separate, delayed interventions. The latter facilitates the participation of persons who are unavailable at their remote terminals at a time convenient for others. Some types of teleconferencing can be programmed to provide a record of what is being said, to catalogue and classify that record as desired, and make it available on demand from any of the terminals. In some systems, participating persons can edit each other's contributions, either in real time or off-line.

(b) Interactive video computer-based systems for education. An example is the PLATO educational system, developed by the University of Illinois. In this system knowledge is greatly enhanced by the student's total visual involvement with the subject matter. It would appear such systems offer more than substitution of live teachers and real classrooms; they can offer an improvement.

Although these advanced applications are far more expensive than other applications, with effective utilization they can offer very impressive results whenever they are affordable.

D.   Conclusions

Transfer of technology from developed to developing countries is an
extremely complex process and involves wide-ranging issues of a social and
political nature as well as technical difficulties. In the case of
computer technology, the objective is to provide a systematic way of utilizing
computers as tools to assist in meeting clearly identified goals. This is
a difficult task, requiring appreciation of the basic goals to be achieved,
understanding of the detailed technical issues to be resolved, and an awareness
of possible undesirable consequences. The technological support systems that
make up the infrastructure needed for computer use, are particularly critical
to success. This includes the legal, economic and social arrangements through
which computer technology becomes available and is controlled. As the
infrastructure in developing countries differs greatly from that in developed
countries, great care must be exercised in the application of technology
transfer.

A cost-benefit analysis of an Electronic Data Processing (EDP) system in
developing countries may point out that it is not economically justifiable,
especially in high labour low-capital cost countries. This paradox, as
indicated by Sharif, is that "an EDP system, particularly in a developing
country, justifies itself by its capacity in providing management services,
enhancing management capabilities and proving its value as a managerial tool.
Otherwise, it is a misplaced investment at worst or an investment in a vacuum
at best." 9/ For management, computer systems will directly enhance the control
capability of central management.

The installation of a computer system may induce movement into more
sophisticated areas of computer applications. Computers could act as a
modernization mechanism, as a means of changing the thinking of managers, and
in improving the organizational climate and affecting change in organizational
and management practices.

Many data communications applications with their powerful facilities can be
appropriate to the needs of developing countries. Using data communications
techniques will result in:

(a)   Reducing the cost of many important services;

(b)   Location of activities in many centres within a country where
adequate maintenance and technical personnel exist;

(c)   Developing countries having access to the best and most advanced
technical data banks and information bases, plus a better type of training;

9/ Fouad Sharif, "Modernization of public administration systems in
developing countries and the use of electronic data-processing", technical
paper presented at the United Nations Interregional Seminar on the Uses of
Modern Management Techniques in the Public Administration of Developing
Countries, held at Washington, D.C., 27 October - 6 November 1970 (United
Nations publication, Sales No. 71.II.H.7), vol. II, p. 136.

(d) A further type of co-ordination between developed and developing countries – a world-type system similar to that proposed by Mesarovic and Pestel, a total system to close the gap.

E. Recommendations

1. National Governments of developing countries should establish a central computer offices centre to conduct the necessary planning and guidance for nationwide computer use.

2. The responsibilities of a central office/centre would include:

(a) National central planning, co-ordination and formulation of policies;

(b) Establishing regulations and/or guidance for hardware and software acquisitions;

(c) Recommending or regulating of areas influencing computer use such as customs duty, import tariffs, rate structure, etc.;

(d) Identifying and removing barriers to computer use;

(e) Identifying and stimulating the infrastructure necessary to support the use of computer technology;

(f) Responsibility for development and implementation of plans and controls of computer use by national Government offices.

3. National computer educational plans should be developed which include the identification of needs, assignment of priorities, and outlines of programmes leading to a national awareness of computer technology, whether through special seminars or courses and programmes at universities.

4. Special educational efforts should be undertaken within government to orient managers to the power of Management Information Systems and existing available program packages.

5. Standardization programmes should be introduced including: software, hardware, data communication, applications, and other acquisitions standards.

6. Transfer of computer technology internally (among different governmental or private sector departments) or internationally (with other countries to exchange information and experiences), should be encouraged.

Bibliography

Dunkerely, Harold B. The choice of appropriate techniques: finance and development. London, McMillan, 1976.

International Bureau for Informatics. Policy considerations on informatics/telecommunications. Rome, 1976.

Martin, James. Telecommunications and the computer. Englewood Cliffs, New Jersey, Prentice-Hall, 1969.

Robinson, P. Computer/communications policies for development. Canada, Department of Commerce, 1975.

Shuman, J.M. The policy implications of interactive computer systems. Proceedings of the Society for General Systems Research, 1975 (Washington, D.C.) 1975.

Twiss, Brian. Managing technological innovation. London, Longman, 1974.

United Nations. Committee on the Peaceful Uses of Outer Space. Report of the Working Group on Direct Broadcast Satellites on the work of its fifth session. 2 April 1974 (A/AC.105/127).

United Nations. Committee on Science and Technology for Development. Application of computer science and technology to development. Report of the Secretary-General. 2 January 1976 (E/C.8/37).

Wallenstein, G.D. Sound and image in interactive telecommunication. Proceedings of the Society for General Systems Research, 1975 (Washington, D.C.) 1975.

INFORMATION SYSTEMS IN PUBLIC ADMINISTRATION
D. Eade, J. Hodgson (editors)
North-Holland Publishing Company
© *DFD, 1981*

REMOTE SENSING TRENDS AND THEIR IMPLICATIONS
ON THE PUBLIC SECTOR*

Joachim Schafer**

Abstract

This paper is intended to highlight some of the current trends in the
development and application of remote sensing technology, mostly as they apply
in the United States of America. Emphasis is placed on discussing the
anticipated effects these trends will have on public sector planning and
administrative activities. Technology development trends, user and application
characteristics, and factors which will affect future R & D and application
are discussed.

A. Technology

Since the launch of Landsat I in 1972, there has been a continuous
growing stream of photographic and digital earth resources data available.
These data have been available from Landsats 1, 2 and 3, Skylab, the Heat
Capacity Mapping Mission, and Seasat. Sensors aboard these satellites have
provided photographic data (colour, colour infrared, and multi-spectral black
and white), digital data (multi-spectral scanner, return beam vidicon, and
thermal scanner), and radar data (microwave radiometer and synthetic aperture
radar). All of these data have been utilized extensively in research
programmes in the United States of America and in foreign countries. Some
operational uses of the data have also been made, particularly in foreign
countries, but space-acquired remote sensing data has so far failed to
approach early optimistic estimates for its utilization in routine earth
resources investigations.

Over the next several years, a number of additional sensors are proposed
or scheduled to be launched by the United States and foreign countries. Among
these are Landsat D, Magsat, Large Format Camera, Shuttle Imaging Radar,
Tethered Magnetometer, Multispectral Linear Array, Gravsat, Stereosat, NOSS,
SPOT (France), and the JEOS series of five satellites (Japan). These
satellite sensors will continue to provide both digital and photographic data

---

* This paper was prepared with the generous support and extensive
co-operation of METRICS, Inc. The information presented in the paper is
partially based on recent findings contained in a 1979 METRICS' report entitled
"Landsat remote sensing market forecast: 1979-1990". This report is available
from METRICS, Inc., 290 Interstate North, Suite 116, Atlanta, Georgia 30339,
United States of America.

**Dokumentations und Ausbildungszenthrum für Theorie und Methode der
Regionalforschung (DATUM e.v.), Bonn, Federal Germany.

J. Schafer

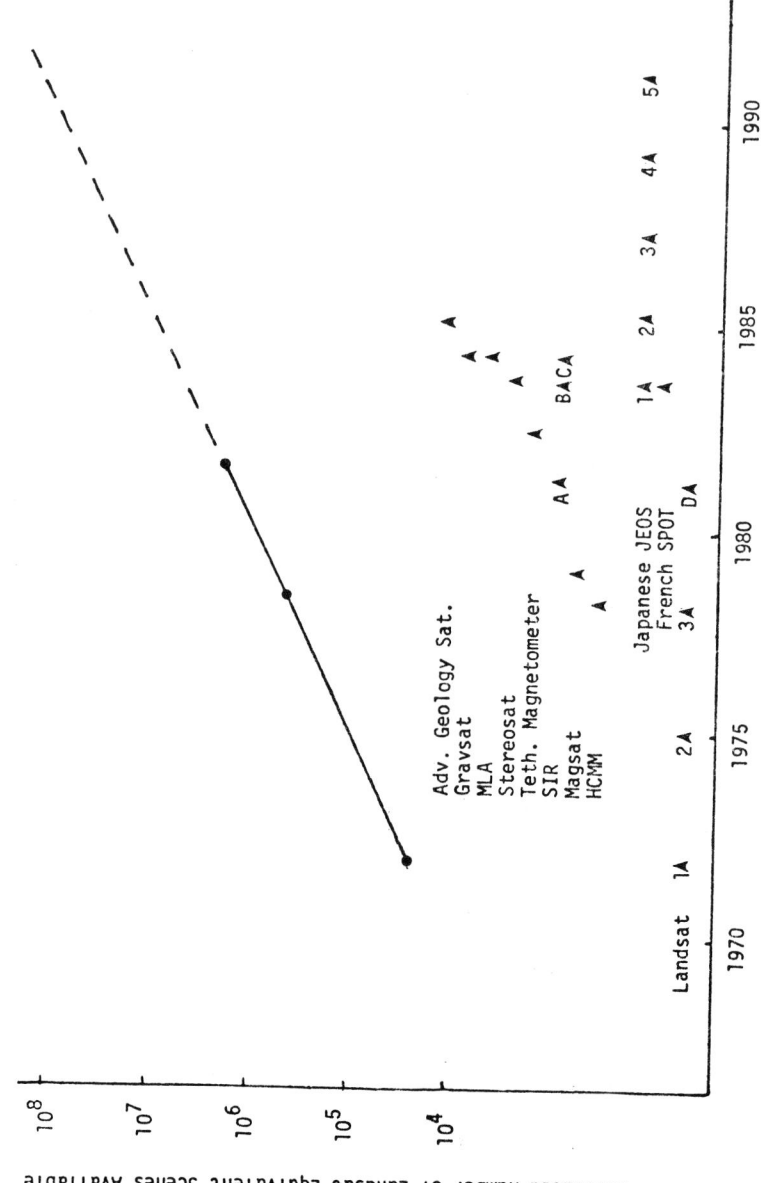

Figure XLVII. Estimated Growth of Data Suitable for Digital Image Processing

for earth resources investigations.

It appears that few, if any, organizations have fully evaluated the impacts of Landsat D and other earth resource satellites on their remote sensing operations. As can be seen in figure XLVII, the amount of satellite earth resource data suitable for digital processing that should become available in the near future is truly phenomenal. The available data are expected to increase by more than three orders of magnitude by 1990 - to the equivalent of more than 10^8 Landsat scenes.

Landsat D will have a particularly large effect on the use of Landsat data. The resolution on Landsat D will much more closely approximate that currently available from medium and high altitude aircraft. Thus many federal, state, and local agencies (as well as other organizations) will be able to use Landsat data to satisfy needs that formerly could only be provided by aircraft data. Landsat D will also have a particularly large impact on mineral resource exploration firms because of the addition of the 2.2 micron band.

Stereosat, if approved, and SPOT will also have significant effects on the use of satellite remote sensing data and therefore on the market for remote sensing equipment and services. Both of these satellites are scheduled to provide data at a 15 meter resolution - nearing the limit of civilian data resolution as approved by President Carter in 1978. Stereosat and SPOT data can be used in conjunction with Landsat data, thereby expanding the Landsat-related markets.

That tremendous amounts of new, space-acquired earth resources data will soon become available is a virtual certainty. However, the extent to which these data will actually be analyzed and interpreted for solving "real-world" problems remains uncertain. At one extreme, these remote sensing data will be used almost exclusively for research purposes. At the other extreme, space remote sensing data will be the predominant data type utilized in virtually all research and operational earth resources investigations. The direction that remote sensing data use takes will obviously have a make-or-break impact on the relatively young, relatively small remote sensing industry.

In the past there have been only two space programmes which have had a significant, continuing impact on day-to-day activities - communications satellites and weather satellites. In the next decade remote sensing satellites should take their place alongside communications satellites and weather satellites. By the end of the 1980s, satellite remote sensing will develop and mature into a vastly expanded, viable industry covering new application areas.

Five events can be listed in support of this forecast:

(a) Launch of Landsat D;

(b) Operation of improved data distribution systems;

(c) Launch of many satellites providing geologic data;

(d) Launch of earth resources satellites by many countries;

(e) Establishment of a world-wide network of ground stations.

All of these events will have a significant, positive impact on the use of Landsat data and the development of new Landsat applications.

B. Users and applications

Landsat data users can be grouped into four categories: federal government, industry, state and local governments and foreign organizations. In order to provide an overview of the primary applications of Landsat technology before discussing user characteristics, the following lists show the major applications for which Landsat data are currently being used and for which they are expected to be used in the future.

Geology

        Mineral exploration
        Earth resources exploration
                Petroleum on shore
                Petroleum off shore
                Coal
                Shale oil and tar sand
                Geothermal exploration
        Environmental geology
                Earthquake damage
                Landslides
                Subsidence and cave-ins
                Volcanic eruptions
                Foundations and construction materials
        Geologic mapping and interpretation
                Orthophoto map preparation
                Mapping rock types
                Structural mapping
                Mapping geomorphic features
                Linear, circular, and long lineament mapping
                Arctic Sea ice mapping

Water resources (hydrology)

        Snowcover and runoff forecasting
        Hydrologic impact of coniferous forest cover changes
        Soil moisture levels
        Groundwater supply
        Lake and reservoir mapping
        Water quality
        Lake ice conditions
        Sediment levels
        Estuarine dynamics
        Inundated areas and shorelines
        River forecasts
        Steamflow modelling
        Urban hydrology
        Ocean rainfall mapping

Agriculture

        Soil moisture estimates
        Soil salinity and drainage
        Nutrient deficiency
        Disease detection
        Insect damage
        Infrequent stress (for example fire, flood, frost)
        High-water tables
        Irrigation management
        Water storage

Water distribution systems (for example canals, pipelines, natural
 channels)
Wastewater disposal (for example evaporation ponds)
Seed germination requirements
Weed infestations
Land erosion potential
Crop surveys - acreage and yield
World-wide crop production estimation

Land inventory

Natural resource inventory
Wetland mapping and inventory
Coastal zone and shoreline mapping and inventory
        Surface circulation and currents
        Shoreline changes
        Charting of reefs, islands, and shoals
Mapping and cartography
Surface mining extent and reclamation monitoring
 and inventory
Urban environments
Change detection

Forestry, range and wildlife

Vegetation stratification
Seasonal change detection and monitoring
Habitat investigation
Forest mensuration
Rangeland productivity measurement
Biomass surveys
Disease detection
Forest fire mapping

1. Federal government

From the standpoint of applications, this market segment is currently
and is expected to remain the most diversified. As can be seen from the lists,
the federal government's applications for Landsat data include all categories.
The largest applications at present are crop forecasting, water resources
management and forestry and range applications. These are likely to remain
major federal applications, but future use of Landsat data will expand in other
applications areas including crop monitoring and management, siting and safety,
and land inventory.

As the demand increases for the world's natural resources, they will be
increasingly exploited (non-renewable resources) and become more intensively
managed (renewable resources). This trend will be especially apparent in the
United States of America, thus leading to increasing federal involvement with
natural resources management. With this increased federal responsibility for
managing the nation's resources will come an increased need for resource data
and information. Landsat, particularly Landsat D and later satellites, will be
in a unique position to supply some of these data on a regular basis. Thus,
there will be a continuing increase in the use of Landsat data by federal
agencies.

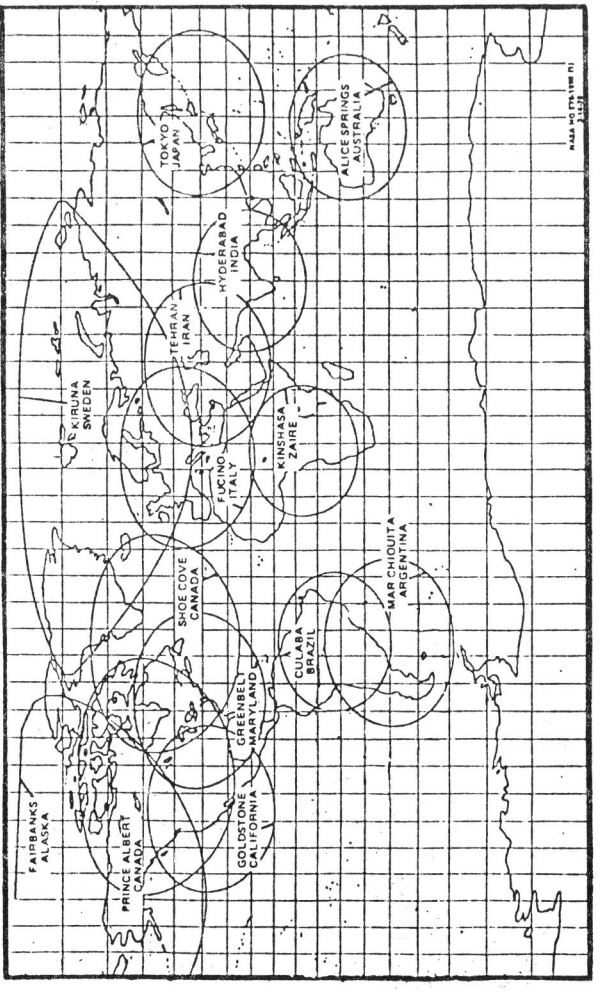

Figure XLVIII. Currently Operating and Planned Landsat Ground Stations

Stations planned for Mexico (1980), Upper Volta (1980),
Philippines (1981), Thailand (1981), and China are not
shown. The Zaire Station will probably not be built by 1981.

2.   Industry

The overwhelming majority of industrial applications for Landsat data will be in the geologic applications area. Two other important areas of Landsat data use will be environmental investigations and agricultural development plans for foreign Governments, but these will be significantly smaller than the geologic applications areas.

3.   State and local government

Land inventory will be the primary applications area for which state and local government agencies use Landsat data. The major uses of Landsat data to date in America have been in connexion with the Environmental Protection Agency (EPA) 208 and Housing and Urban Development (HUD) 701 programmes. A few states, among them Georgia, have had major, statewide land use mapping projects, but no state as yet can be said to have a truly operational Landsat programme.

While this market segment has failed to develop as rapidly as once expected, its development should accelerate within the next three to four years - approximately coinciding with the launch of Landsat D. The timing of this increase coincides with the increases expected in the industry segment, but for somewhat different reasons. Previously, the 80 meter resolution was too coarse for many applications of state and local governments. The 30 meter resolution on Landsat D, however, will make the data suitable for a much wider range of applications.

4.   Foreign organizations

As might be expected, the applications for Landsat data worldwide are extremely varied. They range from simple base mapping in least developed countries to sophisticated environmental investigations in developed countries. Therefore, it is difficult to generalize about the foreign applications to the same extent as with the other market segments. However, the results of a recent survey of foreign remote sensing activities indicate that approximately 40 per cent of foreign applications are related to geology, approximately 40 per cent to agriculture and forestry and approximately 20 per cent to all other applications.

The developed countries currently constitute the largest portion of the market, but the use of Landsat data by the least developed countries is growing faster than that of developed countries. Many of the Landsat-related projects in least developed countries are funded by aid programmes of the United States or of the United Nations and other international bodies.

It is expected that the development of a world-wide network of ground stations (figure XLVIII) will considerably increase the utilization of Landsat data by foreign organizations.

C.   Factors affecting future R & D and applications

Several events are now taking shape which will tend to have impact on the future use of remote sensing data. Although not necessarily obvious at the present time, one event in America of the past year is already having an impact on the use of Landsat data by state and local government agencies. "Proposition 13", with its attendant threat of budget cuts, or at least slower growth in state budgets, is causing many states to take another look at Landsat data. Although present Landsat data are not "ideal" for many agencies, these data are relatively inexpensive and are expected to continue for several years. Thus many agencies, which in the past would have performed their own

separate data collection projects, are now co-operating on data collection
and in many instances are substituting Landsat data for higher resolution
aircraft data and/or windshield surveys.

Another event which is in the process of occurring is the apparent
failure of Landsat-3 and the probable failure of Landsat-2 prior to the launch
of Landsat D. While some fear has been expressed that these events would
"kill" the Landsat programme, the opposite effect is more likely. Any gap in
the availability of data would dramatically demonstrate the "research" nature
of the current earth observation programme. Furthermore, the lack of
available, current data would substantially increase the pressures from all
major market segments for an operational earth observation programme.

Fourteen future events which will have an impact on space remote sensing
markets are discussed below.

1. Launch of Landsat D. With the launch of Landsat D now scheduled
for 1981, the "second generation" era for earth resources satellites will
begin. While the 80 meter resolution on Landsats 1, 2 and 3 has proved
sufficient for many purposes, it has been totally inadequate for other tasks
such as urban/regional planning. Moreover, improved spatial resolution will
benefit most tasks which are now being accomplished with Landsat data.

Thirty meter resolution is only the next step. The French SPOT system is
scheduled to have one band with a 15 meter resolution as are the Multispectral
Linear Array and Stereosat, if approved. Approval of Presidential Review
Memorandum 23 (now Policy Directive 37) by President Carter virtually assures
future data at a 10 meter resolution which is the limit specified for civilian
space remote sensing instruments. It also raises the possibility that some
currently classified military data may be made available.

Landsat D will have a particularly large effect on the over-all use of
Landsat data. The resolution on Landsat D will much more closely approximate
that currently available from medium and high altitude aircraft. Thus many
federal, state, and local agencies will be able to use Landsat data to
satisfy needs that formerly could only be provided by aircraft data.

2. Operation of an improved data distribution system. Several
possibilities exist for improved Landsat data distribution. The EROS Data
Centre has plans for using a domestic communications satellite (DOMSAT) for
receiving data from GSFC as part of the planned NASA Tracking and Data Relay
Satellite System (TDRSS)/DOMSAT data distribution plan. Many potential
applications of Landsat which are time-critical with respect to receipt of the
data from the satellite have failed to materialize because of the long time
delays inherent in the current data distribution system.

Once the proposed data distribution system is in operation, Landsat data
become more valuable for several existing applications such as range and
forestry management. Furthermore, many new applications which have been
widely discussed but never implemented on anything other than an experimental
base become possible. Examples of these new applications include agricultural
studies and, possibly, disaster evaluation studies. Agricultural studies,
particularly, will benefit from improved data distribution methods.

3. Landsat programme made operational. This event, were it to occur,
could have as great an impact on the remote sensing market (particularly
in the United States) as all of the other events combined. Many organizations
not currently making commitments to use Landsat data because the programme is
still "experimental" would begin to use the data. Other organizations currently
using Landsat data would increase their use of the data if continued

availability were assured. The importance of this event for market development
cannot be overemphasized.

Several bills have recently been introduced in the United States Congress
which would establish some form (either private or government operated)
of operational earth observation satellite programme. Also, the Administration
is professing to be committed to an operational programme but has yet to
propose a definitive plan of its own. It seems likely, however, that some
time during this session of Congress a bill will be passed authorizing some
form of operational earth resources satellite programme. It remains to be
seen how much of the operational programme will be turned over to private
interests.

4. Land resource planning bill passed. This event would probably bring
the largest number of new Landsat data users into the market. Any such bill
would likely result in a co-operative planning effort with most, if not all,
states and political subdivisions involved. Since few local or regional
planning agencies could justify the purchase of extensive hardware systems,
the impact would probably be greatest in the services market.

5. Launch of many satellites providing geologic data. This event is
obviously related to other events such as the launch of Landsat and the launch
of earth resource satellites by many countries.

6. Launch of earth resources satellites by many countries. France,
India and Japan all have plans to launch earth resources satellites in the near
future. Other countries and international organizations (for example the
European Space Agency) have also indicated an interest in launching earth
resources satellites. The launch of these satellites by many countries virtually
insures an increasing world-wide interest in satellite earth resources data.
Furthermore, with data from several satellite systems available, more nearly
complete world-wide coverage (and in many instances, more timely data) will be
available.

Since each satellite may have a unique advantage over the other, it is
probable that data of a particular area will be obtained from several satellites
and analyzed. For example, SPOT, when it is launched, may have the best spatial
resolution available (15 meters). Other satellites may have unique bands which
make the data valuable for use with other data products.

7. Establishment of a World-wide ground station network. For several
years a network of ground stations under international sponsorship was seriously
discussed by the United Nations. No action has been taken to date on this
particular issue, but many countries and/or international development
organizations have built and planned their own. If construction proceeds on
schedule, by 1981 there will be 17 ground stations world-wide capable of
receiving Landsat data of which 5 are in the United States and Canada and
the remaining 12 spread around the world; currently there are 8 ground stations
in operation.

As in the case of an increased earth resources satellite population, an
increased number of ground stations improves the prospects for more complete
and more timely world-wide coverage. Both of these improvements would tend to
increase use of the data because many areas are poorly covered.

8. World food shortage. While a world food shortage does not seem
imminent as it did a few years ago, a slight reduction in world food supplies
could precipitate a substantial increase in the use of Landsat data for
world-wide agricultural studies. Many of the agricultural development projects
currently underway around the world have a remote sensing component. The Food

and Agriculture Organization of the United Nations provides technical
assistance to many of these projects and conducts several remote sensing
training courses each year.

Another large United Nations programme which is closely linked to the
food problem is its desertification studies. In Africa in particular, many
thousands of square miles of farm crop and range lands are becoming deserts.
A large-scale effort is underway to study and, if possible, reverse this
condition. Because of the lack of other data sources, Landsat data is being
used extensively in these studies.

Many other international development organizations are also sponsoring
agricultural projects with a remote sensing component. Among these are the
World Bank, the Interamerican Development Bank, and various United Nations
regional commissions. All of these organizations are expected to continue
to increase their support for agricultural-oriented remote sensing projects,
but particularly large increases are anticipated if a food shortage threatens.

9. <u>Water supply crisis</u>. If current predictions hold true, the United
States can expect a water shortage by the year 2000. In many western states
this shortage has already appeared.- on a state-by-state basis more water
is allocated from the Colorado River than is available. Therefore, water
resources are expected to be much more intensively managed in the future than in
the past. More intensive management requires more data and Landsat is expected
to provide a portion of these data.

10. <u>Natural resources crisis</u>. Several people have predicted a severe
shortage of many of the world's natural resources before the year 2000. This
includes both renewable resources (for example forests) and non-renewable
resources (for example fuels and minerals). To forestall such a crisis, most
recommendations include more intensive management of renewable resources and
increased exploration for non-renewable resources. Landsat data can be
utilized in many of these management and exploration programmes.

11. <u>Landsat programme cancelled</u>. As time goes by, this event is
becoming less likely, and furthermore, even if the Landsat programme were
cancelled, the increasing number of foreign countries planning to launch earth
resources satellites would mitigate any negative impacts. It is also becoming
increasingly likely that private interest groups would develop and launch their
own satellites.

While the Landsat programme has not yet become operational, continuing
data is assured through about 1985 with the planned launch of Landsat D in late
1981. (A gap in data availability would occur if Landsats 2 and 3 both fail
prior to the launch of Landsat D.) By then (if not much sooner), it is
probable that the programme will be made operational, thereby assuring many
more years of data availability.

12. <u>Environmental restrictions relaxed</u>. As with most of the negative
factors, little likelihood seems to exist for a major reversal in the trend
toward more environmental restrictions and environmental monitoring programmes.
Consequently, there seems to be reason to expect that the use of Landsat data
for such purposes will continue to grow. While much experimentation has been
done with all types of environmental monitoring using satellite data, the
only quasi-operational programme was the Environmental Protection Agency (EPA)
208 planning process. However, Landsat data proved to be entirely adequate for
the land cover identifications needed for the 208 plans (except in urban areas),
and satellite data is likely to be used again for similar environmental
planning processes.

Indeed, it appears that Landsat data will be used extensively for monitoring strip mine reclamation activities in the United States. The new Office of Surface Mining Restoration and Enforcement in the Department of Interior has been experimenting with the use of Landsat data for monitoring purposes. It appears that the use of these data will become an integral part of the agency's monitoring and enforcement activities.

13. National resistance to "spying". This was, and still is to some extent, a topic of much serious debate within the United Nations. Many third world countries tried to pass a resolution requiring that space-acquired earth resources data be made available only to the countries over which it was taken. Most of these countries were concerned that the data would be used to exploit their natural resources by more advanced countries possessing superior technology for analyzing the data. Alternatively, some countries were concerned that neighboring countries would use the data for spying on their territory. At the present time, however, it seems that the United States position on this subject will prevail, that is, all data should be made available to any nation that desires to purchase it.

Two additional factors have probably helped to reduce the seriousness of this threat to open data dissemination. Firstly, many of the countries which opposed the data dissemination policy (for example Brazil) have acquired the technology to process the data in the same way that the United States does. Secondly, the approval of Policy Directive 37 (which limits the resolution of civilian space imagery to 10 meters) should alleviate, to some extent, the fear that such data will be used for spying. At the present time, this does not seem to be a substantial threat to the earth resource satellite programmes of the United States and other nations.

14. Significant federal spending cuts. For many years the prevailing mood in the United States has been that federal spending cuts should come out of the "technology" budget, for example, the National Aeronautics and Space Administration (NASA), the Department of Defence (DOD), etc. Recently, however, sentiment seems to have shifted toward more expansionary policies with respect to the United States technology base. There is convincing evidence that technologically the United States is falling behind many industrialized nations, including West Germany and Japan. Consequently, any major federal budget cuts are, for the first time in many years, more likely to come in social rather than technological programmes.

This, coupled with the positive benefits that have been and are being derived from the NASA earth resources programme, makes cuts in the Landsat programme unlikely. Moreover, with other nations planning to launch earth resources satellites of their own, it would probably take a severe world-wide recession or even a depression to cancel all of the earth observation satellite programmes planned.

D.   Conclusion

The current trends in remote sensing promise an increased applicability of Landsat technology and data in the public sector, particularly in urban environments. Higher resolution, growing detail and amount of data, and the increased reliability and accuracy of data classification systems make Landsat technology a prime data source for urban and regional planning activities in the future.

Considerable cost savings at a similar or better data quality level compared to conventional data acquisition methods can be expected from an increased utilization of Landsat technology. This is certainly one of the main factors for a growing utilization of remote sensing data at the local and regional level.

Bibliography

Faust, N.L. and Spann, G.W. Landsat information for state planning.
Technical report, Engineering and Experiment Station, Georgia Institute of
Technology (Atlanta, Georgia), June 1977.

Spann, G.W. Landsat remote sensing forecast: 1979-1990. METRICS Inc.
(Atlanta, Georgia), June 1979.

INFORMATION SYSTEMS IN PUBLIC ADMINISTRATION
D. Eade, J. Hodgson (editors)
North-Holland Publishing Company
© *DFD, 1981*

FINAL REPORT OF WORKING GROUP 8*

A. Summary

The technology is not an end in itself

There is danger of putting too much emphasis on new technology. When considering the use of the technology of information in any society one has to be very careful. Emphasis has to be placed on "real" or "basic" needs in judging the use of new technology. People must be encouraged and helped to formulate their own needs. The user must also be assisted in obtaining relevant information and in examining alternatives to the solution of his problem.

The tide of technological development cannot be stemmed

It is necessary to find a good balance between needs and the technological opportunities which are becoming increasingly available at lower cost from hardware and software suppliers.

The goals of standardization, integration and co-ordination are moving targets which are difficult to achieve in the short term. However, the new technologies provide an opportunity which can be used to help meet the goals in government information systems.

New technology is helpful

 (a) in solving problems that could not be solved before;

 (b) in finding easier and cheaper ways of solving old problems.

By comparing new technologies with old, with respect to advantages, disadvantages and efficiency, the benefits can be achieved through selection of alternatives.

---

* Participants: A. Aranyi, Hungary ; H. Buur, Denmark ; M. Diouf, Senegal ; A. Douglas, Great Britain ; J. Fobes, U.S.A. ; C.C. Gotlieb (Chairman), Canada ; P. Lieskovsky, Czechoslovakia ; A. Mustafa, Sudan ; T.V. Natarajan (rapporteur), India ; J.P. Nigoghossian, France ; A. Owolabi, Nigeria ; H.C. Price, Great Britain ; O. Rateau, France ; P. Robinson, Canada.

Adapting the technology to the specific environment

An experimental approach is needed. The challenge is to combine
components to meet real needs. There will be great diversity in inventiveness
and design at this level in combining elements of technology. Communication
must be improved between the places of production and the society that needs
the products or services.

Draw upon experiences when introducing new technologies

There is now substantial evidence about undesirable secondary effects
resulting from the introduction of some new technologies, including computer-
based technology. Such evidence argues against widespread application of
new, expensive technology, in either developed or developing countries, without
careful experimentation.

Education is a prerequisite

The public is not sufficiently aware of the nature and impact of advances
of information technology. There is a need for training for the use of the
technology, and especially for the application of microprocessors.

B.   Preamble to the recommendations

Bearing in mind the universal impact of the technological changes taking
place in the field of computers and communications and the experimental nature
of the applications of this technology, the Group believes that participation
in the preparation, observation and evaluation of applications should be
encouraged. It is recognized that this participation will involve additional
cost in respect of individual projects, but it is felt that the universal
benefit which would flow from international involvement would commend itself
to the international community and would be accepted as a charge by those most
easily able to bear it. Moreover, within each Government there ought to be a
willingness to encourage an experimental approach involving international
co-operation in order to mobilize to the greatest extent possible the relevant
experience in the service of development. In this regard, the Group believes
that there is a role for agencies which are seen to be competent and independent,
in evaluating proposals, in reviewing and assessing projects and in
disseminating information on the results. The Group strongly recommend that
DFD aspire to such a role. There are many executive agencies involved in
international co-operation in the field of computers and communications. The
Group notes with approval that UNESCO recently convened an international
conference on national information policies (SPIN), that the International
Federation for Information Processing (IFIP) has formed a special committee for
development, and that the United Nations is sponsoring a conference under
the aegis of the Committee for Science and Technology for Development. They
welcome these important evidences of international participation and concern.

The Group also believes that the formation of national policies in many
countries and the establishment of national focal points and institutions,
such as national computing centres, contribute towards the objectives set out
above. It also welcomes the initiative of the French Government in convening
an international Colloquium on Informatics and Society this year. The Group
welcomes similar initiatives which have been taken by other Governments.

C. Recommendations

1. The Group recommends that UNESCO intensify its efforts to urge its member states to take full advantage of the opportunities for development offered by computer and communications technologies, and also recognize the fundamental impact of their introduction and the need for careful evaluation of potential social implications and cultural impacts.

2. Having regard to the need for greater public awareness of the problems, possibilities and general implications of the new information technology and for increased training in respect of its utilization, the Group recommend:

(a) That UNESCO include in its programme on science and society the subject of informatics and enlarge its support for training in that field;

(b) That IFIP and appropriate other non-governmental organizations increase their stimulation of and support for the expansion of education in informatics.

3. Believing in the important role which can be played by international non-governmental professional and technical associations in studying and applying the new information technology, the Group recommends that UNESCO and the International Bureau for Informatics (IBI):

(a) Seek suggestions from non-governmental organizations concerning all programmes relating to informatics;

(b) Call upon such associations for assistance in the conduct of studies, seminars and training; and

(c) Provide support for the strengthening of these practical channels of international co-operation.

4. The Group recommends that DFD strengthen its role in assisting developing countries through evaluating proposals, reviewing ongoing progress, assessing completed projects and disseminating information. The work would be carried out by:

(a) DFD members; 1/ and

(b) A small core of resident DFD staff.

Financing would come from specially designated funds in projects carried out by executing agencies.

1/ It is expected that DFD members would contribute their services without cost, when travel is not required.

5.   The Group recommends that in projects supported by United Nations specialized agencies and bilateral aid organizations, funds be designated for:

(a)   Project evaluation;

(b)   Progress review;

(c)   Assessment of results;

(d)   Dissemination of reports.

6.   Recognizing the role that IFIP can play in helping developing countries, the Group recommends that IFIP, in collaboration with the UNESCO Committee on Informatics for Development:

(a)   Assist DFD in any role it undertakes in project evaluation and assessment;

(b)   Make available the expertise of its technical committees and working groups.

Table 24. Technological tools in computers and communications

Tools	Sector applications	Comments
Facsimile Electronic mail Message management	1,4	Telecommunications design must accommodate these modes Telecommunication administrations must be responsive to user needs
Satellite communication	1,5	More channels will be available Prerequisite to modern technology International control needed
Remote sensing	2,3,6	Transborder data flow problem Sovereignty issue Widespread in three to four years Assistance for utilization needed
Text retrieval Word processing	5 1,4	Being marketed aggressively Assess employment consequences Language problems will be handled
Video disk Video display	1,4,5 1	Likely to be dominated by entertainment market May meet specialized requirements
Viewdata based on telephone and television	1	Educational opportunities important Low priority for developing countries
Software packages	1 to 6	Can aid technology transfer Offers an opening in informatics for developing countries Continuing maintenance and support needed Beware of manufacturer's application packages
Computer aided instruction/design	1,4,5	CAI is a luxury CAD useful in specialized areas
Data management systems	1 to 6	Currently oversold Watch developments

Table 24 continued overleaf

Teleconferencing		Cannot replace human contacts Psychological barriers to acceptance Could reduce travel
Voice imput	1	Highly experimental Much desired
Triggered radio/television	1,5	May be useful for isolated communities
Digital transmission	1 to 6	Fundamental to new telecommunication infrastructure
Microprocessors	1 to 6	Will be ubiquitous Use will not be limited by hardware costs Software costs must be considered
Minis and large main frame computers	1 to 6	Use will be limited by costs

Note to Table 24

References are made in column 2 to the first six working groups of this seminar. The tools are regarded as being applicable to both modern and traditional sectors of soeciety.

Tools in the above list may serve one or more stages or aspects of data and information handling, for example:

(a) Collection;

(b) Classification;

(c) Storage;

(d) Retrieval;

(e) Processing;

(f) Presentation;

(g) Dissemination.

It may help in evaluating the utility of a particular tool to consider its role for one or more of these categories of information handling.

ANNEXES

ABDERRAHMEE, Cheikh O Sidi	Statistics Directorate, Mauritania
ARANYI, Attila	Central Statistical Office, Hungary
ARVAS, Christer	National Central Bureau of Statistics, Sweden
ARZOO, Mir S.	Ministry of Planning, Bangladesh
BASAVE AGUIRRE, Leonardo	Secretaria de Hacienda, Mexico
BECA, Raimundo	Mission à l'Informatique, France
BERESFORD, John	Data Use and Access Laboratories, U.S.A.
BRACKETT, James	US Agency for International Development, U.S.A.
BUUR, Hans	Danish State Computer Centre, Denmark
CHIARAMONTI, Claude	Institut National de la Statistique et des Etudes Economiques, France
CLARK, Kenneth	United Nations Economic and Social Commission for Asia and the Pacific
COHEN, Jean-Claude	Centre d'Etudes et d'Expérimentation des Systèmes d'Information, France
COINER, Jerry	City University of New York, U.S.A.
CROWTHER, Warren	Instituto Centroamericano de Administracion Publica, Costa Rica
DIAZ-ZULOAGA, Luis	Ministerio del Ambiente y de los Recursos Naturales Renovables, Venezuela
DIOUF, Magatte	Bureau Organisation et Méthodes, Senegal
DOUGLAS, Sandy	London School of Economics, United Kingdom
DUMAS, Philippe	Université de Toulon, France
EIGBEFOH, Alfred	Federal Capital Development Authority, Nigeria
EVERS, Jeannine	Data Use and Access Laboratories, U.S.A.
EVIOTA, Elizabeth	Institute of Philippine Culture, Ateneo de Manila University, Philippines

FOBES, John	Duke University and University of North Carolina, previously Deputy Director General of UNESCO
FRANCHET, Yves	Ecole Nationale de la Statistique et de l'Administration Economique, France
FRIEND, Anthony	University of Sussex, United Kingdom
GHANI, Modh. Nor	Socio-economic Research and General Planning Unit, Malaysia
GONZALES DIAZ, Violeta	National Statistics, Office of Peru, Peru
GOTLIEB, Calvin	University of Toronto, Canada
GUESNIER, Bernard	Institut d'Economie Régionale, France
GUNERATNE, Dharmasiri	Department of Census and Statistics, Sri Lanka
HAKIM, Catherine	Department of Employment, United Kingdom
HENDERSON, Kenneth	Overseas Development Administration, United Kingdom
HERNANDEZ DE PITTI, Ana	Ministerio de Planificacion y Politica Economica, Republic of Panama
HERR, Harvey	Central Bureau of Statistics, Kenya
JONES, Ken	Norwegian Institute of Urban and Regional Research, Norway
JORSSEN, Vernon	International Development Research Centre, Canada
KEKOVOLE, John	Ministry of Economic Planning, Kenya
KENNERLEY, John	United Nations Economic Commission for Europe
KOPPEL, Harry	Centro Distrital de Sistemas, Columbia
LAIHONEN, Aarno	Central Statistical Office, Finland
LEDERER, Alain	International Standards Organization
LIESKOVSKY, Peter	Computing Research Centre, Czechoslovakia
LOUVET, Gérald	Centre d'Etudes Pratiques d'Informatique et d'Automatique, France
LYDERSEN, Sisdel	Central Bureau of Statistics, Norway
MARTIDES, Leandros	Ministry of Finance, Cyprus
MENDELSSOHN, Rudolph	U.S. Bureau of Labor Statistics, U.S.A.
MUSTAFA, Abubaker	National Council for Research, Sudan

NATARAJAN, T.V.	International Federation for Information Processing
NIGOGHOSSIAN, Jean-Pierre	Centre d'Etudes et d'Expérimentation des Systèmes d'Information, France
OSBERT, Gérard	Institut National de la Statistique et des Etudes Economiques, France
OWOLABI, Amole	United Nations Educational, Scientific and Cultural Organization
PEZANT, Paul	Ministry of Public Works, Indonesia
PINES, James	New TransCentury Foundation, U.S.A.
POMERANCE, Deborah	Data Use and Access Laboratories, U.S.A.
PRICE, Hugh Caton	Western and Charing Cross Teaching Hospitals, United Kingdom
RATEAU, Olivier	Intergovernmental Bureau for Informatics
ROBINSON, Peter	Department of Communications, Canada
RODRIGUES, Marcos	Instituto de Pesquisas Tecnologicas, Brazil
RODRIGUEZ DE ORTEGA, Virginia	Direccion General de Estadistica y Censos, Costa Rica
SABATIER, Jean-Paul	Institut National de la Statistique et des Etudes Economiques, France
SALIH, Kamal	Universiti Sains Malaysia, Malaysia
SALMONA, Jean	Centre d'Etudes et d'Expérimentation des Systèmes d'Information, France
SALOMONSSON, Owe	Nordic Institute for Research in Urban and Regional Planning, Sweden
SARINO, Cesar	Economic Development Foundation, Philippines
SARR, Makha	United Nations Economic Commission for Africa
SCHAFER, Joachim	Dokumentations und Ausbildungszenthrum für Theorie und Methode der Regionalforschung, Federal Republic of Germany
SHAH, S.M.	Planning Commission, India
SHIO, Martin	East African Management Institute, Tanzania
SICRON, Moshe	Central Bureau of Statistics, Israel
SRI POEDJASTOETI, Tuti	Central Bureau of Statistics, Indonesia
SUHARTO, Sam	Central Bureau of Statistics, Indonesia

TERJANIAN, Antoine   Statistics Canada, Canada

TOURE, Oumar   Ministère de l'Economie, des Finances et
                                      du Plan, Ivory Coast

TREILLE Jean Michel   Groupe d'Analyse et de Prospective des
                                      Systèmes Economiques et Technologiques, France

TSHIBAMBE, Kabamba   Service Présidentiel de l'Informatique, Zaire

WARD, Michael   Institute of Development Studies, United
                                      Kingdom

ZIEBINSKI, Michael   Electronic Data Processing Center, Poland

ZULETA GARCIA, Hugo   Oficina Central de Estadistica e Informatica,
                                      Venezuela

AGENDA

MONDAY 18 JUNE

Morning session : Plenary   Chair : J. Fobes
                                       Rapporteur : Y. Franchet

9.00   Introduction   J. Salmona
       DFD Programme 1971-1980

9.30   The Kenya pilot project   H. Herr

10.00 The Tunisia pilot project   J. C. Cohen

11.00 The Senegal pilot project   M. Diouf

12.00 Methodological implications of the first phases   J. Hodgson
       of the three pilot projects   J.C. Cohen

Afternoon session : Plenary   Chair : G. Bager
                                       Rapporteur : Y. Franchet

14.00 Objections to information systems co-ordination   P. Lemoine
                                                   R. Beca

14.15 The Bolivian approach   W. Crowther

14.45 A presentation of the Malaysian project NIDAS on   K. Salih
       the rationalization of public data

15.15 Setting priorities for information systems A. Laihonen
       development projects in public administration

16.15 Round table discussion of the day's presentation - R. Beca
       identification of issues for further discussion in J.C. Cohen
       groups on Tuesday morning   W. Crowther
                                                   M. Diouf
                                                   D. Guneratne
                                                   K. Salih
                                                   J. Salmona

TUESDAY 19 JUNE

Morning session :

9.00 - 12.30 Group discussions

Afternoon session : Plenary   Chair : L. Basave Aguirre
                                          Rapporteur : K. Henderson

14.00 - 16.00 Group reports

16.00 - 17.00 Keynote paper - "Development problems and   M. Ward
              data collection requirements"

17.00   Address   J. Fobes

18.00   ESCAP information systems project   K. Clark

WEDNESDAY 20 JUNE

Morning session

9.00 - 12.30 Group dissussions

Afternoon session

14.00 - 17.30 Group discussions

THURSDAY 21 JUNE

Morning session : Plenary   Chair : M. Diouf
                                          Rapporteur : J. Hodgson
9.00   Group reports

11.00   New trends in computer applications and   P. Robinson
              associated government policies

11.30   The future of packages   A. S. Douglas

11.50   Statistical data-system architecture   A. Aranyi

12.10   User aspects of statistical information   P. Lieskovsky
              systems

Afternoon session

14.00 - 17.30 Group discussions

FRIDAY 22 JUNE

<u>Morning session</u>

9.00 - 12.30 Group discussions

<u>Afternoon session</u> : Plenary   Chair : J. Salmona
                                          Rapporteurs : H. Herr, P. Dumas

14.00   Group reports

16.30   Closing discussion
              Proposals for follow-up work

17.30   Close of seminar